Style in Language

Style in Language

Edited by

Thomas A. Sebeok

THE M.I.T. PRESS
Massachusetts Institute of Technology
Cambridge, Massachusetts

COPYRIGHT © 1960

BY

THE MASSACHUSETTS INSTITUTE OF TECHNOLOGY

———

All Rights Reserved

*This book or any part thereof must not
be reproduced in any form without
the written permission of the publisher.*

Second printing, August 1964
Third printing, first MIT Press paperback edition, August 1966
Fourth printing, January 1968
Fifth printing, September 1971
Sixth printing, July 1975
Seventh printing, July 1978

ISBN 0 262 19007 9 (hardcover)
ISBN 0 262 69010 1 (paperback)

Library of Congress Catalog Card Number: 60–11729

PRINTED IN THE UNITED STATES OF AMERICA

Foreword

When literary critics of different schools of thought come together to discuss basic principles and their application, there is often vigorous debate, even though they are speaking the same critical language (more or less). Although their basic positions may differ widely, they have a common fund of experience and are working with essentially the same materials. The situation is quite different, however, if the literary critics are joined by linguists, psychologists, and, for good measure, a few cultural anthropologists, each speaking his own professional language, each starting from at least a somewhat different base than the others. The problems of communication, to begin with, are manifold, and the difficulties of developing common understandings are enormous.

This book is a record of such a meeting and reflects these problems. But it also reflects a genuine attempt by a group of scholars from several disciplines to bring their special resources of knowledge to bear on one problem: the nature and characteristics of style in literature.

Under the auspices of the Social Science Research Council, such a conference was held at Indiana University in the spring of 1958 to explore the possibility of finding a common basis for discussing and, hopefully, understanding, particularly among linguists, psychologists, and literary critics, the characteristics of style in language. Out of such discussions, it was hoped, might come a clearer perception of what literature is and what the constituent elements of style are. If literature is an aspect of behavior, is there any way in which these groups can reach a meeting of minds on the nature of this behavior and its place in human culture? How can the understandings of one group be used to shed light on those of other groups and on the whole problem of style in literature?

To ensure as large a measure of understanding as possible and to give as much common basis for discussion as possible, each of the members of the conference (except some of those summarizing the papers) submitted in advance a paper discussing aspects of style that particularly interested him. These were in turn distributed to the whole group well before the conference. However much or little agreement there may have been, at least there was a large body of common material to serve as a basis for the discussions.

As would be expected, the participants spoke different languages, yet they brought to light important issues and basic differences of approach. There was a clear difference in method and in understanding in the treatment of the questions whether problems of style (however it might be defined) might be treated quantitatively like problems of social behavior, whether literature is amenable to truly scientific analysis, whether the scientific analyses proposed were really meaningful to the literary critic. Although the group never arrived on common ground as to the nature of style, at least the difficulty of definition—or rather, the wide diversity of definitions—came to be fully recognized.

On a smaller but no less intense scale there was discussion of the nature of poetic language and of metrical form, even of the minutiae of statistical analysis of presumably significant characteristics. And inevitably there was concern for the nature of the creative process. This reached its high point in a discussion by I. A. Richards of the composition of one of his own poems, "Harvard Yard in April/April in Harvard Yard."

If no final agreements and perhaps no common language or common purpose came to be recognized by the whole group, nonetheless it was clear that each participant was stimulated to a new awareness of fields outside his own and of the differences in methods and ends in those fields. Perhaps more important still is the fact that, partly through this awareness, new suggestions for further research in the nature of the literary process and in the functions of literary criticism were opened up by the frank and vigorous discussions which characterized the conference and are recorded in this book.

John W. Ashton

Bloomington, Indiana
May 1960

Acknowledgments

The compelling need for an interdisciplinary Conference on Style became apparent in a proseminar on poetic language conducted jointly by Sol Saporta, Edward Stankiewicz, and myself. Our cooperation made planning the conference a great pleasure, and I am deeply indebted to them both for their gracious and dedicated collaboration.

Primary financial support for the conference came from the Social Science Research Council; in addition, we acknowledge the generous assistance of Indiana University which made available special funds through the (former) Division of Student and Educational Services and the Departments of Philosophy and Psychology. The burden of paper work leading up to and following long after the conference was carried by the clerical staff of the University's Research Center in Anthropology, Folklore, and Linguistics, and I would particularly like to thank Rosemary G. Cronk, Frances Anderson, and Nancy R. Pride for their motherly devotion to this job. I also sincerely appreciate the help of Ann Shannon (University of Kansas) in checking reference materials for this book, and Nancy E. MacClintock's meticulous attention to the index.

For providing me with a year's leisure to carry out various studies in poetic language, and incidentally enabling me to work uninterruptedly on the preparation of this manuscript for press, I am much obliged to the John Simon Guggenheim Memorial Foundation.

THOMAS A. SEBEOK

Bloomington, Indiana
May 1960

Biographical Notes

MONROE C. BEARDSLEY (b. 1915), after completing his studies at Yale University, taught at Yale and Mount Holyoke and then at Swarthmore, where he is now professor of philosophy. His many publications reflect his interest in the theory of knowledge, aesthetics, and social and political philosophy.

ROGER BROWN (b. 1925) received his academic training at the University of Michigan. After teaching there and at Harvard, he joined the faculty of the Massachusetts Institute of Technology, where he is now associate professor of psychology. His experimental studies have included problems in phonetic symbolism, linguistic determinism, and the child's acquisition of speech. He has recently published a general treatment of the psychology of language entitled *Words and Things*.

JOHN B. CARROLL (b. 1916) owes his interest in linguistics to his early acquaintance with the linguist Benjamin Lee Whorf, whose writings he compiled many years later for publication in *Language, Thought, and Reality*. During his studies at the University of Minnesota, Mr. Carroll became interested in various problems of the psychology of language and quantitative linguistics. He has taught at Mount Holyoke, Indiana, and Chicago and has served as research psychologist for the government. Since 1949 he has been at .the Graduate School of Education at Harvard, where he is now a professor of education and Director of the Laboratory for Research in Instruction.

SEYMOUR CHATMAN (b. 1928) was a student at Wayne University and the University of Michigan, after which he worked at Cornell on a project for teaching English as a foreign language. After a year's study in Holland and teaching experience at Wayne, Mr. Chatman joined the faculty at the University of Pennsylvania, where he is now assistant professor of English. His many articles and reviews are largely concerned with problems of literary and linguistic theory and pedagogy.

RICHARD M. DORSON (b. 1916) taught briefly at Harvard after completing his doctorate in American civilization, and then went on to the history department at Michigan State University. After a year in Tokyo he became, in 1957, professor of history and folklore at Indiana University and Chairman of the Committee on Folklore. He is editor of the *Journal of American Folklore.*

ALBERT GILMAN (b. 1923), whose scholarly interests center on Elizabethan drama, studied at the University of Michigan and is now an assistant professor of English at Boston University.

FRED H. HIGGINSON (b. 1921) studied chemistry and mathematics as an undergraduate at the University of Wichita, and then took a doctorate in English and linguistics at Minnesota. Since 1950 he has taught at Kansas State University. His publications include poetry and articles on jazz and Joyce, and he is now engaged in further studies on Joyce, a bibliography of Robert Graves, and investigations in nineteenth-century British philology.

ARCHIBALD A. HILL (b. 1902) studied at Pomona, Stanford, and Yale, and has taught at Michigan, Virginia, and Georgetown. Since 1955 he has been professor of English and linguistics at the University of Texas. His chief professional interests are in linguistics, stylistics, and literary analysis. He is Secretary of the Linguistic Society of America.

JOHN HOLLANDER (b. 1929), after studying at Columbia and Indiana, taught at Connecticut College and became a junior fellow at Harvard. He is now a member of the English department at Yale University, and has published literary criticism and poetry in many journals. His first volume of poetry won the award of the Yale Younger Poets Series in 1958.

FRED W. HOUSEHOLDER, JR. (b. 1913) was a student of classics at Vermont and Columbia and has taught classics, linguistics, and literature at Columbia, Allegheny College, and, since 1948, at Indiana University. His major interests are grammatical theory, the early history of Greek, and the structures of Greek, Latin, and English.

BENJAMIN HRUSHOVSKI (b. 1928) is a native of Wilno, Lithuania, who lived in the Soviet Union during World War II and then became a citizen of Israel. Since 1949 he has studied and taught Hebrew literature and modern poetry at the Hebrew University, Jerusalem. He has recently been on a leave of absence, working in the field of comparative literature at Yale.

DELL H. HYMES (b. 1927) has been a student of literature, anthropology, and linguistics at Reed College and at Indiana University. He is now assistant professor of social anthropology at Harvard and a research fellow in anthropological linguistics at the Peabody Museum. His major field of study is native North America, and his major concerns are with historical perspective and symbolic forms.

ROMAN JAKOBSON (b. 1896), a native of Moscow, took degrees at Lazarev Institute of Oriental Languages (Moscow), Moscow University, and Prague University. He has held professorships and visiting lectureships at Moscow Dramatic School, Masaryk University (Brno), Copenhagen, Oslo, Uppsala, École libre des hautes études (New York), and Columbia. He is a member of many academies and learned societies and holds many academic honors. He serves as Samuel Hazzard Cross Professor of Slavic Languages, Literatures, and General Linguistics at Harvard, and at the same time as Institute Professor at the Massachusetts Institute of Technology. A bibliography of his publications (in general linguistics and poetics; Slavic philology, literary history, and folklore; and Paleosiberian languages) appeared in *For Roman Jakobson* (The Hague, 1956, pp. 1–12). Mr. Jakobson's *Selected Writings,* in seven volumes, are being published by Mouton and Company.

JAMES J. JENKINS (b. 1923) was trained in physics at the University of Chicago, in psychology at William Jewell College and the University of Minnesota. He has been on the staff of the University of Minnesota since 1950 and is now a professor of psychology. His research has been largely concerned with the psychology of verbal behavior and communication.

JOHN LOTZ (b. 1913), a native of Milwaukee, studied philosophy, Germanic languages, and Hungarian at the University of Budapest, Ph.D. 1935; then he taught Hungarian language and literature at the University of Stockholm as Director of the Hungarian Institute. Since 1947 he has been at Columbia University, currently as professor of linguistics. Mr. Lotz is also Director of Research, Uralic and Altaic Program, American Council of Learned Societies.

GEORGE A. MILLER (b. 1920) studied in the speech department at the University of Alabama and took his doctorate in experimental psychology at Harvard. During the war he worked on military voice communication systems at the Harvard Psycho-Acoustic Laboratory. He has taught at both Harvard and the Massachusetts Institute of Technology, and is currently professor of psychology at Harvard.

CHARLES E. OSGOOD (b. 1916) has studied psychology and anthropology at Dartmouth and Yale, and has taught at Yale, the University of Connecticut, and the University of Illinois. He is now Director of the Institute of Communications Research and professor of psychology at the University of Illinois. His fields of special interest and research are the psychology of language behavior, psycholinguistics, and human learning more generally.

I. A. RICHARDS (b. 1893) read moral sciences and taught English literature at Cambridge. He is at present a university professor at Harvard. His television presentations include *Sense of Poetry* and *The Wrath of Achilles: a Version of the Iliad*. He has traveled widely, living for years in Peking. A large part of his time has been spent climbing mountains, an account of which may be found in *Climbing Days* by his wife, Dorothy Pilley. Poetry, the author holds, can be an instrument of inquiry into ways of thought and feeling closed to other sorts of discourse. Without disparagement of prose comments, he supposes that poetry may best be studied in and through poetry. A poem gets its meaning, he thinks, from the language it uses: the reader cannot put anything into the poem unless the language agrees. Nevertheless, even the most admirable readers will be found, if we look, to differ in their perception of almost any line they read. Language has power to defend itself from misreading, however, and poems, he hopes, will increasingly avail themselves of such protection. Meanwhile the current identification of the author with his work heavily cramps them both. The widespread decline in knowledge of the language is the chief danger to poetry.

SOL SAPORTA (b. 1925) studied at Brooklyn College and took his doctorate in Spanish linguistics from the University of Illinois. Since 1955 he has been assistant professor of Spanish and linguistics at Indiana University. His major fields of interest are Hispanic and general linguistics. He is currently engaged in research on certain aspects of child language.

THOMAS A. SEBEOK (b. 1920) is a native of Budapest who has lived in the United States since 1937. At the University of Chicago he studied literary criticism, anthropology, and linguistics, and at Princeton he earned his doctorate in Oriental languages and civilizations. Since 1943 he has been a member of the Indiana University faculty in linguistics, and for the past five years has served as Chairman of the University's Research Center in Anthropology, Folklore, and Linguistics, as well as of its Program in Uralic and Altaic Studies. Currently a fellow of the Center for Advanced Study in the Behavioral Sciences, he has held visiting appointments at several universities, having most recently been professor of anthropology and linguistics and Associate Director of the Linguistic Institute at the University of Michigan. His major research interest centers on the Uralic languages and peoples; his list of publications includes books on Hungarian and Finnish and a series of monographs on the Cheremis.

EDWARD STANKIEWICZ (b. 1920), a native of Poland, studied at the University of Rome, came to the United States in 1950, and took degrees in linguistics at the University of Chicago and in Slavic languages and literatures at Harvard. Since 1954 he has taught Slavic languages and literatures and general linguistics at Indiana University. His interests are in Slavic phonology, dialectology, metrics, morphology, and kinship terminology.

C. F. VOEGELIN (b. 1906) became successively interested in psychology (Stanford), anthropology (University of California), and linguistics (Yale). His early interest in travel and study abroad found later expression in field work among American Indians (in California, Oklahoma, Ontario, Alberta, and in the Southwest after 1953), with associated work at several linguistic institutes at Ann Arbor, Chapel Hill, and Bloomington. He has taught in anthropology departments at De Pauw, Northwestern, and, after 1941, at Indiana University, where he also serves as chairman of the department, editor of the *International Journal of American Linguistics,* and Director of the Archives of the Languages of the World, as well as of the university's summer school field station in Arizona.

RENÉ WELLEK (b. 1903) grew up in Prague, where he received a Ph.D. from Charles University in 1926. After a year in England Mr. Wellek came to the United States in 1927 as a fellow in the graduate school of Princeton, and then he taught German at Smith College and at Princeton. In the 1930's he taught at the University of Prague and London University. In 1939 he returned to this country as a member of the English department of the State University of Iowa, and then in 1946 moved to Yale where he is now Sterling Professor of Comparative Literature and chairman of the newly created Department of Comparative Literature. He has been a visiting professor at Harvard, Minnesota, and Columbia, and is a member of many learned societies and has received many academic honors. He is the author of *A History of Modern Criticism 1750–1950* (of which two volumes were published in 1955 and two more are to follow shortly).

RULON WELLS (b. 1919) took his B.A. from the University of Utah in 1939 and his Ph.D. from Harvard, in the philosophy department, in 1942. During the war he taught the Bengali, Japanese, and Korean languages at the University of Pennsylvania and at Yale. He is now associate professor of linguistics and philosophy at Yale. His special interests are Indic languages; philosophy of the Vedas, Brahmanas, and Upanishads; comparative Indo-European linguistics and philology; synchronic and diachronic semantics; and language typology.

WILLIAM K. WIMSATT, JR. (b. 1907) was originally trained at Georgetown University and began his academic career as a teacher of English and Latin in the 1930's; later he took his doctorate at Yale. He has held many fellowships and offices in scholarly societies and has written numerous historical and critical works. He is now professor of English at Yale.

VALDIS J. ZEPS (b. 1932), a native of Latvia, has lived in the United States since 1950. Formerly a graduate student at Indiana University in general linguistics, East European languages, and sociology, Mr. Zeps is now working on the application of computer techniques to psycholinguistic problems as a National Science Foundation postdoctoral fellow at the Center for Advanced Study in the Behavioral Sciences.

Contents

Introduction

THOMAS A. SEBEOK

The Conference on Style was one of a series of work conferences[1] on selected research problems sponsored by the Social Science Research Council's Committee on Linguistics and Psychology (appointed in 1952). Members of the Committee—all of whom therefore shared in the planning of the conference—were John B. Carroll (Harvard University), Joseph H. Greenberg (Columbia University), James J. Jenkins (University of Minnesota), Alvin M. Liberman (University of Connecticut), Floyd G. Lounsbury (Yale University), Charles E. Osgood (University of Illinois), Thomas A. Sebeok (Indiana University), Rulon Wells (Yale University), and, representing the Council, Joseph B. Casagrande.

The conference was held at Indiana University, in Bloomington, April 17–19, 1958. Preparations for the conference, however, were made far in advance: almost a year earlier a group of scholars, representing a variety of relevant disciplines, were invited to draft work papers, to be duplicated and circulated to all conference participants at least three months before the meeting itself was to take place. The following is the list of the work papers received and distributed.

Roger Brown (Massachusetts Institute of Technology) and Albert Gilman (Boston University), "The Pronouns of Power and Solidarity"

John B. Carroll (Harvard University), "A Factor Analysis of Literary Style"

Seymour B. Chatman (University of Pennsylvania), "Comparing Metrical Styles"

Richard M. Dorson (Indiana University), "Oral Styles of American Folk Narrators"

---

[1] Five work conferences have been sponsored to date, of which the Conference on Style was the latest. The others were: Research on Bilingualism, Columbia University, May 10–11, 1954; Techniques of Content Analysis, Allerton House, University of Illinois, February 9–11, 1955 (cf. **319**); Associative Processes in Verbal Behavior, University of Minnesota, April 25–26, 1955 (cf. **209**); and Dimensions of Meaning— Analytic and Experimental Approaches, Yale University, May 17–18, 1956.

Fred H. Higginson (Kansas State College), "Style in Finnegans Wake"
Archibald A. Hill (University of Texas), "A Technique for the Definition of Literature"
John Hollander (Connecticut College), "The Metrical Emblem"
Benjamin Hrushovski (Hebrew University), "Free Rhythms in Modern Poetry"
Dell H. Hymes (Harvard University), "Phonological Aspects of Style: Some English Sonnets"
James J. Jenkins (University of Minnesota), "Commonality of Association as an Indicator of More General Patterns of Verbal Behavior"
John Lotz (Columbia University), "Metric Typology"
Charles E. Osgood (University of Illinois), "Some Effects of Motivation on Style of Encoding"
I. A. Richards (Harvard University), "Variant Readings and Misreading"
Sol Saporta (Indiana University), "The Relation of Linguistics to Poetic Language"
Thomas A. Sebeok (Indiana University), "A Cheremis Sonnet" and (with V. J. Zeps) "An Analysis of Structured Content, with Application of Electronic Computer Research, in Psycholinguistics"
Edward Stankiewicz (Indiana University), "Expressive Language" and "Linguistics and the Study of Poetic Language"
C. F. Voegelin (Indiana University), "On Distinguishing and Comparing Casual and Noncasual Utterances"
William K. Wimsatt, Jr. (Yale University) and Monroe C. Beardsley (Swarthmore College), "The Concept of Meter: An Exercise in Abstraction"

Three colleagues—a linguist, Fred W. Householder, Jr. (Indiana University), a psychologist, Roger Brown, and a literary critic, John Hollander—were then asked to prepare formal comments, evaluating and discussing the entire range of the work papers submitted. Each of these statements opened one conference session, and the formal remarks were followed by informal discussions in which authors, discussants, rapporteurs, and others at the round table[2] participated. Everything that was said was recorded on tape.

An evening session was devoted to a special lecture, open to the public, by I. A. Richards, on "Poetic Process and Literary Analysis," which constitutes Part One.

[2] Joseph B. Casagrande, Douglas G. Ellson (Indiana University), Joseph H. Greenberg, Mac Hammond (University of Virginia; now at Massachusetts Institute of Technology), Robert Hoopes (American Council of Learned Societies; now at Michigan State University, Oakland), and Harold Whitehall (Indiana University). Two authors, Albert Gilman and Archibald A. Hill, were not at the conference.

Roman Jakobson (Harvard University and Massachusetts Institute of Technology), George A. Miller (Harvard University), and René Wellek (Yale University) presented over-all summaries of the results of the conference and its implications. These concluding talks were also tape-recorded.

Immediately after the conference was over, the tape recordings were transcribed verbatim and the transcripts duplicated, and both were sent to every participant. The author of each work paper was requested either to revise his study before its publication in this book or, if he preferred to publish it elsewhere, to furnish an abstract thereof. These essays and abstracts, which incorporate revisions made in the light of what was said at the conference, constitute Parts Two through Eight of this volume.[3]

The placement of these papers under seven principal headings seemed to provide convenient clusters of topics roughly corresponding to high points as they could be gathered from the discussions; of course, the arrangement is somewhat arbitrary, and several alternative schemes—some of them suggested by the formal discussants and rapporteurs themselves—would have been equally feasible. Thus my own paper, although now grouped with Wells's in a section called Grammatical Aspects of Style, could almost as well have been shifted to the section devoted to the Phonological Aspects of Style, or (as Mr. Wellek points out) to Metrics, or even placed with the group of papers presenting various Linguistic Approaches to Verbal Art. Again, the papers by Dorson and Voegelin were juxtaposed—for different reasons—by Householder ("in both cases we find an area where it is rather difficult to draw the line between what we might call 'style of delivery' and 'inherent literary style'"), and by Wellek ("the two anthropological papers"); but here they are put in two different sections because Voegelin's paper seemed to be discussed more often, on the whole, with those of Saporta and Stankiewicz than with that of Dorson. So also, the essay by Brown and Gilman was labeled a "socio-linguistic" study by one of the speakers, and by another "the most linguistic-seeming of the contributions of the psychologists"; but here it is set side by side with Richards' "Variant Readings and Misreading" on the ground that these two papers more than any others deal with semantic problems. The classifications that I have used, then, were suggested, to a great extent, by what seemed certain focal points around which the arguments—although with unequal emphasis and something less than self-consistency—crystallized.

Professors Jakobson, Miller, and Wellek also revised their respective

---

[3] Rulon Wells's "Nominal and Verbal Style" was received after the conference, and hence was not discussed.

oral reports; these the reader will find, together with the revised versions of the three introductory discussions, in Part Nine.

We had never intended to publish the transactions of the conference as such; they were meant merely to stimulate our contributors to reconsider their position. However, the editor's close work with the manuscript convinced him that many of the exchanges provoked in the heat of the interdisciplinary debate—although they lacked continuity and sometimes even coherence—were, of themselves, of public interest and hence well worth preserving. The procedure followed was to identify the principal plots of our drama, pick up their threads wherever they chanced to lie, and recreate them into congruent, relatively polished and tightened sets of dialogues, while at the same time attempting to preserve their flavor of spontaneity as far as possible. These comments were then assembled at the ends of the sections to which they seemed most pertinent. (The editor, of course, remains entirely responsible for any distortions of intent that may have been introduced by his drastic selection from and rearrangement —regardless of chronological sequence—of the original record.)

The nearly five hundred references made by the authors were brought together in a single place, despite obvious disadvantages, for two reasons which seemed to outweigh these: first, bringing them together enabled the editor to reduce the number of footnotes to an essential minimum, for the pleasure of the reader who wishes to proceed without undue hindrance; and, second, the grouping permits the hope that the references may together constitute a relatively rich working bibliography of at least those aspects of style in language treated in this volume. Parenthetic boldface numerals, in text or note, refer to the corresponding entry in the terminal list.

The significance of the Conference on Style can perhaps best be expressed by the same evocative metaphor which T. S. Eliot once applied to Paul Valéry's meditations on poets and the art of poetry (**426**): "The tower of ivory has been fitted up as a laboratory." In our conference, and in this book which embodies its results, a deliberate and self-conscious attempt was made to initiate a departure from the perpetual humanistic engagement in the solution of a subtle and elusive puzzle—the fluid and dissonant notion of style—by offering an opportunity for experts in philosophic speculation to commingle (if not outrightly collaborate) with men of scientific temperament. To assemble this particular collocation of scholars—philosophers, critics, folklorists, cultural anthropologists, linguists, and psychologists; to bring together some whose primary concern is with the systems of accepted norms in relation to which we speak and write—in a word, tradition—with others who are more fascinated by problems of method was decided upon in the light of this conception.

It would be unreasonable to expect in these essays a solid unity of approach and treatment; but if the dialectic we helped set in motion has perhaps not yet led to a higher synthesis, at least we have come a long way since the project for extracting sunbeams from cucumbers was undertaken at the Grand Academy of Lagado.

PART ONE

Poetic Process
and Literary Analysis

I. A. Richards

Poetic Process
and Literary Analysis

I. A. RICHARDS

My title, I notice, can seem to break my subject up into two halves. I would therefore like to begin by suggesting that it would be unfortunate if we let any clear-cut division, much less any opposition or contrast, form *too early* in our thought. ?Poetic Process? . . . ?Literary Analysis?:[1] Each phrase can be highly elastic, each serves to name many very different things. And their boundaries can shift very suddenly. What I would wish on this occasion to be concerned with chiefly is the fruitful inter-actions of the energies so describable (Poetic Process—the activities through which a poem comes into being; Literary Analysis—the attempt to anatomize a poem) with side glances only at the possibilities of mutual frustration. A good deal of Poetic Process consists in, and advances by, Literary Analysis and, on the other hand, Literary Analysis is often Poetic Process attempting to examine and appraise itself.

One other preliminary: there are sayings that truly deserve to be called "ever memorable" in the sense that the more constantly we bear them in mind the more error we shall be spared. Among these, should we not give a high place to Coleridge's "Do not let us introduce an Act of Uniformity against Poets"[2]? There are many ways of passing Acts of Uniformity: one is by framing definitions. Here are four lines in which Wordsworth reminds Coleridge that they are no friends of

> that false secondary power, by which
> In weakness, we create distinctions, then
> Deem that our puny boundaries are things
> Which we perceive, and not which we have made.[3]

It will be only to some Poetic Processes, occurring in some poets only, and on some occasions only, that what I may contrive to say will apply.

---

[1] The marks ?———? mean 'query'. Cf. fn. 1 to "Variant Readings and Misreading."
[2] Coleridge, letter to Thelwall, December 17, 1796.
[3] Wordsworth, *The Prelude*, (1805–1806) Book II, 221–224.

9

Similarly with Literary Analyses: there are more ways than one of exploring our enjoyments.

Among our more obvious sources of information upon Poetic Process, where shall we place the poet's own account of the matter? It is customary at present to play it down—although any scrap of paper carrying any reference, however oblique, to circumstances of composition or any gossip about occasions is hoarded for the record as never before. Poets of standing—whatever their friends and relatives may be doing—remain as sparing of explanations as ever: to be mysterious and unforthcoming about his own work seems a part of the poet's role. Those who have departed from it have often seemed to feel the need of a cloak. Stephen Spender, in his *The Making of a Poem* (**389**), is one of the few exceptions. Edgar Allan Poe (**317**) uses both cloak and mask: in explaining how "The Raven" came into being he begins by dressing the revelation up as a mere "magazine paper." Coming from such a "magaziner" as Poe, this is surely an ambivalent phrase.

I have often thought how interesting a magazine paper might be written by an author who would—that is to say who could—detail, step by step, the processes by which one of his compositions attained its ultimate point of completion. Why such a paper has never been given to the world, I am much at a loss to say—but perhaps the authorial vanity has had more to do with the omission than any other cause.

We may perhaps linger on this phrase "authorial vanity." We are on ticklish ground here as Poe very well knows. He goes on:

Most authors—poets in especial—prefer having it understood that they compose by a species of fine frenzy—an ecstatic intuition—and would positively shudder at letting the public take a peep behind the scenes, at the elaborate and vacillating crudities of thought—at the true purposes seized only at the last moment—at the innumerable glimpses of idea that arrived not at the maturity of full view—at the fully matured fancies discarded in despair as unmanageable—at the cautious selections and rejections—at the painful erasures and interpolations—in a word at the wheels and pinions.

Alas, we find nothing of all this in what follows. Instead we are given an ostentatious parade of allegedly perfect adjustment of selected means to fully foreseen ends. Poe, so eager—in Harry Levin's phrase—"to convince the world of his self-mastery," spares no pains to make this clear.

It is my design to render it manifest that no one point in its composition is referable to accident or intuition; that the work proceeded, step by step, to its completion with the precision and rigid consequence of a mathematical problem.

What species of "the authorial vanity" is this? Who shall say? But, however "The Raven" may in fact have been written, we know that most poems are not composed so; the authors' manuscripts, where first drafts are available, at least show us that.

Now to the group of questions with which I am most concerned. It is time to state them, and in somewhat provocative form, so that—whether or not I can do anything toward answering them—the questions themselves may be strikingly posed for your consideration. "What, if anything, have its occasion, origin, motivation, its psychological and compositional history to do with the being of the completed poem?" I am trying to pose this group of questions in such a way that—for readers with the scatter of prepossessions which you, I conjecture, enjoy—a sizable section will reply at once with (a) "Why, *everything*, of course!" and another sizable section with (b) "Why, *nothing*, of course!" and yet another with (c) "Well, it depends, of course!" And I will be happy if those in the last section outnumber those in the first two.

I will try now to bring the problem into better focus in two very different ways: *first*, by sketching some of the reasons that may prompt a thinker to reply with *a* or *b* or *c; secondly*, by taking a short poem[4] for which I have special information—since I wrote it myself—and detailing some of "the elaborate and vacillating crudities of thought . . . the true purposes seized only at the last moment . . . the painful erasures and interpolations," in a word the sort of thing Poe left out of his account of the composition of "The Raven." I am doing this in the hope of making the problem as concrete as possible, so that we may possibly be able to put our fingers on questions about the Poetic Process which concern the Being or Nature of the poem and separate them from questions where "the answer little meaning—little relevancy bore." That is the program.

First, why should anyone answer "Why, *everything* . . . !"? Chiefly—don't you think?—because he takes the questions historically, or psychologically or biologically, as asking "By what steps, through what causal sequences, has the poem come to consist of these words in this order?" If so, the occasion, the motivation, the psychological and compositional history do have *everything* to do with the poem.

Then, why should anyone answer "Why, *nothing* . . . !"? Chiefly—don't you think?—because he takes the question linguistically, or stylistically, as asking: "Given these words in this order, what gives them the powers they have?" Asked so, we can see, I think, that the poet's biography need have nothing to do with the powers of the poem.

Finally, the deliberations and discriminations of those who might answer "It depends . . . !" are more complex to describe. Here come in questions about the kind of poetry it may be and its relations to the rest of the known poetry of the author, to his other utterances, to the literature and colloquial of the period, to possible sources, to echoes, and so forth.

[4] "Harvard Yard in April/April in Harvard Yard," which has now appeared (**329**).

Perhaps I can best summarize these considerations by remarking that the author in his Poetic Process, in his actual work on the poem, is an imaginary construct—a handsome creation of the imagination—based on our understanding of the poem. Such is the normal case, the type situation. We then use this imaginary construct—the poet at work—to help us in further interpretation, and we often forget meanwhile that he is our theoretical invention.

Let me turn now to the unusual, the abnormal case, the nontypical situation when we *have* access through the author's testimony—made from the best of his knowledge and belief—about what went on in the Poetic Process. After looking at this poem and at the privileged commentary or explanation, we may, I hope, be in a better position to ask certain questions about what Literary Analysis can tell us of *what is* and *is not* in the poem.

A poem may be regarded as a suitcase (I regret that my metaphor is so old-fashioned) which the poet may think he packs and the reader may think he unpacks. If they think so,

> They know not well the subtle ways
> I keep, and pass, and turn again.

So, at least, the poem, I think, is entitled to retort.
Here is the poem:

HARVARD YARD IN APRIL
APRIL IN HARVARD YARD

Or rather, here is not the poem but only its title—otherwise I should not tax your patience long. It was, I believe, said of the library at Yale "This is not the library; the library is inside!" In a moment I will be putting on the page what? . . . not the poem itself but its lines. A "poem itself" is a most elusive thing, I suggest, that can never be put on any screen or page. Can we even put the words of a poem on a page? I wonder. We can put a notation for them there. But there are many linguists and the like about these parts these days, and I know better than to use the word lightly.

When I put a notation for the words of my poem on the screen, I shall avail myself of another of my authorial privileges *and read them.* That is, I shall give you, through the auditory channel, another notation: an acoustic notation ?'parallel'? (but we must question this word) to the optical notation. This reading, of course, acts as a most powerful persuader as to how the words are to be taken—much more subtle, penetrating, and comprehensive than the glosses and comments which follow. But, I need hardly point out—or need I?—that an author's reading (like any other reader's) has no authority which does not derive from the poem itself. These readings, these renderings, these vocal interpretations are ways of packing, or finding, in the poem what may or may not be there. The author no more than his reader, I submit, can wish things into his poem—or wish them out. Consider the title. It is supposed to have a great deal to do with the poem. But I (as author) cannot settle that. No more can you (as reader). It is something to be settled between the poem and its title. They settle it; we do not. With its duplications and the time-space shift of "in," and the quasi-personification of April and the seesaw of emphasis, the title was added after the poem was finished. It was added partly to summarize, partly to give warning of, certain balancings within the poem.

Words in titles operate in a peculiar suspension and here we have a name within the title. "Harvard Yard," in particular, and "yard" in more general uses, will be charged very differently for different readers: for alumni of different universities and for American and British usage. For the British a yard is a rather humbly useful, limited, outdoor working space, unlike a garden and with no suggestion—with almost an anti-suggestion—of groves academic or sacred. Echoes of "prison yard" I would expect to be weak, although certain lines in the poem might invite them.

But it is time now for the poem.

HARVARD YARD IN APRIL
APRIL IN HARVARD YARD

> To and fro
> Across the fretted snow
> Figures, footprints, shadows go.
>
> Their python boughs a-sway
> The fountain elms cascade
> In swinging lattices of shade
> Where this or that or the other thought
> Might perch and rest.
>   And rest they ought
> For poise or reach.
> Not all is timely. See, the beech,
> In frosty elephantine skin
> Still winter-sealed, will not begin
> Though silt the alleys hour on hour
> Débris of the fallen flower,
> And other flowery allure
> Lounge sunlit on the Steps and there
> Degrees of loneliness confer.
>
> Lest, lest . . . away!
> You may
> Be lost by May.

The poem began, I recall, as a not-at-all wish-fulfilling dream of spring flight from Harvard—in lines in part contained in the *coda:* something like

> Happiest they
> Who would away
> Who may be gone
> By May.

These and similar tentatives were nursed awhile in traverses through the Yard to and from my office—the Yard's character as a pre-eminent locus of "to-and-fro-ing" (physical and spiritual) not coming into clear consciousness until the poem was almost finished. Only then, argument and counterargument (often not meeting) came to mind as a ground justifying some comparing of the fretted snow with tracked and retracked sheets of paper, together with a feeling that "figures" (line 3) could be numerals. There was earlier an echo from a lecture remark I had made: "The printed words of a poem are only its footprints on paper."

> To and fro
> Across the fretted snow
> Figures, footprints, shadows go.

"Shadows," on the other hand, in actual composition looked forward from the first to "shade" (line 6). Afterward, as confirmation and support, I thought of de la Mare's

> When less than even a shadow came
> And stood within the room ... ,

also of

> Coming events cast their shadows before them ... ,

and of T. S. Eliot's **(110)**

> The lengthened shadow of a man
> Is history, said Emerson.

and, beyond all, of F. H. Bradley's **(37,** p. 14**)** "The shades nowhere speak without blood and the ghosts of Metaphysic accept no substitute. They reveal themselves only to that victim whose life they have drained and to converse with shadows he himself must become a shade."

How soon the day-by-day doings of the trees with the coming of spring began to belong to the poem I cannot clearly recall: "fountain" from my very first sight of American elms had seemed the obvious descriptive word; but only after 21 years and through the poem did I learn it is just that, the obvious descriptive word.

Python boughs: in and for the poem the peculiar writhe of boughs, at once sinuous and angular, emphasized itself. Early drafts played with "snakey," but, with "a-sway," "cascade," and "shade" present, another vowel seemed desirable, and since "lithe" and "writhe" were highly active in attempts to describe what was striking me, "python" felt final.

A-sway: the slighter motions of bare boughs are more visible before leafage comes, and in spring, when the eye is watching for every advance, there is more occasion than in winter to observe them. Winter gales agitate them, but with spring breezes they seem to stir of their own will as an outcome of the mounting sap.

Cascade: the thickening fringes and tassels of budding leaf and flower on outermost pendent sprays were green or golden drops defining the outline of the fountain's fall; their "shade," although thin, softening and cooling the glare of sunlight on the snow.

Perch: comparison of thoughts with birds seems inevitable. Trumbull Stickney's grand lines, for example:

> Sir, say no more. Within me 'tis as if
> The green and climbing eyesight of a cat
> Crawled near my mind's poor birds.

Timely: when thoughts turn to trees, in academic groves at least, Mother Eve and her Tree of Knowledge are not far off. I would like to think that the poem contained originally a suggestion that the Tree (python boughs) was itself the Tempter, but that was an afterthought.

Silt the alleys: "silt" proposed itself as suggesting sand—product of breakup, unlubricative, arid, unfruitful; "alleys," channels for to-and-fro-ing, worn into grooves, out of true, and clogged by the grit of work.

Débris: hourly wastage of new, ungerminated, uncared for ideas, which may choke the channels; the wreckage and waste of "essential omission"—to use Whitehead's phrase—the saving neglect, which strains (and trains) the academic.

Allure: a lure is an apparatus used to recall hawks, a bunch of feathers within which, during its training, the hawk finds its food. Catachrestically, it can be both a snare and a mark to be shot at. The young scholar might be glad to borrow Cupid's bow to use on selected members of Radcliffe who at this season begin to decorate the chapel steps in their spring fabrics.

Degrees of loneliness: very different from the degrees that are conferred on those very steps at commencement. The line consciously echoed Donne's "The Extasie" (l. 44): "Defects of loneliness controls"— "Degrees of loneliness confer."

Lost: in terms not only of the allure but of examination results and the perplexities of study. The coda uses, as I have mentioned, what was the temporal germ of the poem.

Now from such detail, what, if anything, of general import can be extracted? How far can knowledge of what went on in the process of composition, however faithfully or tediously reported, serve as evidence of what is or is not *in the poem?*

You will recognize, I believe, that all this is chiefly a device—somewhat elaborate, I grant—for directing our attention to this tricky phrase "in the poem." If you can bear it, let us look through this little collection of samples of things I must aver *were* in the process of composition and ask of some of them whether and how they may not also be IN THE POEM.

First, this impulse—spring fever, nostalgia for the beyond, itchy-footed-ness—what I describe as a "not-at-all wish fulfilling dream of spring flight" out of which the poem started and with which, in the coda, it ends: if any of this feeling has got in, it will not be—will it?—simply because it is talked about, mentioned, or even, in any obvious sense, implied—as by

> away!
> You may
> Be lost by May.

We plainly have to, and do, make a distinction between the overt or manifest content—the inventory of items that should not be omitted in a paraphrase—and what is truly operative in a poem. We would all agree that things may be mentioned and even insisted upon in a poem and yet remain perfectly inert, helpless, and noncontributive. (We should not, however—should we?—conclude that because they are inert (mere dead matter) they are therefore *always* unnecessary and better away. They may serve as catalysts or supporting tissue.)

This distinction between what is overt or manifest and what is operative —whether overt or not—is dangerous, of course. It lets us allege things about poems and deny things about them too easily. It opens the doors, typically, to allegations about the Unconscious.

For example, a friend to whom I had shown this poem and who had liked it—which pleased me because he is an admirable and well-recognized poet—was disappointed by and most suspicious, I believe, of the annotations I have been offering you. They did not, for him, contain the right sort of revelations of hidden passions in me. Alas! Is it any good my saying that *although there may be that sort of thing in the poem* there was nothing of the sort anywhere in the process of composing it. There may be murder in a poem without the author himself being either murdered or a murderer. But, no, once certain dealings with the Unconscious are on the tapis, the best-informed denial turns into additional evidence.

To talk of evidence, what sorts of evidence are really available for the presence or absence of X (whatever it may be) in the poem? This, to me, is the central question, as important as it is difficult to answer. And it is my hope that I may find support for the view that the best, if not the only, sorts of evidence are fundamentally linguistic—have to do with relations of words and phrases to one another—and furthermore (to retort with suspicion to suspicion) that evidence from a poet's alleged biography or psychology is seldom competent in any honest court.

To return to my example, if there *is* spring fever in this poem, it is there as outcome of a very complex set of mutual influences among its lines: in their movement as far as that is a derivative from their meaning, and in their meaning, in and through such things as the optative "might" in

> When this or that or the other thought
> *Might* perch and rest

in and through the fatigued flaccidity of "this or that or the other thought," in and through the alliterative pattern of

> perch and rest.
> And rest they ought
> For poise or reach.

in and through the subjunctives following "though"

> silt   lounge   confer.

Mind you, I am painfully aware that it is easy enough to allege such things: to pick this or that out of the inconceivably complex fabric of an utterance and say that here are more particularly the conveyers of this or that impulse and part of the poem. It is quite another matter to *prove* anything of the sort. We do not, I imagine, even know what the criteria of good proof in such matters would be. We can, of course, consent—agree to find them there—but that falls far short of proof.

On the other hand, the sorts of agreement which I am pointing to with this word "consent" are indispensable. Proof in these matters, if we ever attain it, will be by consent rather than by compulsion. Moreover, it is through such agreement about how words work together—the minute particulars of their cooperations—that discussion, analysis, and criticism must proceed. When two readers *differ*, they can discover and locate and describe their differences of interpretation only thanks to their consent together on other points.

Here let me touch on a misconception which, nowadays, I think—in my experience as a teacher—frustrates more potentially good readers of poetry than any other. To the word "shadow" (and "shade") a few minutes ago I appended a little string of quotations from de la Mare, a proverb, T. S. Eliot, and F. H. Bradley. These were uses of "shadow" that the Poetic Process considered in fixing—although not in forming—its third line "Footprints, figures, shadows go." But, of course, of course—I mean it *should* be of course—no sort of identification of these particular quotes and references is required for the understanding of the line. They belong to the Poetic Process, not to the Literary Analysis. None the less, Literary Analysis, in trying to bring out the force of a word such as "shadow" in such a setting, very often finds it necessary to adduce a number of such other uses. Poetry cannot and does not use such words as though they had never been used before or as though they had only been used in one way. And the teaching of the reading of poetry to students who (somehow or other) have read little poetry anyhow, and very little of it reflectively, does have to play the part of a leisurely dictionary and acquaint students with "this and that and the other" relevant use.

This is a characteristic part nowadays of the technique of Literary Analysis. It is parallel to much that is done for the other arts, a necessary way of helping words to mean more nearly all they should. But,— and here is where the frustrating misconception I spoke of comes in—far too many students somehow suppose that *they*, as readers, ought somehow to have known and thought of just those instances of the use of the word that the analyst has found convenient and illuminating to adduce for his purpose. So Literary Analysis gives rise, by accident as it were, to a set of unreal difficulties and imaginary obstacles quite parallel to those we would have if we supposed that to read aright we must somehow divine all the uses of a word that may have beguiled and guided a poet in the manifold choices of Poetic Process.

This sort of avoidable frustration comes up especially when a Literary Analyst—to bring out the force of a line—sets, say, a passage of Plato beside it. He does not mean necessarily that the poet in the Poetic Process was thinking of the passage, or that the poet need know the passage or even have heard of Plato. All he means is that in the line, in the cooperations among its words, there is active something which can also be exemplified (and often can best be exemplified) in the Plato passage. In brief, he is using a historical reference technique to make what is a linguistic and not a historical point. The "Platonism" he is concerned with is something which is *in the language*.

You remember Emerson's farmer to whom he lent a Republic. The farmer returned it saying "That man has a lot of my ideas!" It was true— if we will allow that the farmer's ideas are the ideas offered him, in some way, through the semantic structure of his language. My ideas are, in a deep sense, *in* my language—in the relations between words which guide me in their use. I have to admit, though, that these phrases, "*in* the poem" and "*in* the language," persuade me that I very imperfectly understand this innocent-seeming little word "in."

Let us look now at another example of relevant relations among words, equally active this time in Poetic Process and Literary Analysis. Among the factors operative in choosing "python boughs a-sway"—in place of, say, "snakey boughs a-sway"—in line 4 were the marginal presence, as I mentioned, of the words "lithe" and "writhe." I may well have thought of "withe" and "scythe," too; and there would also be the less perfect rhyme "alive." For "snakey," on the other hand, there was no such morphemic support; on the contrary: "shakey"—no good at all; "break"—no, no; "fake"—oh, horrors! So "python boughs" it had to be.

I take this as my type specimen of mutual influences among words of the order that is most conspicuously exemplified in rhyme: similarities in sound introducing and reinforcing relevancies of meaning. "Python" was not a rhyme word here, but where rhyme is in use other words than rhyme words do often have their susceptibility to influence from their rhyme field increased.

Now all this, with many other mutual influences among words which need never come into clear consciousness, belongs alike to Poetic Process and to Literary Analysis. In choosing his words, the poet is allowing himself to be guided in ways in which (he hopes) his reader may also be guided. The reader, in turn, may be following—in his awareness of the meaning, in his analysis, and in his appraisal—very closely in the footsteps of the Poetic Process. But the important thing, as I see it, is that both are under the control of the language, both are subject to their understanding of it.

Contrast, now, this happy and healthy condition with the sad state of a reader who is trying to guess—he knows not how—about what some poet at some precise, but unidentified, minute of his mortal journey may have been undergoing.

Of course, we all know that much in criticism and commentary which seems to be discussing the poet and reads as if it were about what he was doing as he wrote, *is not* really about that sort of thing at all. No, it is about what the poem has done and is doing to the critic—the critic who is inventing and projecting a poet's mental processes as a convenient way of talking about something else.

Mr. T. S. Eliot remarked—in his BBC talk, "Virgil and the Christian World"—that for a poet "his lines may be only a way of talking about himself without giving himself away." Well, a great deal of criticism which looks like microscopic biography—a minute by minute, line by line, blow by blow account of the poet's battle with his poem—is no more than the *critic's* way of talking about *himself* without giving the critic away either. Thus a reviewer will quote a line: "One wondered whether the loaded earth . . ." and go on to wonder: "Did one (i.e., the poet, who should be *I*, not *one*) really wonder that, or did one think one ought to wonder something?" This looks like an almost insane attempt to nose into another person's private reflections, but it is not. It is merely the reviewer's way of trying to indicate that the line does not seem very good to him.

Sometimes, however, the biographic assumption hardens: "Even when the pioneer work was completed anybody attempting a fresh critical appraisal of Wordsworth's poetry was faced with some dispiriting machete work if he was to establish the biographical detail to which the criticism would have to be referred."

A *fresh critical appraisal* of poetry *having to be referred* to *biographical detail:* doesn't that make you feel a little uncomfortable? Suppose some barrelful of papers were to roll out of some attic in Stratford-on-Avon. Could it really force us to revise our critical appraisal of *King Lear* or could another batch of Dead Sea Rolls or Scrolls demote the poetry in *The Book of Job?* Personally, I would be extremely sorry to learn one more fact about either author. And I confess that, if I were to be granted such opportunities in the next world, I would as lief *not* meet Homer as any man.

To be more serious, if possible: what I am hoping to suggest is that some of the criticism of Literary Analysis which seems so often nowadays to be pegged to the poet's personality would be more profitable if it discussed the linguistic grounds—the powers in the words and movement of the poem—which make the reader invent and project spiritual characteristics and spiritual adventures for the poet. In short, I have a hope that in time this amalgam of the gossip column and the whodunit will become a less dominant ingredient in criticism. Poetry is so much more than a source for low-down on the lives of poets. To let a thing of the seeming scale of *Ulysses* become chiefly a ground for speculations about Joyce's sexual history—is that not rather a sad comedown from more important sorts of concern with literature? I know, of course, that to an individual nothing can seem more important than his own sexual history. But are we not in some danger of forgetting that general communications should be about matters of general interest?

To take as a minute, a tiny, innocuous, example the second line of "Harvard Yard in April":

> To and fro
> Across the *fretted snow*

fret: eat; eat away; consume; torture by gnawing; gnaw at; wear away by friction; chafe; roughen; cause to ripple, as a breeze frets the surface of water; tease; vex; worry . . . (OED).

Over this "fretted snow" a reader could, if he cared, *either invent* a particularly disgruntled, impatient, spring-fever-beset author who projects his own discomfort even on the very snow, and so on, *or* let the word "fretted" itself—as a highly charged meeting point of various meanings—come to livelier life. The dictionary spreads the meanings out for us. But I am thinking of how the word can strike us before we separate such things—if, indeed, apart from dictionaries, we ever do. The dictionary adds a comment apropos of "gnaw at" which pleased me when I saw it. It says "Now only of small animals." A mouse, I suppose, can fret a bit of cheese (as a fret saw does plywood); but when a grizzly bear chaws up a man, that is not fretting. I liked that; it seems to offer my line "Across the fretted snow" a sort of bonus of meaning I had not been clearly enough aware of. It turned the people who had been leaving all those tracks on the snow into only small animals after all and gave a diminishing-glass sharpness to the scene.

But my point is that "fretted," if it has this power, gets it from its relations to other words—as a node of possibilities of meaning—not from the fact that an author (me in this case) had been pumping petulance into it. No matter how fevered, or how cool, the author may be, he cannot do anything with the word unless the language lets him, unless it is willing to work for him so: "For words it is not poets make up poems."

Perhaps I have overlabored this plea for the emancipation of Literary Analysis from biographic explorations or conjectures. I realize that it will not be welcome everywhere: it looks like an attempt to put a great many people out of their jobs. I would like before I close, to turn to another aspect of contemporary literary analysis—an increasing tendency to read meanings into poems at random, regardless of linguistic limits. I have a small but choice exhibit of awful warnings to show you—all written by people who were at the time of their writing doomed of their own choice to hard labor for the rest of their natural lives—no, I mean for the rest of their employable lives—teaching helpless children in classrooms how to be discerning readers.

The first two lines of Mr. Eliot's "A Cooking Egg" read:

> Pipit sate upright in her chair
> Some distance from where I was sitting.

There has been, as you know, some discussion among critics about what sort of a person Pipit may best be supposed to be *in the interests of the poem as a whole.* Views have ranged from taking her as a retired nurse or governess to taking her as a Bloomsbury *demi-vierge.* The discussion came to a climax in an appeal from Dr. E. M. W. Tillyard, Master of Jesus, to the poet to explain the poem and set our minds at rest, an appeal to which Mr. Eliot, very wisely I think, has not responded.

However, one of my students, being faced with the problem, bethought her of the dictionary. There she found grounds for this:

> Pipit sate upright in her chair . . .

According to Webster's New Collegiate Dictionary, "sate" may mean "to satisfy or gratify to the full a desire" or "gratify to the point of weariness or loathing, satiate." Pipit has obviously satisfied the "I" for she sits upright, at a distance; a state of satiation has occurred.

It is an interesting point in *linguistics* to consider why we are sure that words in such an instance do not work like that.

Or consider this. The last verse of Donne's "The Extasie" reads

> And if some lover, such as wee,
>   Have heard this dialogue of one,
> Let him still marke us, he shall see
>   Small change, when we'are to bodies gone.

To bodies gone: there is an ambiguity in the phrase; is it "gone away from our ecstasy to our bodies" or "gone (in respect) to bodies"—gone entirely away from them? I think this ambiguity is operative.

Another comment on these same last three words of the poem:

To bodies gone: "to" may be a play on words: if read aloud and thought of as "two," it signifies the sacrifice of spiritual union necessary for two people to indulge in physical love.

Observe that both these teachers-to-be feel free to ignore the rest of the line:

> he shall see
> Small change, when we'are . . . .

Their prepossessions enable them to find a meaning accurately opposite to "I must not say 'that which Donne put there'—(I don't know anything about that) but 'that which the rest of the poem expressly requires.'"

Compare another commentator who, perhaps, moves toward the point—but by what strange means!

Let him still marke us: the word "still" can mean "without moving" and the sense of the line is changed to "let him notice that we are quiet and motionless."

Are you completely worn out? Or may I show you another double right-angle swivel?

An important movement in Coleridge's "Dejection: An Ode" begins

> Hence, viper thoughts, that coil around my mind
>   Reality's dark dream!
> I turn from you, and listen to the wind
>   Which long has rav'd unnotic'd.

The poet retunes himself by *turning* inward to his soul . . . . He is coming through a storm which has made him hear the tune. His horror upon noticing makes him *turn* from the world of the senses and the outside.

Lastly, the last verse of Marvell's "The Garden" opens with the lines:

> How well the skilful Gardner drew
> Of flow'rs and herbes this Dial new

First, the word "well" draws its meaning from a pun. It seems to mean how carefully constructed the world is. It would seem to me that "well" has the connotation of a source of water, a deep hole in the ground. That is, nature is a well which has great depth and from which deep and eternal meanings and values can be drawn.

All very true, no doubt, but not anything that the semantic texture of the language will allow the two lines to mean or that the rest of the poem will invite us to understand here. Surely a teacher-to-be should have a better sense than this of what is and is not admissible in an interpretation.

What can have been happening to cause this alarming condition, this reckless disregard of all the means by which language defends itself? I have not been exaggerating; such things are far too frequent in the English studies of those who are likely to become teachers. My instances could be duplicated by every teacher of teachers. Some essential control over interpretation seems to have been relaxed.

At an occasion on which so many authorities in linguistics, criticism, and related studies are gathered together, it seemed appropriate to offer evidence that their work may have more immediate, practical relevance to education than is sometimes supposed.

Comments to Part One

LOTZ: I would like to ask Mr. Richards two questions, if I may, concerning the title of his poem. Is it to be regarded as a metric text like the rest of the poem, or as a sample of prose? And why is the quality of the title so much better as it stands than if we reverse the two phrases and read "April in Harvard Yard/Harvard Yard in April"?

RICHARDS: Well, now, let me see whether I can remember about these things—they meant something. [Laughter.] Following Jakobson's electrifying contrast between a rapt soul and the crypt analyst, in which of my capacities—as rapt soul or crypt analyst—am I to reply? It seems to me I must use a little history here. I think I called it, after the poem was written, something very flat-footed indeed: "Harvard Yard in Spring." That wasn't anything more than a label and then something made me feel that more ought to be done, and against a lot of critical resistance by people who had got attached to "Harvard Yard in Spring" (that always happens; any emendation, I think, always meets resistance from people who at all approve of the first form), I tried this. But the question of which phrase should come first, I think, is crucial. It seems to me unquestionably in the right order now, but reverse it and you begin to analyze and here's where the crypt analyst raps the rapt soul. The crypt analyst comes forward and invents, I'm quite sure, as much as he finds. "Harvard Yard in April"—well, Harvard Yard is a queer block of speech. It is an awkward name—"Harvard Yard." I am perhaps haunted by the number of people I have met in different parts of the world who pronounce Harvard in other ways. There is some tension around that. I have very good friends who ought to know much better and who have visited the place yet go on saying "How are things at Harvard?" [Laughter.] Harvard Yard—how monotonous! When it recurs it is much more monotonous. It has a finality because of its having been initial. There is a great contrast, it seems to me, between "Harvard Yard" and "April." "Harvard Yard in April" is just a temporal and locating phrase, no more. But when we reverse it it seems to me that April, in slight personification, has changed its function. It is no longer mere location. It's what she's up to, and April has become a she instead of a month. What she's up to in Harvard Yard has something to do with the nostalgia of the persona, the mask for the speaker. Well, that's the best I can do.

JAKOBSON: What is repulsive in the suggested inversion "April in Harvard Yard/Harvard Yard in April"? The title of Richards' poem displays a clearcut metrical integrity: it begins and ends with a word stress and consists of two hexasyllabic parts, each with an initial and two further stresses. All six stressed syllables of the title are separated from each other, in four instances by a single unstressed syllable and in one case by two. The whole is both opened and closed by the same leading phrase "Harvard Yard." An inverted order of the two sentences would abolish their rhythmic continuity by a clash of two stressed syllables " . . . Yard/Harvard . . . ": such an inversion would destroy the symmetry between the stressed onset and end of the title and its penult stress would discord with the final stress in all subsequent lines of the poem. The figurative, metonymic tinge of the sequence "April in Harvard Yard" is particularly palpable when preceded by the nonfigurative, literal meaning of the reverse construction "Harvard Yard in April."

PART TWO

Style in Folk Narrative

Richard M. Dorson

Oral Styles
of American Folk Narrators

RICHARD M. DORSON

Since folklore became a field of learning in the first half of the nine-teenth century, collectors have given their primary attention to the dis-tribution and origin of texts. Especially for the folktale has the pattern set by the Grimm brothers in their *Kinder- und Hausmärchen* been endlessly repeated, a volume of collected tales, somewhat "improved" for the reading public, with the human sources suppressed. At best, an appendix will provide a bare list of names and ages of the storytellers. The great fallacy in this approach is the divorce of texts from the folk artists who alone give them life. One notable exception is Russia, where A. F. Hil-ferding (1831–1872) established the principle in folklore studies of centering attention on the *byliny* performer, and furnishing the maximum information about his biography, repertoire, and creative talent (**386**, p. 128; cf. **194**, pp. 631–656). But Russian folklore science, now propagandizing the class struggle, has failed in this one commendable respect to influence Western folklorists. Rarely does an article appear in Western publications like James H. Delargy's "The Gaelic Story-Teller," singling out individual narrators for discussion (**88**; subsequent considerations of Gaelic story-tellers appear in **104, 260**). We find occasional descriptions of storytellers by the excellent British folklorists of the late nineteenth century; Hartland discussed "The Art of Story-Telling" in general terms, and Campbell of Islay gave pleasing detail about his Highland bards (**152**, ch. 1; **56**, Introduction). Recently Bowra in his lucid examination of *Heroic Poetry* (**36**) devoted considerable attention to techniques of composition and presentation used by folk poets in scattered cultures who recite verse narratives of stirring adventure.

The fact remains that folklorists have only incidentally and sporadically concerned themselves with problems of folk-narrative style. Archer Taylor has said (**409**) that we know less about the structural details than

about almost any other aspect of the folktale. Stith Thompson in survey-
ing our knowledge of folktale style reported (**412**, pp. 449–461) mainly on
problems still to be studied. Olrik's general laws of epic style are one
positive accomplishment and appear to cover all forms of oral narration:
the oral tale is simply told, it contains no subplot, it opposes a good and
an evil character, it contains much repetition, two persons only appear in
a scene, the weakest character triumphs (**412**, pp. 455–456, from **299**).
When it comes to any discussion of individual storytelling styles, however,
Thompson must turn to the Russian folklorist Azadovsky and his analysis
of three principal types of raconteurs: the specialist in the obscene, the
precisionist anxious to relate every detail of the tradition accurately, and
the embroiderer who fills in the structure of the tale with the realism and
pathos of everyday life (**412**, pp. 451–453, from **11**).

Anthropologists have infrequently looked at myths and songs of nonliterate peoples for their qualities of style as well as their ethnographic
content. Boas, for all his concern with tales as a mirror of culture, did
call attention to their formal and aesthetic elements (**33**, pp. 491–502).[1]
His student Reichard analyzed "The Style of Coeur d'Alene Mythology"
in terms of plot, action, motivation, characterization, and stylistic devices,
although she used only two informants and admitted that the Coeur
d'Alene were not especially adept storytellers (**327**, pp. 5–35). Usually the
anthropologists comment on general characteristics of tribal style rather
than on the creative role of individual narrators. One difficulty, of course,
for the anthropological student of style is the translation barrier.[2] In my
own fieldwork with bilingual Ojibwa, Potawatomi, and Sioux, I have
collected fluent English narratives in which the Indian storytellers act as it
were as their own interpreters. In such texts, however, we should study
acculturated rather than native style. This field experience strengthened
my conviction that only certain gifted individuals, whether Indians or
anyone else, are the storytellers, and hence that oral style should be
considered individually as well as tribally.

The American folklorist faces a considerably different field situation
from that of the European folklorist or the anthropologist. They confront
a unified culture where storytelling is ritually formalized and transmits a
stable body of narratives which furnish cultural sanctions and aesthetic
satisfactions (**83**). American civilization has produced informal yarns and

---

[1] A linguistic approach and references to other stylistic studies of North American
Indian tribes are given in **437**, notes 3 to 7, p. 149.

[2] Reichard writes (**327**, p. 25), "The story *Cricket Rides Coyote* owes its humor to the
fact that combinations of comic sounds are repeated until the story becomes side-
splitting. This is only one of many examples which shows how impossible it is to carry
over the spirit of the tale into a language like English, which has no machinery for the
expression of such an effect."

anecdotes and tall tales and personal experiences, rather than elaborate creation myths or heroic sagas or night-long wonder tales. We cannot speak of *the* culture but rather of a score of ethnic, regional, and occupational subcultures which form the chief targets of the folklorist. Storytellers and folktales are less easily spotted in the United States than in Europe or among nonliterate cultures. Are jokes and anecdotes folktales? Can a true storyteller flourish among the mass media? Yet the very complexity of American civilization makes possible a broader inquiry than is possible in a simpler culture. We can search out storytellers who represent a wide variety of folk groups, from tradition-directed pockets to other-directed societies in American life.

Two younger American folklorists, Jansen and Ball, have recently published provocative papers on the problem of folk style. Jansen asks for a distinction between folk aesthetic and art aesthetic, and for proper recognition of the artistic folk performer above his ordinary fellows who merely remember or half-remember (**206**). In view of the vital living context of folk narration, Jansen even suggests a classification of verbal performance, based on the degrees of casualness and formality in the storytelling situation (**205**). Ball continues this plea with a demand for good collecting of good performers, to portray in full dimension the "dynamic relationship among style, story, teller, audience, and culture." The culture, the tale, and the teller each contribute to the style of a given text (**12**).

Folk aesthetic does indeed differ from art aesthetic, but still a student of oral narration can borrow some concepts from literary criticism. He, too, is scrutinizing a text and considering its qualities of structure and language. However, the texts he handles are not composed by their speakers or singers, and they do not possess a constant form. The text is in continual flux, even when repeated by the same narrator. Yet the gulf is not so enormous as it appears; literary texts too undergo revision, the folk narrator like an author composes within a tradition, and folklore and literature continually feed each other themes and plots and characters and phrases (cf. **386**, pp. 10–14). A crucial difference lies in the audience; the writer writes for a private reader, the teller speaks to visible listeners. Before he sets his creation in type, the author can prune and polish and perfect, but the narrator delivers his piece as the words pour from his mind, and even though he may have told the tale often, when they are literally recorded many imperfections appear—false starts, circuitous sentences, tangled grammar. Such faults little affect the response of the listening circle, for the speech of first-rate folk narrators is fresh, clear, and vivid, and the flaws that may vex the pampered reader vanish in the excitement of the living text. An added physical dimension enters into the elements of folk style; the narrator employs voice and body as well as words to dramatize his text. Facial expression, hand gestures, intonation and inflection, and the whole human presence mold the recitation. The audience, too, conditions the performance, and so do external factors of time and place. The critic of folk style must necessarily also be the collector-observer, and if he invites others to discuss the style of his narrators, he is bound to furnish facts about the manner of their delivery, along with the texts of their tales.

NARRATORS IN THE FIELD

In the present paper I propose first to discuss the styles of seven folk narrators from whom I have collected sizable bodies of tales, and who reflect five storytelling traditions within American civilization. They include two Southern-born Negroes whom I met in Michigan, J. D. Suggs and John Blackamore;[3] two Yankee lobster fishermen from Maine, Jim Alley and Curt Morse; and from Michigan's Upper Peninsula, a Polish immigrant and a Swedish immigrant who had worked as miners, lumberjacks, and farm hands, Joe Woods and Swan Olson; and an auto mechanic of French-Canadian background, Burt Mayotte. All qualify as outstanding narrators, from a folklore collector's point of view; they told tales fluently and graphically. For each I will give some biographical and repertoire data and discuss a characteristic text.

The Narrators

James Douglas Suggs was my number-one informant. In the course of my visits to him in 1952 and 1953 in Calvin, an all-Negro farming township in Cass County, Michigan, he related 170 folk narratives and sang a score of folksongs. Sixty-five years old when I met him, Suggs had grown up in northern Mississippi and roamed widely about the country in various occupations. Although only a day laborer with ten children to feed at the end of his life, he possessed uncontrollable high spirits and delighted in talk and company.

John Blackamore was thirty years old when I found him in Benton Harbor, Michigan, in 1952, where he had lived for nine years after moving north from Kentucky and Missouri. He was adapting himself successfully to Northern business ways, working in a foundry, driving his own truck, and renting rooms. Stolid and burly, he gave no outward appearance of

---

[3] In **99**, ch. 2, I discussed individual styles of six Negro folk narrators, including Suggs and Blackamore. Here I wish to contrast them with narrators from other subcultures.

possessing the narrative gift, and yet he could recite lengthy stories for hours on end.

In the little town of Jonesport and neighboring Machias high upon the Maine coast I met two raconteurs in July, 1956, who had spent their lives as lobstermen in the coastal waters. James Alley at seventy-six scraped out a living knitting heads for lobster traps, shucking clams, and delivering papers. He lived on a tiny road known as Alley's Lane where a number of related Alley families had moved from Head Harbor Island in the bay nearly half a century before. James had low status in the community and was referred to as "Dirty Jim" from his seedy appearance and alleged immorality, nor was he known as a storyteller. But I found him sensitive and sharp-minded and an inexhaustible fountain of anecdotal tales.

By contrast, the reputation of "Uncle" Curt Morse as a humorist and a character had spread through the county. Although he lived at the end of a country road in Kennebec overlooking a scenic cove, he spent every afternoon lolling along the main street of Machias, the county seat five miles away, and he frequently visited in Jonesport, where indeed I first met him. Curt at seventy did a little clamming, but principally he enjoyed his local fame as wag and entertainer. Curt had never left Maine.

Joe Woods migrated to the United States in 1904 at the age of twenty-one, from Csanok, province of Galicia, in Austrian Poland, where he was born Joseph Wojtowicz. He had traveled through many of the northern states, working in the woods and on the harvest, but he lived most of his years in Michigan's Upper Peninsula where the iron mines offered fairly steady work. Mine dampness gave him rheumatism, and he was invalided from 1930 to 1936, in the state mental hospital at Newberry. This fact may have led to local talk of his being a teller of crazy stories, the scent that led me to him in Crystal Falls in 1946, and back again in 1947. But I found him perfectly clear-headed and a narrator of well-known European tales.

Swan Olson also came from the Old Country, in his case Sweden. I met him accidentally in a barbershop in Negaunee in the Upper Peninsula, where I heard him recounting an incident about being served fly pie. Though a gentle old man of seventy-three in 1946, Swan bristled with experiences of his life in America, working on farms, in lumber camps, and down in the mines. He still worked, as mason, plasterer, bricklayer, and carpenter. At seventeen he had left Stockholm, in 1890, and taken his first job in Litchfield, Minnesota.

Burt Mayotte was born in Michigan but retained his French-Canadian identity. One branch of his family had come from Alsace-Lorraine. His grandfather was a pioneer in Keweenaw County, the lonely finger of the Upper Peninsula thrusting into Lake Superior and a preserve for

French-Canadians come down from the lumberwoods of Quebec. Burt was an auto mechanic at Sault Ste. Marie when I met him in 1946, a wiry, energetic youngish man under forty.

Traditions

1. The Southern Negro tradition of Suggs and Blackamore is more casual than Negro recitation in the West Indies, where the formal style of African storytelling persists. There we find, say in Beckwith's collection from Jamaica, ending formulas and cante-fable structure (songs included within the tales), which are only fragmentarily preserved in the United States. The animal tales so prevalent in the West Indies cross over to the mainland, but they blend with tales based in slavery, supernatural experiences borrowed from the Whites, American anecdotes and tall tales, and European folktales. In spite of these diversified sources, a corpus of Southern Negro tales can be recognized; the same tales are collected again and again from Negro storytellers. This wide range of story materials permits different selections of content by individual tellers. For instance, one informant may specialize in brief, punch-ending jests, and another may indulge in extended, circumstantial relations.

2. European immigrants coming to the United States have brought with them the fictional folktales made famous by the brothers Grimm and known as Märchen or fairy tales. These complex and elaborate tales of wonder, adventure, and magic possess substantial structures and special stylistic features. The long tale will often be divided into equal and symmetrical episodes—say in the Cinderella-type narratives where the three sisters perform identical tasks in succession—which are sometimes linked by interrogations addressed to the listeners. Märchen furnished entertainment for the unlettered peasantry of medieval Europe, and deal with kings, castles, treasure, ogres, witches, and lucky youths of low birth. Joe Woods provides a case, rarely recorded by collectors, of the immigrant relating Märchen in his new tongue. Although the Celtic people of Ireland and Scotland have a wealth of fairy tales, the English are nearly barren of Märchen and contributed few to America.

3. Along the Maine coast, where an isolated Yankee stock gains a bare living from the lobsters, herring, and clams in the coastal waters, a homogeneous culture rich in folklore persists. A good deal of indigenous American yarnspinning flourishes here, drawing its materials from supernaturalism of sea and land and the humor of native character. The tall tale, the local anecdote, the marine legend abound, and specialists can be found for each vein. Here the natural requirements of storytelling under American conditions shape the style, rather than inherited narrative conventions. These requirements are keyed to the informal, gregarious

group; hence the tale must be relatively brief, conversational, topical, and pointed toward laughter or shock. Even Old World plots, when they turn up, will be trimmed to this mold. Curt Morse and Jim Alley yarn within this tradition.

4. In the Upper Peninsula of Michigan a special form of humorous dialect story has developed from the close proximity of foreign-born and native-born Americans. The sons of the immigrants mimic the daily mistakes in grammar, pronunciation, and vocabulary made by adults forced to acquire English as a belated second tongue. At the same time they ridicule the cultural shock and mishaps of the newcomer, who becomes a stock fool character. In the Peninsula several types of comic dialect are found, chiefly the French, Finnish, and Cornish, and secondarily the Swedish and Italian, reflecting the nationality groups of the area. Each neighborly town in the Peninsula vaunts at least one "dialectician" of repute, who entertains at lodge meetings and church socials, and most of the American-born Peninsularites can tell at least a few dialect jokes. Walter Gries, a well-known mining company executive, has told his dialect stories throughout the state in after-dinner speeches and at high school graduations. The linguistic features of each dialect are based on the relation of the parent tongue to English and the common mistakes that ensue when a speaker of that language attempts to master English. Mimetic ability is at a premium, and this extends to facial expression and hand gestures. However, length may vary from a two-line joke to an adventure of several thousand words. Dialect stories appear throughout the United States wherever a nationality group lives in close contact with American-born generations. Danish dialect tales have been recorded from Ephraim, Utah; in the Southwest the Spanish-Mexican dialect blossoms, in Pennsylvania the German, in big cities the Jewish.

5. The stories of Swan Olson are not usually classed as folktales. They purport to be accurate autobiographical experiences, albeit of a hair-raising nature. As oral narratives they interest the folklorist, and they appear to represent a pattern of storytelling especially fertile along the frontier, or in communities like the Upper Peninsula with frontier characteristics. Here exists a society reminiscent of Heroic Age cultures, where individual strength and daring are the admired virtues, and heroes boast of their feats. In the Peninsula I encountered other autobiographical saga men like Swan, whose derring-do, physical prowess, and violent humor echo *The Narrative of David Crockett*, which rests on an oral, heroic, autobiographical base. The successful personal saga evokes belief, suspense, and admiration. On examination its episodes show resemblances to tall tales and hero legends.

Individual Repertoires and Deliveries

Suggs told me about 170 narratives during my visits with him over the course of two years.[4] They covered every theme of modern Negro tale telling: speaking animals (23), Biblical and moral lessons (14), Old Marster and clever John (10), hoodoos and fortune telling (11), spirits and hants (10), social protest (5), exaggeration (15), Irishmen (5), preachers (13), humorous anecdotes (10), with a scattering of migratory fictions, folk history, and supernatural beliefs not easy to classify. In his varied life he had worked for a year with a touring "minister" (minstrel) show and still retained some instinct of the stage performer. Suggs possessed an infectious good humor and ebullience, which spilled over into his narration; he talked with animation and gusto, and laughed from tip to toe at his jest, or mine. Yet he had his somber side, too, and spoke of occult mysteries with solemn conviction. Whichever kind of tale he related, he projected himself completely into the situation, sometimes changing from third to first person in the course of the relation, as he identified himself with the chief actor. His animation compensated the Northern listener bothered by his thick Mississippi Delta dialect. A sweeping range of inflection enabled Suggs to simulate the shrieking woman at revival meeting with a high-pitched electric shout, and in a breath he was back to the rumbling tones of the preacher. Telling a personal experience with a ghost train, he conveyed the mood in short, staccato sentences with his volume turned low. Two special features of a Suggs rendition were his tendency to recapitulate the tale, or its final episodes, in a swift, excited summary immediately upon its completion; and his inclination to moralize upon the story, sometimes even adding an incident from his own personal knowledge which confirmed the lesson of the piece.

John Blackamore told me 29 tales during the same period I was collecting from Suggs (**101**). They included humorous animal, Old Marster, and Irishmen and preacher narratives, but no supernaturalism. His texts are exceptionally long, a good deal longer than usual variants of the same tale type. Several of his stories reach 1800 words, a remarkable length for American Negro texts. Blackamore will take a short anecdote familiar in the Negro repertoire and clothe it with panoramic detail of daily life. Up in the North this storytelling style no longer holds an audience, and a few of his buddies left the room in boredom while he was dictating to me. But in Charleston, Missouri, he used to indulge in all-night sessions. Blackamore delivered his meaty narratives in monotone, with no attempt at inflection. Unlike other of my gifted Negro informants, he seemed to lack any singing ability and recited the story of Billy Lion and Stagalee,

[4] Of these 59 have been printed in **99** and the remainder in **100**.

which is customarily sung as a ballad, in rhyming couplets. He knew his texts faultlessly and dictated them to me with never a miscue.

Joe Woods related eighteen tales to me during my two visits in 1946 and 1947 (**102**). Besides Märchen (6), he told satirical jests of priests and Jews (5), one heroic and one local legend, one novella, a comic Devil and a comic fright tale, an exaggeration, and an unusual true story, all of obvious European origin. The length of his longest Märchen, over 3000 words, is not surprising since Märchen are extended adventure stories, although we rarely encounter full-bodied examples in the United States. Woods claimed seven languages ("Polock, Russian, Croatian, Bohemian, Serbian, Slavish, English") and had narrated his fictions and jests in Polish and Slavish to his countrymen in the mines and the lumber camps. In recounting them to me in English, his errors of pronunciation did not hamper the ease of his delivery. After reading the artificial language of fairy tales in children's books, I was relieved to hear his fresh, colloquial, idiomatic speech. He was obviously a practiced craftsman, knowing his involved plots faithfully and presenting them confidently. He handled dialogue with great ease, spaced his incidents in natural paragraphs, and carried his story line forward with clarity and directness.

In one collecting session in a tavern that lasted from 9 P.M. to 2 A.M., Swan Olson reeled off to me half a dozen sensational experiences that had befallen him in the northwoods country (**95**, pp. 250–257). The episodes seemed sharp and clear in his mind, and he told each one as a unit, although all were connected as segments of his autobiographical saga, and they even repeated each other. He had two accounts of whipping his boss Eric Ericson, two of driving off robbers, two of mine mishaps. The violence of the stories contrasted oddly with Swan's gentle demeanor and ascetic features; his head swung continually from side to side from age, and he doddered when he walked. Contrary to popular belief, old people are not necessarily good informants, who must all possess keenness of mind and lucidity of speech. An old man's reminiscences may prove unbearably tedious, rambling, and disjointed. But Swan wasted never a word; he had searched out the spectacular incidents of his life in America and arranged them into neat episodic shockers. What influences had shaped his style, in the absence of any conventional form of saga tale, could only be conjectured, but this kind of storytelling based on personal adventure and exploit flourished in the Upper Peninsula, and men of the woods, mines, and lakes relished matching such experiences.

During a three-week stay in Jonesport, Maine, I saw Jim Alley nearly every day, and by the time I left he had narrated 143 tales (only 4 of them published so far, in **96**) into my tape recorder. Many of these were brief Irishmen jokes, which turn up with astonishing vitality in the Negro South, the Kentucky mountains, and the New Jersey piney woods. But he also knew a store of anecdotes about odd local characters, several Old World comic tales which he also told anecdotally, and supernatural legends of the Jonesport area. Although Jim uttered his tales with great assurance, none of his kinfolk and townsmen thought of him as a storyteller, except one neighbor woman whom he habitually visited to pour out his troubles. Alley had household problems, usually looked severe and troubled, and was easily offended. He gave forth his stories positively, almost raspingly, whereas his older brother Frank spoke soft and low. Stories came to his mind easily enough if I triggered him off with a tale of my own, or if Frank were on hand to prime his memory, and once under way he kept stimulating himself in an endless flow. He preferred the pithy, compressed, economic anecdote and indeed never gave me a narrative longer than 500 or 600 words. His authoritative air and humorless mien made one think of a very seedy professor delivering a lecture, rather than of a storyteller of the folk regaling his cronies.

On the other hand, the name of Curt Morse was given to me immediately I reached Jonesport and inquired for storytellers. Everyone knew Uncle Curt. I met him accidentally when he visited a home in Alley's Lane, much in character, being the worse for beers, with a couple in tow who screamed with laughter at his every word. Curt lived for his audience and was constantly on display, exuding gags, tall tales, comical expressions, and jocular pieces. He eventually gave me 61 narratives (4 of them printed in **96**, and 6 in **98**), nearly all humorous, save for one local legend and some heroic exploits of Barney Beal, the strong man of Beal's Island. Curt had done a stint on Gene Hooper's Cowboy Show that toured through Maine, been publicized in the county newspaper, and owned a reputation he felt compelled to maintain. Hence Curt played for the laugh with a showman's touch. Nevertheless he knew his countryside and its legends faithfully and had stories a-plenty about the old characters, the witch Sal Joe, and a wild man of the woods called Yo-ho. He made more out of a tale about a local character than did Jim Alley, adding descriptive details of appearance and behavior and smaller jokes along the way to build up the yarn. Frequently he inserted himself into comic personal experiences, thus extending his role as funnyman from storyteller to protagonist. In such narratives as the description of his trip, riddled with mishaps, to Aroostook County to dig potatoes, he played a comic counterpart of Swan Olson's hero.

Two meetings with Burt Mayotte, one quite brief, yielded five dialect stories, four in French and one in Finnish (**97**). His prize narrative, "Paree at the Carnivalle," he claimed to have composed from his grandfather's retelling in broken English of Burt's own misadventures at a carnival.

This ran to 1200 words, and his version of the immigrant's first visit to a baseball game, a dialect favorite, was even longer. As *raconteur* for the Allouette singers, the local French-Canadian club of Sault Ste. Marie, Burt held a semiprofessional status, evident in the poise and ease with which he delivered his pieces. In the act of reciting he simulated the *Canadien* with darting eyes, nervous twists of head and shoulders, and gesticulation of hands, all adding up to a spasm of physical activity that suggested the befuddled, excitable Gallic character of his tales. Burt's phrases fell into a rhythmic beat as he poured forth the story, the French nasal intonations providing neat upswings on which to pause. The vibrancy and lilt of his speech further animated the narration. All five of his texts portrayed a scene—a carnival, a ball game, a hunting trip—and even an ignorant Finnish cop giving a city speeder a ticket took on the dimensions of a little tableau. Furthermore, he set several of his recitations in a frame of straightforward prefatory remarks that explained the situation and the background quite astutely.

The Tales

1. "The Farmer and the Snake" (J. D. Suggs) (**99**, pp. 196–197) is a version of the tale known in the Aarne-Thompson Type-Index (**1**) as "The Ungrateful Serpent Returned to Captivity," Type 155, and Motif J1172.3 (**413**). This was one of Aesop's fables and has enjoyed world-wide currency. It is reported from Europe, Africa, India, China, Indonesia. Joel Chandler Harris has it in *Nights with Uncle Remus*. In one common subtype the serpent is returned to the original position from which he was rescued by a third animal called in as judge.

Suggs gives the story a realistic setting on a Southern farm. Accurate details are included: the reason for the farmer's plowing, the appearance of the snake. The factual background sharpens the comic fantasy of the talking snake; the tale is given matter of factly as an actual occurrence. A Br'er Rabbit influence appears, as Suggs personalizes the snake, calls him Mister, and puts idiomatic conversation in his mouth. Suggs's range of intonation proved especially effective in the dialogue parts, where he simulated the snake's whining pleas and the farmer's dubious tones. His plastic voice conveyed the initial pity of the farmer, the sternness of the deceitful snake, and the final resignation of the fatally bitten farmer. This is a moral tale, and Suggs always seized on the moral for a personal footnote. In this instance he gives an illustration from his own knowledge documenting the moral, just the sort of application to human conduct that Aesop was suggesting. The story of Dan Sprowell is more than half the length of the folktale and is told in a different manner. There is no narrative structure, but a sequence of astonishing facts with cumulative impact. Suggs ends the piece with racy phrases—"he was as crooked as a barrel of scales"—and a character judgment that brings him back to the moral of the folktale. No conflict develops between Dan Sprowell and some particular individual who befriends him, although Uncle Jack Suggs might have played the farmer to Sprowell's snake. However, the two sections are meant to stand together; the fiction and the reality enhance each other, and their union is a mark of narrative imagination and moral insight.

2. "Coon in the Box" (John Blackamore) (**99,** pp. 51–53) is usually told in a dozen sentences or so, even by Suggs. It is one of the most popular Southern Negro tales in the Old Marster cycle. Actually the Negro tale is one episode extracted from a European story complex known as "Doctor Know-All" (Type 1641), in which a poor peasant named Crab (Cricket, or Rat) purchases a doctor's garb, pretends to be omniscient, and manages through luck to detect thieves. He is then put to the test to divine what is hidden under a dish and says "Poor Crab!" in despair; he has guessed right. In the American Negro form the colored man always refers to himself as "coon." Blackamore takes the initial idea, that the clever slave has a reputation for uncanny wisdom, and gives it depth and dimension by the logical device of having Jack hang around his master's quarters and eavesdrop. Next Blackamore fills in the script with three examples of the sort of thing a field hand might very well hear his master talk about in connection with the next day's farming chores. The incident where Jack's boss bets with a rival planter he sets in a council meeting, to introduce the skeptic Carter. Other Southern Negro tales contain scenes where masters put their best slaves to the test, and in the final episode Blackamore strokes this in with a crowded barbecue gathering for the backdrop. He ends the tale with a formula couplet, a convention disappearing from modern Negro narratives. The milieu and cast of characters are drawn from young Blackamore's life in the new South: Old Boss and Jack the handy man replace Old Marster and John the clever slave from plantation times; crackers talk at a council meeting; Jack knows the tractor and fertilizer of the modern farm. Blackamore relies on no oral effects of intonation: for instance, he states that Jack answered his boss "rather slowly," where Suggs would have actually dragged out the words with exaggerated slowness. He does employ considerable dialogue, between Old Boss and Jack, and Old Boss and Carter. Blackamore's talent lies in the supplying of elaborate details of everyday life to clothe the story outline.

3. "The Rich Landlord and the Poor Shoemaker" (Joe Woods) (**102,** pp. 39–47) has enjoyed considerable distribution in Europe, where it is commonly known as "The Master Thief" (Type 1525). Like Doctor

Know-All, it appears as one of the Grimms' household tales but is a good deal longer, containing four or more distinct adventures in which the clever thief steals possessions of the lord who has commanded him to attempt the thefts. Woods refers to each thieving episode as a "proposition" and gives six thefts: of dogs, bull, wife's sheets, wife's ring, stallion, and finally abduction of the priest. No doubt this division into similar episodes, characteristic of Märchen, assists in the considerable feat of memorization; the narrator need keep firmly in mind only the six objects stolen. One of the problems encountered by the collector is seen in Woods' refusal to tell me completely the proposition involving the theft of the wife's ring, which took place in her bedroom. Earlier he apologized for another indelicate incident, saying that was how he had heard the story. Oral tales are invariably expurgated when presented to any large reading public. One stylistic device in this tale, employed as a connective between the episodes, and commented on by Thompson (**412**, p. 458) as a convention of Märchen, is the direct question addressed to the audience: "Why can't they find the shoes? The shoemaker has picked them up when he hang up the dummy"; "Well, what's shoemaker going to do? Is he going to steal that horse?"; "Can you guess what he gonna do, that priest, with the minister?" Woods ends with his own salty moral, but in other tales he uses a formula ending. He reproduced plaintive, subdued, and angry tones. Frequently he omitted the bothersome prefaces of "He said." Often oral narrators inject "say" several times during one quoted conversation, to indicate the speaker is still talking, and they experience trouble too with personal pronouns, repeating "he" instead of the personal name, so that the reader of the text becomes confused. Woods steers clear of these blemishes with a clear, straightforward story line. Although he follows the plot of the tale type consistently, he uses his own muscular and pungent language to tell the story. The action moves forward swiftly. Yet Woods paints in a detailed setting, describing the barn scene minutely, setting down precisely all the objects and trappings involved in the shoemaker's machinations. The effect of realism is enhanced by his asides, emphasizing the typical European style of the barn and the life and death power of the lord over the peasants as remembered by his grandmother. Although his accent was thick and his pronunciations often incorrect, Woods never floundered or groped for a word. The total effect was one of complete control over a complicated text.

4. "My First Job in America" (Swan Olson) (**95**, pp. 251–254, untitled) differs from the preceding tales in that it does not belong to a definitely known folktale type and does not even qualify as a folktale, since it purports to be a true personal experience. Often, however, folktales will

be told in the first person, and were more of these autobiographical sagas collected, we might find the same motifs and themes reappearing. In any event, since this is an oral narrative by a folk narrator, it does interest the folklorist. This account has the symmetry of a folktale, with its series of separate but parallel episodes, in which the brutal Eric Ericson gets severely mauled: plopping in a ditch, getting knocked down with his own gun, being smashed with the stove pipe and whaled with a ramrod. The unsavory character of Eric is demonstrated regularly, to create a satisfaction in the listener at all this mauling. Eric is introduced as a wild man drinking straight alcohol and abusing his family; we see him again drunk in a bar, trying to shoot Swan with no reason; we find him in the act of beating his second wife; we are told he never paid his hired men. In addition to the major sensations there are minor matters to startle the listener, such as the cheapness of eggs at two cents a dozen, and the snake bedfellows in the hay loft. Finally there is the beautiful O. Henry climax, with Eric rewarding the man who had pummeled him all through the preceding day. The smaller touches of realism, like the description of the Old Country chest, and the statement that only silver dollars then circulated, contribute to the effect of authenticity. But the tautness and coherence of the piece, combined with the heroic role of Swan, and the evidence of other similar tales related by him—although not so fully rounded—indicate elements of composition here. Even if it all happened, the narrator must select, arrange, describe, connect the parts. If Swan had been retelling the narrative since 1890, repetition could have perfected it in the course of half a century; and if he had begun to relate it as a septuagenarian reminiscence, his memory could have clutched the feats of other saga men. He used no verbal tricks of intonation to heighten his tale, but let it speak for itself.

5. "The Duck Hunt" (Burt Mayotte) (**97**, p. 127) is a tall tale in dialect. Actually it combines three episodes that could be told separately. The first incident, of a Frenchman on a raft or boat who says in the morning, "Bah gosh, we ain't here, we seven miles from here," is widely told as an independent anecdote about the simple *Canadien* who twists phrases comically. The second and third actions belong to the pervasive American tall-tale tradition of remarkable hunting and shooting. The Motif F 638.3, "Man is waiting for bird to fall that he had shot eight days before," is also known in India. Two humorous figures, here Joe and Curley, frequently occur in dialect stories, under various names, as a pair of comic foils who speak to each other in mangled English and match each other's oddities. Mayotte employs a framework to introduce them and carry on the narrative between comic incidents, but suddenly he switches from the role of

objective narrator speaking perfectly good English to the dialectician who is telling about Joe and Curley in their own *Canadien* speech. This switch comes immediately after a rather literary phrase, "with grave aplomb," which provides a rhythmic lilt to end a sentence and suggests the sober appearance of the Frenchmen, thus intensifying the ludicrousness of their behavior.

The humor of dialect is present throughout. Instances are the use of aspirated h's before consonants, homemade synonyms ("two-pipe shoot-gun" for "double-barreled shotgun"), nonsense construction ("nobody see some more ducks"), and *Canadien* expletives ("maudit," "sapré"). Although obviously farcical, the tale remains true to the local culture; the place names and manner of duck hunting and reference to the *chantier* are all accurate, and the French-Canadians do exist and perform in a way to invite mimicry and caricature. This tale, like all of Mayotte's, relies considerably on verbal effects, both of dialect and rhythm; the sentences are broken into unit phrases with clear pauses in between, making almost a singsong: "So we h'all go hinside / han' Joe cook de pan*cake*/han' heverybody h'eat." "You know/ Cur*lee*/ Hi'll have haim/for his neck." Some creative writers employing the French-Canadian *habitant* speech, like William Henry Drummond, have chosen verse as a vehicle for dialect humor, to capture the verbal rhythms.

6. "Clever Art Church" (Jim Alley)[5] is not a single tale but three independent anecdotes told about the same local wag. Anecdotes of local characters comprise a large section of American folk narrative but have never been seriously collected or systematically studied. Art Church was an actual person, but the tricks he played are similar to those credited around the country to locally celebrated pranksters and fastened onto the Yankee in the newspaper humor of the 1830's and 1840's. The first trick belongs to the theme of the literal contract based on a double meaning. Uncle Josh took "best part" to mean most, but Art pointed out that the two sticks of hardwood were indeed the best part of the cord he sold Uncle Josh. The next supposedly true happening, where Art is asked to lie and says he has no time because so-and-so has just had an accident and he must get a doctor—which is a lie—is an international folktale attached to various American yarnspinners, such as Gib Morgan, the tall-tale bard of the Pennsylvania oil fields (**34**, pp. 29–30; Motif X905.4). The third anecdote is a variation on the Yankee trick to outwit a creditor. Alley presents the meat of the brief stories without trimmings or elaboration, to achieve the terse, pithy quality that gives the anecdote—as distinct from a casual yarn with deliberate build-up—its impact.

[5] Tape recorded in Jonesport, Maine, July 10, 1956. Printed here for the first time.

Direct, idiomatic dialogue in each anecdote sharpens the pace and gives a sense of immediacy, as if Jim himself had been there as witness. Quoted indirectly, the dialogue would lose its bite. Each little tale ends with a statement of chagrin by the dupe. This seems unnecessary in the hardwood story, which could stop with Art's triumphant explanation of the literal sale, but the triumph is sharpened by having the last word a lament from Art's victim. Brief as they are, the anecdotes contain a certain amount of repetition: the phrase "the best part of it was hardwood" in the first; "I ain't got time" in the second; and the parallel utterances and actions of Art and McFall in the third. These repetitions give form to the anecdote; they impress salient points on the listener unfamiliar with the personalities or the situation, who could easily lose the sense of the rapid-fire tale, perhaps hinging on a wordplay, if his attention were not arrested and riveted to the key idea. Alley's positive, even authoritative, delivery contributed to the success of the anecdotes, which become blurred and confused if the speaker falters or stumbles. In a long story a lapse can be picked up without much damage.

7. "The Horse Trade with Bill Case" (Curt Morse),[6] which he told as a personal experience, falls within an honored cycle of American trickster yarns dealing with horse trades. The formula requires that a trade be agreed on and a sorry animal be fobbed off by a Yankee sharper, who adds insult to injury in his subsequent explanation. Here Curt makes himself out to be the Yankee, projecting himself into the story according to his wont. Jim Alley would simply relate the comical saying or deed of the character Bill Case, but now attention is shifted from comical Bill Case to crafty Curt. Curt elaborates the yarn with incidental humor, as in the reference to Bill and his sisters' being "rolled-oat eaters," and the graphic description of Bill's nose. Like Alley, Morse salts the story with natural-sounding dialogue, not only between the traders but also between Bill Case and his sister, and he too ends the tale with a wry comment by the dupe. A humorous vocal effect in the present piece is Curt's reproduction of the snuffling whistle that punctuated Bill Case's speech, formed probably by a sharp intake of breath through a slightly open mouth. Curt used his throaty voice and timbre for doleful and lugubrious inflection.

Both verbally and structurally Curt contrives a continuously humorous piece. Bill Case himself is a comical-appearing and sounding character; he has a humorous exchange with Curt, and another with his sister, and then finally comes the jest of the second swap. Humorous improvisation is by now instinctive with Curt; when he was listening to a playback of another

---

[6] "Curt Gets the Best of Bill Case in a Horse Trade." (Tape recorded in Kennebec, Maine, July 13, 1956. Printed here for the first time.)

tale he had told about an eccentric hermit, he was surprised to hear himself say the hermit could play "The Mocking Bird" on his violin "so real that you'd have to take a stick to keep driving off the birds from the strings." In the course of narrating his yarns Curt can easily insert gags and comic expressions which he repeats regularly in his everyday banter.

. . .

Do these seven folktale texts, selected by the personal taste of the collector from the vagaries of his own field encounters, show any common stylistic features? One point that had escaped me until they were placed on the dissecting table is their plentiful use of dialogue. The tale becomes fresher, livelier, and clearer when natural conversation is introduced, and avoids a tedious and confusing trait of folk narratives, the ambiguous use of indirect quotation.

Throughout their stories the speakers avoided garnishment from literary words and highbrow allusions. Although only three of the seven narratives purported to be true—and these contain highly dubious points (Olson, Alley, Morse)—each teller gave his story the maximum appearance of reality, through use of background detail, internal conversation, personal comments, and earnestness of delivery. This earnestness comes from an act of identification with a protagonist of the tale: Suggs with the trusting farmer against the snake and the confidence man; Blackamore with the handy man against the cracker bosses; Woods with the shoemaker thief against the rich landlord; Swan with his own role as hired man against maniacal Eric Ericson; Mayotte with the comical Frenchmen against the alien Yankees; Alley with clever Art Church against his dupes; and Morse with himself as a shrewd Yankee trading against Bill Case. There is conflict in the tales, sometimes merely a lighthearted battle of wits in the serious business of swapping and trading (Morse, Alley), and again a grim struggle between landowner and serf (Blackamore, Woods, Olson) cloaked in comic sparring. Whether in fairy tale, saga, or jest, the tellers are committed to their tales and communicate their passion and sympathy.

These texts do conform to Olrik's laws for oral narrative. They are simple and unsubtle, they pit together a good and a bad character, and they contain repetitions, even the short anecdotes. But these laws, binding as they seem, still permit considerable play to the talents of individual folk artists.

LINCOLN AS FOLK NARRATOR

The approach suggested here for analyzing the oral style of superior folk narrators has been applied to living storytellers encountered in the field.

Now I shall try it on Abraham Lincoln. From the wealth of Lincoln material we find far more data on storytelling style and repertoire than exists for most folktale tellers of the present day. Lincoln biography fully accepts the fact that Lincoln was an engaging and masterful raconteur, and numerous observers, acquaintances, and friends have described his delivery and written down his texts. In his own lifetime the daily press and Abe Lincoln jokebooks circulated around the country endless yarns, sayings, and witticisms attributed to him, many of them apocryphal. Enough, however, are authenticated, by reliable authorities, so that we can recognize Lincoln tales. Carl Sandburg's six-volume biography (**345–346**) pays special attention to the yarns and sayings and skillfully weaves them into the life. In spite of all the attention given Lincoln as humorist and narrator, no one has seriously analyzed his relation to folk tradition. I am convinced that the evidence proves Lincoln to be an artistic folk narrator and performer on the order of Suggs and Curt Morse and Jim Alley.

Background

Lincoln grew up in Kentucky, Indiana, and Illinois after the first wave of pioneers had opened the country, when farmers were beginning to break the soil and settle the land. He was born in a log cabin in Kentucky, moved after seven years, in 1816, to Little Pigeon Creek in southern Indiana, and in 1831 trekked 200 miles west to New Salem on the Illinois prairie, where a dozen families had founded a town. Here in Illinois he made his permanent home and traveled around the state as a circuit lawyer, gossiping and swapping tales in taverns. Lincoln grew from what folklorists like to call a folk background, a setting in which the formal instruments of learning have scarcely appeared and society is much influenced by time-honored beliefs, word-of-mouth reports, and the natural environment. In time, of course, other influences played upon Lincoln. By the mid-nineteenth century the earlier currents of frontier humor were being submerged by a new breed of professional funny-men writing in urban newspapers—Petroleum V. Nasby, Artemus Ward, Orpheus C. Kerr—and Lincoln read and repeated their manufactured jokes. But the stock of humorous tales on which he drew most frequently and intimately came from his youth on Indiana and Illinois pioneer farms. He said that his best stories came from country folk (**440**, ch. 10).

Delivery and Repertoire

Most persons raised in the midst of a folk tradition never become expert folktale narrators. Only certain individuals with the flair and the relish to remember and perform the tales are themselves remembered for such talent. Lincoln said that he always recalled every story he heard and admitted that he was a mere "retailer" of yarns—a valuable clue to their folklore nature. Witnesses have testified to his enrichment of a story with mimicry of characters and acting out of parts; he reproduced a stutterer's peculiar whistle between syllables (like Curt Morse), gyrated his arms and legs in accompaniment to the text, and twanged in dialect. Under the spell of the tale his melancholy countenance glowed with animation and he seemed transformed, almost handsome. At the Capitol he was soon recognized as a champion yarnspinner (**345**, Vol. 2, p. 302; **346**, Vol. 5, pp. 61, 322, 335). "His favorite seat was at the left of the open fireplace, tilted back in his chair, with his long legs reaching over to the chimney jamb. He never told a story twice, but appeared to have an endless repertoire always ready, like the successive charges of a magazine gun" (**345**, Vol. 1, p. 357, quoting a newspaper reporter). One observer stressed the dry chuckle, the gesture of rubbing the hand down the side of the long leg, the gleam in the eye (**346**, Vol. 4, p. 285, quoting the English author-correspondent Edward Dicey). Lincoln tremendously enjoyed relating his fables. "I can't resist telling a good story," he said. Once he got up in the middle of the night to rouse a sleepy friend and tell him a yarn that was tickling him irresistibly. When he met another tale teller he responded immediately with a matching yarn—again a sure sign of the folk raconteur. An office seeker topped Lincoln's parable with a splendid folk yarn of his own, whereon Lincoln promptly gave him the job. He appreciated the painter Conant for one especial tale he borrowed himself, and he would introduce him as the author of "the Slow Horse story" (**346**, Vol. 5, pp. 323, 329, 339; Vol. 4, pp. 56–57).[7]

John Hay guessed that Lincoln knew a hundred stories. Any such surmise is problematical. Sandburg lists 135 in the index to *The War Years* and gives a score more in the less well-indexed *Prairie Years*. Beyond a doubt Lincoln possessed an extraordinary repertoire (cf. **272**; and a modern collection of recollections, **167**), rarely equaled by folk narrators currently being recorded in the field. He specialized in the humorous anecdotal yarn, "neither too broad nor too long," said Horace Porter. His texts are fuller than the brief anecdotes of Jim Alley, but pointed and concentrated on a single incident so that they never wandered off into a rambling yarn, in the fashion of Mark Twain's garrulous talkers.[8] Apparently he adapted his stories to differing situations, and variants

---

[7] It was Anthony J. Bleecker who matched Lincoln with a tale of a converted Indian praying for his enemy, in order to heap coals of fire on his head and "burn him down to the stump."

[8] Jim Blaine's story of the old ram in *Roughing It*, which never does get to the point, is a good example of the discursive yarn.

appear for certain ones, in distinction to separate versions of the same yarn recorded by different bystanders.

The Tradition

The particular folk tradition represented by Lincoln is not immediately clear. He does not belong to the backwoods vein of Davy Crockett that branched through the Kentucky and Tennessee canebrakes in the early years of the nineteenth century, producing tall tales of bear hunting and Indian fighting and melees between boasting bullies. The scene of Lincoln's stories is the prairie farm, not the forest clearing; the setting is in cornfields and country stores, not in the isolated cabin. His aphorisms and expressions grow from pioneer farm life and concern hogs and ploughs, blacksmiths and circuit preachers. Crockett is the solitary hunter, tangling with occasional eccentrics who penetrate to the backwoods, like Yankee peddlers or uncouth squatters. Some backwoods anecdotes do turn up in Lincoln's repertoire, but few, and they are told *on* degenerate log cabin families, rather than *by* the intrepid backwoodsman, as in Crockett's yarns.[9] Lincoln comes a stage later than the Kentucky hunters and Mississippi keelboatmen who pioneered the West and brought forth hero legends of Crockett and Mike Fink. His folk are farmers. Folklorists have collected surprisingly few farm tales, considering the importance of America's agricultural past and present. Therefore we cannot find many variants to Lincoln's farm stories, but they bear all the internal marks of folktales. Several choice examples follow.

And this reminds me [Lincoln's dream of death] of an old farmer in Illinois whose family were made sick by eating greens. Some poisonous herb had got into the mess, and members of the family were in danger of dying. There was a half-witted boy in the family called Jake; and always afterward when they had greens the old man would say, "Now, afore we risk these greens, *let's try 'em on Jake. If he stands 'em,* we're all right." Just so with me. As long as this imaginary assassin continues to exercise himself on others I can stand it. [**346,** Vol. 6, p. 245; a variant is in Vol. 2, pp. 299–300, placed in Indiana.]

The glib representations of one military report, concealing disgrace and defeat involved, reminded Lincoln of the young fellow who shouted at the plowing farmer, "I want your daughter!" The farmer went on plowing, merely shouting over his shoulder, "Take her," whereupon the youth stood scratching his head; "Too easy, too durned easy!" [**346,** Vol. 5, p. 328.]

"R[aymond], you were brought up on a farm, were you not? Then you know what a *chin fly* is. My brother and I . . . were once ploughing corn on a Kentucky farm, I driving the horse, and he holding the plough. The horse was lazy; but

[9] Backwoods stories are in **346,** Vol. 5, pp. 8, 328, 639–649 (a traveler in a thunderstorm asks for less noise and more light; a pioneer woman tells a Bible salesman, "I had no idea we were so nearly out"; a traveler denied food by a niggardly couple stirs up the ash cake hidden in their hearth fire).

on one occasion rushed across the field so that I, with my long legs, could scarcely keep pace with him. On reaching the end of the furrow, I found an enormous *chin fly* fastened upon him, and knocked him off. My brother asked me what I did that for. I told him I didn't want the old horse bitten in that way. 'Why,' said my brother, 'that's all that made him go!' "

"Now," added Lincoln, "if Mr. C[hase] has a presidential *chin fly* biting him, I'm not going to knock him off, if it will only make his department go." [**346,** Vol. 4, p. 638; a variant follows, pp. 638–639.]

They [United States Marshals] are like a man in Illinois, whose cabin was burned down, and according to the kindly custom of early days in the West, his neighbors all contributed something to start him again. In his case they had been so liberal that he soon found himself better off than before the fire, and he got proud. One day, a neighbor brought him a bag of oats, but the fellow refused it with scorn. "No," said he, "I'm not taking oats now, I take nothing but money." [**346,** Vol. 5, p. 326.]

Some of Lincoln's yarns are recognizable folktales. Mrs. Vallandigham, wife of the Copperhead leader, said she would never return to Ohio except as wife of its governor, a statement reminding Lincoln of a story about a candidate for the county board in Illinois who told his wife on election morning that she would sleep with the township supervisor that night. After the returns came in, she dressed up to sleep with the victor, her husband's rival. I heard the same anecdote told on an unpopular old fellow in Munising, Abe Artibee, during a field trip I made to upper Michigan in 1946 (**346,** Vol. 4, p. 379; **95,** p. 160). An odd horse tale of Lincoln's dealt with a balky animal traded off by its owner as good for hunting birds; it squatted in the middle of a creek, and the owner called out to the dupe: "Ride him! Ride him! He's as good for fish as for birds" (**345,** Vol. 2, p. 300). This popped up in recent years in the cycle of "shaggy dog" stories and was told me in pretty much the same form as this by a colleague at Michigan State University, LeRoy Ferguson, save that the horse sat on grapefruit instead of birds. A superb yarn about a blacksmith hammering a big piece of heated wrought iron into successively smaller tools and finally throwing it into the water to make a "fizzle" out of it, suggests another shaggy dog favorite about the" cush-maker," which has an early variant (**380,** pp. 79–80).[10] The boy sparking the farmer's daughter who is chased by her father with a shotgun and outruns a rabbit falls into the tall-tale theme of fast runners who outrace ghosts and rabbits (**345,** Vol. 2, p. 296).[11] The tearful deathbed reconciliation of Old Brown with his sworn enemy, to be voided if the sick man recovers, is told the same way by Shepherd Tom Hazard in his recollected traditions of South

[10] Jansen reported (**207**) the analogue between Crockett's story and the current shaggy dog jest, relying on **3**. The story does not appear in Crockett's Autobiography (cf. **346,** Vol. 6, p. 150, from Horace Porter; a variant by Grant follows, pp. 150–151).

[11] Baughman cites examples of "Lies concerning speed" under Motif X1796, in **17**.

County, Rhode Island (**346**, Vol. 3, p. 368; told on Sylvester and John Hazard, in **162**, and **163**, pp. 165–166). Lincoln used the anecdote to express his feelings at having to release the Confederate envoys Mason and Slidell to Great Britain. Hearing of a young brigadier general who was captured by the Confederates with his small cavalry troop, Lincoln said "I can make a better brigadier any day, but those horses cost the government $125 a head." So does a Maine sea captain mourn the loss of a couple of dories over that of one sailor and a couple of "Portygees," and a Michigan lumbercamp boss is pleased that a lumberjack rather than a teamster's horse is killed by a falling tree (**346**, Vol. 4, p. 38; **21**, p. 130; **95**, p. 197). Commenting on Douglas's scrap with Buchanan over slavery in Kansas, Lincoln told of the backwoods wife who found her husband in a savage tussle with a bear and cheered both on impartially: "Go it, husband, go it, bear." A Joe Miller Jokebook carried this tale in 1865, and later in the century the sensitive reporter of Vermont folk life, Rowland E. Robinson, placed it in the mouth of one of his raconteurs: "Go it, ol' man, go it, bear, it's the fust fight ever I see 'at I didn't keer which licked" (**318**, p. 263; **227**, p. 207; **338**, p. 191).

Individual Style

As Sandburg remarks, Lincoln's talk was salted with new American words and twists of speech soaking into the language. Lincoln had the gift—as does Harry Truman—for employing the homely barnyard metaphor and earth-drawn proverb to nail his point. "Small potatoes and few in a hill" he said of a signal rocket that fizzled out. Of the Gettysburg address he fretted to Ward Hill Lamon, "Lamon, that speech won't scour," using a figure of speech derived from mud sticking to the mold board of a plow and hindering its movement. "I don't amount to pig tracks in the War Department," he remarked ruefully. "As they say in the hayfields he requires a good man to 'rake after him,'" was one of his farming saws applied to a sloppy worker. From his father he gained the proverb "Every man must skin his own skunk." "Why, I could lick salt off the top of your head," he said to a short man, and of a blowhard he commented, "the only thing you could do would be to *stop his mouth with a corn cob.*" Lincoln used the comparative exaggerations still current in rural speech, and called an argument of Stephen A. Douglas as thin as "soup made by boiling the shadow of a pigeon that had starved to death." As War President he remarked: "Some of my generals are so slow that molasses in the coldest days of winter is a race horse compared to them. They're brave enough, but somehow or other, they get fastened in a fence corner, and can't figure their way out." Country words continually arrested the attention of his associates, who were startled when he asked,

"My young friend, have I *hunkered* you out of your chair?" (**346,** Vol. 5, p. 321; Vol. 4, pp. 472, 305, 299; **345,** Vol. 1, p. 296; Vol. 2, pp. 246, 293, 302; **346,** Vol. 5, p. 331; Vol. 4, p. 203.)

Obviously such dialect words and expressions sauced Lincoln's yarns and added a barnyard aroma to his farming stories. Here, unfortunately, the texts are at their weakest, since reporters of longer narratives would hardly remember the racy turns of phrase that stuck in their minds when used in proverbs or single utterances. Still some of the tales, as that of the rival powder merchants (**346,** Vol. 5, p. 62), convey authentic flavor of speech.

Structurally the chief characteristic of Lincoln's storytelling style is his application of the yarn to an immediate political or social situation. A genius shines forth here, in the uncanny aptness of his illustrative anecdotes. As Seward and others remarked, his little tales were fables and parables of wisdom. Aesop, we know, appealed to Lincoln. The perfection of his folktale lies in its moral lesson. So in the Middle Ages did priests relate exempla to make their point. Whereas Suggs moralized on his tale after telling it, dipping into his past experiences with sinners, Lincoln broke into his story from a live situation—frequently when beset by importunate office seekers. Examples here would include most of his known repertoire, but two felicitous instances are his story of the boy hoping his captured coon would escape so that he would not have to kill it, which Lincoln told when asked what disposition he intended to make of Jeff Davis; and his anecdote of the farmer who trapped nine skunks and then let eight go because the one he killed made such a stench, in reply to the query why he did not fire his whole cabinet and not just Cameron (**346,** Vol. 6, p. 237; Vol. 4, p. 284; a variant is given in **345,** Vol. 2, p. 447).

The tale of "The High- and the Low-Combed Cock" can be cited to illustrate characteristic elements of Lincoln's storytelling style.[12] The political problem posed by the Kentucky Senator, how to woo the shifting factions in Kentucky, prepares the way for the President's yarn, and the moral emerges crystal-clear upon its completion. This was Lincoln's customary framework. The tale itself contains a backcountry scene from Lincoln's own folk experience, in this case a cockfight in Kentucky, and so contrasts sharply with the huffing political arena of the White House. Still fable and crisis are neatly linked, for both pertain to Kentucky, and the weaselly Squire, who hedges his bets until the winning cock is determined, symbolizes the mass of shifting Kentuckians. No doubt the original text would show racier speech, but dialect is rendered, in the Squire's quoted words. The yarn is delicious by itself, limning the shallow

[12] Text from **346,** Vol. 5, p. 327, "as published in the *Philadelphia Times* and other newspapers, and credited to (Colonel James Sanks) Brisbin."

fraudulence of the puffed-up Squire. He resembles one of the sharpers and scapegraces whom Baldwin, Hooper, and other antebellum Southern humorists loved to portray. Much of Lincoln's humor was aimed at such solemn frauds. The narrative possesses enough detail to depict the scene and engage the listener's interest but avoids extraneous description that could overload the story and smother the moral. As Horace Porter said (**346,** Vol. 5, p. 61), Lincoln's tale was neither too broad nor too long.

APPENDIX

CLEVER ART CHURCH

DORSON: You were telling me that this Art Church was quite a fellow. Who was Art Church?

JIM ALLEY: Oh, a fella lived up Injun River.

DORSON: What was he known for?

JIM ALLEY: Well I don't know.

FRANK ALLEY: Oh he was a nice fella, clever.

JIM ALLEY: Clever.

FRANK ALLEY: As clever a fella as you ever see. But if he got it in for you, boys look out. He'd lie to you just as quick as flies.

DORSON: Didn't he play a trick on your uncle Josh?

JIM ALLEY: Yes, he sold Uncle Josh a cord of wood and he told him the best part of it—he'd find the best part of it was hardwood. And Uncle Josh paid him for it and when he went out and looked he had just two sticks of hardwood. And Uncle Josh got after him about it and he said, "I told you the best part—the best of it was hardwood." "Well," he said, "I only got two sticks of hardwood."

DORSON: Now that that whistle has stopped blowing, perhaps you'd tell us one of Art Church's lies.

JIM ALLEY: Art Church was going downtown by Porter Cummings, and Porter hollered "Art, come in." He says, "I ain't got time." He says, "Come in long enough to tell me a lie." He says, "Well, I'm in a devil of a hurry, I ain't got time." Says, "Your father, I just come down by him and he's cut himself awful and I'm after a doctor." Well Porter jumped into his wagon—no automobiles then—and rushed up there and his father hadn't cut himself at all. And he said "The devil, he told me a lie right on the road."

DORSON: What's that one about the other time he wanted to get a receipt in full?

JIM ALLEY: He owed McFall a bill and McFall tried to git it. And he wrote him and wrote him and Art didn't pay no attention. And at last Art started from Machias and he got up Mason's Bay and he met McFall a-comin'. Art says, "I'm just comin' over to pay that bill." Well McFall says, "I'm just comin' over at your house after it." McFall's horses headed toward Jonesport and Art's headed toward Machias. "Well," Art says, "write me out a receipt and I'll pay you." He wrote him out a receipt and Art grabbed it and started his horse and McFall turned around and tried to get him, but said, "It's no use, he's got the receipt and that's all there is to it."

CURT GETS THE BEST OF BILL CASE IN A HORSE TRADE

DORSON: Who was Bill Case?

CURT MORSE: Bill Case was an old fella lived here with his sister. She was an old maid and he was old bach and they lived together. I guess they was kind of rolled-oat eaters, they'd eat sour apples and rolled oats, didn't cost 'em more than thirty cents a year to live. They was a comical pair. Fact, Bill had one of them great wide long transparent noses you look right through it. He was comical, but an awfully good old fella.

DORSON: Talked funny, eh?

CURT MORSE: Yeah he talked funny. So he says to me, he says "[sucking noise] Devil," he says, "How'll we trade horses?" he says, "[sn] I like the looks of your horse." "Well," I says, "I don't know, I got a good horse." Says "[sn] I got a better one." But I said, "Before we trade I'll have to have your harness, your wagon and the hames, corn, brush, and blanket, and them six hens and that Plymouth Rock rooster." Well he looked at me and he says, "[sn] Want the ell off the end of the house too?" Anyhow we hit up a trade, I guess he was kinda lazy about lookin' after the horse. Well that horse I let him have had the blind staggers. So the next day I heard him hollerin' at me to come over and see what ailed the horse, and I went over and he said, "The horse has got a shock." I says, "Well you know, anybody's apt to have a shock." Just then his sister looked through the little hole in the barn door and she says, "William, don't you sell that Plymouth Rock." He says, "Hallelujah [sn], you go in the house or I'll knock your devilish head off." Well anyhow, we got the horse outdoor she kinda straightened up, and he says, "[sn] Want to buy her?" And I says, "No, I'll give you the six hens you give me yesterday for her." And Bill says, "[sn] You bought her, bring my six hens back." I got both horses and the whole outfit for the six hens he give me. Never come to him till the next day, Bill says, "[sn] Great trader I am."

Comments to Part Two

CARROLL: Roger Brown asked why I had not tried to investigate the enduring characteristics of style in individuals. Actually, I hope to do just that, but not until I have established the basic dimensions of style. Only then can we start to test the validity of the saying "Style is the man." Nevertheless, there is a problem here: where would we look for the enduring, invariant characteristics of style in an individual writer? It would be very simple if all the literary output of a given writer were to be found uniform, "unconsciously" shaped in certain directions or with certain peculiarities, for then we would merely have to draw out a suitable sample of this output and study it. Perhaps this would work for some writers. But it is frequently true that a literary artist is an artist by virtue of the fact that he has certain skills at his command, certain ways of selecting materials and techniques to suit a particular end. Thus "style" will reside not so much in particular samples of a man's output as in the way he more or less consciously and artfully selects a particular style. On the other hand, Jenkins' study reminds us that a more enduring kind of personal style might be found, not in the artful creations of the persons but rather in the more casual kind of material represented by spontaneous conversation, personal letters, and other sorts of unstudied, nondeliberate materials. Perhaps we should look at all these possible sources of enduring personal style and their interrelationships and interactions.

STANKIEWICZ: I would like to ask these questions of Mr. Carroll. How would you know that each instance is not a representation of a type? How would you know that this is the style of the man and not the style of the group or, say, of the period?

CARROLL: Well, I think that that would come only by the study of many instances, not only "within" an author but also between authors. We have in statistics the notion of among-group variances and within-group variances. I think this is partly a problem of that sort. It is somewhat like the problem of whether you have an idiolect or a dialect.

DORSON: I wonder if I could speak on the point Mr. Stankiewicz raised, about how one distinguishes between the individual and the group, since this is something that comes into folk literature, and I, myself, have been concerned with it. In the past we have supposed that most people in a group, in a subculture, told about the same tales in the same way and that the style was uniform for all members of the group. But when we look into it a little more closely and begin to consider individual performers, we see that there is a good deal of difference, variation, and individual style. So it seems to me that we can make such a distinction once the group repertoire has been established. Take the tales of Southern Negroes. There is a very definite repertoire which is common to Southern Negro storytellers. They tell the same tales, they use similar gestures—like this (claps hand)—which means that the rabbit runs away fast. Every storyteller has command of this particular gesture. And then they will use the cante-fable verse interspersed in the tale. That is a regular feature of Southern Negro stories. I would say that every Southern Negro informant has such features in common with other members of the group. But when we examine the individual storyteller more closely, we see certain variations from one to another. Some people have a very rapid-fire delivery. I remember I collected from one husband and wife—the wife spoke very quickly and the husband had a very rambling, circuitous delivery. You would think that they would hardly be able to talk to each other. Both of them were excellent storytellers with the same repertoire but with completely different individual styles. That is the sort of thing I have become more conscious of in the field.

JAKOBSON: The folklorists of the late nineteenth and early twentieth centuries, in particular the Russian investigators, were the first to focus their attention on the role of the performers of folk poetry and on their inventive import. There was, however, a dangerous temptation to identify the role of such performers with the role of creative writers. The impact of preventive collective censorship is incommensurably higher in oral tradition and, in this respect, the life of folklore can be compared rather with such social phenomena as language. In any popular tradition there are several stereotyped styles of performances and corresponding selections of epic or lyric genres, and from among these "stock types" (*emplois*) the individual chooses the one particularly suited to him. Likewise, the observers of language are often prone to exaggerate the imprint of personality. We could easily quote amusing lapses such as a psychologist's attribution of individual imprint to so typical a social phenomenon as the incomplete assimilation of a foreign language. The strong tendency of the individual to adapt his language to the milieu, and in any dialogue to approach his interlocutor, considerably reduces the notion of the so-called "idiolect."

PART THREE

Linguistic Approaches
to Verbal Art

Casual and Noncasual Utterances within Unified Structure

C. F. VOEGELIN[1]

There is nothing new in the recognition, within a given language, of a distinction between common usage and uses of the language for more restricted purposes and often enough, perhaps characteristically, more elevated purposes. The monolithic nature of English is not questioned when literary essayists like Emerson contrast poetry and common speech. The latter is recognized in America to be the proper subject for the investigation of linguists who, however, now show some incipient inclination to investigate poetry, too, and other noncasual utterances in a given language.[1]

It is not yet certain that the results will be interesting. Classically, when elevated noncasual texts provided the proper standard of grammars, casual utterances were treated as a deviation from the standard. The new inclination of linguistic interest in America is in no danger of returning to the classical view, of completing the circle. If figures of circles are suggested, they are rather like expanding concentric circles, with the outermost circle representing recent investigations of noncasual utterances by linguists.

If these budding investigations in America develop in the direction of unified structure, they may well attest the monolithic hypothesis about language, or contribute new hypotheses concerned with the interdependence of diverse structures within one language. The final part of this

---

[1] The subject of this paper was also the subject of a symposium at the annual meeting of the American Anthropological Association (Chicago, 1957), published in part (**103, 124, 190, 457**); and a combined anthropological and linguistic faculty in the 1957–1958 academic year found a score of problems concerned with noncasual versus casual utterances in a wide variety of languages (Ethnolinguistic Seminar, Indiana). I am happy to acknowledge that I received both corrective and perspective benefits from the members of the seminar and, subsequently, from the participants of the Conference on Style.

paper considers the consequences of a unified structure for both casual and noncasual utterances and for accommodating diverse dialects and idiolects.

If, on the other hand, the expansion of linguistic interest into noncasual areas eschews the construct of a unified structure, the investigators may increasingly continue to list deviations of noncasual from casual; thus the verb in a given Turkish poem is found not only in clause final, as in common speech, but also in other positions, which can be listed as one kind of deviation from Turkish structure, peculiar to one kind of poem; and so on. The model for such deviant listing is apparent in some dialect studies; here the deviations listed are those that vary from the "standard" of a favorite geographic dialect, or from a first or favorite informant, when unwritten languages are involved. I have already criticized this deviant listing elsewhere (**433**).

However weak, the method of deviant listing from a casual utterance corpus permits linguists to maintain the hypothesis, intuitively accepted by nonlinguists, that language is, by nature, monolithic: for every given language there is one structure, carved out of the common speech of the language. Even as a fiction, this hypothesis would remain operationally useful in linguistic analysis, since it permits the postponement of the question of "selection"—freedom of speaker's choice in alternate ways of combining morphemes, as well as in making substitutions among particular morphemes in the same combination—until after a single structure is set up in which possible combinations are discovered for classes of morphemes rather than for particular morphemes. In other words, the very interesting possibility exists that linguistic selection may throw a sharp but narrowly focused light on the large but diffuse problem of free will. This possibility cannot be explored directly in linguistics, since the first prerequisite to a study of "selection" is a knowledge of "structure." The procedurally secondary position of selection is justified technically in another paper (**432**).

An enormous difficulty is encountered at this point. It turns out (1) that problems of selection can be approached only after the monolithic structure of a language is discovered and, then, (2) that the corpus which served so well for discovering structure is too unwieldy or unbounded to serve the study of selection.

In order to obtain identifiable boundaries, a given problem of selection can be conveniently restricted to a specific corpus in a given language—much as in the practice of European scholarship. My colleague, Alo Raun, an exemplar of the European tradition, would merge the casual with the noncasual as a continuum of aspects of "style study"; for example, he says:

... there is something like *time* style, characteristic of a certain moment or period, and having its own conditioning. There is also a *space* or geographic or area style, restricted to an isolated community, or, as a contrast, spread over an immense area. Then there is a *genre* or work style which is relevant here, causing the difference between *chant, song* and *ordinary prose* styles . . . .

This list of the aspects of style is not intended to be complete. You can also speak of a *personal* style with its special conditionings, etc . . . .[2]

But this practice—in theory, continuum; in application, corpus by corpus—does not resolve the paradox: linguists carve out their monolithic structure from the casual utterances of a language and are then, indeed, able to study selection, but, alas, only to find that in the interest of selection they need to start all over again and work inductively toward carving out a satellite structure from each specific noncasual corpus. Linguists are unable to use immediately the structure carved out of the casual utterances for their new noncasual interests—unless, as already mentioned, they are willing to use it as the standard from which to list deviations.

The "enormous difficulty" noted above can, of course, be bypassed by merely leaving out of consideration the problem of selection, but not by merging the casual with the noncasual and then considering selection for a language as a whole. When this is attempted (as in Chomsky's important book, **64**), it results in denigrating certain utterances in the language under investigation (English); for example, "Colorless green ideas sleep furiously."[3] This utterance, to be sure, would not be recognizable in English as a possible casual utterance—it would have zero probability of selection; on the other hand, not only would it be possible in English as a noncasual utterance but it has, in fact, been so used as the title and for the coherent theme of a poem—it has here a high probability of selection.

---

[2] In notes given me by Alo Raun after the Ethnolinguistic Seminar in which I presented the first version of this paper. John Yegerlehner and I were still under the influence of this traditional continuum theory when we wrote **437**. The anthropologist, Edward A. Kennard, in a paper (**228**) given at the Chicago Symposium, would merge the casual with the noncasual as a continuum, not unlike the linguist, Alo Raun. Kennard argues that the distinction is tenuous since kinship terms, for example, are used in casual as well as noncasual utterances; this is of course true and is one reason why a unified structure for both casual and noncasual is considered in the final section of the present paper. Kennard regards casual utterances set up by categories alone as a residual category, as I do not, since it is possible to show linguistic distinctions in spoken Hopi between spontaneous conversation and deliberative narrative, for example, or, more generally, between varieties of casual utterances. For varieties of noncasual utterances Kennard gives a broader ethnographic survey than that given by Euler and myself (**436**).

[3] This is the title of one of two poems written in the summer of 1957 (the title of the second is "The Child Seems Sleeping") under the heading "Two for Max Zorn," by Dell H. Hymes.

Examples such as this could easily be multiplied to show that a distinction between casual utterances and noncasual utterances is natural and important in languages generally. For one example, the selection made in counting coup by an Arapaho warrior (noncasual) shows the repeated use of certain person markers not used when the same Arapaho warrior is engaged in casual conversation. For another example, the two tones that need to be written—if the record is to be reversible—in Hopi chants and in certain narratives (noncasual folktales) occur neither in casual narratives nor in casual conversation. Examples like this do not permit us to say that person markers will distinguish the noncasual from the casual in all languages because they do so in Arapaho; nor that all instances of noncasual Hopi are characterized by a two register tone system, even though it may be said that the prosodic system of all casual utterances in Hopi may be transcribed by marking stress and junctures and omitting tonemes. (As a monolithic structure, then, is Hopi to be classified as a tone language, or not?) Since no single definition of the word "word" has, so far, been successfully formulated for fitting all known language types (despite notable attempts), it is not surprising that no single linguistic definition adequately serves to distinguish casual from noncasual utterances in languages generally.[4]

Faute de mieux, we seek cultural criteria to distinguish casual from noncasual utterances in languages generally. But we return, in another paper, to a more or less adequate linguistic differentiation in Hopi specifically—linguistic features diagnostic of spoken Hopi and chanted Hopi within a unified structure for both.

CULTURAL RECOGNITION OF THE DICHOTOMY

The person-in-the-culture has less difficulty than the investigator in distinguishing between noncasual and casual, whether nonverbally or verbally. This is reflected less in the literature produced by linguists than in that produced by ethnographers. The latter, having gathered the data, might consider it reasonable to make a general cross-cultural distinction between casual and noncasual on three points, as follows, with some critical reservations on the applicability of each in every culture.

[4] Martin Joos would have succeeded in doing this, however, if (although I explicitly disavow it) "literature" were always equivalent to my "noncasual"; Joos argues, in personal communication and in Linguistic Institute lectures, that literature can be said to be utterances or groups of utterances over a certain minimum length which are—or are likely to be—repeated in identical or nearly identical form. Insofar as casual utterances are included in literature, the probability of identical repetition is reduced; this is in general attested in folklore, in so-called "unwritten literature."

1. It is surely reasonable to say that noncasual utterances are restricted to particular times (as when an Islamic muezzin calls people to prayer, or when a Hopi chanter announces a rabbit hunt) and to particular places (as chanting from a minaret or from a roof top); these particular utterances would seem inappropriate at other times and in other places. The weakness of this cross-cultural generalization is that a converse generalization for casual utterances (unrestricted and hence universally appropriate) is clearly not applicable to all cultures. Perhaps the most that can be said is that this converse generalization is approximated in some cultures. Among the Hopi, casual utterances are unrestricted, except for extent of the utterance: a brief conversational exchange is possible in the performance of an elaborate dance-song ritual, and is said, at least by some Hopi, to be essential when some hitch occurs that cannot be righted silently—as when certain parts of costume become disarranged. In other words, casual utterances in Hopi are appropriate at all times and in all places: either in overlap with some noncasual utterances in an emergency, or in an interlude; or, exclusively, where noncasual utterances would seem inappropriate—most of the time and in most places.

2. When a noncasual utterance—as a rollicking ditty—is sung in the wrong place or by the wrong person, persons-in-the-culture find it shocking or humorous, just as they do when some nonverbal behavior is actualized by the wrong person or in the wrong place: it is more appropriate to kneel in church than in an administrative office. There is wide general agreement among persons-in-the-culture in judging appropriateness of noncasual utterances. To satisfy cultural expectation, a given noncasual utterance will be judged not in respect to any single criterion for appropriateness, but rather in respect to a set of four criteria: (a) a particular kind or variety among available noncasual utterances is required (e.g., although two kinds of chants are available, the chant for announcing a Hopi rabbit hunt is always the kind that is addressed to people and never the kind that is addressed to the supernaturals); the other criteria are (b) a particular place (roof top for Hopi chanting), (c) a particular person (either a chant chief or another Hopi acting in the role of chanter), and (d) a particular time (as the night preceding a rabbit hunt). For casual utterances, on the other hand, persons-in-the-culture do not require the whole set of four criteria in judging what is appropriate; and even when some casual utterance is asserted to be shocking or humorous (because it fails to meet cultural expectation according to one criterion), the assertion is likely to be controverted by others. Accordingly, a tentative cross-cultural generalization seems possible: persons-in-the-culture—in many diverse cultures—have either less agreement among fewer criteria, or less awareness (or both) in respect to appropriateness criteria for judging

casual utterances than they have for judging noncasual utterances. This is not to say that a perceptive informant will be unable to discuss the proper times, places, and persons involved in making different kinds of casual utterances, as greeting and parting formulas, or conversation and monologue narrative for recounting recent experiences. But if the informant is really perceptive, he will admit two things: that a good deal of substitution or switching among different varieties of casual utterance is actually done by persons in his culture, and, secondly, that some kinds of casual utterances—as certain greetings or politeness forms—are appropriate any place and any time, although perhaps not appropriate for every person or role. (Speaking now as a person-in-the-culture, I note without amusement that one of my colleagues, upon meeting me, substitutes a monologue narrative of his recent experiences for an answering greeting; others, who have noted this also, find it amusing; still others have had the repeated experience of having their greetings answered by my colleague's monologue narrative without being aware of the switch from one kind of casual utterance to another.)

3. Neither formal training nor specialized interest contributes—in any excluding or including sense—to the proficiency of different varieties of casual utterances.

Thus, all little Hopi speak a baby language variety of casual utterances, and no one says that one child is more proficient than another; children are surrounded by adults who use shorter or suppletive morpheme alternates for kinship terms (and other terms) in the presence of the little ones; this is the only model children have until they are old enough to follow the conversations that adults hold among themselves. A somewhat greater freedom in the distribution of phonemes is found in the idiolect of children which includes words beginning in the labial spirant /v/; later on, the growing child will more or less abandon children's idiolect—except when addressing the generation beneath him—in favor of one of the adult idiolects which restrict the spirant /v/ to word-medial, with the labial stop /p/ appearing initially (in casual utterances).

Again, all little Hopi girls follow their mother's casual utterances for "thanks," "beauty," and other sex-differentiated terms, and Hopi boys imitate the older males' usage. No unusual interest attaches to learning this; it is learned by imitation without deliberate instruction as a matter that is sex-determined, like dressing as a boy or girl, for which there is virtually no individual choice or variation.

In dialect and idiolect differences of casual utterances, there is even less patent choice: you naturally talk as others in your village talk, but since there is visiting among villages, you learn that diversity is possible, and that there may be a shift in referent expressed by the dialectically alien speaker who uses the same morphemes you do; thus, /pɨʔ/ is an interrogative on First Mesa ("*did* he . . . ?") but a connective on Third Mesa ("*then* he did . . ."). Since some words are restricted to one dialect or one generation, it follows that in a conversation between persons from different Hopi villages, or persons from a grandfather and a grandchild generation, communication does occasionally strain over a half-empty word—a word full of significance to the speaker from another village or from an older generation, but empty to the other villager or the younger person who recognizes the word as one he has heard before but without remembering what the other speaker means by the particular word. The word might, accordingly, be identified as "heard but not spoken."

So also in a conversation between two English speakers, the first having book learning, the second not; the first may utter words that have been previously heard but never spoken by the second. For example, in a discussion of political short-sightedness, "myopic" may be the key word in the first idiolect but a half-empty word in the second idiolect.

Varieties of casual utterances, as in the examples just given, are not necessarily distinguished by special labels in every language, although they are commonly distinguished by labels in European languages. Besides "*Kindersprache*" and "patois" and "archaic" and "learned," we can find matching terms or titles or sociological tags for the characteristic speakers of each variety. Thus children speak *Kindersprache*; an out-group speaks a patois; and old scholars use archaic words, but all scholars use learned words. We might expect that such labels would in general be less commonly found for casual utterances and their speakers than for noncasual, since speakers of noncasual utterances are often enough officially invested with high-sounding titles by church or state. But there is, surprisingly enough, no widespread cross-cultural difference when we turn from labels for varieties of casual utterances (and their characteristic speakers) to varieties of noncasual utterances (and their characteristic speakers). An example of the latter in English (and Hopi) is 'chanting' /cáʔlawɨ/, which is done by a 'chanter' /cáʔ+lawqa/, besides a 'chant chief /caʔákmoŋʷi/. We cannot distinguish casual from noncasual utterances by the fact that one is labeled in a given language and the other is not—both may have labels, as exemplified here. And in some languages labels may be lacking for one or another variety of casual or noncasual utterance, or a label may be found for a variety but may be lacking for the characteristic speakers of that variety.

A very literal reading of this ethnographic commentary on labels might well blind one to the ethnographic realism underlying it—to what people do besides what they say—when they have a predilection for some kinds of noncasual utterances. Labels are, to be sure, often inconclusive. Just the same, if a Hopi man is given a fine title, like *chant chief*, he is supposed to accept as an inseparable part of the complex of this or any job described as "chief" (e.g. *village chief* and a host of others) certain associated preparatory obligations and standards of performance (e.g., in the case of a chanter, to memorize well and sometimes even to mimic the speaker who requests a particular announcement to be made). And quite aside from labels, noncasual utterances imply an audience which favors some chanters or singers or raconteurs more than others. The audience is thereby selective. But the chanter or singer or raconteur may be self-selective in the sense of training himself, or being willing and able to be trained in some formal preparatory period.

Conversely, say in gossip or in reminiscences, some speakers may stimulate conversational exchange more than others, but such stimulation is not reflected in opportunities given or withdrawn for making casual utterances. Some Hopi gossip notoriously, and they are listened to politely; some reminisce (without a hint of gossip), and they too are listened to politely. One individual is said to gossip occasionally, another to gossip endlessly, but no one is said to be lacking in ability or training or opportunity for gossip; this kind of criticism is reserved for noncasual utterances.

Training, or else unusual ability and special interest—in the sense of autodidactic interest—is prerequisite to proficiency in noncasual utterances; but conversely, it is not prerequisite to proficiency in casual utterances. This is our final cross-cultural generalization.

The favorite binary distinctions made at Indiana in the SSRC Conference on Style opposed metric and nonmetric utterances, poetic and nonpoetic language, literature and nonliterary discourse. None of these oppositions is exactly equatable to the other; there is, though, a general inclusion of the first two mentioned within the largest class, literature. Some of the conferees equated casual with nonliterary utterances and noncasual with literature, but I do not make this equation. Some fictive literature, as the modern novel, characteristically strives to replicate casual utterances, both in narrative description and in conversation. And from that large part of literature which is noncasual, more than occasional utterances are liberated for the enrichment or the banality of casual utterances.

If my opposition of casual and noncasual utterances were equatable with what is not and what is literature, it would be trivial in the sense of adding nothing but terminology to the subtle problems discussed by literary critics. The nontrivial contribution of the opposition is to the monolithic-unified-structure problem; the data for this problem must be found in the large anthropological scope of all utterances, in culture as a whole, in the perceptive response of unspecialized as well as specialized persons-in-the-culture. Contrary to the Boasian assumption of uncon-sciousness of linguistic structure on the part of preliterate peoples, it turns out that unspecialized persons-in-the-culture react critically—like literary critics—to their own identifications of noncasual utterances, but have less discrimination (hence the Boasian assumption seems to hold here)—or at least say less discriminating things—about casual utterances which, of course, have a variety or diversity of their own, whether or not we choose to comment on them in the same sense that everyone does comment on varietal or stylistic or linguistically formal differences in a given kind of noncasual utterance (e.g. Hopi chants, **436**).

UNIFIED STRUCTURE

"All grammars leak." The leakage is in part due to the fact that the grammars of natural languages represent the structure of casual utterances whose speakers also know from hearing (if not always from speaking) noncasual utterances; an unwitting influence from one or another non-casual corpus that is excluded from the formulation of the grammar may sometimes account for the leakage.

Sapir's words ("All grammars leak.") are cited (after "We take con-solation in . . .") by Lambek (**240**); there would obviously be more nonsense than consolation in a parallel statement "All mathematics leaks." If mathematics includes constructed languages, whose constructions can be assigned to known authors, then of course there are fewer leaks in languages of mathematics than in natural languages since the former are constructed to avoid leaks. Blame for the leakage in the grammars of natural languages is ascribable to one or more of three sources; the last is discussed in detail.

1. Imperfection in natural languages themselves; this kind of criticism is found in logic and mathematics rather than in linguistics.

2. Inadequacy of analytical models followed by grammarians; this criticism, whatever its truth value, may serve (or serve also) as a strategy for urging the adoption of preferred analytical procedures, as in **64, 245, 432a,** and **434.**

3. Two questionable assumptions in linguistics (as identified, for example, in **435**) that (*a*) native speaking informants give us sufficient data for constructing a grammar when they are making casual utterances; and that (*b*) noncasual utterances can be later structuralized as deviations from the structure based on casual utterances—as constellations of non-casual structures surrounding the central and statistically predominant structure hereinafter termed "the grammar."

According to this last view, "the grammar" of a given language is less than a unified structure. Then, however, whenever a deviant construction derived from noncasual utterances appears—with low statistical probability, to be sure—in our corpus of casual utterances, the grammar (up to this point not counting with this particular host) may be found to leak. We may blame the language for the leakage (1); we may, more reasonably, blame our analytical procedures and by restatement of the grammar plug up a particular hole responsible for a particular leakage (2); or we may construct an expanding grammar which includes not only data from casual utterances (3), but also from noncasual utterances for purposes of formulating a unified structure and thereby enlarging the scope of anthropological linguistics (4). Examples for (4) precede a reconsideration (5) of assumption (*a*) in the preceding paragraph.

4. For illustrating (4), we return now to some of the examples cited in the first section of this paper.

In the unified structure of Turkish, there are two sentence types, the common one with verb in clause final (casual), the less common one with verb in other positions than clause final (noncasual).

So also, all person markers are included in the unified structure of Arapaho, with the interesting result that the number of isosemantic paradigmatic sets is increased.

So also, the alternation of stress system of Hopi is expanded to include information on tones; tone in Hopi then turns out to be structured in more than one way. The first of these is more commonly encountered than the second. (1) Tone can be represented in notation for most utterances by dangling juncture (//) or terminal juncture (#) at the end of contours; and then the notation for stress needs to be written only once, at its first occurrence in each contour span. Subsequent stresses follow on syllables whose mora count is odd-numbered, whereas syllables beginning with even-numbered mora counts are unstressed, that is, have weaker stress. (2) Tone can be represented in notation for other utterances not only by single junctures, as just shown, but also by compound junctures (marked // #, and // //) for paragraph final; and then the notation for stress-tone within the contour span falls on syllables for odd-numbered moras, as above, but needs to be written for each stressed syllable rather than once only on the first stressed syllable in each contour span. Stress follows the same alternation in all utterances, but when stressed syllables are either high tone or low tone, they are then marked /'/ and /`/ respectively.

5. The assumption that the casual utterances of native-speaking informants constitute a sufficient basis on which to construct a grammar is too general. It holds only when it is restricted to "class grammar."

("Class grammar" is used as a cover term for any—even diverse—model-directed structuralizations which have in common this minimum concern: to provide formal definition of classes in morphemics as well as in phonemics.) Under this assumption Sapir could say that language is massively resistant to change, although culture is not. What is so massively resistant or so unchanging in language is at bottom the classes which can indeed be discovered from casual utterances, as can be shown from the actual production of many class grammars.

This assumption cannot be extended to selection in the grammar or to the ever-changing resources in the dictionary; and since selection and lexical resources are interdependent, the dictionary turns out to be relevant to the notion of unified structures, of an expanded grammar. Both Sapir's warning not to confuse the "dictionary" with the "language" and Bloomfield's injunction to list regularities in the "grammar" and irregularities in the "dictionary" apply to the concept of a massively resistant class grammar, which treats neither the problem of selection nor the problem of linguistic acculturation. But the latter is only a special instance of languages in contact—or, more generally, of speakers in contact.

In a homogeneous speech community, the speakers in contact do not speak identically, one exactly as the other. The notion of a speech community has to accommodate itself to the fact that there are idiolectic differences among speakers. In a speech community in which mathematicians speak to nonmathematicians, the latter may borrow combinatorial possibilities characteristic of discourse in mathematics; and such discourse, even when exemplified by the purest mathematician, includes some casual utterances. Still, two grammars could be constructed for this community, a noncasual grammar of mathematical discourse and the usual grammar based on casual utterances. But one unified grammar for both would be more realistic, for it would account, by class and by selection, for all utterances made both in mathematical discourse and in nonmathematical conversation, whereas the separate grammars would wholly account for neither.

In speech communities that are largely bilingual, with unidirectional borrowing, the donor language is often enough not reflected in the scholarly report simply because speakers do not include borrowings in casual narrative texts. The report gives, then, the unacculturated American Indian (as Hopi or Shawnee), or Dravidian language (as Kannada), and notes the paucity of borrowings from English. But such borrowings are, in fact, densely included when the same speakers are engaged in casual conversations with each other—conversations now obtainable for analysis by tape recording. The analysis reveals new dimensions of selection and thereby expands the grammar as well as the dictionary. Only middle-aged and younger bilingual Hopi are known to switch from unacculturated Hopi to expanded or acculturated Hopi. The latter, in a special sense, is a second dialect for such speakers.

One phonemic inventory serves for all dialects in the unified structure of Hopi. The chief differences among village dialects then, between adult and baby language, between girl talk and hypermasculine expression—aside from small word lists which are includable in particular dictionaries—turn out to be in interphonemic specification and in allophonic specification. The unified formula for *woman*, for example, is /wɨ(h)ti/; the dialects may be characterized—allowing for more than occasional imitations of, or influences from other dialects—by the common inclusion or noninclusion of preconsonantic /h/ (/wɨ·hti/ or /wɨ·ti/).

Linguistics and the Study
of Poetic Language

EDWARD STANKIEWICZ

The problems of poetic language are complex and seem to be relevant to a number of disciplines.[1] The sociologist, philosopher, linguist, psychologist, historian, and other specialists all share an interest in verbal art. Attempts to explicate poetry from the various points of view specific to different disciplines are always present. The literary historian himself often assumes all the roles of these specialists when he endeavors to interpret a literary work or the nature of poetic language in general. He thus behaves (to paraphrase an analogy used by Jakobson in his study on Khlebnikov, 201) like a detective who tries to track down his suspect, following every scent and leaving no lead unexplored. As a result, he investigates a great number of suspects, all somehow implicated in the case; yet the real culprit may escape his grasp. It may seem presumptuous for the linguist to assert that he, of all the specialists, is best qualified to solve the matter and so reveal the essence of poetic language, yet it is quite clear that the study of verbal art is intimately connected with, and must be based on, the study of language—the linguist's discipline.

It is the purpose of this paper to indicate to what extent the study of poetic language, especially of verse, is related to linguistics.

Since poetic language derives its material from the colloquial language, the competence of the linguist may at first seem similar to the role of the chemist in art history when he deals with the quality of pigments in a painting, or to that of the geologist when he describes the quality of stone in a sculpture. However, a chemical or geological analysis examines a work of visual art as a physical object and not as a work of art, that is, as a fact of nature, not as an artifact of culture. Techniques that yield data about the physical nature of works of art (e.g. macrophotography,

---

[1] This paper grew out of a proseminar on poetic language, given jointly with Mr. Saporta and Mr. Sebeok. Its polemic passages reflect primarily the atmosphere of discussion and inquiry which existed in the classroom.

X-rays, chemical analysis of the pigments) may be useful for the art historian but are divorced from his basic methodological problems, since they have nothing to do with his analysis of the work as an "aesthetic object," as a product of culture. However, even if we provisionally agree to view the linguist as a specialist who is not at all concerned with the aesthetic quality of poetry, his position differs fundamentally from that of the chemist or geologist, inasmuch as the facts of language are in and of themselves facts of culture. Whereas the "material" of language forms an integrated and hierarchically organized system, the pigments or the quality and texture of wood or of stone acquire systematicity solely because of and within the artistic product. By themselves, that is, separated from the work of art, they are "raw" and unintegrated, whereas poetic organization is completely embedded in language and is fully determined by its possibilities. By taking into account the underlying linguistic structure, the study of poetic language becomes thus a study of a certain type of rearrangement and modification of the elements of everyday spoken language.

It may, however, be questioned whether ordinary language and the language of poetry are really different though interdependent types of verbal organization, or whether poetic language is not merely a less systematic variety of ordinary language. Some linguists are, indeed, of the opinion that the study of poetic language falls entirely within the realm of linguistics. The only difference, they argue, between "casual" language and poetic language lies in the former's being subject to systematic and rigorous description, whereas the latter deviates, or rather shows various degrees of deviation, from the linguistic norm. Thus the definition of poetic language as "casual" language in its less systematic form would reduce the study of verbal art to a mere appendix to the study of language, and at that a highly unruly appendix. Such an approach may, no doubt, hold special appeal to theorists who contend that poetry is the realm of individual creativity, of freedom from binding rules, achieved through "violence of language." However, poetic language need not violate any rules of language and still remain what it is, that is, a highly patterned and organized mode of verbal expression. As I shall try to show, poetic language takes full cognizance of the rules of the linguistic system, and, if it admits "deviations," they themselves are conditioned by the language or by the given poetic tradition.

Another approach may assume that the linguist who has managed to bring objectivity and precision of statement into his own field of inquiry may provide the literary scholar with theoretical insights and a rigorous methodology. The student of poetry who knows the literary facts would thus appear to be in the position of the neighbor who owns the ammunition, whereas the linguist is the neighbor who owns the gun. When the two join their resources, they may expect a successful hunt. This view is oversimplified. As long as the linguist does not clearly realize to what body of facts his theory is applicable, his analysis of poetic language will not transcend the limits of traditional linguistic analysis. We could cite the case of the old philologist who studied an ancient literary masterpiece and was, indeed, moved to tears, not by its artistic value but by its archaic grammatical features. The literary scholar, on the other hand, never deals with "naked" facts. His facts are invariably selected within a framework of some theoretical assumptions and evaluations. If the collaboration of the linguist with the student of poetry is to be fruitful, the linguist must be aware of the problems pertaining to poetic form and tradition, and the literary scholar must attend to the methods and achievements of modern linguistics.

In order to clarify the interrelation as well as the autonomy of the two disciplines, linguistics and poetics, it is convenient to examine the constituent elements of speech. The following dimensions can be singled out in any linguistic utterance: (1) the *subject matter*, that is, the thing spoken about, the referent, or, in Charles Morris' terms (**286**), the "semantic dimension"; (2) the *participants*—speaker and addressee; (3) the *speech act*, that is, the concrete physical event, the delivery of the message; (4) the *code*, that is, the language in which the message is transmitted; and (5) the *message*. By the last we mean the form of presentation of the subject matter, the arrangement of the verbal material. All these dimensions enter into poetic language as they do into "casual" speech. In poetic language they are, however, differently organized, and some of them assume a different significance from what they have in prose. It is interesting that each of them has been claimed to contain the essential characteristics of poetic discourse. We shall therefore examine each of them in turn in an attempt to specify how they function in poetry.

1. Within the study of poetry, or more generally of literature, the problem of subject matter has frequently been phrased in terms of its dependence on external factors; art, it has been argued, is a reflection of life, of a cultural milieu, or of the spirit of a nation. We need not dwell on the last, since the spirit of a nation is unanalyzable and its relationship to art is a matter of belief. If by life or cultural milieu we mean all aspects of human experience, present and past, remote and immediate, poetry is certainly a reflection of these, as well as a part of life itself. If, however, we mean life in the narrower sense, that is, important events, various contemporary ideologies, and social trends, these may or may not constitute the subject matter of poetic works, even though they assume special importance in

some of its forms, as in didactic literature or works of propaganda. In these literary forms, however, the aesthetic function is frequently suppressed or is incidental to the work. When limitations are externally imposed on the selection of subject matter, poetic creativity is drastically narrowed and threatened.

But although poetry quite often draws its themes from the stream of everyday life, the problem of subject matter cannot be viewed simply as a matter of establishing the external correlates of literary topics. Literary themes and motives are known to recur within poetic traditions, and the development of a single theme may constitute the "topic" of an entire, even quite long, poetic work. The poet may simply present the theme from various points of view, manipulate it, or describe his attitude toward it. The same theme may also be differently developed and integrated with other elements in different works. Since poetic creativity never appears in a literary vacuum, the same holds for the treatment of themes within entire literary traditions. We can easily envisage the construction of a typology of themes, or a theme index, similar to Thompson's motif index (**413**), for certain literary periods or in certain cultures. The requirement of adherence to a single theme is, moreover, not obligatory in poetic works. Ordinary discourse is generally monothematic (if it is to be coherent), whereas the switching from subject to subject proceeds without any inner connection. In poetry, on the other hand, themes are frequently developed and interpreted by means of other themes, even if the transitions between them are often blurred. Within a single work the basic theme may alternate with rival themes, and their hierarchic relationship may be quite complex. Without the existence, however, of some link between the various constitutive themes, the literary work loses its essential characteristic, its unity.

Related to the problem of thematic development is the use of tropes, especially of metaphor and of metonymy, which concern transpositions between related semantic domains. Metaphor develops the meaning of terms along the line of semantic similarity; metonymy interprets meaning along the line of contiguity. Both have the function of introducing multiple semantic dimensions. If we view the problem of subject matter from an internal point of view, that is, as it is presented within the work itself (or within a certain tradition), the requirement to relate subject matter to external referents appears to be a side line of literary interpretation. For what matters semantically in literary works is obviously not the selection of an inherently "poetic" subject but rather the formal and thematic treatment of whatever subject the poet may choose. Thus the problem of subject matter turns out to be one of the semantic relationships within a work, that is, the problem of metalanguage. Although the theory of meaning is so far the least-developed field of modern linguistics' attempts to study semantics without reference to external correlates are presently being advanced by philosophers and linguists and promise a more refined methodology also for the study of meaning in poetry, where the problems of semantic organization appear in even sharper focus than in everyday language.

The treatment of subject matter and of tropes is not, however, a purely semantic problem. Form and content are inseparable in poetry. Formal requirements determine and modify content to a far wider extent than in everyday speech, in which the primary purpose is transmission of information. In poetic discourse, in which the transmission of information is secondary to the manner of presentation, content itself is defined and limited by the formal organization of the message. This becomes apparent if we consider the thematic restrictions imposed on various literary genres, for example, on epic, dramatic, and lyric poetry. Epic poetry in its purest form deals with the presentation of important past events, dramatic poetry with the presentation of conflicting present events which are heading toward some solution, whereas lyric poetry has no thematic or temporal limitations. The different treatments of subject matter and of time in these genres entail a different emphasis on the narrative (reported) events and on the speech events, and different assignments to the participants of the narrative and of the speech event. The participants of the speech event may themselves become the subject matter of some forms of poetry, as for example in lyrical poetry which hinges on the poet himself, that is, a fictitious addressor, or in charms, prayers, and magic formulas, in which the emphasis shifts to an imaginary or ubiquitous addressee. Concomitant with these limitations upon the subject matter, time, and participants are different requirements of meter, of stanzaic form, which in turn imply a different treatment of rhyme, of figures, of syntactic phrasing, and of orchestration (or phonic instrumentation). Aside from fulfilling purely rhythmic functions, the use of rhymes and of figures such as anaphora or paronomasia has a decisive effect on the development of a theme, on the choice of grammatical forms and lexical items, no matter how differently these problems are treated by various poets or within various literary traditions. The extent to which form and meaning are interconnected is well known from the traditional assignment of different meters for different genres (such as the hexameter for the epic, free verse for fables, etc.), or, in the case of parodies, through the clash of meter and content. Meaning, then, far from being extrinsic to the study of poetic language, can be analyzed and explained only with relation to the other elements of poetic organization. The requirement that the components of a structure be analyzed with relation to each other, that problems of form be constantly correlated to problems of meaning, is indispensable in the study of language, as well as in the analysis of poetic language.

2. The roles of the participants of the speech event, of the speaker and listener, correspond in poetic language to the relationship between the author and the audience. Students of poetry tend to approach this problem with a one-sided bias; at the center of their interest has always been the poet. This approach leads to investigations concerning the psychological or biographical background of the poet and ignores the fact that the poet writes for an audience which sanctions or proscribes his work. Even when the author rejects the judgment and values of his contemporaries, he writes for a future or imaginary audience, and his work is part of a tradition toward which he takes a positive or negative stand. A similar bias to the one held toward the poet in literary studies has also been known in linguistics. Linguists have often maintained that "language is a fiction" and concentrated their attention on the idiolect, on the speech of the addressor, as of some biological entity, ignoring the fact that language is a social phenomenon and that there is no individual speech outside of socially given norms.

The main shortcoming of the biographical or psychological approach in literature (and, for that matter, in the other arts) lies in shifting the emphasis from the work of art as an autonomous product to the producer, to the creator. The inadequacy of this approach would by itself seem quite obvious and harmless if it were not, in the study of poetic language, connected with a more important methodological question. Poetic works, unlike sculptures and paintings, are not tangible, concrete things. They depend on their implementation, on reading or oral delivery. It is understood that the graphic rendering of a poem bears only a partial relationship to the work as a form of verbal expression, although our typographic conventions do justice to certain elements of poetic organization, such as the division into lines and stanzas. Some typographic devices are, on the other hand, destined only for eye effect. But if poetic works are implemented only by reading, the question may arise: whose reading or recitation is valid as the basis of our analysis? This question has often been asked, although put in this form it is misleading.

3. Although it is undeniable that the aesthetic effect of poetic works is heightened by artistic delivery (not by chance are epics sung or recited by bards or "singers," dramas performed by actors, lyric poems read by actors and poets), the subjective interpretation of a poem cannot be taken as a measure of its objective properties. It is apparent that there may be various oral interpretations for a given poem. Some readers may emphasize the metric pattern of a poem (through "scansion"), others the

semantically important words (through the use of so-called "logical stresses"), or syntactic phrasing. It may therefore appear that if a variety of performances is possible with respect to the same poem, the reading that would have to be decisive is that of the poet himself (as was argued by Sievers, **375,** who divided readers into two categories, *Autorenleser* and *Selbstleser*). The shortcoming of this approach lies in the identification of the poem, which constitutes a replicable, invariant structure, with its acoustic implementation in the concrete performance.

Poetic language differs from prose primarily through the rules of organization of the message, which "acquires autonomous value" and which must be distinguished from the individual and nonreplicable speech act. Every poem constitutes a specific type, composed of invariable elements, whereas the various deliveries constitute its tokens. A poem is, in other words, an organized message, the elements of which must recur in any performance. The study of these constant elements alone constitutes the science of versification, whereas the study of the variations of delivery (where we may, in turn, discern certain dominant types) constitutes the art of declamation. To the modern linguist the distinction between these two branches appears similar to that between phonemics and phonetics. And it is not surprising that versification was considered a branch of experimental phonetics at a time when the functional aspect of language was ignored and when the study of the phonetic minutiae of individual pronunciations was identified with the study of the relevant elements of language.

4. We may now consider the problem of the linguistic code in poetic language.

It has been observed that poetry operates with some linguistic features which do not occur in "casual" language. The use of the phonemes /ŋ/ and /l/, which do not occur in Nootka spoken language, has been observed by Sapir in Nootka chants and songs respectively, and Voegelin indicates (**436**) that Hopi chants utilize certain accentual features not known in "casual" language. It may therefore appear that the difference in the phonemic inventory, or more broadly in the linguistic system, constitutes one of the distinctive characteristics of poetic discourse. Such a conclusion would, however, be unwarranted, considering that some poetic works, or even entire literary traditions, show a strict adherence to the prevailing synchronic norm. "Deviations" from the accepted norm or norms of the spoken language are, on the other hand, not only tolerated but even expected within various poetic traditions, periods, and genres. Such "deviations" must not be viewed as poetic license and individual creations; they are, rather, the result of manipulations of available linguistic material and the skillful utilization of the possibilities inherent in the spoken language. This is apparent if we recognize that no linguistic system has only one norm. For descriptive, and especially for prescriptive purposes, we restrict ourselves synchronically to the analysis of one basic norm. Actually, however, in every speech community there are at least two competing norms, an innovating and a more archaic one, and the vocabulary of any language contains competing forms from different social strata or regional areas. The utilization of heterogeneous elements, pertaining to different systems or layers of language, often becomes in poetry a purposeful, artistically exploited device. In languages that have a variety of norms, each may be assigned a different poetic function. This was, for instance, the case in classical Greek poetry, where epic, lyric, and dramatic works were written in different dialects. The pseudoclassical tradition elaborated the concept of various "styles" suitable to different genres of literature (e.g., the theory of three "styles" developed by Lomonosov for the Russian literary language of the eighteenth century). If there is one recognized standard language, a departure from the norm may often be restricted to only one of its levels or to some of its elements. Quite common is the utilization of lexical items which pertain to different systems or to different strata of one system. This is achieved by the introduction of dialectal or archaic words, of foreignisms or of specialized, technical terms. The Romantic poets had, for example, a predilection for exotic words (e.g. Hebrew and Arabic in the poems of Heine and Mickiewicz) or for a regional and archaic vocabulary, whereas the modern poets often operate with scientific and urban terminology.

Other forms of "deviations" from the norm (which generally coincides in culture languages with the literary standard) may affect also the grammatical and phonemic patterns of the language. This kind of manipulation of language, which is also encountered in child language or in situations of dialect mixing, is in poetry intentionally utilized and integrated with the other elements of poetic organization. Besides yielding neologisms (such as new derivative forms), it may also produce unusual word combinations or sound sequences such as are found in nonsense words. This play with language is, however, based on the poet's intuitive knowledge of the abstract patterns of the language and of the rules of permissible sequences. It could hardly move in the direction of introducing new phonemes or of creating new distributional patterns. Although the exploitation of linguistic resources is thus an important poetic device, the types of neologisms that enter into poetry vary according to the possibilities of the language. Neologisms based on word derivation are, for example, much more common and acceptable in Slavic poetry than neologisms based on compound formation. It is also interesting to notice that attempts to depart drastically from the given linguistic system (such as the "trans-sense" experiments of the Russian futurists) remained only a curious episode in the history of literature.

By full exploitation of the resources of the linguistic system, the poet is able to arrange his themes or the formal elements, such as rhyme and syntactic parallelism, to coincide with phonemic or grammatical opposi-tions. In the Slavic languages, for example, thematic contrasts can be highlighted by the use of different aspects or genders. Rhymes may hinge on similar derivational and grammatical suffixes or may emphasize certain phonemic features at the expense of other, more marginal features (e.g. length, voicing, or palatalization in some Slavic languages).

5. The clearest distinction between poetic discourse and everyday casual language or prose is in the periodic organization of the message. There are no doubt literary works which are difficult to place in a prose-poetry dichotomy, but the study of twilight zones, of transitional types, cannot help us in the identification of properties that mark diametrically opposed phenomena. Methodologically we have to begin our analysis with types that exhibit their characteristic properties in the extreme. The highest form of poetic organization, verse, differs from prose in its rhythmic pattern. Rhythm implies the recurrence of certain elements within regularly distributed time intervals. The rules of distribution of these elements along the syntagmatic axis, which are obligatory for a given language or for a given period, constitute the system (or systems) of versification. When the student of poetry examines the principles of selection of the periodic signals and of their arrangement along the time axis, he cannot avoid consideration of the linguistic code, which deter-mines both the selection and distribution of these signals. It is due to the work of linguists, and especially of the linguistically minded formalists, that the questions of rhythmic patterning have been put in the proper perspective.

The schoolmasters brought up on the models of Greek and Latin verse have for centuries repeated the formulas of the ancient grammarians about the prosodic types which they applied indiscriminately to poetry written in various languages. Dactylic, iambic, or anapestic meters were for them universals, like the grammatical categories of Greek and Latin which were supposed to fit the most divergent languages. Modern studies in versification have shown that certain metrical systems are incompatible with some linguistic systems. What is more important, they revealed that meter itself is only a theoretical construct, an abstract scheme that is never fully implemented, somewhat like a phonemic pattern with empty slots. The implementation of the metrical scheme is in turn conditioned by the underlying linguistic system. Thus it is known that no versification system can be based on prosodic elements which are not relevant in the language, and that changes in the phonemic pattern of a language lead ultimately to innovations in its metrics, even though some conservative metrical systems may be artificially cultivated by writers-scholars.

The dependence of the metrical scheme on the linguistic system can be illustrated by comparing the versification systems of Russian and of Polish. Russian poetry is based on a system which utilizes the phonemic stress of the language as the main element of periodicity, because the Russian "rhythmic vocabulary" lends itself easily to a free arrangement of its stresses. The ultimate constituent of Russian meter is therefore the *foot*, in which the *heavy* (*in principle* stressed) syllable alternates with one or two *light* (*in principle* unstressed) syllables (e.g. trochaic or dactylic feet), or vice versa (e.g. iambic or anapestic feet). Polish, on the other hand, could hardly select stress as an element of periodicity, since Polish words, invariably stressed on the penultimate syllable, could only with difficulty fit into long strings of trochaic and dactylic feet, and even less so into iambic or anapestic feet, which require final stressed syllables. The ultimate constituent of Polish versification could without difficulty, however, be a unit higher than the foot, the line or hemistich, which is defined by a number of signals. The most *constant* of these signals in Polish poetry has been an equal number of syllables per line, delimited by rhyme. The systems that have shown the greatest vitality and longevity in Polish and in Russian have thus been isosyllabic and isotonic meters respectively.

However, Russian learned poetry has for some time employed a versification system based on the Polish model. This shows that various metrical systems may coexist within one language, and that cultural factors are of great significance in the adoption of a meter. The system was nevertheless not suitable for Russian, because it did not exploit the possibilities with which Russian could invest prosody and it was in contradiction to Russian folk poetry. It was also quite differently implemented than in Polish, since it led to an overemphasis and artificial pronunciation of the unstressed vowels and an underemphasis of the stressed vowels. Polish poetry, on the other hand, in the nineteenth century adopted the accentual principle, in imitation of classical meters and of a native melic tradition (the folksong) in which it owed its stability to the support of music. However, the principle of alternating *heavy* and *light* syllables has been employed in learned poetry as an element of variation of the lines, rather than as a strictly observed and basic principle. Metric principles transplanted from foreign systems can, however, be variously utilized, since metric systems employ a variety of elements which fulfill different functions. Besides the example of modern Polish verse, we can cite Czech versification in this connection. Its system is syllabo-tonic, that is, the lines have an equal number of stresses and of syllables. The Czech meter is, nevertheless, quite different from the Russian syllabo-tonic system, since in Czech the distribution of stresses coincides with the word boundaries, Czech stress being automatically restricted to the initial syllable of the word. In Russian, in which stress is independent of word boundaries, the distribution of word boundaries, or phrasing, serves as the principle of rhythmic variation, whereas in Czech variation between the lines is introduced by the skillful alternation of long and short vowels. Cultural as well as linguistic factors have been responsible for the fact that phonemic length has not become the basis for Czech versification.

The foregoing reflections lead us to conclude that the basic constituents and the efficiency of metrical systems are determined by the linguistic system in question. This is even more apparent if we examine the different realizations of the same metrical schemes. Russian, German, and English poetry employ isotonic (or syllabo-tonic) meters, which involve stress as the basis of periodicity. The rhythmic pattern of Russian verse is, however, quite different from that of English or German, as is indicated by the different impression the latter make upon a Russian: German verse seems to him too monotonous, and English verse lacking in rhythm. This impression is due to the fact that German binary meters (trochaic and iambic feet) show little deviation from the metrical scheme, whereas English binary meters tolerate far greater deviations from the metrical scheme than do Russian iambs and trochees. If we study the stress patterns of the respective languages, we see that German employs secondary stresses in compounds and in auxiliary words (the so-called "Nebenton"), whereas English admits a variety of stresses in its syntactic constructions, which are comprised mainly of strings of monosyllabic or disyllabic words. The rhythmic vocabulary of Russian consists, on the other hand, of a large number of polysyllabic words which admit only one stress. Russian polysyllabic words can therefore enter into binary meters only under the condition that some metric stresses be omitted. The vocabulary of Russian has only a limited number of words with a 1 : 1 ratio of stressed and unstressed syllables. The permissible omissions of metric stresses yield, however, a 1 : 2.8 ratio of stressed versus unstressed syllables, which corresponds to the ratio of stressed versus unstressed syllables in ordinary prose. Thus we see that the actual distribution of stresses which determines the rhythmic pattern of verse and which "deviates" from the abstract metrical scheme is in agreement with the distribution of stress within the spoken chain of the ordinary language.

These remarks on meter and on rhythm would seem to suggest that the creative initiative of the poet is highly restricted and, as far as verse is concerned, there is very little room for artistic originality. But such a conclusion would be correct only if by originality we understood freedom from norms. Originality is, however, most clearly achieved within the framework of regularity and of limitations. This idea was lucidly expressed by Goethe:

> In der Beschränkung zeigt sich erst der Meister
> Und das Gesetz nur kann uns Freiheit geben.

Every poem is an autonomous unit of higher organization which is based on a set of generally observed norms, but which also admits areas of relative freedom. Within the areas of freedom we can, further, discern certain tendencies which are more or less observed and are therefore statistically regulated. The relationship between the constants and tendencies is never absolute but is in a state of dynamic tension, which may historically result in a series of structural transformations. Within the versification system (or systems) itself there are *in nuce* tendencies, which determine their further direction. The rearrangement of the constants and of the elements of variation is, at first, always a daring step on the part of some great innovators. When sanctioned, what were first daring innovations constitute new norms, but these in turn contain the elements of further development. The history of Russian versification since the end of the eighteenth century may exemplify the different treatment of the obligatory elements or *constants*, and of the statistically measurable *tendencies*. In eighteenth- and early nineteenth-century poetry, the omission of stress on the light syllables and the compulsory stress on the last heavy syllable of a line were constant. From the time of Pushkin, Russian binary meters exhibited a tendency to omit word stresses in each odd heavy syllable, and an even stronger tendency to omit them on each even heavy syllable, counting backward from the last compulsory stress. Toward the end of the nineteenth century, the situation changed. Within the new ternary meters, the observation of the heavy syllables became compulsory. This led to a rhythmic pattern which adhered very closely to the metric scheme. This system was felt to have too many constants, and during the twentieth century the requirement to have an equal number of unstressed syllables between heavy syllables was abandoned. In this meter the number of stressed syllables per line became compulsory, and the number of syllables per line variable.

The different treatment of meter also entails a different treatment of other rhythmic elements, such as the intonation contour of the lines, the possibilities of enjambment, the distribution of the caesura, the functional burden and the type of rhymes. Since all these elements are hierarchically integrated, the poem constitutes a structure of various interacting levels.

The arrangement and integration of these levels are subject to individual variation, since their combinatory possibilities are indeed enormous. The great poet is the man who possesses an intuitive mastery of the rules that are obligatory within his own poetic tradition and language, but who also can manipulate these rules in accordance with his own artistic intentions and who can surpass the limits prescribed by his tradition. For this reason original poetry, as any good art, always strikes us by its freshness and unexpected turns. However, poetic works are unthinkable outside the rules of language and of a given tradition, which explains why translations of poetry are much more difficult (if not impossible) than those of prose. For any good translation is a work of creative reinterpretation in accordance with the set of rules which govern different poetic systems and in accordance with the different possibilities of variation which these allow.

In conclusion, we can say that the student of poetry is in no position to describe and to explain the nature of poetic language unless he takes into account the rules of language which determine its organization, just as the linguist cannot properly understand the forms of poetic expression unless he considers the forces of tradition and culture that affect the specific character of poetry. The understanding and explication of an original poetic work is, however, always a matter of insight and intuition on the part of the analyst. And since the object of our analysis is broader than our descriptions, which are always of a provisional character, no analysis can be fully exhaustive. Nor can it replace the aesthetic and emotional impact produced by a work of art itself. The poet is therefore basically right when he says: "Grau, teurer Freund, ist alle Theorie, Und grün des Lebens goldner Baum."[2]

[2] The following is a selected list of references appropriate to this paper: **50, 91, 115, 141, 184, 195, 197, 201, 233, 288, 292, 305, 348, 351, 375, 406, 417, 420, 421, 442,** and **462.**

The Application of Linguistics to the Study of Poetic Language

SOL SAPORTA

THE PROBLEM: THE RELATION OF LANGUAGE TO POETRY

Before we make any statements about the application of linguistics to the study of poetry (or literature, or noncasual language), we must make explicit one fundamental assumption about the nature of poetry and its relation to the other kind(s) of linguistic phenomena, that is, prose (or colloquial language, or casual language).[1] Let us assume that there is a class of phenomena, however defined, which we may call *language* and which is the proper domain of linguistics. There is (at least) one class of phenomena which is not language, and which, by definition, is outside the domain of linguistics. Let us assume that this second class includes such things as music, paintings, etc., and that we call these phenomena *art*. In discussing the relation of *poetry* to language and to art, there are only three possibilities: (1) Poetry is language, that is, what we call poetry lies completely within the class of phenomena we call language and is a subclass thereof. It therefore lies within the proper domain of linguistics. (2) Poetry is not language but art, that is, no part of what we call poetry is language, but rather what we call poetry lies completely within the class of phenomena we call art and is a subclass thereof. Poetry therefore lies outside the proper domain of linguistics. (3) Poetry is the overlap between language and art, that is, there are certain phenomena which are simultaneously members of the class we call language and the class we call art, and it is this dual membership which characterizes poetry.

Now, if we assume case 1, to say that linguistics (or linguistic methods) may be applied to poetry is, in a sense, to assert the obvious, since nothing

[1] This paper has benefited from numerous lengthy discussions with George N. Sholes, and many of his suggestions have been included. In addition, I am indebted to Fred W. Householder, Jr., for his criticisms of an earlier draft. The author's research was supported in part by grants from the National Science Foundation and the Institutes of Mental Health.

is gained by maintaining that linguistic methods may be applied to language, that is, to what is the proper domain of linguistics, or so it would seem at first.

If we assume case 2, to say that linguistic methods may be applied to poetry is to assert what would seem to be a contradiction, namely, that linguistic methods are applicable to phenomena outside the domain of linguistics. Or, if it is not a contradiction, it at least implies that the linguist, in studying poetry, has abandoned his role as linguist. There is one sense in which we might profitably speak of the application of linguistic methods to something which is not language, namely, where *linguistic* is in some way taken to be the equivalent of *scientific* (or, perhaps, *more scientific*). This problem is touched on in the next section.

Case 3 would seem to have a sort of intuitive appeal. It makes some kind of sense to classify poetry as verbal art; and yet, to the linguist, the appeal is illusory, since such an assumption may be objected to for precisely the same reason that case 2 may be objected to. The linguist cannot study poetry as art without abandoning his position as linguist; he can only study poetry as language. He is therefore forced to assume case 1, if only to ultimately reject it as being in some way inadequate. On the other hand, it may turn out that the analysis of poetry as language will in some way correlate with, or be a complement to, the analysis of the same phenomena as art, at the same time utilizing more precise techniques. Underlying any linguistic analysis of poetry is the hypothesis that there will be some significant correlation with the results of other, more intuitive methods. The results must in some way coincide with our intuitions about the nature of the phenomena, or we are obliged to doubt their validity. When our analysis does not coincide with our intuitions, usually we find it necessary to modify our analysis; only rarely do we find it necessary to modify our intuitions. Terms like *value*, *aesthetic purpose*, etc., are apparently an essential part of the methods of most literary criticism, but such terms are not available to linguists. The statements that linguists make will include references to phonemes, stresses, morphemes, syntactical patterns, etc., and their patterned repetition and co-occurrence. It remains to be demonstrated to what extent an analysis of messages based on such features will correlate with that made in terms of value and purpose.

A linguistic approach to style, then, will be based on some such assumption as that expressed in case 1, that is, that all poetry is language but not all language is poetry. However, it does not follow from this relationship that language is to poetry as stone is to sculpture, as has sometimes been suggested (e.g. **442**, p. 177). The fact that language can be "manipulated" to serve an aesthetic purpose depends on the communicative function of language which is part of its definition. Stone has no such function, so that no one has seriously suggested that a knowledge of petrology could make anything but the most trivial contribution to the understanding of sculpture. If such analogies are fruitful, perhaps it is more useful to compare the relationship of language to poetry to, say, the relationship between fire and a furnace. It is the heat-giving characteristic of fire, present by definition, that enables its being utilized for cooking or ceramics. The understanding and critical analysis of a furnace would presumably be incomplete without an awareness of the nature of fire.

Now, it is in theory pointless to assert that linguistic methods may be applied to poetry, once we have defined poetry as a subclass of language. However, in practice, linguists have by and large operated on precisely the opposite assumption, namely, that a grammatical description need not accommodate poetic messages. Indeed, it has usually been implicit in most grammars that the occurrence of a particular sequence in poetry alone is sufficient grounds for classifying it as "ungrammatical" or in some way marginal. The danger of circularity is obvious. How do you know this sequence is ungrammatical? Because it occurs only in poetry. How do you know this is poetry? Because where else could you find such an ungrammatical sequence?

The circularity can perhaps be avoided by developing some such notion as Noam Chomsky's suggested *degrees of grammaticalness* (**63**). One example may illustrate. Let us assume that speakers of English will agree that there is a sense (other than statistical and/or semantic) in which "The boy fears the night" may be said to be more grammatical than "The night fears the boy." Similarly, "The night frightens the boy" is in some way "more English" than "The boy frightens the night." One way to account for this feeling of grammaticalness, if it exists, is to establish two subclasses of English nouns, animate, including "boy," and inanimate, including "night," and two classes of verbs, class 1, including "fears," and class 2, including "frightens." All four sequences will fit a general formula of the type Noun Phrase + Verb Phrase + Noun Phrase. However, more specific formulas such as Animate Noun + Verb 1 + Noun or Noun + Verb 2 + Animate Noun will fit "The boy fears the night" or "The night frightens the boy," but not the other two. Now, if sequences can in some way be ordered as to the degree of grammaticalness, it may be possible to characterize the language of poetry in terms of the density of these sequences of lower-order grammaticalness. Thus, "The night fears the boy" and, similarly, "The trees whisper" are more likely to occur in poetry than elsewhere, whereas "The boy fears the night" and "The boys whisper" are just as likely to occur elsewhere.

The question of grammaticalness is discussed further later in the paper; suffice it to say at this point that to linguists the application of linguistics to poetry means essentially the reintroduction into the corpus of a body of data that had been excluded, in part arbitrarily, for the purely practical reason that it complicated the writing of grammars.

This relates to a question discussed during the conference, namely, "Why does a linguist want a definition of poetry or literature?" A partial answer seems to be that, as a writer of grammars, a linguist wants to be able to identify poetry for the same reason that he needs to identify unassimilated loan words or slips of the tongue, namely, as justification for not including them in his grammar. For example, an English poet includes a line with "inverted" word order, say, Subject Object Verb. The transformational rule required for generating such a sentence will also generate a very large, perhaps infinite, number of sentences like "John Mary loves," "I the boy see," and "The fellow in the corner booth a ham sandwich wants," sentences which somehow seem unacceptable. It is more economical to devise a grammar that fails to generate the line in the poem.[2]

LINGUISTICS, STYLISTICS, AND THE SCIENTIFIC METHOD

It has been suggested that the application of linguistic techniques to poetry might in some way be more "scientific," whatever that may be, than the nonlinguistic techniques, whatever they may be. In other words, the justification for a different approach may be either that it reveals new aspects of the data, or that it reveals the old aspects in a more precise, replicable (i.e., scientific) way, or both. The following two quotations may serve as a basis for discussion:

"Poetry is different from science." James Sledd (**382**).

"Linguistics is an art, not a science, and the best linguist is the man with the best hunches, the best natural talent for the job, and the best unreasoned and inescapable feel for language." Fred W. Householder, Jr. (**183**).

The first statement, if taken literally, is true, but trivial. The phenomenon is always different from the method used to describe it. To say that poetry is different from science is like saying that the stars are different from astronomy. *Scientific* is usually meant to apply not to the phenomenon but to a way of talking about any phenomenon. What makes astronomy a science as opposed to astrology is not that it necessarily deals with different kinds of phenomena, but that it makes different kinds of statements about the same phenomena. We assume Sledd's statement to mean that the scientific method has little to offer to the understanding of poetry, that

[2] The problem arises whether such "coexistent systems" can be identified by purely internal evidence such as low frequency, asymmetry in the inventory, etc., or whether some external evidence is required; cf. **127**.

there is some inherent difference between stars and poetry, which makes one amenable to scientific study and the other not. If such is the intention of Sledd's statement, then it is premature, since it would appear that it has not yet been demonstrated. One way to demonstrate whether the statement is true, perhaps the only way, is to apply the scientific method and show wherein it is inadequate.

Now, we have assumed two things: (1) poetry is language, and (2) any phenomenon, including poetry, may be approached scientifically. Therefore, if poetry is language and linguistics is the scientific study of language, linguistics is also the scientific study of poetry.

But there seems to be an essential difference in the aims and consequently the results of linguistics and what can be called stylistics. A linguistic description is adequate to the extent that it predicts grammatical sentences beyond those in the corpus on which the description is based. Now, stylistic analysis is apparently primarily classificatory rather than predictive in this sense. The validity of a stylistic analysis of poetry does not depend on the ability to produce new poems. Put differently, the result of a linguistic analysis is a grammar which generates unobserved (as well as observed) utterances. The aim of a stylistic analysis would seem to be a typology which would indicate the features shared by a particular class of messages as well as the features by which they may be further separated into subclasses. Ideally, each different message would be uniquely defined in terms of a certain set of these defining characteristics.[3]

If such a view does reflect the purpose of stylistics, how can the reliability and validity of the techniques involved be determined? By reliability in this connection we mean that the bases for classification should be made explicit so that they are applicable unambiguously. The validity is tested essentially by the usefulness of the classification or its agreement with that obtained by less precise judgments. Specifically, we ask what features are shared by the members of a class other than the features forming the basis of the classification. It is here that the linguist—now as an analyst of style rather than as a writer of grammars—must eventually rely on the critic's notions about poetry, since the latter's notions serve as a test of the validity of the linguist's results. The linguist's classification, based on the kind of structural features mentioned earlier, will presumably include types the members of which share nonstructural features to be furnished and defined by literary critics.

But we find Householder's statement which seems to say that linguistics cannot achieve the desired replicability. However, as Householder (**181**) and Chomsky (**64**) have since pointed out, replicability is not required of

---

[3] This view of stylistics as essentially classificatory in nature seems to form the basis of two other papers in this volume, the ones by Lotz and Carroll.

the steps leading to the discovery of grammars but only to the steps involved in their validation. Similarly, we require of stylistics only that the basis for classification be specified so as to assure maximum agreement among analysts, and that the criteria for evaluating alternate classifications be made explicit.

We must now indicate what kind of statements linguists generally make, and the model that Charles Morris has suggested (**286**) may serve as a framework. We may distinguish, as Morris proposes, three areas: (1) *syntactics*, the study of the relationship of sign to sign, (2) *semantics*, the study of the relationship of sign to designatum, and (3) *pragmatics*, the study of the relationship of sign to user. Syntactics will coincide with what is generally understood by distributional analysis or combinatorial linguistics or linguistics without meaning. We need not discuss whether, as some linguists maintain, syntactics equals linguistics, but it is surely clear that, at the present stage of development, we are capable of achieving a greater degree of precision in our statements about the relations between signs than we are in those about the relations of signs to designata, if, indeed, these latter statements are relevant to the problems of writing grammars.

However, it seems that there may be an interesting relationship between the syntactic rules, that is, the distribution of a sign, and its semantic rules, that is, meaning. In spite of certain difficulties, it seems reasonable to hypothesize that there are distributional correlates to semantic relationships such as synonymy, etc. As Zellig Harris suggests (**150**), "if we consider words or morphemes *A* and *B* to be more different in meaning than *A* and *C*, then we will often find that the distributions of *A* and *B* are more different than the distributions of *A* and *C*. In other words, difference of meaning correlates with difference in distribution." Thus we may be able to use some function of the distributional data as an approximation to the meaning.

STYLE

The emphasis on distributional statements suggests some such notion as the one proposed by Bernard Bloch (**32**): "The style of a discourse is the message carried by the frequency-distributions and transitional probabilities of its linguistic features, especially as they differ from those of the same features in the language as a whole." Such a view suggests that whereas linguistics is concerned with the description of a code, stylistics is concerned with the differences among the messages generated in accordance with the rules of that code. The analysis of style essentially involves the identification and calibration of the various dimensions along which messages may differ.[4] Or, to state the same relationship in a different way, linguistics deals with types, stylistics with tokens, or at least types of a lower level. Stylistics and linguistics differ in two other aspects. Stylistics may utilize frequencies and transitional probabilities, but these are by and large irrelevant for the writing of grammars, where all sequences are generated once. And, whereas the maximum unit in linguistics is the sentence, a larger unit, the text, serves as the basis for stylistic analysis (**148–149**).

Bloch's definition contains two terms that need elaboration, *linguistic features* and *language as a whole*. In addition, the nature of the deviations in frequency distributions and transitional probabilities must be made explicit.

The Relevant Linguistic Features

It is clear that there are certain aspects of any speech event which are more conveniently described as belonging to something other than the message. This something else is usually referred to as the *performance* or *delivery*. The problem is perhaps phrased best as that of determining when a particular utterance token is to be considered as a repetition of another, that is, as representing the identical message, since if style is a characteristic of messages, and not of utterance tokens, all variants of the same message by definition will have the same style. For example, a decision must be made whether the difference between "There's a big bear in the woods" and "There's a BI::G bear in the woods" is of the same order as those that distinguish messages from one another or whether the difference is like that between variants of the same message. It seems desirable to distinguish the so-called expressive features from linguistic features that will be relevant to a discussion of style. This is not to imply that there is no difference between the two tokens, but only that the difference is best treated as something other than a stylistic one.[5]

Similarly, a particular message is used in two different situations. A beggar wanting something to eat and a child who wants to postpone going to bed at night both say "I'm hungry." Is the difference in situation sufficient to establish a difference in style? We think not. The style of a

[4] Miller (**276**, ch. 6) talks about verbal style in reference to "differences that exist among people." It is not clear to what extent the notions of style as a characteristic of messages and style as a characteristic of individuals are compatible. The fingerprint analogy suggested during the conference by Roger Brown is probably not to be taken to mean that all messages of a particular individual share certain characteristics absent from any and all messages by other individuals.

[5] Some of the recent discussions about metrics would seem to be based on a similar disagreement on what constitutes a feature that distinguishes messages, as opposed to one that is assignable to the performance (cf. **60, 61, 325, 398** and **445**).

message will be described in terms of the relations of the linguistic features to one another, not in terms of the relations of linguistic features to non-linguistic features, so that questions of truth, intention, etc., will fall in a different area of literary analysis. Just as a particular message has a variety of performances, so on the other hand it has a variety of *interpretations*. Both seem to lie beyond stylistics in this admittedly limited conception of what constitutes style.[6] That such a view has limitations is obvious. For example, it seems doubtful that it can readily account for such literary features as irony, humor, etc. However, we may hope and reasonably expect that as a structural semantics develops it will furnish methods applicable to the analysis of the meaning of poetic language as well. For the time being, it is merely suggested that the study of formal relationships be distinguished from the study of semantic relationships, and that it may be convenient to limit the term *stylistics* to the former.

One linguist has suggested that a poem is a long idiom, an idiom being understood to be a sequence of morphemes (or words) the meaning of which is not predictable from the meanings of the individual parts. Thus, "kick the bucket" when it means "die" is an idiom. The difference, however, is that idioms recur in various contexts and presumably we find that some of the contexts in which "kick the bucket" occurs are identical to contexts in which "die" occurs: thus, "He had been sick for a long time before he finally ———." There is usually some purely formal evidence from which the meaning of an idiom can be inferred. But poems do not usually recur in different, larger linguistic contexts; their "idiomatic" meaning cannot be inferred. If, for example, the nursery rhyme about Humpty Dumpty refers to a particular English nobleman, this fact is not discoverable by purely linguistic techniques. In fact, it is not even clear how we would determine that Humpty Dumpty is an egg. The identification and analysis of "private symbols" may be relevant to the genesis and interpretation of the poem but not to the stylistic analysis of the poem itself.

The relation of formal or syntactic analysis to semantics has another aspect. It is sometimes maintained that for ambiguous constructions, that is, constructions permitting of alternate interpretations, an accurate formal analysis provides an insight into the meaning, that is, it resolves the ambiguity. Now, all languages seem to have homonymy on several levels, for example, word homonymy, constructional homonymy, etc. A word may belong to two classes; for example, "cover" is either a noun or a verb. A sentence may belong to two constructions; a telegram "Ship sails today"

---

[6] The exclusion from style of questions of performance and interpretation is analogous to the division between linguistics proper and phonetics on the one hand and semantics on the other.

may be either a command, Verb Object Adverb, or a statement, Subject Verb Adverb. In other words, a particular sequence of words is simultaneously a member of two constructions and thus permits of two structural interpretations and hence of two meanings. It is certainly true that if we have information indicating which construction was intended, we can eliminate one of the meanings. But in an example such as this the identification of the construction of a particular token will often depend on whether or not it is an expansion or transformation or in some way related to a different sequence which is unambiguous: for example, whether the ambiguous "Ship sails today" is related to "Ship the sails today." or "The ship sails today." However, in poetry this other unambiguous sequence is not immediately available. It is its absence that makes the original sequence ambiguous. It seems likely, however, that certain sequences may be resolved with the aid of the metrical analysis, that is, one syntactic construction may imply a distribution of stress which is contrary to the established metrical scheme (**382**).[7]

The reverse is equally true: a knowledge of the meaning will resolve the ambiguity of the construction. If we know that the referent of "ship" is, say, a particular freighter, we can infer the syntactic construction. We have, however, excluded appeal to meaning as a basis for stylistics. We conclude, then, that the formal analysis of poetry can usually only reveal alternative interpretations based on syntactic ambiguity but can rarely decide for one over the other.

We have tried to indicate that there are sentences which are best interpreted as examples of a many-to-one relationship of utterance tokens to message, for example, "There's a big bear" and "There's a BI::G bear." In addition, there is a one-to-many relation between messages and situations. Sometimes the ambiguities are describable only in terms of nonlinguistic features, for example, the beggar's and the child's versions of "I'm hungry"; other times the ambiguity may be described in terms of linguistic features, for example, the different interpretations of "Ship sails today." We suggest: (1) that the two occurrences of "big/BI::G" be considered a difference in performance, hence not a difference in style; (2) that the difference between the two occurrences of "I'm hungry" involves other than linguistic features and hence is not a difference in style; (3) that the different meanings of "Ship sails today" is a function of a constructional ambiguity, and that stylistic analysis will include the identification of such alternatives, even if it may not be able to decide in favor of one over the other. Indeed, it is precisely the use of ambiguous sequences that will be one of the features for characterizing different styles.

[7] Some of the examples of ambiguous constructions frequently cited may be—but need not be—differentiated by stresses and junctures; see **383** for such examples.

The Language as a Whole

The second term that needed defining in Bloch's definition was *the language as a whole*. Clearly, the role of a linguistic feature depends on the frequency (among other things) with which it occurs in ordinary speech. The fact, say, that each line in a particular Cheremis folksong ends in a verb can only be evaluated in the light of the structure of Cheremis sentences in general (**357**).

The delimitation of the language as a whole involves at least two dimensions, which correspond roughly to the difference between synchrony and diachrony. We have already suggested that poetry is part of the language as a whole. Any statements about the frequency of a feature in a language must be based on a random sample of messages, including the poetic ones. But a language may also be viewed as having depth in time, and it is clear that the frequencies and transitional probabilities of certain linguistic features change. A particular message, encoded in accordance with the rules of a seventeenth-century code, is also more or less decodable in terms of a partly overlapping twentieth-century code. Since the description of the message is in part dependent on the code with which it is being compared, changing the code changes the description (cf. **442**, p. 180).

Related to this, perhaps, is the problem of translation. A message is encoded according to the rules of a given code and is describable in terms of it. But the translated version is encoded according to the rules of a different code and can only be described in terms of *it*. The stylistic description of the translation will be independent of the description of the original. There is no reason to suspect that the descriptions will be in any way convertible. A whole set of problems are raised which can only be given a label, such as "comparative stylistics." The discussion of these problems will presumably be based on some notion of universals in stylistics such as rhyme, genre, etc., whereby formal properties in one language can be identified with similar properties in another.

The Nature of Deviations

A given message may deviate from a norm in two ways. First, the message may include features that do not occur elsewhere, or, phrased differently, certain restrictions on messages may be suspended or eliminated. This is usually what is meant by agrammatical or ungrammatical sequences. But, as we have suggested, there may be degrees of grammaticalness. Thus certain utterances in poetry, for example, "A rose is a rose is a rose," can be accommodated into only the most general formula for English sentences,[8] say a formula with only one class of words. Any more specific

[8] Householder points out that such a sentence may be viewed as being of the same type as "*A horse is a mammal*" *is a statement.*

formula fails to accommodate it. On the other hand, "The trees whisper" fits into many of the more specific formulas for sentences, like Noun Phrase + Verb Phrase, or Article + Noun + Intransitive Verb, etc. It is only when we subdivide nouns into animate and inanimate and further divide verbs into subclasses, stating the restrictions on the co-occurrence of certain nouns with certain verbs, that this sentence violates a restriction. Thus a sentence that violates a very general rule may be said to be less grammatical than a sentence that violates only a more specific rule. Any discourse, then, may be described in terms of its grammaticalness, that is, the generality of the rules which are suspended and the frequency with which they are suspended.

The second way in which the message may deviate from the norm is in introducing additional restrictions beyond those of the general grammar. The most obvious example is rhyme. There is no way in which rhyme, as opposed to metaphor, may of itself be said to be ungrammatical. However, when a feature which is optional (perhaps *accidental* is a better word) in the code becomes obligatory, such a feature is obviously relevant to the style of the discourse. Occasionally these additional restrictions themselves become optional in certain positions, and it is this feature that distinguishes what have been called *tendencies* from *constants*. The greater the number of tendencies and constants, and these need not be restricted to phonological phenomena, the more organized is the discourse. The poetic end of the continuum is characterized by messages that are optimally organized, that is, maximum number of tendencies and constants plus optimum ungrammaticalness in the sense described earlier.

During this conference there have been attempts to identify *grammaticalness* as used herewith either *banality* on the one hand or *literalness of meaning* on the other. According to the view proposed by Chomsky and adopted here, such identifications seem unwarranted. For example, "Misery loves company," although at least as banal, is less grammatical than the synonymous "People who are miserable love company," owing to the different classes of nouns represented by "misery" and "people." Similarly, semantic notions would seem to be irrelevant since both grammatical and ungrammatical utterances may be equally nonsensical. One possible view of degrees of grammaticalness is that the notion corresponds to the degree of difficulty with which a particular sentence may be incorporated into the grammar (cf. the last paragraph of the first section). Although grammaticalness may show high correlations with statistical notions (like banality) or semantic notions (like literalness of meaning), the three are to be distinguished and measured independently.

SUMMARY

We have tried to suggest the following: (1) The application of linguistics to poetry must assume that poetry is language and disregard whatever else poetry may be. (2) Syntactic statements, that is, distributional statements, are to be explored before semantic, if only because they seem to afford the desired degree of precision. (3) Stylistics is in some way dependent on linguistics, since style cannot be clearly defined without reference to grammar; but, whereas the aim of grammatical analysis is essentially predictive, the aim of stylistic analysis is primarily classificatory. (4) Every message may be said to deviate from a norm in two ways which are independent in that one or the other or both may be present. The two ways involve the elimination of certain restrictions and the introduction of new ones.

It is obvious that such an approach will have limitations and require redefinition of established terms. For example, many questions about the meaning of a poem go unanswered and, indeed, unasked. Private symbols, irony, humor, etc., seem not to be discoverable, except by recourse to other than linguistic evidence. The analysis of parody poses a problem since the description of the style of the parody would seem to be incomplete without reference to the model. It is hypothesized that from this approach some useful definition of terms like literary genre should emerge, namely, that a typology based on the kinds of deviations will yield clusters that correspond to such notions as sonnets, epic poems, etc. On the other hand, it is by no means clear how comparisons across languages are to be made, nor what the criteria might be by which we could say that any two languages both had, say, epic poems, even in the extreme case in which one is a translation of the other.

A Program for the Definition of Literature

(abstract)

ARCHIBALD A. HILL

This paper presents not a formal definition of literature or works of literature but rather a program whereby a definition can be worked out. The basic assumption is that literature is defined in our culture by comparison between given works and the "institutionalized great books" of Western Europe. The "institutionalized great books" are the works of such men as Homer, Virgil, Dante, and Shakespeare, whom it is impossible for any educated member of the culture to reject. The contemporary works are then compared with these, and if they share formal characteristics with them, it is usually assumed that the work in question is in fact literature. On occasion, however, a less satisfactory approach is adopted. In this less satisfactory approach it is assumed that it is essentially the values which we find in literature that define it for us, so that a critic occasionally will attack a given piece of writing as not valuable enough to form a genuine piece of literature.

This paper proposes a corpus of utterances for study. The definition of this corpus depends on the fact that all known societies have created utterances which they have regarded as of sufficient importance to preserve permanently. It is true that not all these permanently preserved utterances are necessarily of great literary value, and it is also true that there are many utterances of literary value, which, through accidents of history, do not achieve permanence. For these reasons, permanence cannot itself be used to define a given utterance as a work of literature; rather permanence is what defines the corpus for study. Once this corpus for study has been defined, it is then possible to find within it utterances that have formal characteristics which can be used as diagnostic for definition. For instance, none of us would doubt that a work such as *Abie's*

Irish Rose is both a play and an example of literature, since it formally resembles such a work as *Hamlet*. Similarly, the *Ormulum* can be defined as a poem and an example of literature since it formally resembles the *Aeneid*. It is through study of these formal characteristics that we may hope eventually to work out definitions, not necessarily of literature as a whole but of the various species of literature, which may then later be classified into genera and eventually into orders.

This paper has been published in its entirety (**173**).

Expressive Language

(abstract)

EDWARD STANKIEWICZ

The problems of style in language and literature are still in a rudimentary state of investigation. The studies produced by the adherents of the so-called Neo-Idealistic school (of the Croce, Vossler, Spitzer brand) have not contributed significantly to the exploration of style problems because of their programmatic disinterest in theoretical concepts and in a strict methodology. They have also failed to distinguish the problems of literary style that concern the utilization of linguistic forms and constructions in various literary genres and traditions from the problem of different styles in language. These styles may be viewed as coexisting linguistic norms which fulfill different functions in the process of communication (formal, familiar, emotive, explicit, lento, allegro, technical, professional, etc.).

The study of expressive language deals with the description of the elements of the linguistic code (or codes) that are endowed with an emotive function, that is, elements that serve to express the speaker's attitude toward his collocutor or to the thing spoken about. The expressive elements cannot be studied outside of their relation to the distinctive and redundant elements of language. They must also be considered with relation to other styles, which are emotionally neutral. The consideration of the diachronic aspect contributes likewise to a better understanding of the relationship of the expressive and nonexpressive elements, inasmuch as they may exchange functions in the course of history.

The study of expressive elements goes beyond the phonemic level, on which level it had been partially investigated by structural linguists (Laziczius, Trubetzkoy, Jakobson). On the phonemic level we may distinguish expressive features (e.g. the prosodic features of length, intonation, stress), expressive phonemes (e.g. /h/ in French), and expressive distribution (e.g. nonfinal stress in French or the expressive use of tone in Norwegian). Expressive alternations include phenomena which accompany morphophonemic alternations or which have a purely expressive function (e.g. truncation of stems before suffixes, vocalic or consonantal alternations, such as English "food : shmood," Old Russian *baran/maran*, Polish *doktorzy/doktory*).

One of the most widespread expressive devices is the formation of expressive derivatives (e.g. pejorative, affectionate, diminutive). These formations vary greatly, depending on the derivational possibilities of the languages in which they occur. Expressive derivation may also be achieved or accompanied by a different distribution of affixes (e.g. German *Kind-er-lein*, Bulgarian (plural) *glasov-c-e*). On the syntactic level, expressive nuances may be obtained through variations in word order (in languages with a so-called "free" word order) and through different types of sentence intonation.

It appears that the expressive function may be rendered either through special "expressive" forms or through forms which are also endowed with other functions (i.e., distinctive or redundant) but which occur in different environments.

This paper is now being prepared for publication in a modified and extended version (**394**).

Comments to Part Three

WELLEK: I am not convinced that Mr. Householder's substitution of the term "banality" is an improvement over Mr. Saporta's "grammaticalness," and I think that the various definitions of literature proposed here miss the point. The terms "casual" and "noncasual" would allow law and ritual to be literary. These would allow even a telephone book to be literature, because it is produced at great expense [laughter] and is carefully elaborated. I don't think that any one of these definitions face the issue, which I think is an aesthetic one, one that has to be judged even in terms of a word that has not been mentioned here, which is "fictionality." Mr Saporta's use of "grammaticalness" seems to be a strange way of turning things around; to say that "trees whisper" is nongrammatical is to imply that an animating metaphor is the center of poetry, which I think is a very doubtful generalization.

OSGOOD: I read Saporta's paper with interest and care. This banality question: I take it, Mr. Householder, you are referring to *un*banality, the deviation from the ordinary conversational norm?

HOUSEHOLDER: I was just substituting another word. I am not going to argue. [Laughter.]

OSGOOD: I think in a way, though, the term you selected did tend to lead us away from what I consider a very penetrating point in Saporta's paper which gets at the heart of the problem of defining style or the difference between styles. In ordinary casual or conversational speech there are a large number of levels or points at which there are varying degrees of freedom for the individual speaker. Now as I understood Saporta's paper, he was saying that in defining any particular style—situational style—there are two things happening: at some points it decreases in freedom, in the degree of free variation, but at other points or levels, in a sense almost compensating, there is increased freedom. Since in casual conversation we do not ordinarily talk about trees—whatever they were doing . . . .

WELLEK: Whispering.

OSGOOD: . . . whispering, yet we can in poetry; this means that here we have, in a sense, an area of increased freedom. But this is compensated by restrictions in other areas. To me this was an intriguing notion, and I'd like to see the linguists here carry this on a bit. Is this a feasible way of looking at and distinguishing different styles? And in this case we would be dealing not with individual variations in style but with what I would call situational styles—writing a letter, writing a will, writing a poem, and so on. Is this feasible? It seemed intriguing to me as a psychologist, but I don't know enough about the linguistic aspects of it to carry it further.

SAPORTA: What I was trying to suggest is that it seems unlikely we will find any one feature, the presence or absence of which will serve to separate out everything that we feel is literature, for example, sonnets, plays, novels, etc., and everything that we feel is not literature, for example, colloquial speech, telephone books, law, etc. Instead of looking for such a dichotomy, it may be feasible to order messages along a continuum; or at least if the categories are to be discrete, it may be possible to provide more than two of them. The insistence on an either-or definition seems too exacting; the notion of degrees is more flexible and also allows for finer subdivisions; it accommodates, for example, the variations observed within metrics. Incidentally, what I mean by degrees is perfectly compatible, I think, with Mr. Lotz's types; the difference is that I am adding an ordering of the types. Now, as linguists, it seems to me that we are obliged to restrict our statements about literature to the same kind of statements that we make about nonliterature; and these statements are essentially about grammaticalness, especially in terms of restrictions on the combinatorial possibilities. Now from one point of view there are no degrees of grammaticalness. There either is or is not a restriction. However, it seems likely that the kind of restrictions we might set up in a grammar which accounts for colloquial language are suspended or "violated" in messages we somehow feel are poetic or literary, etc. Messages can then be ordered in terms of the additional restrictions, like meter, and the nature and frequency with which other restrictions, like word order, are suspended.

JENKINS: It seems to me that in the approach suggested by Saporta there is a terribly powerful way to get at some of these things behaviorally. There is a tendency, I think, for the conference to stick on "grammaticality" here as if this were the sole thing at issue. I think we would all concede that this is a multidimensional affair. When you step into style, as somebody at Illinois once remarked, you walk into a multidimensional buzz saw and you get chopped up into infinite numbers of pieces. The use of completion techniques may very well begin to give some leverage into the predictability, let's say, of a given piece of literature. I don't mean simply in terms of just saying "*A* has a certain probability of following *B* across all the English language" and then stopping. I think we all agree that this is fairly sterile. Suppose we begin by taking small units, as Osgood suggested, and examining how much predictability we get by completion techniques. From the telephone book we would get a degree of completion which is pretty low. For example, we can predict the class of item 1—it will be a name. We can predict for a tremendous number of hits what letter it will begin with, we can predict it will be followed by a set of numbers, but we can't predict which ones at all, and so on. We would clearly find one level of sequencing here. As we approach something that has more and more a literary flavor, we presumably reach some sort of a higher level of predictability; as we get to absolutely sterile literature, or stuff that isn't literature at all, we may even achieve 100 per cent predictability. No one would regard such material as having any literary value. But along the way the predictability will be modified by different variables. We might take a subject who can't perform very well on the completion test and give him more experience with the form, the verse class, and so on. We would expect his prediction skill to increase. By systematically manipulating the sorts of stimuli and experiences that we give him, we would expect to learn something about the dimensions that are apparently important in being able to handle, understand, and appreciate the material. I think this is a sufficient support for the approach.

MILLER: In connection with what Mr. Jenkins was saying about predictability, and to a certain extent what Saporta said, the general notions of ungrammaticalness and unpredictability seem to me to be related. I have often felt that there is a quality of unpredictability in interesting reading, but that unpredictability was probably neither necessary nor sufficient to make it interesting reading. One of the characteristics of humor is to set up a very definite expectation and then at the last minute change it. I think that unpredictability is not what we want to maximize, because I don't know whether when we have maximized this we will come out with something great or something funny. It seems to me that the kind of unpredictability, the quality of it, is a very important characteristic.

OSGOOD: I should also like to say something about the problem of unpredictability in relation to literature and the other arts. Roger Brown puts his finger on what, to my mind, is one of the very basic notions of what constitutes aesthetic enjoyment—in literature, music, or any other form. Many people have mentioned this in the field of aesthetics—the idea of variations on a theme, and so on. However, I think there is much of interest to linguists, psychologists, and literary critics in this fundamental notion. With too low a degree of unpredictability there is just plain dullness. It is not good literature, it is not good music, or what have you. The rock-and-roll tunes that my two teen-agers play hour after hour are characterized by extreme lack of—well, extreme predictability. Everything has to be said three times: "You send me, you send me, you send me. Honest, you do, honest, you do, honest, you do." If you listen to this day after day, month after month—well, pieces like this have a very rapid rise in popularity and a very rapid descent, with a very short duration to their popularity. On the other hand, take something in the popular field like "Stardust," which is for American popular music a relatively unpredictable pattern with a great many unusual sequences; this tune seems to live. Now, in my own experience, the same thing happens with classical music. Tschaikovsky for me loses interest with relatively few listenings. Now something like Sibelius' Second is sufficiently unpredictable. It took a long time to get to like it, but I can let it go for a relatively short time—and let my nervous system lose its matching, if you will, lose its capacity to predict—and then it becomes very enjoyable again. In other words, I am suggesting that as compared with my teen-agers I have a more mature nervous system; I make predictions much more readily. Rock-and-roll music isn't enjoyable for me. It's too redundant. To them it is not; it is about the optimum of unpredictability. I think the same thing might apply in literature. For most of us, writings like those of Stein, or Joyce's *Finnegans Wake*, are so unpredictable that we get beyond the point of optimum enjoyment and it becomes chaos. However, as one steeps oneself in this—and isn't steeping oneself in Joyce at least in part developing more and more of a matching of one's nervous-system predictions, if you will, with the patterns of redundancies in the message?—Joyce becomes more familiar, to the point where it can be fully and maximally enjoyed. Presumably, great literature—like, forgive the analogy, "Stardust"—has a sufficient degree of unpredictability that it has this lasting character. It doesn't have this sharp upcome and then downgo. It has a lasting character because it is sufficiently unpredictable. All we have to do is wait for a little while and the unpredictability, from the general level of the English language, is sufficient to bring a great work of literature back to the point of optimum aesthetic enjoyment.

JAKOBSON: The idea of higher and lower grammaticalness recalls Orwell's joke about animals being more equal and less equal. In grammar there is, however, an obvious stratification. Kuryłowicz spoke in this connection about primary and secondary function. The metaphorism or metonymism is apparent not only on the lexical level but also in grammar: while a construction—animate subject plus transitive verb plus inanimate object—is neutral, unmarked, the similar syntactic construction with an inanimate subject and animate object carries a figurative tinge. This difference plays a considerable role both in synchrony and in diachrony. In our languages the active construction is primary versus the secondary passive construction. In the latter there is a latent figurative shift: the actor becomes a marginal, omissible part of the sentence. This grammatical imagery plays a substantial role in poetry, especially in such typically "grammatical" languages as the Slavic ones. If the situations in which a given word appears in certain grammatical forms or constructions are relatively infrequent, there is no reason to devaluate or to deny their grammaticalness, as when a Russian dictionary states that the adjective "pregnant" has no masculine form.

STANKIEWICZ: I would like to return to the question raised by Mr. Wellek which approaches the problem phrased here in terms of "grammatical" and "nongrammatical" from a new angle. It seems to me that we have here not only the problem of the metaphor but, ultimately, that of meaning. Even the problem of fictionality is that of meaning, of the immediate versus the remote or displaced reference, and I think we cannot avoid this issue in a discussion of literature. I don't think we should view the problem as one of additional freedom compensated by additional restrictions. In literature (and especially in metrics) there are certain areas of freedom and variation, just as they exist also in colloquial, nonpoetic language. The notion of fictionality can be viewed as the juxtaposition of themes, their development, and presentation. In poetics we have not only the problem of certain restrictions—itself largely a matter of semantics such as the metaphor and the metonym—but also that of the juxtaposition of varying contents or of the development of themes. This again ties up with purely formal problems, for instance, the opposition of epic to lyric genre, and the like.

WIMSATT: Yes, Mr. Wellek spoke of fictionality as a possible norm to define literature. I was reminded that Mr. Beardsley, as it happens, recently gave a very excellent lecture on exactly that topic, fiction, and my thought on it is roughly this: it is a very good, plausible, or possible norm (remember the affinity of fiction for metaphor) as long as we don't make the mistake of supposing that fiction and nonfiction, fictive and nonfictive, is the same as true or not true—I'm not sure whether any of us do or not. Take the telephone book. That is distinct from literature not because it's true but because it is not worthwhile using except in respect to it's being true or not true. If it is false, it's no good; if it's true, it's useful. But many true things conceivably could have fictive quality.

HOLLANDER: Mr. Stankiewicz' point is very well taken.

WIMSATT: Yes, I saw the relevance in that.

BEARDSLEY: And I also agree with what Mr. Stankiewicz said before about the necessity of bringing in considerations of meaning. One of the things that troubled me was the notion of "degree of formality," apart from what I think is a rather unusual way of using the term "formality." But now this won't distinguish, will it, examples like "The night fears the boy" from examples of nonsense like Russell's "Consanguinity drinks procrastination." Here is a case free of ungrammaticalness, but here we have something more than an unusual combination of words. We have a mixture of speech categories or something similar. In "The night fears the boy" we don't have just nonsense, we have a metaphor; two levels of meaning are played off against each other, adding a little bit of interesting complexity to the semantics of it. So it seems to me that we have to start talking about meaning and how meanings are complicated; "degree of formality" will not explain it.

WELLEK: I want to return to the notion of literature viewed in terms of deviations—style as a degree of ungrammaticalness. Stylistics thus becomes a kind of counter-grammar. Is this not a tautology? It seems to me that it leads to an extraordinary overemphasis on pure innovation, or tricks, or something that has not been established in the language. I don't think "deviation" can be accepted as an official definition of style and stylistics.

HYMES: Sentences like "The night fears the boy" are simply a challenge to the imaginative person to try to figure out some context in which he can use them.

HOUSEHOLDER: It looks to me as if the line about consanguinity could also fit very beautifully into a poem. I don't think we can rule anything out of literature on the ground that taken by itself it's nonsense.

BEARDSLEY: Of course, I didn't say it couldn't be a part of a sensible expression, but I said that by itself it is not.

SAPORTA: I think we might try to indicate the fact that messages differ from one another in several ways. First, in the statistical approximation to normal or colloquial or some other kind of language, where it will appear that some messages are more frequent, etc. But there will be no one-to-one relationship between an ordering in terms of frequency and a classification based on semantic notions. This is the second dimension along which messages may differ—I don't know whether it is a continuum or not; I don't know whether one talks about more or less meaningful, or more or less nonsensical. The point is that there are these two dimensions, and although they may be related, they are not isomorphic. And finally, there may be a third dimension, a dimension of grammaticalness, which is related to, but different from, both. In other words, messages can be described independently as to their statistical properties and their semanticity—I don't know what kind of words you would use—and their grammaticalness; it would probably turn out that these three are correlated, but not 100 percent correlated. The very fact that we can talk about grammatical nonsense means that they are not correlated 100 percent.

BEARDSLEY: Well, the nonsensical ones will be infrequent, but they'll be infrequent because they are nonsensical.

SAPORTA: Right. There will be this relationship, so that nonsense has low frequency, but some sense will also have low frequency. And ungrammatical sequences will have low frequency, but so will some grammatical sequences; all combinations are possible.

BROWN: I have the sense that the permanence criterion is used as a more accessible version of what we really have in mind, that there is some language which is treasured or admired. This is perhaps a good deal harder to spell out in terms of behavior, but I think it is clearly the ground on which we reject, in many instances; thus the telephone book is preserved but not treasured. I wonder whether it is a reasonable expectation that those language products that are admired even in one society should have a common denominator. That is, I wonder whether we can be confident that there is anything to be found that will predict admiration, perhaps even within a clique within the society.

WELLEK: What about the Constitution—the Constitution is highly admired but is not, I think, literature. [Laughter.]

RICHARDS: I want to raise a very subversive question indeed as to whether it is likely that a conference of this nature, if it really were frank and stated its views clearly, could possibly agree upon the demarcation of literature. Isn't this really the test, if we take seriously the sort of doctrine that says we want a definition *for some purpose*? We want a definition but what is a definition? It's a means to further work. Now what the linguists want is a definition of literature that will further linguistics. What René Wellek and I, and some others perhaps, want is a definition of literature that will further literary criticism or further the production of literature. These are very different ultimate aims. I now say quite seriously that discourse is divided up in this way, according to the diverse purposes that human beings entertain. So I would rather like to shift this discussion, as it were, to the practicability of arriving at universal definitions for words that can belong to such different universes of endeavor.

GREENBERG: It may well be that the linguists and literary critics here are discussing different things, and this may be the cause of some of our trouble in talking about the characteristics of literature. Some linguists have, as we have seen, been making a distinction between casual and noncasual language. For example, meter was discussed at considerable length (see Comments to Part Five) on the assumption that anything which was metrical was noncasual, and I would agree. Thus, M. Jourdain could have been talking prose all his life, but hardly metrically. Let us suppose we have a didactic metrical poem devoid of literary value. The linguist would consider this an example of noncasual language since it forms part of a corpus which he can distinguish by formal criteria from the normal pragmatic use of language in everyday life. In fact, there will be a large overlap between the linguist's corpus of noncasual language and what literary critics call literature. But some casual language, for example novels, will be literature, and some noncasual language, for example some didactic poetry, will not be literature. Since then the linguist and the literary critic are not talking about the same body of linguistic material, they are also bound to be talking about different things when they talk about the style of these linguistic corpuses.

STANKIEWICZ: I would like to raise here the problem of what we mean by predictability. The notion of predictability, I think, implies two concepts; one is a kind of forward-looking predictability, and one is retrospective predictability. If we speak of, for instance, alliterations and repetitions which appear in a poetic text, we cannot predict that they are going to be repeated in a certain systematic order, if they aren't regulated in a very high measure. They occur here and there, or they *may* occur here and there. Their recurrence will lead us to expect some kind of statistical regularity. This type of predictability will, I think, vary very greatly according to the literary tradition, or the genre, and such factors. For instance, metaphor may not exist at all in some literary forms or poetic traditions that have a kind of thematic straightforwardness. What kind of predictability can we establish there? Rather a retrospective one: after we have gone through the piece, we can start counting certain things and establish certain stylistic devices, a certain abundance or density of phenomena, but it is entirely different from the other kind of systematic predictability, in which recurrences of certain elements—as in meter—are obligatory. In other words, I argue we should make more explicit this notion of predictability because it ties in with the notion of systematicity in literature.

BROWN: It seems to me that, from one point of view, the problem of defining literature would almost be the problem of specifying groups who have admiration for some literary products, and then trying to find out why they admire it. The reasons would vary greatly from one group to another. In one case, it would be because they had been told by a group of higher status, and so forth. On that level, it's a sociological sort of problem. I think we are not interested in that. I think perhaps we are interested more in having a definition of literature for some purpose or other, but we keep defeating offered definitions on the criterion that they do not satisfy one or another member's denotation of the class of literature, and it seems to me that this isn't the appropriate criterion, because if we chose to define a class of phenomena for study, I don't see why we need meet the expectations of the community, in general, about how that class ought to be defined. And if we mix the two things, I think we have nothing at all.

WELLS: Mr. Richards is doubtless right that we wouldn't all agree on a definition of literature, but we might each of us make up his mind on two questions. This would, by cross classification, give four classes in all, and within each of the four classes I would expect greater agreement. The first question is whether we look for a definition that will sharply and in a clear-cut way distinguish literature from nonliterature. The second question is whether within literature we admit the good-bad dichotomy, or whether, on the other hand, literature *means* good literature. With these two questions cleared up, we can divide into four possible groups; a preliminary step will have been taken.

CHATMAN: Isn't it possible to distinguish between criticism and analysis? Cannot value be dispensed with for certain purposes, particularly where there is some possibility that it will impair the clarity with which we may wish to examine the text?

WELLEK: I suppose one can write a history of poetry from the point of view of the light it throws on the history of law; and there are all kinds of other ways. I don't say that they are valueless on their own, but in valued literature we are confronted with the aesthetic problem and this, it seems to me, is completely and constantly neglected by most of the linguistic students who try to be descriptive.

OSGOOD: I would certainly go along with this notion. I would like to be able to say that there is value, in one sense of that term, in good literature—but I hate to see the "good" be part of the definition of what the style is. I would much prefer to have a way of defining the "style" of a language sample that is quite independent of whether we like it or don't like it, whether it is good or bad. Now if we can then go further, in terms of either subjective of objective methods, and show that these kinds of criteria, these kinds of discriminations, correlate with what people who know, who have had a lot of experience, say is good and bad, that is even better. Throughout these discussions, it seems to me, we've been skittering around the problem of art versus science. There are some of us who feel that there is a definite area of the activity of, let's say, the literary critic which is an art, involving value judgments of what is good and what is not good. There are others of us who feel that there is, perhaps, potentially or ultimately, no impregnable area of art, that in the ultimate analysis of extremely complex mechanisms it may be possible to determine, even in a quantitative way, what laws are operating. And this has been pushed even into what, at least in my experience, has always been the most sensitive area of conflict between art and science—that is, where the bold and brash scientist plunges into the actual creative process of the artist himself, the actual process whereby his subjective decisions, which are the essence of his talent, are formulated into overt expressions.

It seems to me that Carroll has made a little start toward an analysis of what may go on in the interpretive behavior of a critic. Graduate students in English were the "critics," and they were given, to be sure, a sub-subtreasury of a vast variety of things, many of them certainly not great literature. But, nevertheless, the kinds of dimensions, of judgments, on the subjective side that Carroll asked the students to make them, were those which, at least in my reading, seem to be used in literary criticism—such judgments as whether a piece is superficial or profound, whether it is awkward or graceful, affected or natural, impersonal or personal, rational or emotional, or even good or bad. Carroll asked these young critics to make these kinds of judgments, but he also analyzed a large number of structural variables in the selections. Now, presumably, in the process of making a judgment like awkward or graceful, these critics were not counting anything. This was a job done by other people. But, nevertheless, the results demonstrate certain relationships between structural and subjective variables. For example, as the proportion of personal pronouns increases, there is an increasing number of subjective judgments of vigorous, intimate, interesting, opinionated, vivid, personal, emotional, pleasant, and not serious but humorous; looking at the frequencies of descriptive adjectives—just the sheer frequency with which descriptive adjectives occur, and again presumably not counted in any sense by the young critics reading the messages and making judgments—we find that as the number of descriptive adjectives increases so do judgments of profound, abstract, not succinct, lush, elegant, unnatural, complex, and florid. Now, I'll confess to the bias that all the critic is responding to are certain events happening out here as he reads the novel, or the poem, or whatever it may be, and certain associations that these produce. Am I way off the beam when I say that this is, to be sure, a very crude and rough attempt to get at something of what are the relations between the kinds of interpretations critics make and what is happening event-wise in the messages?

CARROLL: There were, of course, certain limitations in my study—for the most part I had to use neophyte critics rather than the professional kind. Nevertheless, I regard it as interesting and provocative that I obtained a single "evaluative" factor. In interpreting this finding, let me refer to Richards' remark that the evaluation of a piece of literature is basically one of whether it "achieves its ends." But how are we to decide what its "ends" are? Won't this also be a matter subject to the variation of personal tastes and preferences? It must be that there are different bases for evaluation: some of my raters perhaps stressed precision and clarity, others originality, or "nonbanality" as Householder called it; some of them probably displayed certain likes or dislikes for certain kinds of content. The disagreements among the raters show up in the somewhat lower reliability coefficients for the evaluative scales. Nonevaluative scales like those concerning seriousness and abstractness are highly reliable—raters know what they mean and can agree on their ratings, but raters cannot agree so well on what it means to say that a piece of literature is good, graceful, pleasant, and so on, and therefore the statistics show lessened reliabilities for these scales. Now I had a very heterogeneous sample of "literary" passages. It included advertising copy, wills, legal documents, and all sorts of things besides literary passages of a more conventional kind. We would have thought that the "ends"—the communicative purposes—of such a wide variety of items would have been clearly evident to the raters, but the evidence suggests that the raters tended not to agree very well on the ends that these pieces sought to achieve or on the extent to which the ends were actually achieved. Does this lead us to a counsel of despair? Perhaps it does, if we continue to insist that we must hold always and everywhere to some single canon of the "good" in literature. Is there not a place for the variation of individual preferences—*de gustibus*, let us remind ourselves! And this is the province of the psychologist. For the psychologist, literary criticism becomes a problem of discovering how pieces of literature interact with personal tastes and of noting the values that people find in literature. The problem of evaluation moves to another plane, that of evaluating tastes, or perhaps the tasters, but it then becomes a sociological rather than a literary problem.

Phonological Aspects
of Style

Dell H. Hymes

Phonological Aspects of Style:
Some English Sonnets

DELL H. HYMES

I

To speak of *style* implies a universe of discourse, a set and its stylistically differentiated components.[1] This universe may be of any magnitude, as broad as the set of civilizations (**237**) or as the set of all natural languages: Whorf successfully characterized the cognitive style of Hopi in contrast to some European members of that set, whatever we may think of his epistemology (**447**; see also **160**, ch. 10).

Style may be investigated, both as deviations from a norm and as "a system of coherent ways or patterns of doing things."[2]

Linguists usually speak of style in reference to the universe of a single language, and emphasize deviation. Thus, from Bernard Bloch: "The style of a discourse is the message carried by the frequency distributions and transitional probabilities of its linguistic features, especially as they differ from those of the same features in the language as a whole" (**32**, p. 42). But it should not be forgotten that to some "sources," especially poets, style may be not deviation from but achievement of a norm. And if some stylistic universes are hierarchical, comprising a general norm and

---

[1] By devising efficient methods for tabulating and checking data, and by helping in their use, my wife Virginia has been invaluable. I am indebted to Fellows of the Center for Advanced Study in the Behavioral Sciences (1957–1958) for discussion of sounds and sonnets, and especially to John Tukey and John Gilbert for statistical discussion. Mary Girschik valorously computed chi-squares for a coordinate study of these twenty sonnets; its results are omitted here to conserve space and unity. The account of procedures and results has been severely cut, and the original data and tabulations are also omitted, in this revision of the original work paper.

[2] Kroeber (**237**) intends this as a pointer, not as a formal definition. He states: "A style is a strand in a culture or civilization: a coherent, self-consistent way of expressing certain behavior or performing certain kinds of acts. It is also a selective way: there must be alternative choices, though actually they may never be selected" (p. 150). The fit to natural languages is obvious.

individual deviations, some are egalitarian, comprising a set of norms, such that it would be arbitrary to choose one norm as a standard from which the others depart. Hopi and English differ in cognitive style, but which is norm, which departure?

In literature, verbal art, both ways of regarding style are appropriate.

This paper analyses a universe of twenty English sonnets, ten by Wordsworth and ten by Keats. The analysis relates to the general question of the role of sound in poetry. A specific aim is to balance concern with style as norm and deviation, as what is common (to a language, author, genre), with concern for style as the accomplishment of the individual poem.[3]

II

It is a commonplace that the short poem or lyric depends heavily on the specific properties of language. Thus, from Suzanne Langer:

> The fullest exploitation of language sound and rhythm, assonance and sensuous associations, is made in lyric poetry . . . it is the literary form that depends most directly on pure verbal resources—the sound and evocative power of words, meter, alliteration, rhyme, and other rhythmic devices, associated images, repetitions, archaisms, and grammatical twists. It is the most obviously linguistic creation, and therefore the readiest instance of poesis . . . the lyric poet uses every quality of language because he has neither plot nor fictitious characters nor, usually, any intellectual argument to give his poem continuity. The lure of verbal preparation and fulfillment has to do almost everything (**241**, pp. 258–259).

Such dicta can be taken as questions to be explored. In what sense can the exploitation of sounds in a poem, by participating in the lure of verbal preparation and fulfillment, be said to be appropriate to it? Or the use of some sounds in some poems? Put structurally, has a lyric, such as a sonnet, a structure of sounds which contributes with other structures to its lyric unity?

Two scholars who have recently tackled this problem in linguistic terms are Lawrence Jones and James Lynch. Jones has analyzed the distinctive features in successive lines of poetry. When applied to passages from Shakespeare's plays, his method has shown that utilization of distinctive features differs in different passages, and this in a way that seems appropriate to the tenor of the lines. Since Jones' work has not been published, I will not go into it further.

Lynch has analyzed the phoneme occurrences of whole poems. His goal is "first, to discover the total effect of the poem's euphony or tonality

---

[3] I want especially to thank both Fred W. Householder, Jr., and Alfred Kroeber, who have made suggestive computations of their own from the tabulations of the original work paper.

or musicality, or what Professor Wellek, following the Russian Formalists, calls 'orchestration,' and second, to relate its findings to 'meaning' in such a way that it can be seen how the poem's phonemic totality supports and contributes to its prose and poetic statement" (**259**). His key example is the Keats sonnet "On First Looking Into Chapman's Homer." After determining the dominant phonemes, and comparing them to "Silent," the word whose trochee begins the last line, he finds: "the word we found to occupy such an important position for numerous reasons, which in fact sums up the theme of the sonnet, also sums up its dominant sound structure. The poet's 'sixth sense,' whether operating consciously or unconsciously, led him to consummate his poem not only in terms appropriate to his meaning, but also in terms which climax the workings of the lyrical faculty on its most basic level, sound" (**259**, p. 219).

Certainly this result fits Langer's phrase, "the lure of verbal preparation and fulfillment." It and its underlying approach, however, must be related to two general problems: the nexus between sound and meaning, and the statistical properties of language. How does such a result, fixing "silent" as summative in both meaning and sound, fit a definition of language as "arbitrary vocal symbols" (**404**, p. 2)? How does it take account of "chance as the ever-present rival conjecture" (**166**, p. 5)?

On the Nexus between Sound and Meaning

Many insist on its arbitrary nature. The minor role of onomatopoeia is stressed, its dependence on the pattern of particular languages noted, and classrooms encouraged to titter at "bow-wow" theories of language origin. This matter of origins, however, points to confusion back of a simple insistence on "arbitrary."

One confusion involves scope. Appropriateness of sound may be conceived as (A) universal, in fact or tendency, as (B) a fact of a given speech community, or as (C) pertaining to a given source. Another confusion involves level. In language, sound may be deemed (1) inherently appropriate to meaning or (2) contextually appropriate, in terms of (a) a phoneme, (b) a word, (c) a set of words, (d) a sequence of words, from a single line to a whole poem or text. (The context may be the immediate linear context or the substitution possibilities at a given point.) These distinctions, scope and level of reference, crosscut. Briefly, some putative examples are: (A1a) *m* is a sound of acceptance,[4] high vowels are smaller, low vowels are larger (**349**, pp. 61–72); (B1a) schwa is a phonestheme in English monosyllables (**182**); (A1b) many or most languages have a term

---

[4] Burke (**53**, Vol. 2, p. 81), following Sir Richard Paget; but note Burke's view (**54**, p. 13) that "Paget's theory should be presented as a contribution not to philology, but to poetics."

for a bird of the raven group with back stop and low central vowel (cf. **191**) (B1b) Zuni *z ʔilili* expresses "be a hot day with the noise of insects" (**293**, p. 48); (B2b) of English words for headdress, because of rhyme associations, "cowl," not "toque" or "wimple," suggests something sinister or bad (**35, p. 123**); (B2c) in the history of English, "glare, gleam, glow, gloom, glimmer, flimmer, flare" and other blendings have accumulated and come together (**404**, pp. 111–112).[5] (B2d) Tennyson's "The murmuring of innumerable bees in immemorial elms."

Even the existence of universal sound symbolism cannot be dogmatically denied. There have been rash excesses, such as that of Johannesson, who explains supposed resemblances between Semitic and Indo-European by Paget's gesture-origin theory (**215**);[6] but the matter can be empirically investigated. Most recently, Brown and others have done so; their results show that it is rash to deny the existence of universal, or widespread, types of sound symbolism (**47**).

As for sound symbolism within a language, speech community, or text, it simply misses the point to repeat that *cheval, pferd, misatim,* and *kiutan* all mean 'horse.' Consider the individual growing up in a particular speech community, ignorant of the ultimate origin of its linguistic forms but acquiring and exploiting them as indissoluble complexes of sound and meaning. It is his common error in thinking one language's particular set of complexes natural and universal that the linguist attacks with the slogan "arbitrary." But this "error" is just the point. From the standpoint of origins, it is truly an error, but from the standpoint of speech behavior, dismissing it is a form of genetic fallacy. If we are to understand a fair part of linguistic change, comprehend the use of language in speech and verbal art, take account of all the varied speech play in which a competent speaker may indulge, and to which he can respond, we must study his real and lively sense of appropriate connections between sound and meaning.

We can satirize the argument that high vowels are little, low vowels large, "as in *big* and *small*"; but such a pattern is the basis of much popular use and coinage, for example, "Poopsquawk—that's an elderly pipsqueak."[7] Tennyson's line certainly does not suggest bee sound if the meaning is slightly changed—even more slightly than John Crowe Ransom changed it, to "the murmuring of *e*numerable bees"; but in the

---

[5] Cf. **35**, p. 130: "It is generally recognized that English contains a pool of forms interrelated through rime and assonance. What is not appreciated is the vastness of the pool."

[6] Johannesson (**215**, p. 15) believes that many of the forms "must date from the first period of man's attempt to speak."

[7] Cited by Bolinger (**35**, p. 136, n. 44), after a popular radio program.

poem the particular nexus of sound *and* meaning seems appropriate and effective to English speakers. Bolinger has assembled many examples of the goings-on of association between sound and meaning in English (**35**, *passim*), and Louis Finkelstein has recently written on the great importance of the sound-meaning nexus in the Hebrew Bible (**121**).

Insistence on the arbitrary nature of the connection between sound and meaning simply cuts off inquiry into a very real aspect of speech and language. For the relation of sound to meaning in poetry, two main points are to be made. First, any and all the various types of sound-meaning association may be utilized by a particular poet in a particular language and may be responded to by his audience. In a recent review (**175**, p. 251) the statement is made:

> The second way in which Guiraud's slighting of the linguistic groundwork is unfortunate, is that it leaves him open to the seductive voices of Jespersen and Grammont in discussing sound symbolism. It is true that he begins with caution, but when he says . . . "*La Dormeuse*, full of shadow, languor, and of silence, is softened, veiled, and muffled by nasalization and labialization," he has left his caution behind him.

This cuts off inquiry into two important questions of fact: how prominent are nasalization and labialization in the particular poem, absolutely and in relation to other poems and French in general, and do speakers of French associate these sound qualities (by themselves or in a set of words bearing them) with the effects to which Guiraud alludes? Such facts can be established and are important to poetic style, whether or not there is any universal or original connection between nasalization, labialization, shadow, languor, and silence. In fact, Guiraud determines the percentage of sounds belonging to a variety of sound types for each of the three poems he analyzes in detail, and compares the results for each poem to the results for the other two and the mean for poetry of the period (1880–1920). Thus, "La Dormeuse" is said to be characterized by labialization, because 43.7% of its sounds are labials, compared to 21% and 24.5% for the other two poems and to 32.5% for the period mean (**144**, p. 89).

Second, if as a result of long-term speech experience the sound-meaning complexes of a language induce a sense of appropriateness in speakers, it is possible that the very short-term experience of sound-meaning complexes in a particular poem may also induce a sense of appropriateness. The first may have permanent effect: analogy, contamination, blending are familiar processes in the history of a language. Use can induce a sense of appropriateness that etymology does not justify, regarding the strands of similarity in sound and meaning running through a group of words. The second is a temporary effect. As I interpret Lynch's proposal, the use of words in a particular poem may bring certain meanings and sounds into prominence, so that it may then be sensed as appropriate for the two strands of prominence to come together. A word that sums up the theme of a sonnet may be felt as also appropriate to the sonnet's particular aggregate of sound.

If this is the case, incidentally, it poses the possibility of inappropriate use of sound in the closing part of a sonnet. And I would suggest that an important part of the difference in value between Wordsworth's "Composed on Westminster Bridge" and his "At Dover" (sonnets 2 and 10 of this study) lies in the appropriate culmination of one and the inappropriate culmination of the other, regarding the two sonnets' dominant sounds.

In general, then, I argue that the mass of naive and linguistically unsophisticated reports about sound-meaning connections should not be dismissed (nor uncritically accepted), but should be taken as evidence of a very real linguistic phenomenon, the native speaker's sense of sound-meaning appropriateness; and this phenomenon should be investigated. Such study will be of value to the study of style in verbal art. One kind of induced appropriateness is implicit in the approach proposed by Lynch and is tested in Sections III, IV and V.

On Chance as the Rival Conjecture

Lynch does not place his results in a context of other information about the frequency or dominance of sounds, whether in other poems, in other works by the same author, or in the language generally. (He does indicate in a final footnote the difference in rank order for the sounds in the Keats sonnet from two computations for American English.)

This may be defended as adequate, as near the perspective represented by Leo Spitzer's procedure (as described by Hatzfeld **161,** p. 66):

Spitzer has no preestablished system, he even ignores the implications of the *langue* in his study of the *parole*. He simply starts reading, as he says, and is fascinated by something which strikes him. He jumps at once from description to an attempt at interpretation of the first discovered trait, i.e. of its possible psychological root. Only after having discovered this "radix" does he return to the collection of other traits eligible for the same interpretation. If all the traits investigated lead to the same conclusion, Spitzer declares, then he has found the informing principle of a literary work of art.

The response of the trained mind and congruity of pattern are important tools; and Kroeber states (**237**) that judgment, recognition of style is primary, its analysis and statistics secondary. Yet many will be troubled by another perspective, exemplified in a statement by Herdan: "What before were regarded as quite unique events, the products of willful creation, appear now when studied quantitatively as mere variants of typical expenditure of linguistic material, or as samples of one basic distribution of such material" (**166,** p. 2).

Being so troubled, I have brought to bear on Lynch's approach some increment of additional information. It is by no means a question of complete and controlled analysis, which would require more than my resources permit. Indeed, beyond the sheer work, there are unresolved and fundamental questions of how to apply and interpret statistical methods for such a purpose as the stylistic investigation of a particular poem.

The additional information obtained here is simply the data yielded by the sounds of twenty sonnets, regarding their frequency, and the amount of weighting in stressed syllables, both in terms of absolute values and rank order. Essentially, the basis of interpretation has been broadened so that the significance of a sound and its use can be assessed relative not to just one sonnet but to twenty.

Chance, then, has not been statistically eliminated as a source of the particular frequencies taken as significant in the particular poems. I can state that the /ay/ of "silent" occurs more often in the Keats sonnet on Chapman's Homer than in any of the Wordsworth ten, more often than in all but two of the Keats ten. I can state that by the criteria used it has more weight in the sonnet on Chapman's Homer than it has in any other of all twenty. I can add that /ay/ achieves a relative rank order of weighting in this sonnet which is higher than any it achieves in the Wordsworth ten, as high as any in the Keats ten.

All this points toward importance for the sound as used in this sonnet. But it cannot demand conviction by statistical test. If, as one mathematician proposed, a good test for the importance of /ay/ in the Keats sonnet is to see how many /ay/'s can be put in a sonnet, it is disheartening that a dashed-off sonnet with 70 /ay/'s can be read and its trick go undetected by someone devoted to poetry. On the other hand, frequency and its associated statistical analysis is probably relatively insensitive, a vague mirror, when the focus is on the individual poem. It may well be that the sheer data, usefully arranged, is about as good a kind of statistics as we can get. The occurrences of the sounds do in fact differ from sonnet to sonnet, poet to poet, as the data state, and the stylistic critic can make of this what he can. Perhaps it is simply not worthwhile to attempt significance tests with regard to the importance of sounds in individual poems; perhaps a much more relevant test of significance is fit with other aspects of the poem, especially its structure of meaning.

Certainly the goal of stylistic analysis must be the comprehension of the individual work and its value; for otherwise, why pick on Keats instead of Robert Southey? But it is in the areas of broad comparison between whole bodies of work that statistical tools have the most to contribute. There they are in the forefront, but for a single sonnet they become background. When the focus is the individually valuable work, then no matter how intriguing the broader stylistic matters along the way, statistics is helpful but insufficient. We should push it as far as it will go but not expect it to go all the way. In this study, it is but one of three parameters in the interpretation of the individual sonnets.

The apparatus of charts, tables, and frequencies, then, should not mislead anyone into thinking that my concern is to test a statistical hypothesis about frequency of phonemes. I am *not* testing as a null hypothesis that the dominant phonemes of a sonnet are those that would be the most frequent in a same-size sample of English drawn at random. I am concerned with the stylistic achievement of particular sonnets. If it is useful to speak in such terms here, *the null hypothesis is threefold:* that in any same-size sample of English drawn at random (which meets the requirements of the sonnet form for meter, rhyme, and meaningfulness), some of or all the dominant sounds will (1) co-occur in (2) a word placed toward the end of the sample which (3) expresses a theme found in the whole. In point of fact, if this null hypothesis were found to be true, it would be a finding of the greatest interest. So far as twenty sonnets tell, it is not true; the satisfying of all three conditions is an aesthetic fact about particular sonnets, not about the sonnet form.

III

Space does not permit a detailed account of the procedure used. Brief comment must suffice.

The *transcription* derives from the Trager-Smith analysis of English, guided by my own speech, as subordinated to the "General American" norm. Like Lynch, I treat syllabic nuclei as units for the present purpose. The *weighting* follows fixed rules. I was not able to reduce to rules the weights Lynch assigns in his published example, but my assumptions are much the same as his. A sound is assumed to be given prominence by prose stress, metrical stress, and repetition. By "prose stress" is meant normal occurrence of primary or secondary stress. Metrical stress refers to the abstract metrical pattern of iambic pentameter, as interpreted for the four English stresses by Whitehall (**445,** p. 418; **446,** pp. 142–143). The two kinds of stress often coincide but need not. Repetition subsumes rhyme, alliteration, assonance, consonance, and a few other phenomena.

The domain of a stress level is a syllable, but syllable boundaries are not always clear-cut. Of consonants occurring between nuclei, a single consonant has been counted in the preceding syllable if its nucleus is a simple vowel, not if its nucleus is a diphthong. Of two or more consonants between nuclei, the last has been counted in the following syllable but not in the first.

In assigning metrical stress, I have been guided by the four principles for exceptions to regular iambic succession which John Crowe Ransom has stated (**325**, pp. 471–472). I have not found the weighting of sounds so sensitive, or permissible metrical alternatives so common, that a different choice, where one has had to be made, would alter the dominant ranks in a given sonnet. For two sounds adjacent in rank and slightly different in total weight, an alternative choice might cause them to exchange places, but it does not seem able to make dominant a sound that otherwise was not, or to remove from among the dominant sounds one that otherwise ranked high. Of course, the relation between weights is not arithmetic, and difference in weight for two sounds is an indication of their relative importance, not a measurement of it. (There is thus no automatic procedure for interpretation; we must look at all the high-ranking sounds and not be tempted to use the numerical indices as absolute differences.)

Given a decision as to stressed-syllable membership, a weight of 1 has been assigned for each of the following circumstances: (1) occurrence with primary or secondary "prose stress"; (2) occurrence with metrical stress; (3) recurrence in stressed syllables within a line, syntactic phrase, or rhyme scheme; (4) recurrence in a stressed syllable of a sound in the immediately preceding unstressed syllable. These weightings (1–4) are taken as independent and totaled as they occur. Some lesser types of repetition have been noted (5–7) but are counted as giving weight only when not duplicating the first four: (5) recurrence three times in a line in the same syllable position (nucleus, before nucleus, after nucleus) if the third occurrence is stressed; (6) exact repetition of a word or syllable in parallel syntactic circumstances; (7) recurrence of the same sound(s) before and after a given stressed nucleus. In principle, any kind of repetition and patterning of sound might contribute to dominance. In practice, as Householder has shown (see his formal discussion), only the major patterns are needed to approximate the results fairly well.

Consonants and nuclei are ranked separately, rather than in one order as Lynch ranks them. The phonetic and structural differences between the two classes justify this, and the almost two-to-one greater frequency of consonants would obscure the significance of the nuclei if both were combined in a single order. It should be noted that nuclei are more sensitive to variation between poems than the consonants.

For interpretation, two tables were prepared, one showing for each poem the rank order of sounds within it, the other showing for each sound the ranks it achieved in the various poems. The dominant sounds were listed, for the whole poem and for octet and sestet separately; separate lists were made of sounds whose weight was predominantly in the octet, predominantly in the sestet, and proportionately about even in both. Lists were made of those sounds whose rank in the given poem was the highest achieved in the ten by the particular author; of those whose rank in the poem was the second highest achieved; and of those whose rank was third highest achieved. The original sheets on which the frequency and weighting of the sounds had been recorded line by line were also examined to detect clustering and trends.

An interpretation of the theme of the poem was made, any contrast between octet and sestet being noted. The sonnet was examined for a word or words fulfilling three criteria: (1) on the level of sound, containing sounds dominant in the poem and/or much higher in rank than usual; (2) on the level of meaning, expressing the theme of the poem (or octet or sestet); (3) regarding position, placed so as to have a culminating effect. When all three criteria were met, the result has been termed a *summative* word. When only the first two criteria were met, the result has been termed a *key* word.

IV

There is a clear case for summative words in six of the twenty sonnets: (1) these, (2) still, (5) first blood, (12) silent, (15) unrest, still, (18) soul.

I would consider as key words: (7) forlorn, (14) never, (16) friendliness, (17) blind, name, (19) let, constrained. These occur in five of the sonnets.

Sometimes there is approximation to summative effects, instances that seem not clear-cut but still show something. Such are (3) inner shrine, (4) on herself, (6) great, away, (7) out of time (in the octet), (8) Sleep, joyous health, (9) voice, thee, (14) nothingness. These occur in seven of the sonnets.

In five cases I found no positive result at all: (9), (10), (11), (13), (20).

Some of the detailed analysis for each sonnet is summarized in the following paragraphs.

1. Wordsworth, "I Grieved for Buonaparte." The final word "these" has this strength: /iy/ is the dominant nucleus in octet, sestet, and the whole sonnet; /ð/ ranks eleventh among consonants, the highest it achieves in relation to other Wordsworth sonnets, in which its average rank is 17.1; /z/ ranks fourth among consonants here, the highest it achieves relative to the Wordsworth ten, in which its average rank is 12.7. This is the only sonnet of the twenty in which /z/ ranks in the top four

consonants. It is steadily weighted through lines 4 to 14, having the most weight of any sound in the sestet. (Householder has noted that it is in excess in the sonnet, although we would expect its weighted rank to be lower than its frequency rank; see his formal discussion.) The word has syntactic prominence from the last three lines: "these are . . . , this is . . . , are these."

I sense an antithesis both in sound and meaning between "Buona*parte*" (line 1) and "true *Power*" (line 14). The contrast of masculine Buona*parte* and feminine Wisdom and the theme of courtship rather than of conquest give sexual import to "true Sway doth mount," "the stalk true Power doth grow on," and the suggestion of "rites" by "rights". To the extent that "these" sums up the proper "rights/rites" by anaphoric reference, the relative strength of its sounds makes it an appropriate final word, emphasized by repetition, syntactic parallel, and closure of the sonnet pattern.

2. Wordsworth, "Composed upon Westminster Bridge." The final word of the octet, "air," has its two dominant phonemes /e r/. In meaning, "smokeless air" may be seen as the basis of the whole scene and Wordsworth's delight in it; this is perhaps the only poem in which he responds to the city as a part of nature, with the kind of response he otherwise reserves for natural phenomena.

The final word of the sestet, "still," has the four dominant phonemes of the sestet, /l s t/ and /i/, and seems to sum up the essence of the sonnet; Wordsworth follows "still" with an exclamation mark. In the whole sonnet, /l s/ are the two top consonants, /t/ is the fourth consonant, and /i/ is the second nucleus. Although /e/ is the dominant nucleus, it does not occur after "very" of line 13; it is relatively evenly weighted in both octet and sestet, whereas /i/ rises in weight in the sestet (11 in the eight lines of the octet, 16 in the six lines of the sestet). (Indeed, as scored by Lynch, /l/ would be the dominant nucleus, for Lynch adds one point for each occurrence to the points for weighting; /i/'s 22 occurrences plus weight of 27 would give 49, and /e/'s 30 plus 12 would give 42.)

For the octet "air" and for the sestet and whole sonnet "still" may be seen as summative words.

3. Wordsworth, "It Is a Beauteous Evening, Calm and Free." (The strength of /i/, greatest in the poem and rising in the sestet, may lend some prominence to "with" in line 14.) The best approximation to a summative word or phrase for the whole sonnet is found in "inner shrine" (line 13); it has the two top consonants of sestet and sonnet, /r/ and /n/, and the top nucleus, /i/. The rank of /ay/ is fourth in the sonnet, second in the sestet, and it has here its second highest rank of the Wordsworth ten; it is well sustained through the poem, acquiring more weight in the sestet, and its first prominence is in "The holy time is quiet as a nun." As for /š/, this is

its only occurrence in the sonnet; it may lend prominence, not by culmination but by contrast.

4. Wordsworth, "London, 1802." The words "on herself" have some cumulative force. The two stressed nuclei contain the dominant nucleus of the poem, /e/, and that of the sestet, /a/. (/a/ occurs only in the sestet.) The four dominant consonants of the sonnet are found in it (/r s l n/), whereas /h/ has in this sonnet its highest rank relative to the Wordsworth ten; /f/ has its second highest rank relative to the Wordsworth ten (7 compared to an average rank of 12.2). The word "duties" may have some prominence from contrast, this being the only weighted occurrence of /uw/ in the sonnet; this may set off the following words.

The theme of the poem may be taken as revolving about the opposition of "we are *selfish* men" (line 6) and the "lowliest duties *on herself* did lay." If so taken, "on herself" sums up the poem both in meaning and sound rather well.

5. Wordsworth, "It Is Not to Be Thought of." The words "[we are] sprung from earth's *first blood*" seem to culminate the poem both in sound and meaning. The words "first blood" contain the dominant five consonants of the sonnet, /d r s t l/, and the dominant nucleus of the sestet, /ë/. Were the sonnet transcribed by Lynch, identifying /ɨ/ and /ë/, the effect would be striking, making /ë/ the dominant nucleus of the whole poem. As it is, /ë/ has here its highest relative rank in Wordsworth's ten and the second rank in the poem. This is the only time /d/ ranks in the top four consonants in Wordsworth's ten, and here it is first.

The water imagery of the poem is caught up in "blood." This imagery starts with "flood" (line 1), whose sound is echoed in "blood"; indeed, the association of /l/ and /d/ is strong throughout the poem (flood, world's, flowed, old, hold, held, blood, manifold).

The dominant nucleus of the sonnet, /iy/, last appears in "we" (line 13), and this, plus the intentional setting off of the phrase by dashes, adds to the force of the whole. In imagery, theme, and sound, then, this phrase, especially "first blood," is summative.

6. Wordsworth, "On the Extinction of the Venetian Republic." The last word of the octet, "sea," contains its dominant consonant and vowel, /s iy/. Of the nuclei, /iy/ is dominant in the octet, /ey/ in the sestet, and this parallels the contrast between the octet's description of the glories of Venice, the sestet's comment on her fall. (Note, incidentally, "Venice" in the octet, "vanish" in the sestet.) Since /iy/ dominates seven of Wordsworth's ten, while /ey/ achieves second rank only in this, against an average rank of 7.1, I take it as the most significant nuclei. In this sonnet /w/ also achieves its highest rank relative to Wordsworth's ten, fifth against an average of 9.5, outranking /d/ and /n/. This relative prominence can be

seen as giving force to the sonnet's final stressed syllable in "away." Its force is heightened by the fact that, after appearing in the octet's rhyme scheme, /ey/ completely takes over the rhyme scheme of the sestet.

Some effect is obtained by the recurrence of "once" in lines 1 and 14, but of its phonemes only /w/ and /s/ have strength in the sonnet. "Great" and "away" have some summative force, contributed chiefly by /ey/, backed by consonant strength either absolutely in this poem (/t r/) or relative to others by Wordsworth (/w g/), and abetted by alliteration ("grieve-great," "once-away").

7. Wordsworth, "The World Is Too Much with Us." In the octet "out of tune" is summative, having the two dominant nuclei /aw/ and /uw/ and the two dominant consonants /t/ and /n/. Note that the strength of the back diphthongs is confined entirely to the first eight and a half lines; after dominating these, and achieving their highest relative rank in Wordsworth, neither /aw/ nor /uw/ recurs in a weighted syllable.

In the sestet, /iy/, /ay/, and /ə/ come into prominence; /r l n/ dominate the sestet, and /r l n/ come to be dominant in the sonnet as a whole. No clear and strong instance of summative effect is found for the sestet or the poem. The final words, "wreathed horn," involve the dominant consonants (/r n/) and the dominant nucleus (/iy/) of the sonnet, but there is no connection with the theme of the poem in a summative way. The three dominant consonants of the sonnet and its sestet occur in the stressed syllable of "forlorn," together with the sestet's second-ranking nucleus.

In sum, there is a sharp contrast between the two parts of the poem in the use of nuclei. The octet has a summation in sound and meaning in "out of tune"; some key to the sestet is found in "forlorn," whose metrically stressed consonants (but not its nucleus) dominate the poem as a whole.

8. Wordsworth, "To Sleep." The dominant nucleus, reckoned for the whole sonnet, is /iy/, but its strength ends with the apostrophe to "Sleep!" in line 10. This is a summative effect within the sonnet.

In the sestet /e/ is dominant; all its sestet occurrences follow "Sleep" in line 10, and it emerges second-ranking nucleus in the poem. Of the consonants, /l/ is firm throughout the poem and is dominant. This gives some force to the final rhyme of the poem in "health." The most effect is achieved however, by contrast; neither /j/ nor /oy/ occurs in the poem until they occur together in the last line in "joyous health." What force the edning has, then, comes from a combination of contrast ("joyous") and culmination ("health").

9. Wordsworth, "Thought of a Briton on the Subjugation of Switzerland." Both sestet and octet end with "heard by Thee," although the sestet has also a following exclamation mark. In octet, sestet, and the

poem as a whole, /iy/ is the dominant nucleus. Although /d/ ranks only twelfth among the consonants of the poem, this is its second-highest rank relative to Wordsworth's ten, against an average rank of 17.1.

The other prominent word of the sonnet is "voice." Both /v/ and /oy/ have their highest ranks relative to Wordsworth's ten, seventh against an average rank of 12.7 for /v/, eighth against an average rank of 14.2 among vowels for /oy/. (/oy/ does not even occur in six of Wordsworth's ten.) The word, of course, is part of the subject of the poem, signaled by its repetition in lines 1 and 2.

Both "Thee" and "voice," then, have prominence by word repetition and phoneme rank relative to Wordsworth's other ten; "Thee" also has the dominant nucleus of the whole poem. The dominant consonants of the sonnet have no culminative force.

10. Wordsworth, "At Dover." In the sestet "cease" has its dominant nucleus and consonant, /s iy/, and "wonder" sums up and concludes the strength of /w/ and /ë/, both high in the octet and limited to it.

In the octet the final word "sin" has the two dominant consonants of the sonnet, but its nucleus, /i/, is only fourth in rank. The word "deaden" sums up a surge in the strength of /d/ in the sestet, and the whole sonnet strength of /e/, its second-ranking nucleus. I sense a rise in the poem with "speaks from out the sea" and "shrieks of crime." This probably is due, first, to the dominance of /s/ and /iy/ in the poem as a whole, and second, to the fact that /p k s ay/ have here their highest ranks relative to Wordsworth's ten, whereas /r/ is high throughout the sonnet.

Although these words may be prominent from the point of view of sound, none of them seems summative with regard to the meaning of the sonnet. In fact, there is a sharp disharmony between the theme, which is that of hush and peace, and the funneling of most of the sound into "speaks" and "shrieks of crime." (But René Wellek's interpretation of the sonnet would make "sin" summative—see his formal discussion.)

11. Keats, "Written in the Fields." The dominant nucleus of the sonnet, /e/, is spent in the octet, where it monopolizes the rhyme scheme. (It is the nucleus most often dominant in the ten Keats sonnets, having first rank six times.) Although it overwhelms other nuclei in the octet, it does not enter with the octet's dominant consonants, /t r n l/, into any summative word.

Several points can be made about the final words. Taken together, "clear ether silently" has the six dominant consonants of the sestet (including /k/) and the five dominant consonants of the sonnet; it has also the three dominant nuclei of the sestet, and /i iy/ do not contrast in their position in these words, (/ir/, /iy#/), so that their effect may seem pooled. (The dominant vowel of the poem, /e/, has been spent in the octet and is commonly dominant in Keats anyway.) All this points to considerable force for the sound of these words, but I am unable to generalize their meaning to the theme of the sonnet.

12. Keats, "On First Looking into Chapman's Homer." In the octet "bold" has two consonants and a nucleus whose weight is largely or wholly confined to the octet; /d/, third in rank for the sonnet, is first for the octet, but only in a four-way tie for eighth rank in the sestet. Both /b/ and /ow/ are weighted only in the octet.

By a slight margin /e/ is the sonnet's dominant nucleus, but it is dominant in neither octet nor sestet alone. This is another instance of Keats' preference for /e/. The octet is dominated by /iy/, the sestet by /ay/. Note that /ay/ is dominant at the moment it occurs in "silent" in line 14, for /e/ has a fair part of its total weight yet to come in "Darien."

Of the dominant sounds, the two chief consonants and two chief nuclei, /n l/ and /e ay/, have in this sonnet their highest rank relative to the Keats ten. My ranking for the consonants is in the order /n l d s t/; this differs from the ranking Lynch reports, /n d l t s/. Lynch, however, ranks the sum of added weights and number of occurrences, whereas I rank only the added weights. If the weights and number of occurrences I obtain are summed, and the sums ranked, the resulting order is the same as that of Lynch. This is encouraging, since it suggests that for this sonnet some differences in weighting and ranking do not obscure what may be considered true dominance.

In view of all this, it is fair to say that my procedure confirms Lynch, finding in "silent" a summative word, both in sound and meaning. It denotes the key emotional response to the poem's theme, as analyzed by Lynch in his paper (although, as Wimsatt has observed may happen, there is no simple English word for the theme itself).

13. Keats, "Happy Is England." None of the results show an integration of sound and meaning in the closing lines of the sonnet.

14. Keats, "When I Have Fears." We can read this sonnet and find "love," "fame," and "nothingness" key words: "love" pointing to the first four lines of the sestet, "fame" to the theme of the octet, and "nothingness" denoting not only the threat of annihilation to both but also the result of contemplating the threat. (The nucleus of "fame" also echoes the rhyme scheme of the octet.)

The word "never," repeated in lines 10 and 11, has the two dominant consonants of the sestet and sonnet /r n/, the dominant nucleus of the sestet and sonnet /e/, and a consonant /v/ which achieves in this poem its highest rank relative to the Keats ten. Since /n l/, the second-and third-ranking consonants of the sonnet, stay relatively strong throughout, and /ë/ emerges sharply in the sestet, "love" and the principally stressed syllable of "nothingness" are given strength, and "love" is repeated in the sestet, the first time occurring before an exclamation mark and a dash (line 12). The relative strength of sounds in "unreflecting" makes it also a suitable key word, contrasting "love" to the reflecting part. The only culminating force that I can clearly see is in the sustained strength of /n/, through the repetitions of "never" into "nothingness" in the final line. The sounds in "never" qualify it as a key word, but its position does not give it a summative role.

15. Keats, "Bright Star." The dominant nucleus of the octet is /a/, but it has only one weighted occurrence after that, whereas /e/ is the dominant nucleus both of the sestet and the whole sonnet. In the sestet /i/ rises sharply, acquiring second rank here and reaching third rank in the whole sonnet.

As to consonants, /s t l r/ dominate the sestet, but the order of dominance in the whole sonnet is /t s r l/. Omitting /a/ as confined mostly to the octet, these dominant sounds are found in the stressed syllable of "unrest" (line 13) and the succeeding words "still, still" (line 14).

The theme of the sonnet is a contrast between motionlessness and motion, between observing the moving waters and feeling a soft fall and swell. (The contrast between observing water and being in it runs through several Keats sonnets.) Between negatives ("not . . . no") the octet describes the unwanted state of motionlessness and apartness, and the sestet describes the wanted state of consummation. The stressed syllables, "rest" and "still," have the same meaning, motionlessness and apartness, yet here each is used with urgency regarding consummation. The words can be seen as expressing the tension between the octet and sestet states (for Keats was against his will in the situation of the "bright star"), or as "immersing," transforming the octet state.

Thus we can see "unrest" and "still, still" as summative both in sound and meaning.

16. Keats, "Keen, Fitful Gusts." In line 9 "friendliness" has the six consonants that are dominant in the sonnet, /r l s d f n/, and its dominant vowel /e/. It is a turning point between the immediate scene and the literary solace, a catalyst for the final lines and hence a clear key word. Of the interweaving of sounds and patterns in the sestet, none emerges as culminative.

17. Keats, "Written in the Cottage Where Burns Was Born." The dominant consonants of the sonnet are /n d m/; these and /b/ achieve here their highest rank relative to the Keats ten, and this is the only sonnet of the twenty in which /m/ achieves rank among the first four. The dominant nuclei of the sonnet are /ae ay ey/; these achieve here their highest rank relative to the Keats ten.

Despite its strength in the last two lines of the octet and the first five of the sestet, /ae/ has no concentrated force. The other dominant sounds are represented in the final words of lines 12 and 13, "blind" and "name." Both relate to the theme of the sonnet. Of course "name" involves the apostrophe "O Burns" in line 2, "pledging a great soul" in line 6, and the idea of "fame" in line 14. We can see "blind" in relation to Burns' infant state, "Happy and thoughtless of thy day of doom!" and to Keats' drunken state, "I cannot see" (line 7) from drink and from thought (line 12). Insofar as these words are taken as identifying two main aspects of the sonnet, they have some summative force, before the apostrophe of the final line, which rings out the poem's theme, identification with the famed poet.

18. Keats, "To Sleep." In the sestet the two dominant nuclei of the sonnet, /i ay/, are relatively weak and have no concentrated force; most of their weight stems from use in the octet. The dominant nucleus of the sestet is /ow/, which ranks third in the whole sonnet, the highest rank it achieves relative to the Keats ten. The two dominant consonants of the sonnet are /s l/. These and /ow/ occur together in the sonnet's final word "soul."

Note that /z/ and /s/ achieve here their highest ranks relative to the Keats ten; /z/ is notable in the rhyme scheme of lines 6 to 13. This and the absolute dominance of /s/ may reflect phonesthematic associations of English speakers with these sibilants.

I see a connection between "soul" (possibly also "seal") and the theme of the sonnet. This is suggested by the religious terminology of "this thine hymn," "wait the Amen," "save me"; the association of "curious conscience" with the (Prince of?) darkness; the association of saviour Sleep with a key; and the implication of fate after death in the opening and closing lines: "O soft *embalmer* of the still midnight" and "And seal the hushed *casket* of my soul," as well as in "forgetfulness divine." All this indicates a carrying-out through the sonnet of a metaphoric treatment of Sleep as saviour of the soul.

19. Keats, "On the Sonnet." We note that the three dominant consonants of the poem are those in the word "sonnet," /t s n/. We see also that the six dominant consonants of the poem and of the octet (except /l/, the fifth) and the dominant nucleus of the octet /ey/ are found in the stressed syllable of "constrained" (line 4). (And /ey/ achieves in this sonnet its highest rank, third, relative to the Keats ten.) Both these words involve the poem's theme, that is, the constraints proper to an English sonnet.

Of words that occur in the sestet, "let" has the poem's dominant consonant and nucleus, and /l/ itself emerges as the dominant consonant of the sestet. The word itself recurs in lines 4, 7, 11, and 13, organizing much of the poem syntactically. Its appropriateness in this role is seconded by the fact that English has come to refer to two opposed meanings by this one phonemic sequence, permission and hinderance.

In both sound and meaning, then, "constrained" and "let" are appropriate key words.

20. Keats, "The House of Mourning." The dominant nuclei of the sonnet are /i a ey i/, all four of which achieve their highest rank relative to the Keats ten. The first three are dominant in that order in the octet as well, whereas /ay/ is dominant in the sestet but has no weighted occurrences outside it.

The dominant consonants of the sonnet are /r t d p n/; /p/ achieves its highest rank, fourth, relative to the Keats ten, and this is the only time in all twenty that it is among the top four. Of the consonants, /d/ acquires strength in the last three lines in "damned, Wordsworth's, Dover, Dover, *could*." The other dominant consonants occur in "write upon," together with the sestet's dominant nucleus /ay/ and /a/, whose strength has been noted.

Despite some summative force in sound, these words have little summative force in meaning, given the organization of the sonnet. Several of its disjunct items do concern writing, but there is no cumulation. Given the derogatory tone, it is amusing that the final word of the octet, "pot," has sounds which achieve such strength in this sonnet, and that the dominant vowel of the sonnet, /i/, last occurs weighted in "pit" (line 11). More significant is the way the prose stress seems to force metrical stresses into juxtaposition: "to a *friend's cot*," "a *curst lot*," "a *cold cof*fee pot," "a French *bon*net," "who *could write* upon it?" The piling up of ionic feet seems to underscore the display of a collection of vile curiosities.

V

In this section I shall evaluate the approach, relating it to other uses of sound in lyric poetry, in order to see its value and limitations.

As a preliminary, it is necessary to survey the other results obtained by the approach. In his article Lynch reports on analyses of poems by Wordsworth, Arnold, Spender, Collins, Marlowe, Raleigh, and Donne. I have experimented with the approach on a few pieces by William Carlos Williams and one of my own.

Perhaps the results obtained in some of the poems, yielding a summative word, depend on particular forms or conventions, such as lines of fixed length or rhyme. Suspecting that any short poem might exploit sound occurrences in this way, I analyzed several pieces by William Carlos Williams. Only the first resulted in a neat correspondence between dominant sounds and the theme in a summative word. The poem is "Flowers by the Sea":

> When over the flowery, sharp pasture's
> edge, unseen, the salt ocean
> lifts its form—chickory and daisies
> tied, released seem hardly flowers alone
> but color and the movement—or the shape
> perhaps—of restlessness, whereas
> the sea is circled and sways
> peacefully upon its plantlike stem.

It turns out that /s/ is by far the dominant consonant, /iy/ by far the dominant nucleus. Although the word itself occurs but once, these sounds of course form "sea." (And "restlessness" and "peacefully" are second in containing dominant sounds.)

In the other pieces by Williams, "To Waken An Old Lady," "A Sort of Song," and the final stanzas from "To A Dog Injured In The Streets" and "Choral: The Pink Church," the results direct attention to the unobtrusive skill and pattern by which Williams composes a "machine made of words" but do not point to summative or key words. In "A Sort of Song," the high rank of /k/ does direct attention to a series of words (snake, quick, strike, quiet, reconcile, compose, saxifrage, rocks). The dominance in "To Waken An Old Lady" of /s d n/ warns against the excesses to which such a method could lead, if guided by fertile imagination; for we might argue that this delicate waking song specifically avoids the word and thought "sudden," and that repressing the word has forced its consonants into prominence.

Analysis of a poem of my own (**189**) revealed an organization I had not suspected. The final word "ministry" summed up the dominant phonemes, and, as it turned out, provided a key to the poem's four stanzas, each of which could be seen as expressing a form of ministry.

In his analyses, Lynch has had complete success, although not uniform results. Out of six cases, he found three with summative words (the Keats sonnet, Wordsworth's "I Wandered Lonely as a Cloud," Spender's "Moving through the Silent Crowd"). In one poem difference within the poem matched other facts about it (Arnold's "Dover Beach"); in other poems differences between them matched differences in attitude (Marlowe, Raleigh, Donne); in one (Collins' "Ode Written in the Beginning of the Year 1746") the absence of a summative word was found to correspond appropriately to the poem's thought.

In a sample of twenty sonnets I found that a part clearly had summative words, a part had near-summative words, and a part did not have them at all. Some instances of key words were also found.

On the positive side, then, this can be said. Some short lyrics are so organized that the dominant sounds appear together in a word, appropriately placed, which sums up or gives expression to the subject or theme —there is a coming together both of sound and meaning. For most short lyrics this is probably not true, but charting and totaling the frequency and weighting of sounds directs attention to words and patterns that might be overlooked. It objectifies the occurrence and succession of phonemes and so provides materials the stylistic critic must take into account. If any appeal beyond personal taste is to be made, regarding the significance of sound in a poem, nothing short of a full account of the use of phonemes in the poem will do as a reference point.

It is the grave limitation of the purely intuitive approach (as exemplified by Spitzer) that it takes no such full, objective record into account. But it is equally the grave limitation of a purely statistical approach that it may forget it is dealing with an object, an aesthetic object.

I must reiterate here that this approach does not depend simply on the statistical frequency and weighting of sounds. There are three criteria for a putative summative word to meet; only their successful intersection in the same word is accepted. We may attribute entirely to chance the different dominant sounds among sonnets, although no poet will; it may be that each sonnet by chance will contain one or more words made up of several of its dominant sounds. That this word may also be placed at the end of the sonnet and also sum up the sonnet's theme—this clearly is not an artifact of the sonnet form and the English language; it happens only in about one-third of the twenty cases.

As his formal discussion shows, Fred Householder has subjected the data to a penetrating analysis. He points out that the summative or near-summative words almost always contain the consonants which are normally most frequent in English. But it must also be pointed out that the nuclei show much greater variation, among poems and between poets. Moreover, we must face the theoretical alternatives. A poet works with already structured material, language. But though he is not free to choose sounds at random, are we to believe that he can have no effect at all? One literary critic has said that the words considered summative by this approach are also those that his own response to the sonnets would pick out. Moreover, there are aesthetically two different ways to exploit sounds. The poet may work against the structure inherent in his language, so as to give prominence to sounds otherwise less important. Thus, Wordsworth makes /z/ the fourth most important sound in "I Grieved for Buonaparte," despite the fact, pointed out by Householder, that weighting would be expected normally to decrease its importance. The poet may also work with the structure inherent in his material, as the sculptor or carver may work with the structure inherent in his. If the dominant sounds of a poem must always include some or all of a small set of consonants, the poet may choose a word summative in theme which contains them and place it strategically so as to exploit the cumulative effect which his language unavoidably offers.

Finally, as Householder points out, the sounds below the dominant range may be ones to watch especially. Although not attaining dominance in a given poem, because English does not offer this possibility without a bizarre choice of words, such sounds may occur sufficiently in excess of their normal use to deserve notice. (Such are /v/ and /oy/ in Wordsworth's "Thought of a Briton on the Subjugation of Switzerland.")

In general, the comments on the use of words made in a recent review can be applied to the use of sounds:

> [certain words in Mallarmé] seem characteristic because of their absolute frequency in the text, which catches the eye, and not because of their relative frequency, which is not within the reach of linguistic consciousness. This consciousness will be sensitive to a hapax or a rare word but will become less and less discriminating as the words grow more common. That is, its absoluteness is enough to make a frequency visible and stylistically valid; if the frequency happens also to be relative, this interests the linguist but no longer the stylistician. In my opinion, this concept of *stylistic* consciousness as perception of the relation between a fact and a delimited context—not between a fact and the norm of language—makes the interpretation of frequencies more complicated than Guiraud realizes . . . (**335**, p. 326).

Some considerable limitations of the present approach must now be mentioned. Obviously no such approach can say much about long works. As to a poet's general style, the relative frequency and weighting of sounds are, of course, important: perhaps Eliot has a predilection for dental stops, Yeats and Williams a preference for labial stops, in alliterative patterns, perhaps not, but this can be determined. Presumably, though, the longer the work or passage, the less any particular selection of sounds can escape being submerged by the normal frequencies of the language. The longest test and success are the twenty-four lines of Wordsworth's poem on the daffodils.

Related to this is the question of the domain of an effect. I have had recourse to more limited domains than that of the whole sonnet in analyzing these poems, for example, the culmination of /iy/ in "Sleep!" in the tenth line of Wordsworth's sonnet. One domain or delimited context is clearly the octet and next half-line in Wordsworth's "The World is Too Much With Us."

A further important limitation is that this approach can take account of stylistic effects that depend on cumulation but not those that depend on contrast. I have given some notice to the effect of contrast, or noncumulation, in remarks on "rejoice" in Wordsworth's "To Sleep" and the initial consonant of "shrine" in Wordsworth's "It Is A Beauteous Evening, Calm and Free." But this approach provides no way to assess objectively the relative *non*cumulativeness, "surprise" value, of the sounds within or between poems, except for the rare sound used but once and then at the climax in a poem. It does not touch the giving of prominence to sounds in more limited domains by contrast with other sounds.

Another limitation which, as far as I know, all stylistic approaches share is the making of untested assumptions about the psychology of poet or audience. Many of these assumptions are reasonable and intuitively correct to the student or practitioner of verbal art. But we do not in fact know that the use of a sound in one part of a poem has any effect on a reader in a subsequent part; we have no "just noticeable differences" for the prominence of sounds by repetition in a sonnet. Rather, we analyze the poem, construct an interpretation, and postulate (or instruct) the reader's response.

The Lynch approach taps only one part of the use of sound in lyric poetry. The tonal organization may operate on levels both above and below that of the phoneme. We can study the use of distinctive features: of series, such as stops, continuants, vowels; of orders, such as labial, dental, velar; of classes, such as front vowels versus back vowels, low vowels versus high vowels. There is no reason to exclude from experimental study any dimension along which sounds can be grouped. Any may turn out to be utilized by one or more poets for particular effect in a particular poem or as a general stylistic trait. Of course, so-called suprasegmental features are important. Insofar as we wish to keep to the norm of the poem, rather than focus on a particular performance, the role of secondary and tertiary stresses in relation to the abstract metrical pattern is of the utmost significance (**61**, pp. 424–425). This role inheres directly in the poem's structure in a way that can be ascertained fairly objectively, whereas voice qualifiers and the like seem much more susceptible to individual difference and momentary performance.

The role of stresses in relation to metrical pattern, Chatman has observed, may involve "the close interplay of sound and meaning" (**61**, p. 437). And this illustrates a kind of appropriate sound-meaning nexus more general than any Lynch's approach has led us to consider so far. The nexus may simply inhere in the sustained lyric effect of the whole poem, rather than be focused by culmination or contrast at a particular point. Regarding phonemes, the dominant sounds might show greater concentration in some lyrics than in prose; that is, they might account for a significantly greater proportion of occurrences. Or the poem might be a succession of brief domains and local effects, even using patterns of interplay more intricate than have been scored in this study, but none dominating the whole.

Finally, Lynch approaches the poem primarily as a quasi-simultaneous object. It would be equally possible to approach the use of the sounds primarily in terms of successiveness. Such an information theory type of approach would be very informative about the statistics of prominence by contrast and prominence by repetition.

What, then, of style in relation to value in the individual lyric? Wimsatt has argued "every good poem is a complex poem and may be demonstrated so by rhetorical analysis . . . and further it is only in virtue of its complexity that it has artistic unity" (**448**, p. 275). Helmut Hatzfeld has argued that "A literary work is good, if the style elements fuse into a style compound as the discovered realization of the author's artistic intention; it is bad, if the style elements are contradictory in themselves, do not fuse into an entity, and do not translate the artistic intention of the author" (**161**, p. 65).[8] In a lyric either the complexity and unity of a "concrete universal" or a style compound presumably comprehends the use of sound along with its other components. In some sense, then, there must be appropriateness to the nexus of sound and meaning if the poem is to be regarded as good. It is noteworthy that the positive results obtained by Lynch's approach tend to be in the most highly regarded of the sonnets.

Still, the results of this approach are not themselves a criterion of value. They constitute neither a necessary nor a sufficient condition because they comprehend only a part of the use of sound in lyric poetry. I would say that a sonnet which showed no unity of sound and meaning was not a good one, but there are many ways in which unity can occur. So the absence of a summative word is not critical, and its presence does not guarantee the unity of the other dimensions in the use of sound.

I would say that the results of this approach are indications of value (positive in Wordsworth's "Westminster Bridge," negative in his "At Dover"), but that they are not decisive.

[8] Hatzfeld (**160**) adds a second check, reference to parallels and literary theory.

Metrics

Metric Typology

JOHN LOTZ

This paper presents a general theory of metrics, founded on phonetics and oriented toward structural linguistics. It includes in a unified framework the diverse systems of versification known from various cultures. The material is obviously not intended to be exhaustive. The presentation is concentrated on the central core of the phenomenon and does not follow up the tangents which can lead off at every single aspect of this most deliberately formulated, and experimentally varied, use of language. The article is focused on metric systems which present a complete regulation of texts, though differing in the norms regulating the versification.[1] The material is presented in three sections: (1) linguistic foundation, (2) metric superstructure, and (3) sample analyses.

(1) LINGUISTIC FOUNDATION

1. In some languages there are texts in which the phonetic material within certain syntactic frames, such as sentence, phrase, word, is numerically regulated.[2] Such a text is called *verse*, and its distinctive characteristic *meter*. *Metrics* is the study of meter. A nonmetric text is called *prose*.

2. Numerical regulation may refer to a variety of phenomena, and, therefore, verse and prose are distinguished not as two sharply differentiated *classes* but rather as two *types* of texts. (This, however, should not obscure the fact that verse and prose are *polar opposites*.)

Numerical regulation can mean a strict determination of the occurrence of the syllabics and, in some cases, also of certain prosodic features, as exemplified later. This regulation can be relaxed in various ways.

---

[1] A metric typology was first presented by the author in **255**; a revised summary was published in **253**, p. 376, fn. 22. General metrics are discussed in **84** and **85**, where a select bibliography is also given. Important new ideas are discussed in **199**, with bibliographical references.

[2] The term "text" is used, although it refers primarily to writing, in order to avoid a more cumbersome expression, such as *language product* or the like.

For instance: In some types of Hungarian poetry a metrically relevant phrase can contain six *or* five syllabics; such a variation can be even wider, as in West Siberian folk poetry.[3] Also, the numerical regulation can refer only to one part of the text, as when prose and verse are mixed in the same literary work. But a text can be even more intricately interwoven, as in Indo-European verse, where the beginning of the line was fairly free, whereas the substantial final portion was regulated. In certain types of classical rhetoric texts only a small final portion was determined. (The difference between the two is rather a question of degree than of absolute nature.) Furthermore, such a numerical regulation may refer to the strict determination of the syntactic units with a wide variation in the phonetic material. Free verse often tends to move in this direction. In Ghê there are texts which are repetitions of units consisting of five or three syntactic phrases bound together by rhyme.[4] Such "rhythmic" texts result also in the enumeration of basketball scores on the radio (team–score—team–score).

All these types represent texts which deviate from straight prose, and the deviation can be put in terms of numerical regularity. We could argue about where verse ends and prose begins, or whether or not we should introduce new intermediary types, or whether there is such an intercultural phenomenon as verse at all.

3. In the following, however, we shall concentrate only on texts in which the entire phonetic material in its syllabic, and sometimes also prosodic, aspect is regulated. Such strictly formalized verse gives a contrasting background to other less regulated phenomena where they do occur. Also, the proper typological evaluation of bound texts in languages where strictly regulated verse does not occur is possible only by such comparison.

Examples for such strictly regulated texts are

A. MORDVINIAN DECASYLLABIC VERSE. (1) Word boundary after each 5th syllabic pulse; (2) phrase boundary after each 10th syllabic pulse; (3) sentence boundary after a small number of such decasyllabic stretches; (4) song final after an indeterminate number of stretches characterized in 1 through 3.

B. NORMALIZED SAPPHIC VERSE. (1) Word limit after the 11th, 22nd, and 33rd syllabic pulses; (2) sentence limit after the 38th syllabic pulse; (3) syllabics number [(1, 3, 5, 8, 10) + (0, 11, 22)] and 34 and 37 either long or diphthongal or, if short, followed by at least two consonants; (4) syllabics number [(2, 6, 7) + (0, 11, 22)] and 35 and 36 short and not followed by more than one consonant; (5) poem ending after a certain number of such stretches as described in 1 through 4.

C. BLANK VERSE. (1) Word limit after every 10th or 11th syllabic pulse; (2) sentence limit after a certain number of such decasyllabic or hendecasyllabic stretches (number undetermined); (3) syllabics in even

---

[3] See **10** for a thorough linguistic analysis of such a verse type.
[4] Oral communication by Joseph H. Greenberg.

number position relatively heavier than syllabics in odd number position (as a thoroughgoing tendency); (4) text ending after an indeterminate number of stretches described in 1 through 3.

D. TᶜANG DYNASTY METER. (1) Sentence boundary after each 28th syllabic pulse; (2) syllabics number 2, 6, 11, 18, 23, and 27 belonging to an even tonal class; (3) syllabics 4, 9, 13, 16, 20, and 25 belonging to a noneven tonal class (rising, falling, or abrupt); (4) identical phonetic material (rhyme) in the syllabic and the coda at the phrase endings 7, 14, and 28; (5) poem final after a certain number of units described in 1 through 4.

4. It is typical for polar terms that their referential coverage is dissimilar. (In phonological terminology one is more specific, *marked*, the other more general, *unmarked*.) Among the several possibilities of such marked-unmarked pairs, the *verse-prose* opposition represents an extreme, as prose has no defining mark, except that it is a text which lacks meter.

5. Verse is a purely formal notion. It refers to the language signal alone without reference to function and can correspond to a variety of functions. For instance, even in our culture, where the role of meter is predominantly literary-aesthetic, verse is used in advertising jingles. In Old Germanic law verse was used to prevent alteration. It is, of course, possible to subsume verse under a single psychological label, such as attention getting, or under a logical reflexive sign-to-sign relation, but a labeling of the extension does not mean an intensive definition of a term.

6. Since all metric phenomena are language phenomena, it follows that metrics is entirely within the competence of linguistics. If there were a uniform function behind verse, it would be possible to approach metrics from this point of view and regard the language aspect as differentiating. Since there is no such uniform function, it is impossible to define verse from any other single point of view, such as art or literature.[5]

7. Since metrics is entirely within the scope of linguistics, it presupposes the linguistic analysis of the utterance. For metrical purposes, however, not all aspects of language are relevant, and even among those that are relevant, we have to distinguish the basic constitutive factors of meter and the additive-variative ones. The principle according to which we select the metrically relevant linguistic phenomena is the *principle of metric*

---

[5] I do not intend to say, however, that linguists are metricians *per se*, or that literary critics, psychologists, etc., do not often understand more about relevant features of verse and language than many linguists do.

relevancy in analogy with the principle of relevancy in phonological and grammatical analysis;[6] for example, length of the syllabic is metrically relevant in Classical Greek, whereas intonation patterns are not metrically relevant in English.

8. The language material used in verse might differ from the "normal" use of the language. The study of these phenomena constitutes the domain of *poetic grammar*. This includes all aspects of linguistic analysis, such as phonology (elision, etc.), morphology (the prevocalic accusative *hort* in Latin), and verse syntax.

9. The linguistic study of meter includes two sections, (A) study of the linguistic constituents and (B) study of the metric superstructure.

A. STUDY OF THE LINGUISTIC CONSTITUENTS. This again is subdivided into two divisions: (1) the *phonological constituents* of meter, (2) the *syntactic* (also called *grammatical* or *semiotic constituents* of meter).

1. PHONOLOGICAL CONSTITUENTS. All strictly regulated metric systems are founded on *syllabification*,[7] existing on the physiological, physical, and psychological levels of speech transmission. It is, however, the existence of a syllabic pulse, characterized by a dominant syllabic rather than the syllable as such, that is metrically relevant. (Syllable implies both culmination and delimitation; this latter is not relevant metrically. Even in the so-called "quantitative" meter, as in Classical Greek, the metrically relevant stretch is not identical with the syllable, as is shown later. It is possible, however, to use syllable as a portion of sound determined by one syllabic crest, where the boundaries are not necessarily definite.)

In addition to syllabification some metric systems make use of the *prosodic features*,[8] those of *pitch*, *intensity*, and *duration*.

[6] First formulated by Bühler (**52**), based on Trubetzkoy's phonological theory.

[7] The notions "syllable," "vowel," and "consonant" are among the most obscure in phonemic theory. In our opinion they belong to the aspect of phonemic analysis which precedes the contrastive-distinctive comparison of speech stretches and could be called a *matching* operation. For instance, in "stake" and "takes" we do not start with a phoneme by phoneme comparison, but rather by matching the syllabic peaks. This problem will be discussed in the Report of the 10th Georgetown Round Table Meeting.

[8] The definition of prosodic features as suprasegmentals does not characterize the group of phenomena aimed at; for example, distinctive voicing in English is suprasegmental, whereas an inherent tone in a monophonemic word in Chinese is segmental. The definition of these features as relative features, in opposition to the absolute features, as proposed by Noreen—and since then accepted by many structuralists—is also unsatisfactory since the same burst can be evaluated as belonging to different phonemes dependent on relative arrangement, as has been shown experimentally. In **256**, p. 378, a definition of prosodic features was attempted, by characterizing them as *frame* features in opposition to the *shape* features in the time-frequency-intensity display of speech.

Metrics does not use all the phonemic features available for verse. On the other hand, a tonal metric system, as in Chinese, can only be based on phonemically distinctive tones. (English intonation, although a "pitch" phenomenon, is different from this kind of distinctive tone, and, therefore, tonal meter is impossible in English. The failure to distinguish between the distinctive and configurational aspects of phonological functions makes the single-level phonemic analysis into segmental phonemes, stresses, intonations, junctures, etc., less suitable for metric purposes.)

Metrically relevant features are in general selected among the phonemically distinctive features. But if a phoneme includes both syllabic and nonsyllabic allophones (i = j, l = ḷ), this subphonemic distinction is relevant for the verse.

The numerical regulation refers to the phonological aspects of language.

2. SYNTACTIC CONSTITUENTS. *Sentence* and *word* (comprising various kinds of morpheme groupings in different languages, marked differently) seem to be always relevant metrically. In some languages, especially in folk poetry, cohesive word groups (phrases) may also play a role; such a word group is called a *colon*. (A colon must be cohesive, since discontinuous stretches obviously cannot be utilized for metric purposes. Cola occur in relative degrees of hierarchy: "very big" is a colon; so is "very big house.") The smallest unit, the morpheme, does not figure primarily in meter, although it may be used to indicate verse structure, as in parallelism.

The syntactic constituents provide the frame for which the numerical regulation of the phonological material can be stated.

B. STUDY OF THE METRIC STRUCTURE. The metric units are those syntactic frames for which the numerical regulation of the phonological material can be stated. A metric utterance, the poem, can be constructed repetitively of shorter units, called *lines*,[9] or it can be constructed more freely, *astichic verse*. Lines may be organized into higher-order constructs in the poem, such as *strophe*, *cycle*, and may have an internal organization into *segments* characterized by certain types of word boundaries called *caesurae*.

The relation among comparable elements in the metric structure is called *response*. Where there is only one line in a poem, such as a single hexameter, this response may refer to other examples of such metric structure given in the culture.

10. Besides the necessary elements which are constitutive for meter, there may be added phonological and grammatical features which underline and emphasize the metric structure. These, however, do not create meter and may also function independently in prose. Such notions are

---

[9] Again, line refers to the graphic medium of presentation.

assonance or *alliteration*, which can function as an indicator of cohesion in the line; *rhyme*, which is usually correlated with inner response in the metric structure; *refrain*, which often indicates a higher order of construction; and *parallelism*, which shows a correspondence in the grammatical structure of responsive lines.

(2) METRIC SUPERSTRUCTURE

1. This metric typology is based on the utilization of the phonological material for metric purposes, that is, the regulation of syllabification and, in some metric systems, also of the prosodic features. Thus, we have basically two types of meter:

A. PURE-SYLLABIC METER. Only the number of syllabics within the syntactic frames—word, colon, sentence—is regulated. Example: Mordvinian verse.

B. SYLLABIC-PROSODIC METER. The occurrence of certain types of prosodic features is required, in addition to the number of syllabics. According to the kinds of prosodic features, three subclasses can be distinguished:

1. DURATIONAL METER (commonly called "quantitative"). In some positions the "quantity" of the syllabics and also, in some cases, the complexity of the following consonant cluster are regulated. Example: Classical Greek and Latin verse.

2. DYNAMIC METER. Besides the regulation of the number of syllabics, heavier and lighter syllabic pulses are required in some positions. Example: English and German verse.

3. TONAL METER. In certain positions well-defined tonal classes, for example even and changing, representing classes of distinctive pitch phonemes of the language, are required. Example: Classical Chinese.

2. In the syllabic-prosodic meter the notion of the syllabic alone will not suffice; a second concept has to be introduced, the organization of the syllabic material according to certain prosodic features, called *base class*: *long* and *short* base for durational meter, *heavy* and *light* base for dynamic meter, and *even* and *changing* base for tonal meter.

It is interesting to note that the phonological elements are grouped into only two base classes, never into more, although in principle much finer gradations would be possible. For example, in English more than two stress levels could be utilized, but, apart from the tendency in the so-called *dipodic* meters, there are never more than two classes utilized systematically; in Classical Greek the length of the syllabic and the following consonant clusters would have allowed a large number of classes, but only two types of bases were utilized for metric purposes, the short and the long; in Classical Chinese there were nine (or six) phonemic tones, but for metric purposes there was only one opposition, that between even and noneven tones.

In syllabic-prosodic meters the numerical regulation refers to the base classes as well; that is, in certain positions only one definite base class is allowed. This necessitates the introduction of *positions* as a second numerical principle, besides *quantity*, which is the sole characteristic of the pure-syllabic meter. There are positions which have to be filled out by a definite base class; these positions are called *fixed*. The other positions, which allow variations, are called *free*. There are no syllabic-prosodic systems in which all positions are fixed. In free positions the fitting may be either of the two base classes (*anceps*), or there may be more complex substitution classes (e.g., in a hexameter certain positions can be filled either by one long base or by two short bases). There may be even further restrictions in the filling of adjoining free positions (e.g. Corinna's *anaclasis*).

3. There is a synaesthetic transfer between the base classes of the durational and dynamic metric types, a long base corresponding to a heavy base and a short base to a light one. This correspondence might be called *accentual*. (There is a historical link between these two types in medieval Latin poetry.)

4. Besides these "pure" types—as general in typologies—intermediate or mixed metric types can be found. Also, there are in certain metric systems marginal phenomena of this kind. For example, French meter is basically "pure" syllabic, but the final syllabic in a segment, not counting a final *e-mute*, must be heavy; in early Byzantine hexameter, when quantity was disappearing in the spoken language, the prefinal base had to be *oxyton*; or, in some Hungarian verses, a *choriamb* was superposed on a pure syllabic structure. If *ictus* was used in some Classical Greek or Latin "quantitative" verse—a hotly debated issue—this would provide another example of such a mixture.

5. This typology (summarized in Figure 1) seems to be the most important for metric purposes. It would be possible, of course, to use other aspects of verse for erecting different typologies. For instance, we could set up a typology of syntactic frames utilized in verse. (Greek hexameter was delineated more clearly by words and word groups than Latin hexameter; free verse—when it is still verse—has often a firm syntactic composition; folk poetry often uses cola as units.) Or, we could make a typology of the numerical regulations imposed on the meter (strict,

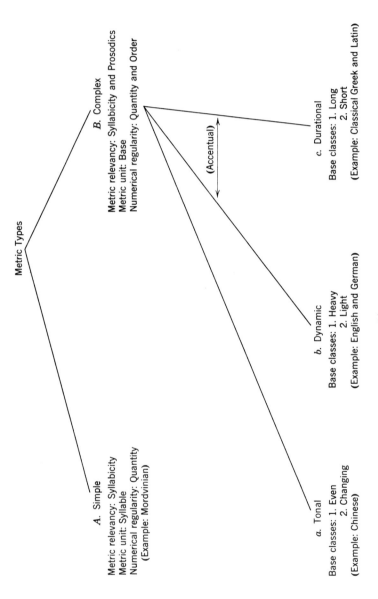

Figure 1

loose, permissible variations; for examples see the beginning of this chapter). These typologies, however, would probably turn out to be less informative and, often, trivial.

(3) SAMPLE ANALYSES

In the following, examples are given for the four metric types. The main emphasis is on the numerical aspect present in the metric scheme. The treatment, obviously, is very sketchy, except for Mordvinian verse which is described in greater detail. Means for notation conclude each section.

1. Pure-Syllabic Meter

Mordvinian [10]
A. LINGUISTIC CONSTITUENTS.   1. PHONOLOGICAL. *Syllable* (a stretch of sounds containing one syllabic, irrespectively of the separation of such pulses).

2. SYNTACTIC. *Word, colon* (contiguous phrase), *sentence*.

B. METRIC STRUCTURE.   RULE 1.   In a metric text there are an integral number of partial stretches which are not shorter than a colon and not longer than a sentence.

Definition 1.1. A partial stretch as in Rule 1 is called a *verse*.

Definition 1.2. A verse within the metric text is identified by its ordinal number in the sequence of the verses in the song.

RULE 2.   In each verse there are two to four partial stretches not shorter than a word and not longer than a colon.

Definition 2.1. A partial stretch as in Rule 2 is called a *segment*.

Definition 2.2. Verses containing two segments are called *minimal*, three segments *medial*, four segments *maximal*.

Definition 2.3.1. The segments in the verse are identified by their ordinal number in the sequence.

Definition 2.3.2. The segment with the highest ordinal number is called *final*, that with the lowest *initial*.

Definition 2.4. Segments with the same ordinal number in different verses are called *responding*.

RULE 3.   A segment contains three to five syllables.

Definition 3. A segment containing three syllables is called *minimal*, four syllables *medial*, five syllables *maximal*.

RULE 4.   Responding segments contain identical numbers of syllables.

RULE 5.1.   The initial segment is never minimal.

RULE 5.2.   If the final segment is medial, all segments are medial.

---

[10] This material, in a different form, was presented in **203** and **204**. The presentation here differs mainly in regarding the alternating verse as a single line comprising four cola.

RULE 5.3. In medial verse, if the final segment is maximal, the first two segments contain identical numbers of syllables.

RULE 5.4. In maximal verses, the first two segments contain identical numbers of syllables, the final segment is never minimal, and the third segment is medial.

RULE 6. There are texts that contain added nonmetric elements at segment breaks.

These rules describe all the existing meters in Mordvinian. It is interesting to note that the numbers involved are low, and that, where variations are permitted, the ratio does not exceed 1 : 2 (Rules 2–3).

Notation.   It is enough to note the number of syllables in the segments with special marking for the ends of the lines (|).

5543 |		444 |
5543 |	or	444 |
5543 | etc.		444 | etc.

2.1. Tonal Meter

Classical Chinese [11]

A. LINGUISTIC CONSTITUENTS.   1. PHONOLOGICAL. The syllables are organized into two base classes for metric purposes: (*a*) *even*, which includes the phonemically even tonal classes (in high and low register); (*b*) *changing*, which includes the rest of the phonemically relevant tonal classes: rising and falling in high and low register and entering in high, middle, and low register. (The phonemic system described here is that of Cantonese, which is probably very archaic and closer to the phonemic system on which this metric principle was originally founded. Most of the dialects have a simpler tonal structure. I understand that this metric technique is today at variance with phonological facts in many dialects, and its practice reflects tradition. I do not have any information about the role of syllabic quantity in Chinese meter.)

2. SYNTACTIC. Since there is an overwhelming correlation between single syllables and morphemes, only syntactic constructs of higher order, such as *sentence*, or perhaps *colon*, can be metrically relevant.

B. METRIC STRUCTURE. On the basis of the available material the following generalizations can be made:

1. A certain (odd?) number of bases are repeated within the frame of a sentence throughout the poem. Such a metric unit is called a *line*.

[11] Cf. **258.** I am indebted for assistance to Miss Diana Kao and Mr. Tung, who kindly supplied translations of Chinese sources and provided samples of Chinese poetry. Professor Jakobson informs me that there are recent theories advancing the idea that Chinese meter was "quantitative." If this view is correct, our typology would be simplified further.

2. In a line there are *fixed positions*, which have to be filled out by a certain base class, and *free positions*. These two positions alternate in the line. The even-numbered positions seem to be the fixed ones.

3. The two base classes alternate in subsequent fixed positions.

4. Different lines "mirror" the fixed base classes in various arrangements.

5. In addition to the tonal-metric pattern, rhyme schemes, occurring in various arrangements, are also used to organize the lines into *strophes*.

Notation. Here follow two metric schemes:

✕ one of the two base classes	(r) rhyme
○ the other base class	(—) no rhyme
. any base	

. ✕ . ○ . (r)	. ✕ . ○ . ✕ . (r)
. ○ . ✕ . (r)	. ○ . ✕ . ○ . (r)
. ○ . ✕ . (—)	. ○ . ✕ . ○ . (—)
. ✕ . ○ . (r)	. ✕ . ○ . ✕ . (r)

2.2. Dynamic Type

English and German

A. LINGUISTIC CONSTITUENTS. 1. PHONOLOGICAL. For metric purposes the syllabics are divided into two base classes: (a) *heavy* and (b) *light*. The assignment of syllabics to either of these classes allows a great deal of freedom, and the syllabic in the same morpheme can be assigned to different base classes, depending on its relative position and its correspondence to the other units in the metric scheme. Stressed syllabics of root morphemes (there are usually more consonants here) are always heavy. Unstressed syllabics following these are light. The syllabics in other types of morphemes, or syllabics in longer words, may be assigned according to the inner correspondences within the metric scheme.

2. SYNTACTIC. Word, colon, sentence.

B. METRIC STRUCTURE. 1. Bases in various arrangements do not usually allow more than two light bases and do not favor two heavy bases in immediate succession (in modern usage).

2. Bases are organized in various metric levels into *lines, strophes,* and *cycles*. Rhyme often indicates the higher-order metric constructs and the separation of the lines. (*Segments*, owing to the general shortness of the words, play only a minor part.)

3. From the point of view of determining positions, there are two types of lines: (a) *isosyllabic lines*, where the position of heavy and light bases can be determined by giving the ordinal number in the sequence (deviations, especially in the beginning of the line, are not infrequent); (b) *isodynamic*

lines, where the number of heavy bases is determined and their position fixed. In free positions either one heavy syllabic may occur or a varying number of light syllabics, in modern usage usually only one or two.

4. Lines in the same poem often show a difference in the number of added light syllables at the end of the line, most often zero versus one (*catalex*).

Notation. The metric structure of a line is described, if the number of contiguous light syllabics is enumerated and their occurrence at the beginning and at the end of the line is indicated, even if they are absent. For example (metrically light syllabics are underlined):

It is an ancient Mariner,	1 1 1 1 0
And he stoppeth one of three.	2 1 1 0
"By thy long gray beard	
and glittering eye,	2 1 1 2 0
Now wherefore stopp'st thou me?"	1 1 1 0

(This notation has advantages over the traditional symbolizations for statistical and other purposes. For instance, the increasing number of 2's symbolizes clearly the growing tension and the fright of the child in Goethe's "Erlkönig.")[12]

2.3. Durational Type

Classical Greek and Latin[13]

A. LINGUISTIC CONSTITUENTS. 1. PHONOLOGICAL. The sequence of phonemes is subdivided into partial stretches, beginning with the syllabic and including the following clusters of consonants, if any, up to the next syllabic. Such a unit is called a *base*. For example (/ indicates base boundary),

Arm/a v/ir/um qu/e c/an/o Tr/o/iae qu/i pr/im/us/ab/or/is/

For metric purposes there are two classes of bases: (*a*) *long* and (*b*) *short*. A long base is a base which contains a long syllabic or a dipthong, or a short syllabic and at least two consonants in the base. That it is the base and not the syllable which is metrically relevant can be shown by the fact that the initial part of *stratos* is counted as a metrically short base, whereas that of *esti* as a metrically long one. (Such a stretch probably corresponds to a certain type of psychological organization of attention.) The phonetic material is in various ways adjusted for metric purposes; for example, certain consonant clusters, like those involving a stop and a

---

[12] The notation of the Germanic verse was treated *in extenso* in **254**, where the complete metric scheme of Goethe's "Erlkönig" is also presented.

[13] For discussion and corrections, I am indebted to Messrs. Householder, Porter, and Knapp. For general bibliography, see **385**, p. 1.

liquid, may be evaluated as a single consonant. There are also various syllabic adjustments, such as *elision, aphaeresis, krasis, synezesis, syncope, etc.*

2. SYNTACTIC. Sentence and word. (Colon plays a role only in a certain type of poetry. Word is defined as an accent unit including proclitics and enclitics.)

B. METRIC STRUCTURE. 1. The bases are organized into stretches varying in length. Such metric stretches can either be short and regularly repetitive (*stichic*, or *line* construction), or they can be very intricate and long (e.g. in Pindar).

2. These units might form various constructs of higher order, such as *strophe, strophe group*, etc.

3. The syntactic organization within the line is strictly regulated; at certain points word boundaries are required (*caesura*), and at other points boundaries have to be avoided (*zeugma*).

4. In the metric unit some places have to be filled by a definite base class, long or short; other positions are free. There are various possibilities:

a. A position can be filled either by one short or one long base (*isosyllabic meter*).

b. A position can be filled either by one long or two short bases; here the notion of *mora* could be introduced, establishing the short base as one mora and the long base as two morae (*isomoraic meter*).

c. A position can be filled in a more complex manner (e.g., short-long versus two short; short versus two short, etc.).

5. In the last syllable of the metric unit the opposition between short and long base is neutralized; that is to say, either of them may occur (*anceps*).

Notation. Long base 2, short base 1; in free positions the alternants are given. Anceps is noted by 2, followed by space.

Examples	Metric Scheme	Number of Syllabics	Number of Morae
1. Sapphicus minor	$2\ 1\ 2\ \frac{1}{2}\ 2\ 1\ 1\ 2\ 1\ 2\ 2$	11	(17–18)
2. Hexameter	$2\ \frac{11}{2}\ 2\ \frac{11}{2}\ 2\ \frac{11}{2}\ 2\ \frac{11}{2}\ 2\ \frac{11}{2}\ 2\ 2$	(12–17)	24
3. Comic trimeter*	$\begin{smallmatrix} 1 & & 1 & & 1 & & 1 & & 1 & & \\ 2 & 2 & & 2 & 2 & 2 & 2 & 2 & 2 & 2 \\ 11 & 11 & 11 & 11 & 11 & 11 & 11 & 11 & 11 & 11 & 11 & 12 \end{smallmatrix}$	12–22	18–23

* Extreme values are not found.

It is significant that even in the most varying line, in the comic trimeter, the syllabic variation is within the ratio of 1 : 2, and the moraic variation within the ratio of 2 : 3. Besides the metric-phonological scheme indicated, these lines have also a strict syntactic scheme (e.g., in hexameter a word boundary between the third and fourth long bases; never a word boundary if there is a succession of short bases in certain stretches in the comic trimeter). The interaction of these two factors *together* constitutes Greek verse.

Comparing Metrical Styles

SEYMOUR CHATMAN

I

Meter might be defined as a systematic literary convention whereby certain aspects of phonology are organized for aesthetic purposes.[1] Like any convention, it is susceptible of individual variation which could be called stylistic, taking "style" in the common meaning of "idiosyncratic way of doing something." The goal of metrical stylistics, like that of the stylistics of other features, is to analyze these variations and to determine what they mean in the design of the whole work of art. Since variations imply norms, however, it seems difficult to analyze styles without establishing some outside reference point. A convenient way of doing this is to compare the styles of two literary figures.

As an exercise in methodology, I have attempted to compare some particulars of the metrical styles of John Donne and Alexander Pope. Donne wrote a group of satires in the 1590's, two of which Pope imitated: Satire II, "Sir; though (I thank God for it) I do hate" (on lawyers writing poetry), and Satire IV, "Well; I may now receive, and die" (on courtiers). Pope "versified" (his own word) Donne's satires because he seems to have felt, with Warton, that Donne had "degraded and deformed a vast fund of sterling wit and strong sense" by harsh diction and faulty meter. Thus we have an instance of a poet consciously attempting to revise another poet's work into his own style (or at least a style acceptable to his period's taste).

My primary intention is to describe the differences between the metrical styles of these poems. However, conclusions of a purely descriptive sort, although linguistically acceptable, will seem trivial to the literary critic; to gain weight they need to be correlated with the whole effect of the poem. In the last section of the paper, therefore, I shall present a brief survey of some recent critical opinions concerning these poems.

[1] I am very grateful to James Sledd for his thoughtful and searching criticism of this paper.

There is no suggestion that my descriptions unearth any startlingly new insights into the styles of either poet. Many features are quite predictable from what we know about the differences between Metaphysical and Neoclassical poetic theory and from our impressions in reading these poets' other works. My chief purpose is to devise and test an application of strictly descriptive techniques to prosodic style; as a test, it is hoped that the reader will forgive what may at times seem like proclaiming the obvious.

Before the comparison, however, it is necessary to make some observations concerning the general relevance of phonemics to metrical structure. In the transmission of literature in English orthography, it is plain that a reader's vocal representation of segmental features (the individual sounds in sequence, like /p/, /t/, /k/) is more narrowly controlled by the text than his representation of suprasegmental features ("covering" patterns of stress, pitch, and juncture) and metalinguistic features (voice qualification, vocalization, etc.).[2] The reader must follow the author's sequence of segmental phonemes (if not individual phonemic actualizations and distributions) if he is to read correctly; for even if he does introduce dialectal variations, these may be disregarded as irrelevant to the text (e.g., Hamlet speaking with a North Georgia accent is still Hamlet). But since suprasegmentals are signaled much less adequately than the sequence of segmental phonemes in English, and metalinguistic features less adequately still, much is left to the reader's judgment in these matters. Presumably he chooses the suprasegmentals and metalinguistic features which in his opinion fit the whole context; we might call these his vocal "interpretation." Thus most people would not giggle or shout when reading Hamlet's soliloquy but would try to use metalinguistic features which signal the quiet and complex desperation of the moment. But differing insights and consequently differing interpretations are bound to arise (and these may admit semantic indeterminacies between the performer and his audience). Besides, there are the differing linguistic and metalinguistic styles of the readers themselves which will add to the complexity (e.g., two readers may agree that a line suggests a specific metalinguistic feature, but they may have different ways of signaling it; this also may prompt indeterminacy). So it seems necessary to distinguish the style of the poem from the performer's interpretation (his selections of appropriate

[2] For "juncture" see fn. 6. The metalanguage is taken to be the system of vocal features, not included in the linguistic system, which operates concurrently with it and signals meanings about the speaker rather than about the lexical message he is presenting. The term "style," however, is not equivalent to "metalanguage"; it is taken to mean *individual variation*. Thus we may speak of "linguistic style" (e.g., the unique way an individual makes his /k/'s or the range in cycles between his highest and lowest pitch levels) or of his "metalinguistic style" (the particular way in which he drawls when indecisive or uses overhigh pitch when excited). See **314** and **384**.

suprasegmentals and metalinguistic features) and the performance style (the way in which he presents these).

It may be objected that, if this is so, we can never adduce the poet's style without introducing our own interpretation and performance style. This may be true, but it does not, I feel, invalidate the distinction. It seems clear that personal style can be excluded from many sorts of considerations; for example, two readers, although they disagree on a wide variety of matters in the interpretation of Shakespeare's sonnets, may still agree that certain stylistic features are typically Shakespearean. Similarly one reader, reading Shakespearean and Spenserian sonnets, can discount, so to speak, his own performance style and still make an intelligible comparison of poetic styles.

II

In the analysis of segmental phonological effects, it is important first to decide what the subject of inquiry is. I have suggested elsewhere (59) that sound symbolism as such—the assumption that individual phonemes have expressive functions over and above their signaling functions in morphemes —is either without objective foundation or is too subliminal to be very useful in linguistics or stylistics. I do not think that the *quality* of individual sounds is productive as a meaningful feature, except insofar as certain conventional associations have grown up around them—that is, by their occurrences in words which they partially evoke when they are uttered alone: for example, /s/ may call up "snake," "smooth," or "soft" (depending on the train of thought the subject finds himself interrupted in); or by suggesting nonlinguistic activity performed by the same parts of the vocal apparatus which create the phoneme: for example, Burke's association of /p/ and /pf/ with spitting. If such associations were to be accepted by the speech community, the phoneme might even achieve the status of morpheme.

We are left with the *quantities* of segmental sounds. (Most of the conventional sound figures, like rhyme and alliteration, are quantitative contrivances.) Again, however, the limits of inquiry must be determined. Raw computation, like counting the total number of phonemes a poet uses in a poem and comparing *that* profile with norms for the language and for other poets, seems somewhat barren as a piece of research. Its validity is in doubt because the reader can hardly become aware of the total effect of "normal curve disruption" when it is diffused over the entire poem; the capacity of eliciting *awareness* of distributional peculiarity seems essential for a feature to emerge as a literary convention. Quantitative effects work only at close range, over two or three words, or in certain conventionally fixed positions in lines, for example, at the end, in the rhyming position. So most style analyses of segmental phonemes have been limited to close-range distributions, and there seems to be no reason for changing this procedure.[3]

Here is a representation of the more usual schemes in their ordinary definitions. (Following Wellek and Warren, **442**, p. 183, I will refer to segmental phonemic effects as "schemes," in contrast to "tropes" which are vocabulary or rhetorical effects.[4])

A. REPETITION SCHEMES

WORD-INITIAL

1. *Consonant alliteration.* Repetition of the same initial consonant in several adjacent syllables, usually coinciding with word stress: "furrow follows free."

2. *Vowel alliteration.* Repetition of the same initial vowel or diphthong in several adjacent syllables, usually coinciding with word stress: "empty effort." (In some systems *any* vowels may alliterate.)

WORD-FINAL

1. *Rhyme.* Repetition of final stressed vowels and final consonants and consonant clusters, if any, but *not* of initial consonants in the syllable: "be:agree."

2. *Feminine rhyme.* The above, plus any additional unstressed identical syllables: "taker:maker" (but not "taker:sicker," for which see 5 below).

3. *Assonance.* Like vowels, different consonants: "fame:late."

4. *Consonance.* Like consonants, different vowels: "pressed:past."

5. *Homeoteleuton.* Repetition of whole final unstressed syllables where the stressed syllables preceding are consonant: "fission:motion." (Hence, a kind of "defective" feminine rhyme.)

6. *Eye rhyme.* A kind of assonance in which the letters are identical, although they represent different vowels: "blood:mood."

B. JUXTAPOSITION SCHEMES ("On Musicality in Verse," in **52**)

1. Chiasmus. Reversal of phoneme sequence: /u/ :/i/ : :/i/ :/u/— "dupes of a deep delusion."

[3] For an important discussion of what constitutes relevancy in style analysis, see **404a**. Stutterheim's position, in his own summary, is: " . . . this is certain, that some formal element, which *is* brought to light through statistical investigation, but cannot be grasped by the consideration of the total experience of this totality, cannot be a stylisticum."

[4] In a recent mimeographed paper entitled "Sound-Repetition Terms," David I. Masson of the University of Leeds has offered some impressive and subtle distinctions between the various sorts of schemes. It is to be hoped that this paper may soon find its way into print.

    2. Augmentation. CC → CVC: "That s̲lid into my s̲oul."
    3. Diminution. CVC → CC: "But s̲ilently, by s̲low degrees."
C. SYLLABLE CONTROLLING SCHEMES (for definitions, see pp. 162–163)
    1. Apocope.
    2. Aphaeresis.
    3. Vowel and consonant syncope.
    4. Synaeresis.
    5. Monosyllabification (synizesis, synechphonesis).
    6. Pseudo-elision.

It is important to distinguish between *structural* uses of schemes, that is, between regular recurrences which form the basic structure of the verse (alliteration in Old Germanic poetry, assonance in Old French) and *occasional* uses. Whether a scheme is structural or not is arbitrary and conventional within the individual verse tradition. In English verse, line-end rhyme and near-rhyme are usually structural. Intralinear or word-adjacent rhyme is occasional, as is alliteration. All the syllable-controlling schemes are structural insofar as they assist in metrical arrangements.

The function of rhyme in English verse is primarily metrical, that is, to help mark line endings. Sometimes, however, it may also have a quasi-lexical function. Professor Wimsatt has shown this very clearly in his paper on rhyme (in **449**). He has proposed a consideration of the "counter-logical" properties of rhyme, the surprise that we feel in observing the curious cooperation in sound that two disparate words have in common. One function of this surprise, as I understand it, is to fix or cement the meaning in a more unified and aesthetically satisfying way than could occur by mere juxtaposition. But in its lexical function, rhyme, like metaphor or epithet, limits meaning by asking us to consider suddenly the connection of two things whose sound shapes happen to be resemblant. In Professor Wimsatt's example, from "The Rape of the Lock,"

> Whether the nymph shall break Diana's law
> Or some frail China jar receive a flaw . . . ,

the rhyme (along with the syntax) requires us to ask in what respects breaking Diana's law and marring a Chinese vase are similar: the implied answer is that in the rarified society of which Belinda is a member, losing one's virginity is somehow similar to being so clumsy as to scratch a precious vase—both are simply marks of bad taste. In this way, the rhyme actually may provide information by limiting the possibilities of interpretation, just as the vehicle of a metaphor forces us to limit the possible interpretations of the tenor ("not *all* x's, or the whole of x but only those x's or parts of x which resemble the vehicle y in some important respects").

Another way of saying this is that rhyme's structural property is to disturb the normal phonemic distribution expectancies by a superimposed pattern which may itself signal in an almost lexical way.

It is of interest to observe in detail the differences between Donne's and Pope's rhyming practice, particularly in relation to their metrical patterns. As is well known, Pope is very uniform: in the vast majority of instances, his end rhymes occur in metrically accented syllables, or to use a term which I prefer, the tenth syllable is a "metrical point." The only exceptions are very occasional occurrences of rhyming feminine syllables, for example,

> as a Still, with Simples in it,
> Between each Drop it gives, stays half a Minute   (126–7).[5]

Donne has about the same number of feminine rhymes, but his practice differs chiefly in rhyming stressed and unstressed syllables (e.g., the final syllables of polysyllabic words, or unstressed function words like prepositions and articles); for example,

> O Sir,
> 'Tis sweet to talke of Kings. At Westminster   (73–4).

Some other pairs in Donne's version are "alone:fashion," "one:prison," "yet:merit." It is possible to watch Pope avoid this sort of rhyme, even where he sticks fairly closely to the original. Thus, Donne's

> Now; Aretine's pictures have made few chast;
> No more can Princes courts, though there be few
> Better pictures of vice, teach me vertue;   (70–72)[6]

[5] All passages from Donne are taken from **93**, pp. 149–154 and 154–158. The passages from Pope are taken from **320**, pp. 27–49 and 132–145. Parenthetic numerals refer to line numbers. All examples are from Satire IV, unless otherwise indicated.

[6] The question has been raised whether "virtue" and other words of the sort might not have been pronounced with the accent on the second syllable, as undoubtedly they had been in the Middle Ages. Jordan, **219**, p. 192, indicates that the stress had already shifted to the first syllable by the thirteenth or fourteenth century in the colloquial language, but in poetry the alternation between the two stress patterns continued "bis ins 15. Jarh. und länger"; in fact "noch Byron kann in Nachahmung alten Gebrauches *virtúe*: *pursúe* reimen (English Bards 1218)." It is thus difficult to be certain about the pronunciation in verse of French loan words of this sort, but the following points might be made in defense of assuming the colloquial pronunciation. (1) Donne uses the word "virtue" 65 times in his poetry (see **72**, under "virtue"). There are as many as ten instances in which the syllable is represented in Grierson's text as eliding into the next word (e.g., "Like Vertue' and truth, art best in nakednesse," in "Epithalamion at Lincoln's Inn," l. 128), something which could hardly happen if it carried word stress. (2) In 41 instances there seems to be little question that the stress pattern is "vírtue," since any other pronunciation would introduce a metrical inversion where there is otherwise no reason to assume one; typically the "vir-" falls on an even-numbered

becomes, in Pope's version,

> Tho' in his Pictures Lust be full display'd,
> Few are the Converts *Aretine* has made;   (94–5).

Another example is

> Ran from thence with such, or more haste than one
> Who fears more actions, doth haste from prison.   (153–4)
> Ran out as fast, as one that pays his bail
> And dreads more actions, hurries from a jail.   (182–3).

Pope is most attracted to those lines in Donne which end in full masculine rhymes. An example which he follows closely is

> With his tongue . . .
> In which he can win widdowes, and pay scores,
> Make men speake treason, cosen subtlest whores,   (45–6).

The poets also differ in the way they use rhymes to construct their couplets. In the majority of Pope's couplets the second rhyme coincides with punctuation marks suggesting end-stoppage, whereas the first line runs on. In Donne, on the other hand, the majority of the lines are couplets only in the sense that the final syllables rhyme; that is, the couplet structure is not regularly confirmed by punctuation suggesting terminal junctures at the end of second lines. In actual count 77 per cent of Pope's lines are junctural as well as rhymic couplets, in comparison to less than half that number (36 per cent) in Donne. Furthermore, 15 per cent of Donne's couplets signal stronger junctures at the end of the first line than at the end of the second. The difference can be seen graphically

---

syllable in an even-syllabled line: "Then vertue or the minde to admire" in "Negative Love," line 4. (3) In ten instances the word appears as the first word in the line, where it seems easier to assume a simple case of metrical inversion than the pronunciation "virtúe." (4) In only four cases, then, outside of the present one, does the question of the pronunciation "virtúe" arise. In one, the balanced syntax and caesura seem to suggest the normal stress on the first syllable: "Falsehood is denizen'd. Vertue is barbarous" in "To Sir Henry Wotton," line 34. Two other instances occur in the poem "A Letter to the Lady Carey . . ." (ll. 30 and 39): "Have through this zeale, Vertue but in their Gall" and "For, your soul was as good Virtue, as she"; the word occurs eight other times in this poem with an indicated pronunciation of "vírtue," so it would seem probable that these are metrical inversions. The last occurrence of "virtue" where there is doubt occurs, interestingly enough, in a line from Satire I (41) which otherwise contains obvious metrical inversions of the extreme sort which typifies Donne's satirical meter: "Hate vertue, though shee be naked and bare?" which has stresses either on syllables 1, 2, 5, 7, 10 or on 2, 4, 5, 7, 10 if we assume "vírtue." All in all, these statistics, plus the fact that we know that it was part of Donne's style to sound colloquial, suggests the pronunciation "vírtue" in the present instance.

by examining Pope's revisions. Of nineteen sets of rhymes that Pope keeps, more than half are changed to closed couplets. Consider, for example,

Donne: to have been Interpreter
            To Babells bricklayers, sure the Tower had stood.
            He adds, If of court life you knew the good,
            You would leave lonenesse. (64–7)
Pope: "For had they found a Linguist half so good,
            "I make no question but the *Tow'r* had stood." (84–5)
and

Donne: Like a bigge wife, at sight of loathed meat,
            Readie to travaile: So I sigh, and sweat
            To heare this Makeron talke: (115–17)
Pope: Like a big Wife at sight of Loathsome Meat,
            Ready to cast, I yawn, I sigh, and sweat:
            Then as a licens'd Spy . . . (156–8).

Finally, Pope's rhymes are much more likely to affect lexical meanings either redundantly or ironically. For example,

            who got his pension Rug ["safe"]
        Or quicken'd a Reversion by a *Drug*? (134–5)
    Who in the *Secret*, deals in Stocks secure,
    And cheats th' unknowing Widow, and the Poor? (140–41)
    Why *Turnpikes* rise, and now no Cit, nor Clown
    Can *gratis* see the *Country* or the *Town*? (144–5).

Ironic juxtapositions like "Rug" and "Drug," "secure" and "Poor," and "clown" and "Town" are to be found only in Pope. They do not seem to be a part of Donne's satirical style.

When we turn to occasional effects, the picture is less clear, but there are indications of differences similar to those already discussed. The stylistic impetus that makes Pope prefer accurate, full rhymes as a structural feature seems to require him to make equally sure that no chance collocation of sound runs afoul of his meaning. This is the negative job of inhibiting mere chance repetitions from occurring: purposeless internal rhymes and alliterations and other distractive sound similarities are guarded against. For example, Donne has (proportionately) twice as many occurrences of alliteration of two syllables in immediate sequence as Pope, whereas Pope has almost four times as many occurrences of an intervening unstress. This means that Pope wants alliteration to cooperate with the meter, not to oppose it. Pope usually prefers to add alliteration where an unstressed syllable will fall in between: he revises Donne's "low fear becomes" to read "base fear becomes," "painted things" to "painted puppets," "fresh and sweet" to "fresh and fragrant," "weak ships fraught" to "frigates fraught," etc. Further, Pope seems to make an effort to avoid immediately contiguous ("ametrical") alliteration, for example, "win widdowes" becomes "cheat widows."

In respect to the structure and meaning of the items alliterated, again Pope shows a greater concern for control. His alliteration of epithet-noun combinations is characteristic and carefully done. Its effect is to strengthen through sound repetitions a favorite pattern of poets writing in an exact style, bisyllabic modifier plus monosyllabic head: "whited wall," "bawling bar," "popish plot," "Gracious God," "Herod's hangdogs," "courtiers' clothes," "liveried Lords," "body's buff," "frigates fraught," "Dante dreaming," "wits so weak," etc. The alliteration gives a rounded or finished appearance to these phrases which was much favored by Neo-classical poets (**415**). Donne, on the other hand, frequently alliterates words that have little structural connection (giving the illusion of mere chance collocation): "dare drown," "leave loneness," "win widows," "hearing him," "saith, Sir," "though there," "bear but," etc.

The same seems to be true of occasional rhyme. Donne has such internal rhymes as "land, and," "I sigh," "those hose," "lords, rewards," and such occasional near-rhymes as "Guinea's rarities," "massacre had sure," "treason couzen," "Jovius or Surius," "courtier and wiser," "either my humor," "waxen garden," etc. Donne's propensity for "jingling" is well known, but his imitator avoids such effects studiously.

All in all, we get the impression that segmental sound effects are more rigidly controlled by Pope than by Donne and that they are more likely to correspond to lexical meanings. In Donne there is little such correspondence; indeed, it is often difficult to remember that we are reading rhymed verse because of the tendency for sound effects *not* to coincide with syntactic and semantic structures.

III

Turning to metrical structure per se, it is important to re-emphasize the necessity of distinguishing between the style of the poem and the interpretation and style of the performer. As far as the style of the poem itself is concerned, the suprasegmental patterns as they are actualized are only relevant insofar as they are possible articulations of the potential that the poet is offering us and *its* style. To keep this clear in my notation, I indicate what I think is the metrical pattern by simply underlining metrical points, while I offer one possible rendition of the lines in phonemic symbols above the line.[7] (When I speak of "meter," then, I always mean *potential* meter.) I make no claims for the adequacy or aesthetic quality of the rendition; other readers, of course, will prefer other actualizations. For example, although I read the first line of Donne's version

$$^{2}\text{Wéll}^{3}\!\uparrow^{2}\text{I máy nòw re}^{3}\text{cêive}\uparrow^{2}\text{and }^{3}\text{díe}^{1}\!\downarrow,$$

some might read

$$^{3}\text{Wéll}^{2}\!\downarrow^{2}\text{I máy nòw re}^{3}\text{cêive}^{2\rightarrow2}\text{and }^{3}\text{díe}^{1}\!\downarrow,$$

or

$$^{3}\text{Wéll}^{2\rightarrow2}\text{I máy nòw re}^{3}\text{cêive}^{1}\!\downarrow^{1}\text{and }^{3}\text{díe}^{1}\!\downarrow,$$

or other versions. But these are all variations in performance style only, and they all develop from the potential

Well! I may now receive and die.

English meter is generally considered to be bidimensional: I refer to one of these dimensions as the metrical point, and to the other as metrical zero, to avoid confusion with the phonemic terms "stress" and "accent." Although some suprasegmental features like stress are organized as potentials in the meter, the meter exists as a system outside the language. It is a rhythmic impulse or set or pattern of impulses in the poet's mind. According to some poets, its genesis precedes the actual composition of the poem; for others, it only becomes accountable in terms of the actual selection of words. But whenever it emerges, it seems to be something apart from the language system. Many people, I am sure, have had the experience of putting down a poem but hearing the "tune" continue. This "tune" I take to be the meter abstracted from linguistic content. Similarly, we can ape the meter by supplying nonlinguistic counters—*te*'s and *tum*'s— to fill the slots. We may assume that the poet picks both his words to fulfill his meter and his meter to fulfill his words, that is, he aims at a reconciliation of the two.

[7] I use a modified version of the Trager-Smith transcription of junctures (**422**, pp. 47–50), in which $/\!\uparrow/$ stands for $/\|\|/$, $/\!\downarrow/$ for $/\#/$, and $/\!\rightarrow/$ for $/\|/$. Junctures may be briefly defined as the boundary phenomena which signal important structural splits in utterances. Thus the two utterances "He came quickly, dispersing gifts" and "He came, quickly dispersing gifts" are distinguished by having the juncture in different positions— i.e., "quickly" goes with "came" in the first example and with "dispersing" in the second. These junctures may be of four sorts: a downward movement of the voice $/\!\downarrow/$, an upward movement $/\!\uparrow/$, an even movement with sustention or delay of some sort $/\!\rightarrow/$, and an even movement without delay $/\!+/$ (the difference between "a name" and "an aim," "that stuff" and "that's tough"). Absence of juncture is called "smooth transition." For a good explanation, see **172**, pp. 21–26. The four stress marks are the same: $/\acute{}\,/$ for primary, $/\hat{}\,/$ for secondary, $/\grave{}\,/$ for tertiary, and no mark for weak.

What complicates the picture is that language has its own patterns and offers some resistance to filling another set of slots. English, for instance, is assumed by many to have four levels of stress, and these must be adjusted to the two-leveled pattern of traditional English meter. It is also assumed to have a four-way junctural system, and one of these junctures must be selected to represent each line ending. If these views are correct, they require us to see "variation" as a more complex matter than has usually been assumed.

It seems necessary, for example, to distinguish between two kinds of variation. First there is purely metrical or intrasystemic variation. This is of two sorts: (1) the occasional displacement of metrical points from the predominating sequence, for example (to use conventional terms only for the moment) a trochee amid iambs; and (2) occasional change in syllable count as the indication of line length (from some traditional norm). These variations occur within the poem itself, regardless of the reader's interpretation or style. To take an example from Pope's imitation:

Thus much I've said, I trust without offence   (II, 125).

In the context this *must* be read as

Thus much I've said . . .

and not   Thus much I've said . . . ,

fixing the metrical point at "thus" to insure a correct lexical and grammatical assignment; that is, "thus" modifies "much" (it answers the question "How much?") and is not a sentence adverb like "as a result." Another instance is the line

There sober thought pursued th'amusing theme

which, if read aloud as

There sober thought pursued th'amusing theme

would suggest a confusion of "there" with "their."

Secondly, there is what we might call countermetrical variation resulting from the superimposition of suprasegmental on metrical system, whenever the poem is performed. This also takes two major forms, involving (1) the choice of the degree of actual phonemic stress used to fill either metrical point or metrical zero, and (2) the selection of actual phonemic junctures to fill the potential juncture points indicated by the punctuation, context, etc., and the correlation of these with line endings. In the second group, what concerns the style of the poem, again, is only what is potential, not what is actualized, for the reasons advanced. For example, consider the line just quoted:

> Thus much I've said, I trust without offence.

This line could be performed as

^{3}Thus múch$^{2\to2}$I've ^{3}said$^{1\downarrow2}$I ^{3}trust$^{3\to2}$without of^{3}fence$^{1\downarrow}$

or ^{2}Thus much I've ^{3}said$^{1\downarrow2}$I ^{3}trust$^{2\to2}$without offence$^{1\downarrow}$

or ^{2}Thus much I've ^{3}said$^{2\to2}$I ^{3}trust$^{3\to2}$without of^{3}fence$^{2\to}$

or in a number of other ways. These are all stylistically different performances, but each fulfills the same potential, namely — U U — U — U — U — .[8]

Thus traditional views of variation have been a little too simple and may have given rise to certain inconsistencies, particularly where aesthetic impressions are involved. For example, the impression of *speed*—insofar as it is not merely a lexically induced illusion—may develop from either pure or contrapuntal variation: in the first case, the effect may be produced by adding a few syllables, as in Pope's

> Flies o'er th'unbending corn, and skims along the main.

In the second, the effect is produced by using light phonemic stresses to fill the metrical points, as in

> Not so, when swift Camillia scours the plain.

The reverse effect is achieved by filling metrical zeroes with syllables capable of secondary stresses:

> When Ajax strives some rock's vast weight to throw
> The line too labours, and the words move slow.

(although another important factor in this example is the heavy consonant clustering). But it must be recognized that there is nothing *intrinsically* "fast" about extra syllables or light actualizations of metrical points or intrinsically "slow" about secondary stresses at metrical zeroes. It is the lexical meaning which induces the perception of speed and gives this feature, like all stylistic features, its "meaning."

---

[8] In general, I work on the principle that a metrical point can be filled by anything from tertiary to primary stress—that what it takes to fix a syllable as a metrical point is not any specific level of stress but a stress that is stronger than that carried by adjacent syllables. James Sledd has suggested that adjacency to a terminal juncture may sometimes be sufficient to permit a minimally stressed syllable to fill a metrical point.

For the purpose of the stylistic analysis of metrics, therefore, there are three kinds of variation that may be considered; the configuration of these peculiar to a poem can be seen as constituting an important part of its metrical style. These variations are in (1) syllable count, (2) the arrangement of metrical points in a line, and (3) the potentials for phonemic phrasing signaled by punctuation marks, context, syntax, etc.[9]

[9] It will be seen that I do not use the concept of "foot" in my description. I avoid the foot because I do not think that it contributes any more information about the meter than is available without it. Since length has not been distinctive in many dialects in English since the Middle Ages, it is questionable whether feet ever marked temporal quantities in English verse as they had in Latin and Greek. Podic segmentation seems applicable in English for only one purpose—to explain the sequential norm and variations of points and zeroes. But I have never been able to discover a good reason for assuming that a metrical accent point has any closer connection with the zero that it follows than with the one that it precedes.

That is, the normal decasyllabic line is

$$1\ \underline{2}\ 3\ \underline{4}\ 5\ \underline{6}\ 7\ \underline{8}\ 9\ \underline{10}.$$

It does not matter whether we take this as

$$1\underline{2}\quad 3\underline{4}\quad 5\underline{6}\quad 7\underline{8}\quad 9\ \underline{10}$$

or

$$1\underline{2}3\quad \underline{4}5\underline{6}\quad 7\underline{8}9\quad \underline{10}$$

or

$$1\underline{2}\underline{4}5\quad \underline{6}7\underline{8}9\underline{10}$$

or

$$1\quad \underline{2}3\quad \underline{4}5\quad \underline{6}7\quad \underline{8}9\quad \underline{10}$$

except as a matter of convenience of arithmetic. The advantage of the first is only that the "units" turn out to be more uniform among themselves—but only for mathematical reasons, not for linguistic or metrical reasons. The trouble begins when readers think that there actually is some kind of equality among these units; the units are equal only because we *take* them to be equal on a false analogy with the classical languages. That is to say, when we learn to scan (and the enormous effort that it requires suggests that this is not in any sense a language-tied system), we learn to take as broadly "the same" quite different phenomena solely on the basis of the relative positions in which these phenomena occur. In the "iambic pentameter" line, for example, the important positions are the second, fourth, sixth, eighth, and tenth syllables. That is, these positions "promote" the syllables falling within their precincts. What I mean by "promote" is this: whatever the actual stress (within the restrictions stated in fn. 7), the syllable is interpreted as a metrical point by the reader. Whether it causes an *actual* increase in vocal amplitude or not is a matter of the style of the performance rather than the style of the poem. If the reader wishes to make much of the meter he may increase the syllable's actual stress beyond the norm. If he adopts a more "prosaic" style he may show the metrical point by giving the weakly stressed syllable a slower or clearer articulation. The same difference in rendition may occur in metrical suppression of stress in metrically zero positions, again according to the effect that the interpreter intends.

Variation in Syllable Count

We first ask then, "To what extent do poets observe a fixed syllable count (in the present meter, the norm is ten to a line); what is the nature of their linguistic adjustments to obtain a fixed count; and what are the consequent effects?"

In analyzing older verse there is frequently a problem in deciding how many syllables a given line actually contains. Our knowledge of the syllabification of words in earlier periods is not particularly good, since it often depends on the same sort of evidence which is under question in prosodic analysis. The consistent use of graphic devices in verse for showing elision (apostrophes, special spelling, and marks) was begun only comparatively late, and often modern prosodists, like Bridges (**42**, pp. 4–36), have felt obliged to work out systems of interpretation that would explain how to read a given poet's verse without making it sound ametrical. This is usually done on the basis of certain tacit assumptions about how "regular" his meter is. And frequently that is precisely what is in dispute. Therefore, comparisons of stylistic variations in syllable count seem to suffer from a certain innate and perhaps unavoidable circularity of method.

The general assumption seems to be that lines should be scanned as regular, wherever possible—that if a decasyllabic line has more than ten syllables, and it is not intentionally or permissively hypermetrical by some approved variation (as, for example, ending with feminine rhyme), its "excess" may be seen as resolved in elision. I take "elision" to mean metrical adjustment by omission and to be a cover term for certain processes which are not always clearly discriminated (cf. **371**, under "hyphaeresis"). I have attempted to describe some of these processes as follows: (1) *apocope:* the loss of a word-final vowel such that the consonant which *precedes* it clusters with the initial vowel or consonant of the following word (for example, "the army" becomes "th'army" and "to write" becomes "t'write"); (2) *aphaeresis:* the loss of an initial vowel such that the consonant which *follows* it clusters with a following vowel or consonant (for example, "it is" becomes "'tis" and "it were" becomes "'twere"); (3) *vowel syncope:* the loss of a vowel such that a syllable is lost without the syllables on either side being affected (for example, "medicine" becomes "med'cine" and "fluctuate" becomes "fluct'ate"); (4) *consonant syncope:* the loss of a consonant such that the syllables on either side are fused, often by the loss of the second vowel, (for example, "seven" becomes "se'en," "devil" becomes "de'l," "by his" becomes "by's" /bayz/); (5) *synaeresis:* the consonantizing of a vowel (usually into /y-/ or /w-/), or the loss of syllabicity of a syllabic consonant, such that it clusters with a following vowel rather than standing alone as a syllable (for example, "many a" becomes /menyə/, "jollier" becomes /jalyər/, "title of" becomes

/taytləv/); (6) *monosyllabification* (or *synizesis* or *synechphonesis*): the reduction of contiguous syllabics to a single nucleus (for example, "idea" becomes /aydiy/, "being" becomes /biŋ/); (7) *pseudo-elision:* the assumption of elision between two consonants that cannot be clustered without one of them becoming syllabic (for example, words ending in "-ism," "rhythm," etc.), or consonant clusters that go against English clustering habits (for example, "th'sea" and "th'loss").

To what extent are or were these elisions actualized? Some prosodists have taken them to be mere orthographic fictions, apostrophes being marked solely to suit the numerical decorum of the eighteenth century and having little reference to actual pronunciation. Bridges, for example, writes that sounds are not really lost; they remain and are "heard in the glide, though prosodically asyllabic." According to the researches of Paul Fussell (**130**), however, this suggests a misunderstanding about the nature of verse performance in the eighteenth century, and Pope's line was probably pronounced as written:

/wandriŋ in menyə šeyd bɪcekəhd grɔt/.

I do not think it is too dangerous to assume that elisions are real things, that they have been observed in some styles of verse performance, and that they can be employed by poets in stylistically characteristic ways. Whether they are to be observed in modern performances or not is another matter.[10]

My count shows that twenty lines in Donne's Satires II and IV are ametrical, that is, do not allow of an explanation by elision; this is about 6 per cent. It is interesting to note that in the text of Donne's poems which appears in the 1735 edition on the pages opposite Pope's versifications, however, eleven lines have been regularized by the editor. A nine-syllable line like 176, for example, "Baloun, Tennis, Dyet, or the stewes," becomes "Baloun or Tennis, Diet, or the Stews"; and an eleven-syllable line (taking "saying" as monosyllabic) "For saying of our Ladies Psalter. But 'tis fit" (217) is adjusted to "For saying our Ladies Psalter. But 'tis fit". In addition, the 1735 edition adds a few apostrophes to show elisions not indicated in the original: "so't" for "so it," "so'are" for "so are", "th'loss" for "the loss," etc.

---

[10] It is not known to what extent Donne and his contemporaries observed elision in their own verse performances. But in his study of Donne's metrical practice, Moloney (**282**) has pointed out that Ben Jonson, although very critical about Donne's treatment of stress placement—" . . . for not keeping of accent, he deserved hanging . . . "—does not object in any way to Donne's "numbers," presumably because he considered them to be adequately adjusted by elision. Moloney goes on to give a detailed account of the importance of elision to Donne, arguing that his verse is no less regular in this respect than Milton's, and placing him in the main stream of the English poetic tradition.

With the exception of aphaeresis, of which Pope has seven occurrences to Donne's one, the relative proportions of *kinds* of elision are quite similar. There is, however, a difference in the number of elisions permissible in a line. Donne regularly allows of multiple elisions, such as:

> Toughly and stubbornly I beare this crosse; But th'houre   (140)
> Nay sir, can you spare me a Crown? Thankfully I   (144).

The latter is characteristic of Donne in that alternatives are possible: we may read the line " . . . my'a Crown? Thankf'lly I" or "me a crown? Thankf'lly'I" (although the latter may not be a permissible cluster in English). Another example is line 214:

> Ten Cardinalls into the Inquisition.

Does one read "Card'nalls" and "the Inquisition" or "Cardinalls" and "th'Inquisition"? Or, as Professor Fred Householder suggests, does *-ion* get two syllables, hence: "Ten Card'nals into th'Inquisition"?

When we consider individual examples, we receive the impression that Pope's elisions are more conventional, Donne's more idiosyncratic. This is demonstrated in two ways: (1) Pope's commoner elisions are more likely to be repeated several times, as if they were well-known and approved methods of controlling the meter (Donne has fewer repetitions); and (2) Donne more frequently employs novel elisions or elisions which seem even to do violence to the convention, for example, "tufftaffaty," "going," "your Apostles," "Makeron," "perpetuities," "torturing I," "Maccabbees," "Heraclitus," etc. Besides, some of Donne's elisions may be taken as unwitting puns: /tum/ for "to whom," /tɔl/ for "to all," /ðerperəlz/ for "their apparels," and so forth. Pope avoids all these except one—he keeps Donne's monosyllabification of "Noah" to the horror of his editor Warton (". . . perhaps the greatest violation of harmony Pope has ever been guilty of"—**321**, Vol. 5, p. 311).

Metrical Point Displacement

The second metrical variable, the relative placement of metrical points in the line, constitutes a great difference in the poet's styles. It goes without saying that Pope places the point normally at the second, fourth, sixth, eighth, and tenth syllables. Less than one-quarter of his lines have any metrical displacement, and of this quarter, two-thirds are simple transfers of the point from the second syllable to the first, giving the pattern 1, 4, 6, 8, 10:

> Talkers, I've learn'd to bear; Motteaux I knew   (50),

and 17 per cent simply transfer the point from the second to the third (thus 3, 4, 6, 8, 10):

> And the free Soul looks down to pity Kings   (187).

There are much fewer transfers in later syllables, only four to the fifth, eight to the seventh, and three to the ninth. Furthermore, Pope rarely has more than one such displacement in a line. Only 4 lines in 403 have two displacements, such lines as the following being quite rare in Pope:

Then as a licens'd Spy, whom nothing can

(1,4,6,9,10)   Silence, or hurt, he libels the Great Man   (159)

(1,5,6,8,10)   Those write because all write, and so have still   (II, 27).

In Donne's verse on the other hand, the majority of lines, 68 per cent, contain displacement, and many lines have two, three, and even four displacements. Unusual combinations like the following are common:

(2,5,7,9,10)   Now; Aretine's pictures have made few chast   (70)

(1,3,6,7,9)   Better pictures of vice, teach me vertue   (72)

(1,3,5,8,10)   Velvet, but 'twas now (so much ground was seene)   (32)

(3,5,7,8,10)   I bid kill some beasts, but no Hecatombs   (II, 108).[11]

Regular lines only occur frequently enough to serve as the barest reminder of what the verse norm is like.

Furthermore, the few lines that Pope takes over intact either are regular to begin with:

As Men from Jayls to execution go   (273)

Jests like a licens'd fool, commands like Law   (271)

He says our *Wars thrive ill*, because delay'd   (163)

or are easily adjusted to a more regular pattern; thus Donne's 1, 4, 6, 7, 10 becomes Pope's 2, 4, 6, 8, 10:

A thing, which would have pos'd Adam to name   (20)

becomes: A Thing which *Adam* had been pos'd to name   (25);

and again,

Which dwell at Court, for once going that way (16)

becomes: Who *live* at *Court*, for going once that Way! (23)

Relationship of Line-Structure to Phonemic Phrasing

The last variable to be considered is the potential relationship between line structure and phonemic phrasing. In a phonemically oriented prosody this involves two things: the occurrence of terminal junctures *intra*linearly—caesura—and the presence or absence of *inter*linear terminal

---

[11] Or, as Householder suggests, 3, 4, 7, 8, 10.

junctures—traditionally end-stoppage versus run-on or enjambment. I think that it is useful to see these as related concepts. In the first instance, suprasegmental features break metrical continuities; in the second, they smooth over metrical discontinuities.

These adjustments of metrical continuity within and between lines are not orthographic facts; they only exist in performances. As such they reflect the reader's interpretation, which is based not only on the meter but on the punctuation, the grammar, and the lexical message as well. But punctuation, grammar, and message are the *causes* of caesura and enjambment, not their manifestation or mode of existence; caesura and enjambment are phonological, not grammatical or lexical entities. In this sense it might be more proper to speak of a line as "suggesting" or "signaling" caesura and enjambment than "having" it.

The strength of the signal is not always uniform. Sometimes we are certain that a given situation—say, the end of a sentence, marked by a period, coinciding with line end—will require a given juncture, say /↓/, or metrically, end-stoppage. And by collecting many recordings of performances we may find almost universal assent in such an ascription. On other occasions, however, the signals are not conclusive, and there is range for personal interpretation. Then it becomes admittedly difficult to distinguish the poetic style from the interpretation and the performance style, unless we are prepared, again, to deal in potentials rather than actualizations. But potentials may be all that really exist "in" the poem as text. If different articulations are possible it would seem prudent theory to recognize that fact; indeed, that a poet frequently allows such choices may itself be a style feature of interest (or it may mean nothing). In this matter, as in all others concerning prosody, it seems futile to propose rigidly one's own performance as if it were the only conceivable one that a given verse allows. This is what causes the confusing proliferation of scansions and systems of scansions and the unfortunate motion toward prescriptivism in many metrical exercises.

Caesura has been defined by Amos R. Morris as "a perceptible break in the metrical line, properly described as an expressional pause" (in **371,** pp. 82–83). For a phonemically based descriptive metrics the term "expressional pause" could be changed to read "terminal juncture." This change is necessary because not all junctures contain pauses, and there seem to be several other kinds of phonetic phenomena, like pitch change, change in intensity (fade), and lengthening of final syllables, which operate in differing combinations to signal terminal junctures. The fact that different idiolects use different combinations of these to express what is structurally the same feature may explain some of the disputes that prosodists have about caesura. So we might revise the definition to read "a perceptible break in the performance of a line, properly described as an intralinear terminal juncture."

The run-on line is defined in Shipley's *Dictionary* as "The carrying of the sense (grammatical form) in a poem past the end of a line. . . ." I am not sure what the parentheses mean: I hardly think that the author intended to give the impression that the "sense" and the "grammatical form" are the same thing. If we interpret the parentheses to mean "and"— "The carrying of the sense *and* the grammatical form . . ."—the definition is still difficult to accept. The "sense" of a line, I presume, is its meaning. But surely the meaning is carried on past the end of end-stopped lines too, for example in Pope's

> I bought no *Benefice*, I begg'd no *Place*;
> Had no new Verse, or new Suit to show; (12–13).

Similarly, as this example demonstrates, the grammar may be carried on beyond the end of an end-stopped line as well; here the subject of the verb "begg'd" is also subject of "Had."

What seems actually "carried on" in a run-on line is the pitch contour, or to use the Trager-Smith term, the *phonemic clause*.[12] This suggests to the ear a carryover of meaning and grammar; however, if we are to have a phonemically sound prosody we must see this as a suggestion only, not as what really occurs. A possible definition of run-on or enjambment is "the occurrence in performance of a phonemic clause (or negatively, the absence of a terminal juncture) across what is represented in the text as line-end." And conversely, end-stoppage is the occurrence of terminal juncture at line end. This would seem to account for such remarks as the following: "Alec Guinness reads Shakespeare's blank verse as if most of the lines were end-stopped." The point is that in Alec Guinness' performance these lines *are* end-stopped, regardless of the meaning or the grammar or what somebody else's interpretation may be; that caesura, end-stoppage, and enjambment can only come into existence in actual performance since they are phonological, not orthographic, phenomena.

Thus we might distinguish three kinds of situations at line end, using quotation marks to emphasize that what is characterized is the line as performed, not as printed.

1. "*Run-on*" *lines*. Most readers would feel that the phonemic clause should not coincide with the line end, so that nothing greater than plus-juncture (i.e., minimally interrupted transition) intervenes between the

---

[12] A phonemic clause has its existence purely in phonology. It is defined (in **422**, p. 49) as "a minimal complete utterance" consisting of only one terminal juncture, "one or more pitch phonemes, one—*and only one*—primary stress, and may have one or more other stresses and one or more plus junctures."

two lines. A punctuation mark would seem practically never to occur at the end of such a line.

> but I have been in___
> A purgatorie, such as fear'd Hell is___
> A recreation to, and scarse map of this.   (2–4).

The feeling for run-on seems to increase greatly when there is a metrical zero at syllable 10, as in line 2 above, or a caesura after a very late syllable:

> As fresh, and sweet their Apparrells be, as bee___
> The fields they sold to buy them;   (180–81)

2. *"Alternative" lines.* Either run-on or end-stopped interpretation seems possible, and there is substantial variety among performances. There is often either no punctuation mark or a comma; for example, Donne's

> My sin___
> Indeed is great,   (1–2)

may be interpreted as either

> ^{2}My ^{3}sín$^{2\rightarrow}$___
>
> ^{2}Indéed ↑ ^{2}is ^{3}gréat^1

or

> ^{2}My ^{3}sîn
>
> Indêed is ^{3}gréat^1

or in other ways.

3. *"End-stopped" lines.* A terminal juncture seems almost obligatory (although *which* terminal juncture is up to the reader's style). The punctuation is usually stronger than a comma:

> as false as they
> Which dwell at Court for once going that way.
> Therefore I suffered this; towards me did run   (15–17).

It is often suggested by literary criticism that enjambment is essentially a linguistic impingement on the meter, and that its extensive use gives such verse the appearance of being closer to everyday speech than verse in which the meter exerts more control on the syntax. As Morris puts it (referring to caesura, but certainly the same could be said of enjambment): "It is essentially an instrument not of metrics but of prose, persisting in the artificial pattern of verse, cutting across the metrical flow with a secondary rhythmic movement of normal speech" (**371,** p. 82). The poet's control lies chiefly in his skill in so adjusting the natural speech movement that it does not cloud but enhances or enriches the verse movement.

Writing in an end-stopped style has a very different effect (**438**). Here the metrical structure restricts the natural speech patterns to a greater extent and consequently controls the reader's choice of phrasing to a finer degree. Each line must suggest that it is itself a full phonemic clause or that it is to be divided in such a way that a phonemic clause occurs at its end.

As an example, compare Donne's first lines with Pope's version:

Donne	Pope
Well; I may now receive, and die;	Well, if it be my time to quit the stage,
My sinne	Adieu to all the Follies of the Age!
Indeed is great, but I have beene in	I die in Charity with Fool and Knave,
A Purgatorie, such as fear'd Hell is	Secure of Peace at least beyond the
A recreation to, and scarse map of this.	grave.
	I've had my Purgatory here betimes,
	And paid for all my Satires, all my
	Rhymes:
	The Poet's Hell, its Tortures, Fiends
	and Flames,
	To this were Trifles, Toys, and empty
	Names.

The meaning is roughly the same: the poet has atoned for his sins *before* dying by visiting the court, a purgatory in comparison to which even Hell loses it terror. But the style differs considerably, and one of the important aspects of that difference seems to be the influence that meter is allowed to exert on the shaping of the rhetoric and the syntax. Donne's lines suggest phonemic clauses running over line end and terminating at varying points within the line—between the eighth and ninth syllables in the first line, between the fourth and fifth in the second, between the fifth and sixth in the third, and between the sixth and seventh in the fourth. The effect is to suggest a forcing of the message into the meter, even the rhymes being reduced to minimal effectiveness as structural units. In Pope's version the metrical exigencies alter the syntactic structures of the original in several ways. In the first two lines Pope revises Donne's abrupt juncture after the eighth syllable and run-on into a full-line modifying clause balancing the following main clause in a perfect end-stopped couplet. Similarly, the run-on

I have been in

A Purgatorie

becomes a full-line main clause followed by a somewhat redundant coordinate clause in line 6:

I've had my *Purgatory* here betimes,
And paid for all my Satires, all my Rhymes.

The end-stopped couplet frequently employs parallels of this sort to satisfy its metrical requirements. Indeed, one very good justification for the heavy use of parallelism and balance in the Neoclassical couplet is that it makes a virtue of a necessity; the necessity to fill out the line and control phonemic phrasing is turned into a source of poetic virtuosity (although this may be a chicken-and-egg matter).

Not only parallel clauses but also parallel phrases have a tendency to appear as full lines. For example,

> My minde, neither with prides itch, nor yet hath been
> Poyson'd with love to see, or to be seene,   (5–6)

becomes:
> With foolish *Pride* my heart was never fir'd
> Nor the vain Itch *t'admire*, or *be admir'd*;   (9–10).

Notice how the rhetorical parallelism implicit in Donne's lines, which runs counter to their metrical structure, finds metrical confirmation in Pope's revision.

Pope's lines 7 and 8 are excellent examples of the mechanism of converting run-on lines into end-stopped lines. Run-on is suggested most strongly where elementary structure points confront each other across the line break without phrasal buffering, for example, in Donne's lines ending "Hell is" and beginning "A recreation" (subject, copula, and predicate noun). Pope obviates this bare juxtaposition by inserting the appositive phrase "its Tortures, Fiends and Flames" and by inverting the verb phrase and the modifying prepositional phrase "To this."

Not only are Donne's run-on lines more numerous than Pope's, but, even more typically, he employs what may be termed a "run-on couplet" (a couplet whose first line is end-stopped and second run-on); for example,

> The men board them; and praise, as they thinke, well,
> Their beauties; they the mens wits; Both are bought.
> Why good wits ne'r weare scarlet gownes, I thought
> This cause . . .   (190–93)

Pope revises these couplets in his version as follows:

> Such Wits and Beauties are not prais'd for nought,
> For both the Beauty and the Wit are *bought*.   (234–5)

IV

By way of conclusion, I should like to consider very briefly some critical views that seem to correlate with the description presented. It seems necessary to seek out such views to give body and meaning to the mere stylistic differential.

It is apparent that Pope's verse displays a different sort of control than Donne's. We have seen that in comparison his rhymes are full and equal, his occasional segmental effects are rigidly controlled to coincide with meter, the meter itself tends to be more regular in terms of syllable count and metrical point placement, and finally his lines and couplets are usually end-stopped, with all that implies about the impact on rhetoric and syntax. Since both poets were writing in the same genre, apparently their notions of what the genre required differed considerably. Critics have called Donne's tone and stylistic practices "rough" or "dark," attributing their cultivation to an imperfect knowledge of classical satire. For one thing, the satires of Persius, which had been couched in equivocal language for purely nonliterary reasons, were taken by Renaissance poets as models. More important, there seems to have been some confusion about the etymology of "satire." Renaissance scholarship derived the word from *satyra* ("a rude mixture of cyclic chorus and primitive drama performed by men dressed in animal skins and tails"), rather than from *satura* (the stuffing of a roast, also *lanx satura* "a full dish or tray," whence "a poetic medley," particularly in respect to variety of versification). This led most of the early English satirists to take crudeness and obscurity to be characteristic of satire as a genre. Thus the "violent and apparently motiveless" style features of Donne's verse (**193**) and its "harshness" (**397**) had the very straightforward dramatic purpose of establishing the poet's tone within the tradition as he saw it. J. B. Leishman writes

[Donne] was . . . imitating . . . the 'harshness' of the Roman satirical hexameter. The fact that many of his lines can only with great difficulty be scanned as five-foot lines is precisely what he intended: he intended the reader to find as much difficulty in reading them as he himself found in reading [classical satires] (**247**, ch. 3).

And Clay Hunt writes

Donne certainly made some attempt in the satires to follow the conventions of the genre of formal verse satire—conventions which were fairly congenial to his temperament . . .

and goes on to refer to the "blunt, crusty, chip-on-the-shoulder moralist . . . snorting his indignation . . . the stock persona of Juvenalian verse satire . . ." (**188**, p. 207).

It is interesting to note that critics consider Pope's style in the satires to be less smooth than his style in some of his other works. The reason (according to Ian Jack) was that he too thought that the genre required a "low" style, although "low" had far different connotations in the eighteenth century than it had at the turn of the seventeenth. The permissible variations were more restricted; the "lowest" that Pope could go was to write some "easy Horation talk" (**320**). Saintsbury sums up the change in taste when he writes of Donne:

> When they [Elizabeth satirists] assumed this greater license, the normal structure of English verse was anything but fixed. Horace had in his contemporaries, Persius and Juvenal had still more in their forerunners, examples of versification than which Mr. Pope himself could do nothing more 'correct' . . . . In Donne's time the very precisians took a good deal of license. If therefore you meant to show that you were *sans gêne*, you had to make demonstrations of the most unequivocal character . . . (**92**).

By Pope's time one could be *sans gêne* by means of much subtler adjustments. That, apparently, is the interesting thing about very restrictive traditions.

The general impression, then, is that Donne's "carelessness" is designed to establish a certain tone and a certain feeling which he takes pains to control. His control lies precisely in his seeming lack of it. In Ben Jonson's phrase, Donne's negligence is to be interpreted as a "diligent kind of negligence," a self-assured indifference toward externals and even a positive contempt for such superficialities as exact meter (**396**, p. 695). As for rhyme, Donne apparently felt that

> it is matter over manner, and the ornamental qualities of rhyme must be made less important; not be allowed to ring and re-echo in full melodious tones and overtones but made to serve a practical function in a new technique of the couplet (**396**, p. 677).

Donne's tone, in short, seems to say "Look, I have no time to be bothered with carefully measuring words and sounds. I take them as they come to me in my divine and angry inspiration. My anger is righteous and sincere, and if I stop to tamper with it, to dissect and to analyze it and to put it into *bons mots*, it will cool into ineffectuality."

Pope, on the other hand, presents a tone which is calculated to demonstrate a merciless competence, a cold ability to demolish neatly what he hates. In this style one strives to give the impression that disposing of the object of one's distaste is analogous and not much more difficult than disposing of the exigencies of one's meter. Pope prefers a stiletto to Donne's blunderbuss.

On Free Rhythms in Modern Poetry

*Preliminary Remarks
toward a Critical Theory
of Their Structures
and Functions*

BENJAMIN HRUSHOVSKI

I

There are two possible ways of facing the fact of the existence of free verse:[1] one is to exclude free rhythms from poetry (since their "form" is supposed not to be "detectable"[2]); the alternative, if we cannot afford simply to dismiss important parts of modern poetry (as well as of Goethe, Heine, Hölderlin, the Bible, and so forth), is to revise thoroughly our old notions on poetic rhythm (as we did for the "ornamental" theories of poetic language) and then to come back to a structural and meaningful description of free-rhythmic phenomena.

[1] The literature in this field (cf. the bibliography in fn. 8) is so heterogeneous that I feel the necessity of arguing points which may to some critics seem trivial and to others unconvincing. This is a first, tentative statement of several general aspects, developed when having in view a descriptive typology of modern European and American free rhythms (in preparation), regretfully unsupported here by concrete illustrations. Only a small part of it was presented at the conference. Still, because of severe limitations of time and space (mainly due to personal circumstances), this paper is, in many respects, not as I would have liked to present it. I am very thankful to Thomas A. Sebeok for his help and support in its preparation.

[2] When D. Stauffer (**395**, p. 204) says "if free verse had form in any real sense, its form would be detectable," we wonder, on the one hand, why "detectable" should mean falling under presupposed strict numerical rules, and, on the other hand, how "detectable" are his other terms: "exact," "intense," "significant," etc. Cf. also Suberville (**405**, p. 158): "il n'y a pas, à proprement parler, de verse sans mesure déterminée." It is to a great extent the fault of free verse, in the eyes of this dogmatic normativist, that the broad public has been estranged from poetry.

We are not saying that such a revision has not yet been attempted, but that it has not yet gone the long way from the happy chaos of ingenious insights to a sound and specific body of knowledge.

Anyone attempting to proceed in this field faces the ungrateful job of plunging into an enormous variety of metrical theories (**442**, p. 168), many of which are estranged from the practice of modern literary criticism, and vice versa. Karl Shapiro—who knows the English writings in this field better than many in his generation—wrote:

One of the most distressing aspects of the study of English prosody, whether as theory of forms or as versification, is the necessity of beginning with absolute fundamentals and working up through an enormous copia of *unscientific scholarship*, analyses which have not even premises in common, and the prejudices of the poets, critics and students of the past three and a half centuries. I do not mean that I have done all this, or intend to, except as an amateur, but I want to point out at the start that if there is any one certainty in this field of study it is that dissension has been the rule from beginning to end" (**368**, p. 77).[3]

I am quoting at length, identifying myself with both parts of these—probably too sharp—statements, since it is easier than undertaking the task of proof. But a similar pessimism was heard recently from a more significant source; J. C. Ransom wrote retrospectively:

It is strange that a generation of critics so sensitive and ingenious as ours should have turned out very backward, indeed phlegmatic, when it comes to hearing the music of poetry, or at least, to avoid misunderstanding, to hearing its meters. The only way to escape the sense of a public scandal is to assume that the authority of the meters is passing, or is past, because we have become jaded by the meters; which would mean that something else must be tried (**325**).

Precisely this is the point: "Something else must be tried." The lack of interest in prosody in literary circles was due to the correct feeling that the mere naming of a meter is as insignificant to the understanding of poetry as classification according to the 250 rhetorical figures and tropes (cf. **226**). A generation which knew so rightly to stress (if not overstress) the organicity of a complex poetic structure could not be interested in what is actually an abstraction, a "prosaic," "scientific," "rational," extremely poor paraphrase of the "music of poetry."

On the other hand, we cannot dismiss prosody as an irrelevant, merely "formal" or secondary question. Generations of poets evidenced the

---

[3] This is certainly exaggerated. There are many intelligent and correct observations in the traditional books, and we should admit that a great deal of collected information can be used, if carefully analyzed and reinterpreted. But sometimes we prefer the laborious task of analyzing anew a vast number of poems because of the questionable reliability of noncritically accumulated facts.

central, poetry-making, significance of rhythm. It is an illusion that poetic language alone—metaphoric, ambiguous, or otherwise—without its peculiar rhythmic embodiment in the structure of a poem, can account for the semantic or "ontological" specificness of poetry. The question is how to translate the feeling of poets and critics into precise, many-sided, and distinguishable observations. When so subtle a critic of poetry as R. Blackmur feels that ". . . it is when words sing that they give that absolute moving attention which is beyond their prose powers" (**31**, p. 369); that "Style is the quality of the act of perception but it is mere play and cannot move us much unless married in rhythm to the urgency of the thing perceived" (**31**, p. 371);[4] when he judges according to these principles, saying, for example, about Wallace Stevens, Marianne Moore, and E. E. Cummings (as compared to Yeats, Eliot, and Pound), that "none of them could ever so penetrate either their prosody or their words that their poems become their own music or their own meaning,"[5] since "it is by prosody alone—by the loving care for the motion of meaning in language —that a poet may prove that he 'was blessed and could bless' " (**31**, pp. 383, 388), he hits at the central points of our problem, although he does not support his metaphoric statements by the kind of concrete analysis he employs in the case of poetic language.

If metaphor is "inevitable in practical criticism" (**452**, p. 750), we have to admit also that it is different from metaphor in poetry, at least in its objective of conveying a less relative order of truth. And in this objective it must base itself on a body of carefully analyzed facts within the structures of poems, which are responsible for the gamut of different rhythmical impacts and functions in poetry, even when we feel that a mere description of a structure does not convey the unique impact of an individual poem. To sum up: "Es ist schon heute nichtssagend, einen Rhythmus lediglich als schön, angenehm, kräftig, weich, markant und wie auch immer zu bezeichnen, ohne dass man die objektiven Gegebenheiten erfasst und darstellt" (**226**, p. 262).

Many of the greatest achievements of world poetry are created in free rhythms (cf. **344**, for a parallel problem in music). A series of the most interesting movements in modern poetry did their worst and their best without strict meters: some are now curiosities of literary history, some turned from revolutionaries almost into classics. Questions of rhythm

---

[4] These two pronouncements are basically close to Tynjanov's (**425**) ideas, expressed in more concrete terms in one of the most interesting modern books on the principles of poetic language.

[5] Cf. Staiger, who asserts (**391**, p. 16) that the lyric poem is an absolute unity of the meaning of the words and their sounds. But how do we know when such occurs and when not?

were central in their arguments as well as in their endeavors.[6] The greatest diversity of rhythmic expression ever seen was tried out almost in one generation. And we cover all this by one negative term, *free verse*, a term created by poets as a slogan against a former literary convention, but meaningless as a single positive description of poets as diverse as Eliot and Cummings, Brecht and Trakl, Majakovskij and Stramm, Rilke and Marianne Moore, H. D. and Wallace Stevens.

Poets knew that the concept was not merely negative. H. de Regnier's remark of 1891 is still a challenge for criticism: "La liberté la plus grand: qu'importe le nombre de vers, si le rythme est *beau*?" (**217**, p. 94). And so are T. S. Eliot's aphorisms: "No verse is free for the man who wants to do a good job. . . . *Vers libre* is a battle cry of a freedom and there is no freedom in art" (**111**),[7] stressing the inner responsibility of the artist in organizing his word material, which is—according to much evidence—more difficult without the support of a metrical framework. In 1942, in retrospect, T. S. Eliot wrote: "Only a bad poet could welcome free verse as a liberation from form. It was a revolt against dead form, and a preparation for new form or for the renewal of the old; it has an insistence upon the inner unity which is unique to every poem, against the outer unity which is typical."

But a criticism, which was so valuable in understanding the "inner unity which is unique to every poem" in the field of meaning or the language of poetry, achieved—if we may generalize—rather poor results in the field of rhythm as soon as a set of traditionally presupposed rules failed to appear.

Despite many valuable insights (often mixed with naive notions on basic matters), there exists no systematic critical analysis of our problem.[8]

[6] For some, rhythm was more than a term of poetry. It was rather a symbol for dynamic forces in life, which they hoped to echo in their poems. The Russian symbolist Blok spoke of the "music of the epoch," "the crushing rhythm of revolution," and the like. The Italian futurist Marinetti proclaimed that paintings are to catch the particular rhythm of every object rather than its outward forms. Pinthus wrote in his preface to the famous expressionistic anthology, *Menschheitsdämmerung* (**313**): " . . . es kommt darauf an, aus den lärmenden Dissonanzen, den melodischen Harmonien, dem wuchtigen Schreiten der Akkorde, den gebrochensten Halb- und Vierteltönen—die Motive und Themen der wildesten wüstesten Zeit der Weltgeschichte herauszuhören." But even those who aimed at avoiding "musicality" and at creating a prosaic illusion in their poems were actually preoccupied with a question of rhythm in its broadest sense, where it is connected with questions of language, meaning, and mimesis.

[7] It should be noted that this was written—in 1917, in a mood of polemic—before Eliot's own more daring departures.

[8] A recent bibliography of writings on free rhythms is available only in German (**281**; see also **165**). In English, **186** covers the polemical stage of the imagist movement. But the writings of this period, although of considerable historical interest, have almost no structural value. With the end of the argument, in the 1930's, the entry "free verse" disappeared from American bibliographies of periodicals. A general bibliography of

Some attempted solutions are very poor; for example, the latest German book in this field (**67;** see **120** for a critique) is chiefly a description of poems and poets who have happened to write in free rhythms. There is a serious literature in German on "classic" free rhythms (e.g. on Hölderlin, **239, 261, 365,** et al.). But the quite different problems of expressionist poetry are almost untouched, except for generalizations. A serious German tradition trying to see in free rhythms a kind of genre (**235, 281, 290**), "die Form der Begeisterung" (Kommerell, **235**), or the like breaks down when confronted with the variety of the modernists. The prominent Anglo-American "New Critics" did not go into the problem (save for essayistic purposes), with one exception, Yvor Winters (**455**), who is limited in his scope and achievements. The gap between criticism and scholarship, the mistrust for "exact" measurement, the lack of continuity of accumulated observations, and the lack of a broad and comparative study of minutiae (which the Russian formalists did carry out) may account for this.[9]

The most detailed studies in free verse were written in French,[10] where the problems of rhythm are much alive in the general theories of literature, and the awareness of rhythmic complexity even in metrical verse is commonly known, or at least has been since the studies of Servien (e.g. **144**). But there the problem is somewhat different, being a freedom from syllabic norms, as opposed to syllabo-tonic, with which I am dealing now (as in English, German, or Russian).

The Russian Formalists (**115, 442**), whose greatest achievements were in metric verse, were stopped in their work too early to be able to solve descriptively the contemporary questions of free rhythmic structures. (Besides, Russian "free" rhythms were not as free as many in German or

---

prosody, with valuable annotations, but not complete, is found in **367.** A most needed bibliography of rhythm analyses in modern practical criticism is not available. In **373,** many Russian writings on prosody are listed, and the book is indexed; for criticism and addenda, cf. **196.** See also **199,** on old Slavic metrics, and **115** for some West Slavic studies. In French, **285** contains a small but essential list; **246,** a strange survey of prosodic studies over the last five centuries, completes the former. There exists also a vast literature on the rhythms in the Bible: for a survey of the main old theories (up to 1905), cf. **68;** and **22** contains a good summary of the subsequent 25 years. For general problems see the surveys and bibliographies in **115, 226,** and **442;** for a recent psychological approach see **123.**

[9] In the vast literature on T. S. Eliot there seems to be no really close analysis of the "music" of his verse and its development, except for mechanistic and often uncritical statistics of fifteen poems and passages (**14;** cf. fns. 16, 17) and a simplifying chapter in **132.**

[10] **285** and **411.** Whether their aesthetic conclusions are well balanced is, of course, a different question.

English.) Moreover, in concrete metric analysis, some of them lost contact with the whole and individual poem. They were less interested in a single poem than in tendencies of generations and looked, therefore, for the dominant rule rather than for local hierarchies of structure (Jakobson's term), which meant—for free rhythms—too vague generalizations. But a few ventures, revealing broader interests than careful syllable counting, are among the most valuable writings in our field, notably Jakobson's analysis of the contribution of semantic elements to Majakovskij's rhythms (**198**), Tynjanov's analysis of the relations of rhythm and poetic language, with a keen understanding of free rhythms (**425**), Brik's remarks on "Rhythm and Syntax" (**43**), Tomaševskij's (**419**) penetrating essay on "Rhythm and Verse"—these, as well as their statistical studies, revealing the complexities of metrical verse, may serve as a departure for a close structural analysis which is bound to bring concrete, valid, and meaningful results if carried out in a broad, comparative way within the framework of a modern understanding of poetry and the complexity and "organicity" of its language (as revealed in "New Criticism" or in writings inspired by German phenomenology).[11]

The best start of a renewed argument would be in a series of thorough analyses of different poems—but only when carried out in a careful, critical perspective. This (as I hope to show elsewhere) will reveal artful organization in what seems to be "natural" writing, and—for criticism— the palpability of what seems to be a matter of indescribable feeling. But since such an analysis must operate with heavily contaminated concepts, I shall try at first to state a few generalizations, which—although far from exhausting the needed clarifications—seem to me to be obvious conclusions from any broad inquiry in the rhythms of poetry. Such a procedure— revealing, I hope, something of the complexity of our problem—must be at the expense of a supported and well-developed argument.

II

We have to distinguish between the concept of meter and the concept of rhythm.[12] Although meter has the value of a traditional norm and

---

[11] In an early attempt (**185**) the author tried to develop methods of structural analysis and a classification of free rhythms, exploring their historical, critical, and linguistic implications in the totality of a relatively little-known body of poetry; cf. **114**.

[12] This distinction is commonly observed on the continent, although variously emphasized (cf. **86, 87, 225–226, 285, 310–311, 419**, etc.). The fact itself is, of course, known to most serious critics. For example, when Y. Winters asserts that "*Miltonic* blank verse is one of the greatest metrical inventions in the history of poetry" and that "he invented it for the sake" of "Paradise Lost," he does not mean merely the meter but, in his words: "the total phonetic quality of metrical language," that is, the rhythm. (Cf. also **113**, p. 37.)

appears as a permanent impulse in the reading of a poem, it is rather an abstraction, one never realized precisely, whereas the rhythmical aspect of a poem implies the whole impact of the movement of the language material in the reading of a poem. By making this distinction, we save, on the one hand, the concept of meter from destruction by exact measurement and avoid, on the other hand, confusing the systematization of meters (which is important in itself) with an understanding of the contributions of rhythmical effects to the whole poem as a work of art.[13]

Poems with the same metrical scheme may have entirely different rhythms and can be rhythmically less alike than poems with different schemes, for example those written by one author. The reason for this is that meter, being a central rhythmical factor, is not necessarily the most important or the most distinctive one. A sonnet by Rilke written in one extremely inverted sentence can be understood as different from a classical sonnet in terms of syntactic structure as a central rhythmical factor in poetry. The revolution here is not less than, and not far removed from, certain syntactical trends in modern free rhythms. But the problems of syntax in its poetic—and, in our case, rhythmic—functions are almost untouched by research (beginnings in **43, 82, 252**), although they involve linguistic elements no less than the number of stresses.

To make a good poem, meter is not enough. This was one of the chief motives in the opposition of free-verse poets to the practice of their predecessors. As Blackmur points out, "This is the chief indictment against that aspect of our poetry which we call verse. Syllable and stress are not enough to make a metric into a style, although they are quite enough to make a doggerel" (**31**, p. 373). It is not only the "resistance of the language material" (as the early Žirmunskij thought) or certain allowances of *licencia poetica* which account for deviations from a smooth metrical order. The difference between poetry and music in this respect is not to the disadvantage of poetry, as it was commonly assumed. Just as we freed ourselves from the fallacy of *ut pictura poesis* to see the peculiar poetic figurative combinations of sensuous—and not only sensuous—elements, so we are to stress the positive values of the

---

[13] I am, of course, far from such absolute dichotomies as were made by the German philosopher Klages (**232**), where a polar opposition between rhythm and *Takt* (i.e., meter) is drawn back to a metaphysical distinction between *Seele* and *Geist*, to the clear disadvantage of the second. His pupil Hellenbrecht writes in his study on free rhythms: "Zur Befreiung gelangt die in den Ketten des Bewusstseins schwingende Seele und befreit wird sie von dem messenden und begrenzenden Prinzip des Geistes" (**165**, p. 33), and, accordingly, he disapproves of Goethe's free rhythms for their relative proximity to regular iambs. No doubt, in most of poetry, meter is the constant organizing factor, around which the local rhythmic configurations as well as the total rhythmic expression are created.

many-leveled expressive variety of rhythm which can be achieved in poetry, with elements of meaning playing a significant role. And, of course, there are poetic rhythms without any meter, as there are poems without any metaphor.

Therefore, a mere naming of the meter is as meaningless for the interpretation of an individual poem as the naming of its general idea; both are abstractions. The matching of form types and theme types on so abstract a level—as has often been done[14]—is largely futile.

A poem cannot be exhaustively decomposed into separate elements, rhythmic, semantic, etc.; to describe the poem we must look at it as a whole from different aspects, the aspect of meaning, the aspect of rhythm, etc. Each of them is but a certain function of the totality of elements of the poem. To use a very simplifying comparison: a poem is like a many-sided crystal; we can observe its inner properties only from one side at a time, but then its whole structure appears through this particular face, showing different emphases in different directions.

If, in reading a poem, we try to listen to its rhythm, we cannot fail to see the participation of the meaning in its creation, nor rhythm's role in the creation of meaning. Thus we can avoid the old fallacy of a form-content dichotomy and yet not give up an approach to poetry through its different aspects. But with one condition: we have to deal with a whole aspect and not merely with a certain a priori known element of it, as an idea, a meter, etc. We have to understand not the mechanical relations of syllables but the dynamic properties of rhythm.

Rhythm is an "organic" phenomenon and can be appreciated fully by a phenomenological approach to the poem, that is, by going within it and moving in a hermeneutic circle from the whole to the parts, and vice versa.[15] Nevertheless, factors contributing to its intersubjective character are detectable. Moreover, we can find characteristic features by which it is possible to describe the rhythmical style of a poem or a poet, or—with more flexibility—of a period or a genre.

We can observe many rhythmical factors: metrical sequences and deviations from their ideal norms; word boundaries and their relations to feet boundaries; syntactic groups and pauses and their relation to metrical

---

[14] For example, Robert Graves and Paula Riding (**140**, p. 24): "Metre considered as a set pattern approved by convention will stand for the claims of society as at present organized: the variations on metre will stand for the claims of the individual." We could compile a book of such pronouncements on the "nature" of free rhythms.

[15] I refer especially to the recently very influential theories of Heidegger and other phenomenologically minded European critics, such as Staiger (**391–393**). With a different philosophical background, American critics often did methodically similar things, because of a similar movement toward the poem as the central object of observation.

groups (line, caesura); syntagmatic relations, word order, syntactic tensions; repetitions and juxtapositions of sound, meaning elements, etc. Practically everything in the written poem can contribute to the shaping of the rhythm—the words in their multidimensional organizations as well as aspects of the whole which arise implicitly from the lines, such as tone, ethos, atmosphere, *"Stimmung"* (a central term in contemporary German literary criticism), or whatever we call them—although each element may, and does, have other functions in the poem too.

Inasmuch as elements of meaning or, for example, syntagmatical relations take part in shaping the rhythm, we have to describe them as real structural elements existing in the written poem. If rhythmic forms and the rhythmic impact are influenced by the feeling of a general ethos or tone, we can detect the choice of words, syntactic patterns, and thematic elements which shaped it. Moreover, there are mutual interrelations of structure, meaning, and function on all levels and between all levels. Structures exist only under these conditions. Stress patterns come to life; decisions about where and how to stress, where and how to "feel" a pause, etc., are made on the basis of a reading of the poem as a whole. In this organization of the language material, rhythmic factors in the narrow sense (as the ways of Gestalt perception) take part, as well as factors of meaning, tradition, and the like.

Not all the existing elements have the same value in each concrete case. We have to determine not only what the distinctive elements are but also how they work together in their concrete configurations in different poems.[16]

We cannot do this by recording readings of poems (1) because there are in a reading subjective elements; (2) because the recording shows the physical, not the psychological, facts, the sounds and not their significations; (3) because a full realization of the rhythm by voice reading is often impossible, as it is often impossible to make a full pictorial realization of the figurative language in a poem. There are tensions that are not realized by a single reading (such as the tension between the factual reading and the metrical norm created during the same reading, as well as "rhythmical oxymorons" or "rhythmical ambiguities"), although their rhythmical role is obvious. But, of course, a rhythm exists only as an "auditory imagination" (even meter does not exist in the text itself, but as a potentiality). We have to analyze the clues which the text provides for the readers for

---

[16] The mere knowledge that there are several kinds of rhythmic elements is not enough. Thus Barry (**14**) analyzes several kinds of "cadence" in T. S. Eliot, without trying to understand their concrete interrelations in different types of poems. Despite some valuable details, it leads to nothing but vague generalizations in the summary. (Cf. also the next note.)

grouping, pausing, emphasis, breathing, etc., looking not for their possible physiological realizations but for their significance in a context and within a tradition.

Moreover, statistical evidence is not enough, although it may help to distinguish certain expressive tendencies in great numbers of poems, as has been shown especially by the Russian Formalists. It may be misleading to show similar numbers for different reasons; or, the more we move away from the normative element, the more we might disregard local variations or local significances.

A style is created not by majorities but by certain conspicuous uses of elements; sometimes one metaphor means by its individual value or function more than ten other "formal" metaphors. And in our field, where the very decision about what is used as a stress must be made in each case (since literary significance is not equal to linguistic significance), the hierarchy of elements, as well as the role of statistical facts, must be judged according to their particular functions.[17] A critical approach is necessary to select and to weigh the effects of possible factors within a given framework. Therefore, a rhythm analysis can be only a part of the

---

[17] A most significant case is the following. Barry, in the only existing book on Eliot's prosody (14), writes: "An examination of Eliot's poems for the purpose of determining to what extent he uses phrasal cadences reveals that only one combination of this sort can be found running through as many as five poems," forgetting that a "phrasal cadence" is, according to her arbitrary decision, a combination of group cadences which occur in at least 15 per cent of the total lines of a poem. So that if it occurs in 14 per cent (say in 7 subsequent lines out of 50), it does not exist. But, furthermore, one "phrasal cadence" happens to consist of two rising dissyllabic groups,—that is, two iambs—and this is an analysis which does not distinguish between metric and nonmetric poems. Would we not be able to suspect before the statistics that a sequence of two iambs may occur in more than one of Eliot's poems? But, moreover, the whole concept of "phrasal cadence" is misleading, since it is an utterly arbitrary group of syllables, without any consideration of its role in the dynamics of rhythm. In a line like "The dove descending breaks the air" (symbolized: OÓ, OÓO, Ó, OÓ), only the words "descending breaks" form a "cadence" (and not the first or last word), simply because in the fourth part of "Little Gidding" there happen to be more than 15 per cent of lines where two adjacent words of this structure occur. Even if it were to occur in 100 per cent of the lines, what effect does it make in a poem? That this is a pure iambic line makes no difference to the author, that word boundaries without relation to the meter make no sense, and that grouping without considering real phrasal groups does not exist in a poem—all this is not even argued by Barry. And then, of course, we discover how few phrases Eliot has, that is, how great is the variety of his rhythms! (A statistical comparison to other poets is out of the question.) So we discover a group like Ó, OÓ in a trochaic poem, and so on. But—what is more important in free rhythms—this exact grouping cannot lead to a perception of repetitions of significantly similar rhythmic groups if they differ in one syllable, a difference which can be unimportant in free rhythms, especially when there is a syntactical parallelism; or simply in a case of a free anacrusis.

"art of interpretation," although it can—and should—be described in exact terms based on the written text.[18]

The foregoing remarks do not imply that a rhythm analysis has to deal with all the problems of the poem, but that it has to keep them in mind and take them into consideration as far as is needed.

Systematizations of elements are helpful. But easily made systematizations should not prevent us from seeing what the rhythm is[19] or lead us to mistake the description of significant elements for the real effect of the whole poetic phenomenon. But, on the other hand, a phenomenological approach has the dangers of an uncritical relativism and impressionism or mystification in description if it does not use structural terms and comparative methods.[20] The latter way is the task of *rhythmology* (as distinct from "metrics"), and this is possible even in free rhythms, where we can always detect the underlying structures if we are not bound by pseudo-classical superstitions.

III

By free rhythms I mean poems which (1) have no consistent metrical scheme, that is, in tonic syllabic poetry have a freedom from the prevalent, predetermined arrangement of stressed and unstressed syllables; but (2) do have a poetic language organized so as to create impressions and fulfill functions of poetic rhythm.

I prefer the German term "free rhythms" to the French "*vers libre*," since the latter implies freedom from the norms of a syllabic system, freedom primarily in the length of the verse line rather than in the relations of stressed to unstressed syllables.

No doubt the first modern impulse toward freedom from metric norms came from France[21] and spread all over Europe. It fits excellently the

---

[18] Staiger (**392**) argues that interpretation of poetry is an art (possibly not the best-chosen term), but the "art of interpretation" is a science, since it carries all the responsibilities of objective proof and can be dismissed if proved incorrect.

[19] We should not be deterred by its complexity, since even "simple" elements are simple merely by a convenient illusion. So is stress, according to a recent definition (**145**), "eine sehr Komplexe Verbindung von Tonhöhe, Tonverlauf, Klangfarbe, Stärke, Dauer," and each of these is, probably, as complex in its turn. Therefore, I prefer phenomenology to an atomistic approach.

[20] So are, to a considerable extent, **165, 310–311,** and many less "rhythmically minded" practical critics; they are usually good in their direct observations but are not concrete and often fail in generalizations if confronted with evidence from wider fields.

[21] In Russia articles on French disputes on free verse, by the French poet R. Ghil, were printed as early as 1903; **428,** which influenced English poets (cf. **408**), was translated into Russian by the "imagist" Šeršenevič.

inner logic of the different "ideologies" of modernistic movements. But, as close analysis shows, this influence was rather confined to slogans, being even less concrete than in figurative language. The use of concrete structural devices—not being formulated in any rational way—was initiated and developed in each language according to its peculiar resources and by each artist according to his habits and poetic needs.

In search for a feeling for concrete syllable relations, word groupings, intonations, etc. (apart from the general tendencies), poets of each language went to their own contemporary speech habits, as well as their own, revised, poetic traditions (although the new free rhythms are not identical with and exceed by far in their range everything known in the past).

Nevertheless, these local developments show similar tendencies, owing to the relation toward the common European cultural heritage, the common functional tendencies of the modernistic movements, as well as certain general human rhythmic properties and limitations. On this ground a comparative study can be much more illuminating than observations of what seems to be "natural" within one language.

The proclaimed tendencies of free rhythmic poetry ran from a search for a more "speech-like," "prosaic" expression to an effort to create individual structures rhythmically more organized than is possible in metrical verse, with preference for local effects rather than for the over-all unity of the poem. Often both polar tendencies appear in the rhythm, as well as in the diction of one poem. Both can be an attempt to escape "musical" fluidity and to regain the value of the single word, even at the expense of—or, rather, by means of—cutting off the stream.

Many misunderstandings stem from a simplified view of the function of meter in poetry, rationalistic views as well as those that detach form from content. By such standards, meter is indispensable. But if we analyze its contributions to the meaning and the "world" of the poem, we see that its functions may be many-sided and vary from one poetic system to another. An important contemporary observation holds that "the influence of meter is . . . to actualize words: to point them and to direct attention to their sound. In good poetry, the relations between words are very strongly emphasized" (**442**). According to my previous distinctions, I should say that meter, by itself, does not cause this "actualization of words"; meter can have the opposite effect (as in "musical," impression-istic poetry). Here "good poetry" means poetry in which the rhythmical factors perform this central, poetry-making task; and this is often what free rhythms aim at. " 'The unity and compression of the verse line' brings words closer to each other, makes them interact, overlap, crisscross, and in so doing, reveals the wealth of their 'lateral' potential meaning"

(**115,** p. 194, quoting Tynjanov). The variety of ways of doing this makes it impossible to speak about free rhythms as one type in any concrete way. In the following I shall outline a few major principles of free rhythms, keeping in mind that their actualizations follow this variety, and are more complex and rich in implications than any all-inclusive principles.

The phenomenological evidence is that free rhythms may have a more "rhythmical" and less "prosaic" impact than many metrical texts. It is possible to show in detail that they are often highly organized and are by no means a border area between prose and poetry. There is a misunderstanding—going back to the Greeks—which requires strict numbers as the only *differentia* of poetry. Strict numbers are not only insufficient (meter without rhythm) but also unnecessary. They can easily limit the flexibility and variety of expression. Moreover, although the numerical relations in free rhythms are a distinctive rhythmical factor, it remains a fallacy to say that the less strict the numbers are the closer we are to prose. As studies in prose rhythm show, it is possible to find prose that is numerically more "regular"—on all levels—than are many poems. Furthermore, prose approaching regularity sounds more "musical" and often more monotonous than many poems approaching prose; (cf. **315,** §71).

Iambic pentameter may sound "prose-like," whereas irregular numerical relations can themselves be a rhythmical factor, merely by being different from regular prose. Thus modern poetry uses as conspicuous rhythmic devices maximal numbers of slacks on the one hand (Majakovskij) and adjacent stresses on the other (Stramm, Majakovskij, Williams, often Eliot). Similarly, juxtaposition of a long line and a very short one is a rhythmical factor, although it is the opposite of numerical regularity, and so on.

Purity of principles is not a feature of poetry (at least when we consider its minutiae). There are many factors that are characteristic of the "pole" of poetry as opposed to the pole of prose. There are characteristic features of poetic language. But it is impossible to name a differentia which will appear in all poetry and which cannot appear even in greater numbers in certain texts of prose. The same applies to numerical relations of groups of syllables or words, if they are not strict. Nevertheless, the rhythmical difference is obvious, and it is first of all an ontological one. For example, much has been written about the "u"-sound of Goethe's "Über allen Gipfeln" as a poetry-making factor; prose is full of such sounds or repetitions of sounds, but their mere number does not mean much if we do not consider their function and the different ontological systems. The same is true of ambiguities, connotations, or any multiplicity of meanings evoked in words of poetry which do not usually function in works of prose.

The differentia of poetry is the verse line; it is hard to overestimate its importance in creating the poetic rhythm and the very being of the poem.

When we rewrite a poem and arrange the lines in a new way we see a striking difference, and when we write a poem as prose we often lose not only the specific rhythm but the poem as a work of art itself. Only careful, close analysis—far beyond syllable counting—reveals the subtle differences that account for this phenomenon (cf. **442**, p. 173).[22]

In the framework of the poem, rhythmic and figurative elements, which appear in other frameworks too, are restressed, reorganized, and reinterpreted in our perception, according to their relative locations and functions; they get another perspective and specific gravity and then play an important role in shaping the "world" of the poem. Our very confidence in the signification of the words depends on these conditions. The mark of this ontologically different framework is the verse line.

Moreover, the verse line can, and does, also fulfill concrete rhythmical tasks. If it is not identical with the syntactic grouping, we have a tension between the two factors that creates or deforms some other factors (especially intonation) and can lead to the restressing of words at both ends of the line, as compared with their prose positions (see especially **252**, p. 94, and **261**). If the sentence is long the verse segments lead to a leveling of phrase divisions and phrase gradations in the sentence, in addition to the leveling of stresses and stress distances, and to a breaking of the sentence intonation and a restructuring of consecutive parts into parallel-related units.

IV

Usually a verse line is a perceptible group of stresses (two, three, or four) or a dipody (or tripody) of such groups. Thus (1) verse lines are correlated units, and (2) within the line the stresses are conspicuous as the main constituents of the unit. Their conspicuous position leads to a leveling of the stress differences and then to a relating of the syllable distances between them whenever possible. Although the principles of this over-all rhythmic organization, according to general tendencies of numeric relationships, require a special argument, I shall try to state the main notions that should be understood as a basis for a discussion of any type of free rhythms.

It has been observed many times that not every possible metrical arrangement, length of line, etc., is commonly used in poetry.

[22] There is an example in **45**, p. 60, although the author, revealing a subtle feeling for the difference, thinks that "it is absurd to suppose that we can explain why and how this happens." For further evidence, cf. **425**, especially pp. 36–39.

As implied from Gestalt psychology, the organization of perceptibly similar elements into groups, similar groups into higher groups, and so forth, is a major tendency of human perception. The rhythmic organization of a poem does not provide any ready order or hierarchy of groupings; it provides merely a possibility for a certain organization, which is realized by the reader. The reader does it in part by habit or agreement (tradition, knowledge of conventions, etc.) and in part by a feeling regulated by human rhythmic properties (rhythmic inertia, rhythmic impulse, etc.). Only on this basis can we speak about "expectations" or "frustrated expectations"; only on the basis of a rhythmic impulse, created by a partial order, does a meter exist; only thus can we understand rhythmic "disturbances," "deviations," or parallels, rhythmic "leitmotifs," etc.

Of course, the tendencies of perception are highly flexible, they are regulated by the enormous variety of structural variations and shades of meaning emphasis, and practically they provide for what seems to be an unlimited range of expressive possibilities.

Therefore, I do not propose to explain rhythm from the rules of Gestalt psychology; rather I shall analyze the structures of a text and ask what kind of reading does this text require, or what are the ways of reading that can bring to life the language of this poem in all its aspects.

Nevertheless, the psychophysiological limitations (or faculties) persist; for example, the average distance between two stresses is limited. This does not mean a precise regularity, as the "musically" minded theorists supposed. But we cannot dismiss it when great differences occur: a great number of slacks tends to provide for a faster reading than concentrations of stressed syllables, or, at least, to be strikingly conspicuous by its wide departure from the normal.

In the field of groupings it seems to me that the evidence of poetry in all different rhythmic systems suggests an over-all rule (the details of which cannot be discussed here) that we organize the language material whenever possible into hierarchies of simple groups. Variations of similar units allow for this grouping of structures; symmetry and asymmetry, length on different levels, interplay of metric groups and language groups, overlappings, and the like, are responsible for the different rhythmic effects. By a simple group I mean a group of two or three smaller units (since two or three are not divisible into smaller groups) and perhaps also of four, which is an innerbalanced composite unit (usually $2 + 2$, but sometimes $1 + 3$). Every constant organization must be built on these principles; only local variations may deviate.

On the lowest level the matter is clear: our metrical feet consist of two or three syllables (or dipodies of such groups). A paeon tends to be read as an iambic or trochaic dipody, unless very strong factors counteract it.

Greater numbers of slacks occur only if they are not regular, that is, in free rhythms or in prose.

I cannot here go into a discussion of the highest level, the structure of stanzas, but it is clear that even on this level a regular stanza can be kept in mind (and perpetuated) only when the rhyme variations are organized so that not more than thrice is the same group repeated; (e.g., in *ottava rima* we have three groups of *ab* and then, to sum up, a couplet *cc*).

There can be several intermediate levels, and this is also true of the structure of the line. It has often been observed that a line of more than four stresses cannot be kept as a single unit and splits inevitably into two groups (**225**, p. 18). The usual explanation is that eight or nine syllables (or so) are the normal syntactical unit ("Kolon," or "syntagma;" cf. **430**, also **223**, and, in poetry, **226**). But although this may be true, it seems clear to me that the factor of grouping is decisive (as for feet where a physiological explanation is given too, but the grouping pattern seems to be the norm). Thus not all pentametric lines split inevitably into two; some can be read as a single unit, for example, "And smooth as Monumental Alabaster" (*Othello*), but this undivided pentameter (in spite of **225**) occurs only when a line can be conceived as a group of three stresses (and not five), even if these are only major stresses.

Whether this is the case in every line is unimportant. The fact remains that major rhythmic differences between poems depend largely on the respective length of the line. Two or three stresses, being essentially a single unit, cannot create a line balanced inwardly and are only a part of greater groupings. The preference for four stresses in different systems, especially in folklore, is obvious. The English pentameter enables the poem to carry content, especially in longer poems, by a constant variation of its inner groupings, avoiding the monotony of a symmetrical unit; whereas the Russians used for the same purpose a four-iamb unit, avoiding monotony by the great variation in the use of word boundaries which is possible in Russian. And so on.

Great as the differences may be, no unit can be kept in mind as a constant norm, unless it is grouped in a perceptible way. We do not remember or "feel" any constant number (say, sixteen syllables) unless it is so grouped. It has been shown (by Servien and others) that in the French classical 6 + 6 verse the organization of stresses (however slight they are) tends to be regular, iambic, or anapestic, although changing from line to line. So the poet (and the reader) does not have to count six syllables. He can feel such a unit as a simple group of simple groups of syllables (2×3 or 3×2). Such a simple group of stresses is, usually, identical with the smallest rhythmic-syntactical unit.

To be sure, these remarks need a great deal of elaboration. For our purposes the fact is useful that perceptibility is more important than constant numbers. This was probably in Tomashevskij's mind when he considered meter merely as an auxiliary device, the measure of equivalence of verse lines (**419,** p. 46).

The poetry of the Hebrew Bible—a "natural" free-rhythmic system—is built, basically, on this principle. A "line" consists of two (or seldom three) simple groups, usually parallel, or partially parallel, in their syntactic and semantic structure. These basic units are not equal; all attempts to correct the text in order to achieve strict numbers make no sense from any textual point of view. (The same is true of attempts to reconstruct exact strophes.) But there is no need of this. The rhythmic impression persists in spite of all "irregularities." The basic units almost never consist of one or of more than four stresses, that is, they are simple groups of two, three, or four stresses, which can be symbolized as *lim 4*. The stresses are strong, being major stresses of words (in a synthetic language) and being reinforced by the syntactic repetition. Thus the groups can be felt as similar, simple, correlated units. As the number of stresses in such a unit is small, they become conspicuous, giving special weight to the words.

Although no regularity of syllables is needed, the distances between stresses are made to be within a limited range by excluding two adjacent stresses and providing secondary stresses for long words.

Although modern poetry is far more complicated, the length of the line is limited here too. W. Kayser complains that the long lines of Stadler (even when metrical) are incapable of being perceived as single units. But we must suppose that at least in the poet's perception they made sense, since Stadler's long lines, as Marianne Moore's or Whitman's (with a few "explicable" exceptions), do not exceed a simple group of simple groups of stresses, that is, $lim\ 4^{lim\ 4}$. But these are the longest lines in poetry; usually we have one or two, or fewer than two, groups of different length and structure. The number of stresses in each of the correlated groups is small and thus conspicuous, which contributes to their leveling and to a tendency toward the characteristic emphasis of each word and a bringing of the local elements into prominence and into relative, temporary independence and isolation from the long linear flow of the sentence.

Under these conditions, when stresses become conspicuous they tend to a relative order, and the syllable distances between them tend to be correlated, which is one of the major tools of local rhythmic expression.

Of course, this can only be done if the meanings and syntagmatic relations of the words support it, for example, if the weight of single words is more important than the statement of a whole sentence and sufficiently independent to resist intonational subordination (the cutting off of the long waves chiefly contributes to this tendency).

As the rhythm of the poem stresses the "density" of the poetic language (Tynjanov), so does the density of an elliptical poetic language underline the poetic rhythm. It is obvious that modern poetry has explored new ways not only in the field of syllable relations but in almost all fields of poetic language. Free rhythms are only a part of these new media and can only be studied as such.

The Metrical Emblem

(abstract)

JOHN HOLLANDER

The most generally accepted contributions of structural linguistics to the analysis of poetry in particular (and literature in general) have involved the overhauling of the analytic vocabulary of metrical criticism, the analysis of the general problem of linguistic sound and sense, and the like. At the same time, some critics and theorists of literature have objected to what they feel are growing "difficulties underlying the identification of literature with its linguistic substance." In an attempt to adjudicate in the dispute between those who claim that literature consists of a certain portion of the population of all linguistic utterances (and is therefore to be identified with "its linguistic substance"), on the one hand, and those essentialists who maintain that language is literally the substance alone of miraculously animated organisms, the old and by now outmoded distinction between "meter" and "rhythm" is introduced.

This division of prosodic analytic concepts distinguishes between the normative prosodic schemata of a poetic convention or form and the actual sound patternings of that poem when interpreted in terms of an actual linguistic performance (or ideal performance based on a generalization of such performative *paroles*). The function and operation of rhythm, the second of these phenomena, has largely been the province of structural linguistics as applied to the analysis of poetry. The role of the first type of prosodic entity (e.g., a purely metrical or normative concept such as the iambic pentameter line, any instance of which would seem to be a deviant) is not as clearly defined, however. Although linguistic methods of analysis seek with some success to show how rhythmic effects can be *expressive* and can operate to reinforce and enforce *meaning*, the study of the meters, the norms, the literary conventions operating historically, has been the province of those who believe that literature is, somehow, "something more" than linguistic utterances.

An exemplary prosodic situation, the enjambment of sound and syntactic patterns across lines of a previously established order, can be shown to have both a rhythmical and a metrical effect. The analysis of a series of enjambments from various periods in the history of English poetry shows that this metrical effect operates in a fundamentally different way than does the other sort. The effects and uses of meter are seen as being "emblematic" in the sense that their function is metapoetic, is directed toward commenting on the poem itself, almost in the manner of a subtitle. This emblematic or "titling" function of meter must needs be analyzed in terms of poetic conventions and, ultimately, in terms of literary history.

The rhythmic and the metrical, like the literary and the linguistic, are thus seen as analytic modes rather than as metaphysical entities, as dimensions along which the effects of certain statements may be plotted rather than as brute "substances" and the mysterious qualities which may inform them.

This paper has been published in its entirety (**176**).

The Concept of Meter:
an Exercise in Abstraction

(abstract)

W . K. WIMSATT, Jr.

M. C. BEARDSLEY

What may be considered the traditional, or classic, account of English meter has been obscured and submerged in some recent prosodic studies. It is in need of clarifying restatement and defense.

I

We begin by presenting in a condensed form the central propositions of this classic account.

1, A poem, as verbal artifact or complex linguistic entity, is, to be sure, actualized or realized in particular performances of it—in being read silently or aloud. But the poem itself is not to be identified with any performance of it or with any subclass of performances; that is to say, not everything that a reader does to the poem in speaking it is a property of the poem itself: a speaker with a Southern accent and a speaker with a Western accent give different readings but are reading the same poem.

2. The meter of the poem is part of, or one aspect of, the sound of the poem, but, again, not every feature of the poem's sound is a metrical feature. English syllable-accent meter inheres precisely in the alternation of stronger and weaker syllables, a stronger syllable, for metrical purposes, being one that is stressed more than its preceding or succeeding syllable. The constant, or nearly constant, alternation of one stronger and one weaker syllable, for example, is both the necessary and the sufficient condition of iambic or trochaic meter.

3. The meter of a line is, consequently, verifiable in the same sense as the

pronunciation of its words is discovered in a dictionary, or by the lexicographer himself. Indeed, there may be meter in nonsense lines, if most of the syllables in these lines are recognized as combinations of English phonemes and are approximate morphemes, subject to acknowledged rules of stressing or leaving unstressed (everyone knows how to pronounce "sporkling warkle").

4. English meters, throughout the history of English poetry, fall into two fundamental types: the syllable-stress meter, the meter of the great English art tradition, in which the syllables are counted and the stressed syllables are followed or preceded by a constant number of unstressed syllables; and the strong-stress meter, the meter of the older poetry and of some contemporary poets, in which the line contains a certain number of stressed syllables of major words but the stressed syllables are associated with varying numbers of weaker syllables.

5. Since poems have other patterns than their meter—syntactic patterns, juncture patterns, and variations in the absolute (as distinct from the relative) stress of the stressed syllables—it is possible for the poet to work out an interplay between the metrical pattern and the other patterns. But this interplay cannot be felt and cannot be analyzed and discussed without discriminating the metrical pattern as such from the other patterns.

II

The foregoing five principles have not so much been openly attacked as simply lost sight of in recent studies, which have approached the problems of meter from two directions.

The *linguistic* approach was especially stimulated some years ago by the publication of Trager-Smith's *Outline of English Structure* (**422**). Trager-Smith claimed to distinguish four levels of speech stress in English speech, and it was thought that to analyze performances of poems with the help of this distinction would throw new light on meter. Such analyses are fruitful in other respects, but it is a mistake to confuse these respects with meter. For no matter how many degrees of stress it may be possible to distinguish, it is only the two basic relative degrees of stress that count in meter—the stronger and the weaker, whether the *next* syllable is stressed more or less than the present one.

The close Trager-Smith analysis of individual performances reveals many subtle variations between one reader and another, but since all the readings may be metrically correct, it is precisely the meter of the *poem* that these studies ignore for the sake of the variations in the *performances*. The case is perfectly analogous to the study of phonetic variations in the production of phonemically equivalent speech elements.

The *musical* theory of prosody has, of course, a much longer history, but it has been enthusiastically revived in recent years. This theory says that the meter of English verse has its necessary and sufficient condition in a principle of equal timing: that a discourse is metrical if and only if some recurrent segment (number of syllables or interval between stresses) is given an almost constant temporal span. It is not ordinarily noticed that this view, in any of its forms, is subject to the same objections that have long been urged against the specific attempt to describe English meter in classical quantitative terms—that is, to account for it according to the temporal length and shortness of syllables.

It may be thought that the correctness of the modern isochronic view is a purely empirical question: we need only devise stop-watch or oscillograph methods for determining whether readers of verse do in fact tend to time their strong stresses equally. At present, the empirical evidence in this matter does not seem to be conclusive, although it inclines to the negative. But in any case it is our main contention that the question is not to be settled this way. For if such equal timing ever occurs, it is part of the performance of the poem, not the poem itself—it is something that can be done to the poem, or done with it, and perhaps for some poems should be done, and for others should not. But the timing of syllables is not a part of the correctness of English speech; it does not belong to the poem as linguistic object; and it therefore cannot be manipulated into the meter of the poem. Some have championed the use of musical notation, with eighth notes and quarter notes, to describe the meter of verse. But given any such description of a line of verse, it is always possible to read the line in some other manner which violates the musical notation but preserves the same meter. The musical notation (although it may accurately and usefully reproduce a given performance) does not describe the meter.

Some of those who have supported the isochronic view with linguistic arguments have defeated their own account by maintaining that *all* English speech tends to be equally timed. Then, of course, equal timing does not distinguish metrical from nonmetrical discourse.

One further mistake that has grown out of both the linguistic and the musical approach, or a conjunction of them, should be noted here. It has sometimes been represented as a prosodic "discovery" that the typical Shakespearean and Miltonic line, always taken by misguided traditional prosodists as being iambic pentameter, is "really" not a pentameter line at all but a four-stress (or sometimes three-stress) line, like the older ballad meter. To this the prosodist should reply that it may be important and interesting to observe that many of these lines do indeed have four stresses that are stronger than the fifth. But given the Trager-Smith four degrees, or any other account of relative stress, it is always highly probable, if not inevitable, that of five stresses one will be weaker than the others. And a line is still pentameter if the weakest of the stronger stresses is stronger than the syllable that precedes it. The pattern of five relative stresses will run throughout even as long a poem as *Paradise Lost*. The pattern of four strong stresses will appear only sporadically. It may also be important that in many lines we can perceive a tension between the basic pentameter pattern and a superimposed pattern of four main stresses; to say this does not refute or outmode the classical prosody but in fact presupposes and vindicates it.

This paper has been published in its entirety (**451**).

Comments to Part Five

WELLS: In basic agreement with the view of Messrs. Wimsatt and Beardsley that meter is an abstraction, I hope to add to its support by a more precise account of this abstraction than they have undertaken to give. This precision is gained by clarifying the relationships between the metrical abstraction and three others: (1) the conventional orthography in which a language is written; (2) a language *tout court*, as contrasted with different periods, different dialects, and different speech varieties (e.g. fast and slow, calm and impassioned) of the language; and (3) the phonemic system of any one dialect of that language at any one time. My account prepares for a rigorous "logical construction" of these four abstractions using the techniques developed by Bertrand Russell.

1. *The recorded poem.* "*The* poem" is never a datum for an interpreter; what is given to him is rather some record of the poem. There is a *first* (*the original*) *record* of the poem, and there is the class of all *exact copies* of the first record. The rules stating the conditions for exactness will vary with the standard. For example, if conventional orthography is the standard, handwriting may be exactly copied by letterpress type and underscored words may be printed in italic type, but the paragraphing, use of capital letters, etc., of the first record must be preserved. Three standards will concern us here: the standard of conventional orthography, the phonemic standard, and the phonetic standard. The first standard applies primarily to written records; the second and third primarily to spoken records.

In modern Europe the first record of a poem is usually a handwritten or typewritten document written by the poet himself. (The case of Milton dictating to his daughters is unusual in these times.) We may switch mediums in the course of making copies: the switch from spoken to written language is commonly called "transcription" and that from written to spoken language "recitation" or "reading aloud." The varieties of transcription that concern us here are conventional orthographic, phonemic, and phonetic.

Relative to a given standard, copies may be exact or inexact, and two kinds of inexactness are worth distinguishing. A copy that *abstracts* in a given respect leaves out a feature falling under that respect; for example, both phonemic and conventional orthographic transcriptions of spoken language abstract in respect to voice timbre (soprano versus tenor, etc.) and so are phonetically inexact. A copy that *embellishes* in a given respect puts in something; for example, relative to both the phonetic and the phonemic standards, the distinction drawn by conventional orthography between "principal" and "principle," or between "higher" and "hire," is an embellishment.

We may now define *the recorded poem* (a more accurate but rather more cumbersome name would be *the record of the poem*) as the class consisting of the first record of the poem and all exact copies of it, and anyone who has the first record or any exact copy of it may be said to "have" the recorded poem. The relation between the recorded poem

197

and its members is that which Charles Peirce calls the relation between Type and Token. (Cf. **298**, pp. 280–281.)

2. *From the recorded poem to the poem.* Can we identify the recorded poem with the poem? Or does it at least *define* (determine, identify) the poem? If it does not, we may say that it is an *inadequate* record of the poem. This could only be true if there are two or more possible poems of which, under the recording rules in use, the recorded poem can equally well be a record. Thus the inadequacy of any inadequate record lies in its being ambiguous.

The position that I would myself take is this: the only adequate record of a poem is a class whose members are (*a*) some one phonemic transcription of a spoken recitation of the poem, and (*b*) all exact copies (spoken or written) of this phonemic transcription. (When linguists disagree about how to phonemicize a given language, their different systems are at least intertranslatable: this justifies the simplification of speaking of *the* phonemicization of the language and dialect in which the poem is composed.) I understand phonemicization to include treatment of prosodic (suprasegmental) features, namely, intonation, stress, and juncture, as well as of the segmental features called vowels and consonants.

No record of a poem written in conventional orthography is an adequate record if judged by the phonemic standard, for, at the very least, its recording of the prosody will be inadequate. It may happen, nevertheless, that from this inadequate record an adequate record may be inferred, owing to the fact that the ambiguities that make the record inadequate are resolved by appeal to the general principles of the language. Or again, it may happen that some inadequacies in the record of the poem can be surmounted with the help of external (i.e., other than orthographic) evidence in the poem. The hypothesis that successive lines rhyme may tell us that the inadequate record *read* represents /rijd/ (because it is rhymed with "deed") rather than /red/ (which it would represent if it rhymed with "bread" or with "said"). Or considerations of meaning may show us which of two phoneme sequences "read" represents by telling us whether it is a nonpast or a past-tense verb.

There remain cases in which the inadequacies of a conventional orthographic record cannot be put to rights by assumptions drawn from generalizations about the language and dialect in which the poem is composed or from hypotheses about the meaning or the meter of the poem. Sometimes the inadequacies are insignificant, other times they are serious.

The upshot of all these distinctions is this. Conventional orthography permits *fairly* adequate records; poems or lines whose conventional recording is seriously inadequate are few. But just those relatively few instances are the ones that provoke so many pages of earnest scholarly discussion. What a needless waste of energy!

3. *The poem and its meter.* I move on now to the stage where the epistemological problem has been solved. The interpreter, I now assume, has inferred an adequate record of the poem; or, at the worst, he has before him a limited set of possibilities, one or another of which must be the true one, and between which the inadequate record available to him does not enable him to choose. What he must do then is work out the meter of each of his possibilities. It may happen, as Messrs. Wimsatt and Beardsley seem to suggest, that all these different possibilities will have the same meter. When that is the case, it can fairly be said that a conventional orthographic record of the poem is adequate to the meter of the poem, even if it is not adequate to the poem. This is one of the ways in which meter is abstract.

The main way, however, in which meter is abstract is this: the meter of a poem can be determined from an adequate record of the poem by (*a*) disregarding all vowels and consonants in the record but retaining the syllable count in each line; (*b*) disregarding intonations and junctures (except that the division between lines is marked by a juncture); and finally (*c*) converting the stress phoneme of each syllable into a metrical accent according to a set of rules.

The rules used are too complicated to be described briefly, but the following crude sketch will make a beginning. These rules are stated in terms of the Trager-Smith system (**422**), with primary, secondary, tertiary, and weak stress denoted by the numbers 1, 2, 3, and 4 respectively.

Rule I. Stress 1 always counts as accented, 4 as unaccented; 2 and 3 are indeterminate.

Rule II. Stresses 2 and 3 are to be taken as accented or as unaccented, in any particular occurrence, whichever way will make the meter of the whole poem most uniform.

These rules only enable us to determine the meter which sets the norm for the poem. They may seem, and in fact are, insufficient to enable a reader to read a poem that is presented to him in conventional orthography. But this is because he has the additional problem, which I am here supposing solved, of inferring an adequate record. And what he does in practice is to cope with two problems simultaneously, the problem of inferring an adequate record and the problem of determining meter. He may use a tentative solution of one problem to help toward the solution of the other. This is what he does when he supposes a "poetic license." Poetic license is the replacement of the usual prosaic lexical form of a word by a different but similar form, for metrical purposes (meter, rhyme, etc.). Thus in the third line of "Westminster Bridge" the final syllable of "majesty "is subject to two replacements: the diphthong /ij/ is replaced by the diphthong /aj/, and (as an automatic consequence of this, since /aj/ with stress 4 does not occur) stress 4 is replaced by 3. Since stress 3 can be construed as accented (Rule II), "-esty" thus altered is fit to be an iamb and to rhyme with "pass by."

The question whether to suppose a poetic license would never confront an interpreter who had an adequate record. The question is only thrust upon him because he has to solve two problems simultaneously. He does it by using a maximization principle: among the possible interpretations of the ambiguous written record that is given him, he picks that one (if there is just one) with the most regular meter (in other words, one that maximizes the regularity of the meter). But it not seldom happens that he can find *two* interpretations, more regular than all the other interpretations but equal to each other, that deviate from perfect regularity in different ways: one by containing a poetic license, the other by containing an exception. This is the case with Milton's line "Immutable, immortal, infinite." In normal stress the syllable "in" has stress 1, "mut-" and "mort-" have stress 2, and all the others have stress 4. The result is a line whose feet are iambic, pyrrhic, iambic, iambic, and pyrrhic respectively—in other words an iambic pentameter line with exceptions in the second and fifth feet. But the conventional orthography equally represents another phonemic possibility: poetic license replacing the stress 4 of the syllables "-ble" and "-ite" by stresses 2 or 3. An adequate (phonemic) record of the poem would not confront the interpreter with the problem of inferring which phonemic interpretation is the intended one (and therefore the true one).

4. *Recitation and style.* The set topic of this conference has been style, but these comments have been about meter. What have meter and style to do with each other?

If style is individual, as opposed to what is common and general, the choice of one meter rather than of another may be a point of style on the part of the poet. But once a poem is composed and published, it is ready to be recited; and the differences between one person's recitation and another's *may* be matters of style. Thus recitational style and the metrical abstraction are complementary to each other. Different recitations of the same poem are allowable. What is common to them all includes the metrical abstractions of the poem (its meters, rhymes, alliterations, assonances, etc.); the features in which they differ include the stylistic individualities of the reciters.

But not every individual difference would usually be called stylistic; for example, the differences between a man's and a woman's voice would not, nor would the differences between different dialects. But the differences between a rapid and a slow tempo would be; so also those between a calm and an impassioned recitation, and between one that emphasized the meter and one that played it down. And then style too is an abstraction, like the poem's metrics and phonemics; for just as the poem is common to all its (admissible) recitations, so the style of a given reciter is what is common to all his recitations of different poems. The two abstractions mesh with each other like warp and woof to form the concrete fabric of recitations.

CHATMAN: I agree with Mr. Wimsatt and Mr. Beardsley that the statement "prosody can resolve the meaning" is misleading. It is not so much the meter—the abstract pattern of alternating metrical points—as the particular vocal interpretation or selection of suprasegmentals the reader makes to fulfill the metrical requirements that may, in some instances, clarify or change the meaning in characteristic ways. I have attempted in my paper to demonstrate as clearly as I could the notion that the meter of a poem must be considered one thing and the performance another.

WHITEHALL: Where I disagree with Mr. Wimsatt and Mr. Beardsley is that the English so-called five-stress line, at any rate, has never been a real five-stress line at all, in its history and even in its production. What we have is a primary stress, according to the Trager-Smith system (**422**), which is always stressed; a zero stress which is always stressless; and a variation of the other two possibilities. Usually it turns out as three or four, most commonly four.

WIMSATT: I am very much suprised at Mr. Whitehall's statement; I just don't understand it. It seems to be a statement without any new evidence adduced, and it amounts for me to no more than a truism that in a line of five stresses, understanding the metrical convention of the weaker and stronger stress, counting the line metrically, four are always bound to be stronger than the fifth. That is the nature of the thing. And so, if you insist on reading the line as an old-type strong-stress line, you can try it, but metrically you'll be defeated. It won't be as satisfactory because of the constantly recurring other patterns which are more precise and inviting. We gave one example— take Pope's line "the proper study of mankind is man" and substitute "the proper concern of *mankind is man*," and we have destroyed the iambic line because we can no longer put a stress on the word "of" because there is too strong a stress just before it. Or take any other example you like: "A little knowledge is a dangerous thing." Change that to "A little advice is a dangerous thing." Or again the example in which the student leaves out the short word, "or Shakespeare's name." Again and again, on the principle of four stresses you could drop a word out of the iambics of Milton, of Pope, and still have the four-stressed line, but it would limp horribly, just as Dryden said that many of Chaucer's verses are lame for want of half a foot because he didn't know about the extra syllable.

WHITEHALL: The reason for Chaucer's feet going that particular way is that Chaucer wasn't even trying to write iambic pentameters.

WIMSATT: Well, I would admit that the iambic pentameter of any two poets sounds very different—Wordsworth, Milton, Pope, Shakespeare, Chaucer—but it also is true that Chaucer's lines read very satisfactorily as iambic pentameter if we remember the extra syllable and employ it except for elision which makes it unnecessary, and so on;

and it seems to me, Mr. Whitehall, that the burden of proof is on you—that you are making an extraordinary and extravagant proposition, and that it wrecks a very understandable and consistent traditional situation in English meter.

WHITEHALL: English poets wrote without the benefit of metrics for centuries.

WIMSATT: It's very possible to write without the benefit of theoretical metrics and yet to write meter.

WHITEHALL: The reason I never use the word "meter" in my article is that any fool can measure the number of stresses in a line—what meter apparently means to most people. But we have another point to think about: I think rhythm is to meter as the allophone is to the phoneme; in other words, the meter is a kind of ideal scheme that we can draw out of the actual occurrences. Now I have no objection whatsoever to using the term meter in that sense. If you want to call it an iambic pentameter, I haven't the remotest objection, although I do know that this theory about English metrics was developed in the seventeenth century, on French models.

WIMSATT: Yes, the theory has changed, but this doesn't necessarily mean that the fact it was trying to describe has changed. The theory may have improved. In other types of English verse, where the strong-stress meter does prevail, we cannot observe this pattern of which I am speaking. But the meter of the poems written in the iambic pentameter tradition is very important; the rhythm is conditioned by the presence of that meter, and your saying that any fool can count a meter is just like saying, observing a man running a hundred-yard dash or a hurdle race, that any fool can stick out one leg after another. [Laughter.] O.K., but let him try running without sticking out one leg after another. [Laughter.] Now I think it is observed in our paper, and we tried to make this as clear as we could, that an understanding of iambic metrics is not a sufficient condition for reading certain kinds of poetry, but is a necessay condition for reading it, just as understanding the English language is not a sufficient condition for understanding Milton, or Pope, but is a necessary condition, and this kind of very regularly repeated convention of form certainly affects and conditions and adds to and controls all these other things that you are talking about. I'm the last person who would want to object to realizing the rhythm and its variations, but I very much doubt that it can be subjected to a system of rules or to a prosody.

WHITEHALL: I find that people schooled in what we might call the traditional metrics—iambs, trochees, dactyls, and so forth—as I was, apparently hear a counterpoint between what is allegedly the theoretical metrical scheme or the actual scheme that we use in reading. Unfortunately, or fortunately, as the case may be, I don't feel that counterpoint.

WIMSATT: Well, I think you lose a lot.

WHITEHALL: Ransom insists, for instance, on the influence of the "meters." And yet, curiously enough, Ransom counts syllables and lets the stresses fall where they may. He once told me that Gerard Manley Hopkins sounded like prose to him.

WIMSATT: That isn't the way he wrote his article (325)! He was letting the stresses fall precisely there. I like to be perfectly clear and honest and show just how simple-minded I am about these things. I maintain that when we have "Rocks, caves, lakes, fens, bogs, dens, and shades of death" and "Immutable, immortal, infinite," both of those lines are iambic pentameter, and if they are not both iambic pentameter, the contrast in their length, their speed, their weight, and all that sort of thing, loses a great deal of its interest. If we find them in a prose composition, there is nothing remarkable about it. It is just the fact that it is very agile—it is very, very gifted in a virtuoso way.

HYMES: I should like to point out that the traditional metrics can account for Pope's line, "The proper study of mankind is man," and without doing violence to normal English stress patterns as analyzed by Trager and and Smith. The only violence done is to one way of mechanically mapping stress into meter. There are four permitted exceptions to a regular flow of iambs in iambic pentameter English verse, according to Mr. Ransom (325). Three were codified by Robert Bridges, the fourth is stated by himself. It is an *ionic* foot, that is, the replacement of two successive iambic feet by a sequence of two metrically unstressed syllables followed by two metrically stressed syllables. In the Pope line, "-y of mankind" is an ionic foot. There are many examples in Shakespeare, Milton, Keats, and others. Thus this line poses a difficulty not for traditional metrics but for a contemporary rule that first describes "mankind" as having two different degrees of stress, and then prescribes that only the strongest of those two adjacent stresses can be a metrical stress (445).

HOLLANDER: I should like to comment on the notion of "counterpointing" that has already been raised. I feel that this is a confusing term. Its musical meaning implies an overlay of two similar processes, that is, melodic lines, which retain their identities rather than blending. But the flows of linguistic stress and of the entities that assign metrical prominence to a syllable (metrical stress in English) are much less alike than are two distinct melodic lines. And to speak of the simultaneous operation of the two as a "counterpoint" of one against the other can mislead us into thinking of them as being identical or similar phenomena. It's obvious that they can characterize the same syllable. But they're not the same sort of thing at all.

CHATMAN: I think I have gone to great lengths to draw a distinction between metrical accent and linguistic stress. I was for a long while confused by this problem, but now it seems to me fairly clear that there are two different systems involved. I further think, as you do, that the word "counterpoint" is misleading (as is perhaps "tension"). A better model for meter may be that of a row of slotted containers, alternating with blanks, but shiftable into certain slightly varied patterns, so long as the fundamental principle of alternation is still recognizable. These slots (metrical points) can be filled by sets of counters (the various levels of phonemic stress) in idiosyncratic ways. But the variability of slot pattern (the metrical style) should be distinguished from the variability in counter selection (which composes a part of the interpretational style, the other parts being selections of pitch patterns, junctures, and metalinguistic features). The first sort of variability is intrasystemic, the second intersystemic.

HOLLANDER: What I want to get back to is this: I think there are many ways of handling a description of something like metrical stress; for example, we might drop the Trager-Smith four-stress levels and adopt a system which requires only one phonemic stress, like that of Chomsky, Halle, and Lukoff (65). This treatment of English stress interprets the structure of the language, as far as I remember correctly, in terms of only one phonemic stress, which is not treated suprasegmentally. In such phenomena as compounds a hierarchy of *phonetic* stresses is nevertheless maintained. This is the kind of situation we have in metrics where the metrical stress and the rhythmic or actual variations correspond to the phonemic and phonetic stress patterns in the system. On the other hand, we might say that metrical stress is simply our expectation that a stressed syllable is going to occur.

WIMSATT: Yes, but it can be defeated. You can write a line that will not submit, and also by the promotion or suppression—two terms that I like very much—it can be fulfilled.

HOLLANDER: This is just what I want to get to: there are different sets of expectations. If I see an English poem printed on a page with lines of a certain length, on a page of a certain size, in a certain type face; if I happen to notice pairs of end rhymes here and there, then even without bothering to count syllables I will make a guess. I will say that these are probably pentameter lines, probably heroic couplets, even though I don't know when they were written, even though I am only glancing at the page (not *reading*, or *counting*). When a sophisticated reader reads iambic pentameter verse, his expectations are going to get more flexible the more of a total stock of iambic pentameter lines he has experienced. He is going to be aware of many kinds of variations. As a matter of fact, if he sees something like "attack attack attack attack attack," he is even going to know it's either a joke, or a heuristic model. He knows that only schemata can be metrically perfect. I would like to be able to interpret metrical stress linguistically, for I often wonder exactly what kind of entity it is.

WIMSATT: We may wonder, but I don't think we need to be skeptical of its existence.

VOEGELIN: I don't want to introduce a new topic, but I do have a question: I miss a discussion of intonation patterns.

HOLLANDER: I presume that the reason this hasn't been mentioned is that the meter of English—which has been by and large the field of most of the discussion of metrics here—doesn't schematize intonational levels.

RICHARDS: Mr. Voegelin brought up what seemed to be a lack in the discussion of intonation. I am a bit conscious of a lack of explicit reference to poems. In many problems of the sort that we have been discussing, the transformation of a line brought in by a pause may be all-important: the sort of pause that is commonly indicated by punctuation. Punctuation is one of the poet's handiest resources. There are all sorts of pauses where he wants to guide his reader. He has, normally, no such direct means, no such notation, for intonation, and so on. So I am wondering about this hay. We have a proverbial expression: "Make hay when the sun shines." With Mr. Householder, I would assume, of course, that in any reading of any fragment of a poem the whole poem, if it is of reasonable length, should be present. Here I'd like to have someone, if anyone can, recite us the Frost poem. I would be much happier then in thinking about this last line. The comments made give at least three readings . . . .

CHATMAN: Frost doesn't pause at all. That was the point.

RICHARDS: Well, I don't take the poet as is, you know. [Laughter.]

CHATMAN: The only point I was trying to make in the article (**61**) was that, as a result of listening to Frost's own reading, a meaning was suggested to me that I hadn't thought of before.

RICHARDS: But what about the future? "I left the job to do," that is, to be done. The hay is still to make. It's an awfully easy interpretation. Somebody else can do it or he himself tomorrow. There are lots of possibilities around that line.

LOTZ: I would like to come back to the problem that Mr. Voegelin raised about intonation patterns. I think we have to distinguish between those linguistic features that are relevant for the metric structure and those that are not, that is, between invariants and variants. Intonation in English is a variant feature; we can have a line with any intonation pattern and the line remains metrically the same. The same is valid for the stress pattern of English. A four-degree stress pattern in itself does not constitute any meter; the stress has to be evaluated for metric purposes. The only thing that matters in English meter is the differentiation between two types of syllabics: the heavier and the lighter. I think we have to make a difference between "suprasegmental" linguistic analysis and the metric analysis of a text.

WELLS: I should like to continue with the discussion of intonation and its place in meter. We have one case before us, at least, where intonation does pertain to meter, namely, the phenomenon of *enjambment*. Mr Hollander has quoted (**176**) from an ode of Ben Jonson's which contains an enjambment that spreads not merely between two successive lines but between the "counterturns" and the following "stand." Now if I ask myself how to read these lines, 1 can only think of two ways to do it. One way makes the word "Ben" end a sentence; conventional orthography would place a period after the word. But then as I read on and see the word "Jonson," I realize that I must go back and revise my reading, say, by putting "comma intonation" on the word "Ben." I agree with Messrs. Wimsatt and Beardsley that the change of reading does not change the meter; but it changes the *metrics*. That is, metrics, as ordinarily used, deals with more than meter.

LOTZ: I would like to go on record as disagreeing with Mr. Wells about the metric role of intonation in English. It is possible to have a counteraction between a metric scheme and an overriding linguistic rendering, such as enjambment, or strophe breaks in Horace, etc. But this can only be done if there is a well-established scheme. I don't think intonation alone would ever make it possible to delineate these lines.

VOEGELIN: In regard to Mr. Richards' remarks about pause, I can see no sensible way of treating a pause in any kind of a linguistic statement unless at the same time the intonational level before the pause is given; that is, to merely stop is sort of meaningless. The stop is either high or low, or going up or down, or something of the sort. I don't want to press the matter of intonation as a part of metrics, but I should like to ask you whether you would say, as you said about intonation also, that you do not want to include pauses in metrics.

LOTZ: I would like to add this one thing about English meter. In some poetic traditions there are tendencies to differentiate three types of syllabics, for example, in "The glory of the garden it abideth not in North," "of" has a medium stress, "glo-" a heavy stress, and "the" a light stress, etc., but this does not constitute any real systematic metric system in English, although in theory this would be possible. But even here we have to distinguish only three levels and not four, and I think a simple transfer of the phonological analysis of stress to metrics is impossible.

WIMSATT: My own feeling, and I'd like to confess it, is that in English there is a kind of continuum of stresses. I don't understand this exactly as four-level stress—it's a decision that we make. We make it for purposes of linguistics: "I will be so accurate and no more accurate. I will recognize unstressed syllables and three levels of stress, and for most phrases that will be enough." But, I'm not at all sure that there aren't cases where there are more than three levels; thus, "lighthouse keeper" is adduced as a good example in its ordinary meaning of the four levels. But suppose I say "drug store manager"; then I think there must be five levels.

STANKIEWICZ: I would like to bring up a problem which is of great interest to the linguist as well as to the poetician. The problem of meter is, of course, a problem of a selection of linguistic units as units of a metrical organization. But even the omissions within the metrical pattern are not merely a matter of individual variation but are again a linguistic problem connected with the given linguistic system. Thus the omissions within the metrical scheme in modern German, let's say, would differ from the omissions or the empty slots in the metrical scheme in modern Russian poetry. This problem has been discussed often enough. I would also like to say that if there arises the possibility of some secondary stresses which are utilized rhythmically, then, as in the case of deviations from the linguistic system, we have to tie it up with other factors that enter into poetic organizations, such as the melic tradition, for instance, the possibilities of transaccentuation or the utilization of secondary stresses which are determined by the use of music in medieval Latin poetry, or the melic tradition of folk poetry in which a certain range of freedom is permitted. In other words, I would detach the whole problem from a purely individual approach and discuss· modifications not only in terms of the metrical systems which depend on the linguistic systems, and on the other factors that determine the given rhythmic patterns and the variations, but in terms of the other subsystems that relate to poetry, such as the melic tradition or music.

WIMSATT: I don't understand your statement as a problem. I don't quite see the question.

STANKIEWICZ: All I tried to say is that, when we speak about meter and rhythm, we should not concentrate merely on the problem of individual variations, but we should relate this problem of so-called individual variations to the linguistic system itself and to the possibilities of omission of metrical stresses in terms of a given cultural tradition.

WIMSATT: I think I understand you now. Let me see if this would make sense. I thought after Beardsley and I wrote our paper that we should have said this: that our conception, at least mine, of meter is that it is made up of real linguistic elements, phonemic elements, yet such as are capable of modification. That is, if we find something that is absolutely necessary in a language, like a certain degree of isochronism, this will not constitute a meter. We would all talk in meter all the time. On the other hand, the meter must not be something that is merely prescriptive, like some quantitative element in English which can be prescribed but can't be found phonemically because it is not a part of right or wrong, in other words is not a part of the dictionary or grammar. Meter occupies this peculiar position: it is made out of linguistic objectivity, but a kind that is capable of modulation, so that a poet can use it this way or that.

STANKIEWICZ: I think it is a misconception to confuse the problem of variation with the problem of meter, as Mr. Lotz indicated here. The point is, when is enjambment possible? In what kind of metrical systems is it permitted? There are metrical systems in which enjambment is impossible. It is impossible in systems that don't have the line clearly defined. It is "liberated" for the effect of variation when the line is determined by other signals, like stress, rhyme, or intonation of the line. Therefore, it functions as an element of variation and not as an element of metrical organization. I think the problem of variation and of the constants is the basic problem in metrics. It was the point I tried to make earlier; I would now go further and say that variation is also coded to a certain extent.

WIMSATT: Yes, I agree with that. I would say that my feeling about the Ben Jonson thing is that it is pretty much an ocular joke. You couldn't pull it off except on the printed-page kind of poetry. Very often with an enjambment there is a certain kind of emphasis, lingering, and hangover which depends a great deal on the printed page. Now thinking of the poetry of Marianne Moore: this seems to me metrical only in that there is an approximate count of syllables, that is where her meter is, and it comes off because she studiously disrupts it by enjambment, curious enjambment, largely ocular. Now one more little point. Mr. Richards' question about "left the hay to make." I don't see that the questions of intonation or pauses, the various interpretations of that phrase, do affect the meter. They affect the rhetoric. It's a much better ending if you understand the stress that comes on the word "make"; otherwise it ends rather lamely, but I would insist again that none of these changes affects the meter.

CHATMAN: I have two comments to make: first, I also do not believe that intonation is relevant to English metrics, at least not in terms of the present analysis of English which separates stress and intonation as different phonemic entities. Neither, to answer

Mr. Voegelin, is pause. Even phonemic stress, as such, is not relevant if we understand metrical pattern to consist solely of arrangements of stress *potential*, rather than actual stresses. Second, there is some necessity of distinguishing between two sorts of variation: metrical, the transposition of potential points in the line, and interpretational, the changes that the individual reader rings in. Metrical displacement exists wherever it is essential, in *any* performance that hopes to preserve the obvious contextual meaning, to pronounce in a way that is contrary to the overriding arrangement of metrical points and zeros. The example I offered for this view was Donne's "Thus much I've said, I trust without offence," which requires stronger stress on "thus" in *any* performance.

WELLS: I would like to carry on with the thought that metrics in the ordinary sense deals with more than meter. We recognize metrical rules, and we recognize exceptions (displacements, as Mr. Chatman called them) to the rules, but we further recognize a higher rule governing the exception, namely, that there mustn't be too many of them. This higher rule, although not a rule of meter, is a rule of metrics. Furthermore, there are other restraints that metrics describes. The line from Donne, just quoted by Mr. Chatman, can be read with interrogative intonation: "Thus much I've said, I trust without offence?" If so read, it indicates, communicates, that you want collaboration from the person addressed. You want him to reassure you. The point I would make here is that this is a legitimate reading that is governed by a rule: lines may end with interrogative intonation, but not too many of them. And thus this very same line, if read interrogatively, illustrates two kinds of exceptions or two kinds of displacements in English. One is illustrated by "*thus* much" (trochee displacing iambus in the first foot); the other is illustrated by the interrogative instead of declarative intonation. Exceptions of both kinds are governed by the same general rule that there mustn't be too many of them.

RICHARDS: Might I add to your rule? You made it very simple: "There mustn't be too many of them." Would you like to add that there must be some reasonable occasion, some justification also? I'm thinking of the remark on kissing that the occasion should be adequate and the actuality rare. [Laughter.] When a rarity factor enters in, I think we may very often expect that it needs justification. I am tempted to suggest that sort of a rule for a great many divergencies.

WIMSATT: Although I am not sure I understood Mr. Wells, I should like to say this: Mr. Beardsley and I did try to make clear in our paper that there is a difference between what we might call substitutions or exceptions to a meter and simply tension against the meter. If we imagine a meter as down and up in a very regular way, a very even difference between the slack syllables and the stress syllables, there is always tension against the meter and, so far as I can see, there are no rules to the limits of that tension. John Donne's meter is so hard and tough that . . . he probably does "deserve hanging," and all that, but it is not the same thing to say that he multiplied the actual substitutions. The substitutions are like the trochaic first foot or the anapest and things like that, and clearly there is a limit to those. I don't know what that limit is, but too many substitutions will destroy the feeling of the meter, and we can also say that certain substitutions or violations are hardly possible at all. Thus the trochaic foot in the fourth or fifth foot of the iambic line is almost an impossibility. It simply destroys the feeling of the line. So we must be careful to distinguish these three different things. The real violation and the substitution which can be done a certain number of times must both be distinguished from the mere tension. And I would add this, that it is not at all clear to me why the trochaic substitution in the first foot is so acceptable in the iambic line. I'm never able to make up my mind whether it is because it just happened, as Mr. Ransom, I think, suggests, sort of got established, or whether there is some peculiar reason. Clearly it is more acceptable in the first than in the fourth or fifth foot, because there we are ending the thing. We don't want to be defeated. At the beginning we can stand more suspension and that sort of thing and finish out strong.

HOLLANDER: By and large, metrical terms have been, up until the past twenty years, persuasively or at least stipulatively defined. Those who have concerned themselves with the bases of meter have been interested in prescribing, in arguing for a particular style, and, implicitly, in making judgments; they have created distinctions and concepts only so that judgment of poems as examples of styles might be made in terms of them. We, on the other hand, are not interested in doing this; we are more interested in showing that we can describe the metrical "style" of a poem, or a poet's corpus, or a group of poets. We are not, I should imagine, interested in the kind of individual metrical observation typified by Ben Jonson's remark about Donne: that he "deserved hanging" for not keeping the accent. The taste of our own age insists that whatever "accent" he violated deserved as much, under the circumstances. Or we might say that we have now decided that accent is not to be as narrowly defined as Jonson meant it to be. This is one of the points where judgment comes in. It enters even at the basis of the most fundamental discriminations made.

LOTZ: I would like to say something about this problem. Since metrics involves a normative scheme, there might be violations of this norm that could be called "mistakes." For instance, in Goethe, the following hexameter with seven feet occurs: "Ungerecht bleiben die Männer und die Zeiten der Liebe vergehen." When Goethe was asked about this he recognized it as an "error" but never corrected it.

HAMMOND: In our discussion of meter and stress, something very elementary is lacking, namely, an appreciation of the subject on which Mr. Hrushovski's paper throws a good deal of light—free verse. If we admit that free verse is poetry, regular meter or stress is not by any means the distinguishing characteristic of poetry or a characteristic which should so exclusively occupy our attention when we are searching for a general definition of poetic style. Meter, stress, and any other collection of recurrent elements in poetry function, perhaps, in the same way and to the same end, because meter, alliteration, rhyme, assonance, and even metaphor all have a common characteristic—equivalence. If we could find a formula based on some general principle of equivalence in poetry, we might arrive at a broader vision of our subject, rather than at this narrow idea of style based on an examination of meter or stress alone, which seems, in the end, to become prescriptive without theoretical support and which makes poetry seem to be not much more than a sophisticated game of ticktacktoe.

. . .

CHATMAN: I have tried to use in my recent work—although perhaps not with complete success—a binary phonemic model. I want to show the existence of two systems in conflict and to allow for the fact that different people reading the same poem are inevitably going to read it differently, although they may both follow the same metrical prescription.

LOTZ: This is not relevant to the problem of meter itself, because the performance is one thing and the scheme another. Scripture tried to establish an objective English metrics on the basis of performance; he didn't get anywhere. In the same way that we are unable to deduce the phonemes from utterances without a number of assumptions, the reduction of the metric system from performance—be it phonetically or phonemically recorded—is impossible.

CHATMAN: I am not attempting to analyze English meter on the basis of performances; to the contrary (and it is apparently a point I cannot repeat often enough) the phonemic notation of a reading is *not* a metrical analysis. It is simply a way of accounting for the differences in readings, all of which may satisfy the same metrical pattern.

LOTZ: But my point is that, apart from the readings themselves, the phonemic notation includes two disparate types of phenomena. If these are distinguished we have a much more powerful model than if we don't distinguish them. These two kinds of phenomena are phonemic features and morphemic frames. If there were a one-to-one correspondence between the syntactic structure and certain suprasegmental border markers, we could replace the grammatical structure by the corresponding phonemic markers, but nobody has shown an exact correspondence. But even so, in metrics the two kinds of phenomena are treated differently: the syllabics are counted numerically and the suprasegmental features serve as frames in which the counting takes place. Moreover, there are countertendencies in verse, for example, enjambment. Therefore, the distinction between "empty" phonemic features and morphemic frames seems to be well motivated already in phonemic analysis, and this dual model distinguishing between "empty" = distinctive = phonemic, and constructional = configurational features is more powerful than a phonemic model with a single set of notions: segmental phonemes, stresses, junctures, and intonation patterns. These two types of phenomena function differently in language and in verse.

JAKOBSON: For the study of verse a phonemic transcription of a poem may be of use only if word distinction and word delimitation, word phonology and syntactic phonology, syntactic phonology and expressive features are strictly discriminated. In these conditions phonemic transcription is highly instructive, but we must remember that it disregards on the one hand the purely graphic elements and on the other the purely morphophonemic equivalences, both of which frequently play a great role in poetic form.

LOTZ: I agree basically with Mr. Jakobson. What I wanted to emphasize is that in order to get at the metric structure we need a double analytical model and not one with a single set of concepts.

·   ·   ·

CARROLL: I was much impressed by Mr. Jakobson's citing of the way in which Serbian bardsmen read their lines of epic poetry with proper stress patterns. The psychologist would want to know how these patterns are learned: are they somehow inherent in the structure of the verse itself, or are they acquired from a folk tradition? I am also wondering whether it might not be fruitful to make empirical studies of the way in which a large number of sensitive people would tend to read such lines as Drayton's "Fair stood the wind for France." To what extent will people prefer to revert to the natural patterns of speech when they are at variance with the metrical patterns? To what extent is this a matter of taste or of training?

OSGOOD: At any particular point in a verse the particular reading that occurs, the particular stress and so on, is presumably a function of some large number of antecedent determinants that, at this particular point, come to focus. Now suppose we were to make tape recordings—taking one particular line of verse on, say, four different levels. We might take a reading recorded of just that line from either, say, sophisticated readers or readers as naive as possible. Take it first as read in the actual context of the poem as it is written and punctuated and everything else; then perhaps, at the second level, take it as read when written continuously as prose. And at the third level, perhaps take it as read when the antecedent material has been translated out of its actual wording, yet preserving the essential meaning, the essential sense, of the situation in which this line occurred. And finally, just the line read by itself without antecedent context. Now if the reading of this crucial line changes particularly when we shift from the poetic structure into any of the other versions, this would suggest, to me at least, that the main effect is one of the rhythmic meter and so on. However, if the change comes when we shift from the antecedent context, even as translated, to just the line itself, this would suggest that the main determinants of a particular reading lie in the sense of the antecedent context, and not so much in anything structural or in anything about rhyme, meter, or so on. This is crude, but you see what I'm trying to get at. And further, if we compare sophisticated with nonsophisticated readers, would there be differences in where the changes in reading occur?

Grammatical Aspects
of Style

Nominal and Verbal Style

RULON WELLS

DESCRIPTION AND EVALUATION

Pronouncements about style are of two sorts, descriptive and evaluative. Description is logically prior to evaluation, in that a reasoned description is possible without evaluation whereas a reasoned evaluation is not possible without description. Some who do descriptive stylistics do it in deliberate abstraction from evaluation, that is, without the intention of proceeding to evaluate; others do the description primarily for the sake of the evaluation which they regard as the end to which description is a means.

What should be a mere distinction is widely regarded as an opposition; a division that should only divide subject from subject too often divides man from man. There is a reason for this. It is not the case, in practice, that the "describers" and the "appraisers" study the same things from different points of view. For the two intents—sheer description, on the one hand, and description conjoined with evaluation—lead to different selections. In principle the appraiser evaluates or appraises all texts, but in practice, in addition to the obvious specialties (texts in French, or English texts of the Elizabethan period, or Latin poetry), he tends to select for study the texts that he will evaluate *favorably*.[1] In particular, he is likely to shy away from spending his efforts on the meaner texts, those that do not even purport to be literature, and to concentrate on belles-lettres, which more vigorously exercise his powers. And equally, the sheer describer, who in principle describes all texts, tends in practice to focus on less pretentious texts precisely because they are less complicated. Experimentalists and statisticians, in particular, are likely to regard belles-lettres as too complicated for fruitful study. The time may come when this limitation is passed beyond, but I am speaking of the present day.

---

[1] At least to the extent of finding them interesting. A critic may pronounce the style of some poem or essay a failure but add that it is a distinguished failure, or a significant experiment, or the like.

In general, then, appraiser and sheer describer tend to study mutually exclusive phenomena or aspects. But there are exceptions. One of these is the degree to which nouns and verbs are used in various styles. Here is a variable of style at once simple and interesting. Nominal (nominalizing) style, the tendency to use nouns in preference to verbs, and the opposite verbal or verbalizing style, which tends to use verbs rather than nouns, are two features that are fairly easy to describe yet are of great interest to appraisers. Those who appraise at all mostly appraise nominal style as inferior to verbal. And yet it crops up again and again, defended on the ground that it is adapted to its purpose.

NOMINAL AND VERBAL STYLE

In this and the next two sections I shall confine my discussion to English, and to written English. The advice to shun the nominal style is sometimes put this way: "Don't use nouns where you could use verbs; don't shrink from the use of verbs." This way of putting it takes two things for granted: first, that nominality and verbality are matters of continuous degree, and second, that the continuum is characterized by the proportion of nouns to verbs in a given text. These presumptions, in turn, seem to indicate a "quantization" (quantitative measure) of our variable, by defining it as a ratio—the sort of thing that might be dubbed the Noun-Verb Quotient (NVQ). Before this indication can be precise, however, three points need to be settled.

1. What is a noun? (*a*) Shall we count pronouns and adjectives as nouns? They share many of the characters that distinguish nouns from verbs. (*b*) Shall a noun phrase count as a single noun? For example, shall "the foot of the mountain" be reckoned as containing one noun or two?

2. What is a verb? (*a*) Do nonfinite forms (infinitives, gerunds, participles) count as verbs, as nouns, as both, or as neither? (*b*) Shall a periphrastic verb like "will do" count as one verb or as two? (*c*) Shall the verb "to be" count the same as other verbs? (The feeling is sometimes expressed that the copula is not a true verb, since it has a purely logical function. On the other hand, it has person, tense, etc., like other verbs. Thus a discrepancy between its form and its meaning is felt. We might recognize this discrepancy by counting occurrences of forms of "to be" one-half, rather than one; or we might take the view that there is no quantitative way of recognizing the peculiar nature of the copula.)

3. The advice might be formulated a little differently. "Keep the proportion of nouns low and of verbs high." An index that would show

whether this advice was being followed would have two parts: a Noun-Word Quotient (NWQ) *and* a Verb-Word Quotient (VWQ). For any given text the sum of these two quotients cannot exceed 1.0 and will only equal 1.0 if there are no other parts of speech in the text, but beyond that there is no necessary connection between the two quotients. It would be interesting to determine experimentally whether there is a consistent inverse relation between them.

The problem of quantizing nominality will not be pursued further here. It might well turn out that some of the questions raised are insignificant, for example, that the NVQ of scientific writers differs markedly from that of literary writers, no matter how noun and verb are delimited. But of course these facts could only be determined by experiment, for which reflections such as those of the present paper are a necessary preamble but no substitute.

There is a further consideration of which any treatment, quantitative or otherwise, should take account. Style is understood to be optional like vocabulary, as contrasted with grammar. So far as the writer of English has a choice, what he writes is *his* diction and *his* style; so far as he has none, it is the *English* language. A treatment that respects this optionality will somehow take account of whether, and in how many ways, a sentence with a certain degree of nominality could be replaced by one with a different degree, for example, a highly nominal by a highly verbal sentence. And of course it is understood that mere variation of style is made not to alter the substance or content of what is expressed but only the way of expressing it; underlying the very notion of style is a postulate of *independence of matter from manner*. If a given matter dictates a particular manner, that manner should not be called a style, at least not in the sense that I have been speaking of. But this postulate does not preclude that a certain matter shall favor or "call for" a certain manner—the so-called fitness of manner to matter, or consonance with it.

CONSEQUENCES OF NOMINALITY

The advice to prefer verbs to nouns makes it sound as though it were a simple substitution, like the choice of familiar words in preference to rare ones, or of short words in preference to long ones. Occasionally this is so, but not in the usual case. In the more nominal phrase "the doctrine of the immortality of the human soul," the particles are different from those in the more verbal phrase "the doctrine that the human soul is immortal"; the one uses prepositions, the other a conjunction. In changing the verb of "He began to study it thoroughly" into the noun of "He began a thorough study of it," we must follow through by a corresponding change of adverb to adjective. The elementary fact of syntax that prepositions and adjectives go with nouns, conjunctions and adverbs with verbs, prevents the contrast of nominality and verbality from being *minimal.*

This fact has two consequences. (1) When nominality is evaluated good or bad, the ground may lie in whole or in part in features entailed by nominality, although distinct from it. (2) And so the nominal-verbal contrast is not a *pure dimension* of style, that is, it is not a variable which can vary without variation in the other basic factors of style.

The aforementioned consequences are necessary ones. Another class must be acknowledged, the probable consequences. From the statistical point of view, necessary consequences appear as those whose probability is 1.0, impossible consequence as those with probability .00, and the less or more probable consequences as those having intermediate probability values.

Even an impressionistic study can estimate some of these probabilities. To facilitate discussion, let us pretend—what is false, but not grossly false —that nominalizing and verbalizing sentences can be paired, so that we can speak of *the* nominal counterpart of such and such a verbal sentence and of the verbal counterpart of a given nominal sentence. The intent of this fiction is to concentrate our discussion on differences as near to minimal as is syntactically possible.

A nominal sentence is likely to be longer, in letters and in syllables, than its verbal counterpart. The greater length in the diction of those writers who favor nominal style results from the fact that the noun corresponding to the verb is likely to be longer than the verb—usually because it is derived from the verb stem by suffixes—and the entailed changes (loss of verb endings, replacement of conjunctions by prepositions, etc.) are not likely to compensate. Compare "when we arrive" with "at the time of our arrival"—fourteen letters (including word spaces) replaced by twenty-six, four syllables by eight.

Another likelihood is that the average number of clauses per sentence tends to decrease (the minimum being 1.0), for nominalization replaces conjunctions by prepositions. The sentence "If he does that, he will be sorry" has two clauses; its nominal counterpart "In the event of his doing that, he will be sorry" has only one.

A third likelihood, entailed by the second and also somewhat likely even in the absence of the second condition, is that the number of distinct sentence patterns will decrease. Compound sentences (both with coordinating and with subordinating conjunctions) tend to disappear, so that only simple (subject-predicate) sentences, more or less swollen by parentheses and modifiers, will be left.

EVALUATION OF NOMINALITY

Nominality is judged bad by some, good by others.

1. Those who judge nominal style bad judge it so for one or more of the following reasons:

a. Nouns are more static, less vivid than verbs. Sometimes this view is defended on deep philosophical grounds. For example, Étienne Gilson (**136,** p. 199)[2] sees in Aristotle's remark (*De interpretatione* 3.16b19) that "verbs in and by themselves are substantival" a revealing clue to his philosophy; not Aristotle but Thomas Aquinas is the one who gives to "is," to existence *in actu exercito*, its full due. And to the argument that the traditional, semantical definitions of noun and verb are of no avail because what one language considers an action, another may treat as a state, the rejoinder might be made that this is just the point: the contrast of action and state varies with the point of view, and one that does not reduce all actions to states is to be recommended. Something like this seems to be intended by Peter Hartmann, to whom I shall refer in the next section.

b. Longer sentences are (on the whole) less vivid and less comprehensible than shorter ones.

c. A text whose sentences are all or mostly of one basic pattern will usually be monotonous. Verbal style allows more diversity, and a good style will exploit the genius of its language.

2. Those who judge nominal style good do so implicitly, for the most part; nominal style is practiced more than preached. The implicit reasons in its favor appear to be these:

a. It is easier to write. Thus it is natural for those who are more concerned with what they say than with how they say it to choose this style, or to drift into it.

b. It helps impersonality. In scientific writing ("scientific" in the broadest sense, including philosophy, and as contrasted with artistic and literary writing), expressions of personality are frowned upon. Now personality can be avoided in various ways. One is the use of the passive voice. Where the seventeenth and eighteenth centuries would have been anecdotal—"I collected sea anemones at low tide"—the nineteenth and twentieth centuries would cast the reporting subject into the shadow of implicitness: "Sea anemones were collected at low tide." Another way to avoid personality is to avoid finite verbs altogether, by nominalizing.

---

[2] On quite different grounds some philosopher mentioned but not named by Aristotle (Physics 1.2.185b28) proposed to replace, for example, "The man is white" by "The man whites," coining a verb for the purpose if need be.

c. Nominality offers another advantage to the scientific writer. The finite verb has not only person but also number and (as does the participle) tense. Of these three dimensions tense is widely felt to be the most fundamental; similarly Aristotle distinguishing the Greek verb from the Greek noun does it on the basis of having or lacking tense (*De interpretatione* 2.16a19, 3.16b6). Now to the extent that a writer can avoid finite verbs and participles (including forms of the verb "to be"), he can avoid commitments as to tense. Indeed, it is partly because of this fact that the pairing of nominalizing and verbalizing sentences is a fiction. "At the time of our arrival" has not one verbal counterpart but two, "when we arrived" and "when we arrive."

d. The very fact that nominality is contrary to conversational style has its value. It sets off the writing as esoteric, specialized, technical. Nominal style in English can be used to play the role (although much less conspicuously and effectively) that Latin played until several hundred years ago.

Certain neutral remarks can be made about these judgments. Those who approve nominal style and those who disapprove it are not in utter disagreement. Its advocates do not claim that it is graceful or elegant, and its critics do not deny that it achieves impersonality and the rest. But after the mutual concessions, a residue of disagreement remains. It is admitted by all that verbal style is harder to write than nominal style; is it *worth* the trouble? This would raise the broader question whether good style is being urged for its own sake (i.e., as an end), or as a means to some other end, or on both grounds. Advocates of nominal style usually defend it as a means to an end; its attackers might argue that it does not achieve its end, and that for the very same end verbal style is more effective. In that case, verbal style would be preferable to nominal both as an end and as a means.

NOMINAL STYLE IN SANSKRIT AND IN GREEK

I have spoken only of noun and verb, neglecting the other parts of speech. It has been a feeling of Indo-European speakers through the ages that noun and verb are the major parts of speech; both Plato (*Sophist*) and Aristotle (*De interpretatione*) take this view, and Plutarch[3] explicitly defends Plato against the charge of neglecting the others, on the ground that they are only like the seasoning in a meat dish. It is curious that the Greeks, of all people, should have taken this view, for they had developed a syntactical device, I mean the definite article, that gave their language a

---

[3] *Moralia* 1010C (*Quaestiones platonicae 10*); cited in **73**, p. 307.

conciseness and flexibility exceeding that of any other Indo-European language. But this device will be better appreciated against the background of some other, similar language.

I pick Sanskrit because of the recent book by Peter Hartmann (**155**).[4] The underlying ideas in his books seem to be that the fundamental distinction of noun and verb is semantical, not formal; that therefore a language may have formal verbs that are semantically nouns (Japanese is his example); and indeed that possession of a true verb is very nearly a peculiarity of the Indo-European family. Against this background, the appraisal of which does not concern us here,[5] he discusses nominality in Sanskrit. Nominalization is a matter of style on the part of Sanskrit writers, which it could not be in any language which lacks a true verb; we have then the interesting phenomenon of a group of writers deliberately neglecting the feature which is most distinctive of their language family. The case is the more interesting because nominal style reaches a higher degree with them than with any other group of writers in any other Indo-European language.

One reason for this is that the verb "to be" can be omitted altogether. Omission of this verb is familiar in Greek and other languages when it functions as the copula, but the Sanskrit nominal style omits it even when it means "exists." For instance (**155**, p. 48), "tasya ca rūpavattvāt karmavattvāt ca dravyatvam [asti]," literally "of-it and from-coloredness from-activeness and materialness [exists]," that is, "And [there exists] materiality of it [sc. darkness] because of coloredness and because of activeness." A still freer and more idiomatic translation that gives the same sense is "And it [darkness] is a material because it has color and because it acts." This same example shows how other verbs are replaced, for example, "acts" by "activeness."

The teleological explanation and historical antecedents of this style are not investigated by Hartmann; but certain facts are obvious. (*a*) This style is very like the "sutra style" in which Panini's grammar, the Vedanta-sutra's of Badarayana, etc., are written, and which therefore (because of Panini's date) goes back as early as about 400 B.C. (*b*) In Panini, it seems to be designed for the sake of brevity. Not only nominality but also many other means are used to this end. Brevity, in turn, seems to have been desired, even at the price of ambiguity and obscurity, in order that the sutras might be memorized entire, and also, later at least, as an elegance. (*c*) The nominal style in question also makes extensive use of compounds. Now a fondness for compounds also marks the literary writers—poets, storytellers, and sometimes dramatists. These compounds are often

---

[4] Part of a series, along with **154, 156–158**.
[5] See a forthcoming review of the series in *Language*.

inherently ambiguous, but the ambiguity is often resolved by the context, and on the other hand it is sometimes deliberately sought as a word play. If the scientific writers do not cultivate ambiguity, at least they do not seem to mind it either.

So the phenomenon of nominal Sanskrit has not yet been explained, but its nature has been made fairly clear. Nominal Sanskrit is possible (*a*) because of the wealth of suffixes by one or another of which an abstract noun can be formed from any part of speech, and (b) because "to be," in either meaning, can be elided.

Classical Greek does not form abstract nouns with quite the freedom of Sanskrit, but it has another resource, its definite article. In fact, the singular neuter article differs formally from the Sanskrit suffix *-tva* in hardly more than this, that it precedes rather than follows what it accompanies. There is a more important semantical difference, namely that the Greek device is sometimes ambiguous. *To leukon* may mean either "the white thing" or "the color white" (**340**, 1. xcii, n. 3). But if an infinitive follows the article, there is not this ambiguity.

That Greek has here an unusual resource was a fact of which the Latin translators were keenly aware. How to translate *to einai* into Latin? Before William of Moerbeke (*ob.* 1285 or 1286), translators had simply complained; but Moerbeke *did* something: he changed the Latin language. He introduced the Romance article *le* to render *to*, and, once or twice, even introduced the possessive *del* to render the genitive *tou: ultra del esse* apparently translates *epekeina tou einai*.[6] His innovation did not stick, but it is an interesting attempt.

That noun and verb will require different definitions in different languages (or more exactly, in those in which the contrast can be found at all) is hardly a controversial proposition nowadays (**337**). The contrast of Sanskrit with Greek is meant to illustrate this fact. In Sanskrit it would be proper to count as verbal a style that used infinitives, but in Greek, owing to its versatile definite article, the infinitive when preceded by the article plays much the same role as the Sanskrit (or English) abstract noun. It is still verbal, though, in that it can have an accusative direct object where the corresponding abstract noun would require a modifying genitive. Thus not only noun and verb, but also nominal style and verbal style, would be distinguished differently in different languages.

[6] See **234**, 28a23-28b26, and 44.26; see pp. xv–xxv on Moerbeke, and p. xxii, n. 3, on the complaints of predecessors.

Decoding a Text:
Levels and Aspects in a Cheremis Sonnet

THOMAS A. SEBEOK

A folksong (like any other song), viewed as a message, possesses the characteristic property of multiple generation: its performance constitutes a concurrently ordered selection from two sets of acoustic signals—in brief, codes—language and music; and often, though optionally, from a set of visual signals (rhythmically organized movements of the body) as well. These are integrated by special rules, indeed an excess of them, which introduce a necessary redundancy serving to increase the chances of the song's being appreciated by the audience.

For the folksinger, of course, text and melody form a harmonious ensemble. Nevertheless, the bond between a specific text and tune is not indissoluble: often the same text is heard sung to a variety of tunes and, vice versa, the identical tune is found to accompany several different texts (**169**, p. 1039).

Traditionally, linguistics and musicology study, in their separate ways, the two codes in question. Such investigations must precede—in fact, are implied by—the study of the two actualized in concert; yet either code can be discovered only by repeated and systematic scrutiny of many individual messages. In attempting to explicate a particular folksong, we may approach it by either of two avenues: we may start with the text (which is sung) or the music (which is verbalized). Both approaches, taken singly, will yield some categories that are obligatory and others that are optional. A unified view must finally be applied, one that displays those additional constraints which govern the interplay of the linguistic and musicological categories, whether these are constant rules or merely tendencies of varying degrees of probability (cf. **199**). The sum total of these categories and of the rules whereby they are combinable, together with the tissue of statements about the function of this particular art form in the culture, would constitute a definition of the Cheremis folksong as a genre. "Genre should be conceived," Wellek and Warren think, "as a grouping of literary works based, theoretically, upon both outer form (specific meter or structure) and also upon inner form (attitude, tone, purpose—more crudely, subject and audience). The ostensible basis may be one or the other . . . but the critical problem will then be to find the *other* dimension, to complete the diagram" (**442**, p. 221).

In the following pages we undertake a detailed examination of one Cheremis song text.[1] Some of our resulting statements will turn out to have a high level of generality: they will be true of any linguistic sample, whether conversational ("unmarked") or poetic ("marked"), whether spoken (coded singly) or sung (coded doubly). Other statements will apply to poetic discourse (which may comprise prayers, proverbs, riddles, charms, and the like, as well as songs), but some of them will be further restricted to this one genre only. Still others may characterize only a certain group of songs, for instance, the type we shall call the sonnet. And, finally, some of our statements will concern this individual message only, and none other. Thus, when we observe that -*eš* is a morph which marks the general indicative third person singular in a given class of verbs, we describe a fact about the Cheremis language. When we add the observation that, whenever it occurs in the text, -*eš* is invariably clause-final and always preceded by no less than seven or more than nine other morphemes, we are clearly dealing with an example of "metered" language. When we discover that -*eš* occurs just seven times in an eight-line text and is absent precisely in the seventh line, we suspect that this reflects a principle underlying the organization of a Cheremis sonnet. When, at last, we remark that the sequence of four morphemes immediately preceding each instances of -*eš* is constant throughout and also identify the actual members of this repeated sequence, our statement relates to this particular message. (The precision with which we are able to assign a statement to its appropriate level of generality in the hierarchy increases, of course, as we approach a sampling of messages which is "adequate," in a statistical sense; see **356** and **364**.)

. . .

The text we propose to deal with here has been taken down twice from the lips of a thirty-two-year-old farmer. The first version was sung, and so

---

[1] On the Cheremis, and the corpus in question, see **360–363**. This paper represents a substantially revised version of **357**. A Fellowship from the John Simon Guggenheim Foundation and National Science Foundation Grant G5556 are supporting different aspects of my current research in problems of linguistics and poetic language.

recorded by a musicologist; the second version was dictated to, phonetically transcribed, and translated (into Hungarian) by a linguist. The two versions are identically represented (**238**, pp. 21 and 81–82).

The informant hailed from the Cheremis village of /iadəkplak/ (in Russian, *Serednyj Jadykbeljak*) and thus spoke the dialect of Uržum, which belongs in the Central Eastern group, or /olək mari/. The phonemic inventory of this dialect, systematized in terms of distinctive features, was given in an earlier article (**359**). The text, now retranscribed phonemically, reads as follows:

iumən kükü ačam kodəldaleš; kükü šuldər abam kodəldaleš; iumən barseŋge izam kodəldaleš; barseŋge šuldər iəŋgam kodəldaleš; keŋež ləbe šol'əm kodəldaleš; ləbe šulder šüžarem kodəldaleš; keŋež saska ške kaialam, saska peledəšem kodəldaleš.

In accordance with the notion of *level*, introduced earlier, it is convenient to establish the foundation for the analysis of the metric system of this text by a prior description of its linguistic organization, or glottic system, in the wider sense. Both levels can then best be studied in two *aspects*, in terms of units that are meaningless, and those that are meaningful. These distinctions yield four groups of topics to be discussed: phonemes, distinctive and configurational features; morphemes; rhythm and meter; images, metaphors, symbols, and the like.

The text, as printed, consists of a string of letters interrupted by spaces and punctuation marks. The letters, of course, bear a one-to-one relation to the phonemes, and the spaces and punctuation marks stand for configurational features of several sorts.

Three kinds of punctuation marks occur: comma (,) and period (.) each once, and semicolon (;) six times. Semicolon and period are allographs, that is, they are different representations of the same juncture (cf. **20**). The former is to be found in text medial, the latter in final position; this grapheme stands for what we have elsewhere (**359**) called terminal (or *A*) juncture. The comma represents suspensive (or *B*) juncture, in opposition to open (or *C*) and close (or *D*) juncture within those groups.

Our sources do not specify the phonetic values of the punctuation marks utilized, but such information is not germane to our purposes. We can discriminate "-etic" graphs from "-emic" ones (cf. **312**, especially ch. 2), and we know that each of the four just identified is opposed to each of the remaining three. We propose to use junctures as border markers in order to delimit frames within which metrically relevant counts can be made. Thus in terms of *A* seven major frames are established, or with *B* as well eight; a frame ending in *A* or *B* will be called a line. A line-by-line transcription yields a form more traditional in appearance:

1. iumən kükü ačam kodəldaleš.
2. kükü šuldər abam kodəldaleš.
3. iumən barseŋge izam kodəldaleš.
4. barseŋge šuldər iəŋgam kodəldaleš.

5. keŋež ləbe šol'əm kodəldaleš.
6. ləbe šuldər šüžarem kodəldaleš.
7. keŋež saska ške kaialam,
8. saska pedəšem kodəldaleš.

Each line, or major frame, is next represented in analytical transcription, that is, as resolved into seven components, manifested in varying proportions at different points in the text (**359,** p. 431 and fn. 4). The assumption here is that the quantitative pattern of the distinctive features of a poetic text deviates significantly from that of the "normal" pattern, that is, the distribution which prevails in the language in general. Each text, furthermore, will presumably be characterized by its individual componential profile, shown in Table 1.

A sequence delimited by an *A* juncture is called a sentence if it includes, minimally, one nonsubordinate clause. The text contains six such minimal, that is, one-clause sentences; these correspond, respectively, to lines 1, 2, 3, 4, 5, and 6. The remaining two lines, 7 and 8 together, correspond to the seventh sentence which, however, is more complex than any of the preceding six, since it consists of two coordinate clauses.

There are several types of clauses in the language, the most common being the predicate clause. This is a sequence delimited by a juncture higher than *C* and including a finite verb (or certain equivalents). The text contains eight predicate clauses, each of them corresponding to one line.

Every predicate clause may be divided into two immediate constituents, the subject-predicate phrase and the expansion of the subject. In turn, each subject-predicate phrase may be divided into two immediate constituents, the predicate and the subject. The predicate, in each of the eight phrases, consists of one finite verb, which functions as the action. The subject, throughout, is a single substantive, which is marked for first person, either lexically (7) or grammatically.

In the last clause only, the expansion of the subject proper is a substantive, /saska/, which forms, with the immediately following subject, an attribute-head construction. In each of the preceding seven clauses, however, the situation is more involved: the subject proper, together with its expansion, form a paratactically coordinated substantive construction which stands, as a whole, in an actor relationship vis-à-vis the action (predicate). The expansion itself consists of a substantive which functions as the head, preceded by another which functions as the attribute; the latter is either in the genitive (1, 3) or in the nominative. Furthermore, the word which

Table 1

```
1.                   i u m ə n k ü k ü a č a m k o d ə l d a l e š
Vocalic              + + - + - - + - + + - + - - + - + ± - + ± + -
Compact              - - - ± - + - + - + + + - + ± - ±   - +   ± +
Grave                - + +   - -       + -         - -
Flat-sharp           - +       + +         +           - -
Tense                + + -   + + + +   +   + + - -   - +   + +
Continuous-strident          - -     ±     - -       + -   + +
Nasal                  + + - -     + - -       -

2.                   k ü k ü š u l d ə r a b a m k o d ə l d a l e š
Vocalic              - + - + - ± - + ± + - + - - + - + ± - + ± +
Compact              + - + - + -   - ± + - + - - + ± - ±   - +   ± +
Grave                  - - + -       + + + -         - -
Flat-sharp             + + + -             +         - - -
Tense                + + + + + +   - -   + - +   + + - -   - +   + +
Continuous-strident  - - + + -   -         - - + -   + +
Nasal                - - - -       - + -         -

3.                   i u m ə n b a r s e ŋ g e i z a m k o d ə l d a l e š
Vocalic              + + - + - - + ± - + - + + - + - - + - + ± - + ± + -
Compact              - - - ± - - +   - ± + + ± - - + + ± - ±   - +   ± +
Grave                - + +   - +       - +   - - -       + -       -
Flat-sharp           - +             - -   - -             +       - -
Tense                + + -   - +   + +   - + - +   + + - -   - +   + +
Continuous-strident            - +     -       +     - -   + +   + +
Nasal                  + + -     -   + -         - + -         -

4.                   b a r s e ŋ g e š u l d ə r i ə ŋ g a m k o d ə l d a l e š
Vocalic              - + ± - + - - + - ± + ± - + ± + - + + - + - - + - + ± - + ± + -
Compact              - + - ± + + ± + -   - ± - ± + + + - + ± - ±   - +   ± +
Grave                +     - - +   - +     - +     - + +     + +       -   -
Flat-sharp                 - -   + -         - +     - +             + -   - -
Tense                - + + + - + + +   - -   + -   - + + + - -   - +   + +
Continuous-strident    - +   - + + -   -       - -   - + -   + +
Nasal                -   - + - -           - + - -       -   -

5.                   k e ŋ e ž l ə b e š o l' ə m k o d ə l d a l e š
Vocalic              - + - + - ± + - + - + + ± - + - + - + ± - + ± + -
Compact              + ± + ± + ± - ± + ± ± - + ± - ±   - +   ± +
Grave                - + -       + - + + + -         - -
Flat-sharp             - - - -       - + +       +           - -
Tense                + + + - -   - + + + -   + + - -   - +   + +
Continuous-strident  -   + +       + +       - +   + +
Nasal                - + - -   - + - -       -

6.                   l ə b e š u l d ə r š ü ž a r e m k o d ə l d a l e s
Vocalic              ± + - + - + ± - + ± - + - + + ± + - - + - + ± - + ± + -
Compact              ± - ± + - - ± + - + + + ± - ± - ±   - +   ± +
Grave                + - + -   - +       - + + -         - -
Flat-sharp           -   - + -       +       + -         - - -
Tense                - - + + + - -   + + - + +   + + - -   - +   + +
Continuous-strident  +     + + - - + +   - -       + -   + +   + +
Nasal                - - -     -       - + - -       -

7.                   k e ŋ e ž s a s k a š k e k a i a l a m
Vocalic              - + - + - - + - - + - + - + - + + + ± + -
Compact              + ± + ± + - + - + + + + ± + + - +   + -
Grave                  - + -   - -   -             - +
Flat-sharp           - - -     -     -   -
Tense                + + + - + + + + + + + + + + + +   +
Continuous-strident  -       + + + - + -   -         +
Nasal                -   + - - - -   - -             +

8.                   s a s k a p e l e d ə š e m k o d ə l d a l e š
Vocalic              - + - - + - + ± + - + - + - + - + ± - + ± + -
Compact              - + + + - ± ± - ± + ± - ±   - +   ± +
Grave                - -   + -   - -     - +   + -
Flat-sharp           - -       - -       -         +       - -
Tense                + + + + + + +   + - - + +   + + - -   - +   + +
Continuous-strident  +   + -     +   +     - +   + +   +
Nasal                - - -   -       - + -   -
```

functions as the head in lines 1, 3, 5, and 7 shifts to the attribute function in lines 2, 4, 6, and 8, respectively.

Word limits are compulsory at *A* or *B* junctures and are delimited, also, at *C* junctures. In this text, every word bounded by either an *A* or a *B* is a verb, and every word bounded by a *C* is a substantive; (particles, the third Cheremis formclass, are not represented). In the last clause there are three words, and there are four in every other.

The last word of a clause is a verb, of which only two tokens occur: /kai-al-am/ 'I go' (7) and /kodə-ld-al-eš/ 'remains' (elsewhere). Three subclasses of substantives are used: one pronoun, eight general nouns, and six kinship terms. The pronoun is the reflexive /ške/ 'ego, self.' The general nouns are /barseŋ-ge/ 'swallow,' /iumə-n/ 'sky's,' /keŋež/ 'summer,' /kükü/ 'cuckoo,' /ləbe/ 'butterfly,' /peled-əš-em/ 'my blossom,' /saska/ 'flower,' and /šulder/ 'wing.'

Elementary kinship terms in this language constitute a partial formclass and may be expanded into a full distribution class in the following manner. There is a derivational suffix, *-i*, which functions as a vocative occurring only with substantives designating persons conceived in the culture as relatives older than ego (/ške/). To this formclass belong, for instance: /ača/ 'father,' /aba/ 'mother,' /iza/ 'elder brother, father's younger brother,' /iəŋga/ 'wife of elder brother, wife of father's younger brother,' etc. Each member of this formclass stands in reciprocal relation with some other substantive designating a person conceived as a relative younger than ego, as, for instance, /šol'ə/ 'younger brother' (reciprocal with /iza/), and /šüžar/ 'younger sister' (reciprocal with /aka/ 'elder sister'), and the like. Although the junior reciprocal substantives make no distinction between addressing in contrast to referential form, they constitute, with the members of the formclass which do, the total distribution class of kinship terms.

In the foregoing paragraphs, all the roots found in this text have been glossed; it remains to provide a list of the suffixes.

Derivational, noun forming—added to nouns: *-ge* (7:1.2,1.), as in /barseŋ-ge/; added to verbs: *-əš* (6:1.1.), as in /peled-əš-em/; verb-forming—added to verbs: *-al* (1:2.1.), as in /kai-al-am/ and /kodəld-al-eš/, and *-ld* (5:2.2,2.), as in /kodə-ld-aleš/.[2]

Person—1st sg.: *-m* ∼ *-em* ∼ *-am*, as in /ača-m/, /aba-m/, /iza-m/, /iəŋga-m/, /šol'ə-m/, /šüžar-em/, /peledəš-em/, /kaial-am/; and 3rd sg.: *-eš* as in/ kodəldal-eš/.
Case—genitive: *-n*, as in /iumə-n/.

---

[2] Parenthetic references in this paragraph correspond to sections of **279.**

In poetry, *-al* and *-ld* usually occur as phoneme sequences devoid of glottic meaning, but they do function on the metric level to isochronize relevant units, namely lines.[3]

We conclude this section with a translation of the text:

1. Sky's cuckoo, my father, remains.
2. Cuckoo wing, my mother, remains.
3. Sky's swallow, my elder brother, remains.
4. Swallow wing, my elder brother's wife, remains.
5. Summer butterfly, my younger brother, remains.
6. Butterfly wing, my younger sister, remains.
7. Summer flower, myself, I depart,
8. Flower blossom of mine remains.

. . .

In glottic analysis, the text was segmented into its constituent parts, and the segments obtained were described and classified. In metric analysis, to the relevant segments—those previously obtained and such additional ones as may be needed—quantitative criteria are applied.

The first aim is to focus on those aspects of the phonic material—distinctive features, phonemes, and syllabic pulses—which recur, with numerical regularity, in various meaningful frames. In other words, we must specify: what unit is repeated, how often, and within what larger segment.

The maximum semiotic frame is the song text (equivalent to the utterance, on the glottic level). It is divided into eight lines (equivalent to the clauses), the last two of which form a line pair (corresponding to a sentence). It will be convenient henceforth to refer to this line pair as the *envoy*, in contradistinction to the six preceding lines, which may together be called the *sestet*.

Matching the grammatical immediate constituent analysis, each line may be divided into two (line-) members: the first member, in each line, consists of the first and second word of the line; and the second member, of the last word plus—except in the last line—the last but one. It is illuminating to reconsider the organization of the line as a sequence of slots, I, II, III, and IV. Slot IV is filled, throughout, by the finite verbs which are, syntactically, predicates. Slot III is taken up either by the subject proper, which is always inclusive of the first person singular marker (*a*) inherent in the root (/ške/, in 7) or (*b*) suffixed to a kinship

[3] One of Y. Wichmann's informants, the Cheremis schoolmaster G. Karmazin (**224**, p. 383), observed that elements such as these are provided "mit der besonderen nuance des schmeichelnden, zärtlichen." Ransom's happy phrase (**325**, p. 468), "mostly a sentimental qualifier, a warmth of language," seems to apply.

term in each line of the sestet; or by the first person singular suffix of a stem which itself belongs to slot II (8). Slot I is occupied by the first general noun which always functions as the attribute to the second general noun occupying slot II. It will be noted that the same word which fills II in an odd-numbered line fills I in the next even-numbered line. The division of the line into two members each corresponds, in general, to the division into slots I–II and III–IV, respectively; but, in the last line, the middle word has an equivocal status: the stem belongs to II, but the first-person-singular marker to III. Table 2 is a graphic representation of the analysis in terms of slots.

Table 2

	I	II	III	IV
1	iumən	kükü	ača-m	kodəldaleš
2	kükü	šuldər	aba-m	kodəldaleš
3	iumən	barseŋge	iza-m	kodəldaleš
4	barseŋge	šuldər	iəŋga-m	kodəldaleš
5	keŋež	ləbe	šol'e-m	kodəldaleš
6	ləbe	šuldər	šüžare-m	kodəldaleš
7	keŋež	saska	ške	kaialam
8	saska	peledəš-	-em	kodəldaleš

The componential profile of a text can be obtained by simple arithmetical operations derived from the data given in the line-by-line analytical transcription. Table 3 provides the percentages of phonemes (ϕ) distinguished by any one feature in any one line:

$$\left(\frac{[\Sigma_{(+)} + \Sigma_{(-)} + \Sigma_{(\pm)}]100}{\Sigma\phi} \right)$$

Table 3

Distinctive Feature	Line							
	1	2	3	4	5	6	7	8
Vocalic	100	100	100	100	100	100	100	100
Compact	91	83	89	83	83	78	95	88
Grave	48	42	59	47	46	41	40	50
Flat-sharp	35	33	37	33	42	37	35	42
Tense	74	79	74	73	71	74	85	83
Continuous-strident	39	50	37	47	46	48	45	50
Nasal	43	42	44	43	42	37	50	46

These figures reflect the profile of one message only, and are, therefore, purely descriptive. To discover what is metrically relevant—that is, to find out how the figures deviate from percentages characteristic elsewhere in the language, whether the frequencies are higher or lower than would be expected by chance—the profiles of many similar messages must be established and compared. This research—involving, as it does, not only questions of a purely linguistic character but numerical considerations as well—is being carried out with use of a general-purpose digital calculator and peripheral equipment. The underlying logic which led us to recast experimentally the structural model of language in terms of machine language, together with a sample of hypotheses being tested, are reported elsewhere (**356**); and so are the results of two pilot projects which had hitherto been successfully carried out (**364**).

Although a full identification of the obligatory categories must await completion of the machine processing, it is possible to observe, if not to interpret with finality, certain tendencies in the system as pictured in Table 3. One such trend is toward covariation for the numbers of phonemes distinguished by any two features. Thus, when the number for the grave feature decreases from 48 to 42 between lines 1 and 2, there is a corresponding drop for the flat-sharp feature from 35 to 33.

Feature-by-feature componential profiles can also be derived from the data. For example, the following is a representation of the text showing the distribution of the grave feature only:

```
1   − + +     −    −     −        +     + −      −        −      ·
2       −     −    +     −        +    +    + −        −        −    ·
3   − + +     − +        − − +    − − −    + +  + −        −      − ·
4   +      − − +      −     + −      −    + −    + + −        −    − ·
5     − + −        + −    +      +    + −      −        −      ·
6      + −    +    −      −        − +  + −      −        −    − ·
7   − + −     −    −           −        −    +,
8   −     −      + −    − −      − +    + −      −        ·
```

Inspection of this message component indicates a sharp decrease in the ratio of (+) to (−) signs for lines 7 and 8 (.33) as against the ratio for lines 1 through 6 (.67).

The study of distinctive features for metrical purposes can be further refined by focusing on their distribution in frames smaller than the line, for instance, in members. The following example represents the text in terms of the continuous-strident feature, with members set off by parentheses:

1	(OOOOO −O −O)	(O ±OO −O −O + −O +O +)
2	(−O −O +O + −O −)	(OOOO −O −O + −O +O +)
3	(OOOOOOO − +OO −O)	(O +OO −O −O + −O +O +)
4	(OO − +OO −O +O + −O −)	(OOO −OO −O −O + −O +O +)
5	(−OOO + +OOO)	(+O +OO −O −O + −O +O +)
6	(+OOO +O + −O −)	(+O +O −OO −O −O + −O +O +)
7	(−OOO + +O + −O),	(+ −O −OOO +OO)
8	(+O + −OOO +O −O +OO)	(−O −O + −O +O +)

The ratio of phonemes distinguished by this feature is somewhat lower in the first member ($37/89 = .42$) than in the second member ($54/110 = .49$). More interestingly, the proportion of "yes" as against "no" responses in terms of this particular feature is roughly constant for the second members (1, 1, 4/3, 3/4, 4/3, 5/3, 1, 1) but increases from the beginning to the end for the first members (0/2, 1/2, 1/2, 3/4, 2, 3/2, 3/2, 2).

The metric significance of phoneme or phoneme sequence repetitions is a function of their position with respect to various junctures. Conventional terms, like alliteration and rhyme—or, more precisely, perhaps, the classical figure of homoeoteleuton—"similar endings," in consequence of morpheme repetition, commonly at the end of parallel clauses (**450**)—may be applied, for example, to recurring identities in, respectively, word-initial and line-final positions.[4] Alliteration groups into three sets the words occupying slot III: /a-a/ (1–2), /i-i/ (3–4), and /š-š-š/ (5–6–7); the endings also constitute a kind of internal rhyme, which includes the /əm/ in 8 but jumps, in 7, to the end of slot IV. Homoeoteleuton binds the lines of the sestet with one another and with 8 (each -*A*), while, at the same time, the uniqueness of 7 (-*B*) is emphasized. The repetition of phoneme sequences which are also words may be called, in nonfinal position, echoing. This phenomenon may be observed in slot I, which is, in fact, filled exclusively with echoed sequences. These are repeated either from a previous instance in the same slot or the next: /iumən/ (1, 3) and /keŋež/ (5, 7) illustrate the former; and the regular alternation between adjacent odd- and even-numbered lines from II to I, as has already been noted, illustrates the latter.

The distribution of syllabic pulses in the relevant frames is as follows: a word boundary comes after no more than four pulses, a member boundary after no more than seven, a line boundary after no more than eleven, and the text ends after 81. Only one word, the pivotal /ške/ "ego," is monosyllabic,[5] and all the rest range from two to four syllables. The number of pulses per member ranges from four to seven, such that, in the sestet, the number in the first is always smaller than in the second, whereas, in line 7, the two are identical and, in line 8, the proportions are reversed: (4 + 6), (4 + 6), (5 + 6), (5 + 6), (4 + 6), (4 + 7), but (4 + 4) and (6 + 4). In lines, the range is from a minimum of eight (7) to the stated maximum (3, 4, 6), with the majority numbering ten (1, 2, 5, 8); no line has nine.

---

[4] A study of alliterative tendencies, shown by the extent to which the initial phonemes in a large sample are not distributed at random, appeared in *Lingua* 8.370–384 (1959) after this book was already in press.

[5] In the sung version, this word might have been dissyllabic, /ᵊške/, but the original transcription does not indicate it. Should our guess be correct, the counts below would need to be slightly adjusted.

If meter is the arithmetical norm, the code, a purely theoretical construct, the sum of its controlled manifestations in this or that particular message may be called its rhythm. Rhythm thus refers to the concrete organization of the material in its phonic aspect, governed by some obligatory rules as well as tendencies to conform to (or deviate from) the norm. The rhythmic system, furthermore, is informed with meaning, a fact that gives rise to the next set of problems to be considered: the semiotic system of the text and how that interrelates with the phonic organization.

This text achieves its thematic unity from the correlation and interlacement of certain pairs of signs. The terms in any given dichotomy are either equated, the minor mode of arrangement; or they are in opposition, the predominant process used. Equations, which occur across members within the same line, are metaphoric; but oppositions, which move from line to line, are metonymic. The pairs themselves are grouped in a multidimensional climactic development which mirrors the hierarchic arrangement of the rhythmic units.

In each of the first seven lines, the subject proper is equated, by paratactic coordination, with its expansion; similarity connects the metaphorical term with the term with which it has been made commutable. The equation becomes still more general, that is, inclusive of line 8, when expressed in slots: $(I + II) \equiv III$. Before examining this formula more closely, it will be useful to inspect the content of both the left side and the right side.

The terms on the left side constitute a class of living things, exclusive of human beings. The members of this class resolve into sets of paradigm-like lexical oppositions, of three degress of inclusiveness: flora (/saska/ 'flower,' in the couplet) versus (alar) fauna, which divides into insect (/ləbe/ 'butterfly,' 5–6) versus birds, which, in turn, divides into swallow (/barseŋge/, 3–4) versus cuckoo (/kükü/, 1–2). The habitat of the butterfly and the flower is specified temporally (/keŋež/ 'summer'), as against the spatial identification of that of the birds (/iumən/ 'sky's').

Another dichotomy then crosscuts all of these. A proportion is established where the wing (/šuldər/) is to the creature as the blossom (/peledəš-/) is to the fruit. This is a transverse synechdoche, where the *pars* in the even-numbered lines stands *pro toto* in the odd-numbered lines.

The foregoing variety of contiguous relationships may finally be reduced to a single underlying dichotomy: superordinate versus subordinate. Each member of the class is superordinate to each successive member, and vice versa.

The terms on the right side, as those on the left, constitute a class of living things; but although the latter excludes human beings, the former consists of elementary kinship terms possessed in the first-person singular (in the sestet), the term for ego (7), and the first-person-singular possessive ending (8).

Four criteria of kinship classification (*a–d*) are accorded recognition in this text. A fifth component (*e*) can also be isolated, but its value is purely poetic. One term, /ieŋga/, names a secondary and affinal relative; all others are primary and consanguineal, except that /iza/ is ambivalent as regards inclusion in the nuclear family.[6]

a. The singer is a male, as we know from the external data. This male ego, who appears twice overtly in the envoy, is distinguished from his six relatives mentioned in the lines of the sestet. The relation of self versus alter is itself explicitly signaled by the morpheme *-m ∼ -em ∼ -am.*

b. The category of sex fragments adjacent lines in the sestet: the odd-numbered ones are "male," in contrast to the even-numbered ones which are "female."

c. The principle of generation aligns ego's own against the first ascending one, to which both his parents (1–2) belong.

d. Difference of age within ego's generation sets off line 3 and (by implication) 4 as older than ego, on the one hand, and lines 5 and 6 as younger than ego, on the other.

e. Finally, the two references to ego in the envoy can be contrasted as full form (7) versus a purely relational expression (8).

The foregoing fragmentary kinship system may also be transformed, by a simple operation, into a single, basic dichotomy: superordinate versus subordinate. As we have shown, slots I–III are filled entirely with signs denoting objects in nature, such that these are human in III but nonhuman in II. Line by line, then, the content of I–II is made equivalent with— becomes a metaphoric substitute for—that of III. Each human being acquires a natural symbol: "my father" is likened to "sky's cuckoo," and "my mother" to "cuckoo wing"; "my elder brother" to "sky's swallow," and his wife to "swallow wing"; "my younger brother" to "summer butterfly," and "my younger sister" to "butterfly wing"; finally, "myself" to "summer flower" and "flower blossom." It is a

---

[6] With respect to criteria *c* and *d*, the position of /iza/ is, more precisely, transitional. The term refers, at once, to ego's father's younger brother and ego's own elder brother; cf. U. Harva's remark that "it is a very common custom" among Finno-Ugric peoples "that the same designation is used for the elder brother and for the father's younger brother, especially as the latter is older than the speaker . . . ," in **159**, p. 57. Our translation as sibling rather than as paternal uncle is arbitrary, since the Cheremis word, of course, ignores this distinction. The interpretation of /ieŋga/ then depends on the translation value assigned to its male counterpart. For a fuller discussion of the latter, particularly sensitive, Cheremis kinship term, see **358**.

consequence of this set of equations that whatever relationships were found to prevail on the left side will also prevail on the right side: for instance, as the cuckoo (the whole) is to its wing (the part), so "my father" is to "my mother"; or as the flower is to its blossom, so the full expression for ego is to its reduced form; and so forth. It will be seen that as all male kin are likened to a winged creature, so all corresponding female kin are likened to the wing of the respective bird or butterfly: as the whole is to the part, so is the male to the female. Category *b*, which figures as a synechdoche, furthermore, stands in complementary distribution with another actualization of the same figure, category *e*: as the whole is to the part, so is the full (lexical) presence of the ego to the mere trace of the self. The two categories are thus also variants of the superordinate versus subordinate dichotomy.

The order in which the couples are introduced is far from fortuitous: members of the older generation precede one's contemporaries, among whom the elder come before the younger—the order of respect dictated by the culture (**159**, pp. 56–60). These two oppositions—ego's parents to his coevals and his seniors to his juniors—once again exemplify the basic dichotomy.

One dyad remains to be observed, namely the content of slot IV. Here we find two antonyms, the Cheremis root for "depart" (7) and its opposite for "remain" (in all the other lines). This lexical contrast between rest and motion, permanence and change, is reinforced by the endings: the source expressly participates in the communication ("I depart") versus the six third persons in the sestet on the one hand, and his subordinate self (8) on the other (he or she or it "remains").

We must now raise the very same question that has often been asked about myths, and other forms of oral literature, the world over: why is this text—as are, indeed, Cheremis song texts in general—so much disposed to multiplication (if not identical repetition) of the same basic opposition? The striking answer was given, in another context, by C. Lévi-Strauss (**248b**, p. 65). To paraphrase him: repetition has as its function to make the structure of the song apparent; the structure "seeps to the surface, if one may say so, through the repetition process."

What is the message this folksinger is conveying? With the diagram completed—"outer" and "inner" dimensions in balance—and with the added support of the following piece of external information at our disposal, an attempt can be made to restate the text. The singer's explicit involvement is an earmark of the lyric monologue, of the so-called Cheremis "traditional" song. The collectors tagged this one as to its function: it was classified with the sizable group of "recruit's songs," associated with one of the acutest traumas in the life of a Cheremis youth—the poignant occasion of his induction into the Russian army, when he is wrenched from amidst his relatives and removed far from his home.

The song sounds one of the most conventional of romantic themes. The sestet pictures man and nature in harmony, the family circle and its village environment coadunate. The images are symbols of order and stability: they are permanent, they "remain." The envoy's preoccupation with the self is also in the romantic vein: "I," too, belong in the landscape, am of nature, and have my proper place in my family. Yet must "I depart." But there is a seeming paradox here: the flower of summer passes away, but its blossom, its essence, "remains." Even so, the outward form of "myself" departs, but (the singer concludes) my essential inward being—my thoughts of you and your memory of me—stays here at home.

Upon a more elevated plane, the song is about death and its denial, immortality, a distillation of the same cultural experience as is epitomized by another instrument in the Cheremis folk repertoire, a proverb: "A man dies, his name remains."[7]

Although superficially different, the present song fundamentally resembles, both in over-all form and theme, a song similarly analyzed at another occasion (**359**). That song we characterized, casually, as a kind of "primitive sonnet." Both of these songs belong with the devices of Cheremis folk literature which some Russian scholars have called (somewhat inaccurately) *protjažnaja pesnja*, a phrase we prefer to render as 'traditional songs' (**362;** cf. **29, 236**). In this large group, "sonnets" constitute a well-defined type. Our use of the term "sonnet," however, calls for an explanation. It is employed here in its genetic sense: the Cheremis vehicle is strongly reminiscent of the medieval Sicilian strambotto, out of which the sonnet familiar to Western literary tradition

---

[7] In **363**, proverb No. 8.3.3. A native Cheremis, Karmazin, **224**, pp. 380–381, gives a moving account of feelings generated among his people at occasions when songs such as the one analyzed here are sung: "Es ist zu bemerken, dass das soldatenleben in Russland eine der allerdrückendsten erscheinungen für die bewohner, besonders für die 'fremdstämmigen' ist. Muss doch der mann seine blühendsten jahre fern von der heimat mit der waffe in der hand unter ständiger harter militärischer disziplin verbringen. Wie ich sagte, ist das soldatenleben besonders schwer für den 'fremdstämmigen.' Im allgemeinen können die 'fremdstämmigen' nicht russisch sprechen, infolgedessen sind sie nicht imstande, alle kommandos und befehle der offiziere genau auszuführen, und mussen sie verschiedene strafen und massregelungen bis zur auspeitschung über sich ergehen lassen. Dabei versteht es sich von selbst, dass die 'fremdstämmigen' und unter ihnen die tscheremissen nicht besonders gern in den militardienst treten und auf jede weise versuchen, sich der dienstpflicht zu entziehen. Werden sie aber zum dienst angenommen, so verlassen sie nur widerwillig ihre heimat und *ihre verwandten, und die angehörigen der rekruten, besonders deren frauen, geleiten sie wie verstorbene* mit weinen und schluchzen" [emphasis supplied]. (On Cheremis beliefs concerning life after death, see **361**, especially pp. 232–233.)

developed. Sung by minstrels, these verses "were eight lines in length, and were divided into groups of two lines each. Divisions of thought often agreed with one or more of these groups. . . . Often a few extra lines were added as a sequel." The lines usually contained eleven syllables. The form was rather flexible and found its way into written literature in a variety of shapes: Cariteo, a fifteenth-century Italian author, continued to favor the octave; in France it grew to ten lines; and "in England the strambotto probably encouraged the writing of many poems resembling the sonnet in nature but varying in length between six and ten lines" (41, pp. 93–94, 111).

The Cheremis sonnet, too, is typically an eight-line song, but this length is not compulsory. Fluctuations are common. Its distinguishing trait lies in the use of a principle of contrast between two parts, the envoy (previously called the focal image) and the introductory matter (previously called the supplementary image) contained in the sestet. The contrast is elaborated analogously in the phonic and the semiotic dimensions.

An Analysis of Structured Content, with Application of Electronic Computer Research, in Psycholinguistics

(abstract)

THOMAS A. SEBEOK

V. J. ZEPS

In contrast to the attempt (reported in the preceding paper) to give as exhaustive a linguistic and poetic analysis of a single text as possible, this paper is based on the premise that it is equally necessary to study the numerical features that are common to many texts in a given corpus; certain linguistic and psycholinguistic hypotheses require information that is readily derived only from the processing of a large body of related materials. The employment of electronic computers makes the testing of such hypotheses reasonably feasible, and, incidentally, the machines also tend to free the investigator of the burden of compiling lists and reference indices "manually." We have tested programming possibilities on a pilot sample. Two programs which have proved successful are outlined: one designed to tally co-occurrences of units within frames, the other to yield inventories of units. As this research is extended and evaluated, it is hoped that from the descriptions of association matrices, studies in metrics and symbolism, and the like, will come applications in cultural anthropology on the one hand and literary theory on the other.

This paper has been published in its entirety (**364**).

Comment to Part Six

SAPORTA: I am a little disturbed by the impression some might have gathered from the discussion in Part Five of whether metrics is somehow independent of the more general problem of style. Mr. Lotz and others pointed out that certain things like intonation or pause may turn out to be irrelevant for the metrics of a certain language, say English. Couldn't we extend this in the opposite direction? I take it that any constants are relevant to the analysis of poetry. Surely these constants are not by definition restricted to the phonological level. The descriptions of certain poems would presumably be inadequate if they failed to indicate recurrent grammatical features on all levels, ranging perhaps from the systematic repetition of certain verbal suffixes to adjective-noun constructions to the repetition of whole sentence patterns. And just as in the phonological features of meter and rhyme, mere repetition is not sufficient for the feature to be pertinent to the metrical analysis; the repetition must be systematic. Put differently, the repetition should be statable in terms of metrical units like line and stanza. The mere fact that clause boundaries and line boundaries coincide in certain poems is relevant to the metrical analysis. The framework for metrical analysis must be broad enough to accommodate these features, and, similarly, these would seem to be the formal features most widely applicable to general problems of style, to problems the psychologists might be interested in, such as motivation, analyzing style and correlating it with the internal states of the senders of messages, and so forth.

Semantic Aspects of Style

Variant Readings and Misreading

I. A. RICHARDS

In this paper I shall later be attempting to construct a definition of [?]misreading,[?][1] and it is a sound rule—is it not?—to consider on such occasions, as closely as we can and as explicitly, what we want the definition for. Such consideration commonly lightens the strains on the definition and can make it relatively less necessary. I would ask therefore that much of the following be read as an account of [sw]misreading[sw] for which it may prove useful and important to have a definition marking it off clearly from [sw]variant readings.[sw] Inevitably, behind this will be a concern with possible meanings for [?]reading.[?] We will be considering what uses we should be endeavoring to make of this term. It is well to note that among them will be normative uses. Every definition no doubt sets up a normative field: uses are either conforming to it or not. But among uses of [w]reading,[w] [w]interpretation,[w] [w]understanding,[w] and so on, there will be some that are normative in a further sense: they lay down rules by which instances may be judged as [?]valid[?] or invalid, as [?]correct[?] or mistaken. Some uses escape this: we may say of a reader that he is reading without raising any question whether he is correctly interpreting what he reads. It appears that there will be a plurality of uses of [w]reading[w] (as of most other important, nontechnical words), uncomfortable though this thought may sometimes feel, and it will be prudent to prepare ourselves for a plurality of definitions.

It is worth remarking that such a paper is inherently circular. Each sentence is attempting to form itself and relate itself to the others so as to reduce the probability of its being misread. Whatever its success, it is itself continuously exposed to the accidents and disasters of which it is professing to supply some account. And it is guiding itself—in part

[1] I resort here to a set of specialized quotation marks whose use will, I hope, be evident: [?]——[?] = query; [sw]——[sw] = what may be said with ——; [w]——[w] = the lexical form ——. See **330,** pp. 66–70; **333,** p. 30.

wittingly, in part unwittingly—by the considerations it is hoping little by little to present.

The occasion for this paper is a conference in which minds are hoping to meet, minds that have undergone different trainings and have thereby developed different patterns of procedure and tendencies toward technicalization. It will not be unwise therefore to allow a margin of our time and attention to boundary questions and to devices for the treatment of misconceptions, which may be expected to abound. Even for so experienced a company I may spend a sentence to note the peculiar importance, theoretical and practical, of improving (if we can) our means of discriminating between variant readings and misreading. This distinction is, I take it, a chief operating assumption in most education, and its application is a prime aim of much discussion: the recognition, on the one hand, of the inevitability and desirability of diverse understandings and, on the other, their sharp contrast with the mistake, the inadmissible interpretation. It is not surprising that the distinction should be somewhat complex and difficult to formulate. What is puzzling is that a matter of such theoretical status and practical moment should be, currently, so little discussed. Possibly the neglect may have a ground in fear. I confess to a feeling of urgency in this. You develop it if you are in a position to observe the linguistic disabilities of many who are going into the teaching of English and the teaching of reading.

Let me set out from an adaptation of a familiar diagram:

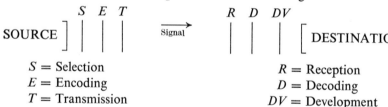

Let me stress first the cyclic mutual dependence, the complexity of feedforward and feedback between S, E, and T.

What is selected is commonly selected in order to be encoded and transmitted. One selection is, indeed, only doubtfully distinguishable from another, except through some encodement. Hence the question: "How do I know what I mean till I see what I say?" This encodement need not be what is transmitted. Many people, in writing and in speaking, use, here and there at least, private codings, ellipses, substitutes, schemata, which would be useless to others; they compose in these, translating thence into public language for transmission. Most people recognize the process describable as ᔆᵂmaking up one's mind to say X rather than Y— without either X or Y being as yet put into words.ᔆᵂ (We may, of course, differ deeply on what account we would prefer to give of this process.) The point here, however, is that priority of X over Y may be, among other things, determined by encodement problems that have not yet explicitly arisen.

A similar cyclic mutual dependence holds between E and T. The encoding is with a view to transmission: a coming tongue twister, or a word that we do not know how to pronounce or spell, can kick back to cause extensive revision, obviously, not only in the encoding but in selecting. More interesting are the modes of composition for which specially exacting conditions to be satisfied in encoding and transmission enforce especially rigorous and revisionary activity in selection: for example, meter and rhyme. As *Hudibras* has it

> Rimes the rudders are of verses
> By which, like ships, they steer their courses.

These courses commonly entail much more thorough and varied search for what is available to be encoded than would occur in prose composition. Thus verse form, as we know, may improve what is being versified. Furthermore, in most composition for which the encoding conditions are exacting, the composer is pressed fairly continuously into a dual role. He has to be his own pilot audience, to be destination as well as source, and go through (with modifications that would probably repay study) R, D, and DV in critical response to his own transmission. Somewhat similar effects may be induced by the restrictions of translation and by composition within limited vocabularies, as in the design of graded language-learning materials. The importance of this dual role is in developing our power to compare what we would say with what we have said is evident.

The reason for noting—even in so summary a fashion—these familiar involvements is that a perhaps important point about our descriptive technique is thereby brought up. It concerns the use—sometimes insufficiently reflective—of the words "encode" and "decode." How much of what sorts of agreement, I wonder, will there be if I suggest that these words are frequently—for example, as I have just been using them—unfortunate because they are too general, because they name alike processes that may need to be recognized as differing importantly from case to case?[2]

---

[2] May I inject here a note of similar suspicion of much use that is currently made of the term ?information?? I have an impression that the term frequently makes it easier for people to overlook and neglect distinctions and connections among types or modes of ?information? that they may, at that point, need to keep their eye on. I hope to be forgiven (by some) if I suggest, further, that mathematical cultivation can sometimes be a handicap. There is the parable of the bridge at Hamburg: Hilbert, the story goes (no doubt, untruly), was shown a famous bridge at Copenhagen. He duly admired it but concluded his praise with "It's exactly like the bridge at Hamburg!" "Nonsense," replied his friend, "How is it like any bridge at Hamburg?" "Why," said Hilbert, "it goes from this side to that side and the river flows under it!"

For example, such an operation as writing down a spoken sentence, or tapping it out in Morse, is extremely different from composing a sonnet, and that again from finding a tactful phrase, and that again from formulating an argument. How much that is useful and not misleading are we saying by calling any of these last ?encodings?? No doubt some reference may be made thereby to the possibility that rules might be found to govern the operation. But in writing something down according to an explicit convention (or in Morsing it), the rules are fully worked out; they are familiar and available to give rulings. In the other cases, in any instance of enterprising and adroit use of language, the rules are conjectural merely and as yet, in fact, barely conjecturable. Meanwhile, however, in more than a little of the talk about coding and decoding that goes on there is present, I fear, a suggestion that Morsing and composing are closely alike. I have listened to "communication theory" being offered to teachers-to-be in such a way that you would suppose that to speak or write well is no more than to emit—in parallel with strings of received notions—the clichés that have the highest probabilities. What is odd is that some have a difficulty in seeing why such a degradation of crude usage theory should be debilitating. An account well suited to the purposes of the communication engineer may be highly misleading as an instrument in teaching writing and reading. I am not doubting that the engineers' formulation has been convenient in phonology, but only whether its extension into higher levels of linguistics may not need the especial attention of critics. I hazard the guess that higher levels can help out lower levels more frequently than lower higher.

All this is a practical objection to much talk about encoding. There are also serious theoretical difficulties, of which we are all more or less aware, as to the status of the ¦message¦ which is said to be encoded. We can, if we like, regard the ¦message¦ as a fictive construct not to be identified with any of ¦its¦ encoded forms, but convenient as a means of referring to certain equivalences or transformation relations and the rules they obey. That may make ᵂmessageᵂ harmless, if we keep strictly to transformation relations: from *ABC* we can pass to *abc* and back again. But, even so, this is a discreditable sort of ghost to have haunting a modern theory, however well its migration from the telegraph office may be understood. And when, as is too likely to happen in even well-conducted discussions, it strays out of transformation theory into attempted explorations of the relations of, say, a Shakespeare sonnet to something else which the lines could be supposed to be an encoding of—where are we? Well over the frontier and inside that very ghostland itself whose inmates are precisely privileged to elude our grasp.

I should attempt to divine and meet objections that will be stirring in some at this point. I prefer as an opinion, and hold to it (in these topics) as constantly as I find I can, that the meaning of a line of Shakespeare is, for linguistics, to be conceived (in some way, at present insufficiently defined) in terms of its relations to other utterances, actual or possible, in English. And I am willing to add that an appeal to some hypothetical event in Shakespeare's ¦mind,¦ or to equally hypothetical events in any readers' minds, is not—unless recognized for the mere stopgap it is—propitious procedure. (Of course, in a novel or play or sermon I would use such appeals unhesitatingly.) And yet I find in myself, and observe (so it appears to me) in others, that when we do really set aside any such appeal we are, to put it mildly, short of means for making and establishing the very distinction between variant readings and misreading that we are here concerned with.

It is time to come down to an example, the second line of Sonnet 66 which I had innocently supposed would be well enough understood by a class of graduate students:

> Tir'd with all these, for restful death I cry:
> As to behold desert a beggar born,

What did I get from a budding Master of Arts in Teaching who will, I fear, be teaching English hard for the rest of her working life? This:

> Weary of these sights, for reposeful death I implore:
> As I see desolate one born a beggar.

Feeling, perhaps, a need for something more, she added a comment: "That one could be born a beggar seems to presuppose that there be someone around to beg from." (ˀDesolateˀ: not ˢʷ*entirely* alone.ˢʷ) No doubt the banishment of beggars from modern streets does make all this more difficult.

Now what can we allege here to confirm our opinion (in which I, for one, am unshakable) that we have here a *misreading*—and not an allowable *variant*?

I do not see how the answers can avoid, at present, a somewhat dogmatic air. We have to seem to be laying down the law with a confidence, schoolmasterly and authoritarian, that deserves to be noted. If our role, for the moment, is not so much to make these declarations as to inquire into our grounds for them, this confidence will, I fancy, strike us as in mysterious and interesting contrast with our difficulty in producing, specifically and explicitly, what will even look like actual and adequate evidence. This observation, I hasten to add, should not in the least make us doubt that our confidence is justified; it is merely the recognition that it is not *easily* justifiable.

In this instance we can be confident, I suggest, that this reader's attempt to take "desert" as here equivalent to "desolate" will not do. We can conjecture—with much less certainty—how she came to think so: probably by equating "desert" with "deserted" and then substituting "desolate." But that is a necessarily precarious guess about an individual's mental process. The solid confidence that the "desert"-"desolate" equivalence will not do is something very different; it is not a guess but an observation, a linguistic perception.

Such perceptions may of course be fallacious: no perceptions, perhaps, are immune from error; but with large classes of these linguistic perceptions risk of error is happily extremely small. Our task in this paper is in part to inquire how risk of error in these perceptions increases and how it may be controlled.

It will be well, though, to note that a linguistic perception may be veridical, and yet the description anyone may offer of what is perceived may be mistaken. The description is an application of theoretical machinery, it is a picture or representation we try to give of certain facts. The facts may be truly observed, even though the account we give of them is defective. It is part of the aim of linguistic studies to improve both literary perception and the techniques of describing what is perceived. I have an uneasy sense that of late they are being more successful in this last.

To return to our example, we had better separate two questions: (1) On what does our perception that ˢʷdesolateˢʷ is a misreading of ʔdesertʔ depend? (2) How would we support or defend this opinion if necessary?

1 In broad outline the answer, of course, is "On our knowledge of English—including the English of Shakespeare's day." And perhaps this very broadness is here a merit; a wide and varied familiarity with how words have been used then and since may serve us better than a more limited, even though more precise, focus on other instances of the use of ʷdesert.ʷ We must put into this ˢʷknowledge of Englishˢʷ knowledge not only of lexical distinctions, overlaps, and so on, but of the varied sentiments (to use a stopgap term) that such lines as these have variously uttered.

"As to behold desert a beggar born." I had better risk my own gloss here, hoping that those who will differ may allow it to me as a variant reading.

Having to see and recognize and admit and deeply realize that Merit, the possession of the highest virtue (of which men of good will should be most regardful, being beholden to and in duty bound to aid and comfort its possessor) may in fact be as little esteemed by the passerby and its subject even be as suspect as one born into the beggar's trade.

I have tried to mix the concrete or literal interpretation: in modern terms "the most gifted child may be most gravely underprivileged" with some of the abstracter, and perhaps optional, metaphoric reaches. How much we personify 'desert,' how far we turn it into a strangely or horribly disguised, perhaps maimed and deformed, presence which, however much we want to avert our eyes, goes on crying out with importunate demands and forces us to be aware of it and take it in; all this, which of it we make focal, which penumbral, which background—these variations I would offer as samples of variant reading.[3] We may dissent from this or that, take the line ourselves another way, and yet not be inclined to condemn even readings very unlike our own *as wrong*—in the fashion in which we can, I think, unhesitatingly reject "As I see desolate one born a beggar."

2. A good deal that may occur to us as confirming our reading (whichever variant it may be) we may have to admit on reflection to be not strictly relevant: etymology, for example. If we were trying to show this reader that she had gone wrong, we might draw her attention to the entries in the nearest dictionary, and this might be an effective way of reminding her of things which, in a less precise way, she perhaps knew already. She would probably not know anything of the etymological detail, but this is not the sort of knowledge of which she is in need. What she did not know was how to see which of the various meanings was present in the line she was reading. The dictionary cannot tell her that, although it may be helpfully suggestive.

The Dictionary (to accord it a capital of respect) often seems to be the contemporary representative of Holy Writ. Its invention should, I suppose, be considered an innovation every bit as momentous as those we associate with Galileo or Newton or even, perhaps, with Einstein. The audience this paper is primarily addressed to is rather sophisticated about dictionaries; it knows more about how they are written than the general public. Nevertheless even great lexicographers may sometimes be observed to adopt devout attitudes toward the institutions they direct. It is perhaps natural, therefore, that today we look to the Dictionary (or to something a Dream Dictionary of the future might embody) for the guidance and even for the validation we are in search of. What a simplification it would be were it to turn out that an interpretation is *wrong*, is a *misreading*, that it conflicts with information stored in that superdictionary.

---

[3] I confess to some skepticism about this type of analysis or explanation. Within my lifetime—I seem almost able to recall a specific beginning—a practice of expressing whatever a line or passage could possibly yield under squeezing has grown up. At first the practitioners were few and some of them became renowned for powerful grasp; but competition jacks up standards. There are fashions in reading as well as in writing. Perhaps questions of relevance are now due for more searching discussion. It seems unlikely that run-of-the-mine students today should really be able to find so much more *in* Shakespeare than earlier readers. Have they learned how to cultivate their garden more intensively or is some of it just a novel conjuring trick?

The solution cannot really be quite as simple; although, with qualifications by no means easy to be clear about, something of the sort is no
doubt in part what we seek. One set of such qualifications must preserve
flexibility. Languages change. New words, new uses of old words,
obsolescences, revivals, shifting fashions in reading, changing types of
invitation to readers, enlarging and dwindling sensitivities to nuance, to
the figurative, to status, to implication, to attitude—limitless variations,
not only in new utterance but in how old utterance may be understood—
all these have to be taken care of. That dream-Dictionary would have to
be much more than a mere storage system, a record of records. It would
have to respect creativity while discouraging crudescence. It would
somehow have to combine the uttermost literary discernment with a
complete freedom from prejudice. And yet, at the same time, it would
have to protect the language from those forms of disabling confusion for
which my "desert"–"desolate" may stand. It is clear enough that this
dream-Dictionary is no actual project but a Platonic idea of the most
ineffable order:

> the unimaginable lodge
> For solitary thinkings, such as dodge
> Conception to the very bourne of Heaven
> Then leave the naked brain.

And yet, even as such, it has something to offer toward the definition of
²misreading² we are attempting to approach.

Can we advance a little by considering further the knowledge a good
reader must have and a bad reader manifestly lacks? The same misreader,
in dealing with the fourth line of Sonnet 66,

> And purest faith unhappily forsworn,

offers us what looks like additional evidence. Here is her paraphrase:

> And the most absolute confidence sadly renounced.

This seems to me to show two related characteristics: (1) isolated word-by
word procedure; and (2) inability to recognize pluralities of potential
meanings and to select from among them.

1. *Purest:* having kept, I fancy, little beyond the superlative (I doubt,
from collateral evidence, whether "absolute," for her, had much of what
made Shakespeare so fond of it, or was more than emphatic)

Faith: lacking the control of ˢʷcompletely sincereˢʷ (for ²purest²), lapsed
from naming a virtue of active engagement to become the passive thing we
associate with confidence men. And then

Unhappily: losing all its august relations—with Fortune, with intellectual activity as, for Aristotle, man's highest happiness—it deteriorates into a mere description of a feeling, [sw]sadly.[sw] Which leaves

Forsworn: undefended (to a reader who can render "cry" by "implore"); all connection with "faith" is missed and what remains is only a change of mind.

2. The failure to select goes along with the word-by-word jumping at the first meaning that turns up.[4] There is a randomness about the process in striking contrast with what, to a better reader, will seem the continual invitation to perceive connection and design, tension and outcome, variously balanced throughout the sonnet.

This failure to connect, word with word and line with line, extends to an inability seemingly even to look for an over-all mutual relevance, a control of whole over part, and beyond that to an impercipience of significant relationships between wholes. Such a sonnet as this is no doubt near the top of a scale on which a laundry list would be near the foot. But if on a scribbled laundry list we found ourselves reading "teas" for "ties" we would know that we were in danger of letting the local point of focus cease to be duly guided by the ambient. Perhaps in such mutual influences between focal point and ambient we can find what is needed to unify the concept of an ideal Dictionary into a definition of misreading.

Two difficulties must be recognized first. This discussion, these approaches, are haunted by the concept of *knowing* and by the concept of *comparing*. Each of them is very likely to get itself represented in our definition in too explicit, too conscious, and too deliberate a guise. This trouble with *know* is, of course, notorious. To know is both the end and, it would seem, the means of intellectual endeavour, and yet who knows anything about knowledge? Here, in the key role in all exploratory activity is an inexplorable, and this admission becomes the more discomforting the nearer we come (as in considering misreading) to asking about what we may know and how.

A similar and closely related trouble attends *comparing*. If advance in knowledge is through comparing—and I suppose the triumphs of linguistics in recent decades to be among the clearest illustrations of the powers of systematic comparison—where is our theory of the comparing of meanings? This may be the place where a Principle of Instrumental Dependence which seems needed everywhere else breaks down. "The properties of the instruments or apparatus employed enter into, and confine, the scope of

[4] I connect this faulty behavior in reading with the grave defects of much current instruction in reading. Word calling of isolated words and the vacuousness, the lack of significant content, of the characteristic texts have their consequences. It is to the very beginnings of the teaching of reading that we must go for a remedy. See **333,** ch. 8; and **134.**

the investigation" (**333,** p. 114). Does this hold too of our key concepts and procedures? Does it hold pre-eminently of them? Or are these questions self-destructive?

Is it not very odd, when we consider on how vast a scale outcomes of comparing are recorded in the Dictionary, how little explicit reflection upon comparing has been recorded? Each article presents vocables which, *in some respects* but not in all, may be compared with the head and found the same in meaning. But how scanty, when set beside all these difficult and hazardous comparings and decisions, is the discussion of the respects (**333,** pp. 25–38). And, as I have remarked above, the readings on which the comparings and decisions are based are strangely confident—strangely, in view of the uncertainties that arise as soon as we try to justify them and the obscurities of any theoretical accounts of how we arrive at the compared meanings. And yet our practical confidence about meanings ought not to surprise us. It may on occasion betray us, but we would understand nothing at all without it; this widespread assurance is the necessary condition for every local doubt.

It should, however, be added—and with some emphasis—that if, with sentences having more than a minimal routine content, we ask for a paraphrase, we will be supplied (as with lines of Sonnet 66) with enough misreadings to make us wonder how high the price we pay for this necessary confidence may be. For example,

> To behold merit born a beggar (without merit)
> To see a wretched beggar getting what he deserves.

misread: to read or interpret wrongly.
wrong: (related to **wring**) having a crooked or curved course, form or direction; twisted or bent—1613.

I must now try to put the parts that have been looked over into some sort of unity, and the uniting idea will be that implied by the undertaking the Dictionary makes to explain any word in a language by means of others. A language, this assumes, is a system such that each part (we need not worry, here, whether these are necessarily ?words,? or how a ?word? should be defined, or whether different languages may not differ as to these parts) has its various duties or tasks under quasi-control by other parts— a quasi-control reflected in the fact that it can be replaced by them (at the price of some adjustment or awkwardness). A word can do, that is, what the rest of the language will let it. The limitations that the system imposes on any component much resemble those that a society imposes on its members or those that an organism imposes on its constituent cells (**330,** pp. 228–232; **328,** pp. 223–226). They are normally inseparable from (commonly reciprocal to) the dependences that every word has (in any sentence) on others. Normally a word works only through the cooperations of other words. These restrictive-permissive, controlling-enabling inter-relations, which tie the utterances possible within a language into a system, give us our means of distinguishing between variant readings and mis-reading. Once again, we must never forget that the system in living languages is nowhere fixed or rigid—though it will, no doubt, be more rigid in certain regions of use than in others. The interrelations correspond to the needs the language has met and is meeting, to the tasks it has attempted and is attempting to perform. As need and task change, the interrelations undergo strain which may be met by adjustment and by growth. Here is where novelty, in phrasing and in interpretation, enters, the opportunity for variant reading and original utterance.

We are not far here from valuative considerations. The analogies I have mentioned with a society and an organism suggest that we may properly be concerned with linguistic *health*—whose connections with "whole" we should keep in mind as well as its forward-looking implication: we would not say anyone was in good health if he were unable to continue so for some while. It may be very deeply doubted whether any great language has ever really been left to its own devices unsubject to effective criticism from those who were, by privilege or by profession or by poetic or social endowment, unusually well able to use it and to judge how it should be used. The language arts, after all, are arts. Perhaps we should not take too seriously those who seem to claim authority from linguistics as a ¹science¹ to tell a rather helpless generation that what is said by enough people thereby becomes what *should* be said. (Are we to think that what is thought by enough people thereby becomes what should be thought?) And yet in this age of the advertiser (¹Everybody's buying it¹) there is occasion for concern. It is not quite enough to leave the matter to the experience of anyone speaking or writing with care, reflection, and intent. In selecting our phrases are we seeking (1) what most people in our situation would most probably say, or (2) what will best do the work in hand? (cf. **331,** chs. 15–16.) Only in a very exalted linguistic community indeed would (2) be in general the same as (1); it would be a diseased community in which there was widespread doubt which to prefer. Similarly with interpretation: what we should seek is not the sense that is, or would be, most widely accepted, but what most fully takes into account the situation the utterance is meeting and the integrity of the language. It was with this in view that I inserted in my diagram DV (development) after D (decoding). There should be—although it may slow reading down—a cyclic mutual dependence between R, D, and DV, as with S, E, and T. In spite of Plato's jokes in the *Phaedrus* the chief service that writing and reading can do us is to help us to reflect, to reflect, *Deo volente*, to some purpose. Counting hands in interpretation cannot do that. Misreadings may, as scholarship frequently discovers, be universal through long periods.

Most speech and writing, and most interpretation, is not, I have urged above, as conscious as the word ?seek? here may suggest. Commonly a series of possible phrases or interpretations offer themselves (more or less schematically), and our choice is not ordinarily guided by highly explicit considerations. It is this that makes a crude usage doctrine dangerous; it can present *the thing to say* in a fashion which blurs the vital distinction between *what I should say here* and *what is said.* And this not only for the form but for the content of the utterance, as ad-men and opinion promoters have noted.

To sum up, a sound account of interpretation must build into itself a duty to be critical. A linguistics that is properly aware of the processes through which language grows in the individual and of the effects that his attitudes to language can have upon its health in him must be concerned with pedagogy and with what sorts of assumptions are spread in the school. Poor pedagogy in the thinking of linguistic authorities is in its own way quite as alarming as bad linguistic doctrine in the classroom.

After all this my definition of ?misreading? will still have to lean on much more than has been said if it is not itself to be most variously misread. In this it corresponds to the statesman, whose responsibilities as guardian expose him to misrepresentation. He does well not to formulate his policies in ways that give handle to his opponents. My definition, too, will be well advised not to do more, seemingly, than advance a modest request: "For the purposes outlined above and on the appropriate occasions, may *misreading* mean the taking of a sentence in such a way that the equivalence relations of one or more of its parts to the rest of the language lapse and thereby, if such taking were to continue, harm would be done to the language—due regard, however, being given in applying this criterion to the necessity for change in language activity with change in the situations to be met, and, in general, to the health of the language."

The Pronouns of Power and Solidarity

ROGER BROWN

ALBERT GILMAN

Most of us in speaking and writing English use only one pronoun of address; we say "you" to many persons and "you" to one person. The pronoun "thou" is reserved, nowadays, to prayer and naive poetry, but in the past it was the form of familiar address to a single person. At that time "you" was the singular of reverence and of polite distance and, also, the invariable plural. In French, German, Italian, Spanish, and the other languages most nearly related to English there are still active two singular pronouns of address. The interesting thing about such pronouns is their close association with two dimensions fundamental to the analysis of all social life—the dimensions of power and solidarity. Semantic and stylistic analysis of these forms takes us well into psychology and sociology as well as into linguistics and the study of literature.

This paper is divided into five major sections.[1] The first three of these are concerned with the semantics of the pronouns of address. By semantics we mean covariation between the pronoun used and the objective relationship existing between speaker and addressee. The first section offers a general description of the semantic evolution of the pronouns of address in certain European languages. The second section describes semantic differences existing today among the pronouns of French, German, and Italian. The third section proposes a connection between social structure, group ideology, and the semantics of the pronoun. The final two sections of the paper are concerned with expressive style by which we mean covariation between the pronoun used and characteristics of the person speaking. The first of these sections shows that a man's consistent pronoun style gives away his class status and his political views. The last section

[1] Our study was financed by a Grant-in-Aid-of-Research made by the Ford Foundation to Brown, and the authors gratefully acknowledge this assistance.

describes the ways in which a man may vary his pronoun style from time to time so as to express transient moods and attitudes. In this section it is also proposed that the major expressive meanings are derived from the major semantic rules.

In each section the evidence most important to the thesis of that section is described in detail. However, the various generalizations we shall offer have developed as an interdependent set from continuing study of our whole assemblage of facts, and so it may be well to indicate here the sort of motley assemblage this is. Among secondary sources the general language histories (**16, 48, 90, 142, 213, 275**) have been of little use because their central concern is always phonetic rather than semantic change. However, there are a small number of monographs and doctoral dissertations describing the detailed pronoun semantics for one or another language— sometimes throughout its history (**133, 139, 216, 353**), sometimes for only a century or so (**229, 401**), and sometimes for the works of a particular author (**55, 119**). As primary evidence for the usage of the past we have drawn on plays, on legal proceedings (**208**), and on letters (**89, 151**). We have also learned about contemporary usage from literature but, more importantly, from long conversations with native speakers of French, Italian, German, and Spanish both here and in Europe. Our best information about the pronouns of today comes from a questionnaire concerning usage which is described in the second section of this paper. The questionnaire has thus far been answered by the following numbers of students from abroad who were visiting in Boston in 1957–1958: 50 Frenchmen, 20 Germans, 11 Italians, and two informants, each, from Spain, Argentina, Chile, Denmark, Norway, Sweden, Israel, South Africa, India, Switzerland, Holland, Austria, and Yugoslavia.

We have far more information concerning English, French, Italian, Spanish, and German than for any other languages. Informants and documents concerning the other Indo-European languages are not easily accessible to us. What we have to say is then largely founded on information about these five closely related languages. These first conclusions will eventually be tested by us against other Indo-European languages and, in a more generalized form, against unrelated languages.

The European development of two singular pronouns of address begins with the Latin *tu* and *vos*. In Italian they became *tu* and *voi* (with *Lei* eventually largely displacing *voi*); in French *tu* and *vous*; in Spanish *tu* and *vos* (later *usted*). In German the distinction began with *du* and *Ihr* but *Ihr* gave way to *er* and later to *Sie*. English speakers first used "thou" and "ye" and later replaced "ye" with "you." As a convenience we propose to use the symbols T and V (from the Latin *tu* and *vos*) as generic designators for a familiar and a polite pronoun in any language.

THE GENERAL SEMANTIC EVOLUTION OF *T* AND *V*

In the Latin of antiquity there was only *tu* in the singular. The plural *vos* as a form of address to one person was first directed to the emperor and there are several theories (**55, 58**) about how this may have come about. The use of the plural to the emperor began in the fourth century. By that time there were actually two emperors; the ruler of the eastern empire had his seat in Constantinople and the ruler of the west sat in Rome. Because of Diocletian's reforms the imperial office, although vested in two men, was administratively unified. Words addressed to one man were, by implication, addressed to both. The choice of *vos* as a form of address may have been in response to this implicit plurality. An emperor is also plural in another sense; he is the summation of his people and can speak as their representative. Royal persons sometimes say "we" where an ordinary man would say "I." The Roman emperor sometimes spoke of himself as *nos*, and the reverential *vos* is the simple reciprocal of this.

The usage need not have been mediated by a prosaic association with actual plurality, for plurality is a very old and ubiquitous metaphor for power. Consider only the several senses of such English words as "great" and "grand." The reverential *vos* could have been directly inspired by the power of an emperor.

Eventually the Latin plural was extended from the emperor to other power figures. However, this semantic pattern was not unequivocally established for many centuries. There was much inexplicable fluctuation between *T* and *V* in Old French, Spanish, Italian, and Portuguese (**353**), and in Middle English (**229, 401**). In verse, at least, the choice seems often to have depended on assonance, rhyme, or syllable count. However, some time between the twelfth and fourteenth centuries (**133, 139, 229, 353**), varying with the language, a set of norms crystallized which we call the nonreciprocal power semantic.

The Power Semantic

One person may be said to have power over another in the degree that he is able to control the behavior of the other. Power is a relationship between at least two persons, and it is nonreciprocal in the sense that both cannot have power in the same area of behavior. The power semantic is similarly nonreciprocal; the superior says *T* and receives *V*.

There are many bases of power—physical strength, wealth, age, sex, institutionalized role in the church, the state, the army, or within the family. The character of the power semantic can be made clear with a set of examples from various languages. In his letters, Pope Gregory I (590–604) used *T* to his subordinates in the ecclesiastical hierarchy and they invariably said V to him (291). In medieval Europe, generally, the nobility said T to the common people and received V; the master of a household said T to his slave, his servant, his squire, and received V. Within the family, of whatever social level, parents gave T to children and were given V. In Italy in the fifteenth century penitents said V to the priest and were told T (139). In Froissart (late fourteenth century) God says T to His angels and they say V; all celestial beings say T to man and receive V. In French of the twelfth and thirteenth century man says T to the animals (353). In fifteenth century Italian literature Christians say T to Turks and Jews and receive V (139). In the plays of Corneille and Racine (353) and Shakespeare (55), the noble principals say T to their subordinates and are given V in return.

The V of reverence entered European speech as a form of address to the principal power in the state and eventually generalized to the powers within that microcosm of the state—the nuclear family. In the history of language, then, parents are emperor figures. It is interesting to note in passing that Freud reversed this terminology and spoke of kings, as well as generals, employers, and priests, as father figures. The propriety of Freud's designation for his psychological purposes derives from the fact that an individual learning a European language reverses the historical order of semantic generalization. The individual's first experience of subordination to power and of the reverential V comes in his relation to his parents. In later years similar asymmetrical power relations and similar norms of address develop between employer and employee, soldier and officer, subject and monarch. We can see how it might happen, as Freud believed, that the later social relationships would remind the individual of the familial prototype and would revive emotions and responses from childhood. In a man's personal history recipients of the nonreciprocal V are parent figures.

Since the nonreciprocal power semantic only prescribes usage between superior and inferior, it calls for a social structure in which there are unique power ranks for every individual. Medieval European societies were not so finely structured as that, and so the power semantic was never the only rule for the use of T and V. There were also norms of address for persons of roughly equivalent power, that is, for members of a common class. Between equals, pronominal address was reciprocal; an individual gave and received the same form. During the medieval period, and for varying times beyond, equals of the upper classes exchanged the mutual V and equals of the lower classes exchanged T.

The difference in class practice derives from the fact that the reverential V was always introduced into a society at the top. In the Roman Empire only the highest ranking persons had any occasion to address the emperor, and so at first only they made use of *V* in the singular. In its later history in other parts of Europe the reverential *V* was usually adopted by one court in imitation of another. The practice slowly disseminated downward in a society. In this way the use of *V* in the singular incidentally came to connote a speaker of high status. In later centuries Europeans became very conscious of the extensive use of *V* as a mark of elegance. In the drama of seventeenth century France the nobility and bourgeoisie almost always address one another as *V*. This is true even of husband and wife, of lovers, and of parent and child if the child is adult. Mme. de Sévigné in her correspondence never uses *T*, not even to her daughter the Comtesse de Grignan (**353**). Servants and peasantry, however, regularly used *T* among themselves.

For many centuries French, English, Italian, Spanish, and German pronoun usage followed the rule of nonreciprocal *T–V* between persons of unequal power and the rule of mutual *V* or *T* (according to social-class membership) between persons of roughly equivalent power. There was at first no rule differentiating address among equals but, very gradually, a distinction developed which is sometimes called the *T* of intimacy and the *V* of formality. We name this second dimension *solidarity*, and here is our guess as to how it developed.

The Solidarity Semantic

The original singular pronoun was *T*. The use of *V* in the singular developed as a form of address to a person of superior power. There are many personal attributes that convey power. The recipient of *V* may differ from the recipient of *T* in strength, age, wealth, birth, sex, or profession. As two people move apart on these power-laden dimensions, one of them begins to say *V*. In general terms, the *V* form is linked with differences between persons. Not all differences between persons imply a difference of power. Men are born in different cities, belong to different families of the same status, may attend different but equally prominent schools, may practice different but equally respected professions. A rule for making distinctive use of *T* and *V* among equals can be formulated by generalizing the power semantic. Differences of power cause *V* to emerge in one direction of address; differences not concerned with power cause *V* to emerge in both directions.

The relations called *older than*, *parent of*, *employer of*, *richer than*, *stronger than*, and *nobler than* are all asymmetrical. If *A* is older than *B*, *B* is not older than *A*. The relation called "more powerful than," which is abstracted from these more specific relations, is also conceived to be asymmetrical. The pronoun usage expressing this power relation is also asymmetrical or nonreciprocal, with the greater receiving *V* and the lesser

T. Now we are concerned with a new set of relations which are symmetrical; for example, *attended the same school* or *have the same parents* or *practice the same profession*. If *A* has the same parents as *B*, *B* has the same parents as *A*. Solidarity is the name we give to the general relationship and solidarity is symmetrical. The corresponding norms of address are symmetrical or reciprocal with *V* becoming more probable as solidarity declines. The solidary *T* reaches a peak of probability in address between twin brothers or in a man's soliloquizing address to himself.

Not every personal attribute counts in determining whether two people are solidary enough to use the mutual *T*. Eye color does not ordinarily matter nor does shoe size. The similarities that matter seem to be those that make for like-mindedness or similar behavior dispositions. These will ordinarily be such things as political membership, family, religion, profession, sex, and birthplace. However, extreme distinctive values on almost any dimension may become significant. Height ought to make for solidarity among giants and midgets. The *T* of solidarity can be produced by frequency of contact as well as by objective similarities. However, frequent contact does not necessarily lead to the mutual *T*. It depends on whether contact results in the discovery or creation of the like-mindedness that seems to be the core of the solidarity semantic.

Solidarity comes into the European pronouns as a means of differentiating address among power equals. It introduces a second dimension into the semantic system on the level of power equivalents. So long as solidarity was confined to this level, the two-dimensional system was in equilibrium (see Figure 1*a*), and it seems to have remained here for a considerable time in all our languages. It is from the long reign of the two-dimensional semantic that *T* derives its common definition as the pronoun of either condescension or intimacy and *V* its definition as the pronoun of reverence or formality. These definitions are still current but usage has, in fact, gone somewhat beyond them.

The dimension of solidarity is potentially applicable to all persons addressed. Power superiors may be solidary (parents, elder siblings) or not solidary (officials whom one seldom sees). Power inferiors, similarly, may be as solidary as the old family retainer and as remote as the waiter in a strange restaurant. Extension of the solidarity dimension along the dotted lines of Figure 1*b* creates six categories of persons defined by their relations to a speaker. Rules of address are in conflict for persons in the upper left and lower right categories. For the upper left, power indicates *V* and solidarity *T*. For the lower right, power indicates *T* and solidarity *V*.

The abstract conflict described in Figure 1*b* is particularized in Figure 2*a* with a sample of the social dyads in which the conflict would be felt. In each case usage in one direction is unequivocal but, in the other direction, the two semantic forces are opposed. The first three dyads in Figure 2a involve conflict in address to inferiors who are not solidary (the lower right category of Figure 1b), and the second three dyads involve conflict in address to superiors who are solidary (the upper left category in Figure 1b).

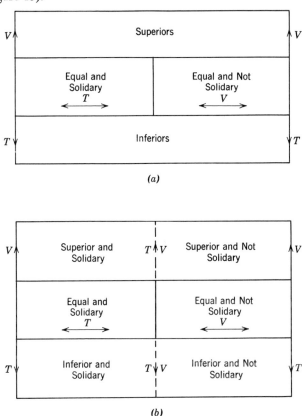

Figure 1. The two-dimensional semantic (*a*) in equilibrium and (*b*) under tension.

Well into the nineteenth century the power semantic prevailed and waiters, common soldiers, and employees were called *T* while parents, masters, and elder brothers were called *V*. However, all our evidence consistently indicates that in the past century the solidarity semantic has gained supremacy. Dyads of the type shown in Figure 2a now reciprocate the pronoun of solidarity or the pronoun of nonsolidarity. The conflicted address has been resolved so as to match the unequivocal address. The abstract result is a simple one-dimensional system with the reciprocal *T* for the solidary and the reciprocal *V* for the nonsolidary.

It is the present practice to reinterpret power-laden attributes so as to turn them into symmetrical solidarity attributes. Relationships like *older than, father of, nobler than,* and *richer than* are now reinterpreted for purposes of T and V as relations of *the same age as, the same family as, the same kind of ancestry as,* and *the same income as.* In the degree that these relationships hold, the probability of a mutual T increases and, in the degree that they do not hold, the probability of a mutual V increases.

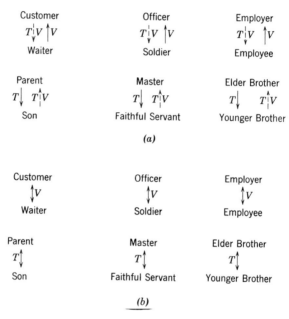

Figure 2. Social dyads involving (*a*) semantic conflict and (*b*) their resolution.

There is an interesting residual of the power relation in the contemporary notion that the right to initiate the reciprocal T belongs to the member of the dyad having the better power-based claim to say T without reciprocation. The suggestion that solidarity be recognized comes more gracefully from the elder than from the younger, from the richer than from the poorer, from the employer than from the employee, from the noble than from the commoner, from the female than from the male.

In support of our claim that solidarity has largely won out over power we can offer a few quotations from language scholars. Littré, writing of French usage, says (**251**): "Notre courtoisie est même si grande, que nous ne dédaignons pas de donner du vous et du monsieur à l'homme de la condition la plus vile." Grand (**139**) wrote of the Italian V: "On commence aussi à le donner aux personnes de service, à qui on disait tu autrefois." We have found no authority who describes the general character of these many specific changes of usage: a shift from power to solidarity as the governing semantic principle.

The best evidence that the change has occurred is in our interviews and notes on contemporary literature and films and, most importantly, the questionnaire results. The six social dyads of Figure 2 were all represented in the questionnaire. In the past these would have been answered in accordance with asymmetrical power. Across all six of these dyads the French results yield only 11 per cent nonreciprocal power answers, the German 12 per cent, the Italian 27 per cent. In all other cases the usage is reciprocal, as indicated in Figure 2*b*. In all three of the languages, address between master and servant retains the greatest power loading. Some of the changes toward solidarity are very recent. Only since the Second World War, for instance, has the French Army adopted a regulation requiring officers to say *V* to enlisted men.

Finally, it is our opinion that a still newer direction of semantic shift can be discerned in the whole collection of languages studied. Once solidarity has been established as the single dimension distinguishing *T* from *V* the province of *T* proceeds to expand. The direction of change is increase in the number of relations defined as solidary enough to merit a mutual *T* and, in particular, to regard any sort of camaraderie resulting from a common task or a common fate as grounds for *T*. We have a favorite example of this new trend given us independently by several French informants. It seems that mountaineers above a certain critical altitude shift to the mutual *T*. We like to think that this is the point where their lives hang by a single thread. In general, the mutual *T* is advancing among fellow students, fellow workers, members of the same political group, persons who share a hobby or take a trip together. We believe this is the direction of current change because it summarizes what our informants tell us about the pronoun usage of the "young people" as opposed to that of older people.

CONTEMPORARY DIFFERENCES AMONG FRENCH, ITALIAN, AND GERMAN

While *T* and *V* have passed through the same general semantic sequence in these three languages, there are today some differences of detailed usage which were revealed by the questionnaire data. Conversations with native speakers guided us in the writing of questionnaire items, but the conversations themselves did not teach us the characteristic semantic features of the three languages; these did not emerge until we made statistical comparison of answers to the standard items of the questionnaire.

The questionnaire is in English. It opens with a paragraph informing the subject that the items below all have reference to the use of the singular pronouns of address in his native language. There are 28 items in the full questionnaire, and they all have the form of the following example from the questionnaire for French students:

1. (*a*) Which pronoun would you use in speaking to your mother?	1. (*b*) Which would she use in speaking to you?
T (definitely) ——	*T* (definitely) ——
T (probably) ——	*T* (probably) ——
Possibly *T*, possibly *V* ——	Possibly *T*, possibly *V* ——
V (probably) ——	*V* (probably) ——
V (definitely) ——	*V* (definitely) ——

The questionnaire asks about usage between the subject and his mother, his father, his grandfather, his wife, a younger brother who is a child, a married elder brother, that brother's wife, a remote male cousin, and an elderly female servant whom he has known from childhood. It asks about usage between the subject and fellow students at the university at home, usage to a student from home visiting in America, and usage to someone with whom the subject had been at school some years previously. It asks about usage to a waiter in a restaurant, between clerks in an office, fellow soldiers in the army, between boss and employee, army private and general. In addition, there are some rather elaborate items which ask the subject to imagine himself in some carefully detailed social situation and then to say what pronoun he would use. A copy of the full questionnaire may be had on application to the authors.

The most accessible informants were students from abroad resident in Boston in the fall of 1957. Listings of such students were obtained from Harvard, Boston University, M.I.T., and the Office of the French Consul in New England. Although we have data from a small sample of female respondents, the present analysis is limited to the males. All the men in the sample have been in the United States for one year or less; they come from cities of over 300,000 inhabitants, and these cities are well scattered across the country in question. In addition, all members of the sample are from upper-middle-class, professional families. This homogeneity of class membership was enforced by the factors determining selection of students who go abroad. The occasional informant from a working-class family is deliberately excluded from these comparisons. The class from which we draw shows less regional variation in speech than does the working class and, especially, farmers. At the present time we have complete responses from 50 Frenchmen, 20 Germans, and 11 Italians; many of these men also sent us letters describing their understanding of the pronouns and offering numerous valuable anecdotes of usage. The varying numbers of subjects belonging to the three nationalities result from the unequal representation of these nationalities among Boston students rather than from national characterological differences in willingness to answer a questionnaire. Almost every person on our lists agreed to serve as an informant.

In analyzing the results we assigned the numbers 0–4 to the five response alternatives to each question, beginning with "Definitely V" as 0. A rough test was made of the significance of the differences among the three languages on each question. We dichotomized the replies to each question into: (*a*) all replies of either "Definitely T" or "Probably T"; (*b*) all replies of "Definitely V" or "Probably V" or "Possibly V, possibly T." Using the chi-squared test with Yates's correction for small frequencies we determined, for each comparison, the probability of obtaining by chance a difference as large or larger than that actually obtained. Even with such small samples, there were quite a few differences significantly unlikely to occur by chance ($P = .05$ or less). Germans were more prone than the French to say T to their grandfathers, to an elder brother's wife, and to an old family servant. The French were more prone than the Germans to say T to a male fellow student, to a student from home visiting in America, to a fellow clerk in an office, and to someone known previously as a fellow student. Italians were more prone than the French to say T to a female fellow student and also to an attractive girl to whom they had recently been introduced. Italians were more prone than the Germans to say T to the persons just described and, in addition, to a male fellow student and to a student from home visiting in America. On no question did either the French or the Germans show a significantly greater tendency to say T than did the Italians.

The many particular differences among the three languages are susceptible of a general characterization. Let us first contrast German and French. The German T is more reliably applied within the family than is the French T; in addition to the significantly higher T scores for grandfather and elder brother's wife there are smaller differences showing a higher score for the German T on father, mother, wife, married elder brother, and remote male cousin. The French T is not automatically applied to remote relatives, but it is more likely than the German pronoun to be used to express the camaraderie of fellow students, fellow clerks, fellow countrymen abroad, and fellow soldiers. In general it may be said that the solidarity coded by the German T is an ascribed solidarity of family relationships. The French T, in greater degree, codes an acquired solidarity not founded on family relationship but developing out of some sort of shared fate. As for the Italian T, it very nearly equals the German in family solidarity and it surpasses the French in camaraderie. The camaraderie of the Italian male, incidentally, is extended to the Italian female; unlike the French or German student the Italian says *T* to the co-ed almost as readily as to the male fellow student.

There is a very abstract semantic rule governing *T* and *V* which is the same for French, German, and Italian and for many other languages we have studied. The rule is that usage is reciprocal, *T* becoming increasingly probable and *V* less probable as the number of solidarity-producing attributes shared by two people increases. The respect in which French, German, and Italian differ from one another is in the relative weight given to various attributes of persons which can serve to generate solidarity. For German, ascribed family membership is the important attribute; French and Italian give more weight to acquired characteristics.

SEMANTICS, SOCIAL STRUCTURE, AND IDEOLOGY

A historical study of the pronouns of address reveals a set of semantic and social psychological correspondences. The nonreciprocal power semantic is associated with a relatively static society in which power is distributed by birthright and is not subject to much redistribution. The power semantic was closely tied with the feudal and manorial systems. In Italy the reverential pronoun *Lei* which has largely displaced the older *voi* was originally an abbreviation for *la vostra Signoria* 'your lordship' and in Spanish *vuestra Merced* 'your grace' became the reverential *usted*. The static social structure was accompanied by the Church's teaching that each man had his properly appointed place and ought not to wish to rise above it. The reciprocal solidarity semantic has grown with social mobility and an equalitarian ideology. The towns and cities have led the way in the semantic change as they led the way in opening society to vertical movement. In addition to these rough historical correspondences we have made a collection of lesser items of evidence favoring the thesis.

In France the nonreciprocal power semantic was dominant until the Revolution when the Committee for the Public Safety condemned the use of *V* as a feudal remnant and ordered a universal reciprocal *T*. On October 31, 1793, Malbec made a Parliamentary speech against *V*: "Nous distinguons trois personnes pour le singulier et trois pour le pluriel, et, au mépris de cette règle, l'esprit de fanatisme, d'orgueil et de féodalité, nous a fait contracter l'habitude de nous servir de la seconde personne du pluriel lorsque nous parlons à un seul" (quoted in **49**). For a time revolutionary "fraternité" transformed all address into the mutual *Citoyen* and the mutual *tu*. Robespierre even addressed the president of the Assembly as *tu*. In later years solidarity declined and the differences of power which always exist everywhere were expressed once more.

It must be asked why the equalitarian ideal was expressed in a universal *T* rather than a universal *V* or, as a third alternative, why there was not a shift of semantic from power to solidarity with both pronouns being retained. The answer lies with the ancient upper-class preference for the use of *V*. There was animus against the pronoun itself. The pronoun of the "*sans-culottes*" was *T* (**133**), and so this had to be the pronoun of the Revolution.

Although the power semantic has largely gone out of pronoun use in France today native speakers are nevertheless aware of it. In part they are aware of it because it prevails in so much of the greatest French literature. Awareness of power as a potential factor in pronoun usage was revealed by our respondents' special attitude toward the saying of *T* to a waiter. Most of them felt that this would be shockingly bad taste in a way that other norm violations would not be, apparently because there is a kind of seignorial right to say *T* to a waiter, an actual power asymmetry, which the modern man's ideology requires him to deny. In French Africa, on the other hand, it is considered proper to recognize a caste difference between the African and the European, and the nonreciprocal address is used to express it. The European says *T* and requires *V* from the African. This is a galling custom to the African, and in 1957 Robert Lacoste, the French Minister residing in Algeria, urged his countrymen to eschew the practice.

In England, before the Norman Conquest, "ye" was the second person plural and "thou" the singular. "You" was originally the accusative of "ye," but in time it also became the nominative plural and ultimately ousted "thou" as the usual singular. The first uses of "ye" as a reverential singular occur in the thirteenth century (**229**), and seem to have been copied from the French nobility. The semantic progression corresponds roughly to the general stages described in the first section of this paper, except that the English seem always to have moved more freely from one form to another than did the continental Europeans (**213**).

In the seventeenth century "thou" and "you" became explicitly involved in social controversy. The Religious Society of Friends (or Quakers) was founded in the middle of this century by George Fox. One of the practices setting off this rebellious group from the larger society was the use of Plain Speech, and this entailed saying "thou" to everyone. George Fox explained the practice in these words:

"Moreover, when the Lord sent me forth into the world, He forbade me to put off my hat to any, high or low; and I was required to Thee and Thou all men and women, without any respect to rich or poor, great or small" (quoted in **116**).

Fox wrote a fascinating pamphlet (**122**), arguing that *T* to one and *V* to many is the natural and logical form of address in all languages. Among others he cites Latin, Hebrew, Greek, Arabick, Syriack, Aethiopic, Egyptian, French, and Italian. Fox suggests that the Pope, in his vanity, introduced the corrupt and illogical practice of saying *V* to one person. Farnsworth, another early Friend, wrote a somewhat similar pamphlet (**118**), in which he argued that the Scriptures show that God and Adam and God and Moses were not too proud to say and receive the singular *T*.

For the new convert to the Society of Friends the universal *T* was an especially difficult commandment. Thomas Ellwood has described (**112**) the trouble that developed between himself and his father:

But whenever I had occasion to speak to my Father, though I had no Hat now to offend him; yet my language did as much: for I durst not say YOU to him, but THOU or THEE, as the Occasion required, and then would he be sure to fall on me with his Fists.

The Friends' reasons for using the mutual *T* were much the same as those of the French revolutionaries, but the Friends were always a minority and the larger society was antagonized by their violations of decorum.

Some Friends use "thee" today; the nominative "thou" has been dropped and "thee" is used as both the nominative and (as formerly) the accusative. Interestingly many Friends also use "you." "Thee" is likely to be reserved for Friends among themselves and "you" said to outsiders. This seems to be a survival of the solidarity semantic. In English at large, of course, "thou" is no longer used. The explanation of its disappearance is by no means certain; however, the forces at work seem to have included a popular reaction against the radicalism of Quakers and Levelers and also a general trend in English toward simplified verbal inflection.

In the world today there are numerous examples of the association proposed between ideology and pronoun semantics. In Yugoslavia, our informants tell us, there was, for a short time following the establishment of Communism, a universal mutual *T* of solidarity. Today revolutionary *esprit* has declined and *V* has returned for much the same set of circumstances as in Italy, France, or Spain. There is also some power asymmetry in Yugoslavia's "Socialist manners." A soldier says *V* and *Comrade General*, but the general addresses the soldier with *T* and surname.

It is interesting in our materials to contrast usage in the Afrikaans language of South Africa and in the Gujerati and Hindi languages of India with the rest of the collection. On the questionnaire, Afrikaans speakers made eight nonreciprocal power distinctions; especially notable are distinctions within the family and the distinctions between customer and waiter and between boss and clerk, since these are almost never power-coded in French, Italian, German, etc., although they once were. The Afrikaans pattern generally preserves the asymmetry of the dyads described in Figure 2, and that suggests a more static society and a less developed equalitarian ethic. The forms of address used between Afrikaans-speaking whites and the groups of "coloreds" and "blacks" are especially interesting. The Afrikaaner uses *T*, but the two lower castes use neither *T* nor *V*. The intermediate caste of "coloreds" says *Meneer* to the white and the "blacks" say *Baas*. It is as if these social distances transcend anything that can be found within the white group and so require their peculiar linguistic expressions.

The Gujerati and Hindi languages of India have about the same pronoun semantic, and it is heavily loaded with power. These languages have all the asymmetrical usage of Afrikaans and, in addition, use the non-reciprocal *T* and *V* between elder brother and younger brother and between husband and wife. This truly feudal pronominal pattern is consistent with the static Indian society. However, that society is now changing rapidly and, consistent with that change, the norms of pronoun usage are also changing. The progressive young Indian exchanges the mutual *T* with his wife.

In our account of the general semantic evolution of the pronouns, we have identified a stage in which the solidarity rule was limited to address between persons of equal power. This seemed to yield a two-dimensional system in equilibrium (see Figure 1*a*), and we have wondered why address did not permanently stabilize there. It is possible, of course, that human cognition favors the binary choice without contingencies and so found its way to the suppression of one dimension. However, this theory does not account for the fact that it was the rule of solidarity that triumphed. We believe, therefore, that the development of open societies with an equalitarian ideology acted against the nonreciprocal power semantic and in favor of solidarity. It is our suggestion that the larger social changes created a distaste for the face-to-face expression of differential power.

What of the many actions other than nonreciprocal *T* and *V* which express power asymmetry? A vassal not only says *V* but also bows, lifts his cap, touches his forelock, keeps silent, leaps to obey. There are a large number of expressions of subordination which are patterned isomorphically with *T* and *V*. Nor are the pronouns the only forms of nonreciprocal address. There are, in addition, proper names and titles, and many of these operate today on a nonreciprocal power pattern in America and in Europe, in open and equalitarian societies.

In the American family there are no discriminating pronouns, but there are nonreciprocal norms of address. A father says "Jim" to his son but, unless he is extraordinarily "advanced," he does not anticipate being called "Jack" in reply. In the American South there are no pronouns to mark the caste separation of Negro and white, but there are nonreciprocal norms of address. The white man is accustomed to call the Negro by his first name, but he expects to be called "Mr. Legree." In America and in Europe there are forms of nonreciprocal address for all the dyads of asymmetrical power; customer and waiter, teacher and student, father and son, employer and employee.

Differences of power exist in a democracy as in all societies. What is the difference between expressing power asymmetry in pronouns and expressing it by choice of title and proper name? It seems to be primarily a question of the degree of linguistic compulsion. In face-to-face address we can usually avoid the use of any name or title but not so easily the use of a pronoun. Even if the pronoun can be avoided, it will be implicit in the inflection of the verb. "Dites quelque chose" clearly says *vous* to the Frenchman. A norm for the pronominal and verbal expression of power compels a continuing coding of power, whereas a norm for titles and names permits power to go uncoded in most discourse. Is there any reason why the pronominal coding should be more congenial to a static society than to an open society?

We have noticed that mode of address intrudes into consciousness as a problem at times of status change. Award of the doctoral degree, for instance, transforms a student into a colleague and, among American academics, the familiar first name is normal. The fledgling academic may find it difficult to call his former teachers by their first names. Although these teachers may be young and affable, they have had a very real power over him for several years and it will feel presumptuous to deny this all at once with a new mode of address. However, the "tyranny of democratic manners" (**77**) does not allow him to continue comfortable with the polite "Professor X." He would not like to be thought unduly conscious of status, unprepared for faculty rank, a born lickspittle. Happily, English allows him a respite. He can avoid any term of address, staying with the uncommitted "you," until he and his addressees have got used to the new state of things. This linguistic *rite de passage* has, for English speakers, a waiting room in which to screw up courage.

In a fluid society crises of address will occur more frequently than in a static society, and so the pronominal coding of power differences is more likely to be felt as onerous. Coding by title and name would be more tolerable because less compulsory. Where status is fixed by birth and does not change each man has enduring rights and obligations of address.

A strong equalitarian ideology of the sort dominant in America works to suppress every conventional expression of power asymmetry. If the worker becomes conscious of his unreciprocated polite address to the boss, he may feel that his human dignity requires him to change. However, we do not feel the full power of the ideology until we are in a situation that gives us some claim to receive deferential address. The American professor often feels foolish being given his title, he almost certainly will not claim it as a prerogative; he may take pride in being on a first-name basis with his students. Very "palsy" parents may invite their children to call them by first name. The very President of the Republic invites us all to call him "Ike." Nevertheless, the differences of power are real and are experienced. Cronin has suggested in an amusing piece (**77**) that subordination is expressed by Americans in a subtle, and generally unwitting, body language. "The repertoire includes the boyish grin, the deprecatory cough, the unfinished sentence, the appreciative giggle, the drooping shoulders, the head-scratch and the bottom-waggle."

GROUP STYLE WITH THE PRONOUNS OF ADDRESS

The identification of style is relative to the identification of some constancy. When we have marked out the essentials of some action—it might be walking or speaking a language or driving a car—we can identify the residual variation as stylistic. Different styles are different ways of "doing the same thing," and so their identification waits on some designation of the range of performances to be regarded as "the same thing."

Linguistic science finds enough that is constant in English and French and Latin to put all these and many more into one family—the Indo-European. It is possible with reference to this constancy to think of Italian and Spanish and English and the others as so many styles of Indo-European. They all have, for instance, two singular pronouns of address, but each language has an individual phonetic and semantic style in pronoun usage. We are ignoring phonetic style (through the use of the generic T and V), but in the second section of the paper we have described differences in the semantic styles of French, German, and Italian.

Linguistic styles are potentially expressive when there is covariation between characteristics of language performance and characteristics of the performers. When styles are "interpreted," language behavior is functionally expressive. On that abstract level where the constancy is Indo-European and the styles are French, German, English, and Italian, interpretations of style must be statements about communities of speakers, statements of national character, social structure, or group ideology. In the last section we have hazarded a few propositions on this level.

It is usual, in discussion of linguistic style, to set constancy at the level of a language like French or English rather than at the level of a language family. In the languages we have studied there are variations in pronoun style that are associated with the social status of the speaker. We have seen that the use of V because of its entry at the top of a society and its diffusion downward was always interpreted as a mark of good breeding. It is interesting to find an organization of French journeymen in the generation after the Revolution adopting a set of rules of propriety cautioning members against going without tie or shoes at home on Sunday and also against the use of the mutual T among themselves (**308**). Our informants assure us that V and T still function as indications of class membership. The Yugoslavians have a saying that a peasant would say T to a king. By contrast, a French nobleman who turned up in our net told us that he had said T to no one in the world except the old woman who was his nurse in childhood. He is prevented by the dominant democratic ideology from saying T to subordinates and by his own royalist ideology from saying it to equals.

In literature, pronoun style has often been used to expose the pretensions of social climbers and the would-be elegant. Persons aping the manners of the class above them usually do not get the imitation exactly right. They are likely to notice some point of difference between their own class and the next higher and then extend the difference too widely, as in the use of the "elegant" broad [a] in "can" and "bad." Molière gives us his "*précieuses ridicules*" saying V to servants whom a refined person would call T. In Ben Jonson's *Everyman in his Humour* and *Epicoene* such true gallants as Wellbred and Knowell usually say "you" to one another but they make frequent expressive shifts between this form and "thou," whereas such fops as John Daw and Amorous-La-Foole make unvarying use of "you."

Our sample of visiting French students was roughly homogeneous in social status as judged by the single criterion of paternal occupation. Therefore, we could not make any systematic study of differences in class style, but we thought it possible that, even within this select group, there might be interpretable differences of style. It was our guess that the tendency to make wide or narrow use of the solidary T would be related to general radicalism or conservatism of ideology. As a measure of this latter dimension we used Eysenck's Social Attitude Inventory (**117**). This is a collection of statements to be accepted or rejected concerning a variety of matters—religion, economics, racial relations, sexual behavior, etc. Eysenck has validated the scale in England and in France on members of Socialist, Communist, Fascist, Conservative, and Liberal party members. In general, to be radical on this scale is to favor change and to be conservative is to wish to maintain the status quo or turn back to some earlier condition. We undertook to relate scores on this inventory to an index of pronoun style.

As yet we have reported no evidence demonstrating that there exists such a thing as a personal style in pronoun usage in the sense of a tendency to make wide or narrow use of T. It may be that each item in the questionnaire, each sort of person addressed, is an independent personal norm not predictable from any other. A child learns what to say to each kind of person. What he learns in each case depends on the groups in which he has membership. Perhaps his usage is a bundle of unrelated habits.

Guttman (**402**) has developed the technique of Scalogram Analysis for determining whether or not a collection of statements taps a common dimension. A perfect Guttman scale can be made of the statements: (*a*) I am at least 5′ tall; (*b*) I am at least 5′ 4″ tall; (*c*) I am at least 5′ 7″ tall; (*d*) I am at least 6′ 1″ tall; (*e*) I am at least 6′ 2″ tall. Endorsement of a more extreme statement will always be associated with endorsement of all less extreme statements. A person can be assigned a single score—*a*, *b*, *c*, *d*, or *e*—which represents the most extreme statement he has endorsed and, from this single score all his individual answers can be reproduced. If he scores *c* he has also endorsed *a* and *b* but not *d* or *e*. The general criterion for scalability is the reproducibility of individual responses from a single score, and this depends on the items being interrelated so that endorsement of one is reliably associated with endorsement or rejection of the others.

The Guttman method was developed during World War II for the measurement of social attitudes, and it has been widely used. Perfect reproducibility is not likely to be found for all the statements which an investigator guesses to be concerned with some single attitude. The usual thing is to accept a set of statements as scalable when they are 90 per cent reproducible and also satisfy certain other requirements; for example, there must be some statements that are not given a very one-sided response but are accepted and rejected with nearly equal frequency.

The responses to the pronoun questionnaire are not varying degrees of agreement (as in an attitude questionnaire) but are rather varying probabilities of saying *T* or *V*. There seems to be no reason why these bipolar responses cannot be treated like yes or no responses on an attitude scale. The difference is that the scale, if there is one, will be the semantic dimension governing the pronouns, and the scale score of each respondent will represent his personal semantic style.

It is customary to have 100 subjects for a Scalogram Analysis, but we could find only 50 French students. We tested all 28 items for scalability and found that a subset of them made a fairly good scale. It was necessary to combine response categories so as to dichotomize them in order to obtain an average reproducibility of 85 per cent. This coefficient was computed for the five intermediate items having the more-balanced marginal frequencies. A large number of items fell at or very near the two extremes. The solidarity or *T*-most end of the scale could be defined by father, mother, elder brother, young boys, wife, or lover quite as well as by younger brother. The remote or *V*-most end could be defined by "waiter" or "top boss" as well as by "army general." The intervening positions, from the *T*-end to the *V*-end, are: the elderly female servant known since childhood, grandfather, a male fellow student, a female fellow student, and an elder brother's wife.

For each item on the scale a *T* answer scores one point and a *V* answer no points. The individual total scores range from 1 to 7, which means the scale can differentiate only seven semantic styles. We divided the subjects into the resultant seven stylistically homogeneous groups and, for each group, determined the average scores on radicalism-conservatism. There was a set of almost perfectly consistent differences.

In Table 1 appear the mean radicalism scores for each pronoun style. The individual radicalism scores range between 2 and 13; the higher the score the more radical the person's ideology. The very striking result is that the group radicalism scores duplicate the order of the group pronoun scores with only a single reversal. The rank-difference correlation between the two sets of scores is .96, and even with only seven paired scores this is a very significant relationship.

There is enough consistency of address to justify speaking of a personal-pronoun style which involves a more or less wide use of the solidary *T*. Even among students of the same socioeconomic level there are differences of style, and these are potentially expressive of radicalism and conservatism in ideology. A Frenchman could, with some confidence, infer that a male university student who regularly said *T* to female fellow students would favor the nationalization of industry, free love, trial marriage, the abolition of capital punishment, and the weakening of nationalistic and religious loyalties.

What shall we make of the association between a wide use of *T* and a cluster of radical sentiments. There may be no "sense" to it at all, that is, no logical connection between the linguistic practice and the attitudes, but simply a general tendency to go along with the newest thing. We know that left-wing attitudes are more likely to be found in the laboring class than in the professional classes. Perhaps those offspring of the professional class who sympathize with proletariat politics also, incidentally, pick up the working man's wide use of *T* without feeling that there is anything in the linguistic practice that is congruent with the ideology.

On the other hand perhaps there is something appropriate in the association. The ideology is consistent in its disapproval of barriers between people: race, religion, nationality, property, marriage, even criminality. All these barriers have the effect of separating the solidary, the "in-group," from the nonsolidary, the "out-group." The radical says the criminal is not far enough "out" to be killed; he should be re-educated. He says that a nationality ought not to be so solidary that it prevents world organization from succeeding. Private property ought to be abolished, industry should be nationalized. There are to be no more out-groups and in-groups but rather one group, undifferentiated by nationality, religion, or pronoun of address. The fact that the pronoun which is being extended to all men alike is *T*, the mark of solidarity, the pronoun of the nuclear family, expresses the radical's intention to extend his sense of brotherhood. But

Table 1. Scores on the Pronoun Scale in
Relation to Scores on the Radicalism Scale

Group Pronoun Score	Group Mean Radicalism Score
1	5.50
2	6.66
3	6.82
4	7.83
5	6.83
6	8.83
7	9.75

we notice that the universal application of the pronoun eliminates the discrimination that gave it a meaning and that gives particular point to an old problem. Can the solidarity of the family be extended so widely? Is there enough libido to stretch so far? Will there perhaps be a thin solidarity the same everywhere but nowhere so strong as in the past?

THE PRONOUNS OF ADDRESS AS EXPRESSIONS OF TRANSIENT ATTITUDES

Behavior norms are practices consistent within a group. So long as the choice of a pronoun is recognized as normal for a group, its interpretation is simply the membership of the speaker in that group. However, the implications of group membership are often very important; social class, for instance, suggests a kind of family life, a level of education, a set of political views, and much besides. These facts about a person belong to his character. They are enduring features which help to determine actions over many years. Consistent personal style in the use of the pronouns of address does not reveal enough to establish the speaker's unique character, but it can help to place him in one or another large category.

Sometimes the choice of a pronoun clearly violates a group norm and perhaps also the customary practice of the speaker. Then the meaning of the act will be sought in some attitude or emotion of the speaker. It is as if the interpreter reasoned that variations of address between the same two persons must be caused by variations in their attitudes toward one another. If two men of seventeenth century France properly exchange the V of upper-class equals and one of them gives the other T, he suggests that the other is his inferior since it is to his inferiors that a man says T. The general meaning of an unexpected pronoun choice is simply that the speaker, for the moment, views his relationship as one that calls for the pronoun used. This kind of variation in language behavior expresses a contemporaneous feeling or attitude. These variations are not consistent personal styles but departures from one's own custom and the customs of a group in response to a mood.

As there have been two great semantic dimensions governing T and V, so there have also been two principal kinds of expressive meaning. Breaking the norms of power generally has the meaning that a speaker regards an addressee as his inferior, superior, or equal, although by usual criteria, and according to the speaker's own customary usage, the addressee is not what the pronoun implies. Breaking the norms of solidarity generally means that the speaker temporarily thinks of the other as an outsider or as an intimate; it means that sympathy is extended or withdrawn.

The oldest uses of T and V to express attitudes seem everywhere to have been the T of contempt or anger and the V of admiration or respect. In his study of the French pronouns Schliebitz (**353**) found the first examples of these expressive uses in literature of the twelfth and thirteenth centuries, which is about the time that the power semantic crystallized in France, and Grand (**139**) has found the same thing for Italian. In saying T, where V is usual, the speaker treats the addressee like a servant or a child and assumes the right to berate him. The most common use of the expressive V, in the early materials, is that of the master who is exceptionally pleased with the work of a servant and elevates him pronominally to match this esteem.

Racine, in his dramas, used the pronouns with perfect semantic consistency. His major figures exchange the V of upper-class equals. Lovers, brother and sister, husband and wife—none of them says T if he is of high rank, but each person of high rank has a subordinate confidante to whom he says T and from whom he receives V. It is a perfect nonreciprocal power semantic. This courtly pattern is broken only for the greatest scenes in each play. Racine reserved the expressive pronoun as some composers save the cymbals. In both *Andromaque* and *Phèdre* there are only two expressive departures from the norm, and they mark climaxes of feeling.

Jespersen (**213**) believed that English "thou" and "ye" (or "you") were more often shifted to express mood and tone than were the pronouns of the continental languages, and our comparisons strongly support this opinion. The "thou" of contempt was so very familiar that a verbal form was created to name this expressive use. Shakespeare gives it to Sir Toby Belch (*Twelfth Night*) in the lines urging Andrew Aguecheek to send a challenge to the disguised Viola: "Taunt him with the license of ink, if thou thou'st him some thrice, it shall not be amiss." In life the verb turned up in Sir Edward Coke's attack on Raleigh at the latter's trial in 1603 (**208**): "All that he did, was at thy instigation, thou viper; for I thou thee, thou traitor."

The *T* of contempt and anger is usually introduced between persons who normally exchange *V* but it can, of course, also be used by a subordinate to a superior. As the social distance is greater, the overthrow of the norm is more shocking and generally represents a greater extremity of passion. Sejanus, in Ben Jonson's play of that name, feels extreme contempt for the emperor Tiberius but wisely gives him the reverential *V* to his face. However, soliloquizing after the emperor has exited, Sejanus begins: "Dull, heavy Caesar! Wouldst thou tell me . . . ." In Jonson's *Volpone* Mosca invariably says "you" to his master until the final scene when, as the two villains are about to be carted away, Mosca turns on Volpone with "Bane to thy wolfish nature."

Expressive effects of much greater subtlety than those we have described are common in Elizabethan and Jacobean drama. The exact interpretation of the speaker's attitude depends not only on the pronoun norm he upsets but also on his attendant words and actions and the total setting. Still simple enough to be unequivocal is the ironic or mocking "you" said by Tamburlaine to the captive Turkish emperor Bajazeth. This exchange occurs in Act IV of Marlowe's play:

Tamburlaine: Here, Turk, wilt thou have a clean trencher?
Bajazeth: Ay, tyrant, and more meat.
Tamburlaine: Soft, sir, you must be dieted; too much eating will make you surfeit.

"Thou" is to be expected from captor to captive and the norm is upset when Tamburlaine says "you." He cannot intend to express admiration or respect since he keeps the Turk captive and starves him. His intention is to mock the captive king with respectful address, implying a power that the king has lost.

The momentary shift of pronoun directly expresses a momentary shift of mood, but that interpretation does not exhaust its meaning. The fact that a man has a particular momentary attitude or emotion may imply a great deal about his characteristic disposition, his readiness for one kind of feeling rather than another. Not every attorney general, for instance, would have used the abusive "thou" to Raleigh. The fact that Edward Coke did so suggests an arrogant and choleric temperament and, in fact, many made this assessment of him (**208**). When Volpone spoke to Celia, a lady of Venice, he ought to have said "you" but he began at once with "thee." This violation of decorum, together with the fact that he leaps from his sick bed to attempt rape of the lady, helps to establish Volpone's monstrous character. His abnormal form of address is consistent with the unnatural images in his speech. In any given situation we know the sort of people who would break the norms of address and the sort who would not. From the fact that a man does break the norms we infer his immediate feelings and, in addition, attribute to him the general character of people who would have such feelings and would give them that kind of expression.

With the establishment of the solidarity semantic a new set of expressive meanings became possible—feelings of sympathy and estrangement. In Shakespeare's plays there are expressive meanings that derive from the solidarity semantic as well as many dependent on power usage and many that rely on both connotations. The play *Two Gentlemen of Verona* is concerned with the Renaissance ideal of friendship and provides especially clear expressions of solidarity. Proteus and Valentine, the two Gentlemen, initially exchange "thou," but when they touch on the subject of love, on which they disagree, their address changes to the "you" of estrangement. Molière (**119**) has shown us that a man may even put himself at a distance as does George Dandin in the soliloquoy beginning: "George Dandin! George Dandin! Vous avez fait une sottise . . ."

In both French and English drama of the past, *T* and *V* were marvelously sensitive to feelings of approach and withdrawal. In terms of Freud's striking amoeba metaphor the pronouns signal the extension or retraction of libidinal pseudopodia. However, in French, German, and Italian today this use seems to be very uncommon. Our informants told us that the *T*, once extended, is almost never taken back for the reason that it would mean the complete withdrawal of esteem. The only modern expressive shift we have found is a rather chilling one. Silverberg (**378**) reports that in Germany in 1940 a prostitute and her client said *du* when they met and while they were together but when the libidinal tie (in the narrow sense) had been dissolved they resumed the mutual distant *Sie*.

We have suggested that the modern direction of change in pronoun usage expresses a will to extend the solidary ethic to everyone. The apparent decline of expressive shifts between *T* and *V* is more difficult to interpret. Perhaps it is because Europeans have seen that excluded persons or races or groups can become the target of extreme aggression from groups that are benevolent within themselves. Perhaps Europeans would like to convince themselves that the solidary ethic once extended will not be withdrawn, that there is security in the mutual *T*.

Style in *Finnegans Wake*

(abstract)

Joyce's well-known stylistic devices in *Finnegans Wake* produce effects
that are interesting in various ways to various disciplines. The linguist is
interested in and often aggrieved by the extremity of the Joycean idiolect;
the psychologist is interested in that idiolect and also in the semantic
density Joyce achieves; the critic is interested in all these things. But it
falls to him to strike a balance between the extremity of method in the
book and its personal structuring of literary experience, between its
trivial materials and its linguistic agility in their manipulation, between
the obsessive perseverance which kept Joyce at it and the concentrated
and vigorous literacy which that perseverance produced. In the last
analysis, any evaluation of the book cannot escape reckoning with its
energetic stylistic belligerence as that relates to linguistic possibility.

The bulk of this paper is a detailed study of the revisions of a single
paragraph of the "Anna Livia Plurabelle" chapter of *Finnegans Wake*,
from first draft to final version. The revisions are shown to be stylistic
in the main, which is to say that they affect principally the language of the
book; and although the narrative or descriptive elements in the book are
also extended by the revisions, there is a sense in which the "story" may
be said to have been there from the first and to have been simply adum-
brated by the revisions. The style of *Finnegans Wake* is shown to be both
a cohesive force which gives the book a basic and centripetal unity and
also a device for reminding us continually that the book is an artifact, a
made thing.

The paper is in substance the introduction to a definitive edition of the
"Anna Livia Plurabelle" manuscripts now in the British Museum; the
edition will be published shortly by the University of Minnesota Press
(of. **171**).

Comments to Part Seven

CHATMAN: My point concerns pedagogical implications suggested by Mr. Richards' splendid paper. There is a serious danger that some of the best minds coming into the university find literature unpalatable because they have picked up the notion, in high school and elsewhere, that poetry is supposed to be very vague and elusive. It goes without saying, of course, that this is quite untrue; that poetic language is not only extraordinarily complex but also extraordinarily precise; that the responsible and successful poet is just as careful about the structure of his discourse as the most thoroughgoing logician; that even in Romantic poetry it is necessary to recognize the difference between vagueness of *feeling* and the precision of language in which these feelings are depicted. (Indeed, the serious undervaluation by some modern critics of Romantic poetry stems less from a close and exacting study of its structure than from a distaste for the role that the Romantic poet typically chooses to assume.) The greatest service modern teachers can perform is to convince our more technically minded students that they do not have to give up any sense of intellectual discipline when they take up a poem; that, far from it, they should be prepared for an experience which is just as intellectually demanding *and* satisfying as that afforded by scientific discourse. And I know of no one who has demonstrated this quite so clearly and persuasively as I. A. Richards.

. . .

JAKOBSON: Brown's interesting research deserves further development. The use of different pronouns designating the addressee is but a part of a more complex code of verbal attitudes toward the addressee and must be analyzed in connection with this total code, in particular with the question whether we do or do not name the addressee and how we title him. There is an essential difference among languages: how often the addressee is supposed to be named in the utterances, is he to be addressed preferably by name (Ivan Ivanovič!) or by a general term (Monsieur!), and whether such a term exists in the given language. Although in French the omission of the vocative noun is impolite (Oui, Monsieur!), in Russian its repetitive use is a feature of servile style. In this respect each language, and each social dialect within a given language, has its own invariants. The variables display different connotations. In the choice of conventional means to designate the addressee, the addresser exhibits his individuality only by an optional preference for one of the eligible etiquettes extant in the over-all code of the given language. In such a research there is a great danger of reinterpreting the data of one language from the point of view of another pattern. The choice between the singular and plural form of the second-person pronoun has quite different connotations and social functions in French, in German, and in Russian. The ranking of addressees follows different patterns: to what degree and in what situations the gestural or pronominal pointing at the addressee is estimated as unceremonious, indecent, or

278

intimate, in contradistinction to the distancing forms like plural and/or third person. The most striking ritual of such a distancing is the prohibition of verbal intercourse between persons who are, or have a right, to be in sexual intercourse: Gilyaks in connubial relations communicate with each other by addressing a third person or a spirit. The use of the second-person pronoun must also be confronted with the whole pattern of personal pronouns; for example, for Czech the absence of the first or second pronoun as a subject in verbal sentences is neutral, and the insertion of these forms is emphatic; on the other hand, in Russian the presence of such pronouns is neutral and their omission emphatic.

PART EIGHT

Psychological Approaches to the Problem of Style

Vectors of Prose Style

JOHN B. CARROLL

The very concept of style implies variation. It takes little argument or evidence to secure agreement that there are different manners of writing, and that these differ among themselves not only by virtue of the content or the subject matter treated but also by virtue of a host of "stylistic" elements which are present in varying degree in samples of prose. But what, exactly, are these stylistic elements? Ever since man discovered the pleasure of commenting upon his own and others' oral and written compositions, he has been seeking a useful set of pigeonholes for classifying style. The tendency has been for the classifications to proliferate without design or system. Literary criticism today does not have any well and sharply defined set of elements by which a sample of prose may readily be characterized.

In 1935, the renowned psychologist L. L. Thurstone published a book (**414**) in which he presented the technique of what is generally known as *factor analysis*—a statistical procedure for identifying and measuring the fundamental dimensions ("vectors") that account for the variation to be observed in any set of phenomena. Since then factor analysis has been a tool widely used by psychologists in studying intelligence, personality, interests, emotions, rates of learning, and even word meanings, but the technique has never heretofore been applied to the study of literary style. If we can study the "personalities" of people by factor analysis, we should be able to study the "personalities" of samples of prose. In the simplest possible terms, factor analysis enables the investigator to apply a large number of measurement procedures to a sample of objects and find out to what extent these measures overlap with each other.

Although the objective study of literary style by means of statistical analysis is not a completely novel endeavor, none of the scholars who have engaged in such study has ventured to ask the question raised here: what are the basic dimensions in which style varies? In contrast to previous statistical studies of style, each of which has fixed attention on one or a small number of the possible ways of measuring style, this investigation[1] examines the relations among a large number of indices of style and attempts to identify the most salient ways of describing stylistic variation in prose.

The notion of attempting to quantify aspects of literary style will be repulsive to many literary critics and outright ridiculous to others. The writer must confess that even he, after completing the study, remains skeptical whether the dimensions identified here adequately represent the aspects of style that truly make the difference between great literature and the not so great, or even the aspects that serve to differentiate some of the recognized styles of writing. Nevertheless, some of the hopes in which the study was undertaken seem to have been realized: the study points to some of the more obvious characteristics of prose which have to be observed, mentioned, and duly noted before the literary critic can really go to work. It injects a semblance of order into the study of "readability" and suggests certain bases for guiding the teaching of English composition in schools. Further, it provides leads toward the psycholinguistic study of the "encoding" processes by which the individual translates nonverbal prelinguistic states of behavior into linguistically encoded output. It lends some support to the notion that certain factors of literary style correspond to predispositional "sets" which govern the emission of large classes of verbal responses—personal pronouns, for example.

PROCEDURES

There are two distinct kinds of problems to be faced in designing any study that seeks to identify the major dimensions of a set of phenomena: (1) how can we obtain a sufficiently heterogeneous sample of the things we want to study, and (2) what measurements shall we take in order to sample

[1] The research reported herein was performed pursuant to a contract with the United States Office of Education, Department of Health, Education, and Welfare. Reproduction in whole or in part is permitted for any purpose of the United States Government. I am indebted to the eight raters used in the study, Zita Gray, Grace Kestenman, Don McCaull, R. Dale Painter, Mrs. Newton Press, Dr. E. H. Sauer, Mrs. Mary G. Seifel, and Mary Alice Tomkins, and to Marilyn Brachman, Mrs. Mary S. Carroll, Arthur S. Couch, Marjorie Morse, Frederic Weinfeld, and Mrs. Marcia Wideman for their help in various aspects of analysis. The statistical computations were performed by means of facilities made available at the Littauer Statistical Laboratory of Harvard University, the Computation Center of Massachusetts Institute of Technology, and the John Hancock Life Insurance Company, and thanks are hereby tendered to each of these organizations. A longer and more detailed report of the study is being submitted for publication elsewhere.

all the significant ways in which the phenomena vary? Practical considerations set certain limits in both of these problems.

The sample of objects studied here consisted of 150 passages from various sources and styles of English prose. Each passage was chosen so as to be more or less self-contained within a little more than 300 words. By selecting passages according to categories—novels (both British and American, both nineteenth and twentieth centuries), essays, newspaper features and editorials, biographies, scientific papers, textbooks, speeches, legal documents, personal letters, and sermons were among the categories used—we hoped to include the widest possible assortment of subject matters and styles. The sample even included several relatively low-grade high-school English compositions.

The measures taken on these 150 passages fell into two classes: subjective and objective. The objective measures involved various counts, indices, and ratios based on the enumeration of certain classes of words, clauses, sentences, and other linguistic entities and included some of the measures used in previous statistical studies of style. Subjective measures were secured partly to help in the interpretation of results for the objective measures, partly to provide bench marks for certain characteristics of style which the objective measures could hardly be expected to describe. It was of intrinsic interest, also, to study the extent to which a group of competent judges could agree in assigning ratings, and to determine the totality of ways they could find for characterizing the passages. In order to make the rating task as simple as possible, 29 adjectival scales were chosen with a view to covering the major qualities and traits of style as far as they could be determined a priori, and 8 expert judges—all with interest and training in English literature—were secured to rate each of the 150 passages on each of the 29 scales, the form of which may be illustrated as follows:

meaningless ___ : ___ : ___ : ___ : ___ : ___ : ___ meaningful

The 8 judgments obtained for each passage on each scale were then averaged.

In all, 68 scores were obtained for each of the 150 passages: the 29 averaged ratings of the 8 judges, and 39 objective measures. The names of the measures are listed in the first column of Table 1; unfortunately, space does not permit a full description of the procedures for obtaining the objective measures. The resulting 68 × 150 scores formed the basis for the ensuing statistical analysis. The correlation of each measure with each other measure was determined—the results being exhibited in a very large table with 68 rows and 68 columns. This *correlation matrix* was then subjected to a factor analysis in order to determine how many fundamental

Table 1. Results for 68 Measures of Prose Style; Reliability Coefficients and Loadings on Six Dimensions (Factors) of Prose Style

Variable	Variable Number	Reliability	General Stylistic Evaluation A	Personal Affect B	Ornamentation C	Abstractness D	Seriousness E	Characterization F
Subjective Ratings								
Profound-superficial	1	.84	.43	−.11	.06	.53	.41	.15
Subtle-obvious	2	.81	.20	−.17	.09	.72	−.09	.15
Abstract-concrete	3	.90	.02	−.01	.18	.64	.11	.16
Meaningful-meaningless	4	.70	.70	−.11	−.04	.04	.41	.03
Succinct-wordy	5	.78	.51	−.15	−.65	−.15	.14	−.01
Graceful-awkward	6	.73	.84	−.01	.07	.17	−.08	.12
Vigorous-placid	7	.80	.26	.63	.17	−.06	.21	−.10
Lush-austere	8	.80	−.01	.43	.55	.07	−.29	.17
Earnest-flippant	9	.87	.06	−.05	−.01	.05	.71	.13
Intimate-remote	10	.87	.10	.82	.02	−.33	.03	−.01
Elegant-uncouth	11	.82	.33	−.29	.44	.40	−.11	.02
Natural-affected	12	.80	.49	.06	−.51	−.26	.29	.08
Clear-hazy	13	.78	.72	.16	−.09	−.45	.10	−.17
Interesting-boring	14	.78	.84	.25	−.04	.12	.01	.06
Strong-weak	15	.64	.88	.21	.13	.00	.11	−.07
Opinionated-impartial	16	.89	−.01	.53	.36	.01	.07	.02
Original-trite	17	.77	.54	−.08	−.04	.44	−.20	.15
Ordered-chaotic	18	.69	.65	−.29	−.04	−.15	.06	−.09
Vivid-pale	19	.80	.61	.54	.07	−.09	−.05	−.01
Personal-impersonal	20	.86	.03	.83	.14	−.26	.00	.01
Precise-vague	21	.71	.64	.00	−.10	−.47	.03	−.17
Masculine-feminine	22	.85	.22	.06	.08	−.08	.58	−.09
Varied-monotonous	23	.75	.75	.22	.04	.20	−.10	.15
Emotional-rational	24	.90	−.05	.77	.22	−.12	−.02	.09
Complex-simple	25	.82	−.09	−.18	.48	.51	−.07	.04
Pleasant-unpleasant	26	.75	.88	.15	−.03	.07	−.11	.08
Serious-humorous	27	.92	.01	−.12	.00	.13	.70	.08
Florid-plain	28	.82	−.08	.33	.66	.16	−.28	.11
Good-bad	29	.74	.95	.01	−.02	.12	−.05	.02

Objective Measures (All based on 300 words)

30 No. paragraphs	—	−.09	−.13	−.50	−.02	−.23	−.03
31 No. syllables	.86	−.10	−.58	.30	.05	.09	−.23
32 No. sentences	.85	.05	−.03	−.61	.13	−.18	.05
33 Standard deviation sentence length	.17	.11	.25	.54	.00	.12	−.01
34 No. clauses	.78	.01	.28	−.60	.26	−.22	.04
35 Clause complexity index	.60	−.08	.18	.39	.02	.18	−.15
36 % noun clauses	—	−.02	.01	−.22	.45	.13	−.25
37 % adjectival clauses	—	−.13	−.07	.19	−.21	.05	.34
38 % adverbial clauses	—	−.11	.09	.04	−.20	−.17	.06
39 % parenthetical clauses	—	−.01	.04	.08	−.01	−.02	−.29
40 % "action" verbs	.76	.06	.11	−.40	−.17	−.23	−.01
41 % "cognitive" verbs	.58	.06	.46	.07	.12	.05	−.06
42 % transitive verbs	.33	.01	−.06	.03	−.15	−.03	−.63
43 % intransitive verbs	.26	−.14	.14	−.09	−.05	−.17	.32
44 % copulative verbs	.44	.04	−.04	.06	.18	.12	.43
45 % Latin-derived verbs	.57	−.06	−.33	.20	.12	.10	−.25
46 % passive verbs	.49	−.06	−.45	.15	−.07	.16	.12
47 Mean tense	.88	−.12	−.15	.11	−.02	−.01	.04
48 Entropy of tense	.42	−.16	.07	−.02	.06	−.04	−.29
49 No. infinitives	—	.04	.16	−.14	−.01	.05	−.02
50 No. participles	—	.08	−.08	.17	−.31	−.07	−.15
51 No. gerunds	—	.13	−.20	−.03	.08	−.04	−.15
52 No. proper nouns	.83	−.04	.01	−.03	.01	−.01	−.38
53 No. common nouns	.74	−.01	−.49	.18	−.22	−.11	.13
54 % unmodified common nouns preceded by "the"	.45	.07	.07	−.50	.10	.03	.18
55 % nouns with Latin suffixes	.69	−.06	−.22	.42	.22	.20	−.22
56 No. articles	.52	.18	−.28	−.11	.01	.04	.20
57 % indefinite articles	.48	.07	−.09	−.10	−.01	−.48	.01
58 No. personal pronouns	.84	.11	.60	−.23	.20	−.10	−.09
59 No. possessive pronouns	.64	−.07	.30	.09	.08	−.21	−.14
60 No. indefinite pronouns	.43	.01	.28	−.18	.14	.21	.27
61 No. indefinite and quantitative determiners	.27	−.10	−.09	.11	−.24	.35	.20
62 No. demonstrative pronouns	.44	−.18	.11	−.05	.05	.22	.13
63 No. numerical expressions	.67	−.01	−.07	−.09	−.49	−.06	−.02
64 No. prepositions	.58	.01	.34	.35	−.01	.09	−.01
65 No. pronouns	.83	−.01	.58	−.26	.18	−.14	−.13
66 No. determiners	.52	−.19	.01	.00	−.45	.34	.25
67 No. descriptive adjectives	.66	.11	−.18	.38	.09	−.10	.20
68 No. participial modifiers	.38	.09	−.05	.33	.01	−.13	−.01

* The positive pole of the adjectival scales is represented by the *first* of the two adjectives specified.

dimensions would be needed, at a minimum, to account for all the inter-relations among the 68 measures.[2]

RESULTS

The formidable appearance and size of Table 1 are due simply to the desire to compress a maximum of the essential results of the study into a single table; the reader is invited to examine it carefully. It contains information bearing on two kinds of questions about the 68 measures. (1) How "reliable" are the measurements? In the case of the 29 subjective measures, this question relates to the extent to which the judges agreed in their ratings. A reliability coefficient of 1.00 would denote perfect agreement, and a coefficient of .00 would denote purely random agreement. In the case of the 39 objective measures, the coefficients given in Table 1 (where they are present at all) refer to the extent to which each measure gives consistent results from the first half of a 300-word sample to the second half. (2) What general trait or traits does each variable measure and to what extent? The data relevant to this question are the coefficients found in the last six columns of the table. All coefficients larger than about .25 in absolute magnitude may be regarded as significant for purposes of interpretation.

The reliability coefficients (in the first data column of Table 1) for the 29 averaged subjective ratings range from .64 for the scale *weak-strong*, to .92 for the scale *humorous-serious*, with a median at .80. Although the figures are high enough to suggest that each measure is sufficiently reliable to give meaningful results, the lack of perfect agreement is particularly noticeable for some scales. Some scales, such as *meaningful-meaningless* and *ordered-chaotic*, have low reliability because, we may guess, judges differ in their conceptions of how these terms apply to prose passages. It is of more than passing interest that scales which (as will be seen later) denote general stylistic evaluation, such as *good-bad, pleasant-unpleasant, strong-weak, interesting-boring, graceful-awkward, varied-monotonous, clear-hazy*, have uniformly low reliabilities, whereas such scales as *serious-humorous, abstract-concrete, emotional-rational, opinionated-impartial, earnest-flippant, intimate-remote*, and *personal-impersonal*, all of which refer to specific and relatively nonevaluative qualities of style, have high reliabilities. Judges can often agree in making descriptive classifications

[2] Of possible technical interest to some readers is the fact that the initial factor analysis was performed by means of Thurstone's centroid method, after which the factors were "rotated" to oblique simple structure by the writer's so-called *normal biquartimin* criterion (57). All these computations were performed with the aid of high-speed electronic computing machines.

of prose passages but they agree less often in making general evaluations of style. Perhaps this is what makes literary criticism exciting.

Concerning the reliabilities of the objective measures, we shall only comment that the figures indicate the extent to which a writer is likely to hold certain formal characteristics of his style constant within relatively short stretches.

We come now to the main findings of the study, the findings that give a provisional answer to the question of what are the dimensions of literary style. Although *seven* dimensions were indicated by the factor analysis technique, it appeared that only six of these could be given meaningful interpretation, and thus the data for the seventh are omitted from Table 1. The order in which the six remaining factors are discussed is actually immaterial, but they are listed in Table 1 as factors *A*, *B*, *C*, *D*, *E*, and *F*, in order of their apparent interest, importance, and relevance in connection with the study of literary style.

The variables having high coefficients in column *A* of Table 1 are in every case subjective ratings. In order of the magnitude of their "loadings" (as the coefficients are often called) they are the scales *good-bad* (29), *pleasant-unpleasant* (26), *strong-weak* (15), *interesting-boring* (14), *graceful-awkward* (6), *varied-monotonous* (23), *clear-hazy* (13), *meaningful-meaningless* (4), *ordered-chaotic* (18), *precise-vague* (21), *vivid-pale* (19), *original-trite* (17), *succinct-wordy* (5), *natural-affected* (12), *profound-superficial* (1), *elegant-uncouth* (11), and *vigorous-placid* (7). All these scales, in differing degrees, denote over-all positive or negative evaluation of a prose passage. We are therefore inclined to identify this factor by the name General Stylistic Evaluation. Notice, however, that some of the scales have significant loadings on certain other factors. Only the first six scales mentioned are unequivocal measures of stylistic evaluation alone. It is cheering to note that not a single objective measure shows any significant loading on factor *A*, General Stylistic Evaluation. Although the style of literary passages can be indexed in certain ways mechanically, it cannot be *evaluated* mechanically!

The key to the interpretation of factor *B* seems to be the presence of the subjective scales *personal-impersonal* (20), *intimate-remote* (10), *emotional-rational* (24), *vigorous-placid* (7), and to a lesser extent *vivid-pale* (19) and *opinionated-impartial* (16). Let us call this dimension Personal Affect. It is also indexed by a number of objective measures, such as number of personal pronouns (58), number of pronouns (65), and (negatively) number of syllables (31). (The negative loading of number of syllables is to be interpreted as indicating that passages with high Personal Affect have a relatively small number of syllables in 300 words, that is, the words tend to be short.) The dimension of Personal Affect is unrelated to General

Stylistic Evaluation: it refers simply to the extent to which a passage uses personal references, emotive terms, and similar devices, without necessarily making for "good" style or for "bad" style, either, for that matter.

Let us proceed to column C in Table 1. If the reader will run his finger down this column he will find high loadings for the following subjective scales: *florid-plain* (28), *wordy-succinct* (5) [reversing the polarity of the scale makes the loading positive], *lush-austere* (8), *affected-natural* (12), *complex-simple* (25), and *elegant-uncouth* (11). The factor is also indexed by long sentences (measure 32), long clauses (34), wide variation in sentence length (33), a relatively high proportion of common nouns which are preceded by adjectival or participial modifiers (54), long paragraphs (30), a high proportion of nouns with Latin suffixes (55), a low proportion of verbs denoting physical action (40), a high degree of use of dependent clauses of various orders (35), and a high number of descriptive adjectives (67). "Ornamentation" (as opposed to "plainness") is clearly a suitable name for this dimension.

The subjective scales having high loadings on factor D are *subtle-obvious* (2), *abstract-concrete* (3), *profound-superficial* (1), *complex-simple* (25), *hazy-clear* (13), *original-trite* (17), *elegant-uncouth* (11), and *remote-intimate* (10). The common element in these scales seems to be a generalized notion of abstractness and obscurity as opposed to concreteness, precision, and perspicuity; for convenience let us call this dimension Abstractness. Like factors B (Personal Affect) and C (Ornamentation), it is independent of factor A (General Stylistic Evaluation); that is, abstractness versus concreteness, the use of personal references versus the failure to use them, and ornamentation versus plainness have nothing to do with whether a prose passage is favorably thought of or with each other. Factor D (Abstractness) can be fairly well measured by several objective indicators: by a low proportion of numerical expressions (63), a low number of determining adjectives and pronouns like "this," "each," etc. (66), a high proportion of noun clauses (36), and a low number of participles (50).

Factor E we call Seriousness. The two subjective scales measuring this factor best are *earnest-flippant* (9) and *serious-humorous* (27). We are somewhat surprised to find, however, that the scale *masculine-feminine* (22) also relates to this factor. Evidently the term "masculine" as applied to literary style connotes earnestness and seriousness, whereas flippancy and humor are associated with femininity. Other scales measuring seriousness are *meaningful-meaningless* (4) and *profound-superficial* (1), and the factor can be indexed objectively by a low proportion of indefinite articles (57), a high proportion of indefinite and quantifying determining adjectives (61), and a high number of determiners (66). Whether these objective measures are intrinsically related to seriousness, or whether the findings are simply a reflection of the particular sample of literary passages used, we do not know.

Factor *F* in Table 1 is measured exclusively by objective measures: a low proportion of transitive verbs (42), a high proportion of copulative verbs relative to all verbs (44), a low number of proper nouns (52), a high

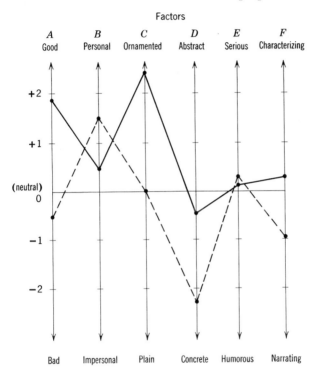

Figure 1. Style profiles of two prose passages: (———) a selection from F. Scott Fitzgerald's *A Diamond as Big as the Ritz*; (– – – –) a selection from Mickey Spillane's *Vengeance is Mine*.

proportion of adjective clauses (37), and a high proportion of intransitive verbs (43). We can make only a tentative interpretation of the underlying significance of this dimension; the evidence seems to point to a dimension of Characterization versus Narration. We would expect passages with high scores on this factor to be those that are more concerned with the "characterization" of entities—either by equating them with other entities through the use of copulative verbs or by describing them through the use of adjective clauses. Passages with low scores on this factor are more likely to be concerned with the reporting of action, most frequently the action of persons; they would thus be found to have a high proportion of transitive verbs and proper nouns.

These, then, are the six independent dimensions of "style" which have been identified in this study: General Stylistic Evaluation, Personal Affect, Ornamentation, Abstractness, Seriousness, and Characterization versus Narration. Just to intimate the possibility of using these dimensions as the basis for a typology of style, we present in Figure 1 the "profiles" of two of the passages measured in the study. One was a selection from F. Scott Fitzgerald's short story *A Diamond as Big as the Ritz*, in which the author paints a vivid picture of the impressions of the hero and his companion as they wander through the diamond palace. The other is a passage from a very different sort of writing, that of Mickey Spillane.

Two questions may have harassed the reader: are all these dimensions really of "style"—are not some of them rather a matter of the content of a passage? And are not some of these "dimensions" merely dimensions of the *meaning* of adjectives, not necessarily dimensions truly inherent in samples of prose? With respect to the first question, we must reply that there is no hard and fast distinction between style and content. Try as we may to define style as the *manner* of treating subject matter, the type of subject matter will in general impose constraints upon the possible kinds of stylistic treatment. In the present study a vain attempt was made to have judges differentiate between content and style: *content* was to be rated with scales 1 through 4, and *style* was to be rated with scales 5 through 29. The results make it abundantly clear that the judges did not differentiate content and style, at least not in their ratings.

With respect to the second question, it must be insisted that even though somewhat comparable results might be obtained by asking raters simply to judge adjectives for similarity of meaning in the abstract, the dimensions of meaning themselves cannot exist without some support in the real world to which the adjectives presumably refer. The reality and substantiality of these dimensions is further attested to by the abundant instances of correlation between subjective ratings and completely objective, quantitative indices which derive meaning only when applied to actual samples of prose.

Some Effects of Motivation
on Style of Encoding

CHARLES E. OSGOOD

A DEFINITION OF STYLE

Any language includes both obligatory and variable features at all levels of analysis, phonemic, morphemic, and syntactical.[1] The study of style concerns the *variable features* of the code. However, the variability need not be completely "free" (i.e., chance, unpredictable); rather, the student of style is interested in the *statistical properties of choices* where there is some degree of freedom in selection. The choices made in speaking and writing can also be characterized as either lexical or structural. Stylistics is generally more concerned with *structural choices* than with lexical choices, that is, in *how* a person talks about something rather than *what* he talks about. Finally, the student of style is usually interested in *deviations from norms* rather than the norms themselves, although the norms have to be determined before deviations from them can be noted and interpreted. However, we must distinguish what might be called situational deviation from individual deviation. Writing a textbook or a poem, talking on the telephone or to one's little children, as situations, produce certain predictable deviations from the over-all norm. Some students of style will be interested in such situational deviations. But in any situation of encoding, individuals will still display variations about the new, situational norm, and other students of style are interested in such *individual variations*.

For the purposes of this paper, then, *style is defined as an individual's deviations from norms for the situations in which he is encoding, these deviations being in the statistical properties of those structural features for which there exists some degree of choice in his code.* The nature of this

[1] This paper is based on research done by the author and Evelyn Walker, using samples of suicide and pseudocide notes provided by Edwin Shneidman, of Los Angeles. (A more detailed report has appeared in **304**.)

definition can be illustrated with one of the more familiar measures of style, *the verb/adjective ratio* developed by Busemann and others: Busemann recorded this measure for a sample of children telling stories; he also compared the ratios of individual children judged as varying in emotional stability (cf. **276**, p. 127). The average verb/adjective ratio for his whole sample would be what I refer to as a situational norm—the ratio most characteristic of children telling stories probably does differ somewhat from that most characteristic of a representative sample of English speaking and writing in general. The deviation of an individual child from this situational norm is an aspect of *his* style.

STYLE AS A PSYCHOLINGUISTIC PROBLEM

It is part of the credo of psycholinguists that the events that occur in messages produced by speakers and writers are dependent on events (states, processes) in these sources—their habits, their intellectual levels, their motivational and emotional states, their previously developed associations, their attitudes, and so on. Many message events depend on common or shared processes in sources—common because they are part of the obligatory structure of the code which various sources must learn if they are to communicate at all. Other message events are to some extent variable, and these are presumably correlated with variations of some sort among sources—either variation in the momentary situation in which they speak or persistent variation in their make-ups as individuals.

The study of style as a psycholinguistic problem, then, involves the following requirements: (1) some *indicator*, preferably objective, in the messages from the source; (2) some *characteristic*, preferably objective, of the individual producing the messages; (3) a *dependency relation* between indicator and characteristic, that is, a nonchance correlation across sources and messages with respect to this relation. The potential indicators in messages are as numerous as the features that display any degree of free variation (e.g., frequency of the first-person-singular pronoun "I," pitch variation in speaking, rarity of the vocabulary items employed, frequency of infinitive constructions, etc.). Equivalently, potential characteristics of human sources that might be indexed are as numerous as the pooled ingenuity of psychologists and other social scientists can make them (e.g., intelligence, anxiety, association structure, social role or status, occupational classification, etc.).

There are two restrictions on our freedom to relate indicators with human characteristics, however. One is embodied in condition 3—a nonchance dependency relation between indicator and characteristic must be demonstrated, and this often proves to be difficult (in part because of the multiple causation of message events). The other reflects one of the major pitfalls in science generally, circular reasoning or tautology. It must be possible to indicate the presence, absence, or degree of the independent variable (here, personal characteristic) *independently* of the dependent variable (here, message event or indicator). To take a ridiculous example, if we hypothesize that the frequency of "I," "me," and "mine" in messages is indicative of a person's "ego anxiety" and then proceed to rank our subjects' "ego anxiety" levels in terms of the frequency of first-person-singular pronouns, we obviously come out with a remarkably high relation, but one that is meaningless scientifically. To get out of this circle, the investigator needs to discover and apply some valid and independent index of "ego anxiety" in his subjects, for example, judgments of clinicians or some special objective test. More subtle circularity can also be illustrated with this example. Suppose the clinicians' judgments of "ego anxiety" actually, upon analysis, come down to their paying attention to the frequency of first-person-singular pronouns in interviews with the subjects—the resultant correlation between the indicator and the supposedly independent criterion of the subject characteristic is still suspect.

There is an essential difference between what may be called *idiosyncratic* and *nomothetic* studies of style. The idiosyncratic method is concerned with describing and interpreting the necessarily unique features of a style, either a situational style (e.g. of children's fairy stories, of eighteenth-century novels) or an individual style (e.g. Shakespeare's plays or particular college students' speech and writing as done in **347**). The investigator of idiosyncratic style may depend on intuitive methods or he may make use of deviations from norms determined by nomothetic methods. It is his goal which is different, being the accurate characterization of a particular style. The goal of the nomothetic method, on the other hand, is the discovery and validation of general dependency relations between message indicators and variables in communicators. The essence of the method is the demonstration of nonchance relations between particular indicators and particular characteristics (independently measured) in a sample drawn from within some specified situation of encoding, for example, from ordinary conversations, from personal letters, or the like. If the situation completely determines the style, correlations will approximate zero across the population of speakers or writers. A variant of the nomothetic method —and the one used in the study to be reported—employs criterion groups presumed to differ sharply on some source characteristic such as intelligence, attitude, or motivation. Then the investigator tries to keep the situation of encoding constant (e.g. letters to relatives and close friends) and uses statistical methods to determine which indicators display significant differences between the two criterion groups.

It will be apparent that there is a close relation between the investigation of style and content analysis in general. In both we are interested in relations between message variables and source variables, and many of the same problems arise. The salient differences, perhaps, are these: (1) Whereas content analysis is concerned more with lexical choices than structural choices (i.e., in what is talked about rather than in how it is talked about), the reverse is true for the study of style. (2) Whereas content analysis is concerned mainly with making inferences *from* message indicators to either source or receiver states and characteristics, stylistics is more concerned with predicting (or interpreting) *to* message indicators or events from knowledge of source variables. In other words, the student of style is mainly interested in describing variations in message structure and showing how these depend on either the situation of encoding or individual differences functioning in the situation.

EFFECTS OF MOTIVATION UPON LANGUAGE BEHAVIOR: THEORY

The experimental study to be reported was designed to test certain theoretical notions about the effects of motivation, or drive, on language behavior. The theoretical analysis was based on considerations developed by Hull (**187**), Hebb (**164**), and Spence and his associates (cf. **388**). This will be presented first in a very abbreviated form—briefly because the general theory is not the immediate concern of this conference. A more complete analysis is given in another paper (**301**).

Language habits, like habits in general, appear to be organized into *hierarchies of alternatives*. At both lexical and structural choice points, to the extent that there *is* choice, certain alternatives will be most probable, others less probable, and others very improbable. Grammatical and syntactical regularities or redundancies place severe restrictions on structural choices, and frequency-of-usage factors have a similar effect on lexical choices (both of these factors contributing to the norm in any encoding situation), but there is still room at many points for modification of the probability structure of hierarchies as functions of situational and individual variables. Increased drive or motivation is assumed to have two distinct effects on selection within such hierarchies: generalized energizing effects and specific cue effects.

Generalized Energizing Effects

Following certain notions expressed by Hebb, the generalized, energizing effects of drive may be identified with arousal of a neural system in the brainstem from which there is diffuse, nonspecific projection into the cortex, these impulses having a facilitative, "tuning-up" function. Assuming, with Hull and Spence, a multiplicative relation between habit strength and drive in producing reaction potential, the effect of increased drive should be to make the dominant alternatives within all hierarchies even more probable relatively. This means that behavior under increased drive, including encoding behavior, should become more *stereotyped*—the alternatives selected at all choice points should tend to be the most familiar, the most often practiced, the most expected. However, since habit strength is assumed to be asymptotic to a common maximum, *extreme* increases in drive should force many competing habits toward equal strength, hence producing interference, blocking, and confusion. This means that behavior under extremely high-drive conditions, including encoding behavior, should become disorganized; the finely adjusted motor skills, the subtle modulation of alternatives in terms of grammatical redundancies, and the selectiveness of semantic choices should break down.

Specific Cue Effects

To the extent that drive states are accompanied by distinctive sensations, such as thirst sensations, feelings of anxiety, sensations of pain, these distinctive cues can become associated with certain alternatives within habit hierarchies through the operation of ordinary learning principles. Therefore the presence of such cues, as directive states, will have the effect of modifying the probability structure of behavioral hierarchies, raising the probability of some alternatives and decreasing the probability of others. This means that behavior under the influence of some specific drive state will be shifted toward those *alternatives appropriate to this drive* in past experience. Finally, if two or more motives are operating, and their cues are associated with selection of different alternatives within hierarchies, we may expect oscillation between the responses appropriate to each state. This means that we can expect increased evidence of *conflict* in behavior, including encoding behavior, where two or more motives are operating simultaneously.

HYPOTHESES AND RELEVANT INDICES

These general theoretical considerations lead to the four hypotheses about language encoding to be given. Perhaps other hypotheses could also be developed. Each hypothesis suggests certain message indicators that should be associated with increased drive states. However, the indicators given here are by no means exhaustive; they were the ones used in our study of suicide notes. Sometimes they relate to the lexical content of messages, not their structural characteristics, and hence are not appropriate to the analysis of style. Each indicator will be described and evaluated in relation to the present problem.

Hypothesis I. The greater the motivation level under which language encoding occurs, the greater will be the stereotopy of choices. This stereotopy should be reflected at all levels where alternatives of varying probabilities are available. *I* (1) *Average number of syllables per word.* Since, as Zipf (**459**) and others have shown, there is an inverse relation between length of words and their frequency of usage, and since we expect encoding under increased drive to involve selection of the more familiar, more frequently used items, it follows that average syllable length should decrease with increased motivation. *I* (2) *Type/token ratio.* This measure is obtained by dividing the number of *different* words by the total number of words in a message. It has been shown to be a good index of lexical diversity, differentiating between education levels, telephone versus ordinary conversations, and so on. Since diversity of vocabulary presumably requires selecting more and more rare, low-probability items, it follows that encoding under heightened motivation should be characterized by less diversity and hence lower TTR's. *I* (3) *Repetitions.* Repetition of phrases (as compared with repetition of single words, indexed by TTR) also reflects redundancy in the message. A person encoding under heightened drive, being less able, in theory, to select equivalent though less probable ways of saying things, should display greater repetitiousness. *I* (4) *Noun-verb/adjective-adverb ratio.* This is a modification of the familiar verb/adjective ratio. It includes nouns with verbs as contributing to simple assertions and includes adverbs with adjectives as contributing to a more discriminative qualification of language. Since we expect people encoding under high drive to be less discriminative, they should yield larger ratios. *I* (5) *Cloze measure.* Taylor (cf. **410**) has devised a measure of predictability or stereotopy in which a message is "mutilated" by substituting blanks for every fifth word, say, and subjects try to fill in these missing items correctly. The more stereotyped the message as a whole (in terms of lexical, grammatical, and syntactical choice made), the better the subjects will be able to replace missing items from context. Accordingly, messages produced under increased drive should yield higher cloze scores. *I* (6) *Allness terms.* If we assume that extreme or polarized assertions are easier to make, are associated with stronger habits than are more discriminating assertions, people encoding under high drive should use more terms which permit no exception: *always, never, forever, no one, everyone,* and so on. All these measures, although they involve lexical items, can be considered stylistic indicators since they reflect *how* one encodes rather than *what* one encodes content-wise.

Hypothesis II. If language encoding occurs under sufficiently high motivation levels, disorganization of language skills will result. General theory here says that moderate drive facilitates performance, higher drive produces stereotopy, and extreme drive produces disorganization. We are all familiar with the speaker who is so mad that he can only sputter, spurt, and stutter. But theory does not tell us at what point the shift from stereotopy to disorganization will occur. *II (1) Structural disturbances.* A message can be highly stereotyped and yet be "correct" grammatically and syntactically. Presumably there is some degree of motivation where the myriads of delicately balanced language habits break down. In written materials this would take the form of misspellings, punctuation errors, grammatical errors, syntactical errors, and even clearly awkward constructions. A person encoding under extremely high drive should display more of these disturbances. *II (2) Average length of independent segments.* Maintaining long, involved, complex constructions in encoding presumably requires much closer attention to the process, much finer discriminations, and longer spans of immediate memory than does encoding in short, simple, child-like assertions. It seems likely that disruptive effects would most readily affect such complex encoding operations. Therefore a person encoding under extremely high drive should tend to operate with shorter and simpler independent segments. By "independent segments" I mean segments of messages that constitute complete sentences in themselves. Compound sentences connected by conjunctions would be separated into their components for counting purposes.

Hypothesis III. Encoding under heightened motivation will be characterized by selection of lexical and structural alternatives appropriate to the particular drive(s) operating. Most of the indicators employed to test this hypothesis were clearly content-oriented and hence do not apply to the study of style per se. These included *III (1), the distress/relief quotient* (DRQ), a ratio of distress-expressing phrases to the sum of these plus relief-expressing phrases; *III (2), number of evaluative common-meaning terms*, terms like "unfair," "sweet," "drunkard," and so forth, on whose denotative and connotative meanings users of the English language must agree if they are to communicate; and *III (3), positive evaluative assertions*, the proportion of all assertions made about ego which associate him with favorable common-meaning or attitude objects or dissociate him from unfavorable common-meanings or attitude objects (cf. **302**). Two measures in this category which seem to reflect structural properties of messages and hence be relevant to style are: *III (4) Time orientation.* A particular motivational state (e.g. suicidal) may direct the interest of the encoder away from the present time, or it may produce an imbalance toward either past or future time. *III* (5) *Mands.* According to Skinner (**381**) a mand is an utterance which (*a*) expresses a need of the speaker and which (*b*) requires some reaction (immediate or delayed) from another person for its satisfaction. It is usually expressed in the form of an imperative, where the verb comes early in the utterance (e.g. "Don't feel too bad about this," or "Please understand me"), but is not restricted to this form (e.g. "I wish I could see you" or "God forgive me!"). The self-stimulation associated with heightened drive (need) of a specific sort should increase the probability of mands whose content would be appropriate to the particular drive.

Hypothesis IV. Whenever there are competing motives operating in the encoder, evidence of compromise and conflict should appear in the messages produced. Compromise will generally appear in qualification ("weaseling") and conflict in oscillation between alternatives satisfying one motive and then the other. *IV* (1). *Qualification of verb phrases.* A person encoding under competing motives might tend to modify and complicate his verb phrases away from simple direct present or past tense, for example, away from "I loved you" toward "I tried to love you" or perhaps "I had to love you." Both of the latter forms do seem to imply the existence of some contrary motivation. *IV* (2) *Ambivalence constructions.* There are a number of forms in English which seem to directly express some degree of ambivalence, conflict, and doubt on the part of the encoder. Examples are the following: *but, if, would, should, because (for, since), well, however, maybe, probably, possibly, seems, appears, guess, surely, really, except,* etc. Certain question forms, like "Must I do it?" have the same effect. Messages produced by speakers under conflict should display a larger number of such forms. *IV* (3) *Percent ambivalent evaluative assertions.* If a person shows perfect consistency or lack of ambivalence, all his assertions relating to each attitude object should have the same sign, positive or negative (cf. **302**). Conflicting motives toward an attitude object, however, should produce ambivalent assertions, for example, "I love you, honey . . . You never trusted me . . . I always quarreled with you . . . I stuck by our marriage, though." Evaluative assertion analysis should reveal larger proportions of ambivalent assertions in messages produced by speakers in conflict.

A COMPARISON OF SUICIDE NOTES WITH ORDINARY LETTERS

Use of the criterion group version of the nomothetic method to study style requires that we select messages from one group known to deviate markedly on the independent variable in which we are interested. On a priori grounds it seems likely that a person penning a suicide note will be encoding under considerable motivation. A sample of 100 genuine suicide notes was available for study, 50 written by men and 50 by women. To control for situational style factors, we need another group producing the same type of message, but without the high level of drive. Since, with few exceptions, suicide notes are written to close friends and relatives, we secured a sample of ordinary letters received from friends and relatives by members of a panel of men and women in the Champaign-Urbana area (a panel that was being used for other purposes).

Since most of the measures we wanted to make made it desirable to have messages at least 100 words long, the total sample was reduced to 40 male suicide, 29 female suicide, 13 male controls, 59 female controls. Each measure was applied as consistently as possible to the total materials. Nonparametric tests of the significance of differences were made, first between sexes within suicide and control groups and then, if no sex differences were found, between total suicide and control groups. Unless specific mention is made later, it can be assumed that sex differences were nonsignificant.

Stereotopy Measures

To obtain I (1), *the average number of syllables per word*, the total syllables per message, as estimated from breath pulses while reading aloud, was divided by the total number of words. Differences between suicide and control notes were not significant but were in the expected direction. I (2), *the type/token ratio*, was obtained by dividing the number of different words by the total number of words in each message. Differences between suicide and control notes were significant at the .01 level and in the predicted direction. The *repetition* measure, I (3), was obtained by dividing the number of repeated words (in phrases of two or more words) by the total words in each message; differences were as predicted and were significant at the .01 level. I (4), *noun-verb/adjective-adverb ratio*, was obtained for each message by dividing the total number of nouns and verbs by the total number of adjectives and adverbs, and defining these categories by substituting message words in linguistic test frames where necessary; again, differences were significant at the .01 level and were as predicted. In estimating I (5), *the Cloze measure*, only ten messages for each group (male suicide, male control, female suicide, and female control) were used, these being selected at random. Each message was mutilated by substituting a blank for each fifth word, and the score was the average number of correct fill-ins when 34 male students and 31 female students tried to reconstitute the original male and female notes respectively. Differences as predicted and significances at the .01 level between suicide and control notes were obtained for male materials, but not for the female materials. *I* (6), *allness terms*, was simply the number of such words (*always, never, everything*, etc.) divided by total words for each message; again, differences were as predicted and were significant at the .01 level.

Disorganization Measures

Neither of the two presumed measures of disorganization of language behavior—*structural disturbances* (errors in composition, when the coder took the role of English teacher) or *average length of independent segments* (obtained by dividing total words by the number of such segments)—yielded differences significant in the expected direction. In fact, male suicides used somewhat longer segments than their controls, significant at the .05 level, and this is opposite to the prediction made.

Directive State Measures

For all the measures obviously dependent on what is talked about in suicide notes versus ordinary letters to friends and relatives—the *distress/ relief quotient*, the *number of evaluative common-meaning terms*, and the *proportion of positive evaluative assertions*—there were highly significant differences, as might be expected. What is perhaps interesting is that, although there are no differences in number of evaluative common-meaning terms for men and women, females in both suicide notes and ordinary letters display significantly more negative evaluation (i.e., higher distress/ relief quotients and lower percentages of positive evaluative assertions) than do males, as if males were more reticent about expressing negative affect. *III* (4), *time orientation*, contrary to our expectations, yielded no significant differences between suicides and controls, either in deviation from present time or in valence toward future or past. *III* (5) Skinner's *mands*, on the other hand, proved to be one of our best measures. Our index was the number of imperatives and related forms (see earlier examples) expressed as a rate per 100 words. Differences between sexes were not significant, but differences between suicide and control letters were significant at the .01 level.

Conflict Measures

Measure *IV* (1), *qualification of verb phrases*, was obtained by totaling the number of excess words in verb phrases (e.g., in "I might have loved you," the words "might" and "have" would be considered excess) and dividing by the number of verb phrases; differences between suicides and normals were significant at the .01 level and were as predicted. *IV* (2), *ambivalent constructions*, was simply the rate per 100 words of terms like *but, if, should, however, possibly*, etc. Here again, differences were significant at the .01 level and in the expected direction. *IV (3), per cent ambivalent evaluative assertions*, was the proportion of assertions relating ego to various attitude objects like the spouse, his children, etc., which were opposite to the dominant sign in each case, positive or negative. Suicides, as expected, showed significantly (.01 level) more ambivalent evaluative assertions.

Our comparison of suicide notes with ordinary letters to friends and relatives may be summarized and interpreted as follows: if we can legitimately assume that suicide notes are written under heightened drive level, most of the predictions from theory are borne out. Suicide notes display greater stereotopy—they are less diversified in vocabulary, more redundant or repetitious, less qualified and discriminative (noun-verb/adjective-adverb ratio), more predictable (Cloze measure) for males, at least, and they employ more polarized, extreme assertions. Suicide notes also reflect the specific motivational character of the suicidal state, both in content measures (by having more distress-expressing phrases, by having more evaluative terms in general, and by having fewer positive evaluative assertions) and in one structural measure (by having more *mands*, commands, demands, requests, pleas, and the like). They do not display the displaced time orientation we expected. Suicide notes also provide clear evidence that the suicide state is one characterized by motivational conflict (e.g., self-praise versus self-blame, spouse aggression versus spouse affection)—there is greater qualification of verb phrases, more ambivalent constructions, and a larger percentage of ambivalent assertions relating ego to significant others in suicide notes. One expectation from theory definitely does not hold up; suicide notes do not display more disorganization of encoding skills, either in structural disturbances or in shortening of sentence segments. This could mean that the drive level of the suicidal writer is not extremely high, that these measures were inadequate, that our samples were not well matched, or that the theory is wrong.

The implications for stylistics are not so clear, for many of the indicators studied here are probably multiply determined. Take the stereotopy measures, for example: There is ample evidence elsewhere (cf. **276**) that vocabulary diversity, verb/adjective ratio, and the like reflect the intelligence and education level of the writer. We have evidence that these measures also reflect the motivational state, and there may be other source states or characteristics to which these same indicators are sensitive. This probably means that, knowing the motivational state of the source, we can make certain predictions about his messages, but given only the message indicators we cannot with any certainty infer the source characteristics responsible. Another limitation is that, whereas we have been dealing with informal, spontaneous messages and relatively momentary states of sources, stylistics is more typically concerned with relatively enduring characteristics of writers as reflected in more formal, planned messages, like novels and sonnets. It seems unlikely that we could infer differences in the general motivational or emotional levels of novelists from indicators such as these.

COMPARISON OF GENUINE SUICIDE NOTES
WITH PSEUDOCIDE NOTES

To what extent can a writer adopt the stylistic features of a character or situation in which he is writing? The materials we had available for study included one set of 33 paired suicide and pseudocide notes, with a key to which member of each pair was which in a sealed envelope. We decided to attempt prediction on a blind basis, using only those measures that had successfully discriminated known suicide notes from ordinary letters in the analysis reported above. We also eliminated the measures that obviously reflected the suicide topic and content (e.g., distress/relief quotient, evaluative terms, and positive evaluative assertions) and the Cloze measure (there being too few notes of sufficient length). Unfortunately, for only thirteen of these paired notes were both members of sufficient length to apply most of our measures meaningfully. A prediction of suicide versus pseudocide was made for each of these thirteen pairs on the basis of which note garnered the most suicide votes on the nine remaining measures. These quantitative predictions were correct in ten cases, which is significant at the .05 level.

However, before opening the sealed envelope, the two investigators independently assigned all 33 pairs to suicide and pseudocide categories on an intuitive basis—one of us (EW) got 31 out of 33 correct and the other (CEO) 26 out of 33! Had we been utilizing the cues developed in our quantitative coding of genuine suicide notes? Had we perhaps developed intuitive sensitivity to the suicidal style? Or is it simply that the human computer is more sensitive than a few, crude, quantitative measures? We had eight graduate students with no prior experience with the genuine notes do this intuitive sorting; they were successful on the average in 16.5 out of 33 cases, which is precisely chance. So it appears that either we had been unconsciously using our own quantitative cues or (as likely) had picked up a feeling for the suicidal style.

Having opened the sealed envelope and thus knowing which were the genuine suicide notes, we now asked which of our quantitative measures successfully differentiate genuine from pseudo notes. This analysis was done in two ways: first, we used only the 13 pairs where both members were long enough for coding; second, we enlarged our sample to 24 suicide and

18 pseudocide notes by scoring all notes of sufficient length, regardless of pairing. Essentially the same results appear in both analyses. The only two measures that differentiated *significantly* (.05 level) *and in the right direction* in both cases were the *noun-verb/adjective-adverb ratio* and Skinner's *mands.* Several stereotopy measures approached significance in the right direction, *syllables per word, repetitions,* and *allness terms.* Of the conflict measures, one, *proportion of ambivalent assertions,* barely missed significance in the right direction and one was clearly nonsignificant (*qualification of verbs*), but the other, *ambivalence constructions,* was significant at the .05 level in the *wrong* direction. As anticipated, the measures dependent on suicidal content (*distress/relief quotient, number of evaluative terms,* and *proportion of positive evaluative assertions*) did not differentiate between genuine and pseudo notes. Finally, it is worth noting that the two measures of disorganization of encoding skills which had failed to differentiate suicide notes from ordinary letters did approach (*structural disturbances*) or reach (*length of independent segments*) significance at the .05 level in differentiating genuine suicide from pseudocide notes.

What conclusions can we draw about the ability of nonsuicidal people to intuit and adopt the encoding content and style of the suicidal person? First, there is no question but what they can intuit the content of the suicidal state, as least as far as our quantitative measures reflect this content. Second, from the general reduction in magnitude of differences in stylistic measures here, as contrasted with the suicide versus ordinary-letter comparison, it is clear that nonsuicidal writers can intuit and encode the style of suicidal people to a considerable extent. And it should be noted that the writers of these pseudocide notes, although matched with the genuine suicides for sex, age, and general social status, were not professional writers in any sense. Whether they were able to imitate the style of suicidal people by generating the heightened emotional state and then encoding accordingly, or simply by adopting a style of encoding available in their repertoire (through extensive reading, listening to plays, or the like) cannot be answered from our data.

On the other hand, there are certain features of the suicidal style which are less easily intuited and adopted. This applies particularly to the *noun-verb/adjective-adverb ratio* and to Skinner's *mands*; it applies somewhat to the *proportion of ambivalent evaluative assertions* and to the disorganization measures, *structural disturbances* and *length of independent segments.* The nonsuicidal person, asked to produce the note he might write just before taking his own life, *fails* to catch the true suicide's emphasis on simple, nondiscriminative action statements, his demanding, commanding, pleading character, his exaggerated emotional ambivalence toward himself and significant others, and his somewhat disorganized or distracted approach to encoding, leading to more errors and shortened, explosive segments. Whether a skilled writer—or perhaps a person who had himself experienced the suicidal state without actually taking his own life—would be able to intuit the suicidal state more completely, and thereby encode the style more faithfully, we do not know.

Commonality of Association as an Indicator of More General Patterns of Verbal Behavior

JAMES J. JENKINS

This paper is an example of one of the ways in which the psychologist approaches the problem of individual style.[1] It attempts to set forth (1) the "context of discovery" in which a style construct was formulated, (2) the development of hypotheses concerning the relation of the construct to observable behaviors, and (3) the process of gathering a variety of empirical data which provide evidence for or against the construct and hypotheses.

The reader will quickly discover that the construct discussed here is of limited scope and that some of the more general sets of hypotheses fare poorly when subjected to test. The major purpose of the paper is to illustrate the methodology. The discussions of the conference have clearly indicated that several participants do not appreciate the need for or usefulness of this procedure as applied by the behavioral scientists. The psychologist, however, must insist on some process such as that employed here to separate the "things every person knows" which are *true* from the "things every person knows" which are *untrue*. The final appeal must be to data wherever possible. That data can hold a tight rein on speculation is amply demonstrated here.

The apparent differences in methodology among the various disciplines may be easily overemphasized. I believe the reader will see that the self-conscious, formal, and, usually, statistical approach used by the psychologists is in principle closely related to "the circle of understanding" discussed in Wellek's summary paper and to Richards' approach to variant readings

[1] This paper was prepared during the tenure of a Social Science Research Council Faculty Fellowship. The research has been supported by a grant from the Graduate School of the University of Minnesota and by a Grant-in-aid for Behavioral Science Research from the Ford Foundation.

and misreadings. There are, to be sure, great differences in the choices of ends, data, and tools of analysis, but the methodology appears to me to be general.

INTRODUCTION

Verbal style impresses all observers as a most complex multidimensional entity (if, indeed, it can be conceived of as an entity at all). The variety of expressive features that may be incorporated in language, whether written or spoken, is manifestly enormous, and the number of combinations of features or patterns is staggering to contemplate. An individual uttering a single sentence makes a surprising number of "choices" in the "simple" act. Although we assume in the case of the untutored speaker or writer that most of the choices are "automatic" or "unconscious," the problem of accounting for them is far beyond the scope of any current theory.

In an effort to begin with a manageable problem, the approach employed by W. A. Russell and myself in the Minnesota studies of verbal behavior has been that of limiting our subjects' behavior to a single-word utterance in response to a single-word stimulus. In short, we have turned to the classic word association situation. Our subjects are told to respond as rapidly as possible with the first word they think of when they see a stimulus. They are also instructed that the response word should not be the stimulus word itself. Under these instructions each subject responds to 100 common English words used as stimuli. Our faith has been that as we learn how these one-word to one-word relations manifest themselves in somewhat different language situations, we will increasingly understand verbal processes and equip ourselves to deal with more complex language units.

In most of our work we have dealt with the relationships between words themselves as our basic data, and we have shown that simple associations can play a major role in recall processes (**211**), perceptual situations (**300**), verbal learning (**341**), generalization (**278**), and transfer (**15, 342**). These findings have encouraged us to pursue a different line of research which deals with the characteristics of people who make the associations: asking whether subjects who produce similar patterns of associations share other verbal and nonverbal behaviors as well. This amounts to asking whether similarity in associations is an index of some aspect of style.

The use of the term style here requires some explanation. In this paper it refers to an individualized characteristic of behavior. In the most extreme view we might speak of the "life style" of an individual—a personal mode of responding which typifies all the behaviors of the person concerned. In a more limited view we might regard style as a trait that manifests itself in some particular set of behaviors (e.g., social behaviors, athletic behaviors, problem-solving behaviors). In a still more limited view style might be thought of as a particular personal modification of a single narrow behavior (e.g., handwriting, dress, articulation), etc. Much of the work of differential psychologists is aimed at finding specific, readily observable behaviors which index, or predict, more general behaviors of greater importance. The studies reported here were conducted to discover whether behavior manifested in the word association situation was indicative of or predictive of past histories, social behaviors, learning behaviors, verbal behaviors, and personal attributes and attitudes of the subjects involved.

Past Work with Word Association as an Individual Characteristic

Word association tests have long been of interest to psychologists as indicators of individual differences. Sir Francis Galton, the first investigator to use the association method, wrote (**131**).

[The results] gave me an interesting and unexpected view of the number of operations of the mind, and of the obscure depths in which they took place, of which I had been little conscious before. . . . They lay bare the foundations of a man's thought with curious distinctness, and exhibit his mental anatomy with more vividness and truth than he would probably care to publish to the world.

The association techniques were widely taken up by the "depth" psychologists and psychiatrists as a means of access to unconscious materials and aids in understanding symbolic processes. Jung and Riklin (**221, pp. 8–172**) took the word association test into the clinic and developed its use in the detection of complexes. In this and in subsequent clinical applications, attention was focused on the content of *deviate* responses. It was discovered that ordinarily there was marked agreement between normal subjects in the choice of a response to a given stimulus word. It was further found that popular responses were given more rapidly than idiosyncratic responses and were repeated more consistently. Clinicians compiled response norms and emotionality indicators to aid in the identification of deviant responses (**230**), and attempted to weave the content of these responses and the stimuli to which they occurred into meaningful hypothetical models of particular personalities. Criminologists made similar uses of association tests, using idiosyncracy of responses to key words along with response time and emotionality indicators as lie-detecting devices. Other investigators explored the relationship of responses to vocational interests, age groupings, sex of the subjects, and a variety of physical and mental conditions.

In spite of this wealth of detail concerning deviation, only a few investigators have raised questions concerning the nature of the continuum from deviation on the one end to conformity on the other. (We have chosen to call this the *commonality* dimension.) In every large sample of normal subjects there is a wide range of commonality of response; to the 100 stimulus words of the Kent-Rosanoff Word Association Test, for example, some subjects will make only two or three of the most common responses while others may make more than 60. That such levels of commonality are more than chance variations has long been established, but the meaning of the levels has not been made clear. Two common hypotheses have been that the commonality dimension is one of *introversion-extroversion* and that it is one of generalized *emotionality*.

O'Connor, who endorsed the first hypothesis most enthusiastically, wrote (**296**):

[He who makes a popular response] concurs with the majority; his first thought identifies him with a controlling percentage of humanity; he is in perfect accord with two hundred and sixty-seven others from every thousand, sympathizes with their mode of expression, foresees their reactions, and feels himself akin with the world; the result is far-reaching. When he speaks, others nod in approval—he has expressed their own thought. He speaks again with more confidence and self-assurance; gradually usurps command; ultimately often dominates.

Of the low-commonality subject on the other hand he says:

His answers epitomize his life; he differs from the multitude; he acts a monologue in the world drama. He fails to comprehend the impulses of the majority, or the tie which binds it together, apparently against him. . . . Modern science calls him the introvert and his antithesis, the extrovert.

Those who endorse the emotionality dimension tend to view it as an extension of the clinical finding. McDougall, for example, wrote (**273**):

. . . it is often found that words which provoke such abnormal replies are words whose meaning is somehow connected with a complex; the word suggests either the emotional nature of the complex or its cognitive content, the object of the complex . . . . The point of theoretical interest is that the abnormality of the response seems to be due to conflict of affects.

Attempts to identify the commonality continuum with either of these continua have uniformly yielded meager results. Commonality has steadfastly refused to be linearly correlated with various scales of intro-version, personality, achievement, and intelligence. At the present time any interpretation of commonality is open to question.

Commonality as a Construct

Several years ago in the course of our research on the role of associative processes in verbal behavior we discovered that high-commonality subjects behaved more predictably in our verbal experiments than low-commonality subjects. We became interested in the matter and somewhat casually ran linear correlations between commonality scores and tests of *rigidity* and *anxiety.* These correlations were low and negative; the predictable behavior reflected neither rigidity nor anxiety. We noticed, however, that some relation existed; the scatter plots were wedge-shaped as if each personality variable exercised a constraint on commonality but was not otherwise related to it. A subject might have low commonality and almost any degree of rigidity, low rigidity and almost any degree of commonality; but, if he were high on either one of the scales, he could not be high on the other. A study of the literature suggested that this same phenomenon was evident in the data of other workers; low negative correlations were the rule almost without regard to the variable selected for correlation against commonality.

These findings and our experimental findings led us to formulate a model of the commonality in the following fashion.

Commonality can be thought of as representing the degree to which one is like the "standard" of the verbal culture. It indexes the number of verbal habits which one shares with others. Because the verbal habits are learned in the context of daily living, commonality must depend on and reflect a wealth of common experiences, common attitudes and common attributes. Its existence is further dependent on the absence of super-normal or subnormal abilities, experience, attitudes or personality traits.

The commonality dimension is not a single primary dimension but rather a resultant of many dimensions. It is best thought of as a sphere which centers at the average of all culturally relevant dimensions. Complete commonality exists at the center of the sphere. As one diverges from the norm on any dimension, his commonality becomes less and less.

Further, as the number of dimensions of divergence increases, commonality decreases. Thus, one could be highly divergent because he was very bright *or* very psychotic *or* very religious; or on the other hand because he was somewhat bright *and* somewhat psychotic *and* somewhat religious.

If this analysis is correct, it is clear that we ought not to expect to find simple linear relations between commonality and any single trait since commonality has a clearly defined meaning at only one end, the high-conformance end; as it diverges it becomes increasingly more complex. High-commonality status is indicative of average status on many dimensions. The archetype is the pollsters' mythical "average man." Low-commonality status indicates divergence from the norm but does not indicate what sort of divergence or even the number of dimensions of divergence.

A number of other implications may be drawn from this model. For example, when the culture is stable, the high-commonality subjects should be stable and consistent in behavior whereas the low-commonality subjects may vary. When the culture shifts, the high-commonality subjects should shift but the low-commonality subjects may not.

The implications of this model for unipolar and bipolar traits may be set forth briefly: only when we are dealing with another unipolar "conformity" trait may we expect to find a high degree of relation between that trait and commonality. If some measure of social conformance or "averageness" were devised, we would expect it to classify high-commonality subjects as conformers or as "very average" people and low-commonality subjects as nonconformers or nonaverage people. If the conformity measures yielded quantitative scores, we should predict differences between the mean scores of the high- and low-commonality groups. (The same kind of reasoning applies to scales that predict only deviation from normality, for example, a scale for schizophrenia.)

To the extent that these conformity traits measure the same factors as those involved in commonality, we should expect large mean differences and high intertrait correlations. To the extent that some other kind of conformity is being measured, we should expect the mean differences between high- and low-commonality groups to disappear and the intertrait correlations to approach zero.

When we deal with a bipolar dimension which discriminates two sorts of deviation from the average, for example, an intelligence test, we should expect the resultant relationship with commonality to be curvilinear with both the high- and low-intelligence groups tending to fall into the low-commonality classification; we should expect the high-commonality classification to contain only persons of average intelligence. The mean intelligence score of the high- and low-commonality groups should be about the same, but the distribution of scores in the high group should be tightly clustered about the average and the distribution of scores in the low group should be widespread.

To the extent that bipolar traits or dimensions are important to commonality, we should expect marked differences in the *dispersions* of high- and low-commonality groups on the trait and strong curvilinear relations. To the extent that such traits are irrelevant to commonality, we should expect the dispersion differences to disappear and the correlations to go to zero.

Supporting Evidence Available before This Study

Various kinds of information already available seemed to give support to the commonality construct as just outlined.

1. Studies of the consistency of word association responses over time showed that high-commonality subjects made the same responses on multiple occasions and remained in the high-commonality group (8). Low-commonality subjects were inconsistent from one occasion to another, giving different but still uncommon responses. An over-all high relationship between consistency and commonality was manifested.

2. High-commonality subjects show a very strong tendency to respond with the same part of speech as the stimulus word, whereas low-commonality subjects tend to respond with a modifier of the stimulus word or with a word which appears in some sequence with the stimulus word in speech. Although this is very indirect evidence for the model, it may be thought of as representing a tendency to give "more of the same" in the one case and "something different" in the other.

3. In general women score higher in commonality than men (**456,** ch. 15). It seems a fair inference from a large body of psychological literature that women are more socially oriented and more conforming than men (**424**).

4. As was stated earlier, personality traits correlated low negative with commonality. Rosen found (**339**) that all the scales on the Minnesota Multiphasic Personality Inventory were negatively related to commonality in normal subjects. Divergence from the norm was associated with low commonality.

5. When we obtained new norms for the Kent-Rosanoff Word Association Test in 1952–1953, we discovered that there was a marked increase in popular responses compared with the Minnesota norms collected in 1929. Further study (**210**) seemed to show that the trend toward higher and still higher popular responses has been characteristic of the norms obtained in this country since 1910. This seemed to be in accord with the trend toward higher conformity, "group-mindedness," and "other-directedness" reported by other disciplines.

Many more examples of such tangential evidence could be cited. It is sufficient here to report that enough such evidence exists to encourage intensive investigation of the commonality construct.

The Case Study

As a first approach to the testing of the construct a joint case study of a high-commonality woman (*H*) and a low-commonality man (*L*) was undertaken. These subjects were studied through a series of thirty experiments. The results were most encouraging. They may be briefly summarized by quoting the summary of the report (**309**):

Perhaps the most striking finding of our study was the widespread difference in a variety of situations of the verbal behavior of the two subjects who had been selected originally by their difference on the commonality variable alone. In nearly every task the subjects were in contrast.

In addition the commonality variable seems to be related to several other characteristics of verbal traits. The high-commonality subject appears highly consistent, highly predictable. Her associations appear to be locked in well-organized, tightly-knit clusters. These characteristics appear to extend even into the unstructured compositions of the subject. The low-commonality subject appears to be responsive to the same general processes as the high-commonality subject (if his own associative material is used, the same phenomena can be demonstrated). But the low-commonality subject seems to be much less predictable and less consistent, than the high-commonality individual.

Very tentatively, the differences between the high-and low-commonality subjects studied here might be sketched by the following paired adjectives:

Conforming—Nonconforming
Consistent—Inconsistent
Redundant—Nonredundant
Predictable—Unpredictable
Associatively fluent—Nonfluent
Social—Asocial
Noninsightful—Insightful
Average—Deviate

The individual differences manifested in these studies have been for the most part attributed to the commonality status of the two subjects. It may be observed that *logically* they might equally have been attributed to the difference in sex, intelligence, school history, values, motivation, etc., of the subjects. While such attribution cannot be denied on the basis of this study, the fact that the differences are consistent with group commonality differences (e.g., in associative clustering) relate meaningfully and consistently with our prior notions about commonality as a "trait," and are internally consistent from situation to situation where commonality might be presumed to have consistent effects, encourages our belief that these case studies shed new light on this variable. That more widespread confirmation is required, of course, goes without saying.

PRESENT INVESTIGATIONS AND THEIR RESULTS

Encouraged by the survey of the literature and the case study, we launched a series of studies which constitute the body of this report. The studies may be divided for convenience into six areas: questionnaire data, extensions of verbal context, nonverbal situations, learning situations, social contexts, and psychometrics.

Questionnaire Data

In attempting to analyze the determinants of commonality we found ourselves speculating fruitlessly about the effects of many variables on the lives of the subjects. We argued, for example, that an "only" child might be expected to be a low-commonality subject because of his somewhat atypical home environment and lack of stimulation from other children. On the other hand we felt that such a child might achieve commonality earlier because of greater exposure to adult, already highly socialized speech. Similarly, we argued that persons who belonged to many social organizations ought to have very common associations; but if an individual belonged to *too* many organizations, that in itself constituted deviate behavior and should relegate him to low-commonality status. Rather than continue such arguments, we decided to let the data speak for themselves.

We administered the Kent-Rosanoff Test to students in an introductory class in psychology and collected data from the students regarding family size, birth order, social activities in high school and college, elected offices held, hours spent in social activities, preferences for social or solo activities, etc. The subjects were divided into four groups on the basis of their commonality scores on the association test: Low, Low Average, High Average, and High. There were approximately forty subjects in each group. The data from the questionnaires were then examined to see where reliable differences could be found which characterized the individual groups.

In general the groups of subjects appeared to be quite similar. Subjects from rural, small-town, and urban origins were evenly distributed across the groups. No differences appeared with respect to desire for social activities, types of activities participated in, "bearableness of being alone," number of dates and parties, and socioeconomic status or indices of family background.

A few small differences emerged. There appeared to be a tendency for subjects in the Low group to spend fewer hours in social activity and more hours alone than subjects in the other groups, although they belonged to a larger number of organizations. The High group, conversely, spent the largest number of hours in social activities but belonged to the smallest number of organizations. "Only" children tended to be overrepresented in the High group and first and later children were evenly distributed in terms of group membership. A careful study of the data suggested that many other variables operate more importantly than commonality to influence social activities and that patterns of relationship between commonality and social behavior may be quite different for various subgroups of subjects.

In data collected by Denuta Ehrlich for another sample the same trends appeared in the main. In addition she found that the Low group had larger dispersions in the "time spent reading magazines and periodicals and (for subjects who had not been in the service) in "time spent in completely new surroundings, away from home and friends." This means that the Low group had both more and less stimulation from these sources than did the High group.

It is, of course, dangerous to generalize from the fragmentary findings of such a "shotgun" approach. The data suggest, however, that the relationship of commonality to biographical and social activity variables is not at all a simple one. At this time it appears fruitful to study further measures of stimulation (media consumption, new and unusual experiences, degree of freedom from family, etc.) and measures of what might be called "degree of commitment to" social activity. The latter attempt is suggested, of course, by the incongruity of hours and activities for the Low group which suggests that they may be "dabblers" in social activity rather than "real participants."

Extensions of Verbal Context

We decided to extend our studies of verbal behavior by varying the complexity of the verbal stimuli presented to groups of High- and Low-commonality subjects and also by increasing the latitude permitted the subjects in the selection of responses. Four different studies were conducted in this area.

First a new association test was devised (The New Association Test). This test was both longer than the Kent-Rosanoff, using 200 stimuli instead of 100, and more varied in terms of the parts of speech employed. The Kent-Rosanoff list is made up almost exclusively of singular nouns and simple adjectives; the new test was broadened to include all parts of speech and to include the "same" words in varied forms (singular and plural nouns, comparative and superlative adjectives, present and past tenses of verbs, etc.). Two hypotheses were involved. The first hypothesis was that subjects classified as High- and Low-commonality subjects on the Kent-Rosanoff would continue to be so classified on the New Association Test. The second hypothesis was that High-commonality subjects selected on the Kent-Rosanoff would tend to give response words which matched the stimulus word with respect to "substitution class" or part of speech on the New Association Test whereas Low-commonality subjects would not.

Second, Carroll's Phrase Completion Test (57) was employed. Instead of a single-word stimulus, this test presented short phrases or sentences with missing words which the subjects were asked to fill in. The hypothesis here, of course, was that High-commonality subjects would tend to choose "popular" responses for phrase completion to a greater extent than the Low subjects.

Third, two essays were taken from the case study, one from each subject. Every tenth word was deleted and the subjects of the present study were asked to fill in the deletions. We already knew from the work of the case study that the essay by the High-commonality subject was highly predictable and easy to complete and the essay by the Low-commonality subject was unpredictable and difficult to complete. The hypothesis being investigated was that the High-commonality subjects would make more successful completions of the essays than the Low-commonality subjects.

Finally, the subjects were asked to write essays on the topic "A Description of the University of Minnesota." The hypotheses were that the Low-commonality group would employ a wider range of words, use more complex words and sentences, and in general write more idiosyncratic and unpredictable essays than the High group.

Subjects were obtained for these four experiments by administering the Kent-Rosanoff Word Association Test to a large introductory class in psychology and drawing subjects from the upper and lower quarters of the commonality distribution. Data for men and women were collected separately, both to avoid confusion of sex differences and commonality differences and to provide double tests of each hypothesis. In the studies which follow there were eighteen subjects in the High Male, Low Male, and Low Female groups and seventeen subjects in the High Female group.

New Association Test. Responses to this word association test were scored for commonality of response and frequency of "same part of speech" or "substitution class" responses. Commonality was scored by giving one point for each item to which the subject gave the most popular response. "Part of speech" or "substitution class" responses were scored by judges. In English, of course, the classification of an isolated word is often ambiguous, and it may even be argued that all words out of context are ambiguous. The scoring represented a compromise. Words that frequently fall into several classes were not scored. In all other cases the judges devised common frames involving the stimulus word and tested the response words by substitution. In general, this resulted in fairly strict classification. Although the system is beset with difficulties, agreement between judges was high and, presumably, the scoring was not biased in favor of either High- or Low-commonality groups.

The results indicated that both measures clearly separated the experimental groups, with little overlapping of scores between the High and Low subjects. The means of the High groups were two to three standard deviations above the means of the Low groups on both the variables. On the average the High groups made twice as many popular responses as the Low groups and made from two to three times as many substitution class responses as the Low groups.

The first two hypotheses may be regarded as being clearly substantiated. Commonality on the Kent-Rosanoff Test is closely related to commonality on the New Association Test. Commonality is not specific to a single set of words but rather represents a general style of associative responding. Similarly, the high relation between commonality and "substitution class" behavior suggested by the Kent-Rosanoff data is clearly evident on the New Association Test where much more grammatical diversity is involved. The style of popular associative responding may therefore be further described as "paradigmatic" or as involving stimulus-response substitutability.

Phrase Completion. Carroll's phrase completion test was scored according to his instructions. No differences were found among the scores of the experimental groups. The means clustered around the 25th percentile on Carroll's norms, however, which suggests either that the relation between commonality and phrase completion is curvilinear (with High- and Low-commonality groups scoring low and Middle-commonality groups scoring high) or that the normative responses have changed since his standardization work. On the assumption that the norms had changed, the scoring was changed to give one point for the most popular response to each item. With this kind of scoring small differences in the predicted direction emerged, but the differences cannot be regarded as statistically reliable.

The third hypothesis, therefore, cannot be viewed as being supported by these data. High-commonality subjects do employ slightly more popular responses in phrase completion, but the differences are not large enough to state this with confidence. A longer and more elaborate phrase completion test might be used in further work to provide clear evidence on this point.

Essay Completion.   The completions of the deleted essays of subjects *H* and *L* were scored for the presence of the exact word used by those writers in their essays. The High-commonality males made more correct predictions than the Low-commonality males for each of the essays. This result is statistically significant. For women no reliable differences were found. The fourth hypothesis must therefore be regarded as only partially confirmed and the relation of commonality to essay completion procedures left as an unanswered question. No straightforward explanation of the one-sided result suggests itself. Further investigation seems to be called for.

Essays.   The essays by the subjects in the experimental groups were scored for (1) number of words, (2) number of sentences, (3) words per sentence, (4) syllables per word, (5) type-token ratio for the first 250 words, (6) number of nouns in the first 250 words, and (7) number of verbs in the first 250 words. No significant differences between the High- and Low-commonality groups were found for any of these measures. The High and Low groups wrote essays of about the same length with the women in both groups writing slightly longer essays than the men. The High groups wrote slightly fewer sentences than the Low groups and therefore averaged slightly more words per sentence. The number of syllables per word was almost exactly the same with the Low Males and the High Females using slightly longer words. The type-token ratios showed no differences, and the number of nouns and verbs were almost exactly alike across all four groups. All hypotheses regarding differences between the essay scores of the four groups lack confirmation. We must conclude that commonality is not related to these measured characteristics of essays. The findings that were so pronounced in the case study for subjects *H* and *L* are not substantiated by group data.

An interesting finding emerged, however, with regard to the predictability of these essays when they were put to that test. The essays were systematically mutilated, replacing every tenth word with a blank, and given to a new group of subjects for completion. Here it was found that the essays of the High-commonality subjects were easier to complete than were the essays of the Low-commonality subjects. On the average about 5 per cent more correct completions were made of the High subjects' essays. It is apparent that somewhat greater stereotypy or redundancy is present in the High essays, even though none of the counts performed shows such a difference. It is also of passing interest to note that within each commonality class the essays by women were more predictable than those by men and that women subjects were consistently better at the essay completion task than were men.

The fourth hypothesis may be regarded as partially substantiated. Although no differences exist between the groups of essays with respect to counts of the formal properties of the writing, the hypothesized differences in predictability of the essays are observed when other subjects attempt to complete the deleted texts.

Nonverbal Situations

In an effort to test the limits of generality of the commonality construct, we tried to construct simple situations in which either the stimulus or the response side was nonverbal. For the nonverbal stimulus case color naming was selected. The subject was presented with a series of color chips and asked to name each of them as if he were describing it to a friend. The hypothesis being tested was that High subjects would tend to choose the most popular descriptive terms whereas Low subjects would show more diversity and idiosyncratic naming.

For the nonverbal response case Osgood's visual semantic differential cards were used. Subjects were given a series of thirteen concepts to rate. The rating was accomplished by having the subject indicate which of two pictures seemed "to go best with a given concept." Ten pairs of pictures were used, each pair involving at least one major contrast of an important scale on the verbal semantic differential (e.g., near-far, large-small, etc.). All concepts were rated on all scales. It was hypothesized that High-commonality subjects would show greater agreement in selecting popular responses (i.e., pointing to the most frequently selected pictures) than would the Low subjects.

Fifteen subjects from each of the experimental groups were given the color naming and the visual semantic differential situations. Color naming was scored on the basis of the number of subjects in each group giving the most popular color name for each color chip. The visual semantic differential was scored by totaling the number of popular responses (determined from Osgood's data) made by each subject and comparing means across the experimental groups. No significant differences were found between the High- and Low-commonality groups, although very appreciable sex differences were found in color naming (with women utilizing a higher variety of names) and both female groups made more popular responses to the visual semantic differential than the male group.

Learning Situations

Learning situations represent an interesting set of the behaviors being studied in that both stimuli and responses are fixed. In other respects the kinds of behavior involved appear similar to word association behavior; that is, a single verbal stimulus and a single verbal response constitute the unit being studied. The subject's problem is to learn a specific set of habits connecting the specified stimuli with the specified responses.

The first learning study, conducted by Rochelle Johnson, consisted of the learning of a single list of paired associates. The paired associates were made up of stimulus-response pairs from the association test itself. The pairs differed, however, in the strength of association involved. High-, medium-, and low-strength associates as well as unrelated control pairs were employed in balanced numbers. It was hypothesized that High subjects would have an advantage over the Low subjects in learning high-strength pairs but that this advantage would disappear or even be reversed for the low-strength pairs and control pairs. Subjects were drawn from the upper and lower quarters of the commonality distribution for the experiment.

The data on speed of learning confirm the hypothesis. High subjects learned high-strength associate pairs more readily than low subjects, and the Low subjects learned the low-strength associates *and* the control pairs more readily than the High subjects.

The second learning study involving a more complex associative chain was performed by James J. Ryan. Two lists of paired associates were learned in sequence. In the first list the subjects simply learned a set of paired associates; that is, to every stimulus, *A*, they had to learn to respond with an appropriate (but previously unrelated) *B*. Then the subjects were asked to learn a new list comprised of the same responses, the *B*'s, but these responses had to be made to new stimuli which may be called *C*'s. One third of the *C* words were known to be connected by popular word associations to the relevant *A* words (the original stimuli), one third of the *C* words were similar in meaning to the relevant *A* words, and one third of the *C* words were neither associated with nor similar to the *A* words. It was hypothesized that High-commonality subjects would learn to make the responses to associated stimuli more readily than to either the similar or control stimuli. The Low-commonality subjects were expected to show the same sort of facilitation but were expected to show it to a lesser degree. Thus, it was predicted that the relative advantage involved in transferring responses to associated stimuli would be greater for the High-commonality group.

Six different sets of learning lists were used in the experiment to avoid effects of specific pairs which might have been particularly easy or difficult to learn. Each test list contained the three kinds of new stimuli to which responses were to be learned; associates, similars, and control words. Each list was learned by approximately equal numbers of High- and Low-commonality subjects. No subject learned more than one of these test lists, so the data for the lists are completely independent.

In four of the six cases the High group learned the responses to *associated* stimuli more readily than the Low group. (Both groups learned responses to associates more readily than responses to either similars or controls). In five out of six cases the Low group learned responses to *similar* stimuli more readily than the High group and, similarly, in five out of six cases the Low group learned the responses to *control* stimuli more readily than the High group.

When the data are put in the form of ratios the difference between groups is even more apparent. The ratio of the number of "associated stimulus–old response" pairs learned to the number of "control stimulus–old response" pairs learned holds an individual's learning skills constant and shows only the relative advantage of one sort of material over another. Over all six lists this ratio was always larger for the High group than it was for the Low group. This holds true whether we consider the first test trial, the first two test trials, or the total number of correct responses over all test trials. This was not true of the ratio of associates to similars which was divided between High and Low groups and varied with the number of trials considered. The results strongly suggest that the High subjects are superior to the Lows in learning responses to stimuli which are associated with old stimuli and that the Lows are superior to the High subjects in the learning of responses to stimuli which are unrelated to old stimuli.

The findings of both of the learning studies are in accord with the construct proposed. The High subjects in both cases show large and predictable facilitation through associative habits. The Low subjects show less facilitation through associative habits and a somewhat greater tendency or ability to form new habit patterns. The notion advanced earlier concerning the stable nature of the High subject's verbal habits and the shifting, changeable nature of the Low subject's habits seems to receive confirmation.

Social Contexts

It was suggested in the model of commonality given that the dimension was one of conformity. We felt that it would be interesting to see whether the High-commonality subjects actually sought conformity or whether verbal conformity simply represented a static state. Accordingly, an experiment was designed which created the impression that each subject was a deviate from the rest of the experimental group with respect to his opinion about the outcome of a particular case of delinquency being studied by the group. It was hypothesized that High-commonality subjects would yield to implicit group pressure and change their opinions and that Low subjects would not. It was further hypothesized that this effect would be greater when the subject expected his opinion to be made public than when he expected his opinion to remain anonymous.

This evaluation of the role of the commonality variable in predicting conformance to perceived group pressures was attempted by Denuta Ehrlich as part of her doctoral research. Although a complete report on her experimentation cannot be attempted here, two findings are relevant and clear. First, the High- and Low-commonality subjects do *not* respond differentially when they "see" that they are deviates from the consensus of the group in the setting in which they believe that their opinions will remain anonymous. Both groups show the same amount of shift toward the group mean. Second, when the subjects believe that their opinions will be made public and identified as their own, the Low-commonality subjects show a greater dispersion in their shifts of opinion than the High-commonality subjects. The average shift in opinion for the two groups is not different, but the Low subjects tend either not to shift at all or to shift very greatly toward the group opinion while the High subjects tend to shift a uniform moderate amount.

These findings contribute little to the notion of the High-commonality subject as a person who seeks to conform or the Low-commonality subject as a chronic deviate. They do add a small amount of evidence favoring the idea that the High subjects are more typical, uniform, and predictable whereas the Low subjects are more atypical and heterogeneous. The complexity of Low commonality as a class seems to be indicated.

Psychometrics

In assessing some of the psychological characteristics presumed to be associated with commonality, conventional psychological tests were employed rather than attempting to devise complex behavior situations in which the behavior itself might be observed. Three kinds of tests were used: tests of values, personality deviation, and interests.

Values. A test of values was selected because our model suggested that the High and Low groups would differ with respect to social values and because the subjects in the case study showed a very great difference in the value they placed on social activities. The test used was the Allport-Vernon-Lindzey study of values which yields scores for six areas of activity preference: theoretical, social, political, economic, religious, and aesthetic activities. The hypothesis was that the High group would show higher social values than the Low group. It was further felt that the High group might be more homogeneous on all values than the Low group.

The results obtained with the study of values show the High and Low groups to be much more similar than different. The hypothesized difference on social values was not confirmed. The only reliable difference between the High and Low groups was found on the aesthetic value scale where Low-commonality men were found to have a higher mean score (higher aesthetic value) than High-commonality men. Although this may provide a clue for future research, it does not appear in the women's samples and should not be seriously interpreted without confirmation in further studies. A study of the dispersion of the scores of the groups on each of the six scales gives no support to the hypothesis that the High groups are more homogeneous than the Low groups.

Personality and Interest Tests. The study of personality variables was undertaken by Theodore Volsky as part of his doctoral research. The major aims of this part of his work were to evaluate the relationship between commonality and ratings of maladjustment based on a personality inventory and to determine the relationship between commonality and stability of test performance over time. The hypotheses derived from the commonality construct given were, first, that appreciable deviations on the personality test indicative of maladjustment would be found more frequently among the Low-commonality subjects than among the High subjects and, second, that there would be a higher frequency of significant changes in test profiles in the repeated testing of the Low group than in the repeated testing of the High group.

The Minnesota Multiphasic Personality Inventory and the Strong Vocational Interest Blank were the tests employed. The sample was drawn from students appearing for testing at the Student Counseling Bureau of the University of Minnesota. Personality tests and retests were collected for 144 males and 92 females. Interest tests and retests were obtained for 185 males. The period between the test and retest varied from six to twelve months. The samples were divided into upper and lower halves on the commonality distribution for comparison.

With regard to maladjustment it was found that the typical rating of the personality profiles of the High-commonality subjects was "No adjustment problem" and the typical rating of the profiles of the Low subjects was "Moderate adjustment problem." Subjects in the upper half of the commonality distribution were about twice as likely to receive ratings of "No adjustment problem" as persons in the lower half of the distribution, and persons in the lower half were about twice as likely to receive ratings of "Major adjustment problem" as those in the upper half.

When judgments of change in personality profile were considered, it was found that the typical rating for the High subjects was "Moderate change" and the typical rating for the Low subjects was "Major change." Subjects in the lower half of the distribution were more than twice as likely to receive ratings of "Major change" as were subjects in the upper half of the distribution. (The findings with regard to judgments of personality adjustment and change were consistent for both male and female subjects.)

With regard to occupational interest (where only males were considered because of the inadequacy of the test when applied to females), Volsky found that a stable interest profile is typical of the High-commonality subjects and "Moderate change" is typical of the Low-commonality subject. Subjects in the upper half of the distribution were two to three times as likely to obtain ratings of "No change" as were subjects in the lower half of the distribution.

It is obvious that these findings are in agreement with the hypotheses advanced earlier and appear to reflect both the deviate nature of the Low-commonality subject and his relative instability, at least with respect to paper-and-pencil test behavior, as compared to the High-commonality subject.

CHANGING THE COMMONALITY CONSTRUCT

The mixed results of this study indicate that the commonality construct proposed earlier in the paper is in need of revision. A brief summary of the results is helpful in considering the nature and extent of such a revision. For our purpose here the results are grouped as confirmations, partial confirmations, and disconfirmations of the original hypotheses.

Confirmations

1. Commonality generalizes to new word association situations. The tendency to make popular or unpopular responses is consistent across varied sets of stimulus words.

2. Commonality score is closely associated with the tendency to make "substitution class" responses. Persons who make popular responses

tend to respond with a word that is of the same grammatical class as the stimulus, whereas persons who make unpopular responses tend to respond with a word that is of a grammatical class which might well follow the class of the stimulus word.

3. High-commonality subjects learn high-strength stimulus-response pairs more rapidly than do Low-commonality subjects, but the latter learn low-strength and unrelated stimulus-response pairs more rapidly than the former.

4. High-commonality subjects show more facilitation in learning to respond to a new stimulus which is associatively linked to an old stimulus than do Low-commonality subjects. Low-commonality subjects show a relatively greater facility in learning to respond to unrelated new stimuli than do High-commonality subjects.

5. Commonality is negatively related to maladjustment (as indicated by ratings of personality test results) and to the judged amount of change in personality and interest test profiles over a test-retest period.

Partial Confirmations

1. Commonality is slightly associated with the ability to complete deletions in essays of other persons. (True for the men in our sample but not for the women.)

2. Although formal counts (number of words, sentence length, word length, etc.) showed no difference between the essays written by the High- and Low-commonality groups, the essays of the subjects in the High groups were easier for other subjects to complete than were the essays written by the subjects in the Low groups.

Disconfirmations

1. Scores on the popularity of responses given on the phrase completion test were not significantly different for the High- and Low-commonality groups.

2. Scores on the popularity of responses given in color naming were not significantly different for the High- and Low-commonality groups.

3. Scores on the popularity of responses given on the visual form of the Semantic Differential were not significantly different for the High- and Low-commonality groups.

4. Biographical information, social activities, and desire for social participation show no clear relation to commonality, although there are slight indications that atypical experiences may be associated with Low-commonality scores.

5. Changes of opinion as a result of perceived difference from the

majority opinion are not directly related to High- and Low-commonality status.

6. Scores on a test of values (with one exception) are not related to High- and Low-commonality status.

Discussion

It is clear that the commonality construct advanced earlier was much too broad in scope. There is little evidence in this study to support the postulated relationships between commonality and social behaviors. High commonality apparently arises in a variety of backgrounds and a variety of social experiences (although great deviations from the norm may make it unlikely). It has little relation to the social activities, social desires, or values of the individual. It is not a useful predictor of reaction to social pressure.

Further it appears that the effects or manifestations of commonality are difficult to find in situations which are either highly structured with respect to the kind of verbal response required (color naming, phrase completion), or which involve appreciable nonverbal components (e.g. visual semantic differential, color naming). It is not clear from our data whether these are separate variables or two reflections of the same variable, namely, amount of structure.

If we turn to the studies in which commonality was shown to be of some importance, a major characteristic seems to be evident in them. Commonality is most apparent as a determining variable in settings which call into play a wide variety of *intraverbal connections* which may be presumed to exist at varying strengths but at the same time settings which do not provide further determinants of the subject's behavior. Here the High-commonality subjects "elect" to stay in the same grammatical class as the stimuli and exercise strong, well-established habits. The Low-commonality subjects, on the other hand, seem to vary responses more and exercise their facility for making new associations. These apparently different behaviors may, of course, be a reflection of a single difference between the subjects. The High subjects may simply have a few strong responses available, the Lows may have many weak ones. The High subjects, therefore, appear stable and consistent, the Lows unstable and inconsistent. When the strong associates are "correct" in an experiment, learning is facilitated for the High subjects (in effect these subjects start with the material partially learned), but when the strong associates are "incorrect" in an experiment, these same habits may interfere with new learning and the Low subjects appear to have an advantage.

Extensions of this line of thinking may be employed in the explanation of all the positive results of this investigation. The psychological tests considered here, for example, have no "right" or "wrong" answers (as opposed to intelligence or achievement tests) and, therefore, may be considered for our purposes simply as opportunities to manifest selected sets of intraverbal connections. The Low-commonality subjects (having more diverse responses to choose from) may be expected to choose, on the whole, somewhat less popular responses. Choosing less popular responses on a standard personality test increases the likelihood that one will appear maladjusted, as the Low subjects in our study did in fact appear. The Low subjects, having lower strengths of intraverbal connections, would also be expected to change more from one testing to the next. This also was in fact observed for both the personality and the interest test. The Study of Values test differs from the others in that the responses from which a subject may choose have previously been balanced and equated for popularity; hence, no particular manifestation of the High-Low group differences can be observed on a single testing. We would predict, however, that the Low subjects would show more change in responses from one testing to the next. It is regrettable that such data were not collected.

The data concerning the completion of others' essays and the predictability of the essays written by the experimental subjects fit moderately well with this narrow intraverbal conception of commonality. The essay completion task is relatively highly structured so that the opportunity to observe the contrast between the strong common habits of the High subjects and the somewhat weaker diffuse habits of the Low subjects is extremely limited. (Here we found a difference for men but not for women.) In the essays written by the subjects themselves there is less constraint, and differences in predictability of *intraverbal sequences* were observed even though the "countable" indices of static complexity showed no differences.

It thus appears feasible to think of commonality as a relatively fragile and limited concept which pervades tasks involving intraverbal habits. The reader will of course observe that this conception retreats entirely from the question of the origins and determinants of commonality and says nothing about such practical matters as the actual adjustment status of the subjects. Low-commonality subjects may in fact be more maladjusted and this may have some causal connection with the character of their verbal habits, but such an explanation is not required to account for the present set of data.

This construct of commonality as we see it at the conclusion of this set of studies is sharply limited to intraverbal behavior. Further, it applies to that behavior only in the *absence* of other sets of stimuli which furnish clues about the desired or correct response. In such situations the behavior of High-commonality subjects is expected to be determined by high-strength, popular responses of a stable and enduring nature. Conversely, the behavior of the Low-commonality subjects is expected to reflect a wide range of responses of relatively low strength which appear to shift and change from time to time. The more completely the situation depends on intraverbal relations alone, the more markedly will commonality manifest itself. The more other determinants are introduced (in instructions, in the use of nonverbal stimuli, in constraints on the response possibilities, etc.), the less will be the influence of commonality. (The interested reader is referred to the work of Siipola and her students (**377**, **106**) for a detailed and insightful study of the interrelations between word association performances under different conditions of administration and the relation of such performances to personality variables.)

Further Research

The construct of commonality, even though severely limited, is by no means clearly understood at this point. Habit structures typical of High and Low subjects have been postulated but not convincingly demonstrated. Alternative explanations for even the intraverbal phenomena can be advanced. The following are typical of the studies which we hope to perform in the near future to help clarify the nature of commonality.

1. A study of "substitution class" behavior. We hope to set up experimental instances of "substitution classes" and "sequence classes" of both nonverbal and verbal natures to see whether these reflect behavior sets rather than simple verbal habits.

2. High- and Low-commonality subjects will be used in verbal learning experiments employing nonsense syllables to determine whether Low subjects have a real advantage in learning new associations or whether the differences so far discovered represent interference from old verbal habits on the part of the High subjects.

3. The stability of verbal habits of High- and Low-commonality subjects will be studied through learning experiments with delayed tests on the material learned given after an appreciable length of time.

SUMMARY

This paper presents the work of a psychologist in pursuit of a general dimension of individual variation or style. The approach to verbal behavior through word association techniques and the history of word association as a measure of individual differences were briefly introduced. A broad construct of commonality (measured by the extent to which individuals respond with popular associations) was presented and elaborated to yield a set of hypotheses concerning various aspects of style. Data were collected through questionnaires, completion tasks, verbal context and nonverbal context situations, essay writing, learning tasks, and social group experiments. The results indicated that the construct of commonality originally presented was much too extensive. A severe reinterpretation of the construct was offered, limiting it to intraverbal tasks. Typical future experimentation was outlined.

Comments to Part Eight

JAKOBSON: Osgood is right in advocating an intense cooperation between psychologists and linguists, but such a cooperation can become efficient only if linguists know enough psychology to avoid psychological mistakes and if psychologists when dealing with questions of language do not commit blunders in linguistic essentials. No use of different methodology and terminology may excuse psychological errors of linguists or mistreatments of linguistic data by psychologists. For example, Osgood states that the study of style concerns the variable features of the code. But besides redundant elements, any grammatical or lexical form is a variable. The code of English gives to its users the freedom of choice between the active "he attacked" and the passive "he was attacked," but the study of style is not concerned with such a selection, while the choice of the active construction "they attacked him" or the passive one, "he was attacked by them," —is a stylistic (or in classic terms which have been rehabilitated by Richards, rhetoric) problem, because both constructions have one and the same reference, and we could not object: "It's not true that they attacked him, but it's true that he was attacked by them." Equally strange is the statement that stylistics is "more concerned with structural choices than with lexical choices," because the choice of synonyms (metaphoric, metonymic, nonfigurative) is a very important area of stylistics. Such a lexical choice precisely indicates "*how* a person talks about something rather than what he talks about." When arguing that the student of style is usually interested in *deviations from norms* rather than in the norms themselves, Osgood forgets that each style of language has its own subcode and consequently a specific norm, for example, the elliptic style has its own norm. The quantitative approach is far from exhausting the problems of stylistics. Osgood's concepts and examples of "situational" and "individual" style are confusing. Eighteenth-century novels, which reflect a historical stage of the given language and which on the other hand display the artistic devices of a certain literary genre and trend, are cited as specimens of "situational style," whereas a typical sample of a local social dialect, as particular college students' speech for a certain year, is supposed to display an "individual style" together with Shakespeare's plays, which, by the way, the paper cites without making the relevant distinction between Shakespeare's poetic pattern and his private parlance. Osgood's comparison of suicide notes with ordinary letters discovers the obvious fact that the choice of lexical and grammatical means is limited by the topic as it is, let us add, in any utterance, for example, in a dialogue between a bartender and the customer. It is self-evident that volition finds expresssion in suicide notes, but what would be actually instructive is the relation between imperative constructions and their periphrastic substitutes. Elementary linguistic mistakes harm the analysis, for example, the arbitrary evaluation of compound verbal forms as "excess words" or of the compound sentences with the conjunctions "but" and "if" as "ambivalent constructions." The foreigner's accent is a social linguistic phenomenon and is by no means a personal style.

CHATMAN: I wonder whether a feature of personal style *is* that it is an enduring characteristic. It seems to me that the styles most readily available to analysis are often ones that are nonce styles—styles put on for the occasion. For instance, it is quite easy to analyze the style of somebody doing a burlesque. Now, in no sense is this an enduring characteristic of the individual, and it seems to me if we are going to insist on enduring characteristics, there is a great deal of what has traditionally been called style that would have to go out the window. Mr. Brown makes the suggestion that it is the function of—I think he used the term—"literary men" to have the values in literature and for other individuals, linguists, to analyze them. I am not at all sure that it is a part of the linguist's equipment or interest to deal with such matters; I should imagine this sort of activity would appeal more to the aesthetican. But even if we grant the possibility, I wonder if there isn't a third role involved. I think that it is becoming increasingly necessary to separate two kinds of activity which are often lumped together as "literary criticism." This, in part, is a result of certain developments in modern criticism, although the distinction may have been valid in the past as well. It has been a tacit assumption of many critics that it is possible to find within the poem certain objectively determinable features which can substantiate value judgments. I am not sure that this is possible, since I have never seen a completely satisfying demonstration. But, in any case, the notion does mean that the modern literary critic typically performs two rather different jobs. One job is that of literary analysis, that is, the discovery and explication of the structure of literary discourse (as opposed to other forms of discourse). This is clearly a literary, not a linguistic, occupation. The other job is literary criticism per se, the judgment of poems and the "improvement of taste." Now I wonder if an individual who chooses on occasion, and for certain purposes, to perform only the first of these tasks is so totally useless a member of society as is sometimes implied. It seems to me rather significant that some of our best critics are far subtler interpreters than they are aestheticians.

JENKINS: I want to talk about Mr. Chatman's question in regard to style. I think that the question has been tremendously amplified by Mr. Jakobson, and that we need to go into this at some length. Let me give you an example of an analogous problem. When the Committee on Psychology and Linguistics met in 1953, here in Indiana, to discuss problems of psycholinguistics, one subgroup of that Committee spent two weeks of mornings, afternoons, and evenings discussing the so-called "Whorfian hypothesis." At the end of two weeks we suddenly discovered that we had been talking about entirely and completely different things, and that the reason we couldn't get any agreement was that we kept "misreading," in a very marked way, what the people from the other discipline were saying. There were two major ways of talking about the hypothesis. The psychologists were talking about habit structures in individuals *within* a given language group; and the linguists were talking about differences *across* language groups, the patterns of the language code. When we finally got that ironed out we didn't have any time left to say anything about Whorf's assertions. Now, we have here *at least* two major groups of style definitions, and within those we have levels and kinds in a tremendous density. Mr. Jakobson wants psychologists and linguists to work together. But superficially, at least, it appears he is only willing to have psychologists and linguists work together within his definitions. I don't believe that such an approach is fruitful. I don't think we will be able to get any kind of synthesis out of such restrictions. I think that we have to start by leaning far over on the permissive side and by moving as far as we can from the prescriptive side. We have the problems here of the "enduring qualities of style," and this has been used in two quite different ways. Mr. Chatman, for example, says the burlesque style can be readily identified, but we don't expect it to persist or endure for the individual. Here we are talking about "style one," a burlesque style which is not to be associated with the individual but rather with the art form. It is in the work and not in the person. We have enduring qualities of style for art forms, and, in the very broad sense that Roger Brown suggested, a language can be considered as a style, novels in the language as a style, poetry as a style, subdivisions of poetry as a style, sub-subdivisions of poetry as a style, etc. These styles have a kind of *construct existence*. They go on, so to speak, whether there are people in this particular year doing any of this or not. These styles have enduring qualities—formal qualities—which are identifiable, so that when one of them occurs we can say "I know what that is. It has the characteristics that belong to the enduring art form." But the psychologists, it seems to me, are saying that we have a little bit different interest in the problem. We are not interested in the work *qua* work. We are not interested in formal characteristics (although we reserve the right to be interested in them at some other time). We *are* interested in "style two," that is, what the individual has done to vary the characteristics of the art form. What we hope to find is some characteristic of the individual, some enduring quality of the man which would pop up in his poetry, in his novels, perhaps in his common speech, perhaps in his gestures, something about him that we could characterize and describe. Then we could say that this is a way that this person characteristically modulates, modifies, or changes standard art forms.

Now this procedure is a terrible gamble. We have no assurance that such characteristics exist. Perhaps when a man goes into poetry he is somehow separated from the rest of his style in a way we don't understand, and perhaps when he is talking to his wife he is in a whole new style class with no transfer between the two. The people who write beautiful poetry *may* treat their wives and speak to their associates in any one of the full range of ways. Psychologists are making the bet that this doesn't happen. Let me invent an example of some sort. Let's suppose that a person is characterized psychologically as being constrained. He is somehow "all tied up." We expect that his utterances will all be of a more or less frugal and worried sort, and we would like to assert that when he writes a short story, or when he tries to write poetry, or when he talks to his friends, this characteristic will somehow intrude on and modify what is in all these. It seems to me we can't talk together unless we keep recognizing whether we are talking about style subone or style subtwo or some others that we may uncover here. It seems to me that we have to make some kind of separation and tolerate both definitions. Mr. Jakobson apparently does not want to treat with enduring personal characteristics, because he keeps saying that this is characteristic of the dialect of the group. College students speak college student language. But the college student himself modifies it in a particular way, and, we hope, in an enduring way. Mr. Jakobson modifies English, even the phoneme, in a persistent and relatively enduring way. He characterizes his speech by certain kinds of markers. Let us take a trivial example: the end of a point is ocularly marked for the rest of us, with a pausal phenomenon and removal of the glasses. This we would think might be a cue for us. We might now move to his lectures instead of the discussion group and see if simply on visual grounds we could get something that would structure for us the language continuum. This would be a trivial example, to be sure, but an example of a kind of enduring characteristic which is associated with a particular person. Now, of course, he never gets that way independent of his culture, or his time, but he has something special which we hope is unique to him. I think this sort of deviation from the norm is what Roger Brown was trying to structure for us initially. One of the nasty problems we face in this conference is that one man's deviation is the other man's enduring personal characteristic. If we look at the art form and say there are some deviations from the art form in which we are not interested—we will throw those out—those are precisely the things that the psychologist comes along and sweeps up so that he can try to put them together and make something of them. He in turn throws something away that the next group will want to pick up and do something with.

osgood: Mr. Jakobson had so many things to say about the suicide paper that I hardly know where to start or what to stress. There are a few things, somewhat along the lines of what Jenkins was saying, I'd like to mention. And this goes back also to Brown's question about the rigor of the prediction of the theory, and so on. I wouldn't claim the hypotheses in my paper were, in any sense, rigorous. I don't think the theory that I am following permits a high degree of rigor, and I have a feeling that few psychological theories of learning, of verbal behavior, do. But the essential notion I had in mind—and this will get to what Mr. Jakobson was discussing, I think—was that when a person is creating a message of any kind, whether in writing or in speaking, more or less simultaneously on a variety of levels, semantic, grammatical, and so on, there are choices among alternatives being made. Well now, at some points, if he is following a given code which he has learned, the choices are essentially zero if he is going to communicate—for example, in what phonemes he will use. But at other points there will be a relatively large number of alternatives, and whatever vocal events occur will be a function of a very large number of determinants operating at that particular point and time. If we were to take a large representative sample of English speakers, let's say, in all kinds of situations, as I've called them, we might get, admittedly, a purely statistical norm of what are the relative probabilities. This might be considered, as I said, a base line from which to assess deviations. But now when people are talking on telephones there are certain characteristics of the medium—the lack of the person addressed as a physical stimulus, the inhibition of walking around for most of us, at least, a whole host of things—which restrict, limit, change, modify the probabilities of choices, presumably to some degree on all levels. Take any kind of measure you wish— let's say something like the choice of active versus passive construction, just for an illustration. We might find that in the telephone situation for most speakers of English this choice will be shifted away from its typical frequency pattern in ordinary conversation to a different level. Now, if we extend this one little example to all kinds of choices— syntactical, lexical, and so on—we have what I meant by *a situational style*. Telephone conversation as a situational style represents a somewhat different pattern of deviations from the usual, or random, sample of English conversations than do novels or poetry, which have their own characteristic patterns as situational styles.

As for *individual style*, what I meant was that even though a person shifts toward a new norm, if you will, a new pattern, dependent on the situation he is in—writing a suicide note, talking on the phone, writing a poem—nevertheless, as Jenkins was saying, it will be characteristic of him as an individual that, in functioning in this new situation, he will still deviate from other individuals in this same situation in some fashion. As he was suggesting, in certain characteristics of style an individual may tend to deviate in the same ways regardless of the situation, whereas for other characteristics of style he may deviate one way in one kind of situation and quite differently in other situations. The latter would not be an enduring characteristic; for example, when he is on the telephone he gets much more nervous than in almost any other situation—particularly if it is long distance—but it would still be a stylistic characteristic of his in this situation. Well now, the college student example then, Mr. Jakobson, was along these lines, essentially. Surely, I agree that being a college student, being in this social group, implies a whole set of deviations from the usual conversational norm of English speakers in general. But on top of that, modulating even that deviation, there are these individual differences between Johnny Jones as a student and Sammy Smith. There are certain characteristics that would differentiate them. The choice of lexical alternatives—*what* a person talks about—I would prefer not to call style, at least to the extent to which this is situationally determined. That is, if, in suicide notes, people tend to talk about "death" more frequently, to use the word "my dearest," to talk about insurance policies, or whatever it may be, I would say that this is not stylistic. Otherwise we would be in the awkward situation of saying that whenever a person talks or writes about different topics, he is necessarily using a different style. However, for something like what Skinner calls "mands" (**381**)—and here I am not going to hold out any strong case for the linguistic adequacy of this particular category, except it was something we felt we could count by following certain rules—there is a difference. It's true that mands in general will increase when a person is writing a suicide note, and, as you said, this is in part a function of the situation. However, the interesting thing, as you may have noticed, was that when we compared genuine suicide notes with pseudosuicide notes— that is, people asked to think about committing suicide and then to write a note for this kind of situation—one of the big differences was in "mands." The true suicides still show a significantly higher frequency of the demanding, commanding, pleading, if you will, kind of behavior, as if this were something which, although situation-determined in part, is further increased by the actual motivational state of the true suicide.

I think there are many differences of this kind relating to the general conception I have tried to follow—individual style versus situational style. I think that Carroll's study also provides some interesting evidence for variations about norms and how these reflect what most of us, I think, at the conference would agree are stylistic. I was very intrigued by some of the correlations between the semantic differential type of subjective judgments and formal characteristics. I think they illustrate that shifts in choices, in this case of a very formal sort, to which the coder does react reliably and consistently, are related to stylistic judgments. In the present example, the stylistic judgments concern whether the selection is *intimate* or *remote* in character. What formal, structural characteristics determine these judgments? Well, the larger the number of syllables per word, on the average—the longer the words—the less intimate the style; the greater the number of clauses, however, the more intimate; the greater the number of action words, the more intimate; the greater the number of cognitive verbs—what are those, Jack?

CARROLL: I think they're verbs of knowing, feeling, and believing.

OSGOOD: Yes, the greater the number of these, the more intimate the style. The greater the number of Latin and Greek verbs, however, the less intimate; the greater the number of passive verbs, the less intimate; the greater the number of common nouns the less intimate. However, the greater the number of personal pronouns, with a correlation of .58, the more intimate. Now remember, the *reader* does not go through and count these things—the coders do that. He just reads the passage and somehow gets an impression—this is an intimate style, others are remote. But something has happened; there is some information being given, and the interesting thing to me is that it seems to be in the choices, the relative frequencies of certain of these rather formal kinds of things. The greater the number of prepositions, the less intimate; but the greater the number of pronouns, the more intimate. Now here is a pattern of varying frequencies of certain choices in messages which does produce very definite impacts upon the reader; and I suspect, because we are all more or less simultaneously speakers and receivers, that for the source, too, this was an expression, if you will, of more intimate intentions.

MILLER: I have followed in my own research some of Mr. Jakobson's ideas. I found it rather profitable to do so, and I think other psychologists have had a similar experience. That is to say, I am more optimistic about a level of collaboration among the several points of view represented than Mr. Jenkins' rather strong statement suggests.

HYMES: I want to comment on two points concerning Mr. Osgood's paper and the discussion of it. First, Mr. Osgood studies the style associated with individuals across different situational contexts. This is only an alternative. From an anthropological point of view, one shared by psychologists such as Roger Barker, it would be preferable to start with situational contexts, discover what is characteristic of them across individuals, and then study individuals within these known contexts. The same data may give quite different results, depending on whether we compare individuals across situations, or situations across individuals, and we can associate *style* with either approach. Second, the words "deviation" and "unpredictability," I suspect, are not as neutral as might be scientifically desirable with regard to the study of style. Regarding deviation, what a poet often has to do, as does a child learning the use of its language, is to achieve a norm, not to deviate from it. In many aesthetic fields, as well as in other contexts, the problem of attaining, of mastering a style, is just as important for study as the problem of deviation from a norm. Regarding "unpredictability," artistic style is not just concerned with the unexpected. Style may also involve the mastery of the expected. In *Counterstatement*, Kenneth Burke brought out the importance of analyzing an art form as rousing, then satisfying, expectations. He used the example of the opening scene in *Hamlet*, where the ghost is anticipated, is about to come, about to come, and finally does come. This business of "teasing" the audience for a while before resolving its aroused tensions may be the whole point.

PART NINE

Retrospects and Prospects

From the Viewpoint of Linguistics

Opening Statement

FRED W. HOUSEHOLDER, JR.

I will begin by explaining part of my procedure. I have tried to say something about everything, but sometimes what I have to say is brief. I hope no one will feel slighted if I do not spend much time on his particular contribution. In preparing what I have to say, I have tried to arrange my discussion in a relatively logical way, proceeding from the more general to the more particular; but running across that arrangement is another one that proceeds from the more literary to the less literary.

I start, therefore, with a few comments on the contribution of Archibald Hill (**173**) in which he considers the question of defining "literature" and appears to reject permanence as a criterion and to argue for something that he calls "stylistics." That seems to include vocabulary choice—partly, at least, in relation to the chain—and co-occurrence patterns over segments of greater length than a single sentence. In addition to those two factors, he also includes under stylistics various formal features of sound, such as meter, rhyme, etc., and suggests a procedure for defining literature by starting with a definition of, for example, a sonnet, and gradually working up. Now in this connection I should like to mention a few criteria that have been proposed, some of which Hill does not mention.

Permanence is certainly one criterion that has often been mentioned; if we make use of the idea of repetition of an utterance, we must define "repetition" in such a way that it includes silent reading, subvocal repetition as well as audible repetition, and, in the case of new works, somehow or other we have to take into account the author's hopes for permanence.

Another criterion that is not mentioned by Hill is length. One might say that any continuous or connected utterance of over a certain length—ten minutes or something of that order—belongs in the domain of literature and then we can argue about whether it is good or bad literature. Or we could set it up negatively, saying that any utterance of less than five syllables is not literature. Each of these restrictions would help to exclude or include certain troublesome cases that have come up in this kind of discussion.

We can take into account structure of a nonlinguistic sort—that is, regularities which are not conditioned by the grammar of the language itself. And, finally, in connection with almost any criterion, we might take into account some kind of similarity of form to items which have already been classified as literature by another criterion.

After I had written this, I noticed that in Voegelin's paper there was something which is closely allied to this. He is concerned there with the distinction between casual and noncasual utterances, and, if we equate noncasual utterances with literature, we might consider his criterion of "restriction to certain times and certain places," (and, it might be desirable to add in a modern western culture, "restriction to certain media of communication," or the like). This, however, seems to be a little too broad for a definition of literature, although whatever class it defines may be a larger class of which literature is a subclass.

I would be inclined to suggest, as a tentative disjunctive definition, that literature includes: (1) all continuous (i.e., excluding catalogs and telephone books, etc.) utterances that are over a certain minimum length and (2), in addition, utterances of any length which are marked by structural regularities not required by the grammar, and (3), in the case of short utterances, some of those that are marked by the characteristic which, in connection with Mr. Saporta's paper, I will rechristen "nonbanality," but which he calls "ungrammaticality" or "ungrammaticalness." And (4), also for the short utterances, I think we would have to take into account in some way permanence or possibility of repetition.

I turn now to Saporta's paper. In this he takes from Chomsky (**63, 64**) the notion of degrees of grammaticalness. I am inclined to doubt the wisdom of using the term "grammatical" in this way. In the long run it seems likely that the term will be more useful if it is defined as an all-or-nothing quality; but the thing that Saporta talks about in these terms we might call by another name, say if you like, "banality." Then we will have degrees of banality, and the subclasses that Saporta talks about in his paper will specify *banal* co-occurrences, and the language of poetry will show a higher density of nonbanal utterances or utterances of a low order of banality; and this nonbanality would represent the kind of stylistic mark that Hill seems to desiderate for literature. It is possible that this system might run into difficulty in that some bad literature might turn out to be not as banal as we would like. But I think that what we run into in bad literature is banality in a more ordinary sense, and I think it would be distinguishable.

A little further on in his paper Mr. Saporta quotes a remark that I once made about linguistics being an art. I would like to take this opportunity of pointing out that in the context in which that quotation occurs (**183**), I say that "as matters now stand, linguistics is an art" and I do not despair entirely of its ever becoming in any way scientific. Further on he considers the matter of effective orthography. A point here which may cause some trouble is that in a language with a defective orthography the very defects are likely to be exploited by the poet, so that improving the orthography might raise as many new problems as it solves old ones.

The next paper I want to comment on is by Mr. Higginson (**171**). In his opening pages he lists three ways in which Joyce minimizes redundancy; I would say that all these are good examples of what I mean by non-banality and perhaps even in some cases they border on what would be considered true nongrammaticalness. The most fascinating thing about this paper on *Finnegans Wake* is that although we have heard talk about language as a coding process, here seems to be an authentic, well-documented case of a process of encoding followed through various successive steps. The method of "perfixing" is mentioned as one of Joyce's main methods, and it is of course available to Joyce because in English we can exploit the phonemic redundancy of the language very readily. This suggests the thought that under extremely noisy conditions the reading aloud of *Finnegans Wake* might be more intelligible than it is as it stands.

The notion of encoding leads me on to Mr. Richards' paper on "Misreading and Variant Readings" which has a number of points of interest to a linguist. First, he discusses a particular line of Sonnet 66 by Shakespeare—and I will impose on your good-will sufficiently to present the sonnet to you now so that you may understand a little better what I am talking about:

> Tired with all these, for restful death I cry;
> As to behold desert a beggar born
> And needy nothing trimm'd in jollity,
> And purest faith unhappily forsworn,
> And gilded honor shamefully misplaced,
> And maiden virtue rudely strumpeted,
> And right perfection wrongfully disgraced,
> And strength by limping sway disabled,
> And art made tongue-tied by authority,
> And folly, doctor-like, controlling skill,
> And simple truth miscall'd simplicity,
> And captive good attending captain ill:
> Tired with all these, from these would I be gone,
> Save that, to die, I leave my love alone.

Now, in discussing a misreading of the second line of this, a linguist wonders why Mr. Richards makes no mention of the parallel structure of eleven consecutive lines here, which all seem, to me at any rate, to depend on "As to behold," all of the form "something good badly treated," or "something bad honored," and all in that same order, subject first and predicate second. Surely, this multiply repeated pattern almost forces us to put "desert" in the class of "something good" and "a beggar born" in the "badly treated" class. Without these parallels in order and sense, it might be possible to understand the line as meaning "to behold a born beggar abandoned." "Desert" does occur as an adjective with that sense (although not in Shakespeare).

A linguist would most naturally consider misreading a special case of misinterpretation, which in general involves inadequate use of the redundancies in the context, and variant readings as special cases of ambiguity or homonymity, whether lexical or constructional—cases where the redundancies are insufficient to settle the issue except in a probabilistic or statistical way. In fact, I think this same line "to behold desert a beggar born" contains an instance of this sort in which my gloss would differ from Richards'. He takes "a beggar born" as a noun phrase, equivalent to "one born into the beggar's trade." I would take it as precisely parallel to the participles in the other ten lines. To recall how those other ten go, they are "trimm'd," "forsworn," "misplaced," "strumpeted," "disgraced," "disabled," "made," "controlling," "miscall'd," "attending," all but two of them past (passive) participles, the other two active (-ing) participles. Since they are all of this same pattern, I would be inclined to render "to behold desert born a beggar" (which seems to be partially like one of the misreadings which Richards condemned)—"to see merit come into the world with as little notice or prospect." The variance is not great enough to lead me to claim that Richards' interpretation is a misreading, and furthermore the net difference of meaning is very slight; consequently, I should class this with variant readings, that is, ambiguities—here constructional homonymity.

Richards, of course, might well class my reading as another misreading (since it does resemble one which he rejects). I don't know what his grounds would be, perhaps the boldness of the figure in this context would add at this point that the same idea, the same phrasing, almost, of the "birth of desert," or "desert being born," does occur elsewhere in Shakespeare, in *Troilus and Cressida*.

I hope that no responsible linguist nowadays says that "what is said by enough people thereby becomes what should be said." A linguist *might* say that whatever is said by enough people is highly likely to become what *must* be said, that is, by anyone who hopes to communicate. The aesthetic or moral question how long and how hard we should fight for a losing linguistic cause cannot, as far as I can see, be answered by linguistics; we all of us have our own private battles of this sort. I will mention some of mine. I fight a strong battle against the substitution of "would have" for "had" in unreal conditions; I fight against spelling pronunciations of all kinds, such as the tendency to pronounce the "l" in palm, balm, psalm, etc; I fight against the use of "presently" to mean "now." But I know they are all losing battles in the end.

As for the dream dictionary, linguists of my own tastes, at any rate, would probably rather have a kind of superconcordance or Thesaurus, listing all or an absolutely representative sample of all the various contexts in which each word occurs. The co-occurrences (both in the grammatical sense—that is, what nouns occur as subjects with which verbs, what adjectives modify what nouns, etc.—and in the stylistic or psychological sense—that is, if word A occurs, which words B are especially prone to turn up in the vicinity, regardless of grammatical relation)—the co-occurrences of words in texts are probably amenable to much more systematic treatment than they have received, and many of our semantic intuitions can probably be related to them. Here is where I would localize the matter of misreading, at least in part, and also, in part, one of the possible consequences of misreadings—semantic and structural change in languages.

I started out with "literature" and "style" in some sort of lexical-distributional co-occurrence sense in the papers by Hill, Saporta, Higginson, and Richards. We come now to a group of papers where certain phonological aspects of style are singled out for study. Here we may adopt the notions used by Stankiewicz and Lotz of "constants" and "variables," and take next a group of papers concerned with variables of this sort, that is, occurrences not primarily determined by a pre-established pattern. One of Stankiewicz's two papers (**394**) gives a kind of general survey of some parts of this field (including a few that go beyond the phonological domain) with many useful and interesting observations. He does not here distinguish, since he is talking about language rather than literature, between the items that are common to all renditions of a poem, for instance, and those that belong more particularly to the delivery. This point he makes clear in his second paper on "Linguistics and the Study of Poetic Language," which we shall discuss a little later.

Now I think we should all be grateful to Dell Hymes's discussion of "Some English Sonnets." We should be grateful because he has carried out this laborious method of phoneme counting and phoneme weighting on a big enough corpus so that we can now say fairly confidently that (in this form, at any rate) it is a waste of time. [Laughter.] Modified from an earlier proposal by Lynch (**259**), it involves ranking the consonants and vowels in order of their weighted frequency and then (1) discovering, if possible, some important word or phrase in the poem made up chiefly of high-ranking phonemes, and (2) suggesting some tentative synaesthetic appropriateness of the high-ranking phonemes to the theme of the poem. In the first place, it should be pointed out that the laborious weighting is largely unnecessary. The only important differences in rank of consonants between the direct frequencies and the weighted count affect the phonemes /d/, /z/, and /ð/, which are lowered in rank by the weighting system for obvious reasons connected with the structure of English (/d/ and /z/ are frequent in suffixes, /ð/ occurs commonly in such weakly stressed morphemes as "the," "with," etc.). In the case of vowels, in Hymes's modified Smith-Trager transcription (**422**) it is /ə/, /ɨ/, and /æ/ which are mainly affected, in the same direction and for similar reasons. In either system, the English consonants fall into three fairly clear-cut groups: high-frequency consonants /r, n, s, t, l/, with frequencies so close together that is is hardly feasible to rank them from any small sample (the investigations cited by Lynch would rank them /n, t, r, s, l/, and it does seem likely that /n, t, r/ form a slightly more frequent subgroup and /s/ and /l/ a less frequent one). Pure frequency counts would also include /d/ and /ð/, but we have seen the reason for demoting them. The second group of consonants includes /m, k, z, v, w, p, t, b, h/ (with the now demoted /d/); here counts even of very large samples differ so greatly that precise order cannot be insisted on; the order is probably roughly that given, except that d should be ranked ahead of them all. And finally, the last group includes the demoted /ð/ and /g, ŋ, θ, š, y, č, ǰ/, again with a rather uncertain internal order. The vowels, after demotion of /ə/, /ɨ/, and /æ/, show a much less definite split into groups: the group used most frequently contains /i, e, iy/, and there seems to be kind of a middle group /ey, ay, æ, a, ə/, and a lower group containing /ow, ɔ, uw, aw/, with /u/ and /oy/ at the very bottom.

Now Lynch and Hymes did not rank their phonemes by excess or defect in comparison with average frequencies or norms of any kind, but rather absolutely; so naturally these same basic rank groups crop up in sonnet after sonnet. We should scarcely be surprised at the frequency of consonants in "silent" in Keats's "On First Looking into Chapman's Homer" (number 12 in Hymes's paper), since /s, l, n, t/ are among the first six consonants in weight rank in thirteen of the twenty sonnets, among the first ten in eighteen of them, and the morpheme "silent" occurs in five of the twenty and an almost equally good word "still" in an additional four (although neither of these occurs in sonnets numbers 3, 8, or 10 where they might seem especially appropriate). If, instead of absolute frequencies or weights, we consider deviation from the average (here I am using the average for all twenty), a deviation greater than a certain amount, say eight for consonants and six for vowels, a quite different rank order will result. In most cases there will be several phonemes ranking above normal and several below. (For example, in excess: poem 1, /z, n, g, m, ð, iy, uw/; 2, /l, e, i/; 3, /i/; 4, /aw/; 5, /d, z, p, ə/; 6, /t, w, ey, iy/; 7, /r, w, uw, aw/; 8, /l, t, z, w, θ, iy, ɔ, e/; 9, /v, oy, iy/; 10, /s, n, š, iy, oy/; 11, /r, l, h, e, i/; 12, /d, e, ay, ow/; 13, /n, æ, e, ɨ, ə/; 14, /r, n, f/; 15, /t, s, p, e, a, uw/; 16, /r, l, f, d, e, ə, i/; 17, /m, d, ð, n, b, æ, ey/; 18, /z, ow/; 19, /t, d, iy, ey, e/; 20, /r, p, a, i, ɨ, ay, ey/. In defect: poem 1, /l, s, e, ay, ɔ/; 2, /n, d, ey/; 3, /s, f, t, p, l, e, ay/; 4, /b, z, m, ay, iy, ə/; 5, /n, ay, e/; 6, /n, k, i, ɔ, a/; 7, /d, f, ay, e, ə/; 8, /æ, ow/; 9, /p, ay, e/; 10, /l, ey, ɔ/; 11, /d, ɔ, ə/; 12, /r, ey, ɔ, i, ɨ, ə/; 13, /r, s, k, ey, ay/; 14, /t, z/; 15, /d, iy, ay, ə/; 16, /t, w, n, ey, iy, æ, ɔ, a/; 17, /s, v, r, i, iy/; 18, /iy, ɔ, e/; 19, / r, h, ɔ, i, æ/; 20, /l, s, n, k, e, iy, ə/.)

But, before we become too enthusiastic about these, let us first tabulate the phonemes that occur as rhymes and those that occur in alliterations, internal rhymes, or repetitions. I have made this tabulation, and, as far as I can see, it will account for every deviation, whether in excess or defect. The defects occur mainly when favorite rhyme vowels (such as iy, a rhyme vowel used in nineteen out of twenty sonnets) are avoided or used only for single rhymes (instead of the four-line rhymes of the octave), or when favorite alliterative phonemes (such as s, used in all but three of the twenty) are not used. The lesson, therefore, is to note and count only the phonemes of rhymes, alliterations, etc., and ignore the rest. If we really want to convert these into figures such as Hymes gives, the laborious counting and weighting process is unnecessary; simply add the figures obtained from counting the rhymes and alliterations to the averages, subtracting where a favorite is avoided, and the result will be pretty close. Taking a look now at Hymes's summative words and key words, we may observe that some combination of two or more of the phonemes /r, s, l, n, t/ occurs in fifteen out of sixteen. A good statistician should have been turned loose on this to give the chance hypothesis a fair shake; but I am willing to bet that he would in no case find any strong reasons for suspecting the operation of factors other than chance. This is, of course, not to deny that there are many relations in languages and in poetry between sound and meaning, such as Hymes well exemplifies in the early part of his paper, and Stankiewicz also. Nor would I wish to question the value and necessity of statistical methods in studying possible cases of sound symbolism in poetry.

In Sebeok's paper on "Decoding a Text" we have to come to a similar conclusion, that there is more promise for analysis on a syntactical level than on the level of phonemes or distinctive features.

Now I will turn to the group of papers that I would consider deal with metrics, by Chatman, Hollander, Lotz, Wimsatt and Beardsley, and Stankiewicz. These seem to be in very remarkable agreement on the differences between metrical form and rhythmical renditions and between constants and variables in meter, and in general on all essential points. There is now a new paper lying before us by Hrushovski, which, as far as I can tell from a hasty glance, may possibly be an exception to this agreement. In discussing these papers, I will limit myself to points of detail, although there is one general point that does seem to merit further study. What are the devices by which a poet in a short poem conveys what basic patterns he is varying, what norms he is occasionally violating? The printed arrangement, of course, does much of the job nowadays, but what about the situation when that is lacking? A long poem allows the listener to acquire the pattern gradually and thoroughly, but it seems conceivable that real doubt might exist for very short lyrics if no external clue were provided. A nursery rhyme may illustrate my point. I have always been worried about the end of Humpty-Dumpty. Should the couplet be read:

> Áll the king's hórses and áll the king's mén
> Cóuldn't put Húmpty-Dumpty togéther agáin

with four weaks between "Hump" and "gether" or

> Cóuldn't put Húmpty-Dúmpty togéther agáin

with one extra "foot" over that in the preceding line? Or should we simply emend (my favorite solution) by dropping out "Dumpty?" [Laughter.] If the poem were sufficiently long we could have some confidence in one or another of these solutions, but here we are in doubt.

It seems, then, that the writer of short poems has an especially difficult problem, best solved by using either a strict, well-established form or a very free form with relatively few constants. It may be a reference to something like this that is intended by Hollander in his paper (**176**) when he speaks of the "emblematic" function of metrical form, but I must confess that his main point escapes me (although I admire the way he makes it). [Laughter.] Lotz alludes to the problem when he speaks of a one-line poem as a "response" referring to other poems in the culture. Lotz's paper in general impresses me as being one of the best and clearest introductions to general metrics I have ever seen, (although I should like also to call attention to de Groot's excellent account, **85**). The notation proposed for English and German verse (that is, indicating the number of light syllables before, between, or after heavy ones) seems to me especially neat, and by using it it is possible to simplify descriptions of variant metrical patterns considerably. Incidentally, a similar notation was proposed (I do not know whether independently or not) for Ancient Greek lyric verse by Miss A. M. Dale (**80**). I think that the main difference is that she uses "s" and "d" instead of 1 and 2 respectively. In Lotz's section on Greek and Latin verse, there do not seem to be quite enough restrictions on the (Greek) comic trimeter. I am sure a 23-mora line of 22 syllables is in fact excluded by an important rule which Lotz omits—namely, even and odd positions ("thesis" and "arsis" in traditional terms) cannot both be resolved—so that we cannot choose to follow his bottom line straight across the paper. This means that the range in number of syllabics should be 12 to 17, not 12 to 22 as given. As for the 23-mora line, there is only one recorded in all of Aristophanes (in a line of 17 syllables), and there are only four 22-mora lines, so that, normally, 21 moras must be considered the maximum.

From a linguist's point of view, Wimsatt and Beardsley's paper (**451**) dealing with English meter is also very satisfying, although to a linguist it seems a little unfair to be assigned in advance to the camp of the wicked. Arguments offered by one or two linguists (or linguisticians, if a derogatory term must be used) do not thereby become the settled dogma of all linguists—or even of the original ones. I think the authors perhaps slightly exaggerate the lack of isochrony in normal poetic reading; certainly "equal" must be interpreted as "equal within a range of variation," but with some such allowance most of the renditions I have measured show a fairly good isochrony, whether they are nursery rhymes or Shakespearean sonnets. However, as they justly observe, this point is not directly relevant to metrics. Some readings of these authors, and many of Chatman's, seem to ignore the known accent patterns of earlier periods of English and produce irregularities which are irregular only for modern readers. Certainly accentuations like "prófuse" and "súpreme" when a stressed syllable followed were normal conversational ones until modern times, just as "úpstairs" and the like still are. And when Chatman collects the harshnesses of Donne, he is increasing them beyond what any contemporary would have heard. When he implies that the verb form "saith" should normally be pronounced in two syllables, this is perhaps due to ignorance. When he asks about the line—and I'll read this very slowly so as not to give anything away—"Ten Cardinals into the Inquisition," he appears to forget that in Donne's day the "-ion" ending was often of two syllables, with a secondary or at least a tertiary on the final, so that the line could be read "Ten Cárd'nals ínto th' ínquisítion" to exaggerate the pattern of the meter. What the phonetic quality of the final vowel was I hesitate to say, perhaps /úwn/. And a good deal of Pope's revisions have as much to do with the development of the modern stress system in the intervening period as they have with Donne's intentional harshness or excessive license, which is admittedly great. Chatman reads almost all the lines on page 154 differently than I would, where, for instance, he ignores the possible accentuation "virtue," the contrastive stress "sóme beasts," and other similar features (but see now fn. 6 of his paper for an answer to this criticism). But in general, I think we must judge that there is little real difference of opinion between Chatman and Beardsley and Wimsatt, most of our doubts lying in the area of uncertainty between misreadings and variant readings.

In Mr. Dorson's interesting paper, we find an interpretation of the term "style" which is rather tangential to that discussed by other conferees; it seems to have its closest affinities perhaps with Mr. Voegelin's paper. The reasons for this are clear enough; in both cases we find an area where it is rather difficult to draw the line between what we might call "style of delivery" and "inherent literary style." Perhaps such a line could be drawn by basing a study on numerous variant renditions of the same oral item, but at present it looks pretty difficult.

I have reserved until the last my comments on the contributions of the psychologists, partly because I am naturally somewhat less at home in this field and partly because they seem to differ strikingly from the others in a variety of ways. Linguists and critics seem on the whole to speak much the same language and inhabit the same world; with the psychologists we both seem equally ill at ease, although perhaps linguists are less repelled by the array of statistics and the apparent triviality of some problems and results.

The most linguistic-seeming of these papers (and I should be inclined to call it almost wholly linguistic except for the ease and sureness with which statistics are manipulated) is that on second-person pronouns by Brown and Gilman. This contains what I should regard as an excellent semantic distinctive-feature analysis, supported by much more and more carefully controlled data than has often been the case. This strikes me as a solid contribution with which I have no quarrel, except perhaps the artificial restriction of the field to exclude other person markers and other phenomena of address (vocatives, imperatives, etc.). I only hope that the investigation can be extended to many other languages where similar phenomena occur. The value both for descriptive and historical studies is great; it is unfortunate that we cannot question informants of earlier periods, but certainly a great deal can be determined from a study of the texts. The connection with any definition of style is somewhat tenuous, however; perhaps the domain of "selection" involved here might be termed "social style," but co-occurrence seems to be only marginally involved.

Carroll's paper speaks of prose style in its title. Since the part that I was able to read before this session contains only the design of the experiment (which I as a linguist would hesitate to criticize, except perhaps that it seems a little bit too big and all-inclusive to be easily manageable), we can only look forward hopefully to the report of the results.

Osgood's paper involves a correlation between style in the grammatical sense and some supposed emotional factors. The results are very interesting and suggest a possible means for distinguishing one sort of bad literature from good, if real feeling or whatever we wish to call it leaves reliable traces in the message.

And, finally, we must be grateful to Jenkins, in the same way as we are to Hymes, for testing a plausible hypothesis thoroughly enough to be sure that it is not correct. The paper starts from the known fact that some people, when they are given free-association tests (i.e., the investigator says a word and the subject responds as quickly as possible with some other word), will respond with a word belonging to the same category, usually a word of the same small form class in fact, whereas other people tend to respond with a word that might be associated in context with that word, that is, a noun that would be suitable for a given adjective to modify or something of the sort. Mr. Jenkins attempted to see whether there were any other measureable traits which were closely correlated with this difference. The net result, although there are a few qualifications to this, is that none of the traits he tested seemed to show much correlation. At the end of his paper he outlines further studies which may well produce more positive results. Paradigmatic associators (that is, those who associate other words of the same type) and syntagmatic associators appear not to show any sort of consistent behavior pattern. Here again it might be worthwhile to test a large number of creative writers to see whether they in general fall into one class or the other. I would be inclined to guess that many poets, at any rate, are paradigmatic associators in some measure.

Closing Statement: Linguistics and Poetics

ROMAN JAKOBSON

Fortunately, scholarly and political conferences have nothing in common. The success of a political convention depends on the general agreement of the majority or totality of its participants. The use of votes and vetoes, however, is alien to scholarly discussion where disagreement generally proves to be more productive than agreement. Disagreement discloses antinomies and tensions within the field discussed and calls for novel exploration. Not political conferences but rather exploratory activities in Antarctica present an analogy to scholarly meetings: international experts in various disciplines attempt to map an unknown region and find out where the greatest obstacles for the explorer are, the insurmountable peaks and precipices. Such a mapping seems to have been the chief task of our conference, and in this respect its work has been quite successful. Have we not realized what problems are the most crucial and the most controversial? Have we not also learned how to switch our codes, what terms to expound or even to avoid in order to prevent misunderstandings with people using different departmental jargon? Such questions, I believe, for most of the members of this conference, if not for all of them, are somewhat clearer today than they were three days ago.

I have been asked for summary remarks about poetics in its relation to linguistics. Poetics deals primarily with the question, *What makes a verbal message a work of art?* Because the main subject of poetics is the *differentia specifica* of verbal art in relation to other arts and in relation to other kinds of verbal behavior, poetics is entitled to the leading place in literary studies.

Poetics deals with problems of verbal structure, just as the analysis of painting is concerned with pictorial structure. Since linguistics is the global science of verbal structure, poetics may be regarded as an integral part of linguistics.

Arguments against such a claim must be thoroughly discussed. It is evident that many devices studied by poetics are not confined to verbal art. We can refer to the possibility of transposing *Wuthering Heights* into a motion picture, medieval legends into frescoes and miniatures, or *L'après-midi d'un faune* into music, ballet, and graphic art. However ludicrous may appear the idea of the *Iliad* and *Odyssey* in comics, certain structural features of their plot are preserved despite the disappearance of their verbal shape. The question whether Blake's illustrations to the *Divina Commedia* are or are not adequate is a proof that different arts are comparable. The problems of baroque or any other historical style transgress the frame of a single art. When handling the surrealistic metaphor, we could hardly pass by Max Ernst's pictures or Luis Buñuel's films, *The Andalusian Dog* and *The Golden Age.* In short, many poetic features belong not only to the science of language but to the whole theory of signs, that is, to general semiotics. This statement, however, is valid not only for verbal art but also for all varieties of language since language shares many properties with some other systems of signs or even with all of them (pansemiotic features).

Likewise a second objection contains nothing that would be specific for literature: the question of relations between the word and the world concerns not only verbal art but actually all kinds of discourse. Linguistics is likely to explore all possible problems of relation between discourse and the "universe of discourse": what of this universe is verbalized by a given discourse and how is it verbalized. The truth values, however, as far as they are—to say with the logicians—"extralinguistic entities," obviously exceed the bounds of poetics and of linguistics in general.

Sometimes we hear that poetics, in contradistinction to linguistics, is concerned with evaluation. This separation of the two fields from each other is based on a current but erroneous interpretation of the contrast between the structure of poetry and other types of verbal structure: the latter are said to be opposed by their "casual," designless nature to the "noncasual," purposeful character of poetic language. In point of fact, any verbal behavior is goal-directed, but the aims are different and the conformity of the means used to the effect aimed at is a problem that evermore preoccupies inquirers into the diverse kinds of verbal communication. There is a close correspondence, much closer than critics believe, between the question of linguistic phenomena expanding in space and time and the spatial and temporal spread of literary models. Even such discontinuous expansion as the resurrection of neglected or forgotten poets—for instance, the posthumous discovery and subsequent canonization of Gerard Manley Hopkins (d. 1889), the tardy fame of Lautréamont (d. 1870) among surrealist poets, and the salient influence of the hitherto ignored Cyprian Norwid (d. 1883) on Polish modern poetry—find a parallel in the history of standard languages which are prone to revive outdated models, sometimes long forgotten, as was the case in literary Czech which toward the beginning of the nineteenth century leaned to sixteenth-century models.

Unfortunately the terminological confusion of "literary studies" with "criticism" tempts the student of literature to replace the description of the intrinsic values of a literary work by a subjective, censorious verdict. The label "literary critic" applied to an investigator of literature is as erroneous as "grammatical (or lexical) critic" would be applied to a linguist. Syntactic and morphologic research cannot be supplanted by a normative grammar, and likewise no manifesto, foisting a critic's own tastes and opinions on creative literature, may act as substitute for an objective scholarly analysis of verbal art. This statement is not to be mistaken for the quietist principle of *laissez faire;* any verbal culture involves programmatic, planning, normative endeavors. Yet why is a clear-cut discrimination made between pure and applied linguistics or between phonetics and orthoëpy but not between literary studies and criticism?

Literary studies, with poetics as their focal portion, consist like linguistics of two sets of problems: synchrony and diachrony. The synchronic description envisages not only the literary production of any given stage but also that part of the literary tradition which for the stage in question has remained vital or has been revived. Thus, for instance, Shakespeare on the one hand and Donne, Marvell, Keats, and Emily Dickinson on the other are experienced by the present English poetic world, whereas the works of James Thomson and Longfellow, for the time being, do not belong to viable artistic values. The selection of classics and their reinterpretation by a novel trend is a substantial problem of synchronic literary studies. Synchronic poetics, like synchronic linguistics, is not to be confused with statics; any stage discriminates between more conservative and more innovatory forms. Any contemporary stage is experienced in its temporal dynamics, and, on the other hand, the historical approach both in poetics and in linguistics is concerned not only with changes but also with continuous, enduring, static factors. A thoroughly comprehensive historical poetics or history of language is a superstructure to be built on a series of successive synchronic descriptions.

Insistence on keeping poetics apart from linguistics is warranted only when the field of linguistics appears to be illicitly restricted, for example, when the sentence is viewed by some linguists as the highest analyzable construction or when the scope of linguistics is confined to grammar alone or uniquely to nonsemantic questions of external form or to the inventory of denotative devices with no reference to free variations. Voegelin has clearly pointed out the two most important and related problems which face structural linguistics, namely, a revision of "the monolithic hypothesis of language" and a concern with "the interdependence of diverse structures within one language." No doubt, for any speech community, for any speaker, there exists a unity of language, but this over-all code represents a system of interconnected subcodes; each language encompasses several concurrent patterns which are each characterized by a different function.

Obviously we must agree with Sapir that, on the whole, "ideation reigns supreme in language . . . "(**348**), but this supremacy does not authorize linguistics to disregard the "secondary factors." The emotive elements of speech which, as Joos is prone to believe, cannot be described "with a finite number of absolute categories," are classified by him "as non-linguistic elements of the real world." Hence, "for us they remain vague, protean, fluctuating phenomena," he concludes, "which we refuse to tolerate in our science" (**218**). Joos is indeed a brilliant expert in reduction experiments, and his emphatic requirement for an "expulsion" of the emotive elements "from linguistic science" is a radical experiment in reduction—*reductio ad absurdum*.

Language must be investigated in all the variety of its functions. Before discussing the poetic function we must define its place among the other functions of language. An outline of these functions demands a concise survey of the constitutive factors in any speech event, in any act of verbal communication. The ADDRESSER sends a MESSAGE to the ADDRESSEE. To be operative the message requires a CONTEXT referred to ("referent" in another, somewhat ambiguous, nomenclature), seizable by the addressee, and either verbal or capable of being verbalized; a CODE fully, or at least partially, common to the addresser and addressee (or in other words, to the encoder and decoder of the message); and, finally, a CONTACT, a physical channel and psychological connection between the addresser and the addressee, enabling both of them to enter and stay in communication. All these factors inalienably involved in verbal communication may be schematized as follows:

CONTEXT

ADDRESSER   MESSAGE   ADDRESSEE

C O N T A C T

CODE

Each of these six factors determines a different function of language. Although we distinguish six basic aspects of language, we could, however, hardly find verbal messages that would fulfill only one function. The diversity lies not in a monopoly of some one of these several functions but in a different hierarchical order of functions. The verbal structure of a message depends primarily on the predominant function. But even though a set (*Einstellung*) toward the referent, an orientation toward the CONTEXT —briefly the so-called REFERENTIAL, "denotative," "cognitive" function— is the leading task of numerous messages, the accessory participation of the other functions in such messages must be taken into account by the observant linguist.

The so-called EMOTIVE or "expressive" function, focused on the ADDRESSER, aims a direct expression of the speaker's attitude toward what he is speaking about. It tends to produce an impression of a certain emotion whether true or feigned; therefore, the term "emotive," launched and advocated by Marty (**269**) has proved to be preferable to "emotional." The purely emotive stratum in language is presented by the interjections. They differ from the means of referential language both by their sound pattern (peculiar sound sequences or even sounds elsewhere unusual) and by their syntactic role (they are not components but equivalents of sentences). "*Tut! Tut!* said McGinty": the complete utterance of Conan Doyle's character consists of two suction clicks. The emotive function, laid bare in the interjections, flavors to some extent all our utterances, on their phonic, grammatical, and lexical level. If we analyze language from the standpoint of the information it carries, we cannot restrict the notion of information to the cognitive aspect of language. A man, using expressive features to indicate his angry or ironic attitude, conveys ostensible information, and evidently this verbal behavior cannot be likened to such nonsemiotic, nutritive activities as "eating grapefruit" (despite Chatman's bold simile). The difference between [big] and the emphatic prolongation of the vowel [bi:g] is a conventional, coded linguistic feature like the difference between the short and long vowel in such Czech pairs as [vi] 'you' and [vi:] 'knows,' but in the latter pair the differential information is phonemic and in the former emotive. As long as we are interested in phonemic invariants, the English /i/ and /i:/ appear to be mere variants of one and the same phoneme, but if we are concerned with emotive units, the relation between the invariant and variants is reversed: length and shortness are invariants implemented by variable phonemes. Saporta's surmise that emotive difference is a nonlinguistic feature, "attributable to the delivery of the message and not to the message," arbitrarily reduces the informational capacity of messages.

A former actor of Stanislavskij's Moscow Theater told me how at his audition he was asked by the famous director to make forty different messages from the phrase *Segodnja večerom* 'This evening,' by diversifying its expressive tint. He made a list of some forty emotional situations, then emitted the given phrase in accordance with each of these situations, which his audience had to recognize only from the changes in the sound shape of the same two words. For our research work in the description and analysis of contemporary Standard Russian (under the auspices of the Rockefeller Foundation) this actor was asked to repeat Stanislavskij's test. He wrote down some fifty situations framing the same elliptic sentence and made of it fifty corresponding messages for a tape record. Most of the messages were correctly and circumstantially decoded by

Moscovite listeners. May I add that all such emotive cues easily undergo linguistic analysis.

Orientation toward the ADDRESSEE, the CONATIVE function, finds its purest grammatical expression in the vocative and imperative, which syntactically, morphologically, and often even phonemically deviate from other nominal and verbal categories. The imperative sentences cardinally differ from declarative sentences: the latter are and the former are not liable to a truth test. When in O'Neill's play *The Fountain*, Nano, "(in a fierce tone of command)," says "Drink!"—the imperative cannot be challenged by the question "is it true or not?" which may be, however, perfectly well asked after such sentences as "one drank," "one will drink," "one would drink." In contradistinction to the imperative sentences, the declarative sentences are convertible into interrogative sentences: "did one drink?" "will one drink?" "would one drink?"

The traditional model of language as elucidated particularly by Bühler (**51**) was confined to these three functions—emotive, conative, and referential—and the three apexes of this model—the first person of the addresser, the second person of the addressee, and the "third person," properly—someone or something spoken of. Certain additional verbal functions can be easily inferred from this triadic model. Thus the magic, incantatory function is chiefly some kind of conversion of an absent or inanimate "third person" into an addressee of a conative message. "May this sty dry up, *tfu, tfu, tfu, tfu*" (Lithuanian spell: **266**, p. 69). "Water, queen river, daybreak! Send grief beyond the blue sea, to the sea-bottom, like a grey stone never to rise from the sea-bottom, may grief never come to burden the light heart of God's servant, may grief be removed and sink away." (North Russian incantation: **343**, p. 217f.). "Sun, stand thou still upon Gibeon; and thou, Moon, in the valley of Aj-a-lon. And the sun stood still, and the moon stayed . . . " (Josh. 10.12). We observe, however, three further constitutive factors of verbal communication and three corresponding functions of language.

There are messages primarily serving to establish, to prolong, or to discontinue communication, to check whether the channel works ("Hello, do you hear me?"), to attract the attention of the interlocutor or to confirm his continued attention ("Are you listening?" or in Shakespearean diction, "Lend me your ears!"—and on the other end of the wire "Um-hum!"). This set for CONTACT, or in Malinowski's terms PHATIC function (**264**), may be displayed by a profuse exchange of ritualized formulas, by entire dialogues with the mere purport of prolonging communication. Dorothy Parker caught eloquent examples: " 'Well!' the young man said. 'Well!' she said. 'Well, here we are,' he said. 'Here we are,' she said, 'Aren't we?' 'I should say we were,' he said, 'Eeyop! Here we are.' 'Well!' she said.

'Well!' he said, 'well.' " The endeavor to start and sustain communication is typical of talking birds; thus the phatic function of language is the only one they share with human beings. It is also the first verbal function acquired by infants ; they are prone to communicate before being able to send or receive informative communication.

A distinction has been made in modern logic between two levels of language, "object language" speaking of objects and "metalanguage" speaking of language. But metalanguage is not only a necessary scientific tool utilized by logicians and linguists; it plays also an important role in our everday language. Like Molière's Jourdain who used prose without knowing it, we practice metalanguage without realizing the metalingual character of our operations. Whenever the addresser and/or the addressee need to check up whether they use the same code, speech is focused on the CODE: it performs a METALINGUAL (i.e., glossing) function. "I don't follow you—what do you mean?" asks the addressee, or in Shakespearean diction, "What is't thou say'st?" And the addresser in anticipation of such recapturing questions inquires: Do you know what I mean?" Imagine such an exasperating dialogue: "The sophomore was plucked." "But what is *plucked*?" "*Plucked* means the same as *flunked*." "And *flunked*?" "*To be flunked* is *to fail in an exam*." "And what is *sophomore*?" persists the interrogator innocent of school vocabulary. "*A sophomore* is (or means) a *second-year student*." All these equational sentences convey information merely about the lexical code of English; their function is strictly metalingual. Any process of language learning, in particular child acquisition of the mother tongue, makes wide use of such metalingual operations; and aphasia may often be defined as a loss of ability for metalingual operations.

We have brought up all the six factors involved in verbal communication except the message itself. The set (*Einstellung*) toward the MESSAGE as such, focus on the message for its own sake, is the POETIC function of language. This function cannot be productively studied out of touch with the general problems of language, and, on the other hand, the scrutiny of language requires a thorough consideration of its poetic function. Any attempt to reduce the sphere of poetic function to poetry or to confine poetry to poetic function would be a delusive oversimplification. Poetic function is not the sole function of verbal art but only its dominant, determining function, whereas in all other verbal activities it acts as a subsidiary, accessory constituent. This function, by promoting the palpability of signs, deepens the fundamental dichotomy of signs and objects. Hence, when dealing with poetic function, linguistics cannot limit itself to the field of poetry.

"Why do you always say *Joan and Margery*, yet never *Margery and Joan?*

Do you prefer Joan to her twin sister?" "Not at all, it just sounds smoother." In a sequence of two coordinate names, as far as no rank problems interfere, the precedence of the shorter name suits the speaker, unaccountably for him, as a well-ordered shape of the message.

A girl used to talk about "the horrible Harry." "Why horrible?" "Because I hate him." "But why not *dreadful, terrible, frightful, disgusting?*" "I don't know why, but *horrible* fits him better." Without realizing it, she clung to the poetic device of paronomasia.

The political slogan "I like Ike" /ay layk ayk/, succinctly structured, consists of three monosyllables and counts three diphthongs /ay/, each of them symmetrically followed by one consonantal phoneme, /..l..k..k/. The make-up of the three words presents a variation: no consonantal phonemes in the first word, two around the diphthong in the second, and one final consonant in the third. A similar dominant nucleus /ay/ was noticed by Hymes in some of the sonnets of Keats. Both cola of the trisyllabic formula "I like / Ike" rhyme with each other, and the second of the two rhyming words is fully included in the first one (echo rhyme), /layk/—/ayk/, a paronomastic image of a feeling which totally envelops its object. Both cola alliterate with each other, and the first of the two alliterating words is included in the second: /ay/—/ayk/, a paronomastic image of the loving subject enveloped by the beloved object. The secondary, poetic function of this electional catch phrase reinforces its impressiveness and efficacy.

As we said, the linguistic study of the poetic function must overstep the limits of poetry, and, on the other hand, the linguistic scrutiny of poetry cannot limit itself to the poetic function. The particularities of diverse poetic genres imply a differently ranked participation of the other verbal functions along with the dominant poetic function. Epic poetry, focused on the third person, strongly involves the referential function of language; the lyric, oriented toward the first person, is intimately linked with the emotive function; poetry of the second person is imbued with the conative function and is either supplicatory or exhortative, depending on whether the first person is subordinated to the second one or the second to the first.

Now that our cursory description of the six basic functions of verbal communication is more or less complete, we may complement our scheme of the fundamental factors by a corresponding scheme of the functions:

REFERENTIAL

EMOTIVE   POETIC   CONATIVE
                     PHATIC

METALINGUAL

What is the empirical linguistic criterion of the poetic function? In particular, what is the indispensable feature inherent in any piece of poetry? To answer this question we must recall the two basic modes of arrangement used in verbal behavior, *selection* and *combination*. If "child" is the topic of the message, the speaker selects one among the extant, more or less similar, nouns like child, kid, youngster, tot, all of them equivalent in a certain respect, and then, to comment on this topic, he may select one of the semantically cognate verbs—sleeps, dozes, nods, naps. Both chosen words combine in the speech chain. The selection is produced on the base of equivalence, similarity and dissimilarity, synonymity and antonymity, while the combination, the build up of the sequence, is based on contiguity. *The poetic function projects the principle of equivalence from the axis of selection into the axis of combination.* Equivalence is promoted to the constitutive device of the sequence. In poetry one syllable is equalized with any other syllable of the same sequence; word stress is assumed to equal word stress, as unstress equals unstress; prosodic long is matched with long, and short with short; word boundary equals word boundary, no boundary equals no boundary; syntactic pause equals syntactic pause, no pause equals no pause. Syllables are converted into units of measure, and so are morae or stresses.

It may be objected that metalanguage also makes a sequential use of equivalent units when combining synonymic expressions into an equational sentence: $A = A$ ("*Mare* is *the female of the horse*"). Poetry and metalanguage, however, are in diametrical opposition to each other: in metalanguage the sequence is used to build an equation, whereas in poetry the equation is used to build a sequence.

In poetry, and to a certain extent in latent manifestations of poetic function, sequences delimited by word boundaries become commensurable whether they are sensed as isochronic or graded. "Joan and Margery" showed us the poetic principle of syllable gradation, the same principle which in the closes of Serbian folk epics has been raised to a compulsory law (cf. **268**). Without its two dactylic words the combination "*innocent* by*stander*" would hardly have become a hackneyed phrase. The symmetry of three disyllabic verbs with an identical initial consonant and identical final vowel added splendor to the laconic victory message of Caesar: "*Veni, vidi, vici.*"

Measure of sequences is a device which, outside of poetic function, finds no application in language. Only in poetry with its regular reiteration of equivalent units is the time of the speech flow experienced, as it is—to cite another semiotic pattern—with musical time. Gerard Manley Hopkins, an outstanding searcher in the science of poetic language, defined verse as "speech wholly or partially repeating the same figure of sound" (**179**). Hopkins' subsequent question, "but is all verse poetry?" can be definitely answered as soon as poetic function ceases to be arbitrarily confined to the domain of poetry. Mnemonic lines cited by Hopkins (like "Thirty days hath September"), modern advertising jingles, and versified medieval laws, mentioned by Lotz, or finally Sanscrit scientific treatises in verse which in Indic tradition are strictly distinguished from true poetry (*kāvya*)—all these metrical texts make use of poetic function without, however, assigning to this function the coercing, determining role it carries in poetry. Thus verse actually exceeds the limits of poetry, but at the same time verse always implies poetic function. And apparently no human culture ignores versemaking, whereas there are many cultural patterns without "applied" verse; and even in such cultures which possess both pure and applied verses, the latter appear to be a secondary, unquestionably derived phenomenon. The adaptation of poetic means for some heterogeneous purpose does not conceal their primary essence, just as elements of emotive language, when utilized in poetry, still maintain their emotive tinge. A filibusterer may recite *Hiawatha* because it is long, yet poeticalness still remains the primary intent of this text itself. Self-evidently, the existence of versified, musical, and pictorial commercials does not separate the questions of verse or of musical and pictorial form from the study of poetry, music, and fine arts.

To sum up, the analysis of verse is entirely within the competence of poetics, and the latter may be defined as that part of linguistics which treats the poetic function in its relationship to the other functions of language. Poetics in the wider sense of the word deals with the poetic function not only in poetry, where this function is superimposed upon the other functions of language, but also outside of poetry, when some other function is superimposed upon the poetic function.

The reiterative "figure of sound," which Hopkins saw to be the constitutive principle of verse, can be further specified. Such a figure always utilizes at least one (or more than one) binary contrast of a relatively high and relatively low prominence effected by the different sections of the phonemic sequence.

Within a syllable the more prominent, nuclear, syllabic part, constituting the peak of the syllable, is opposed to the less prominent, marginal, nonsyllabic phonemes. Any syllable contains a syllabic phoneme, and the interval between two successive syllabics is in some languages always and in others overwhelmingly carried out by marginal, nonsyllabic phonemes. In the so-called syllabic versification the number of syllabics in a metrically delimited chain (time series) is a constant, whereas the presence of a nonsyllabic phoneme or cluster between every two syllabics of a metrical chain is a constant only in languages with an indispensable occurrence of nonsyllabics between syllabics and, furthermore, in those verse systems where hiatus is prohibited. Another manifestation of a tendency toward a uniform syllabic model is the avoidance of closed syllables at the end of the line, observable, for instance, in Serbian epic songs. The Italian syllabic verse shows a tendency to treat a sequence of vowels unseparated by consonantal phonemes as one single metrical syllable (cf. **247a,** secs. VIII–IX).

In some patterns of versification the syllable is the only constant unit of verse measure, and a grammatical limit is the only constant line of demarcation between measured sequences, whereas in other patterns syllables in turn are dichotomized into more and less prominent, and/or two levels of grammatical limits are distinguished in their metrical function, word boundaries and syntactic pauses.

Except the varieties of the so-called vers libre that are based on conjugate intonations and pauses only, any meter uses the syllable as a unit of measure at least in certain sections of the verse. Thus in the purely accentual verse ("sprung rhythm" in Hopkins' vocabulary), the number of syllables in the upbeat (called "slack" by Hopkins) may vary, but the downbeat (ictus) constantly contains one single syllable.

In any accentual verse the contrast between higher and lower prominence is achieved by syllables under stress versus unstressed syllables. Most accentual patterns operate primarily with the contrast of syllables with and without word stress, but some varieties of accentual verse deal with syntactic, phrasal stresses, those which Wimsatt and Beardsley cite as "the major stresses of the major words" and which are opposed as prominent to syllables without such major, syntactic stress.

In the quantitative ("chronemic") verse, long and short syllables are mutually opposed as more and less prominent. This contrast is usually carried out by syllable nuclei, phonemically long and short. But in metrical patterns like Ancient Greek and Arabic, which equalize length "by position" with length "by nature," the minimal syllables consisting of a consonantal phoneme and one mora vowel are opposed to syllables with a surplus (a second mora or a closing consonant) as simpler and less prominent syllables opposed to those that are more complex and prominent.

The question still remains open whether, besides the accentual and the chronemic verse, there exists a "tonemic" type of versification in languages where differences of syllabic intonations are used to distinguish word meanings (**198**). In classical Chinese poetry (**29a**), syllables with modulations (in Chinese *tsê,* 'deflected tones') are opposed to the nonmodulated syllables (*p'ing,* 'level tones'), but apparently a chronemic principle underlies this opposition, as was suspected by Polivanov (**318a**) and keenly interpreted by Wang Li (**438a**); in the Chinese metrical tradition the level tones prove to be opposed to the deflected tones as long tonal peaks of syllables to short ones, so that verse is based on the opposition of length and shortness.

Joseph Greenberg brought to my attention another variety of tonemic versification—the verse of Efik riddles based on the level feature. In the sample cited by Simmons (**379**, p. 228), the query and the response form two octosyllables with an alike distribution of *h*(igh)- and *l*(ow)-tone syllabics; in each hemistich, moreover, the last three of the four syllables present an identical tonemic pattern: *lhhl*/*hhhl*//*lhhl*/*hhhl*//. Whereas Chinese versification appears as a peculiar variety of the quantitative verse, the verse of the Efic riddles is linked with the usual accentual verse by an opposition of two degrees of prominence (strength or height) of the vocal tone. Thus a metrical system of versification can be based only on the opposition of syllabic peaks and slopes (syllabic verse), on the relative level of the peaks (accentual verse), and on the relative length of the syllabic peaks or entire syllables (quantitative verse).

In textbooks of literature we sometimes encounter a superstitious contraposition of syllabism as a mere mechanical count of syllables to the lively pulsation of accentual verse. If we examine, however, the binary meters of the strictly syllabic and at the same time, accentual versification, we observe two homogeneous successions of wavelike peaks and valleys. Of these two undulatory curves, the syllabic one carries nuclear phonemes in the crest and usually marginal phonemes in the bottom. As a rule the accentual curve superposed upon the syllabic curve alternates stressed and unstressed syllables in the crests and bottoms respectively.

For comparison with the English meters which we have lengthily discussed, I bring to your attention the similar Russian binary verse forms which for the last fifty years have verily undergone an exhaustive investigation (see particularly **407**). The structure of the verse can be very thoroughly described and interpreted in terms of enchained probabilities. Besides the compulsory word boundary between the lines, which is an invariant throughout all Russian meters, in the classic pattern of Russian syllabic accentual verse ("syllabo-tonic" in native nomenclature) we observe the following constants: (1) the number of syllables in the line from its beginning to the last downbeat is stable; (2) this very last downbeat always carries a word stress; (3) a stressed syllable cannot fall on the upbeat if a downbeat is fulfilled by an unstressed syllable of the same word unit (so that a word stress can coincide with an upbeat only as far as it belongs to a monosyllabic word unit).

Along with these characteristics compulsory for any line composed in a given meter, there are features that show a high probability of occurrence without being constantly present. Besides signals certain to occur ("probability one"), signals likely to occur ("probabilities less than one") enter into the notion of meter. Using Cherry's description of human communication (62), we could say that the reader of poetry obviously "may be unable to attach numerical frequencies" to the constituents of the meter, but as far as he conceives the verse shape, he unwittingly gets an inkling of their "rank order."

In the Russian binary meters all odd syllables counting back from the last downbeat—briefly, all the upbeats—are usually fulfilled by unstressed syllables, except some very low percentage of stressed monosyllables. All even syllables, again counting back from the last downbeat, show a sizable preference for syllables under word stress, but the probabilities of their occurrence are unequally distributed among the successive downbeats of the line. The higher the relative frequency of word stresses in a given downbeat, the lower the ratio shown by the preceding downbeat. Since the last downbeat is constantly stressed, the next to last gives the lowest percentage of word stresses; in the preceding downbeat their amount is again higher, without attaining the maximum, displayed by the final downbeat; one downbeat further toward the beginning of the line, the amount of the stresses sinks once more, without reaching the minimum of the next-to-last downbeat; and so on. Thus the distribution of word stresses among the downbeats within the line, the split into strong and weak downbeats, creates a *regressive undulatory curve* superposed upon the wavy alternation of downbeats and upbeats. Incidentally, there is a captivating question of the relationship between the strong downbeats and phrasal stresses.

The Russian binary meters reveal a stratified arrangement of three undulatory curves: (I) alternation of syllabic nuclei and margins; (II) division of syllabic nuclei into alternating downbeats and upbeats; and (III) alternation of strong and weak downbeats. For example, Russian masculine iambic tetrameter of the nineteenth and present centuries may be represented by Figure 1, and a similar triadic pattern appears in the corresponding English forms.

Three of five downbeats are deprived of word stress in Shelley's iambic line "Laugh with an inextinguishable laughter." Seven of sixteen downbeats are stressless in the following quatrain from Pasternak's recent iambic tetrameter *Zemlja* ("Earth"):

> I úlica za panibráta
> S okónnicej podslepovátoj,
> I béloj nóči i zakátu
> Ne razminút'sja u rekí.

Since the overwhelming majority of downbeats concur with word stresses, the listener or reader of Russian verses is prepared with a high degree of probability to meet a word stress in any even syllable of iambic lines, but at the very beginning of Pasternak's quatrain the fourth and, one foot further, the sixth syllable, both in the first and in the following line, present him with a *frustrated expectation*. The degree of such a "frustration" is higher when the stress is lacking in a strong downbeat and becomes particularly outstanding when two successive downbeats are

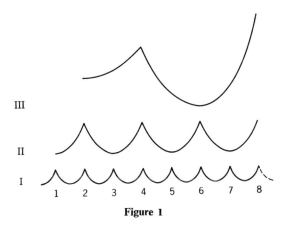

Figure 1

carrying unstressed syllables. The stresslessness of two adjacent downbeats is the less probable and the most striking when it embraces a whole hemistich as in a later line of the same poem: "Čtoby za gorodskjóu grán' ju" [stəbyzəgərackóju grán'ju]. The expectation depends on the treatment of a given downbeat in the poem and more generally in the whole extant metrical tradition. In the last downbeat but one, unstress may, however, outweigh the stress. Thus in this poem only 17 of 41 lines have a word stress on their sixth syllable. Yet in such a case the inertia of the stressed even syllables alternating with the unstressed odd syllables prompts some expectancy of stress also for the sixth syllable of the iambic tetrameter.

Quite naturally it was Edgar Allan Poe, the poet and theoretician of defeated anticipation, who metrically and psychologically appraised the human sense of gratification for the unexpected arising from expectedness, both of them unthinkable without the opposite, "as evil cannot exist without good" (**316**). Here we could easily apply Robert Frost's formula from "The Figure A Poem Makes": "The figure is the same as for love" (**128**).

The so-called shifts of word stress in polysyllabic words from the downbeat to the upbeat ("reversed feet"), which are unknown to the standard forms of Russian verse, appear quite usually in English poetry after a metrical and/or syntactic pause. A noticeable example is the rhythmical variation of the same adjective in Milton's "Infinite wrath and infinite despair." In the line "Nearer, my God, to Thee, nearer to Thee," the stressed syllable of one and the same word occurs twice in the upbeat, first at the beginning of the line and a second time at the beginning of a phrase. This license, discussed by Jespersen (**212**) and current in many languages, is entirely explainable by the particular import of the relation between an upbeat and the immediately preceding downbeat. Where such an immediate precedence is impeded by an inserted pause, the upbeat becomes a kind of *syllaba anceps*.

Besides the rules which underlie the compulsory features of verse, the rules governing its optional traits also pertain to meter. We are inclined to designate such phenomena as unstress in the downbeats and stress in upbeats as deviations, but it must be remembered that these are allowed oscillations, departures within the limits of the law. In British parliamentary terms, it is not an opposition to its majesty the meter but an opposition of its majesty. As to the actual infringements of metrical laws, the discussion of such violations recalls Osip Brik, perhaps the keenest of Russian formalists, who used to say that political conspirators are tried and condemned only for unsuccessful attempts at a forcible upheaval, because in the case of a successful coup it is the conspirators who assume the role of judges and prosecutors. If the violences against the meter take root, they themselves become metrical rules.

Far from being an abstract, theoretical scheme, meter—or in more explicit terms, *verse design*—underlies the structure of any single line—or, in logical terminology, any single *verse instance*. Design and instance are correlative concepts. The verse design determines the invariant features of the verse instances and sets up the limits of variations. A Serbian peasant reciter of epic poetry memorizes, performs, and, to a high extent, improvises thousands, sometimes tens of thousands of lines, and their meter is alive in his mind. Unable to abstract its rules, he nonetheless notices and repudiates even the slightest infringement of these rules. Any line of Serbian epics contains precisely ten syllables and is followed by a syntactic pause. There is furthermore a compulsory word boundary before the fifth syllable and a compulsory absence of word boundary before the fourth and tenth syllable. The verse has, moreover, significant quantitative and accentual characteristics (cf. **199, 200**).

This Serbian epic break, along with many similar examples presented by comparative metrics, is a persuasive warning against the erroneous identification of a break with a syntactic pause. The obligatory word boundary must not be combined with pause and is not even meant to be

perceptible by the ear. The analysis of Serbian epic songs phonographic-
ally recorded proves that there are no compulsory audible clues to the
break, and yet any attempt to abolish the word boundary before the fifth
syllable by a mere insignificant change in word order is immediately
condemned by the narrator. The grammatical fact that the fourth and fifth
syllables pertain to two different word units is sufficient for the appraisal
of the break. Thus verse design goes far beyond the questions of sheer
sound shape; it is a much wider linguistic phenomenon, and it yields to no
isolating phonetic treatment.

I say "linguistic phenomenon" even though Chatman states that "the
meter exists as a system outside the language." Yes, meter appears also in
other arts dealing with time sequence. There are many linguistic problems
—for instance, syntax—which likewise overstep the limit of language and
are common to different semiotic systems. We may speak even about the
grammar of traffic signals. There exists a signal code, where a yellow light
when combined with green warns that free passage is close to being
stopped and when combined with red announces the approaching
cessation of the stoppage; such a yellow signal offers a close analogue to
the verbal completive aspect. Poetic meter, however, has so many
intrinsically linguistic particularities that it is most convenient to describe
it from a purely linguistic point of view.

Let us add that no linguistic property of the verse design should be
disregarded. Thus, for example, it would be an unfortunate mistake to
deny the constitutive value of intonation in English meters. Not even
speaking about its fundamental role in the meters of such a master of
English free verse as Whitman, it is impossible to ignore the metrical
significance of pausal intonation ("final juncture"), whether "cadence"
or "anticadence" (**223**), in poems like "The Rape of The Lock" with its
intentional avoidance of enjambments. Yet even a vehement accumulation of enjambments never hides their digressive, variational status;
they always set off the normal coincidence of syntactic pause and pausal
intonation with the metrical limit. Whatever is the reciter's way of reading,
the intonational constraint of the poem remains valid. The intonational
contour inherent to a poem, to a poet, to a poetic school is one of the most
notable topics brought to discussion by the Russian formalists (**108, 461**).

The verse design is embodied in verse instances. Usually the free variation of these instances is denoted by the somewhat equivocal label "rhythm."
A variation of *verse instances* within a given poem must be strictly distinguished from the variable *delivery instances*. The intention "to describe
the verse line as it is actually performed" is of lesser use for the synchronic
and historical analysis of poetry than it is for the study of its recitation in
the present and the past. Meanwhile the truth is simple and clear: "There

are many performances of the same poem—differing among themselves in many ways. A performance is an event, but the poem itself, if there *is* any poem, must be some kind of enduring object." This sage memento of Wimsatt and Beardsley belongs indeed to the essentials of modern metrics.

In Shakespeare's verses the second, stressed syllable of the word "absurd" usually falls on the downbeat, but once in the third act of *Hamlet* it falls on the upbeat: "No, let the candied tongue lick absurd pomp." The reciter may scan the word "absurd" in this line with an initial stress on the first syllable or observe the final word stress in accordance with the standard accentuation. He may also subordinate the word stress of the adjective in favor of the strong syntactic stress of the following head word, as suggested by Hill: "Nó, lèt thĕ cândĭed tóngue lĭck ăbsùrd pómp" (**174**), as in Hopkins' conception of English antispasts—"regrét nĕver" (**179**). There is finally a possibility of emphatic modifications either through a "fluctuating accentuation" (*schwebende Betonung*) embracing both syllables or through an exclamational reinforcement of the first syllable [àb-súrd]. But whatever solution the reciter chooses, the shift of the word stress from the downbeat to the upbeat with no antecedent pause is still arresting, and the moment of frustrated expectation stays viable. Wherever the reciter put the accent, the discrepancy between the English word stress on the second syllable of "absurd" and the downbeat attached to the first syllable persists as a constitutive feature of the verse instance. The tension between the ictus and the usual word stress is inherent in this line independently of its different implementations by various actors and readers. As Gerard Manley Hopkins observes, in the preface to his poems, "two rhythms are in some manner running at once" (**180**). His description of such a contrapuntal run can be reinterpreted. The superinducing of an equivalence principle upon the word sequence or, in other terms, the *mounting* of the metrical form upon the usual speech form, necessarily gives the experience of a double, ambiguous shape to anyone who is familiar with the given language and with verse. Both the convergences and the divergences between the two forms, both the warranted and the frustrated expectations, supply this experience.

How the given verse-instance is implemented in the given delivery instance depends on the *delivery design* of the reciter; he may cling to a scanning style or tend toward prose-like prosody or freely oscillate between these two poles. We must be on guard against simplistic binarism which reduces two couples into one single opposition either by suppressing the cardinal distinction between verse design and verse instance (as well as

between delivery design and delivery instance) or by an erroneous identification of delivery instance and delivery design with the verse instance and
verse design.

> "But tell me, child, your choice; what shall I buy
> You?"—"Father, what you buy me I like best."

These two lines from "The Handsome Heart" by Hopkins contain a heavy
enjambment which puts a verse boundary before the concluding mono-
syllable of a phrase, of a sentence, of an utterance. The recitation of these
pentameters may be strictly metrical with a manifest pause between "buy"
and "you" and a suppressed pause after the pronoun. Or, on the contrary,
there may be displayed a prose-oriented manner without any separation
of the words "buy you" and with a marked pausal intonation at the end
of the question. None of these ways of recitation may, however, hide the
intentional discrepancy between the metrical and syntactic division. The
verse shape of a poem remains completely independent of its variable
delivery, whereby I do not intend to nullify the alluring question of
Autorenleser and *Selbstleser* launched by Sievers (**376**).

No doubt, verse is primarily a recurrent "figure of sound." Primarily,
always, but never uniquely. Any attempts to confine such poetic conventions as meter, alliteration, or rhyme to the sound level are speculative
reasonings without any empirical justification. The projection of the
equational principle into the sequence has a much deeper and wider
significance. Valéry's view of poetry as "hesitation between the sound
and the sense" (cf. **426**) is much more realistic and scientific than any bias
of phonetic isolationism.

Although rhyme by definition is based on a regular recurrence of
equivalent phonemes or phonemic groups, it would be an unsound
oversimplification to treat rhyme merely from the standpoint of sound.
Rhyme necessarily involves the semantic relationship between rhyming
units ("rhyme-fellows" in Hopkins' nomenclature). In the scrutiny of a
rhyme we are faced with the question of whether or not it is a homoeoteleuton, which confronts similar derivational and/or inflexional
suffixes (congratulations-decorations), or whether the rhyming words
belong to the same or to different grammatical categories. Thus, for
example, Hopkins' fourfold rhyme is an agreement of two nouns—"kind"
and "mind"—both contrasting with the adjective "blind" and with the
verb "find." Is there a semantic propinquity, a sort of simile between
rhyming lexical units, as in dove-love, light-bright, place-space, name-fame?
Do the rhyming members carry the same syntactic function? The difference
between the morphological class and the syntactic application may be
pointed out in rhyme. Thus in Poe's lines, "While I nodded, nearly

napping, suddenly there came a *tapping*, As of someone gently *rapping*," the three rhyming words, morphologically alike, are all three syntactically different. Are totally or partly homonymic rhymes prohibited, tolerated, or favored? Such full homonyms as son-sun, I-eye, eve-eave, and on the other hand, echo rhymes like December-ember, infinite-night, swarm-warm, smiles-miles? What about compound rhymes (such as Hopkins' "enjoy-ment–toy meant" or "began some–ransom"), where a word unit accords with a word group?

A poet or poetic school may be oriented toward or against grammatical rhyme; rhymes must be either grammatical or antigrammatical; an agrammatical rhyme, indifferent to the relation between sound and grammatical structure, would, like any agrammatism, belong to verbal pathology. If a poet tends to avoid grammatical rhymes, for him, as Hopkins said, "There are two elements in the beauty rhyme has to the mind, the likeness or sameness of sound and the unlikeness or difference of meaning" (**179**). Whatever the relation between sound and meaning in different rhyme techniques, both spheres are necessarily involved. After Wimsatt's illuminating observations about the meaningfulness of rhyme (**449**) and the shrewd modern studies of Slavic rhyme patterns, a student in poetics can hardly maintain that rhymes signify merely in a very vague way.

Rhyme is only a particular, condensed case of a much more general, we may even say the fundamental, problem of poetry, namely *parallelism*. Here again Hopkins, in his student papers of 1865, displayed a prodigious insight into the structure of poetry:

The artificial part of poetry, perhaps we shall be right to say all artifice, reduces itself to the principle of parallelism. The structure of poetry is that of continuous parallelism, ranging from the technical so-called Parallelisms of Hebrew poetry and the antiphons of Church music up to the intricacy of Greek or Italian or English verse. But parallelism is of two kinds necessarily—where the opposition is clearly marked, and where it is transitional rather or chromatic. Only the first kind, that of marked parallelism, is concerned with the structure of verse—in rhythm, the recurrence of a certain sequence of syllables, in metre, the recurrence of a certain sequence of rhythm, in alliteration, in assonance and in rhyme. Now the force of this recurrence is to beget a recurrence or parallelism answering to it in the words or thought and, speaking roughly and rather for the tendency than the invariable result, the more marked parallelism in structure whether of elaboration or of emphasis begets more marked parallelism in the words and sense.... To the marked or abrupt kind of parallelism belong metaphor, simile, parable, and so on, where the effect is sought in likeness of things, and antithesis, contrast, and so on, where it is sought in unlikeness (**179**).

Briefly, equivalence in sound, projected into the sequence as its constitutive principle, inevitably involves semantic equivalence, and on any linguistic level any constituent of such a sequence prompts one of the two correlative experiences which Hopkins neatly defines as "comparison for likeness' sake" and "comparison for unlikeness' sake."

Folklore offers the most clear-cut and stereotyped forms of poetry, particularly suitable for structural scrutiny (as Sebeok illustrated with Cheremis samples). Those oral traditions that use grammatical parallelism to connect consecutive lines, for example, Finno-Ugric patterns of verse (see **10, 399**) and to a high degree also Russian folk poetry, can be fruitfully analyzed on all linguistic levels—phonological, morphological, syntactic, and lexical: we learn what elements are conceived as equivalent and how likeness on certain levels is tempered with conspicuous difference on other ones. Such forms enable us to verify Ransom's wise suggestion that "the meter-and-meaning process is the organic act of poetry, and involves all its important characters" (**324**). These clear-cut traditional structures may dispel Wimsatt's doubts about the possibility of writing a grammar of the meter's interaction with the sense, as well as a grammar of the arrangement of metaphors. As soon as parallelism is promoted to canon, the interaction between meter and meaning and the arrangement of tropes cease to be "the free and individual and unpredictable parts of the poetry."

Let us translate a few typical lines from Russian wedding songs about the apparition of the bridegroom:

> A brave fellow was going to the porch,
> Vasilij was walking to the manor.

The translation is literal; the verbs, however, take the final position in both Russian clauses (Dobroj mólodec k séničkam privoráčival, // Vasílij k téremu prixážival). The lines wholly correspond to each other syntactically and morphologically. Both predicative verbs have the same prefixes and suffixes and the same vocalic alternant in the stem; they are alike in aspect, tense, number, and gender; and, moreover, they are synonymic. Both subjects, the common noun and the proper name, refer to the same person and form an appositional group. The two modifiers of place are expressed by identical prepositional constructions, and the first one stands to the second in synecdochic relation.

These verses may occur preceded by another line of similar grammatical (syntactic and morphologic) make-up: "Not a bright falcon was flying beyond the hills" or "Not a fierce horse was coming at gallop to the court." The "bright falcon" and the "fierce horse" of these variants are put in metaphorical relation with "brave fellow." This is traditional Slavic negative parallelism—the refutation of the metaphorical state in favor of the factual state. The negation *ne* may, however, be omitted: "Jasjón sokol zá gory zaljótyval" (A bright falcon was flying beyond the hills) or

"Retív kon' kó dvoru priskákival" (A fierce horse was coming at a gallop to the court). In the first of the two examples the *metaphorical* relation is maintained: a brave fellow appeared at the porch, like a bright falcon from behind the hills. In the other instance, however, the semantic connection becomes ambiguous. A comparison between the appearing bridegroom and the galloping horse suggests itself, but at the same time the halt of the horse at the court actually anticipates the approach of the hero to the house. Thus before introducing the rider and the manor of his fiancee, the song evokes the contiguous, *metonymical* images of the horse and of the courtyard: possession instead of possessor, and outdoors instead of inside. The exposition of the groom may be broken up into two consecutive moments even without substituting the horse for the horseman: "A brave fellow was coming at a gallop to the court, // Vasilij was walking to the porch." Thus the "fierce horse," emerging in the preceding line at a similar metrical and syntactic place as the "brave fellow," figures simultaneously as a likeness to and as a representative possession of this fellow, properly speaking—*pars pro toto* for the horseman. The horse image is on a border line between metonymy and synecdoche. From these suggestive connotations of the "fierce horse" there ensues a metaphorical synecdoche: in the wedding songs and other varieties of Russian erotic lore, the masculine *retiv kon* becomes a latent or even patent phallic symbol.

As early as the 1880's, Potebnja, a remarkable inquirer into Slavic poetics, pointed out that in folk poetry a symbol appears to be materialized (*oveščestvlen*), converted into an accessory of the ambiance. "Still a symbol, it is put, however, in a connection with the action. Thus a simile is presented under the shape of a temporal sequence" (**322**). In Potebnja's examples from Slavic folklore, the willow, under which a girl passes, serves at the same time as her image; the tree and the girl are both copresent in the same verbal simulacrum of the willow. Quite similarly the horse of the love songs remains a virility symbol not only when the maid is asked by the lad to feed his steed but even when being saddled or put into the stable or attached to a tree.

In poetry not only the phonological sequence but in the same way any sequence of semantic units strives to build an equation. Similarity superimposed on contiguity imparts to poetry its throughgoing symbolic, multiplex, polysemantic essence which is beautifully suggested by Goethe's "Alles Vergängliche ist nur ein Gleichnis" (Anything transient is but a likeness). Said more technically, anything sequent is a simile. In poetry where similarity is superinduced upon contiguity, any metonymy is slightly metaphorical and any metaphor has a metonymical tint.

Ambiguity is an intrinsic, inalienable character of any self-focused message, briefly a corollary feature of poetry. Let us repeat with Empson: "The machinations of ambiguity are among the very roots of poetry" (113). Not only the message itself but also its addresser and addressee become ambiguous. Besides the author and the reader, there is the "I" of the lyrical hero or of the fictitious storyteller and the "you" or "thou" of the alleged addressee of dramatic monologues, supplications, and epistles. For instance the poem "Wrestling Jacob" is addressed by its title hero to the Saviour and simultaneously acts as a subjective message of the poet Charles Wesley to his readers. Virtually any poetic message is a quasi-quoted discourse with all those peculiar, intricate problems which "speech within speech" offers to the linguist.

The supremacy of poetic function over referential function does not obliterate the reference but makes it ambiguous. The double-sensed message finds correspondence in a split addresser, in a split addressee, and besides in a split reference, as it is cogently exposed in the preambles to fairy tales of various peoples, for instance, in the usual exordium of the Majorca storytellers: "Aixo era y no era" (It was and it was not) (135). The repetitiveness effected by imparting the equivalence principle to the sequence makes reiterable not only the constituent sequences of the poetic message but the whole message as well. This capacity for reiteration whether immediate or delayed, this reification of a poetic message and its constituents, this conversion of a message into an enduring thing, indeed all this represents an inherent and effective property of poetry.

In a sequence, where similarity is superimposed on contiguity, two similar phonemic sequences near to each other are prone to assume a paronomastic function. Words similar in sound are drawn together in meaning. It is true that the first line of the final stanza in Poe's "Raven" makes wide use of repetitive alliterations, as noted by Valéry (426), but "the overwhelming effect" of this line and of the whole stanza is due primarily to the sway of poetic etymology.

> And the Raven, never flitting, still is sitting, *still* is sitting
> On the pallid bust of Pallas just above my chamber door;
> And his eyes have all the seeming of a demon's that is dreaming,
> And the lamp-light o'er him streaming throws his shadow on the floor;
> And my soul from out that shadow that lies floating on the floor
> Shall be lifted—nevermore.

The perch of the raven, "the pallid bust of Pallas," is merged through the "sonorous" paronomasia /pǽləd/—/pǽləs/ into one organic whole (similar to Shelley's molded line "Sculptured on alabaster obelisk" /sk.lp/—/l.b.st/—/b.l.sk/). Both confronted words were blended earlier in another epithet of the same bust—*placid* /plǽsɪd/—a poetic portmanteau, and the bond between the sitter and the seat was in turn fastened by a paronomasia: "*b*ird or *b*ea*st* upon the . . . *bust*." The bird "is sitting // On the pallid bust of Pallas just above my chamber door," and the raven on his perch, despite the lover's imperative "take thy form from off my door," is nailed to the place by the words /ʒʌst əbʌ́v/, both of them blended in /bʌ́st/.

The never-ending stay of the grim guest is expressed by a chain of ingenious paronomasias, partly inversive, as we would expect from such a deliberate experimenter in anticipatory, regressive *modus operandi*, such a master in "writing backwards" as Edgar Allan Poe. In the introductory line of this concluding stanza, "raven," contiguous to the bleak refrain word "never," appears once more as an embodied mirror image of this "never:" /n.v.r/—/r.v.n/. Salient paronomasias interconnect both emblems of the everlasting despair, first "the Raven, never flitting," at the beginning of the very last stanza, and second, in its very last lines the "shadow that lies floating on the floor" and "shall be lifted—nevermore": /névər flítíŋ/—/flótíŋ/ . . . /flór/ . . . /líftəd névər/. The alliterations which struck Valéry build a paronomastic string: /stí . . . /—/sít . . . /—/stí . . . /—/sít . . . /. The invariance of the group is particularly stressed by the variation in its order. The two luminous effects in the chiaroscuro—the "fiery eyes" of the black fowl and the lamplight throwing "his shadow on the floor"—are evoked to add to the gloom of the whole picture and are again bound by the "vivid effect" of paronomasias: /ɔ́lðə símɪŋ/ . . . /dimənz/ . . . /ɪz drímɪŋ/—/ɔrɪm strímɪŋ/. "That shadow that lies /láyz/" pairs with the Raven's "eyes" /áyz/ in an impressively misplaced echo rhyme.

In poetry, any conspicuous similarity in sound is evaluated in respect to similarity and/or dissimilarity in meaning. But Pope's alliterative precept to poets—"the sound must seem an Echo of the sense"—has a wider application. In referential language the connection between *signans* and *signatum* is overwhelmingly based on their codified contiguity, which is often confusingly labeled "arbitrariness of the verbal sign." The relevance of the sound-meaning nexus is a simple corollary of the superposition of similarity upon contiguity. Sound symbolism is an undeniably objective relation founded on a phenomenal connection between different sensory modes, in particular between the visual and auditory experience. If the results of research in this area have sometimes been vague or controversial, it is primarily due to an insufficient care for the methods of psychological and/or linguistic inquiry. Particularly from the linguistic point of view the picture has often been distorted by lack of attention to the phonological aspect of speech sounds or by inevitably vain operations with complex phonemic units instead of with their ultimate components. But when, on testing, for example, such phonemic oppositions as grave versus acute we ask whether /i/ or /u/ is darker, some of the subjects may respond that this question makes no sense to them, but hardly one will state that /i/ is the darkest of the two.

Poetry is not the only area where sound symbolism makes itself felt, but it is a province where the internal nexus between sound and meaning changes from latent into patent and manifests itself most palpably and intensely, as it has been noted in Hymes's stimulating paper. The super-average accumulation of a certain class of phonemes or a contrastive assemblage of two opposite classes in the sound texture of a line, of a stanza, of a poem acts like an "undercurrent of meaning," to use Poe's picturesque expression. In two polar words phonemic relationship may be in agreement with semantic opposition, as in Russian /d,en,/ 'day' and /noč/ 'night' with the acute vowel and sharped consonants in the diurnal name and the corresponding grave vowel in the nocturnal name. A reinforcement of this contrast by surrounding the first word with acute and sharped phonemes, in contradistinction to a grave phonemic neighborhood of the second word, makes the sound into a thorough echo of the sense. But in the French *jour* 'day' and *nuit* 'night' the distribution of grave and acute vowels is inverted, so that Mallarmé's *Divagations* accuse his mother tongue of a deceiving perversity for assigning to day a dark timbre and to night a light one (**265**). Whorf states that when in its sound shape "a word has an acoustic similarity to its own meaning, we can notice it. . . . But, when the opposite occurs, nobody notices it." Poetic language, however, and particularly French poetry in the collision between sound and meaning detected by Mallarmé, either seeks a phonological alternation of such a discrepancy and drowns the "converse" distribution of vocalic features by surrounding *nuit* with grave and *jour* with acute phonemes, or it resorts to a semantic shift and its imagery of day and night replaces the imagery of light and dark by other synesthetic correlates of the phonemic opposition grave/acute and, for instance, puts the heavy, warm day in contrast to the airy, cool night; because "human subjects seem to associate the experiences of bright, sharp, hard, high, light (in weight), quick, high-pitched, narrow, and so on in a long series, with each other; and conversely the experiences of dark, warm, yielding, soft, blunt, low, heavy, slow, low-pitched, wide, etc., in another long series" (**447**, p. 267f).

However effective is the emphasis on repetition in poetry, the sound texture is still far from being confined to numerical contrivances, and a phoneme that appears only once, but in a key word, in a pertinent position, against a contrastive background, may acquire a striking significance. As painters used to say, "Un kilo de vert n'est pas plus vert qu'un demi kilo."

Any analysis of poetic sound texture must consistently take into account the phonological structure of the given language and, beside the over-all code, also the hierarchy of phonological distinctions in the given poetic convention. Thus the approximate rhymes used by Slavic peoples in oral and in some stages of written tradition admit unlike consonants in the rhyming members (e.g. Czech *boty, boky, stopy, kosy, sochy*) but, as Nitch noticed, no mutual correspondence between voiced and voiceless consonants is allowed (**294**), so that the quoted Czech words cannot rhyme with *body, doby, kozy, rohy*. In the songs of some American Indian peoples such as Pima-Papago and Tepecano, according to Herzog's observations—only partly communicated in print (**168**)—the phonemic distinction between voiced and voiceless plosives and between them and nasals is replaced by a free variation, whereas the distinction between labials, dentals, velars, and palatals is rigorously maintained. Thus in the poetry of these languages consonants lose two of the four distinctive features, voiced/voiceless and nasal/oral, and preserve the other two, grave/acute and compact/diffuse. The selection and hierarchic stratification of valid categories is a factor of primary importance for poetics both on the phonological and on the grammatical level.

Old Indic and Medieval Latin literary theory keenly distinguished two poles of verbal art, labeled in Sanskrit *Pañcālī* and *Vaidarbhī* and correspondingly in Latin *ornatus difficilis* and *ornatus facilis* (see **9**), the latter style evidently being much more difficult to analyze linguistically because in such literary forms verbal devices are unostentatious and language seems a nearly transparent garment. But one must say with Charles Sanders Peirce: "This clothing never can be completely stripped off, it is only changed for something more diaphanous" (**307**, p. 171). "Verseless composition," as Hopkins calls the prosaic variety of verbal art—where parallelisms are not so strictly marked and strictly regular as "continuous parallelism" and where there is no dominant figure of sound—present more entangled problems for poetics, as does any transitional linguistic area. In this case the transition is between strictly poetic and strictly referential language. But Propp's pioneering monograph on the structure of the fairy tale (**323**) shows us how a consistently syntactic approach may be of paramount help even in classifying the traditional plots and in tracing the puzzling laws that underlie their composition and selection. The new studies of Lévi-Strauss (**248, 248a,** also, **248b**) display a much deeper but essentially similar approach to the same constructional problem.

It is no mere chance that metonymic structures are less explored than the field of metaphor. May I repeat my old observation that the study of poetic tropes has been directed mainly toward metaphor, and the so-called realistic literature, intimately tied with the metonymic principle, still defies interpretation, although the same linguistic methodology, which poetics uses when analyzing the metaphorical style of romantic poetry, is entirely applicable to the metonymical texture of realistic prose (**197**).

Textbooks believe in the occurrence of poems devoid of imagery, but actually scarcity in lexical tropes is counterbalanced by gorgeous grammatical tropes and figures. The poetic resources concealed in the morphological and syntactic structure of language, briefly the poetry of grammar, and its literary product, the grammar of poetry, have been seldom known to critics and mostly disregarded by linguists but skillfully mastered by creative writers.

The main dramatic force of Antony's exordium to the funeral oration for Caesar is achieved by Shakespeare's playing on grammatical categories and constructions. Mark Antony lampoons Brutus's speech by changing the alleged reasons for Caesar's assassination into plain linguistic fictions. Brutus's accusation of Caesar, "as he was ambitious, I slew him," undergoes successive transformations. First Antony reduces it to a mere quotation which puts the responsibility for the statement on the speaker quoted: "The noble Brutus // Hath told you . . . ." When repeated, this reference to Brutus is put into opposition to Antony's own assertions by an adversative "but" and further degraded by a concessive "yet." The reference to the alleger's honor ceases to justify the allegation, when repeated with a substitution of the merely copulative "and" instead of the previous causal "for," and when finally put into question through the malicious insertion of a modal "sure":

> The noble Brutus
> Hath told you Cæsar was ambitious;
> For Brutus is an honourable man,
> But Brutus says he was ambitious,
> And Brutus is an honourable man.
> Yet Brutus says he was ambitious,
> And Brutus is an honourable man.
> Yet Brutus says he was ambitious,
> And, sure, he is an honourable man.

The following polyptoton—"I speak . . . Brutus spoke . . . I am to speak"— presents the repeated allegation as mere reported speech instead of reported facts. The effect lies, modal logic would say, in the oblique context of the arguments adduced which makes them into unprovable belief sentences:

> I speak not to disprove what Brutus spoke,
> But here I am to speak what I do know.

The most effective device of Antony's irony is the *modus obliquus* of Brutus's abstracts changed into a *modus rectus* to disclose that these reified attributes are nothing but linguistic fictions. To Brutus's saying "he was ambitious," Antony first replies by transferring the adjective from the agent to the action ("Did this in Caesar seem ambitious?"), then by eliciting the abstract noun "ambition" and converting it into a subject of a concrete passive construction "Ambition should be made of sterner stuff" and subsequently to a predicate noun of an interrogative sentence, "Was this ambition?"—Brutus's appeal "hear me for my cause" is answered by the same noun *in recto*, the hypostatized subject of an interrogative, active construction: "What cause witholds you . . . ?" While Brutus calls "awake your senses, that you may the better judge," the abstract substantive derived from "judge" becomes an apostrophized agent in Antony's report: "O judgment, thou art fled to brutish beasts . . ." Incidentally, this apostrophe with its murderous paronomasia Brutus–brutish is reminiscent of Caesar's parting exclamation "Et tu, Brute!" Properties and activities are exhibited *in recto*, whereas their carriers appear either *in obliquo* ("withholds you," "to brutish beasts," "back to me") or as subjects of negative actions ("men have lost," "I must pause"):

> You all did love him once, not without cause;
> What cause withholds you then to mourn for him?
> O judgment, thou art fled to brutish beasts,
> And men have lost their reason!

The last two lines of Antony's exordium display the ostensible independence of these grammatical metonymies. The stereotyped "I mourn for so-and-so" and the figurative but still stereotyped "so-and-so is in the coffin and my heart is with him" or "goes out to him" give place in Antony's speech to a daringly realized metonymy; the trope becomes a part of poetic reality:

> My heart is in the coffin there with Cæsar,
> And I must pause till it come back to me.

In poetry the internal form of a name, that is, the semantic load of its constituents, regains its pertinence. The "Cocktails" may resume their obliterated kinship with plumage. Their colors are vivified in Mac Hammond's lines "The ghost of a Bronx pink lady // With orange blossoms afloat in her hair," and the etymological metaphor attains its realization: "O, Bloody Mary, // The cocktails have crowed not the cocks!" ("At an Old Fashion Bar in Manhattan"). Wallace Stevens' poem "An Ordinary Evening in New Haven" revives the head word of the city name first through a discreet allusion to heaven and then through a direct pun-like confrontation similar to Hopkins' "Heaven-Haven."

> The dry eucalyptus *seeks god in the rainy cloud.*
> Professor Eucalyptus of New Haven *seeks him in New Haven* . . .
> The instinct *for heaven* had its counterpart:
> The instinct for earth, *for New Haven*, for his room . . .

The adjective "New" of the city name is laid bare through the concate-nation of opposites:

> The oldest-newest day is the newest alone.
> The oldest-newest night does not creak by . . .

When in 1919 the Moscow Linguistic Circle discussed how to define and delimit the range of *epitheta ornantia*, the poet Majakovskij rebuked us by saying that for him any adjective while in poetry was thereby a poetic epithet, even "great" in the *Great Bear* or "big" and "little" in such names of Moscow streets as *Bol'shaja Presnja* and *Malaja Presnja*. In other words, poeticalness is not a supplementation of discourse with rhetorical adornment but a total re-evaluation of the discourse and of all its com-ponents whatsoever.

A missionary blamed his African flock for walking undressed. "And what about yourself?" they pointed to his visage, "are not you, too, somewhere naked?" "Well, but that is my face." "Yet in us," retorted the natives, "everywhere it is face." So in poetry any verbal element is converted into a figure of poetic speech.

My attempt to vindicate the right and duty of linguistics to direct the investigation of verbal art in all its compass and extent can come to a conclusion with the same burden which summarized my report to the 1953 conference here at Indiana University: "Linguista sum; linguistici nihil a me alienum puto" (**249**). If the poet Ransom is right (and he is right) that "poetry is a kind of language" (**326**), the linguist whose field is any kind of language may and must include poetry in his study. The present conference has clearly shown that the time when both linguists and literary historians eluded questions of poetic structure is now safely behind us. Indeed, as Hollander stated, "there seems to be no reason for trying to separate the literary from the overall linguistic." If there are some critics who still doubt the competence of linguistics to embrace the field of poetics, I privately believe that the poetic incompetence of some bigoted linguists has been mistaken for an inadequacy of the linguistic science itself. All of us here, however, definitely realize that a linguist deaf to the poetic func-tion of language and a literary scholar indifferent to linguistic problems and unconversant with linguistic methods are equally flagrant anachronisms.

From the Viewpoint of Psychology

Opening Statement

ROGER BROWN

The Discussant's role is sometimes played very responsibly; he becomes the Representative of a Discipline who picks his words carefully as if a slip might mean war. I had thought beforehand that it would be dishonest to play the role that way because, when I am among psychologists, I do not feel particularly representative. However, now that I am here and have seen the very exotic folkways and sampled the barely intelligible speech of linguists and literary men, I feel myself to be profoundly and irredeemably psychological. What you have, today, is a kind of coarse psychological filter into which some very subtle materials have been fed. The trouble with a filter is that it can only transmit the frequencies to which it is tuned, and not even these, as you will see, come through without some distortion and loss of detail.

Almost everyone had something to say about the concept of style. Almost everyone agreed that the definition of style begins with the identification of something that is not style—some constancy or invariance. With language the immediate data are particular utterances by particular speakers. We cannot hear many of these before we begin to identify recurrences, consistencies of one sort or another. We might settle on the idiolect of a speaker, the dialect of a region, the language of a country, the things written by Americans about to commit suicide, the frequencies of phonemes in a collection of poems, the standard metric in one poem or in many, the second-person-singular pronouns in Indo-European languages. When some invariance has been recognized, a class of phenomena is marked out. All the instances or tokens or particulars manifest the defining characteristic, but there are residual characteristics in which they vary and these are to be regarded as stylistic.

In many ways the fingerprint is a good concretization of the notion of style. We can make a definition of the superordinate class of phenomena as the markings on the ends of the fingers that can be registered by an ink pressing. The resulting data have two important properties. The values for an individual are constant through time—they are an enduring characteristic. To find such linguistic features has been a first problem in studies like those of Yule (**458**) and Herdan (**166**), which try to find *the* style of an author. In the second place the fingerprint data yield unique values for every living person, a single set of dimensions yielding unique and enduring personal characteristics. Nothing of this sort has ever been worked out with linguistic data. Although Yule found certain statistical features to be fairly constant in the works of one author and different from the average of many other authors, he certainly did not find that all authors writing English had unique and consistent values on these dimensions.

Several of our papers are in part concerned with the description of features of personal style. The "perfixing" of James Joyce in *Finnegans Wake* (**171**) seems sufficiently idiosyncratic to pass, not as Joyce's fingerprint (which would be different in pattern from other men's), but more like an eleventh finger that grew on Joyce alone. However, it is not quite that peculiar, for perfixing is after all the process of condensation that Freud found in dreams, jokes, slips of the tongue, and neurotic symptoms. The unwitting exhibitionist who said he was interested in "physible" culture made a perfix. Mr. Dorson's descriptions of styles in folk narration extend the concept beyond literature into a wider sort of noncasual speech. Here we wonder about the normative data. To what extent are these individual styles and to what extent are they styles of a region and a time?

I think, too, that Mr. Carroll's factor analysis of literary products can be understood in terms of the fingerprint analogue. I suppose that if we studied all the details of fingerprints, we should find that there is a certain amount of redundancy or intercorrelation of detail. Not every little swirl and whorl and line would be independent of every other. They would fall into clusters. What a factor analysis does is to identify such clusters, that is, to find out what things go together so that we need not measure them all. The literary works analyzed in this study were produced by a variety of authors, each author represented only once. Consequently, this study cannot tell us whether the writings of a man consistently manifest the same values for the factors identified. A possible next step would be to ask a group of subjects to write themes on a variety of topics. For each factor identified in the first study, we would select one or two of the better indices and apply these to the new themes to see whether each author has unique characteristic values.

One very interesting aspect of Mr. Carroll's study derives from his use of two kinds of data: ratings of each literary production on bipolar scales like "awkward-graceful" and "hazy-clear," objective measures like the proportion of Latin-derived verbs and the proportion of indefinite articles. When a factor shows significant loadings on some judgments and also on some objective indices, the possibility arises that the objective fact is the "ground" of the judgment. Factor *B*, for instance, which Mr. Carroll calls "personal appeal," involves the judgment "personal-impersonal" as well as the objective number of personal pronouns. It seems likely that the latter fact is the basis for the former judgment. This is not certain, however, for some of the objective facts may be incidental correlates of other facts which are the ones actually determining the judgments. The factor analysis cannot establish the "cue" value of an objective fact for a given judgment; it can only put forward likely candidates. In this connection it is of great interest to note that the major factor, called by Mr. Carroll "evaluation," loads many judgments but no objective measure. The implication is that judgments of good and bad style (across 150 literary samples and 8 judges) have no consistent objective foundation. This fact should be of some interest to those who seek to find an objective common denominator in that class of highly valued linguistic productions called "literature."

There are many definitions of style implied by our papers for which the fingerprint is a bad model. Fingerprints, for instance, do not have an "interpretation." They are a genetically determined characteristic which probably has no important correlates among the traits, motives, and attitudes of the person. In this case the style is not the man. However, variations in linguistic behavior rising out of life experience, temperament and intelligence are expected to have such correlates. Some psychologists (Gordon Allport, for instance) hold that uninterpreted personal variations are simply individual differences and ought not be called *styles* at all. Variations are styles insofar as they are associated with a wide range of behavior dispositions in the person. The pronoun study made by Mr. Gilman and myself is one attempt to interpret style—to demonstrate that a personal characteristic of language usage is associated with a general ideology.

Mr. Osgood's study of stylistic differences between suicide notes and letters is also an interpretation of style but of a somewhat different kind. He is not concerned with differences between fixed fingerprints but rather with the way in which people press their fingers on the ink pad when they are "wrought up," in comparison with the way they press their fingers when they are calm. He looks for the tremulous smudge that will mark out the excited group. Characteristically, Mr. Osgood has made a systematic approach to style, keeping in mind the psychologist's goal of a general theory of behavior. How do people change their way of doing something when their level of motivation changes? I am not sure, however, that the specific predictions made for the suicide notes can be strictly deduced from Mr. Osgood's general theoretical propositions. Take the matter of stereotypy. The general proposition is that under high motivation "the alternatives selected at all choice points should tend to be the most familiar, the most often practiced." Two predictions are that the length of words will be shortened (because word frequency and length are inversely related) and the type-token ratio will go down as fewer different words of low probability are chosen. One must ask: Why not predict a sequence of letter "e's" since that is the most commonly practiced letter in written English or, alternatively, the sentence "Now is the time for all good men to come to the aid of the party" since that is a well-practiced sentence? Assumptions are being made about the units of choice in language behavior and about the amount of preceding context that is relevant to the calculation of probability at a choice point and about the governing intention of the person writing the note to say something relevant to his suicide. The question is whether these assumptions can be made explicit and then be justified?

Mr. Jenkins, in his research, has also sought to find an interpretation of a feature of individual style. To stay with my simile, he has noticed that some people have very typical or "modal" fingerprints (high commonality in word association) and others have very unusual fingerprints (low commonality). It certainly is a reasonable hypothesis that high-commonality scores would be generally associated with conforming, "normal" behavior, but after very thorough testing this highly probable hypothesis seems to be generally incorrect. This negative result is really more informative, in the sense that it is more surprising, than a confirmation would have been. The problem now is to find out in what way our thinking about word association and conformity is mistaken. Mr. Jenkins probably has some very good ideas on this subject. The only thing that occurs to me is to wonder whether the low-commonality subjects may not divide into two very different psychological types: those who do not know the high-commonality responses and those who know them well enough but who take the word association test as an invitation to be original. Would it be worthwhile to ask low-commonality subjects to go through the list a second time attempting to provide for each word "the response most people would make"? This would separate knowledge of the verbal norms from conformity to them. I have a suspicion that the verbally creative person knows the norms of many populations but is himself able to eschew banality in favor of the statement that is novel, yet apt.

Now we come to the papers concerned with defining and studying literature. The literary men seem to me to be saying quite frankly: "Some fingerprints are better than others, and we propose to study the best." The psychological studies are a kind of "comparative stylistics," dealing with style among the lesser phyla. The literary man studies the style of Joyce, Milton, Pope, and the other major primates.

Many papers have worked at the separation of noncasual language from the casual and at the isolation of literature from other kinds of noncasual language. Mr. Hill, Mr. Saporta, Mr. Stankiewicz, and Mr. Voegelin have given us good leads here—perhaps too many leads, as I am left uncertain of the criteria for differentiating these kinds of language. My uncertainty centers on the "preservation" criterion. The *fact* of preservation, as in the survival of some routine greeting or courtesy phrase or cliché, seems not to be the criterion we seek. I wonder whether it would not be better to say that some utterances and writings are "treasured"; an *effort* is made to preserve them. This criterion might serve to separate casual language from noncasual, but it does not distinguish literature and poetry from law and science and historical documents. Perhaps this can be done in terms of the attributes of an utterance or document that are treasured or considered worthy of preservation. The Pythagorean theorem and the theory of natural selection are valued, but it seems to be the sense of them that matters rather than the precise phrasing whereas this is not the case with *Paradise Lost* or *Hamlet*. The "acceptable" rephrasings of natural selection can vary on dimensions where no variation is permitted to *Hamlet*. If we reach the point where the very paper on which something is written is treasured, I suppose we have a historical document. The same production might have both literary and historical value, but the two values are separable in terms of the dimensions of the production that are valued.

I think the linguist's use of the *fact* of preservation as a criterion for defining literature represents an almost phobic avoidance of value. Descriptive linguists usually place themselves within the larger discipline of cultural anthropology. Cultural anthropologists have from the beginning quite frankly studied the values of various societies, and I should think that linguists would similarly be interested in valued linguistic productions. Value can be objectively treated. It is only necessary to specify a group for study and an objective way of determining what they value. The danger to behavior science that creates the linguist's phobia is, I think, the possibility that his own values will enter into his identification of "literature" or of "noncasual" language. This would make trouble, for it might mean that linguistic scientists would not agree with other people on the identification of a corpus to be called "literature." This difficulty will not arise if the linguist defines literature and other kinds of noncasual language in terms of other people's values. It must be added that this need not inhibit the linguist from feeling strongly about various kinds of literary productions. Physicians have very strong opinions about various levels of blood pressure and psychologists greatly value certain I.Q.'s and regret others, and this makes no difficulty for either medicine or psychology. The crucial difference is that the values of the individual physician or psychologist do not enter into his assessment of blood pressure or I.Q. Diagnosis must be independent of the values of the diagnostician, but diagnosis can be based on the values of the population studied.

I am suggesting that the linguist and literary man have very different professional roles. It seems to me to be the critic's business to evaluate, to try to establish his preferences, to show how they are based and what benefits follow from participation in his values. The linguist, on the other hand, is in the business of comparing utterances valued by one group with utterances valued by another. Not everyone ought to be a behavior scientist. Not everyone ought to study values. Someone has to have values and, in this area, it is the literary man's business to value.

It is a proper task for linguistic science to examine a body of valued utterances in search of common distinctive characteristics. Mr. Hymes does this in his interesting search for sound symbolism in sonnets of Keats and Wordsworth. The question of sound symbolism interests me very much, and it seems to me that experiment (**47**) has demonstrated that for the members of one language community there is very high consensus on which of two antithetical meanings is more appropriate to a given sound or sequence of sounds. It is not known as yet whether there are sound-meaning linkages which are the same for members of all language communities. Psychological experiments (**46**) also indicate that speakers of English do not ordinarily look for sound symbolism. They expect words to be conventional (not appropriate) tokens and will only reveal a sense of sound symbolism when they are explicitly instructed to make use of it. I would summarize the work to date by saying: within the English-speaking community there is enough consensus on sound symbolism that this could be a means of communication. Probably it usually is not. Whether or not poetry uses sound symbolism and whether the reading of poetry sensitivizes us to sound symbolism, I do not know.

Mr. Hymes's study takes a very fresh line to this topic. He finds that a sonnet tends to give weight to certain sounds which are then combined in a strategically placed word which is semantically central to the poem. I am not sure how to relate this thesis to the more familiar notion of sound symbolism. Are the weighted sounds of a sonnet appropriate to the meaning of the sonnet in the judgment of speakers of English? Two lines quoted by Mr. Richards suggest the associative mechanism that might produce the result discovered by Mr. Hymes:

> Rhymes the rudders are of verses
> By which, like ships, they steer their courses.

Is it possible that the writer of a sonnet starts with an important word or two which must figure prominently in his poem? For Wordsworth writing "Upon Westminster Bridge" the words may have been "air" and "still." Because he was writing rhymed lines he was led to select "fair," "wear," "bare," "hill," and "will." This is not to say that he chose these words for rhyme alone but only that the sound of a word is a more important guide to word selection in writing poetry than it is in writing prose. This would lead to the effect Mr. Hymes observes, but I am not clear in what sense this is sound symbolism. It is sound selection or concentration, but do the sounds suggest the sense of the poem?

A psychologist is not the man to make the most of the many papers discussing metrics, and it is really a tag end of the discussion by Mr. Wimsatt and Mr. Beardsley (**451**), Mr. Lotz, and Mr. Hollander (**176**) that catches my attention. Meter, I gather, is a norm and so generates expectancies. Psychology has been much interested in the role of expectancy in perception. The general design of many experiments involves presenting some complex stimulus to the eye or ear under less than ideal conditions and then noting the fact that identification of the stimulus is distorted by strong expectancies. Unlikely content in rumors is assimilated to some norm (**6**), improbable combinations of sounds or syllables (**277**) are identified as more probable combinations. When perceptual conditions are poor a strong expectancy will override the effect of the stimulus itself. The very interesting difference between these studies and the situation involved in reading or listening to poetry is that in the reading or listening accurate perception is much more likely. The resulting combination of a strong expectancy and an improbable event communicates two meanings rather than one. To take a very crude example, Cummings said in a lecture (**79**) at Harvard: ". . . although [my mother's] health eventually failed her, she kept her sense of humor to the beginning." We cannot help supplying from memory the word "end" meaning death but, at the same time, we cannot help hearing its antonym, the word "beginning" which rebukes our worldly outlook. Here is a new topic for psychological research—the communication of multiple meanings by creating an expectancy so strong that it is bound to be completed and then completing it in unexpected but unmistakable fashion.

Mr. Richards' paper on "Variant Readings and Misreadings" is also concerned with multiple meanings and raises a problem that is as central to psychology as it is to literature. It is a rule of the game of Freudian interpretation that an item in the manifest content of dreams, jokes, phantasy, or symptoms can have more than a single meaning. When M.I.T. students are made acquainted with this rule, I find that they are inclined to understand it as: anything can mean anything in Freudian interpretation. It is very difficult to play the Freudian game or the literature-interpreting game when we have learned that the highest virtue to which a word can attain is univocality. So far as I can judge, there are two psychological shifts that must be made. In the first place there must be some detachment of element from context, since context serves to select one meaning from those that are possible. The word must be isolated so that its various current and archaic meanings, its concrete roots, and its clang associates can come to mind. Misreadings are then to be excluded from these possibilities by a reconsideration of context in the fullest sense. The valid interpretation will be congruent with some interpretation of other items in the full collection of materials. It will be a recurrent theme. Somehow we make a judgment that a given reading is congruent with too many other items to be accidental and so find the acceptable interpretation. No one, now, can make explicit the quality and degree of coincidence that identifies the valid interpretation, but we may be right in thinking that a diagnostic sense can be acquired which operates with elaborate probabilities we cannot specify. To a surprising degree it is possible to persuade others of these interpretations. It is as if there were some common understanding of the degree of congruence that cannot be expected to occur by chance. For the Freudian interpretation there are rough criteria against which the reactions of the patient to the suggested interpretation and his later behavior may be tested. In the case of literature, too, there are rough criteria in the effect of an interpretation on a reader or an author and its congruence with later work of the same author.

In conclusion, let me offer a presumptuous "clinical" observation. As professional participants we can be divided into two groups. In one are the behavior scientists, the linguists, anthropologists, and psychologists. In the other are the literary critics. Each group seems to be unified around a common fear. I have already mentioned the values phobia of the behavior scientists. It seems to be almost balanced by the statistics phobia of the literary critics. One group is afraid to say: "*A* is better than *B*" and the other is afraid to say: "*A* is larger than *B*." Perhaps it is our central problem to discover how these two utterances are related to one another. If we do not manage that, we can take advantage of the ambiguity of natural language and agree to say: "*A* is greater than *B*."

Closing Statement

GEORGE A. MILLER

It is always a pleasure to hear Roman Jakobson, with his scholarship and enthusiasm, discuss topics near to his heart. It is an honor for me to appear here today on the same program with him. I would like, however, to take issue on one point. He began his remarks by saying that one outcome of our discussion these last two days has been to clarify the problems that need to be worked on. I had reached an opposite opinion. As our discussion progressed, I became less clear, more confused, more worried, more puzzled, and more agonized as to what in heaven's name we were talking about.

The major result for me has been confusion. However, I am not worried about this confusion. There are different ways to be confused: some are bad, but some are good ways. Several times during this conference I had occasion to remember another conference held at the Massachusetts Institute of Technology about ten years ago, when Mr. Locke had the happy notion that it would be good to get people together to talk about speech, language, and communication. So he began the conferences on speech analysis, which were attended by communication engineers, mathematicians, psychologists, and linguists. After the first one or two of these speech analysis conferences, I was, as I am today, completely and utterly confused. The linguists talked about some mystic entity called the "phoneme," an abstraction that had never been seen on the face of an oscilloscope. (The fact that they could not agree among themselves as to what a phoneme was added to the mystery.) The engineers had a fantastic idea that they could measure information, but the probabilities and logarithms involved made it certain that nobody really understood what they were saying. And the psychologists kept insisting that the important thing was the perception of speech, which did not impress anybody but the psychologists. After the conference we all felt rather puzzled about how the other groups could talk so consistently and yet so unintelligibly. They must have been talking about something, but we did not know what. Those conferences continued, however, and eventually we managed to educate each other. I can now talk about information theory, and the phoneme does not frighten me quite the way it did. Roman Jakobson will now use words like "source" and "receiver" and "message" and "code." And many engineers are now deeply worried about the acoustic basis of phonemes and speech perception. It was good confusion and, I think, those conferences made an appreciable difference in the subsequent work on speech analysis.

In this way I gradually learned to understand a little of what the linguist has on his mind when he begins to talk; his verbal behavior during these past days has not puzzled me quite the way it once would have. But the critics have some mystic entity called a "poem," or "literature," whose existence I must take on faith and whose defining properties still confuse me. (The fact that they cannot agree among themselves on what a poem is adds to the mystery.) But past conferences have taught me some small degree of tolerance. I assume that if I am willing to live with this confusion, I will eventually learn something. In spite of my cognitive distress and my disagreement with the claim that our problems have been clarified, I feel once again that I have been confused in a good way. I have faith that something productive will come of this conference. But, at the moment, I do not know what I have learned that will make me a better psychologist. Perhaps, if it flounders around in my unconscious long enough, I will eventually come up with some helpful formulation of the psychological problems that are involved.

In trying to flounder around in a conscious way, rather than leaving the analysis entirely to processes I know nothing about, I have tried to state for myself the relation between the three fields that have been represented here. I think of psychology as the study of behavior. I mean behavior broadly conceived. I do not mean just adult, Western European, verbal behavior. I mean to include the behavior of rats and children and psychotics. It is a very large area. When psychologists try to talk about stylistics, they feel they should narrow this broad field in some way; they narrow it down to "expressive behavior," behavior which says something to another organism about the state of the behaving organism. As a psychologist, therefore, I imagine a very large area of expressive behavior, one that includes a great deal more than anyone else at this conference wants to include. That notion was, I think, rather well expressed by Mr. Jenkins when he said that we can find certain consistencies within an individual over a very wide range of expressive behaviors. Such consistencies contribute to our concept of "personality." However, the difficulty in following out these consistencies is greatly increased if we limit ourselves to the highly stylized, extremely noncasual utterances of the sort that go into literature. The psychologist tends to look more closely at spontaneous expressive behavior.

Now, a subdivision of this broad area of expressive behavior is human language, the proper domain of the linguist. So I can imagine that the psychologist's problems include those of linguistics as a special case. And somewhere within the range of language behavior there is a domain that we call literature. So I can imagine, further, the critic dealing with a subbranch of the field of linguistics. Mr. Jakobson eloquently discussed the relation between the linguist's concern and the concern of the poet and critic. Hence I derive a formula: psychology includes linguistics includes criticism. Here is a cognitive structure I can use to hang new things on as I learn them.

However, being a cynical person, I set myself the exercise of completely reversing this formula. It is quite simple to do. A psychologist studies the individual organism; he is not concerned with anything beyond a particular person at a particular time. But the individual belongs to a social group which has agreed on a code for communication. Thus the psychological problem must be set in a larger social context which is the proper domain of the linguist. But the language habits of the group are strongly determined by certain influential people who shape the language, who mold it, change it, give it new freedom, new words, new structure. Thus I can imagine that our critic, in his proper study, must include the work of the linguist as a sort of "special case" of what the language can become in the hands of a great craftsman. And so the formula is reversed.

I offer this double view simply as proof positive that I am confused and that there are many ways my confusion might possibly be structured. I await with some interest to see what my unconscious will make of it. It seems to me that this sort of thing—people talking past each other over the same domain in exactly opposite directions—has been characteristic of many of our hours together.

As I said, it was the literary analysts who were most surprising to me. I have learned the redundancies in the linguist's language and I can make a rough prediction when he says A that he will next go on not to B but to M or N. But when a critic says A I am still unprepared for what will come next. He seems to operate on a basis I am not accustomed to.

I like to work with problems that are well defined. I do not make a fetish of being scientific, but a well-defined problem, to me, is a thing of beauty. By a well-defined problem I mean one for which, if you told me the answer, I would have some way of testing whether or not it was indeed a correct answer. Given a well-defined problem, it is then possible to frame hypotheses—tentative answers—and to check the adequacy of those hypotheses by making observations about how it really is in the world. Hopefully, if I can frame a reasonable hypothesis and if I have made observations appropriate to that hypothesis, I have some chance of deciding whether or not the hypothesis is an answer or not. And I would speak of this approach rather generally in terms of the criteria of *evidence* that a psychologist should insist on before he draws any conclusions about his problem.

Literary questions seldom seem to be of this well-defined sort. For example, I was interested in "The proper study of mankind is man," and I wanted to know what kind of evidence would settle the question raised about the placement of emphasis on "mankind." But, first of all, what *is* the question? That never became clear. Is the problem to discover how Pope said it? Is the problem to discover the way it should be said? Or the way "most people" say it? Or the way "educated people" say it? If I knew what the problem was, perhaps I could understand a little better the kind of evidence a critic would use and the consistency of evidence he will insist on before he is willing to make a statement about that fragment of literature.

I do not understand yet how a critic works, or what kind of evidence he uses. I rather suspect that he is not working with the words "true" and "false" in quite the same way that I would. There is a subjective element of "true for me," or "true for this time," or "true from this point of view." But this, I am told, is a question of relativism versus absolutism, a question I know little about; anything I would say would run into strongly entrenched positions. So, rather than be shot at on that issue, let me display the kind of confusion that results.

I was fascinated to hear I. A. Richards describe the poetic process. I was particularly interested in the "python boughs" versus the "snaky boughs." Being a contrary fellow, I tried to find some associations to "python" that he would not have liked and some associations to "snaky" that he would have liked. The fact that I was not able to may indicate the wisdom of his choice. How could he do that? What goes on in the poet when he makes such a decision? There is no evidence, is there?

Suppose we had Mr. Jenkins conduct word association tests using "python" as the stimulus word. He would find, I am sure, that the most frequent associate to "python" *is* "snake." We know from these tests that semantic associations are, by and large, far stronger than phonetic association. Does not this fact trap the poet in a way that he cannot escape? If he speaks of "python boughs," people will think of "snaky boughs" and along with "snaky" comes "sneaky" and all the unpleasant words he wanted to avoid.

Clearly, this is not what Richards was talking about. I do not think any poet would write a poem by choosing his alternative words at any point on the basis of a word association test given to his friends. He relies on his own associations and on some assumption of communality with the associations of others. In thinking about these words, he pays particular attention to phonetic associations. The fact that "python" suggests "snake" violates the poetic *Einstellung*. The poet announces, by the form in which he writes it, that his product is a poem; the announcement carries an invitation to consider the sounds of these words as well as their meaning. If we wish to participate in his game, we will adopt an attitude of phonetic, as well as semantic, sensitivity to the words he uses.

There is far more to the process than a phonetic sensitivity in the choice of words, however. If I were to press my stupid questions about what the poet is doing, he might eventually explain to me that he is making value judgments. He has developed an extremely high-level skill with language, a skill much harder to develop than that required to knock a baseball over a wall. It may take years of careful reading and studying to cultivate it. Those of us who have not served such an apprenticeship do not really understand the processes involved.

We might reply, I suppose, that a poet does not understand what he is doing either. In the sense that he cannot describe it to nonpoets, we would be right. But there is an interesting fact about the communication of skills. Two people who both possess a particular skill *can* talk to each other about it. Two skiers can talk about how they make this turn or go down that hill. Two golfers can talk about golf—one can give instructions to the other on how to cure his slice—even though neither of them may be competent to describe it to somebody who does not have the skill. Part of my difficulty in understanding the critics at this conference is due to the fact they are talking about a skill that I do not have. People who do can talk to each other and understand what they are saying; those of us who do not have had trouble, in spite of the brilliant efforts of Mr. Richards, to get down to a level where even I could understand what the poet is doing. These random thoughts perhaps explain why communication was not always as successful as it might have been.

A point that has interested me for a long time about the artistic process in general, and one that Mr. Richards did not talk about, is how a poet knows when he is finished with a poem. My question is not confined to the poetic process. How does a painter know when he has finished his painting? How does a composer know when he is through with a symphony? It comes up in psychology occasionally; how do you know when a psycho-analysis is complete? If you ask the analysts, they say, "You just know." You do not have to be told when you are finished. And if you have finished a poem, I suppose you "just know" because you have built up some way of looking at poetry, or novels, or whatever it is you are creating. You are aware of the fact that it is complete because you know what a poem is.

One knows what a piece of literature is in much the same way that I know what a chair is. If I were building a chair, I would know when I had finished it; I have developed a cognitive category of chairs through my experience with such objects and I imagine that, in some similar way, the poet must have a similar sensitivity to this abstract thing, the poem.

I was reminded, in this connection, of some psychological speculations on the mechanism of instinctive behavior. Several years ago Karl Lashley, in his studies of instinct (**243**), described how birds will build a nest. Some birds take just the first steps toward building a nest; they collect some sticks and moss and live in it. Other birds go through that stage but continue to worry the materials until they build up a larger, more elaborate nest. Still other birds go through all these steps and more until they build a very elaborate and beautiful abode. Lashley speculated that the controlling factor in this behavior might lie in the innate characteristics of the bird's perceptual organization: "It is possible that the nest, or other product of activity, presents a sensory pattern which is 'closed' for the animal, in the sense in which this term has been applied to visually perceived forms. The nest might then be built by somewhat random activity, modified until it presents a satisfactory sensory pattern."

Obviously, the pattern of a poem is not something that we receive via our genes and chromosomes. It is something learned. But I suggest that there is a crude analogy between the sensory control of nest building and poetry building. The poet also strives toward a "closed" sensory pattern.

The perceptual controls on literary nest building are acquired by long and patient learning. When we mention this word "learning," psychologists usually prick up their ears with some interest. Learning is a topic we have said a great deal about, some of it mildly interesting. We are very curious to know how a person develops such complex cognitive skills as the ability to recognize a good poem. I wish we had time to discuss how the abstract concepts that critics use can be learned.

How does such learning occur? The best authorities differ. There is a school of psychology which starts from the most basic and simple elements possible, conditioned reflexes, for example, and hopes to build the more complicated structures out of these simple basic elements, much as a modern digital computer is built up out of rather simple electronic components. There is another contrary point of view that says instead that we must begin our analysis with rather elaborate cognitive structures, cognitive maps, schemata, etc., and that we will never understand the individual elements so long as we ignore their superordinate structure.

During the conference I frequently recalled this theoretical contrast as we went from one paper to another, back and forth from a discussion of linguistic elements to discussions of abstract conceptual schemata. We would switch from a very molecular level, where we were dealing with isolated phenomena, to extremely broad, inclusive, and global thinking. It felt to me similar to the conflict that psychologists have been talking about in the field of learning.

If this feeling is correct, I can say, by analogy with the situation in psychology, that it would be impossible to succeed in either of these ventures alone. We must be able to define our units of analysis. But, also, we must have some sort of an over-all, overarching map or guide that tells us where to go, that enables us to see how to fit the individual elements together. I could speak for a long time about this question, but I am not sure it would be relevant to style.

At any rate, as I say, I would like to have heard more discussion about how a person builds up the cognitive concepts that are the necessary armamentarium of a poet and that enable the critic to recognize a poem when he sees one.

Now, in the time I have left, I want to say a word about statistics. A number of papers used statistical methods. The ones I think of, offhand, are Mr. Osgood's, Mr. Hymes's, Mr. Sebeok's, and Mr. Carroll's. These four papers tried to use statistics in order to find some kind of objective basis for subjective judgments of style. To me, this is a very familiar approach to the problem. Ten years ago I would have regarded style as a problem in statistical inference; the way I had seen style discussed was in terms of identifying the authors of controversial works, measuring readability, and trying to make quantitative analyses of the personality of the author (**276,** ch. 6). These problems can, by and large, be stated in terms of statistical inference. Today I feel there is vastly more to style than we can catch in the statistician's net, but I still would argue that counting has many positive virtues.

I think all four of these statistical papers are interesting and, by and large, I feel the conference tended to ignore them. This attitude puzzles me, because statistics is an old, traditional approach to problems of style. Literary analysts have been using it for years, long before psychologists or linguists. We all do it. Statistics are not something new that psychologists brought here for the first time, although perhaps psychologists tend to be a little more sophisticated about statistics than either linguists or critics.

What are we trying to achieve with the statistical approach? I could imagine that there is room for both a science of style and an art of style, much as we have a science of pigments and an art of applying pigment to canvas. But I think it is not the intent of the present work that the statistical analysis should be so peripheral to the artistic essence as the chemistry of paint is to great art.

What is the opinion of this congregated group of specialists and scholars about the value of statistical methods in the analysis of style, assuming that they will be applied with a certain amount of intelligence? For instance, let me raise a specific question. Something that is implicit in Carroll's factor analysis of style is his use of a spatial coordinate system. In thinking about style he assumed that he was analyzing a set of points in a four-dimensional space. These four dimensions characterize the stylistic space. If we state the value that any particular passage has on these four dimensions, we have placed it in the space of different styles and we have stated its distance from all other points in that space. This is a very powerful tool, if it is appropriate.

But the question is, *is* the spatial analogy appropriate? I have received little guidance from you as to whether it is appropriate or not. Mr. Carroll and Mr. Osgood both have needled the linguists and literary analysts to give an answer to this question.

I think linguists do not like to talk about language in terms of dimensions. Dimensions seem to them odd, strange, foreign things. Linguists prefer to talk about rules, or about oppositions, or about phonemic and morphemic units. Their thinking tends to be more algebraic than geometric. Do they feel that it is a distortion of the basic problem to try to embed style in a space? I rather got the impression, since everybody avoided it, that they did not like the spatial analogy, but that they were being polite in not saying so. Or perhaps they feel that the statistician, in his description of what the style is, misses the crucial question of the literary *value* of the texts? Let me try to come at this from a different angle.

Closely related to this question of the value of statistical analysis is the question of the relation between style and predictability. When this question arose in the discussion, it seemed to me to be rather closely related to the linguists' proposal of "grammaticalness" as a characteristic of literature, and since the interest in it may be at least that general, I would like to make one or two comments about predictability.

The suggestion, as Mr. Osgood so well presented it, was that if a sequence of words is too predictable, it becomes banal and we quickly lose interest. At the other extreme, if the sequence is completely unpredictable it becomes confusing and we refuse to go on. Somewhere in between banality and confusion there may be an optimum of predictability. Various amusing incidents may sometimes make you feel that this suggestion might have merit. I read in a newspaper about a prize-winning poem that was later found to have been constructed by a table of random numbers and the Army Ordnance Regulations. I cannot believe that any responsible group of critics would, over any long period of time, assign any permanent value to such a composition, particularly when its source was made known! I heard a radio bulletin about a little girl who won a prize for modern painting. She was eight years old. Her comment was: "They tell me people can't understand modern painting, but it's the only thing I can do." Thus it is possible for a more or less random generator to produce something which a trained audience considers to be of some merit. Perhaps they have accidentally hit the right level of predictability, and all the critics are really looking for is to be surprised enough (but not too much) as they examine it. Perhaps, though I doubt it.

Predictability is a matter of probabilities. I think we could derive the following corollary on the basis of this suggestion: if the probability of utterance X is equal to the probability of utterance Y, the literary value of utterance X is equal to the literary value of utterance Y. If merit is solely a matter of predictability, two things of equal predictability would be of equal value wherever they fell, whether they were banal, or whether they were confusing, or anywhere in between. However, we can easily find examples that are equally predictable but are not of equal value.

Let me set the problem in a different context. Warren Weaver, a mathematician, wrote an article (**439**) in which he discussed the concept of surprise. He discussed it in a mathematical way and pointed out that surprise depends both on probability and on interest. He took an example from bridge. Imagine that you are out for an evening of contract bridge. Someone deals the cards. You pick up your hand and look at it. You know what you will see. It happens to you all the time, more or less. You have no particular name for it—it is just another one of those hands. It doesn't surprise you. But do you realize that the probability you would get that particular hand is 1 in 635,013,559,600? It is a fantastically improbable event for you to have exactly those thirteen cards.

You continue to play for a while and lightning strikes. You pick up a hand and see thirteen spades. (If this *should* happen to you, don't get flustered and bid seven no-trump!) You hold thirteen spades and I think it is safe to suppose that you are surprised. Thirteen spades seems terribly improbable. You have never seen it happen before. Nevertheless, the probability that you would get those particular thirteen cards is exactly 1 in 635,013,559,600—exactly equal to the probability of any other hand that you may hold all evening.

There is no difference in the probabilities. There is a tremendous difference in your surprise. Wherein lies the difference? According to the rules of bridge, there is a vast difference in the *values* of those two hands. A bridge player categorizes hands, not with respect to the particular thirteen cards but with respect to their value in the game.

I hope the analogy with the literary situation is not too strained. Perhaps you could help me with it. I imagine taking a dictionary, printing all the words on cards, then "dealing" a sequence of 100 cards. You look at them to see if this is a sonnet. Think what you would get—time after time—nothing, nothing, nothing. Imagine that something comes along then that really is a sonnet. You would be tremendously surprised. You would be surprised because the string of words has now fallen into a particular class of strings which, by the rules of some game, has value. Your surprise would not depend on the probability of any particular string of words.

What I imagine the linguist and literary critic should tell us are the rules of the game. When we are dealt this particular string of words and we know the rules, we know what its worth is in the aesthetic game. I have not yet found out what the rules of the game are. A great author may invent his own rules, which the critic tries to discover. In any case, I am convinced that there are highly skilled people who do know them, at some level, and that eventually I could learn them, too.

This detour into card games is my way of trying to suggest that any statistical analysis of style must be modified in terms of the cognitive organization imposed by the rules of the literary game. We cannot sneak literary values in by the back door; we must use value judgments to decide what the cognitive organization is in the minds of poets and critics. Perhaps, if this analogy is of any use at all, it may suggest a way to let the statistical and the intuitive approaches to style live side by side.

From the Viewpoint of Literary Criticism

Opening Statement

JOHN HOLLANDER

One of the difficulties that this session in particular must confront is raised by the question of what exactly we mean by literary criticism. We can see that it has already arisen, at least implicitly, not only in discussions but in several of the papers as well. Both Mr. Chatman and Mr. Hymes make a point of concluding their analyses of certain aspects of particular poetic styles with a kind of measured disclaimer. Mr. Chatman "leaves it to criticism" to interpret his results. Mr. Hymes brings up a question of "value," only really to hold it in abeyance, with what seemed to be at least a vague hint that there might be a methodology of some discipline, other than linguistics, ready to take over. Messrs. Wimsatt and Beardsley, by challenging the relevance of certain microlinguistic approaches to the problem of English meter are, I think, raising a fundamental question about the boundaries of the methods of literary criticism, as well as the boundaries of their object of study. Now it is generally true of academic disciplines, I think, that they tend jealously to guard their boundaries. Charges such as "X isn't really doing psychology, he is a physiologist after all" will no doubt be familiar to many. These charges are often applied to a particular problem as a kind of test case, often propounded by some acknowledged watchdog of the discipline. Behind such charges lies a firm consensus of agreement about the object of study and the results to be obtained. But among literary critics we could find no such agreement about results and a suspiciously unacknowledged disagreement about objects of study. I am afraid that there are many critics who would either scorn this whole conference or shun it out of some kind of nameless terror. There are many more who would want to define themselves out of such a gathering, trying to show either that they did not belong here or that, more likely, no one else did.

Perhaps, after all, literary criticism is more than a misleading term for the practice Mr. Richards has called "literary analysis." Many critics, for example, see their function as primarily that of a judge. In Mr. T. S. Eliot's words, the function of criticism is "the elucidation of works of art and the correction of taste": does the "and" here not mean "in order to"? We notice that even Mr. Chatman, during the discussion, seemed to refer to this as the true function of criticism. I do not know whether he was saying that the word "criticism" ought to be applied only to these activities, or whether he was actually stipulating something more than how the word was to be used. A prominent British critic, when asked by Mr. Wellek to unpack a few of his metaphors in order more clearly to define his terms and to ground the basis of his judgments, declared that his questioner was being "a philosopher" and not a true critic, in that he allowed his attention to turn from the critical business of evaluation to such hopeless sophistries. But behavioral scientists are so heavily responsible to just such questions of rigorous terminology and invariant usages that the judge sort of critic, whose primary concern is to praise or blame, might choose to ignore an interdisciplinary discussion like this as being irrelevant to his concerns or to his very notion of "style."

There are, of course, other sorts of critics, others who practice literary analysis either as an end in itself or as a means toward some other end. I might briefly list here the historians, the teachers, and perhaps the analysts pure and simple. For all these, the notion of literary (or even of "linguistic" or "personal") style will have a slightly different significance. But in general they all concur in treating stylistics as a study of the similarities and divergences between individual and families of literary utterances. But even here the problem of herding together and corralling the literary portion of the whole population of speech acts remains a difficult one. There are no visible brands upon their flanks. It is true that literary utterances, if they were treated as if they were nonliterary ones by a linguist, philosopher, or merely another speaker would be considered (1) trivial or (2) too long, (3) unduly excited occasionally, or (4) lying, and (5) often meaningless or tiresomely puzzling; and it is obvious that the process of interpretation, of literary analysis, of talking about these utterances, is going to have to be done in a different way from that in which the analysis of other more casual utterances—conversational, informative, or commanding ones, for example—is done. All that I think I can try to do, in bringing up a few problems for discussion that I feel might be fruitful, is to try to pin down issues that have either come up already in one form or another or seem to have been neglected. These issues, I think, will turn out to involve notions of linguistic and literary "style" common not only to the usage of the word by most critics but by most of us here as well.

The first problem is one that has come up several times in the discussions. (I hope, when the informal discussion starts again, that Mr. Beardsley will say a few words about it; we are fortunate in having a philosopher in our midst, and this is the kind of question that very often requires a philosopher to explore properly.) It is the aforementioned problem of the definition of literature. All explicit treatment of this has been confined to discussion of Mr. Hill's paper, which is summarized by his remark that "The burden of this paper has been to insist that literature has its being in the area of stylistics and the definition of literature must be sought in stylistics." A problem seems to have arisen here about definitions. The definition of a word is usually treated either as a report on how the word is used, or else as a stipulation about how the word *should* be used. A typical problem of literary definition appears in the question "What is a poem?" This can be interpreted either as a request for a description of a class of utterances, or as a request for the definition of a word, in either of the two senses just given. Now *describing* something and *defining* a word, I think, are very different matters; and I should like to suggest that the behavioral scientist and the critic of whatever persuasion, in seeking common criteria for the literary status of utterances, should bear this in mind.

Closely related, if not intimately involved in all this, is the question of value. Mr. Householder, in his opening statement, made a linguist's request for a kind of open definition of literary utterances. That is, he wanted to be able to designate utterances as literary, casual, or what not without this entailing any discussion of "values" at all. I am not sure whether Mr. Householder would have accepted Mr. Jakobson's designation of a poem as a text in which the coding was of greater interest than the message; he might have found it tendentiously "organic," perhaps itself embodying a selective principle. But any such open definition, of course, would have to be extremely general; by not ruling in or ruling out any candidate utterances for literary status, by not saying "X isn't a poem (play, novel, etc.) because a poem really should be thus and so," we might like to call these nonpoems "pseudopoems," "bad poems," etc. A different kind of definition will lead us always to find that others are misusing the word poem, distorting it sufficiently to include, say, those of that proverbial nonpoet Edgar Guest. Now it may very well be that most critics' interpretation of their subject matter (and perhaps, implicitly, of their role) must lead inexorably back to what the philosopher Charles Stevenson calls a "persuasive definition," a readjustment of a perhaps vague common usage so as covertly to urge a choice or enforce a selection. In their desire for operational definitions and other apparatus of a neutral descriptive language, both the linguist and the psychologist must implicitly distrust words so persuasively defined; or rather, must seek to understand, in different ways, the conditions under which such statements of implicit "valuation" or "judgment" are uttered. And it may be that it is the critic's task, remembering what Mr. Brown said in his opening remarks, merely to utter them.

The notion of literary "style" is closely involved with this, I think, aside from a rather badly evaluative usage of the word in which "style," in the abstract, becomes a praiseworthy quality (what lies behind what I seem to recall as Whitehead's remark: "Style is the ultimate morality of the mind"). There remains always the temptation for the stylistic analyst to prescribe. It may be that those who have developed the greatest sensitivity to the nuances of literary styles must somehow be unable to neutralize their judgments in describing; or it may be that they wish only to judge. But I do feel that there are many literary analysts who realize that for such a conference as this, in any case, a definition of a poem, a literary work, as anything that purports to be one will be more useful and less puzzling than any other. The only other alternative is to evaluate in the process of defining or describing. As a corollary problem, we might consider briefly Mr. Saporta's classification, at the beginning of his paper, of three possible ways of interpreting the relation of poetry to language. It is relevant here because it explores the notion that poetry is only language or that it is not made up of language at all, but of something indeterminate called "art," or else, as I understood it, that poetry is somehow made up of both of these things. Now this, of course, brings in the question of what "art" is; it may be that to raise it is merely to raise in another form the same question we have been discussing. But aside from this the metalinguistic, or seemingly nonlinguistic, properties of literary works need not demand that there be created for them a special domain, half in, half out of "language." Or again, perhaps there is an implicit question here about what language itself is, or rather what the proper depth of focus of micro- or macrolinguistic studies should be.

The second question that I wish to bring up for discussion concerns the role of tradition and history. It is a very large question, and, as such, has not hitherto arisen. Perhaps I might introduce it by referring to Mr. Brown's wonderful example of Cummings' *mot*. Now everybody so far has discussed this from the point of view of defeated expectancy, and Mr. Brown made some rather telling comments on exactly how this joke constituted a reproof of the listener for going on believing that the phrase would conclude "she kept her sense of humor until the end." As a literary critic talking about tradition and history, however, I might want to say something else about this. I might want to say it is not so much the reader but a cliché that is being reproved. Perhaps the literary interpretation of this piece of wit would want to invoke a prior linguistic matrix (I will not say a *form*, or *style*, as such)—what we would ordinarily call a cliché: "She kept her sense of humor until the end" or "until the last." I think that much of what happens here depends not only on just the expectation of "end" after "until the" but on the whole pollyannish cliché, about bearing up under adversity with a stiff upper lip "until the very end." I think that an attack on the reader's habitual acceptance of this notion ("people as a rule don't bear up until the end, really") is part of Cummings' intention. He is saying, almost in a very dramatic way, that the facts of life are much grimmer than anything like our folklore, and his trick is played against our ways of talking about life.

Now what does this have to do with tradition and history? I have cited Mr. Brown's example to show what the linguists here understand very well already, namely that a synchronic and a diachronic analysis of the same text will show different things. In this case I have put the text into a conventional or historical frame, and while this may be doing no more than specifying the grounding conditions for a reader's expectations, it retains the advantage of keeping in mind a specific "preparatory set" of prior linguistic acquaintance on the part of a particular reader. For the linguist and psychologist this background is of mutual concern. For the literary analyst it becomes all-important, and he might want to define the literary object as such in terms of the way in which it took up a historical pose or role with respect to its predecessors. One word that nobody, if I remember correctly, has mentioned yet, except perhaps in passing, in some of the papers on metrics, is "convention." In talking about the different ways in which literary critics use the word "style," we should want to mention the idea of literary conventions first of all, for it is certainly basic to most critics' view of what literature is. It seems to have both a synchronic and a diachronic dimension, but these are seldom separated; a literary convention represents historical norms, traditions, as well as currently observable regularities, of formal and semantic elements. We can say that in one sense meter itself, any sort of regularizing of patterns of sound, is conventional. On the other hand, we talk about different meters as representing different conventions. We might recall here the distinction between personal and literary style that Mr. Jakobson drew, the distinction between personal style, Shakespeare's conversation in The Mermaid Tavern, and the style of his plays. The element of difference is that his plays were written against the background of one sort of convention and speech in The Mermaid Tavern was produced against the background of other sorts of convention. There are ways in which people talk to each other. There are ways in which they are Shakespeare: that is, in which they plan and write plays that they hope will be reasonably successful in view of a particular audience's prior expectations.

The example from Cummings, brought up as a question of convention, may be made a little clearer if I compare it with another example of defeated expectation in which I think there is no element of a formal or rhetorical matrix involved and no problem of tradition or historical convention. Let me take the example of a common zeugma: "She came in a sedan chair and a flood of tears." Now here is, to a certain sense, a defeated expectation. We might want to say that it results merely from a pun on "in"; we might want to deal with it in other ways, but at any rate there is a defeated expectation and it does not necessarily resonate against a particular prior utterance. If anything, it is set against a whole class of utterances in the language, actually against the way we use the word "in." Perhaps to say that Cummings' remark is specifically a piece of *wit*, or possibly in a special sense a poem in itself, whereas "She came in a sedan chair and a flood of tears" might only be part of one is to say that there is a convention being invoked in one case and not in the other. Of course, the clear analogy remains between literary or rhetorical conventions and the actual semantic practices of the language itself. Meanings of words are in a sense only conventions of usage: the relevant problem here is that of locating the categorical boundary between them. Among other things, such a boundary would mechanically separate the concerns of the linguist and the literary analyst, without the need of positing some "nonlinguistic" processes assumed to be at work in literature. Here, too, we might return for a moment to the linguist's opposition of synchronic and diachronic dimensions. Some critics might object that literary history and synchronic criticism are two utterly separate, if not hostile, processes. But by and large, even those critics who wish to treat poems as objects rather than as utterances or speech acts agree about the relevance of both literary and linguistic history to an account, description, or "exploration" of a literary work.

A third question that I want to bring up for consideration has already been shown to lie implicit in the first one. This is the question of the role of values in treatments of literary stylistics. Quite a few comments that have already been made indicate that at least two attitudes toward the problem of values seem to be represented here. While literary critics are often interested in dealing with unanalyzed values, most students of human behavior today tend to analyze out values in terms of the interests of particular groups or individuals. But aside from the whole question of critical praise and blame, or of covert praising and blaming that may go on under the guise of classification and description, values may enter into literary discussion in other ways. Some critics, for example, might want to relegate the "proper" or "highest" function of literary works to the embodying or preserving of values, or to the making of statements affirming them. And then there is the undeniable fact that a literature's whole historical dimension depends on the memorization of utterances, or more usually their preservation in inscriptions, because of their valued status. Works that are "great," "important," "perfect of their kind," "optimally representative," etc. and that are agreed to be so by decades of critics may originally have been preserved by some fluke; or because they were praised for very different reasons; or, indeed, may not have been preserved at all but resurrected to fit a waiting set of judgments. Perhaps all this will lead to the question of whether or not there is such a thing as "bad literature," whether or not such a notion is self-contradictory. Most critics, I am sure, would insist that there is by no means anything self-contradictory here, that there *are* bad poems that yet properly remain poems. But the fact that they might have such strenuous disagreements about particular works, and the fact that there nevertheless seems always to be a literary canon, an approved corpus, cannot help but lead the non-literary onlooker to feel that only the already praiseworthy seems to merit "serious" attention.

Now for the matter of metrics. I think that because they are so obviously close to more immediate microlinguistic concerns metrical matters have come up almost immediately and exclusively in the discussions. It is certainly true that in the whole area of sound and sense a lot of confusions have recently been cleared away; and that the poetic organization of speech sounds has been more accessible to analyses based on structural linguistics than to impressionistic gropings of much belle-lettristic "literary appreciation." Despite the attenuated debate on the subject of the applicability of phonemic analysis to critical studies of poetry, following Part Five, it should be clear to what extent there remains considerable agreement between Messrs. Wimsatt and Beardsley, on the one hand, and Messrs. Chatman and Hymes on the other. [There followed a lengthy quotation from, and discussion of, a critical piece (**94**), an article which was held to represent prelinguistic methods of dealing with metrical style. In particular, Mr. Donoghue's comment on two lines from Robert Frost: "Mother can make a common table rear/And kick with two legs like an army mule," to the effect that it was "not fanciful to see the stress on 'like' (demanded by the meter alone, not by the sense) as stiffening the rhythm and strengthening the impression of the kicking table legs," was sharply criticized with a view to pointing out the inadequacies of impressionistic comment of this sort. This digression concluded with the suggestion that linguistic contributions to metrics could surely be justified in so far as they have helped to supplant such implausible methods and interpretations.]

The problem of poetic metrics also seems a nice one with respect to the question of norm and deviation that came up in the discussion of several Parts (especially Part Five). In an almost schematic way, a poem's formal metrical structure is normative, whereas its particular *version* of that structure, or form, makes for what was called its "personal" style. Perhaps it was some of the condemnatory overtones in the notion of "deviation" that caused some objections to its use. But a resolution of any rebuking distinction between norm and deviant certainly occurs in the critical commonplace that poets seem to adopt strict forms and meters *in order that* they may proceed to violate slightly the normal or canonical "we" of that form or meter. (Wordsworth, for example, writing on the sonnet form and its obvious restrictions on a poet dwelling in an age when its use in certain contexts was *not* almost mandatory, remarked "In truth the prison, unto which we doom/Ourselves, no prison is.") But again, this complicated dialectic between the normal and the special—on another level, between the expected and the actual event—has always seemed to literary analysts to be the very stuff of their subject. While metrical styles in poetry seem to be a rather special case, they represent the classic confrontation of the schema and the variant.

Now, one problem that has hardly come up at all is that of the literal versus the nonliteral use of language. I think that this is very close to Mr. Saporta's invocation of Chomsky's distinction between the "grammatical" and the "nongrammatical." Some debate resulted from the fact that Chomsky seems to use "grammatical" in a rather peculiar way; but we might consider for a moment, without invoking this notion, a case cited by Mr. Jakobson, in which "pregnant" was declared to be not a masculine but only a feminine adjective. It is very obvious that there is nothing wrong morphologically or syntactically with saying "That man is pregnant with ideas," for example. There is nothing grammatically wrong with such a sentence in the usual sense; it is just that it cannot be literally true. Now simply to say, "*That man is pregnant*" is a perfectly good false sentence; but that it can never be a true assertion is quite obvious. Perhaps when Mr. Saporta says that such uses are "nongrammatical," he means that there is some peculiar lexical effect at work. As a matter of fact, this comes close to what we might call the *nonliteral*, rather than the *literal*, use of language. Again this is one of those distinctions that seem to be crucial for any consideration of literary utterances in a general linguistic context.

Here also I feel that the notion of *fictionality* which Mr. Wellek spoke about is quite relevant. It certainly has to do with the way in which we agree to take usages and statements of a certain kind, with the whole set of distinctions between usage levels and, even more, between "sentence situations" or types of speech act. These might generally be termed *rhetorical* distinctions. For example, in "I took the money" and "The money was taken by me," the differences are, as Mr. Jakobson pointed out, rhetorical as well as syntactic. But if such rhetorical considerations make up what we might call the prosody, the poetic style, of casual speech, those

404 中 Retrospects and Prospects

of the particular way in which we are to take a speaker's word or sentence or assertion seem to correspond to its mythology. Rhetoric is the study not so much of *what* is said as, in particular cases, of *who* is saying what, and *how*, and to *whom*, and what each thinks about his relationship to the other. It has many provinces, but perhaps the most elusive of these is that of figurative language. Here again the interplay of norm and variant may be invoked, if only in terms of a lexical analysis of nonliteralness that would account for a figurative or metaphorical usage as being less likely and a literal usage as being the more frequent one, given the whole language as a base. But most poetic theory, particularly of recent decades, has remained intent on distinguishing literature from the rest of the written language with respect to just these criteria of metaphor and fictionality. In this view, of course, figurative language has a fragile sort of vitality: if used often enough, a metaphor will "die." The classic example of a "dead metaphor" is "the leg of a table" (where there can be little argument that "leg" is being used figuratively). Such dead metaphors are invoked in contrast to "real" or "fresh" ones in order, very often, to distinguish the features of literary and mundane language.

In any event, the role of this figurative-literal distinction in considerations of literary style is a profound one, and the interpretation of that role is one to which critics, linguists, and psychologists alike have carefully applied their concerns. Given a reader's suspension of normal attitudes and beliefs, a whole range of literary devices, from a figure of speech up to such complex aggregates as fictional plots, characters, the elements of dramaturgy, etc., becomes part of significant fiction. The linguist approaches this with lexical, or even rhetorically contextual, norms in mind. The psychologist may operate with the notion that, through the vehicle of nonliteral utterances, pseudoreports, what are actually legitimized lies, any speaker may reveal more of himself than he might otherwise, even willingly, be able to do. And the critic must try to give the proper attention to both of these approaches, at the same time confronting the fictions as things in themselves.

The last formal topic that I should like to propose for discussion may, after all, seem overly general. The question of the significance of stylistic elements seem to lie close to the general theme of this conference. I am posing it in a purely literary sense, that is, in terms of the old and almost outmoded dualism of "form and content." Let me turn for a second to a sentence in Mr. Hrushovski's preliminary remarks to his work paper, where he points out that free rhythms are a central "ideological" as well as a "structural" aspect of modern Yiddish poetry. In the course of his paper, he makes the valuable point that so-called "free" rhythms are just as conventional as are strict forms and just as significant in their conventionality. Behind this lies the principle that a signal refusal to follow a literary convention is in itself significant with respect to it. The practice of the Imagist poets, for example, of not capitalizing the initial letters of lines of verse had as strictly a signifying or labeling effect as does the conventional capitalization: the sign read "This is an Imagist poem," rather than merely "This is verse." Even as trivial and as "empty" a formal or stylistic device as this may be seen as significant in the deliberate violation of it. Now while the occurrence of such deviant graphematic forms as the lower-case initial would be noted by the linguist, and perhaps its environments tabulated, the whole problem of the kind of deliberateness, of the intention of its use, would be more a matter for literary history and for criticism. For the psychologist, with his broad approach to symbolism, content lurks beneath the surface of all forms. Similarly, for the literary analyst, significance must appear to characterize all but the most nearly random stylistic elements. But this is not to suggest that the expressive, gesturing significance that is usually afforded to the instrumentalization of formal elements is the only kind of stylistic significance. The quasi-titling function mentioned is another one, and there would seem to be a whole family of related functions.

It does seem to be the case that normal styles have the "titling" kind of significance, what Mr. Chatman in discussion called the "metalinguistic" function, and characteristic deviations bear the burden of "expressiveness." Of course, these deviations can only be effective insofar as they do engage the receiver's prior experience. An utterly novel sign would be, in the strictest sense, meaningless.

In conclusion, I should like to pose, with a little hesitancy, a problem that seems to follow from the foregoing. In the statistical analysis of stylistic elements, it is usual to assume that greater expressive prominence is attained by more "surprising" effects, and that these will show up, in a statistical analysis of the flow of events, as being less frequent. That is, studies using information theory in the analysis of language and music seem to equate defeated expectancy (on the part of the receiver) with greater information (in the message). Now what seems to disturb some literary analysts is this interpretation of probability of occurrence of formal elements, in terms of the expectancy-surprise dimension in an audience. Perhaps I can make this clearer with a rather crude but, I hope, helpful musical case. Let us imagine ourselves going into a large concert hall for a performance by a major American orchestra. Upon scanning the program, we recognize a familiar bill of musical fare, starting out with an operatic overture, perhaps. Then comes a contemporary work, and finally, the long, romantic symphony, after the intermission. We see that the modern work is for strings, and we estimate that it will be about sixteen minutes long by reason of its place on the program. We also assume, because it is on a program at a major concert hall, that it is not going to be too extreme a piece—probably not a twelve-tone composition for example—and we wait patiently, wrapped up in our predictions. Finally the conductor picks up his baton and all the strings (there are no winds at all on the stage) commence playing a unison ostinato—*bom bom bom bom bom bom bom*—and this goes on for four minutes and suddenly stops, bringing the piece to an end. [Loud laughter.] My point here is simply that a post-mortem statistical analysis of the repeated notes will show that no matter what we select as the event, that is, the note, or the pair, or the measure, or any other group, they will all carry equal information, and that hence there will be no surprise at all. But of course, this is not what actually happens. As a matter of fact, the fifth will be an incredible surprise, simply because the upper strings did not take up a melodic strain. In other words, the statistical picture did not account for the fact that at the end of the very first group of four repeated notes something else was called for by the prior expectation of the audience, by their history of musical experience. A musical convention, that is, was being engaged, and once it was violated the more sophisticated part of the audience might be able to assume that there would be surprises ahead, such as that of the abrupt cadence. To put it another way, a single event (the first beat, given all the conditions) almost constituted a norm in itself.[1] The problem of the

---

[1] In the course of the discussion, Mr. Brown remarked that with proper choice of the units or elements whose frequency was under consideration, this same situation might be shown to confirm the "notion that the infrequent event causes suprise." He suggested that instead of calculating frequency on the basis of the first two notes, it might be done "on the basis of preceding context," and he implied that this would yield the expected rather than the pathological result.

He is of course correct; but my point here was simply that the choice of the proper element for frequency analysis in all "rhythmic" or "periodic" processes (of which linguistic signals are only one example) is an all-important one. What actually constitutes a signal, then, must be decided in advance of the analysis of all but the most mechanical cases: In the graphic sequence "O-O-O-O-O-O-O-," the question whether there has been an alternation of two signals, or merely a repeated series of "right translations" of one signal (in other words, is the signal a "O" and a "–", or a "O–"?) is more of a philosophical one, about ends in view, than either a visual or mathematical one about methodology.

In the case of language, and particularly in the case of literary language, I merely meant to suggest by my example that such prior or "philosophical" questions must take into consideration the listener's own history with respect to the perception of the sequences of signals, his own "beliefs" or "superstitions" about the boundaries of those signals themselves, etc. In my example, it would have been the history of Western music, and the bit of modern cultural history and sociology that described the particular subject's own record of musical experience, that would have accounted for the fact that the audience *was* surprised because the repeated tones *did* keep up without variation.

statistical investigation of stylistic factors depends on this matter of hidden or prior norms, given expectancies, unstated conditions, or axioms of the literary situation.

Some of the literary critic's normal diffidence in assailing the statistical analyst may indeed result, as Mr. Hoopes suggests, from some quality of literary experience that is alien to mensuration, to quantizing. But I wished to conclude here with the observation that the level at which the counting is done, what categories and regularities of events are selected for counting, is a very treacherous matter, and that an attempt to interpret significance in terms of relative frequencies of occurrence of stylistic elements must often remain as misleading a pursuit as it seems ultimately to be a proper one. Well, I hope that these topics may yield some fruitful discussion. The questions themselves are basic to the concerns of literary critics, no matter what their obligations to judgment, to "the correction of taste," no matter what their very reasons for the "elucidation of works of art" may be.

Closing Statement

In summing up the results of a conference of anthropologists and linguists held here at Indiana University in 1952 (**249**) Roman Jakobson admitted that for a man who closes a conference there are no two-choice situations. "It can never be heard from him that the Conference was not successful." As I am not an adherent of the communication theory, I shall, however, refuse to accept this single alternative and shall rather follow Mr. Richards' example, who, in speaking about the biographical approach to literature, allowed us three choices. We can say that biography has everything to do with literature; we can say that it has nothing to do with it; and finally we can say that "it depends." I shall say about the success of our conference: "it depends."

We can say that the conference has been successful, as we have heard many very ingenious, elaborate, laborious papers on many important subjects. It has been a success in setting forth the different points of view; it has been a success in examining many individual problems. But in my opinion, it has not been a success, or rather it has been only a qualified success if its purpose was to establish a common language and to throw light on its professed central topic, the problem of style and particularly of style in literature and the methods of analyzing style.

I was particularly struck by the fact that the question of style has not been discussed at all in terms of the enormous labor which has gone into it for centuries or in terms even of the theories and methods of the many contemporary practitioners of stylistics who come to the mind of every student of literature. In one paper only (Stankiewicz's, **394**), a brief reference is made to the work of Leo Spitzer, but no mention has been made, to give only a few examples, of the work of Erich Auerbach, or of that of the two Alonsos—Dámaso Alonso at Madrid and the late Amado Alonso, the author of a very fine book (**7**) on the poetry of Pablo Neruda, at Harvard—or of the work of the Italian stylistic school, of Giuseppe De Robertis or Gianfranco Contini. No stylistic analysis of a really literary text was presented except for Mr. Higginson's paper (**171**) on *Finnegans Wake*. Thus some of the most obvious and central problems of the study of style, at least in literature, have never been raised and could not have been brought nearer to a solution.

As I understood my role of rapporteur to be that of a critic of the individual papers, and as Mr. Hollander preferred to adopt a different procedure, I shall go over the papers, classifying them, always strictly from the point of view of literary criticism. My judgments are not meant to be judgments of absolute value but are focused only on the relevance of the papers to the problems of literary criticism.

I agree with Mr. Voegelin that there were actually four disciplines represented, psychology, cultural anthropology, linguistics, and literary criticism. From the point of view of the literary critic, the psychological papers were of least immediate interest. To my mind, they established nothing that could not be predicted from ordinary observation. Mr. Jenkins' paper, for instance, labored to show, by word association tests, that "high commonality" subjects (or persons) are more uniform, more predictable than "low commonality" subjects, who are more heterogeneous, more atypical in their verbal behavior. But this seems a mere tautology drawn out of the very definition of the two categories. On the question of aesthetic value which interests the critic, Mr. Jenkins can come to the conclusion that "Low commonality men are found to have a higher mean score (higher aesthetic value) than High commonality men." It seems to me no great news to be told that less conforming people have greater aesthetic sensitivity. Still, it may be reassuring to know that this can be established statistically.

The same seems to be true of Mr. Carroll's elaborate paper. The laborious calculations based on the opinions of 8 different judges about 150 passages of 300 words, according to 29 different criteria, lead only to such obvious results as that the "humorous-serious" distinction is more reliable than the "good-bad" or "weak-strong" distinction. Similarly, Mr. Osgood's paper on suicide notes tells us only that suicide notes contain more *mands* (**381**), that is demands, pleas, requests such as "take care of the house," "bury me" in this or that cemetery, and more "distress-expressing" phrases than ordinary letters.

I recognize of course that psychologists consider their task as that of quantification, that they believe nothing to be objectively ascertained and verified before it has been reduced to some quantitative ratio. I, as every humanist must, however, argue that this is a false epistemology based on the superstition of behaviorism. It denies the evidence of introspection and empathy, the two main sources of human and humane knowledge.

Among the papers by psychologists that of Mr. Brown is not open to these objections. It is really different in its methodology: it is a sensitive sociolinguistic study which makes fine discriminations between the French and German uses of *tu* and *vous* and *Du* and *Sie*.

Of the two anthropological papers, Mr. Dorson's presents interesting materials, but it is almost purely descriptive and does little to analyze the texts. It is valuable for the stress it puts on the description of the narrator of a folktale, a stress widely observed in studies of Slavic folklore. Mr. Voegelin's paper establishes a point of interest to literary critics. It shows that the rabbit hunt chant of the Hopi Indians does not deviate sharply, in its diction or its phonemic repertory, from ordinary colloquial Hopi language. The differences between the chant and talk about the chant are limited to some free alternations in consonants and a greater allophonic range in vowels. I understand this to be an argument against the conception of a specific Hopi poetic language. Of course, Mr. Voegelin's results apply only to Hopi and can hardly be generalized beyond his modest but securely founded observations.

The next group of papers are those by linguists. I am one of those students of literature who recognize and emphasize the enormous contribution of linguistics to literary scholarship. Especially in the analysis of meter, and especially again in the analysis of the phonemic principle, the contribution of linguistics has been invaluable. There can be no comparative metrics without linguistics. I agree with the linguists about the important role of sound in literature, but I would always argue that there is a point at which literature (and poetry) goes beyond the scope of linguistics. Roman Jakobson said a while ago that he would admit this privately, but, of course, he admitted it publicly, and I welcome such an admission from an eminent linguist who is also a keen student of literary theory. I find the concept of the stratification of a work of literature as it was first elaborated by the Polish phenomenologist, Roman Ingarden (**192**), most illuminating on this point. He recognizes a sound stratum (which must not of course be considered as sounded physically but as merely a potential phonemic stratum) which is present in every work of literature and is absolutely indispensable to it. If a linguist tells us that we cannot discuss literature without its sound stratum, we have to admit that a literary work of art is accessible only through its sound stratum. The sound stratum, besides, can become, as the Russian formalists would say, "actualized" or, in the new terminology, here used by Jakobson, we can draw attention to the "message" itself. Poetry focuses attention on the linguistic signs as such. According to Ingarden, beyond the sound stratum or rather above it, there is the stratum of meaning, or of units of meaning, the semantic stratum, and this stratum in turn gives rise to the stratum of represented objects, to the "world" of the poet. (This corresponds, in the diagram of Jakobson, to the term "referent" but is more narrow, as referent may include not only things but other words.) The world of objects which poetry and fiction build up in our imagination is of course not identical with that of ordinary reality. It is related to reality. For instance, we could describe the world of Dickens, postillions, old inns, fog, etc., or that of Dostoevsky, the dusty slums of Petersburg, the dreary provincial towns, easily enough; but there are other worlds more difficult to describe, like those of Valéry or Rilke. These worlds are obviously highly selective, even idiosyncratic, and they may be quite fantastic structures, distortions of reality like Kafka's world. But still the world of the poet is related to ordinary reality, and we cannot, in literary criticism, escape the issue of this relationship to reality. It must not, of course, be conceived in terms of a copy or exact imitation of reality: it may be a complete distortion of the ordinary world, a topsy-turvy world, a world of dreams or nightmares. But however diverse these relationships may be and however difficult to define and judge, it seems necessary to recognize that the literary critic must go beyond the purely linguistic and stylistic stratum and must thus arrive at a poetics.

Poetics in a wide sense is identical with theory of literature. In English, the word "poetry" is so closely linked up with verse that poetics is often understood to exclude prose fiction. But a coherent theory of literature must refer to all fictive structures whether in verse or in prose.

In commenting on the linguistic papers I can only object that they often forget or ignore the preceding considerations. They claim that the study of poetry is merely a part of linguistics, that literary theory is completely subordinated to linguistics. This was the case in Mr. Miller's first diagram, where criticism appears enclosed by linguistics and psychology, although I recognize that later he reversed the order and drew another diagram with literary criticism enclosing linguistics and psychology. But I would not want to make such grandiose claims for literary criticism at all. I shall be content to think of literary criticism as a discipline that studies the structures and values of literature and uses gratefully the help of linguistics and psychology. Mr. Saporta, in his paper, wants to absorb criticism into linguistics, but finally he comes to the sensible conclusion that "many questions about the meaning of a poem go unanswered" in linguistics. We must simply conclude that many problems of poetics are not susceptible to linguistic analysis.

Mr. Stankiewicz submits two papers. One of these (**394**) is a rather general linguistic paper which concerns, in part, poetics, as poetry certainly uses the devices of expressive language. The second paper, a study of poetic language, expounds the view of the Russian formalists and suggests that there may be a semantics without reference to external correlates. But I have never seen such a science—a semantics without meaning—and wonder whether there can really be any.

As to the strictly literary papers, I shall refer only briefly to Mr. Higginson's fine study (**171**) of *Finnegans Wake*. It examines one device which is usually called the *portmanteau* word. Mr. Higginson shows by examining different versions of a passage how Joyce worked more and more of such puns and ambiguities into his text, or "perfigured" it, as Mr. Higginson would say. Mr. Higginson's method is quite traditional and has been used in all close examinations of style.

Mr. Hymes's paper discusses the general problem of sound symbolism in poetry very perceptively. We seem all agreed that it would be a mistake to dismiss this problem: certainly sound symbolism is a factor in much poetry. We might distinguish three different degrees. There is the actual imitation of physical sounds, which seems to me undeniably successful in cases like "cuckoo" or "meow." Then there is the suggestion of natural sounds through speech sounds in a context, where words, in themselves quite devoid of onomatopoetic effects, are drawn into a sound pattern. An example is Tennyson's line, "And murmuring of innumerable bees," where the word "innumerable" is, out of context, quite neutral but strengthens the pattern in its context. Mr. Ransom has argued that the sound effect depends only on meaning and can easily be destroyed if, as he wittily suggests, we change the phrase to "murdering of innumerable beeves." But we could object that the change made by Mr. Ransom is only apparently slight. Replacing "m" by "d" in "murmuring" destroys the sound pattern "m-m" and thereby lets the word "innumerable" drop out of the pattern in which it has functioned. Then there is a third level of the relation of sound and sense, sound symbolism or metaphor proper: something like a "physiognomy" of words, which in each language seems to have its own established conventions and patterns. There are synaesthetic combinations and associations in all languages, and these correspondences have been exploited and elaborated by many poets. Maurice Grammont has made an elaborate, if somewhat impressionistic, study (**138**) of French verse on this point. There is the general problem of what Miss Elizabeth Sewell has called charmingly "the sound-look" of words. Poets know it, and Mr. Hymes has re-examined the problem sensitively.

He has used statistics to some purpose when he shows that there are "summative" words in these sonnets by Wordsworth and Keats: words which sum up the meaning and at the same time assemble the dominant sounds of the poem. But I am not convinced by his argument that this congruence of sound and meaning is a criterion of poetic value. Mr. Hymes himself concedes that there are "many other ways in which unity can occur," and that the criteria of congruence he establishes comprehend only a part of the use of sound in lyric poetry. Still, he inclines to the view that a sonnet such as Wordsworth's "Westminster Bridge," with its clear congruence of sound and meaning, is superior to the sonnet "At Dover," which, according to his statistics, shows no such agreement. He finds "a sharp disharmony between the theme, which is that of hush and peace, and the funneling of the sound into 'speaks' and 'shrieks of crime.'" But I doubt that, on close inspection, the sonnet can be read as one concerning "hush and peace" at all. The poet looks from the pier at the promenade on the quay of the city of Dover and does not hear the people walking there, not because of any hush or peace but because their "social noise" is drowned out by the voice of the ocean, that "dread Voice that speaks from out the sea of God's eternal Word, the Voice of Time" that deadens "shocks of tumult, shrieks of crime, the shouts of folly, and the groans of sin." A sharp contrast between the voice of God and the shouts of folly and groans of sins of erring humanity is perfectly realized in the sounds of the concluding line. We might dislike the poem on quite different grounds: we might object to the pious or sentimental identification of the voice of the sea with the voice of God and thus rate the poem below "Westminster Bridge." But these are obviously considerations beyond our present concern.

Mr. Chatman's paper makes a careful comparison between the satires of Donne and their revision by Pope. He seems to me in general correct, although his method may be excessively cumbersome: we could easily predict that Pope would regularize the meter of Donne's lines, would introduce endstops, avoid harsh consonant clusters, and so on, just from our knowledge of the poetics of Pope's time, of the whole change from the Baroque to Neoclassicism. But it is good to see it demonstrated in such detail.

I hesitate to say anything very concrete about Mr. Sebeok's paper, since I do not know Cheremis and am not familiar with the statistical techniques he uses. But I am impressed by his attempt to use statistics even for a study of meaning relations. He succeeds because he has found a poem that is highly structured and extremely symmetrical in its internal relations. He would run into much greater difficulties with larger and looser structures. This is a very interesting start, which shows that something can be done by quantitative means to go beyond the mere sound stratum into certain simple meaning relations.

The papers on metrics, surprisingly, show much agreement, and they seem in many ways to have achieved the most secure results. Mr. Sebeok's and Mr. Chatman's papers belong, in part, to metrics. Mr. Lotz gives a very carefully worked out typology of metrics: an excellent descriptive and analytical piece of work which has its critical implications. It allows us to discern the different metrical norms in the main languages. Their history is an enormously complex business, as norms have changed even within one language over the centuries. I agree with Messrs. Wimsatt and Beardsley when they distinguish two main traditions in English metrics: the Old Teutonic or strong accentual and the syllabic accentual prevalent since the time of Chaucer. With Coleridge and the imitation of the Scottish ballads late in the eighteenth century there was a partial revival of the Old Teutonic tradition, and since then there have been compromises and conflicts between the two metric conventions. But we cannot say that only one of them (as Mr. Whitehall wants us to believe) is properly English.

Mr. Hrushovski's paper pleads very persuasively for a "rhythmology," for the study of free rhythms apart from metrics, as free rhythms are characteristic of most modern poetry and have not been analyzed successfully. But he gives us rather a program than a performance.

I was surprised at the general agreement with which the paper of Messrs. Wimsatt and Beardsley (**451**) was received. It scraps musical metrics and returns to older "graphic" metrics, although these are revised and liberalized by the insights of phonemics. When I was a student at Princeton thirty years ago, one of my teachers, Morris Croll, who was, incidentally, one of the finest students of stylistics—especially seventeenth-century prose style—in this country, taught me musical metrics. But I was always restive and could not understand why, for instance, the blank-verse line "Lo, the poor Indian whose untutored mind" should be scored as 3/8, and why "mind" and "in" should be the only half-notes in the line. It seems high time that we got over a theory which ignores the metrical pattern and reduces all verse to a few types of monotonous beats.

Mr. Hollander raises the questions of tradition, of genre and of convention in metrics by speaking of "the metrical emblem" (**176**). He takes us into general poetics and suggests many questions far beyond the confines of linguistic style. He uses the term "code," but "tradition" would seem preferable, as it is a wider term which includes nonlinguistic elements.

We can, no doubt, analyze the literary work of art according to Jakobson's diagram. But for literary purposes it may be advisable to rechristen some of the terms. There is the "sender" or "speaker," who might be rather called "the poetic self." The "I" of the poet must not of course be confused with his private personality. Even the "I" of a lyrical poem is dramatic. Croce, in his essay on Shakespeare (**75**), drew the distinction between the "private" and the "poetic" person very clearly. Obviously we know, for instance, hardly anything about the private individual Shakespeare, but we do know a great deal about his poetic personality. We cannot dismiss this problem of personality in literature even where there is no biographical evidence of any kind. There is a quality which may be called "Shakespearian" or "Miltonic" or "Keatsian" in the work of these authors, to be determined on the basis of the works themselves, although it may not be ascertainable in their recorded lives. There are, no doubt, connecting links, parallelisms, oblique resemblances between life and art.

There are degrees of self-expression which may allow us to rank literary figures on a scale. On one end there is a poet such as Byron who displayed his ego, cultivated his poetic personality quite deliberately, and on the other end there are naturalistic novelists who completely disguise their personality, cultivate objectivity, and pretend to be cutting only a slice of life. Thus we can speak of "personal" style.

A similar distinction can be made in the emphasis on the addressee, the conative or pragmatic side of our scheme. There is plenty of writing which appeals directly to the reader to do something or, at least, to change his mind about something. It seems to me false to say that didactic poetry or a novel with a purpose is necessarily bad art. Much art is, in a wide sense, propaganda art. It wants to change the views and habits of its readers, and surely literature has had an enormous social influence throughout history. True, it is sometimes very difficult to define this influence, to isolate the channel. How can we, concretely, prove that the essays of Addison had any influence on people's manners and attitudes? Was Mrs. Stowe really the "little woman who made the great war"? Has *Gone With the Wind* really changed the Northern reader's attitude toward Mrs. Stowe's war? It seems impossible to answer such questions with precision. Still, they do suggest that important historical changes have come about through the insidious influence of books, slowly, deviously, in inextricable combinations with other factors.

Such books would be on the one end of the scale of effect on the reader. On the other would be the poet indulging almost in a monologue, writing for himself, addressing himself, keeping his poems in a drawer for years, or a diarist like Pepys, who concealed his jottings under a cipher. But even such a writer writes for some audience, even if only for his own later self, or for his own present self, which he wants to define or redefine for himself in writing. This whole relation to the reader could come under the category of "rhetoric" or "rhetorical style."

Another term in our diagram is "code." This might better be called "convention" or "tradition" in literature. This has been discussed here under the term of expectancy and its disappointment or under the contrast between novelty and banality. The curious notion of the "ungrammaticalness" of poetry used by Mr. Saporta seems another formula for this problem. To my mind, the criterion of novelty is much overrated in literary history. It would make Marlowe a greater writer than Shakespeare because the former was the innovator and initiator. But we must distinguish between historical merit, temporal primacy, "novelty" if you like, and aesthetic value. Shakespeare, although less novel than Marlowe, is more complex, more diverse, or simply more perfect. We could again devise a scale that would reach from the most extreme innovators such as futurists to the most conforming traditionalists. In both directions extremes would be impossible. Complete novelty would be incomprehensible; complete conformity would be banality, tautology, nonart. In stylistics, all problems of convention, "genre," and "period" style belong to this part of our scheme.

If we turn now to the "message" on the diagram, we can make again analogous distinctions. The term "message," which refers, in Jakobson's scheme, to the actual text of a work of literature, is unfortunate in literary criticism, as it has been used for ages for the overt statement of the author's purpose, and all critics have warned us against "message hunting." But the emphasis on the message (in Jakobson's sense) is precisely on what is peculiarly "poetic," on the devices themselves, particularly the sound stratum. I would not consider "I like Ike" poetic, but I can see that it illustrates one of the devices of poetry: one end of a scale. There is poetry like that of Gerard Manley Hopkins which forces us to pay attention to the surface of words, to their sounds, to what Hopkins himself called quaintly their "inscape;" and, on the other end of the scale, there are writers in whom language becomes almost diaphanous, where we hardly seem to notice the verbal surface. Many novels seem not to require any close attention to style. But even a novel by Dreiser is either written well or badly, and unobtrusively the verbal surface will influence our feelings and finally our judgment. This is the place for the style of an individual work, the "work style."

The last place on our diagram, the "referent," has been touched upon before. We see now more clearly that it cannot be discussed in isolation: that not only is there a direct relationship of the work of art to the world of objects it projects, but that this world is determined also by the kind of artistic "code" or tradition which the work uses. Realistic art, supposedly mirroring reality with exactitude, is only one special convention, not necessarily superior to others. Realism often means not only objectivity, contemporaneity, and the like, but also the exclusion of older conventions. For instance, Ibsen avoided asides, soliloquies, eavesdropping, sudden unmotivated appearances of new characters, chance encounters; but he introduced his own very marked conventions. The relation to reality has to be defined differently in every age or artistic style: it runs the whole gamut from extreme stylization to apparently naive imitation.

Historically, one of the chief meanings of "style" has been this relation of the work of art to reality: the sort of thing which was discussed, for instance, by Goethe in a famous essay on "Einfache Nachahmung, Manier, Stil" (**137**). We have heard nothing of this crucial relation of style to reality. Nor have we discussed style in many of the other senses I have indicated. One speaker has used it so broadly that it could refer to the peculiar way we eat grapefruit and drive a car, and no doubt the term "style" is used far outside the realm of language and literature. We speak of style in architecture, in painting and music, and of course of style in dress, where it simply means fashion. For our purposes here, we should limit ourselves clearly to verbal style, but verbal style is also a far wider concept than style in literature. Literary style is to my mind not exhaustible by linguistic analysis: it needs analysis in terms of the aesthetic effects toward which it is aiming. Style may include all devices of speech that convey the attitude of the speaker (all "expressive language") and all devices that aim to achieve rhetorical ends, all devices for securing emphasis or explicitness, metaphors, rhetorical figures, syntactical patterns. Clearly, style embraces all speech and all writing. But stylistics as part of a science of literature must be concerned with much more special problems. No doubt, there will be a wide coincidence between general studies of verbal style and studies of literary style in particular. There are many transitional forms and genres in which literature, in the sense of imaginative literature, shades off into science, philosophy, political thought, religious meditation, and the like. We cannot, I think, escape discriminations that make Homer, Virgil, Dante, and Shakespeare the center of literature, and we shall have to recognize great historians such as Gibbon or moralists like Emerson as representing only intermediate forms between the mere conveyance of knowledge and the fictive act of imagination. A text like Gibbon's *History* or Emerson's *Essays* does present problems of style, of structure and overall form, but the central quality of literature, its "fictionality," its "illusion," is missing.

The coincidence between linguistic study of style and literary analysis will occur in the study of even the greatest poets. We can, for instance, write (there are such books) a grammar of Shakespeare's language. We can compare Shakespeare's grammar with, say, the grammar of Ben Jonson. We can make a comparison of traits, concluding that certain traits are shown in common, whereas others differ, diverge, or even contrast. Authors nearly related in time, place, and genre will obviously yield very similar grammars. An attempt can be made, by statistical methods, to discriminate the frequency of certain devices used by two or more authors: words and their distribution or any other stylistic trait. But we wonder whether the result will be very meaningful for criticism. Statistical frequency necessarily ignores the crucial aesthetic problem, the use of a device in its context. No single stylistic device, I believe, is invariable: it is always changed by its particular context. Literary analysis begins where linguistic analysis stops. The danger of linguistic stylistics is its focus on deviations from, and distortions of, the linguistic norm. We get a kind of countergrammar, a science of discards. Normal stylistics is abandoned to the grammarian, and deviational stylistics is reserved for the student of literature. But often the most commonplace, the most normal, linguistic elements are the constituents of literary structure. A literary stylistics will concentrate on the aesthetic purpose of every linguistic device, the way it serves a totality, and will beware of the atomism and isolation which is the pitfall of much stylistic analysis. It will distinguish the style of a work of art and proceed from there to such problems as the style of an author, the style of a genre, the style of a period. Style is a historical phenomenon; it evolves and changes with society, in history.

Two papers of very general nature still remain to be commented upon. Mr. Hill's on the definition of "literature" (**173**) does not, it seems to me, get very far. He himself, at the end, admits that he has not excluded law and ritual. As long as the term is defined so inclusively, it is of little use for literary criticism.

Mr. Richards' paper on variant readings and misreading should be highly welcome as a plea for the importance of the problem of relevance and correctness in reading and interpretation. It is particularly helpful because some of Mr. Richards' early writings are concerned with elusive patterns of impulses, with psychic effects of literature, so exclusively that the text is somewhat neglected. But correctness and interpretation concern the text itself and are obviously the central problem for the teacher of literature. If we do not believe that some interpretations are right and others are wrong, we must all step down from our dais and throw up our hands in despair. There are many theories about Hamlet. One of them tells us that Hamlet was a woman, and I am sure that this is wrong. There are theories that would be more difficult to refute, but clearly Mr. Richards has the clue to the solution of the problem when he appeals to the context, to an imaginary ideal dictionary. Mr. Richards talks largely about individual words such as the word "desert" in the sonnet by Shakespeare, but obviously the very same problem arises and the same remedy offers itself in interpreting a scene or a character in a novel. The only way of refuting and correcting misinterpretations is to point to the context. To quote an example: in the *Brothers Karamazov* Ivan tells the "Legend of the Grand Inquisitor" to his brother Alyosha. After the great speech of the Grand Inquisitor, the Inquisitor waits for some time for Jesus to answer him. But Jesus "suddenly approached the old man in silence and softly kissed him on his bloodless aged lips. That was all the answer." Some students and even critics say that Christ has nothing to say in refutation of the speech and by his kiss accepts the arguments of the Grand Inquisitor. Why is this a wrong interpretation? If we read on, we hear that soon afterward Alyosha got up and softly kissed Ivan on the lips.

"That's plagiarism!" cried Ivan. He knew that Alyosha had answered him in the same way Christ had answered the Grand Inquisitor. Christ (and following him, Alyosha) has given the only answer of religion to atheism: the silent answer, the answer of forgiveness. We could buttress this interpretation by going beyond the immediate context: we could appeal to other parts of the novel, to the preachings of Father Zossima, or the last scene with Alyosha promising the boys immortality. We could go outside the particular work and study the other novels of Dostoevsky and finally draw on his journalistic writings, his professed statements of intentions. Somewhere beyond the writings of Dostoevsky an appeal may have to be made to the literary and religious tradition to which he belongs, and finally we might feel that the whole history of thought and even the whole history of humanity provides a context. We might even dream not only of an ideal dictionary as Mr. Richards does but of an ideal dictionary of terms, ideas, themes, even situations and characters. But for practical purposes we need not postpone understanding to a distant future.

In reading with a sense for continuity, for contextual coherence, for wholeness, there comes a moment when we feel that we have "understood," that we have seized on the right interpretation, the real meaning. The psychologists might say that this is a mere hunch, a mere intuition. But it is the main source of knowledge in all humanistic branches of learning, from theology to jurisprudence, from philology to the history of literature. It is a process that has been called "the circle of understanding." It proceeds from attention to a detail to an anticipation of the whole and back again to an interpretation of the detail. It is a circle that is not a vicious, but a fruitful circle. It has been described and defended by the great theorists of hermeneutics, by Schleiermacher and Dilthey, and recently by one of the best living practitioners of stylistics, Leo Spitzer. Interpretation, understanding, explication, analysis are not, at least in the study of literature and art, separate from evaluation and criticism. There is no collection of neutral, value-proof traits that can be analyzed by a science of stylistics. A work of literature is, by its very nature, a totality of values which do not merely adhere to the structure but constitute its very nature. Thus criticism, a study of values, cannot be expelled from a meaningful concept of literary scholarship. This is not of course a recommendation of pure subjectivity, of "appreciation," of arbitrary opinion. It is a plea for literary scholarship as a systematic inquiry into structures, norms, and functions which contain and *are* values. Stylistics will form an important part of this inquiry, but only a part.

Comments to Part Nine

WIMSATT: I would like to move back for a minute or two to some of the general aspects of Mr. Brown's introductory remarks, just to remind us where we are in some of our orientations. I was much pleased with what I thought was one general drift of his discourse, namely, that the psychologist or the psychoanalyst can legitimately pursue certain concerns, and the literary critic can pursue others, legitimately, with neither necessarily threatening or trying to engulf the other. This seems to me very just and encouraging. Particularly, of course, I was interested in his acknowledgment that it is up to some people, or that some people have the right, to be valuing things while others are trying to describe things from a neutral point of view, simply to enumerate and record the values of others and not their own. Now in the end this will lead us back to the question whether a literary critic trying to define literature is involved in the notion of value in his definition. I'm one of those who believe he is, but I'm content to defer that topic. Right now I would like to make a slightly more precise comment on this matter of style. I was disturbed when Mr. Brown began talking about style as a matter of constants and variables—the difference between a constant and a variable. That may be the useful way for psychologists to talk about it, or even for linguists; I am not sure. But I would like to point out that the literary tradition has not been like that. We have a distinctive, different tradition. I think Mr. Jakobson certainly believes this and implied it. Style may be one of the most constant things in a writing. For example, Alexander Pope characteristically writes in the heroic couplet, and that is a feature of his style. But as he himself argued in his "Epistle to Dr. Arbuthnot": "Soft were my numbers; who could take offence While pure Description held the place of Sense?" Then later he began to talk about "gentle Fanny" and "Sappho," and they all took offense, but he was using the same style, in one sense. One important feature of his style was the same, the content had varied. That's a noticeable fact about literature. Now why is that? How is that accounted for by the literary critic? It is accounted for, I think, in this way—by distinguishing levels of meaning and kinds of meaning. In the classical tradition the style was thought to be roughly a sort of ornament or elegance, and if I understand the progress of stylistics in our time, represented say by the book of Mr. Richards, *Philosophy of Rhetoric*, borrowing partly from linguistic ideas, we now have to say that these things are more like levels of implicit meaning, implication (with a strong personal reference). Paralinguistic reference, I think, to use Mr. Chatman's phrase in his paper, cuts across these too. It's a difficult line to maintain, I would certainly grant, this difference between a style and a content, the definable stated dictionary kind of meaning, scientific meaning in some sense, strict discourse, message. But roughly a difference is something like this in an example used by Pope in his *Peri Bathous*, "Shut the door," and "The wooden guardian of our privacy quick on its axle turn," statements which at some level mean the same thing. [Laughter.] But in various ways they have additional meanings; the more complicated form means something different. Now I don't think a literary critic is very willingly going to relinquish that

420

conception, doesn't want to start talking about style as deviation. It doesn't make much sense to him because a deviation can occur at the deeper levels, the more abstract levels, too—more readily perhaps than at the stylistic levels. Mr. Brown himself said it would be a good idea if style could be thought of as corresponding to, as having a relation to, something broader, wider, deeper, or more like a message meaning, and that certainly is the way the literary critic likes to think. His levels of meaning are a structure from one point of view, from the dramatic or dramatistic point of view, when the means and end in the pragmatic or rhetorical purpose are seen as a structural fact. So it must be a little disturbing to a literary critic to hear this constant worry here whether style is a deviation, a personal deviation, or a group deviation, or something like that. It doesn't quite make sense, and I think that we have a better insight. We've been worrying about this longer than the psychologists have.

BROWN: Let me ask whether the use of the heroic couplet would be regarded as part of style if there were not those who did not use the heroic couplet.

WIMSATT: If everyone used it? Surely it would still be a part of style.

BROWN: Then it is simply a question, it seems to me, of setting a level of invariance and then saying it is a part of this writer's way of working to use the heroic couplet, and that it is a part of his style because there are those who do not.

WIMSATT: Let me answer this way. The variation always brings out characteristics. If everything were absolutely the same, we would know nothing, but that distinction applies to the level of stated meaning or content as much as it does to the level of style.

WELLS: I want to offer, if not a definition of a key term, at least a clarification of it. Style has been characterized in terms of a contrast between the variable and the constant. But this constant is relative. That is, something is variable against one background or in one context which is constant in another. For instance, if Pope uses the heroic couplet, this is variable against the whole background of the English language, and even against the whole background of the available verse forms of his day. On the other hand, it is a constancy in Pope that he writes in heroic couplets, so we can say once and for all that Pope writes in heroic couplets. This is stylistic about Pope as opposed to somebody who writes ballads, you might say. But then within that, within this constancy, there will be room for new variables as Pope grows older, say, or as he writes in a more humorous or in a more philosophical vein. Let me give a somewhat different example, the styles used by various philosophers of antiquity. Before Plato, a philosopher, we may say, had no choice about how to write. If he was going to write philosophy, he had to write a poem—Parmenides, Empedocles, and so on. Aristotle said (*Poetics* 1447b18) that Empedocles and Homer had nothing in common but meter. This was his recognition, I take it, that there was no creativity in Empedocles's poetry as there was in Homer's. Homer shows creative style, but Empedocles adopts or borrows a style. What I am trying to do is bring together the notions of style, choice, and variability. Plato deviated against a previous background of constancy. He made, or introduced, a variation—the dialogue. After his time people had their choice. Aristotle wrote dialogues in his youth and later shifted to the straight expository style. After Aristotle philosophers in Greece wrote in the expository style, and it had ceased to become a variable in the context of philosophy. It became a constant, and we might, for that very reason, say it was no longer a stylistic matter. I want to go back to put the question: wouldn't it be normal usage among literary theorists to say that, in such a case, it was not a stylistic matter that Empedocles wrote poetry, or that Aristotelian philosophers wrote expository prose? I think then that some agreement has been brought about between those who have stressed variation and constancy and those speaking from the point of view of more traditional literary theory.

WIMSATT: I have only a short retort to Mr. Wells. He's sure that style could come under the rulebook of the constant or the variable, and that everything else could come under this rule. If he means more especially that the style in Empedocles is probably bad because it is metrical style and that was already established, I think he is wrong. Many people have repeated metrical style. Virgil, for example, came off pretty well.

BEARDSLEY: We have employed at this conference, I think, two very different uses of the word "style." First we speak of the style of such and such where such and such might be a particular discourse or a collection of discourses. Here we get into the problems of deviations from the norm, and so on. But I think the second usage is really the more fundamental one, and if we could clear that up, the first one wouldn't give us much trouble. For the second usage we speak of a difference in style. So I wonder if we couldn't get at it best by taking certain small scale models, so to speak, pairs of expressions or sentences that differ in some way. Model *A* might be Mr. Saporta's example: "There's a big bear in the woods. There's a BI:IG bear in the woods." Model *B* might be Mr. Jakobson's "I took the money," or "The money was taken by me." Model *C* might be something that would occur in the suicide notes: "*X* died," versus "*X* passed away," and so on. Now which of these differences are we going to count as differences in style; which of them are differences not in meaning at all; which of them are such big differences in meaning that we don't count them as differences of style? It might be that by this method we could agree that certain minimal, or subtle, or detailed differences of meaning are to be counted as differences of style. And, perhaps, this definition of differences of style would suit not only literary critics but also at least some purposes of linguists and psychologists.

WIMSATT: It seems to me that most persons at this table—all the psychologists, and perhaps all the linguists—are interested in talking about style in a way that makes it mean nothing more than a trait, a character, or a complex of traits and characters, a type, a class, or something similar. Then they want to ask themselves a question: "Can I distinguish between an individual style and a group style?" And, of course, we really can't on those terms. It's the same as the logical problem whether we can describe an individual. As soon as we start describing him we have to classify him. And what the literary critic says, I think, on that score is that each literary work is unique, individual, but as far as we attempt to analyze it or describe it, we put it in classes and we don't hope to exhaust it. We only hope to approximate it like squaring a circle. But why should we be lost in these basic logical kinds of arguments? We want something more specific, something which is specific to the nature of language or literature. We want to ask a question about style which relates to verbal style and not to other kinds of style, like the style in haircuts or style in clothes. (They would be just the same; we could discuss them in the same terms that we have been using to discuss literature.) I propose that Mr. Beardsley has given us a good model. It hinges on the question of whether there are any different levels of expression, referential or external kinds of expression, and how far certain things like metaphor would fall into one or the other class. Broadly speaking, put it this way: does style include everything that is expressed in a poem? Or is nothing that is expressed in a poem style? Or is the style a part of what is expressed and therefore different from something else? That is a fruitful sort of question which will lead us into relations of technique and content, whereas the other one merely leads us into endless quarrels about the possibility of classifying.

RICHARDS: I would like to continue with the expectation and frustration theme that Mr. Brown finished up with. I want to start with his excellent example from Cummings (**79**, p. 12): the substitution of "to the beginning" for "to the end," where we get a sudden jolt to a very definitely developed expectation. There seem to be two possibilities, at least. One is that there is no outlet—we have to take it; and another is that there is a clear path somewhere, or a variety of paths of radiation by which we escape, as it were, with a very different step. Now, clearly, in the Cummings instance there was a beautiful path of escape for the frustrated expectations, and that is in the academic institution of Commencement. The substitution here of a beginning for an end is one of the things that most shocks strangers to this country when they first meet it. They take what is very solemnly called "Commencement" in this country as a termination. It is one of the things they have to get used to—calling this a Commencement and trying to think of it so. I once had a very distinguished pupil, the late Ahmed S. Bokhari of the United Nations, one of the great wits of our time. He used to put every year on his Christmas card: "A. S. Bokhari, born ——, died ——." The dates were those of his coming up to and going down from Cambridge. You see the death notion coming in here. I am trying to illustrate what I think is the action of expectation and frustration of expectation, or twisting of expectation and release or check, as a large part of—what shall I call it, poetry or literature. I'm a little tempted to go as far as to say literature, but in the literary man's sense of literature which Wellek and Wimsatt have been particularly drawing our attention to. If we have to use a variety of definitions, are we really forced to be disturbed, distressed? Are we to sense danger? I listen in these discussions for words of alarm and discomfort that seem to be used. Sometimes instead of saying something sparks we say it is dangerous. Are we really doing something very, very different on these two occasions? Or is it a part of our strategy and so on? Now, the point is this: are we really unable as versatile individuals to have a definition of style for linguistic purposes; and another definition of style for psychological purposes; and a third, fourth, fifth, and sixth definition for critical purposes? A literary critic who is orientated *historically* would need a definition of style which is distinctly different from that of one who might be given the label "new critic," a breed of critic for which I have never been able to find any differentiating marks at all. But I would urge here that to accustom ourselves to using a variety of definitions (especially in these juncture conferences, these conferences where different disciplines are meeting), to acquire a habit of expecting and being able to operate freely with a variety of definitions without fear, finding these differences between people's needs, as expressed in their definitions, instructive and not perturbing, is what we should collectively aim at. Therefore, I rejoiced in Jakobson's point about the diversity of uses of norms. I think that is fundamental. As I would say, every definition attempts to set up a norm, and if so it is reasonable that we should use a variety of definitions for different sets of interests organized as fields of inquiry. The profit from a conference such as this is chiefly in increased recognition—among all the participants—of the necessity of deviations in the uses of their key terms, recognition of how other people are using them, although they themselves wouldn't actually so use them in their work.

WIMSATT: I would like to interject a few words on the matter of definition before we drop it. I have in mind both Mr. Hollander and Mr. Richards. Now it would seem to me that if we are willing to limit ourselves, if we set out to limit ourselves, to a kind of dictionary or semantic inquiry in the use of terms, then either we report the meaning that we can discover, or we stipulate how we think it would be useful or helpful to use the term, or we do both. I think that all dictionary definitions are of that sort. They say this is the state of affairs, and if you would be correct or communicate with those of your community, use the words this way. But having observed that much, surely we all are very much intent upon going on to something else, and to continue to talk in that idiom is only to try to obstruct some further inquiry that we don't like. Really, we are all asking about reality. We are all asking some sort of analogical question about what used to be called, in old-fashioned terms, "real definitions." Whether they can be exact, or more exact, or less exact in this particular discipline, or not, is not quite relevant. We have a term, or set of terms. We have what tools we can find—what semantic tools we can find—and with them, in a more or less clumsy and obstructed way we are trying to get at something deeper. I would take it for granted that none of us is willing to go from this room and say that all we were doing is talking about compiling a dictionary of terms, or talking about the meaning of words. We are talking about something beyond that. The difficulty comes because it is a reflexive and more or less self-consuming inquiry. What we are talking about is the way in which words work.

This very fact sometimes confuses the inquiry and disguises the resemblance of our activity to the various other sciences and inquiries, which brings us back to the question of the value of definition. Is it appropriate to talk about that now, or is it reserved for some later point? Mr. Richards himself observed, in his "Poetic Process and Literary Analysis," that there are various kinds of interests in literature, and that one person wants to define literature from the point of view of linguistics and another person from the point of view of psychology; still Mr. Richards and Mr. Wellek agreed later on that we are interested in defining literature from the point of view of literature. That would be the definition. And I don't believe it means putting literature in the predicate. It means trying to find a predicate—a more analytic set of terms—which will explain the term "literature." Now my view of how this enters into value is somewhat like this. It is convenient to set up a kind of neutral, intermediate, tentative sort of definition. We recognize that the thing has rhymes and meter and features of that sort—also that it deals with a lot of warm values. This isn't just a set of instructions, such as we would have to build a cabinet, or a set of traffic rules. We make such tentative, half-way definitions, and we can call them neutral, and then we add to that *value*. But it's a rather clumsy process if we really think there is a clean division between that neutral setup and the value. I remember very well a passage in Mr. Richard's fine book, *Coleridge on Imagination*, to the effect that Coleridge first defined imagination in such a way as not to imply that it had to be *good* imagination, that then he was embarrassed and went on and tried to redefine it so as to require *real* imagination to be *good* imagination. That is what I've constantly been doing for about fifteen years now, and I think Mr. Richards, too, has been doing it. That's why I've always admired his books, because they gave me entrances into the study of literature as value. So, as I see it, we have this little platform up there of practical definition which is an area we are going to talk about for convenience's sake. I mean anybody can tell an apple from a coal mine, but it is harder to tell an apple from a false apple or a poem from a false poem. These temporarily and neutrally defined poems, if they are no more than that, are really fake poems. I like that conception of the expressionists—the idea of a falsity. I don't mean that the test is spontaneity on the part of the author. I mean the genuineness and depth of the article when we examine it. The idea of a good poem which we erect beyond the neutral has a sort of analogical relation to the neutral platform, is pointed or shaped with regard to an ideal. The platform is merely temporary, and it withholds the sense of value. So, in fact, "bad literature" is not quite a contradiction in terms, but it *tends* to be a contradiction in terms. [Laughter.]

And now I want to say something about the topic of expectancy and defeat; this has indirect relevance to both the metrical problem and the problem of value and definition. It strikes me that a good deal of this talk about expectancy and defeat of expectancy is carried on at far too simple a level in a way that would seem to imply that any kind of upset, any kind of bungle, can be admired. As a poetic rule, this would be utterly disastrous. Either a man gets it right and then we praise him for getting it right, or he gets it wrong and we call it irony. I have an approximate solution to that problem. It has always seemed to me that the kind of defeated expectancies which we consider valuable, which we call witty, which we call ironic, have a kind of smuggled-in extra dimension. They have a sort of special appropriateness packed into them, and I think I can illustrate that first with a very childish example of my own supplying, and then I will return to Cummings' joke and add something that no one has said. Suppose I should go over to that blackboard and start writing on it an injunction "No Smoking," and I wrote it in such big letters that when I came to the right side of the blackboard I still had to write "-ing" and therefore wrote it down the side of the blackboard. That would show a defeated expectancy. I hadn't planned and didn't get it on the board. It would not be particularly funny. It would just be a mistake. But there is a kind of comic sign that you can buy in some stores which starts out and says "Plan Ahead," and it goes across and then the letters get smaller and smaller and tumble down the side. [Laughter.] The person who is giving this advice "Plan Ahead" has not himself planned ahead. This is a modest example of the reflexive or extra, smuggled-in dimension which characterizes poetic wit. If applied to meter, for example, this would have something to do with interaction of the levels of sense, meaning, and meter. Now take the Cummings joke: I was thinking it over, and at first it didn't seem very funny to me. "My mother lost her health but kept her sense of humor until the beginning" is not what we would expect, but what special quality does it have? It's just that and that's all. It's a rather silly little joke. And I'm not sure it's so good now, but I think I *could* say just this much more in its defense, about why it probably strikes us as funny. The first part of it (all but the last word) represents a form of optimism, a cliché of optimism which we might call worldly optimism. "She kept her sense of humor until the end." As Mr. Hollander observed, most of us don't or would not. We die rather miserably. The second half (the last word), the substitution, represents the other-worldly kind of optimism, as if this cynical person is saying, well, if you really have this view of things, then you shouldn't say "end," you should say "beginning," because those things go together, the worldly sense of optimism and a faith in the other world. That's what sustains a person, probably, keeping his sense of humor—the other-worldly sense of optimism. So it is a joke on optimism, I take it. If it is not, it is just a rather trivial disappointment of expectancy.

WELLS: I want to continue with the issue upon which Mr. Wimsatt ended, whether bad literature is a contradiction in terms or anything like that. I wanted to indicate my agreement with Mr. Wimsatt that there is something very odd about speaking of bad literature, and further to indicate some parallels and also some reasons. First, as for parallels, there is something odd in speaking about a bad tool, or a bad knife, for example. So far as it is a bad knife, we might argue it just isn't a knife. It may look like a knife, it may be shaped like a knife, but it doesn't cut. Again, if we speak of someone as a bad father, we mean not that he is not a father biologically, but that he is not a father socially. He doesn't play his role in education, in rearing, and, in consequence, he just is not a father. To that extent, "bad" works like the word "false" (a false friend, a false poem); also it works like the word or prefix "ex-," or "former." (The ex-mayor is simply not the mayor; he was once the mayor, but he is not the mayor.) These are parallels. Now for reasons why it should be odd to speak of a bad poem, or a bad father—the reason why we are tempted to is that we use another criterion for poetry or fatherhood, as the case may be, the criterion of intention. Something is a poem, or is a knife, or is a father if it is designed to be one—if it claims to be one. So I move on to my next point that, in agreeing that it is odd to speak of a bad poem, I do so on the ground that it involves the intentional fallacy. It makes reference to intention. To speak of a bad poem is to say that this is a poem as shown by its intention (its intended purpose), but that it carries out the purpose badly. May I turn now to a different point, the question of a real definition (granting that we want a real definition) of poetry, literature, and style? There is still a question about what that definition would exclude. In particular, granting that Shakespeare, say, is real literature and suicide notes perhaps are not, barring an occasional exception, we still have to raise the question whether the study of suicide notes would be of help to the seeker for a real definition of literature or style. What of the suicide note, or the one-word-to-one-word association test, or the simple matter of selecting one pronoun rather than another for use in social relations? It should not be overlooked that possibly the study of these would be pertinent to the literary theorist, even if his final definition of literature, style, poetry, and so on, excluded them.

CHATMAN: I would like to say something about this subject of intention brought up by Mr. Wells. If literature is, as I believe, a special kind of human discourse, any definition of literature would necessarily involve distinguishing the discriminata of literature from those of other types of discourse. In this connection, essential discriminata may themselves be signaled, and, in part, the intention along with them. If we take a broader view of semiotic to include nonlinguistic as well as linguistic signals, we might find certain discriminata which can at least get us started. Many things may be signaled by signs from the *non*linguistic context, or the *setting*, to use a technical definition of that word for which we are indebted to Mr. Richards. For example, the stanzaic form may be taken as a nonlinguistic sign which signals to us that the author wishes to be considered as, at the least, a verse writer, perhaps even a poet. If we go to a church and a man stands up in the pulpit, the setting announces to us that the form of discourse is to be religious. If we are reading a newspaper and we see among the lines of print a box with a certain kind of drawing, more often than not multicolored, this is a sign that the discourse contained within that box is of the order of advertising. So that these nonlinguistic signs, I think, can be very useful in distinguishing the intention, which according to Mr. Wells needs to be taken into account in the act of judgment. After we have identified the form of the discourse, we can search it for the structural discriminata which may or may not satisfy the claims the poem makes on our attention. This seems to me a very useful way of proceeding and of avoiding a number of the difficulties involved in the search for commonly acceptable definitions.

GREENBERG: In the course of the earlier discussion it became obvious, I think, that one of our difficulties was that people from different disciplines use the word "style" in different ways. So I began to consider what I, as a linguist, meant by style and what the psychologists and literary critics intended by this term. Could one arrive at reasonable definitions, at least for each field separately? Having arrived at definitions which, if not completely satisfactory, might at least be considered fair approximations, I came to certain pessimistic conclusions which might be stated in the following manner, that it was only the delightful ambiguity of the word "style" that made this conference possible. However, on more sober reflection, it seemed to me that the conference had indeed been fruitful. Perhaps also behind this ambiguity there lies a higher synthesis. Why do we use this word "style" for apparently different things? This is an old problem. For example, Plato in discussing Justice is not satisfied with a multiple definition. We have a feeling that the use of a single term in ordinary language points to some unitary significance, even if we cannot verbalize it easily. So I decided to seek a definition of style that might cover all the varied usages that we have encountered here in our discussions. The definition is in very general logical terms and indeed it comes close to what Mr. Brown was saying. Let us define style as that set of characteristics by which we distinguish members of one subclass from members of other subclasses, all of which are members of the same general class. This is simply a way of saying that style is diagnostic like a fingerprint. We are asking within a whole set of things how we can categorize in a way that will allow us to put things in one box rather than in another. As a matter of fact, even in literature we give the student passages with the author's name omitted, and we ask him to assign it to the subclass of utterances of the true author rather than some other. However, if stated in this general logical way without reference to subject matter, there will be some strange results. Thus we might say that hydrogen has a certain style since it has its individual way of behaving and combines with other elements in unique ways not duplicated by any other element. In this case the chemist's qualitative analysis of a new substance is a stylistic analysis. So, likewise, is that of the doctor diagnosing a disease. However, all of us here are concerned with linguistic utterances, and this qualification of our logical definition will probably give us what we want. But regarding psychology, as we shall see, there is very likely some question of the validity of a restriction to language behavior. One other factor of a logical nature should be pointed out, and that is that the characteristics which define the style may be quantitative or, on the other hand, may be all or nothing or comparative predicates. If it is quantitative, the center of distribution may be called the norm, and noncentral values may be called deviations. In this sense we can say that a particular style may be marked by a deviation as against the more general norm of the class of which it is a subclass. This kind of statement then led those here who do not think in statistical terms and who take norm in some valuational way to rise up in arms against the notion that style is a deviation. To say that anything is a deviation from a statistical norm is, of course, not to say that it is morally wrong. In view of the general tendency among behavioral and other scientists to exalt the quantitative, it might be pointed out that nonquantitative diagnostics where attainable are likely to be more useful than statistical norms based on a sample because it is an unfailing criterion, whereas with statistical norms we can only state regarding a particular example that it has a certain probability of belonging to the subclass.

With this as a preliminary, what can we say about the use of the term "style" by psychologists, linguists, and literary critics? The psychologist, perhaps out of deference to the interests of others present, has employed the term "style" in reference to verbal behavior. This is no doubt an important aspect to him, but it is still not the primary one. The psychologist is interested in the individual, and the style of the individual is his personality. Here he has only been considering the verbal personality, the style insofar as it has linguistic expression. For example, Jenkins earlier was talking about constricted personalities. Now, to him, either verbal or nonverbal behavior is evidence relevant to the same problem. Further it may be pointed out that the psychologist is not satisfied with mere description of diagnostic characteristics. He tries to work out a more comprehensive concept based on an over-all typology that makes some sense of personality so that it becomes a unity such that having learned about certain aspects of it as symptoms he can make predictions about the rest. What about the linguist? As his name implies he is interested in language as such. Therefore he confines himself to linguistic expression and tries to define, within the corpus of linguistic production of a community, subcorpuses with definable characteristics. This can be done in a number of ways. Thus we have the idiolect of a particular individual. When its characteristics are analyzed we can identify the sender of the message. On the other hand, we might take certain utterances within the speech community common to a number of individuals, like a particular literary genre, and derive its linguistic characteristics.

This can also be done for social classes or regions. When we come to the literary critic, we have a much greater difficulty in describing what he is doing.

The problem is this: the psychologist knows he can try some objective criterion, separate out the class of utterances whose stylistic characteristics he wishes to study, and so can the linguist. However, the critic is bothered precisely about what his corpus is. He keeps asking, "What is literature?" To study the stylistics of literature, we must first determine what this literature is that we are studying. Some would react by saying simply that they don't want such questions to be raised by other people. Let us just work with the things we have been calling literature all along. They assume the corpus, and on the whole they are very successful about this, but of course there are individual differences of opinion. One man's literature is not always another man's. But each one has his own fairly satisfactory corpus which he considers to be literature. However, when he describes it stylistically he is generally operating on a subtler plane than would be the case for people with other backgrounds. Consider as an example of this latter the study by Yule, a statistician, of the writing of Thomas à Kempis. It is the kind of thing that the linguist would do, but, on the whole, the literary critic isn't very interested. He doesn't care how often Thomas uses nouns as compared to adjectives. The literary critic feels that such things are obvious anyway, so why should some outsider come along and start counting? The best they can do is tell me I'm right when I knew it all along. Or they can tell me something upsetting which I probably wouldn't like to hear. A critic will rather say, for example, that a work is rich in imagery of a certain kind and, at the most, that some item is particularly frequent if any quantitative judgments are to be made at all. All these are the sorts of things that the linguist on the whole could not measure because he doesn't have the experience and capabilities for this kind of analysis. Further, for literary critics, so far as I can make out, the matter of style is only a very small part of the job. If by style we mean the characteristics that distinguish one writer from another or one literary genre from another, it is only practically important in freshman classes or if there is an historical document and we don't know who wrote it—in other words, questions of literary scholarship. What the critic is interested in is what Mr. Richards was talking about as literary analysis, and in literary analysis such stylistic investigations are of little help.

HOOPES: I agree with Mr. Wimsatt that any definition of literature will and must include a statement or statements about the value of literature. Mr. Jakobson spoke of the essential impersonality of the drama as an art form, and he implied that it was therefore impossible, or at least extraordinarily difficult, to detect anything about the style of the man who creates this impersonal form. I would reply first of all that I think the style of the dramatist as dramatist is indeed identifiable. If we were to place dramas, for example, by Shakespeare, Marlowe, Webster, Tourneur, Etheredge, Congreve, and Ibsen before a person who had not studied them, it would be quite possible to educate him to their stylistic differences. He might bring himself to such an awareness without instruction. The fingerprint analogy that was mentioned by Mr. Brown is simply another version of that chestnut of literary criticism, "The style is the man." Teachers of literature must believe in it or else they wouldn't give spot passages on their examinations—and not only passages that the students have read but others that they have not read from the same authors. The whole point is to see whether the students have developed some sensitivity to the particularities of the author's style. But to return to the drama. If we take some very bad dramatists, say Arthur Wing Pinero and Henry Arthur Jones, we find that it is practically impossible to distinguish between their styles. And not just because they are alike, because of the sameness of their clichés, but because of the banality of their clichés, because they are so bad. In effect, they are not worth comparing. What I am suggesting is that the stylistic avenue is a partial avenue toward demonstrating the inextricability of the two concepts of definition and value of literature. As a contrast to Jones and Pinero, consider Elmer Rice's play *Street Scene*. Here the author has set out deliberately to create a cast of characters in which no one is really distinguished from anyone else. The title itself is revealing, and the result is an artistic achievement. Jones and Pinero simply couldn't do it. Finally, I should like to add that I don't really believe that stylistic elements in literature are in any way susceptible to what I would call mensurated accounting. Everyone likes to prescribe required reading when he talks with his contemporaries and peers, and in this context I have learned much from Lionel Trilling's essay on the nature of a literary idea and from Mr. Wellek and Mr. Warren's book (**442**). In different ways these authors are saying that a literary idea is not a literary idea until it is transmitted by metaphor, image, what-have-you. It simply is not a literary idea until it has become a constituent element of a work of art. When we try to restate it in a propositional or conceptual form, it ceases to be a literary idea. And this is why I suggest that in their fullest sense stylistic elements cannot be dealt with in a mensurated manner. They can be counted, but the numbers don't really mean very much. And I sense a real incompatibility of angles of approach in this conference, with the psychologists isolating and counting and the literary critics making an effort to deal with the literary or artistic idea in its total complexity and integrity.

· · ·

STANKIEWICZ: Mr. Hollander raised a number of questions and I think that, as in the Russian fairytale, we are coming closer and closer to the target. But I am unhappy about some vague formulations like the one by Mr. Hollander, I believe, that poetry is actually language. Or about Mr. Saporta's question whether art is not something more than language. And I think that here, in this context, we could try to define more explicitly what we really mean and where our discussion of stylistics and poetic language is moving. I would like to present here some points on the relationship of language to poetic language or to literature in the broader sense. It ties up with the problem of synchronic-diachronic raised by Mr. Hollander and with the problem of grammaticalness which was brought up by Mr. Saporta [see also Comments to Part Three]. I will start with the problem of grammaticalness. When we say something is grammatical or agrammatical we should add the question "on what level." If I take a passage like "'Twas brillig," it is perfectly grammatical from the point of view of the distribution of the phonemes, but it is "ungrammatical" as far as the lexicon is concerned. We can find similar examples on the levels of morphology and syntax. Linguistic innovations and archaisms often introduce such conflicting elements into a poetic text, which are "grammatical" on one level and "ungrammatical" on another level. The linguistic problem may enter into poetry and may be utilized poetically, but it is, by no means, a prerequisite of poetic discourse. For poetry the linguistic deviations are a marginal problem. I think that what is crucial is the problem of the organization of the message and not the problem of the linguistic code. We have a certain message to deliver, a certain amount of cognitive or emotive information, and we are free to arrange it in various ways. We are forced to use the existing linguistic units and to arrange them according to the pattern of the given language We observe the syntactic arrangement imposed by the language, but we are free to choose synonymous lexical items and to arrange them into higher units which are independent of the linguistic system, such as feet, lines, stanzas, paragraphs, etc. The linguistic code is found in our grammars and in our dictionaries, but the selection of lexical items, their juxtapositon and distribution, is largely a matter of the poet's intention. The problem of synchrony and diachrony, raised by Mr. Hollander, is also pertinent here, because it shows the difference between nonpoetic language and poetry. Mr. Hollander says that poetry is something synchronic and should be discussed in synchronical terms. I think that the notion of synchrony is not applicable in literature. I think that since we always quote authors like Chaucer and Shakespeare, and since we study and know by heart the older literature, we constantly live with tradition. Poetry is in a sense asynchronic. Every literature builds on poetic traditions of various times with which we maintain an intimate contact, especially, I suppose, this group.

Mr. Hollander brought up the problem of poetry as a convention. Language is a convention, too. It is a convention in the sense that language is a norm, but the rules of the poetic and nonpoetic conventions are different. In poetic language the main problems are those of selection and of arrangement—the arrangement, let's say, according to a metrical scheme and the selection of synonyms or of metaphors. These cannot be confused with the problem, for instance, of idiomatic expressions or of a fixed linguistic order. A "hot dog" is nothing but the idiom a "hot dog," but if we were to place it in a new context it might become metaphoric and "poetic." The problem of synchrony in poetic language is different from the one in everyday language. Poetic traditions are immersed in diachrony. Synchrony comes in only in our attitude toward diachrony, in our acceptance or rejection of the poetic traditions which have been transmitted to us. And that's where the problems of values come in. I think that the attitude we take toward particular traditions leads to continuous innovations. But again, we may distinguish between purely linguistic innovations and conservatism and conventionality or innovation in the poetic sphere. We return often to poetic traditions. Nonpoetic, ordinary language knows no returns; it is a progressive development in time. Synchrony in poetry, especially if we consider also the openness of poetry to foreign influence, is by no means similar to synchrony in language. If we switch in everyday language from English to French, we use two languages, but if we switch from one poetic system to another, we only vary the poetic expression. Because of the constant coexistence with foreign systems as well as with more archaic systems, poetic norms show a high degree of fluidity and of independence with respect to linguistic norms. In connection with this we must also consider the audience. I think we cannot provide a simple definition of value because the audience varies as much as traditions do. What is good poetry for one group may be bad poetry for another. I don't think we can adopt an optimal norm which is determined by an intellectual nobility. If we are going to be more objective about it, we should consider and compare coexisting values of various social groups or literary audiences. To continue, briefly, with this problem of norms, which I see as connected with the problem of values, I will now tie up what I have to say with the comments of Mr. Brown about the linguist describing and the literary historian having values. I think that the linguist describes what is given to him by the literary historian, or what is transmitted by tradition. He does not go into the description of works that have been ignored by literary historians—he may not be aware of these things. Norms or values present a shifting or continuous scale, since the things that yesterday had value may not have value today, whereas forgotten authors, on the other hand, may be revived. This is true not only in literature but in the other arts as well. I suggest that the whole problem of value must be approached relativistically in the sense of measuring values against our own values, against those of our own time, in other words, of constructing a frame of reference. This relates to the problem of predictability. If we remember that certain poetic traditions at a certain period such as the Neoclassical put a premium on predictability, the highest achievement, the "best" work, would be those that stick strictly to a chosen norm. Basically, it relates to Wölfflin's dichotomy of the romantic and classical, or to the other terms which were applied to designate opposite traditions or tastes. The romantic "taste" puts a premium on variation or tension, whereas the classical tradition puts a premium on constants and homogeneity. We can view the problem of variables and of constants also in the sense of a sliding scale, or rather of a hierarchy of constants, because the variables relate to the things that are regular or invariant. The whole problem, for instance, of symmetry becomes interesting if we ask the questions where is symmetry required and in what areas of a literary work are variation and asymmetry permitted. In other words, if there is a premium on variation or on the lack of variation, it is important to examine the areas in which they are found. The evaluation of these phenomena varies, however, according to our own standards, so that we have always, at least, two norms which affect our judgment: the one of the time or of the author in which the work originated and the other of our own time, which may revive or reactivate works that have been forgotten. Mr. Jakobson has said that the study of literature should not be merely a study of famous generals in literature, of the great authors. Significant innovations are sometimes introduced by mediocre authors, whereas some time-honored works lose their significance if they don't correspond to our own concepts of value. It is impossible to avoid a historical and relativistic approach in the study of art, of aesthetic products.

BEARDSLEY: I am not sure what Mr. Hollander had in mind, but I would like to stick up for the separation of evaluation and definition. I foresee that this is going to be an issue and there are just a few points I would like to suggest about it. I think Mr. Hollander is right that in order to cope with this question we must keep a clear separation between the process of recording existing usage and deciding on a new usage of our own. If we ask whether the word "literature" is a normative term, whether it carries a value concept in ordinary usage, or in literary usage, I think we would have to say yes. When you say this is literature, that is a commendation of it. So that perhaps we will have to set aside the word "literature" and use some term like "literary discourse," and say we are distinguishing literary from nonliterary discourses. But I should think the term "literary discourse" is pretty neutral even if "literature" isn't. I think Mr. Richards' question "What do we want the definition for?" is crucial, and it seems to me that what we want it for is to mark out in a rough way some area for consideration. The definition, in other words, is not going to be the conclusion of the inquiry, but merely a way of getting it started. It seems to me when we are making such a definition of "literary discourse" there are really three distinctions that cause the trouble, and probably the best way to approach it would be to separate these three problems. There is first the distinction, as I see it, between those metrical discourses (verses) that we want to call poems and those that we don't want to call poems. Mr. Hill says (173) that "thirty days hath September" is something that he has no hesitation in saying is both an example of poetry and literature. But I think literary critics in general would want to include in their definition of poems, although not in their definition of verse, some kind of complexity, or playing against each other of different levels of meaning. Second, I think we want to distinguish fiction from nonfiction. And third, within the class of assertive discourses, that is, of essays, in a very broad sense, I think we would want to distinguish some as literary essays and some to set aside. Then if we did this we could give a disjunctive definition of "literary discourse"—a literary discourse is anything that is a poem or a prose fiction or a literary essay. This might seem circular, because it might turn out that the very features we selected for distinguishing poems from other verses were features that were counted in favor of saying that they have literary value. But I think this doesn't mean that we included value in our concept of poem. It really means that the thing that makes a verse a poem is also something that later on helps to make it a good poem to some degree.

RICHARDS: May I also go back to Mr. Hollander's division into two of the descriptive accounts of how words have been used, and to that kind of dictionary effort which Mr. Beardsley mentioned, as well as the other thing which he put into terms of stipulation. I would like to linger for a moment on stipulation. It can range very, very widely, it seems to me, from a mere request to something that becomes a sort of an obligation imposed which the recipient of the invitation is not really free to decline. There is quite a subtle order of different types of definitions lost behind the phrase "stipulation." I would suggest that just where you freeze it, as it were, how fluid your invitation is, how optional the option really is, and so on—all this makes a great deal of difference to the practical outcome of any discussion. That's why it's an important point linguistically, I think, to observe this range of moods here from a pure request to a disguised order with the interrogatives all around, too: "Don't you want to?" All that kind of thing is very important in the strategy of discussion. I think this will go from the pure case of the mathematician laying out his matrices, and so on, to what will look sometimes like large historical generalizations disguised as how the word has been used and always will be used by all sensible people. You see there is always something like: "By all sane characters," in the background. [Laughter.] Behind the request: "Please let us use X in this way!" there has historically been also an attempt to state briefly *the distinguishing truths about X.* "Do agree with me, please, on this occasion, to use X in this way for *this is what X is.*" We have actually and literally a stake in the historical facts behind that maneuver. It is the serious attempt to return to life. We accept a request—in part to see what will come of it—and then find ourselves thereby seemingly committed to accepting something about the inner being of X. There is a universal tendency to begin with sort of a survey of what people have meant by the word—very sketchy, probably very inaccurate.

This is one thing that the dictionary is supposed to do. The dictionary is a thing I think we appropriately can linger over for a moment. I happened once to be a member of a committee I think numbering just as many as we have here. It was the BBC's committee on spoken English. Fortunately for the English language, the scope of the decisions of the committee was limited to the pronunciations of certain words by BBC's announcers. Our chairman, George Bernard Shaw, vigorously sustained a defensive operation against many people who wanted us to deal with more important matters of usage, the barring out of certain connotations as vulgarisms, and so on. We could stamp certain pronunciations of separate words as vulgarisms, but that was all. I got in hot water for wanting some permission for the pronunciation *of-ten* in addition to *of'n.* I was squashed because *of-ten* was a vulgarism, but I continue to use it on suitable occasions as an alternate. [Laughter.] We had the editors of the major dictionaries—about seven were represented there—at first without their dictionaries. But soon somebody took the precaution of looking up their rulings in their dictionaries. I am sorry to say that we *of-ten* found [Laughter] the editor quite at variance with his own work. After that we had able secretaries stationed at the actual works all laid out before us, and anything that the editor said was at once checked. After a bit the editor would begin by going into cahoots with the secretary. [Laughter.] This business, the descriptive account of how the word has been used, is, of course, a matter of extreme difficulty and delicacy. Anybody looking carefully at the *Oxford Dictionary* will see that the quality of the work differs enormously from article to article; different people have been assigned different letters, have had different interest in different parts, and so on. It is very patchy and reflects frequently the date at which the article was written.

Well, perhaps that is enough about, first, the idea of having a descriptive set of definitions adequate to the occasion; secondly, of having behind it as clearly formulated a set of requests as mildly made as may be; and thirdly, recognizing the grave danger of smuggling into the request a whole doctrine instead of just sufficient to enable that word to be used consistently up to the point where we will find deviations between the two uses. However, that is the great danger: the putting of eternal truth in as a supporting statement behind the description of the request. Well, now, so much for that. Now, I want to say that it delighted me to hear Mr. Hollander twice refer to THE definition of literature. But you see on the position he is taking there is no such thing as *the* definition of *X*, whatever *X* may be. There are definitions subject to negotiation between people who want to make their interests engage and to pursue a common task. This phrase, "*the* definition" is a sort of alarm clock bell which tells us that at the moment we are being less sophisticated than need be.

Now I want to take up as a second branch, and it is very closely related to Jakobson's words about rhetoric, and with the problem of the presence of value and valuation. I would like to say that not only with *literature*, under whatever definition we assign to it, and with *style*, no matter what definition we assign it, but with *X*, unrestrictedly however defined, value-packed questions will enter. That's a big philosophical assumption, but I hold it merely as a working hypothesis—until I see something too tricky for me to handle coming up. Now take this, for instance. Suppose we consider "good"—the word itself is a notorious wanderer, perhaps one of the most versatile of all words offering more opportunities for different definitions on different occasions than any other word—one of the supreme wanderers. But suppose, for our purposes in this conference, I put forward an old doctrine, that good is efficiency. A good act, operation, code—a good *X*—is one that will reach its end. This old definition of rhetoric is from Isocrates. "Rhetoric is the art by which discourse is adapted to its end." It's as simple as that. It is very pragmatic: good discourse, for Isocrates, is discourse that works. No more than that. But that I think is very fundamental. Consider the reviewer: for his purposes he wants to say this is a good book and this is a bad one. We may all differ from him no doubt, but what he is trying to say, I would suggest, is that this book will do for its audience what it set out to do. Its audience may be mistaken in thinking that it's the right book for them, but that's a rather broad picture of what's behind the phrase "a good book." What's behind "a bad book" is the converse: it will not achieve its purpose. And this meets, I think, Mr. Saporta's opening framework which Mr. Hollander was referring to in connection with science and art. I'd like to generalize the notion of art as widely as this. There will be an art in every activity. It's either an activity which is being so conducted that it will reach its end, or it's an activity so conducted that it will fail—through its own fault, as it were, it will lapse. So we would have, you see, good literature and bad literature; we would have good exposition and bad exposition. I'm not begging any questions about whether exposition is literature. One of the uses of the word "literature" which has not been mentioned at this table is the phrase that perhaps most of us use most often—"the literature of a subject." Now, for psychology: I've met, you know, literary men in my time who would say that literature and psychology are incompatibles. If you mentioned them together they would look as though you were giving them an emetic. [Laughter.] My last remark is just a footnote. Two footnotes, if I may, the first on grammatical and nongrammatical. It seems to me there is a great deal in the literature of psychology of late—at least, many people would like there to be a great deal in the literature of psychology of late—which has avoided and renounced what is known as mentalism. Now unless I am deceived, in the very structure of a great many languages, including English, mentalism enters extremely deeply. The understanding of enormous classes of verbs and other parts of the language depend on the assumption that a spiritual agent, a unique soul, in fact, is doing something, and to translate that into nonmentalistic language amounts to a very great departure from the governing principles, as it were, that the speech community is unconsciously, like Jakobson's rapt soul, obeying. My last footnote is on your dead metaphor, your leg of the table and the unlucky critic **(94)** whom Hollander quoted to us (I do wish I thought he was as out of date as you do). The unlucky critic you quoted to us introduced a nice example of reviving a dead metaphor, precisely the leg of the table which got up and kicked like a mule. [Laughter.] We never can say for sure that a metaphor is dead. In a poet's hand it may come to life.

OSGOOD: As Mr. Richards was speaking, I began to worry because we are not sticking by clear definitions but are defining good literature in terms of what achieves the ends set by the author. I had the horrible thought that if this were true, if this were accepted, we would have to conclude that among the best literature we have in the present day is advertising. This fits the definition perfectly.

WIMSATT: This is a point that I have been wanting to speak on for some minutes. I should like to enter a mild protest, a gesture of protest. Certainly I believe in ends and means in all the dualistic, realistic concerns of our existence. But I think that there is a sense in which the end is always modified by the means, that sense merges into the senses where the end and the means are the same, in certain situations, and with words the literary situation is that situation. This is just commonplace as part of idealistic aesthetics, expressionistic aesthetics, that we don't have ends and means in a poem but are constantly changing meaning with changes in form, in style, and so on. I think all psychological end-means talk about poetry should always be set against some extreme idealistic expression like that of Croce, just as I think Croce needs to be set against the other. And I don't think either is a complete truth. But surely a poem is a verbal engine, a verbal expression, which has no end except to be known. That is its end. A poem like Mr. Richards' "Harvard Yard in April" accomplishes its end in being known. We can't talk about the style as a means of promoting the end. And so it happens that these correlation tables of the sort that abstract off some neutral aspect of a pragmatic composition in words, like its number of sentences or number of words, have a very limited value to the literary inquiry. (They might have a relation to a rhetorical study of either advertising or the speeches of certain demagogues, say the speeches of Hitler during the last war.) Mr. Richards himself did employ a certain amount of means-and-ends vocabulary in his *Principles of Literary Criticism*, but it seems to me this did not stand up; the terms were reduced finally to a system of appreciation of poetic knowledge, which is much like that in expressionism.

RICHARDS: Mr. Wimsatt and I are not in disagreement.

References

1. Aarne, A., and S. Thompson. *The types of the folk-tale.* Helsinki, 1928
2. Abbott, J. S. C. *David Crockett: his life and adventures.* New York, 1875.
3. Abercrombie, L. *Principles of English prosody* Vol. 1. London, 1923.
4. Allen, C. "Cadenced free verse," *College English* 9.195–199 (1948).
5. Allen, G. W. *American prosody.* New York, 1935.
6. Allport, G. W., and L. Postman. *The psychology of rumor.* New York, 1947.
7. Alonso, A. *Poesía y estilo de Pablo Neruda.* Buenos Aires, 1940.
8. *Annual technical report,* ONR contract, N8 onr 66216, University of Minnesota. Minneapolis, 1955.
9. Arbusow, L. *Colores rhetorici.* Göttingen, 1948.
10. Austerlitz, R. *Ob-Ugric metrics. Folklore fellows communications* 174 (1958).
11. Azadovsky, M. *Eine sibirische Märchenerzählerin.* Helsinki, 1926.
12. Ball, J. "Style in the folktale," *Folk-lore* 65.170–172 (December 1954).
13. Bally, C. *Linguistique générale et linguistique française.* Berne, 1944.
14. Barry, Sister M. M. *An analysis of the prosodic structure of selected poems of T. S. Eliot.* Dissertation, Catholic University of America. Washington, 1948.
15. Bastian, J. R. "Response chaining in verbal transfer," *Technical report* 13, ONR contract, N8 onr 66216, University of Minnesota. Minneapolis, 1957.
16. Baugh, A. C. *A history of the English language.* New York, 1935.
17. Baughman, E. W. *A comparative study of the folktales of England and North America.* Doctoral dissertation, Indiana University. Bloomington, 1953.
18. Baum, P. F. *The other harmony of prose: an essay on English prose rhythm.* Durham, 1952.
19. ———. *The principles of English versification.* Cambridge, Mass., 1922.
20. Bazell, C. E. "The grapheme," *Litera* 3.43–46 (1956).
21. Beck, H. P. *The folklore of Maine.* Philadelphia and New York, 1957.
22. Begrich, J. "Zur hebräischen Metrik," *Theologische Rundschau: neue Folge* 4.67–89 (1932).
23. Beloof, R. L. *Cummings, the prosodic shape of his poems.* Microfilmed dissertation, Northwestern University. Evanston, 1945.
24. Belyj, A. *Ritm kak dialektika.* Moscow, 1929.
25. ———. *Simvolizm.* Moscow, 1910.
26. Benn, G. *Frühe Lyrik und Dramen.* Wiesbaden, 1952.
27. ———, ed. *Lyrik des expressionistischen Jahrzehnts.* Wiesbaden, 1955.
28. Benoist-Hanappier, L. *Die freien Rhythmen in der deutschen Lyrik.* Halle, 1905.
29. Berdnikov, V. M., and E. A. Tudorovskaja. *Poètika marijskix narodnyx pesen.* Joškar-Ola, 1945.
29a. Bishop, J. L. "Prosodic elements in T'ang poetry," *Indiana University conference on Oriental-Western literary relations.* Chapel Hill, 1955.

30. Bernštejn, S. "Èstetičeskie predposylki teorii deklamacii," in *Poètika*, Vol. 3. Leningrad, 1926.

31. Blackmur, R. "Lord Tennyson's scissors," in *Form and value in modern poetry*, pp. 369–388. Garden City, 1957.

32. Bloch, B. "Linguistic structure and linguistic analysis," in A. A. Hill, ed., *Report of the fourth annual round table meeting on linguistics and language teaching*, pp. 40–44. Washington, 1953.

33. Boas, F. *Race, language and culture*. New York, 1948.

34. Boatright, M. C. *Gib Morgan, minstrel of the oil fields*. Texas Folklore Society. Austin, 1945.

35. Bolinger, D. L. "Rime, assonance, and morpheme analysis," *Word* 6.117–136 (1950).

36. Bowra, C. M. *Heroic poetry*. London, 1952.

37. Bradley, F. H. *Essays on truth and reality*. Oxford, 1944.

38. Brecht, B. *Gedichte und Lieder*. Berlin, 1956.

39. ———. "Über reimlose Lyrik mit unregelmässigen Rhythmen," *Versuche* 12, pp. 143–147. Berlin, 1953.

40. Brenner, R. *Ten modern poets*. New York, 1930.

41. Brewer, W. *Sonnets and sestinas*. Boston, 1937.

42. Bridges, R. *Milton's prosody*. Oxford, 1921.

43. Brik, O. M. "Ritm i sintaksis," *Novyj LEF* 3.15–20, 4.23–29, 5.32–37, 6.33–39 (1927).

44. Brooks, C., and R. P. Warren. *Understanding poetry*. New York, 1950.

45. Brower, R. A. *The fields of light*. New York, 1951.

46. Brown, R. W. Review in *Language* 31.84–91 (1955).

47. ———, A. Black, and A. Horowitz. "Phonetic symbolism in natural languages," *Journal of abnormal and social psychology* 50.388–393 (1955).

48. Brunot, F. *Histoire de la langue française*. Paris, 1937.

49. ———. *La pensée et la langue*. Paris, 1927.

50. Budzyk, K. *Stylistyka teoretyczna w Polsce*. Warsaw, 1946.

51. Bühler, K. "Die Axiomatik der Sprachwissenschaft," *Kant-Studien* 38.19–90 (Berlin, 1933).

52. ———. *Sprachtheorie*. Jena, 1934.

53. Burke, K. *Attitudes to history*. New York, 1937.

54. ———. *The philosophy of literary form*. Baton Rouge, 1941; New York, 1957.

55. Byrne, Sister St. G. *Shakespeare's use of the pronoun of address*. Dissertation, Catholic University of America. Washington, 1936.

56. Campbell, F. J. *Popular tales of the West Highlands*. Edinburgh, 1860.

57. Carroll, J. B. "Biquartimin criterion for rotation to oblique simple structure in factor analysis," *Science* 126.1114–1115 (1957).

57a. ———. *A factor analysis of verbal abilities*. Doctoral dissertation, University of Minnesota. Minneapolis, 1941.

58. Châtelain, É. "Du pluriel de respect en Latin," *Revue de philologie* 4.129–139 (1880).

59. Chatman, S. "Linguistics, poetics, and interpretation: the phonemic dimension," *Quarterly journal of speech* 43.248–256 (1957).

60. ———. "Mr. Stein on Donne," *Kenyon review* 18.443–450 (1956).

61. ———. "Robert Frost's 'Mowing': an inquiry into prosodic structure," *Kenyon review* 18.421–451 (1956).

62. Cherry, C. *On human communication*. New York, 1957.

63. Chomsky, N. *The logical structure of linguistic theory*, mimeographed. Cambridge, Mass., 1956.
64. ———. *Syntactic structures*. 's Gravenhage, 1957.
65. ———, M. Halle, and F. Lukoff. "On accent and juncture in English," in *For Roman Jakobson*, pp. 65–80. The Hague, 1956.
66. Clemens, S. L. *Roughing it*. Hartford, 1872.
67. Closs, A. *Die freien Rhythmen in der deutschen Lyrik*. Bern, 1947.
68. Cobb, W. H. *A criticism of systems of Hebrew metre*. Oxford, 1905.
69. Coculesco, P. S[ervien]. *Essai sur les rythmes toniques du français*. Paris, 1925.
70. ———. *Les rythmes comme introduction physique à l'esthétique*. Paris, 1930.
71. ———. *Science et poésie*. Paris, 1947.
72. Combs, H. C., and Z. R. Sullens. *A concordance to the English poems of John Donne*. Chicago, 1940.
73. Cornford, F. M. *Plato's theory of knowledge; the Theaetetus and the Sophist of Plato*. London and New York, 1935, 1951.
74. Costello, Sister M. C. *Between fixity and flux*. Dissertation, Catholic University of America. Washington, 1947.
75. Croce, B. *Ariosto, Shakespeare and Corneille*, D. Ainslie, tr. Mimeographed. London, 1927.
76. Croll, M. W. *The rhythm of English verse*. Princeton, 1929.
77. Cronin, M. "The tyranny of democratic manners," *The new republic* 137.12–14 (1958).
78. Cummings, e. e. *Poems*. New York, 1955.
79. ———. *I. Six nonlectures*. Cambridge, Mass., 1953.
80. Dale, A. M. "The metrical units of Greek lyric verse, 2," *Classical quarterly* 1 (n.s.).20–30 (1951).
81. Dauzat, A. *Défense de la langue française*. Paris, 1912.
82. Davie, D. *Articulate energy: an enquiry into the syntax of English poetry*. New York, 1958.
83. Dégh, L. "Some questions of the social function of storytelling," *Acta ethnographica* 7.91–146 (1957).
84. De Groot, A. W. *Algemene versleer*. The Hague, 1946.
85. ———. "Phonetics in its relation to aesthetics," in L. Kaiser, ed., *Manual of phonetics*, pp. 385–399. Amsterdam, 1957.
86. ———. "Der Rhythmus," *Neophilologus* 17.81–100, 177–197, 241–265 (1932).
87. ———. "Zur Grundlegung der allgemeinen Versbaulehre," *Archives néerlandaises de phonétique expérimentale* 8–9.68–81 (1933).
88. Delargy, J. H. "The Gaelic story-teller," *Proceedings of the British Academy* 31.177–221 (1945).
89. Devereux, W. B. *Lives and letters of the Devereux, earls of Essex, in the reigns of Elizabeth, James I, and Charles I, 1540–1646*. London, 1853.
90. Diez, F. *Grammaire des langues romanes*. Paris, 1876.
91. Długska, M. *Studia z historii i teorii wersyfikacji polskiej*. Cracow, 1948.
92. Donne, J. *The poems of John Donne*, E. K. Chambers, ed. London, 1896.
93. ———. *The poems of John Donne*, H. J. C. Grierson, ed. Oxford, 1912.
94. Donoghue, D. "Yeats and the clean outline," *Sewanee review* 65.202–225 (1957).
95. Dorson, R. M. *Bloodstoppers and bearwalkers*. Cambridge, Mass., 1952.
96. ———. "Collecting folklore in Jonesport, Maine," *Proceedings of the American Philosophical Society* 101.270–289 (1957).
97. ———. "Dialect stories of the Upper Peninsula," *Journal of American folklore* 61.121–128, 136 (1948).

98. Dorson, R. M. "Mishaps of a Maine lobsterman," *Northeast folklore* 1.1–7 (1958).

99. ———. *Negro folktales in Michigan.* Cambridge, Mass., 1956.

100. ———. *Negro tales from Pine Bluff, Arkansas, and Calvin, Michigan.* Bloomington, 1958.

101. ———. "Negro tales [of John Blackamore]," *Western folklore* 13.77–79, 160–169, 256–259 (1954).

102. ———. "Polish wonder tales of Joe Woods," and "Polish tales from Joe Woods," *Western folklore* 8.25–52, 131–145 (1949).

103. Dozier, E. P. "Cultural matrix of singing and chanting in Tewa pueblos," *International journal of American linguistics* 24.268–272 (1958).

104. Draak, M. "Duncan Macdonald of South Uist," *Fabula* 1.47–58 (1957).

105. Drew, E., and J. L. Sweeney. *Directions in modern poetry.* New York. 1940.

106. Dunn, S., J. Bliss, and E. Siipola. "Effects of impulsivity, introversion and individual values upon associations under free conditions," *Journal of personality* 26.61–76 (1958).

107. Èjxenbaum, B. *Anna Axmatova.* Leningrad, 1923.

108. ———. *Melodika stixa.* Leningrad, 1922.

109. Eliot, T. S. "The borderline of prose," *The new statesman* 9.157–159 (1917).

110. ———. *The complete poems and plays 1909–50.* New York, 1952.

111. ———. "Reflections on vers libre," *The new statesman* 8.518–519 (1917).

112. Ellwood, T. *The history of the life of Thomas Ellwood.* London, 1714.

113. Empson, W. *Seven types of ambiguity.* New York, third edition, 1955.

114. Erlich, V. Review in *Comparative literature* 8.254–255 (1956).

115. ———. *Russian formalism.* 's Gravenhage, 1955.

116. Estrich, R. M., and H. Sperber. *Three keys to language.* New York, 1946.

117. Eysenck, H. J. *Sense and nonsense in psychology.* Harmondsworth, Middlesex, Baltimore, 1957.

118. Farnsworth, R. *The pure language of the spirit of truth . . . or "thee" and "thou" in its place . . . .* London, 1655.

119. Fay, P. B. "The use of 'tu' and 'vous' in Molière," *University of California publications in modern philology*, 8.227–286 (1920).

120. Feise, E. "Closs, A.: Die freien Rhythmen . . . ," *Modern language notes* 65.127–130 (1950).

121. Finkelstein, L. "The Hebrew text of the Bible: a study of its cadence symbols," in L. Bryson et al., eds., *Symbols and society*, pp. 409–426. New York, 1955.

122. Fox, G. *A battle-doore for teachers and professors to learn plural and singular.* London, 1660.

123. Fraisse, P. *Les structures rythmiques: étude psychologique.* Louvain, 1956.

124. French, D. "Cultural matrices of Chinookan non-casual language," *International journal of American linguistics* 24.258–263 (1958).

125. Friedmann, H., and O. Mann, eds. *Deutsche Literatur im zwanzigsten Jahrhundert.* Heidelberg, 1956.

126. ———. *Expressionismus.* Heidelberg, 1956.

127. Fries, C. C., and K. L. Pike. "Co-existent phonemic systems," *Language* 25.29–50 (1949).

128. Frost, R. *Collected poems.* New York, 1939.

129. Frye, N. *Anatomy of criticism.* Princeton, 1959.

130. Fussell, P. *Theory of prosody in 18th century England.* New London, 1955.

131. Galton, F. *Inquiries into human faculty and its development.* London, 1883.

132. Gardner, H. *The art of T. S. Eliot.* London, 1949.

133. Gedike, F. *Über du und sie in der deutschen Sprache.* Berlin, 1794.
134. Gibson, C. M., and I. A. Richards. *First steps in reading English.* New York, 1957.
135. Giese, W. "Sind Märchen Lügen?" *Cahiers S. Puşcariu* 1. 137ff. (1952).
136. Gilson, É. *Being and some philosophers.* Toronto, second edition, 1952.
137. Goethe, J. W. "Einfache Nachahmung der Natur, Manier, Stil," in *Goethes sämtliche Werke*, E. von der Hellen, ed., Vol. 33, pp. 54–59. Stuttgart and Berlin, 1902.
138. Grammont, M. *Le vers français, ses moyens d'expression, son harmonie.* Paris, 1913.
139. Grand, C. *"Tu, voi, lei;" étude des pronoms allocutoires italiens.* Ingebohl, 1930.
140. Graves, R. *Contemporary techniques of poetry: a political analogy.* London, 1925.
141. Greenwood, D. *Truth and meaning.* New York, 1957.
142. Grimm, J. *Deutsche Grammatik*, Vol. 4. Gütersloh, 1898.
143. ———. *Über den Personen-wechsel in der Rede.* Berlin, 1856.
144. Guiraud, P. *Langage et versification d'après l'œuvre de Paul Valéry.* Paris, 1953.
145. Habermann, P. "Akzent," in P. Merker and W. Stammler, *Reallexikon der deutschen Literaturgeschichte*, W. Kohlschmidt and W. Mohr, eds., pp. 16–21. Berlin, second edition, 1955.
146. ———, and W. Mohr. "Hebung und Senkung," in P. Merker and W. Sammler, *145*, pp. 623–629.
147. Hamm, V. M. "Meter and meaning," *Publications of the Modern Language Association of America* 69.695–710 (1954).
148. Harris, Z. S. "Discourse analysis," *Language* 28.1–30 (1952).
149. ———. "Discourse analysis: a sample text," *Language* 28.474–494 (1952).
150. ———. "Distributional structure," *Word* 10.146–162 (1954).
151. Harrison, G. B., ed. *The letters of Queen Elizabeth.* London, 1935.
152. Hartland, E. S. *The science of fairy tales.* London, 1891.
153. Hartmann, M. *Das arabische Strophengedicht: Ergänzungshefte zur Zeitschrift für Assyriologie. Semitische Studien* 13–14. Weimar, 1897.
154. Hartmann, P. *Einige Grundzüge des japanischen Sprachbaues.* Heidelberg, 1952.
155. ———. *Nominale Ausdrucksformen im wissenschaftlichen Sanskrit.* Heidelberg, 1955.
156. ———. *Probleme der sprachlichen Form.* Heidelberg, 1957.
157. ———. *Wortart und Aussageform.* Heidelberg, 1956.
158. ———. *Zur Typologie des Indogermanischen.* Heidelberg, 1956.
159. Harva, U. "The Finno-Ugric system of relationship," *Transactions of the Westermarck Society* 1.52–74 (1947).
160. Hatzfeld, H. *A bibliography of the new stylistics.* Chapel Hill, 1952.
161. ———. "Stylistic criticism as art-minded philology," *Yale French studies* 2.62–70 (1949).
162. Hazard, T. R. *The Jonny-cake letters.* Providence, 1882.
163. ———. *The Jonny-cake papers of "Shepherd Tom."* Boston, 1915.
164. Hebb, D. O. "Drives and the C.N.S. [conceptual nervous system]," *Psychological review* 62.243–254 (1955).
165. Hellenbrecht, H. *Das Problem der freien Rhythmen mit Bezug auf Nietzsche. Sprache und Dichtung*, Vol. 48. Bern, 1931.
166. Herdan, G. *Language as choice and chance.* Groningen, 1956.
167. Hertz, E. *Lincoln talks, a biography in anecdote.* New York, 1939.

440 *References*

168. Herzog, G. "Some linguistic aspects of American Indian poetry," *Word* 2.82 (1946).

169. ———. "Song: folk song and the music of folk song," in M. Leach, ed., *Standard dictionary of folklore, mythology and legend*. 2.1032–1050. New York, 1950.

170. Heusler, A. *Deutsche Versgeschichte*. Berlin, 1925–1929.

171. Higginson, F. H. *Anna Livia Plurabelle: the making of a chapter*. Minneapolis, 1960.

172. Hill, A. A. *Introduction to linguistic structures*. New York, 1958.

173. ———. "A program for the definition of literature," The University of Texas, *Studies in English* 37.46–52 (1958).

174. ———. Review in *Language* 29.549–561 (1953).

175. ———. Review in *Language* 31.249–252 (1955).

176. Hollander, J. "The metrical emblem," *Kenyon review* 21.279–296 (1959).

177. Holthusen, H. E., ed. *Ergriffenes Dasein: deutsche Lyrik, 1900–1950*. Ebenhausen, 1953.

178. ———. "Vollkommen sinnliche Rede," *Akzente* 2.346–356 (1955).

179. Hopkins, G. M. *The journals and papers*, H. House, ed. London, 1959.

180. ———. *Poems*. W. H. Gardner, ed. New York and London, third edition, 1948.

181. Householder, F. W. "Accent, juncture, and my grandfather's reader," *Word* 13.234–245 (1957).

182. ———. "On the problem of sound and meaning, an English phonestheme," *Word* 2.83–84 (1946).

183. ———. Review in *International journal of American linguistics* 18.260–268 (1952).

184. Hrabák, J. *Úvod do teorie verše*. Prague, 1956.

185. Hrushovski, B. "On free rhythms in modern Yiddish poetry," in U. Weinreich, ed., *The field of Yiddish*. New York, 1954.

186. Hughes, G. *Imagism and the imagists*. Stanford and London, 1931.

187. Hull, C. L. *Principles of behavior: an introduction to behavior theory*. New York, 1943.

188. Hunt, C. *Donne's poetry*. New Haven, 1954.

189. Hymes, D. H. "I do what I can," *Accent* 15.68 (1955).

190. ———. "Linguistic features peculiar to Chinookan myths," *International journal of American linguistics* 24.253–257 (1958).

191. ———. "The supposed Spanish loanword in Hopi for 'jaybird,' " *International journal of American linguistics* 22.186–187 (1956).

192. Ingarden, R. *Das literarische Kunstwerk*. Halle, 1931.

193. Jack, I. "Pope and 'the weighty bullion of Dr. Donne's satires,' " *Publications of the Modern Language Association of America* 66.1009–1022 (1951).

194. Jakobson, R. "Commentary," in *Russian fairy tales*, N. Guterman, tr., pp. 631–656. New York, 1945.

195. ———. "The kernel of comparative Slavic literature," *Harvard Slavic studies* 1.1–71 (1953).

196. ———. "M. P. Štokmar: Bibliografija rabot po stixosloženiju," *Slavia* 13.416–431 (1934).

197. ———. "The metaphoric and metonymic poles," in *Fundamentals of language*, pp. 76–82. 's Gravenhage, 1956.

198. ———. *O češskom stixe preimuščestvenno v sopostavlenii s russkim* (= Sborniki po teorii poètičeskogo jazyka, 5). Berlin and Moscow, 1923.

199. Jakobson, R. "Studies in comparative Slavic metrics," *Oxford Slavonic papers* 3.21–66 (1952).

200. ———. "Über den Versbau der serbokroatischen Volksepen," *Archives néerlandaises de phonétique expérimentale* 7–9.44–53 (1933).

201. ———. "Viktor Xlebnikov," in *Novejšaja russkaja poèzija*, pp. 3–68. Prague, 1921.

202. ———, and M. Halle. "Phonology in relation to phonetics," in L. Kaiser, ed., *Manual of phonetics*, pp. 215–251. Amsterdam, 1957.

203. ———, and J. Lotz. *Axiomatik eines Verssystems am mordwinischen Volkslied dargelegt.* Stockholm, 1941.

204. ———, and J. Lotz. "Axioms of a versification system exemplified by the Mordvinian folksong," *Acta Instituti Hungarici Universitatis Holmiensis, Series B. Linguistica* 1.5–13 (Stockholm, 1952).

205. Jansen, W. H. "Classifying performance in the study of verbal folklore," in W. E. Richmond, ed., *Studies in folklore*, pp. 110–118. Bloomington, 1957.

206. ———. "From field to library," *Folk-lore* 63.152–157 (Sept. 1952).

207. ———. "The klesh-maker," *Hoosier folklore* 7.47–50 (1948).

208. Jardine, D. *Criminal trials*, Vols. 1–2. London, 1832–1835.

209. Jenkins, J. J. *Associative processes in verbal behavior: report of the Minnesota conference*, mimeographed. Minneapolis, 1959.

210. ———. "The change in some American word association norms in the twentieth century," Paper presented at the Fifteenth International Congress of Psychology. Brussels, 1957.

211. ———, and W. A. Russell. "Associative clustering during recall," *Journal of abnormal and social psychology* 47.818–821 (1952).

212. Jespersen, O. "Cause psychologique de quelques phénomènes de métrique germanique," *Psychologie du langage.* Paris, 1933.

213. ———. *Growth and structure of the English language.* Leipzig, 1905.

214. ———. *A modern English grammar*, Vol. 2. Heidelberg, 1914.

215. Johannesson, A. *Origin of language.* Reykyavik, 1949.

216. Johnston, O. M. "The use of 'ella,' 'lei' and 'la' as polite forms of address in Italian," *Modern philology* 1.469–475 (1904).

217. Jones, P. M. *The background of modern French poetry.* Cambridge, England, 1951.

218. Joos, M. "Description of language design," *Journal of the acoustical society of America* 22.701–708 (1950).

219. Jordan, R. *Handbuch der Mittelenglischen Grammatik.* Heidelberg, 1934.

220. Joyce, J. *Finnegans wake.* New York, 1939.

221. Jung, C. G., and F. Riklin. "The association of normal subjects," in *Studies in word association*, ch. 2. London, 1918.

222. Jünger, F. G. *Rhythmus und Sprache im deutschen Gedicht.* Stuttgart, 1952.

223. Karcevskij, S. "Sur la phonologie de la phrase," *Travaux du cercle linguistique de Prague* 4.188–223 (1931).

224. Karmazin, G. "Tscheremissiche Lieder," *Mémoires de la société Finno-Ougrienne* 59.373–476 (1931).

225. Kayser, W. *Kleine deutsche Versschule.* Bern, 1946.

226. ———. *Das sprachliche Kunstwerk.* Bern, second edition, 1951.

227. Kempt, R., ed. *The American Joe Miller.* London, 1865.

228. Kennard, E. A. "The context of song and chant in Hopi culture," Paper presented

442

at the Symposium on Casual and Non-casual Language, American Anthropological Association meeting. Chicago, 1957.
229. Kennedy, A. G. *The pronoun of address in English literature of the thirteenth century.* Stanford, 1915.
230. Kent, G. H., and A. J. Rosanoff. "A study of association in insanity," *American journal of insanity* 67.37–96, 317–390 (1910).
231. Kenyon, J. S. "'Ye' and 'you' in the King James version," *Publications of the Modern Language Association of America* 29.453–471 (1914).
232. Klages, L. *Vom Wesen des Rhythmus.* 1931.
233. Kleiner, J. *Studia z zakresu teorii literatury.* Lublin, 1956.
234. Klibansky, R., and C. Labowsky. *Plato Latinus, Volumen III. Parmenides ... necnon Procli Commentarium in Parmenidem ....* London, 1953.
235. Kommerell, M. *Gedanken über Gedichte.* Frankfurt am Main, 1943.
236. Koukal', V., K. Četkarev, and F. Rubcov, eds. *Marij kaḻk muro.* Leningrad and Moscow, 1951.
237. Kroeber, A. L. *Style and civilizations.* Ithaca, 1957.
238. Lach, R. "Tscheremissische Gesänge," *Gesänge russischer Kriegsgefangener,* Vol. 1:3. Vienna and Leipzig, 1929.
239. Lachmann, E. *Hölderlins Hymnen in freien Strophen: eine metrische Untersuchung.* Frankfurt am Main, 1937.
240. Lambek, J. "Mathematics of sentence structure," *American mathematical monthly* 65.154–170 (1958).
241. Langer, S. *Feeling and form.* New York, 1953.
242. Lanz, H. *The physical basis of rime.* Stanford and London, 1931.
243. Lashley, K. S. "Experimental analysis of instinctive behavior," *Psychological review* 45.445–471 (1938).
244. Lasker-Schüler, E. *Die gesammelten Gedichte.* München, 1920.
245. Lees, R. Review in *Language* 33.375–408 (1957).
246. LeHir, Y. *Esthétique et structure du vers français d'après les théoriciens du 16ième siècle à nos jours.* Paris, 1956.
247. Leishman, J. B. *The monarch of wit.* London, 1951.
247a. Levi, A. "Della versificazione italiana," *Archivum Romanicum* 14.449–526 (1930).
248. Lévi-Strauss, C. "Analyse morphologique des contes russes," *International journal of Slavic linguistics and poetics* 3 (1960).
248a. ———. *La geste d'Asdival.* École Pratique des Hautes Études. Paris, 1958.
248b. ———. "The structural study of myth," in T. A. Sebeok, ed., *Myth: a symposium,* pp. 50–66. Philadelphia, 1955.
249. ———, R. Jakobson, C. F. Voegelin, and T. A. Sebeok, *Results of the Conference of Anthropologists and Linguists.* Baltimore, 1953.
250. Lewis, B. R. *Creative poetry.* Stanford and London, 1931.
251. Littré, É. *Dictionnaire de la langue française,* Vol. 4. Paris, 1882.
252. Lockemann, F. *Das Gedicht und seine Klanggestalt.* Emsdetten, 1952.
253. Lotz, J. "Kamassian verse," *Journal of American folklore* 67.369–378 (1954).
254. ———. "A notation for the Germanic verse line," *Lingua* 6.1–7 (1956).
255. ———. "Notes on structural analysis in metrics," *Helicon* 4.119–146 (Budapest, Leipzig, 1942).
256. ———. "The structure of human speech," *Transactions of the New York Academy of Sciences,* Ser. II, 16.373–384 (1954).
257. Lowell, A. "Whitman and the new poetry," in *Poetry and poets,* pp. 60–87. Boston and New York, 1930.

258. Luh, C. W. *On Chinese poetry.* Peiping, 1935.

259. Lynch, J. J. "The tonality of lyric poetry: an experiment in method," *Word* 9.211–224 (1953).

260. MacLean, C. I. "Hebridean traditions," *Gwerin* 1.21–33 (1956).

261. Maeder, H. "Hölderlin und das Wort: zur Problem der freien Rhythmen in Hölderlins Dichtung," *Trivium* 2.42–59 (1944).

262. Majakovskij, V. *Polnoe sobranie sočinenij.* Moscow, 1939.

263. ———. *Sobranie stixotvorenij.* Leningrad, 1950.

264. Malinowski, B. "The problem of meaning in primitive languages," in C. K. Ogden and I. A. Richards, *The meaning of meaning*, pp. 296–336. New York and London, ninth edition, 1953.

265. Mallarmé, S. *Divagations.* Paris, 1899.

266. Mansikka, V. T. *Litauische Zaubersprüche. Folklore Fellows communications* 87 (1929).

267. Marbe, K. *Über den Rhythmus der Prosa.* Giessen, 1904.

268. Maretić, T. "Metrika narodnih naših pjesama," *Rad Yugoslavenske Akademije* 168, 170 (Zagreb, 1907).

269. Marty, A. *Untersuchungen zur Grundlegung der allgemeinen Grammatik und Sprachphilosophie*, Vol. 1. Halle, 1908.

270. Matthiessen, F. O. *The achievement of T. S. Eliot.* New York, 1947.

271. ———, ed. *The Oxford book of American verse.* New York, 1950.

272. McClure, A. K. *Lincoln's yarns and stories, a complete collection of the funny and witty anecdotes that made Abraham Lincoln famous as America's greatest storyteller.* Chicago and Philadelphia, n.d.

273. McDougall, W. *Outline of abnormal psychology.* Chicago, 1926.

274. Meyer, H. "Vom Leben der Strophe in neuerer deutscher Lyrik," *Deutsche Vierteljahrschrift für Literaturwissenschaft und Geistesgeschichte* 25.436–473 (1951).

275. Meyer-Lübke, W. *Grammaire des langues romanes*, Vol. 3. Paris, 1900.

276. Miller, G. A. *Language and communication.* New York, 1951.

277. ———, J. S. Bruner, and L. Postman. "Familiarity of letter sequences and tachistoscopic identification," *Journal of genetic psychology* 50.129–139 (1954).

278. Mink, W. D. "Semantic generalization as related to word association," *Technical report* 17, ONR contract, N8 onr 66216, University of Minnesota. Minneapolis, 1957.

279. Minn, E. K. *Studies in Cheremis* 4, *derivation.* Bloomington, 1956.

280. Minor, J. *Neuhochdeutsche Metrik.* Strassburg, 1902.

281. Mohr, W. "Freie Rhythmen," in P. Merker and W. Stammler, **145**, pp. 479–481.

282. Moloney, M. F. "Donne's metrical practice," *Publications of the Modern Language Association of America* 65.232–239 (1950).

283. Monroe, H. *Poets and their art.* New York, 1926.

284. Morgan, F. "William Carlos Williams: imagery, rhythm, form," *Sewanee review* 55.675–690 (1947).

285. Morier, H. *Le rhythme de vers libre symboliste étudié chez Verhaeren, Henri de Regnier, Vielé-Griffin, et ses relations avec le sens.* Genève, 1943–1944.

286. Morris, C. *Signs, language and behavior.* New York, 1946.

287. Mukařovský, J. "Intonation comme facteur de rhythme poétique," *Archives néerlandaises de phonétique expérimentale* 8–9.153–165 (1933).

288. ———. *Kapitoly z české poetiky*, Vols. 1–3. Prague, 1948.

289. Müller, D. H. *Komposition und Strophenbau.* Wien, 1907.

290. Müller, G. "Die Grundformen der deutschen Lyrik," *Von deutscher Art in Sprache und Dichtung* 5.95–135 (1941).

291. Muller, H. F. "The use of the plural of reverence in the letters of Pope Gregory I," *The Romanic review* 5.68–89 (1914).

292. Naess, A. "Toward a theory of interpretation and preciseness," in L. Linsky, ed. *Semantics and the philosophy of language.* Urbana, 1952.

293. Newman, S. *Zuni dictionary.* Bloomington, 1958.

294. Nitsch, K. "Z historii polskich rymów," *Wybór pism polonistycznych* 1.33–77 (Wrocław, 1954).

295. Nykl, A. R. *El cancionero del . . . Aben Guzmán (Ibn Quzmān).* Madrid, 1933.

296. O'Connor, J. *Born that way.* Baltimore, 1928.

297. O'Donnell, M. J. *Feet on the ground, being an approach to modern verse.* London and Glasgow, 1946.

298. Ogden, C. K., and I. A. Richards. *The meaning of meaning.* New York and London, fifth edition, 1938.

299. Olrik, A. *Folkelige afhandlinger.* Copenhagen, 1919.

300. O'Neil, W. "The effect of verbal association on tachistoscopic recognition," *Technical report* 4, ONR contract, N8 onr 66216, University of Minnesota. Minneapolis, 1953.

301. Osgood, C. E. "Motivational dynamics of language behavior," in M. R. Jones, ed. *Nebraska symposium on motivation.* Lincoln, 1957.

302. ———, S. Saporta, and J. C. Nunally, "Evaluative assertion analysis," *Litera* 3.47–102 (1956).

303. ———, and T. A. Sebeok, eds., *Psycholinguistics: a survey of theory and research problems.* Baltimore, 1954.

304. ———, and E. Walker. "Motivation and language behavior: a content analysis of suicide notes," *The journal of abnormal and social psychology* 59.58–67 (1959).

305. Panofsky, E. *Meaning in the visual arts.* New York, 1955.

306. Peacock, R. "Probleme des Musikalischen in der Sprache," in *Weltliteratur: Festgabe für Fritz Strich zum 70. Geburtstag.* Bern, 1952.

307. Peirce, C. S. *Collected papers,* Vol. 1. Cambridge, Mass., 1931.

308. Perdiguier, A. *Mémoires d'un compagnon.* Moulins, 1914.

309. Peterson, M. S., and J. J. Jenkins. "Word association phenomena at the individual level: a pair of case studies," *Technical report* 16, ONR contract, N8 onr 66216, University of Minnesota. Minneapolis, 1957.

310. Pfeiffer, J. *Umgang mit Dichtung.* Hamburg, 1936.

311. ———. *Zwischen Dichtung und Philosophie.* Bremen, 1947.

312. Pike, K. L. *Language in relation to a unified theory of the structure of human behavior,* Vols. 1–2. Glendale, 1954–1955.

313. Pinthus, K., ed. *Menschheitsdämmerung.* Berlin, 1920.

314. Pittenger, R. E., and H. L. Smith, Jr. "Basis for some contributions of linguistics to psychiatry," *Psychiatry* 20.71–74 (1957).

315. Pjast, V. *Sovremennoe stixovedenie.* Leningrad, 1931.

316. Poe, E. A. "Marginalia," *The works,* Vol. 3. New York, 1857.

317. ———. "The philosophy of composition," in *The complete poems and stories of Edgar Allan Poe with selections from his critical writings,* A. H. Quinn, ed. pp. 978–987. New York, 1951.

318. *Political debates between Abraham Lincoln and Stephen A. Douglas,* Cleveland, 1894.

318a. Polivanov, E. D. "O metričeskom xaraktere kitajskogo stixosloženija," *Doklady Rossijskoj Akademii Nauk,* serija V, 156–158 (1924).

319. Pool, I. de Sola, ed. *Trends in content analysis.* Urbana, 1959.
320. Pope, A. *The Twickenham edition of the poems of Alexander Pope*, J. Butt, ed. Vol. 4. London, 1939.
321. ———. *The works of Alexander Pope, Esq.*, W. Roscoe, ed. London, 1824.
322. Potebnja, A. *Ob'jasnenija malorusskix i srodnyx narodnyx pesen.* Warsaw, 1 (1883), 2 (1887).
323. Propp, V. *Morphology of the folktale.* Bloomington, 1958.
324. Ransom, J. C. *The new criticism.* Norfolk, Conn., 1941.
325. ———. "The strange music of English verse," *Kenyon review* 18.460–477 (1956).
326. ———. *The world's body.* New York, 1938.
327. Reichard, G. A. *An analysis of Coeur d'Alene myths.* Philadelphia, 1947.
328. Richards, I. A. *English through pictures.* New York, 1945.
329. ———. *Goodbye earth and other poems.* New York, 1958.
330. ———. *How to read a page; a course in effective reading.* New York, 1942.
331. ———. *Interpretation in teaching.* New York, 1938.
332. ———. *Principles of literary criticism.* New York and London, 1924.
333. ———. *Speculative instruments.* Chicago, 1955.
334. Riding, L., and R. Graves. *A survey of modernist poetry.* London, 1927.
335. Riffaterre, M. Review in *Word* 12.324–7 (1956).
336. Rilke, R. M. *Sämtliche Werke*, E. Zinn, ed. Wiesbaden, 1955.
337. Robins, R. H. "Noun and verb in universal grammar," *Language* 28.289–298. (1952).
338. Robinson, R. E. *Danvis folks.* Rutland, 1934.
339. Rosen, H. *Correlations between the Schellenberg free association test and the Minnesota multiphasic personality inventory.* M.A. thesis, University of Minnesota. Minneapolis, 1944.
340. Ross, W. D. *Aristotle's Metaphysics. A revised text with introduction and commentary.* Oxford, 1924, 1953.
341. Russell, W. A., and L. H. Storms. "Implicit verbal chaining in paired-associate learning," *Journal of experimental psychology* 49.287–293 (1955).
342. Ryan, J. J. III. "An experimental comparison of response transfer facilitated by meaningfully similar and associated verbal stimuli," *Technical report* 21, ONR contract, N8 onr 66216, University of Minnesota. Minneapolis, 1957.
343. Rybnikov, P. N. *Pesni*, Vol. 3. Moscow, 1910.
344. Sachs, C. *Rhythm and tempo.* New York, 1953.
345. Sandburg, C. *Abraham Lincoln, the prairie years*, Vols. 1–2. New York, 1927.
346. ———. *Abraham Lincoln, the war years*, Vols. 3–6. New York, 1940.
347. Sanford, F. H. "Speech and personality," *Psychological bulletin* 39.811–45 (1942).
348. Sapir, E. *Language.* New York, 1921.
349. ———. "A study of phonetic symbolism," in *Selected writings of Edward Sapir*, D. Mandelbaum, ed., pp. 61–72. Berkeley, 1949.
350. Saran, F. *Deutsche Verslehre.* München, 1907.
351. Schlauch, M. "Language and poetic creation," in *The gift of tongues*, pp. 227–259. New York, 1942.
352. ———. *Modern English and American poetry.* London, 1956.
353. Schliebitz, V. *Die Person der Anrede in der französischen Sprache.* Breslau, 1886.
354. Schneider, F. J. *Der expressive Mensch und die deutsche Lyrik der Gegenwart.* Stuttgart, 1927.
355. Schramm, W. L. *Approaches to a science of English verse.* Iowa City, 1935.

356. Sebeok, T. A. "Approaches to the analysis of folksong texts," *Ural-Altaische Jahrbücher* 31.392–399 (1959).

357. ———. "Folksong viewed as code and message," *Anthropos* 54.141–153 (1959).

358. ———. "Levirate among the Cheremis as reflected by their songs," *American anthropologist* 53.285–291 (1951).

359. ———. "Sound and meaning in a Cheremis folksong text," in *For Roman Jakobson*, pp. 430–439. The Hague, 1956.

360. ———. *Studies in Cheremis 5, the Cheremis.* New Haven, 1955.

361. ———, and F. J. Ingemann. *Studies in Cheremis 2, the supernatural.* New York, 1956.

362. ———, and E. Lane. "The Cheremis folksong: a Soviet viewpoint," *The Slavonic and East European review* 28.139–151 (1949).

363. ———, and others. *Studies in Cheremis 1, folklore.* Bloomington, 1952.

364. ———, and V. J. Zeps. "An analysis of structured content, with application of electronic computer research, in psycholinguistics," *Language and speech* 1.181–193 (1958).

365. Seckel, D. *Hölderlins Sprachrhythmus.* Leipzig, 1937.

366. Selvin, H. C. "A critique of tests of significance in survey research," *American sociological review* 22.519–527 (1957).

367. Shapiro, K. *A bibliography of modern prosody.* Baltimore, 1948.

368. ———. "English prosody and modern poetry," *ELH* 14.77–92 (1947).

369. ———. "Prosody as the meaning," *Poetry* 73.336–351 (1949).

370. Shengeli, G. *Traktat o russkom stixe.* Odessa, 1921.

371. Shipley, J. T. *Dictionary of world literature.* New York, 1943.

372. Shirman, J. "Poet contemporaries of M. Ibn Ezra and Yehuda Halevi," in *Studies of the Research Institute for Hebrew Poetry* 2.132–135 (Berlin, 1936). [In Hebrew.]

373. Shtokmar, J. *Bibliografija rabot po stixosloženiju.* Moscow, 1933.

374. Sievers, E. *Grundzüge der Phonetik.* Leipzig, 1901.

375. ———. *Rhytmisch-melodische Studien.* Heidelberg, 1912.

376. ———. *Ziele und Wege der Schallanalyse.* Heidelberg, 1924.

377. Siipola, E., W. N. Walker, and D. Kolb. "Task attitudes in word association, projective and nonprojective," *Journal of personality* 23.441–459 (1955).

378. Silverberg, W. V. "On the psychological significance of 'Du' and 'Sie' " *Psychoanalytic quarterly* 9.509–525 (1940).

379. Simmons, D. C. "Specimens of Efik folklore," *Folk-Lore* 66.417–424 (1955).

380. *Sketches and eccentricities of Col. David Crockett of West Tennessee.* London, 1833.

381. Skinner, B. F. *Verbal behavior.* New York, 1957.

382. Sledd, J. "A note on linguistics and literary study," *The comparative literature newsletter* 8. Mimeographed. Cambridge, Mass., 1956.

383. ———. Review in *Language* 31.312–345 (1955).

384. Smith, H. L., Jr. "The communication situation," multilithed. Washington, D.C., 1955.

385. Snell, B. *Griechische Metrik.* Göttingen, 1957.

386. Sokolov, Y. M. *Russian folklore,* C. R. Smith, tr. New York, 1950.

387. Sonnenschein, E. A. *What is rhythm?* Oxford, 1925.

388. Spence, K. W., I. E. Farber, and H. H. McFann. "The relation of anxiety (drive) level to performance in competitional and non-competitional paired-associates learning," *Journal of experimental psychology* 52.296–305 (1956).

389. Spender, S. H. *The making of a poem.* London, 1955.

390. Spies, H. *Studien zur Geschichte des Englischen Pronomens im XV und XVI Jahrhundert.* Halle, 1897.

391. Staiger, E. *Grundbegriffe der Poetik.* Zürich, 1951.

392. ———. *Die Kunst der Interpretation.* Zürich, 1955.

393. ———. Review in *Erasmus* 6.212–213 (1953).

394. Stankiewicz, E. "Expressive language" (forthcoming).

395. Stauffer, D. *The nature of poetry.* New York, 1946.

396. Stein, A. "Donne and the couplet," *Publication of the Modern Language Association of America* 57.676–696 (1942).

397. ———. "Donne's harshness and the Elizabethan tradition," *Studies in philology* 41.390–409 (1944).

398. ———. "Donne's prosody" and "A note on meter," *Kenyon review* 18.439–443, 451–460 (1956).

399. Steinitz, W. *Der Parallelismus in der finnisch-karelischen Volksdichtung. Folklore fellows communications* 115 (1934).

400. Stern, S. M. "Influences of Arabic muwaššahs on Hebrew poetry in Spain," *Tarbitz* 18.166–186 (1947). [In Hebrew.]

401. Stidston, R. O. *The use of ye in the function of thou: a study of grammar and social intercourse in fourteenth-century England.* Stanford, 1917.

402. Stouffer, S. A., L. Guttman, et. al. *Measurement and prediction.* Princeton, 1950.

403. Strich, F. *Deutsche Klassik und Romantik.* Bern, 1949.

404. Sturtevant, E. H. *An introduction to linguistic science.* New Haven, 1947.

404a. Stutterheim, C. F. P. "Modern stylistics," *Lingua* 3.52–68 (1952).

405. Suberville, J. *Histoire et théorie de la versification française.* Paris, 1956.

406. Taranovski, K. "Metode i zadači savremene nauke o stihu . . . ," *III congrès international des Slavistes* 4.109–132 (1939).

407. ———. *Ruski dvodelni ritmovi.* Belgrade, 1955.

408. Taupin, R. *L'influence du symbolisme français sur la poésie américaine.* Paris, 1929.

409. Taylor, A. "Some trends and problems in studies of the folk-tale," *Modern philology* 37.19 (1940).

410. Taylor, W. L. "Recent developments in the use of 'Cloze procedure,'" *Journalism quarterly* 33/1 (1956).

411. Thomas, L. P. *Le vers moderne.* Bruxelles, 1943.

412. Thompson, S. *The folktale.* New York, 1946.

413. ———. *Motif-index of folk-literature.* Bloomington, 1955–1958.

414. Thurstone, L. L. *The vectors of mind: multiple-factor analysis for the isolation of primary traits.* Chicago, 1935.

415. Tillotson, G. *On the poetry of Pope.* Oxford, second edition, 1950.

416. Timofeev, L. J. *Poètika Majakovskogo.* Moscow, 1941.

417. ———. *Teorija literatury.* Moscow, 1945.

418. ———, and L. M. Polak, eds. *Tvorčestvo Majakovskogo.* Moscow, 1952.

419. Tomaševskij, B. *O stixe.* Leningrad, 1929.

420. ———. *Russkoe stixosloženie.* Petrograd, 1923.

421. ———. *Stix i jazyk.* Moscow, 1958.

422. Trager, G. L., and H. L. Smith, Jr. *An outline of English structure.* Norman, 1951.

423. Trakl, G. *Die Dichtungen.* Leipzig, 1917.

424. Tyler, L. *Psychology of human differences.* New York, second edition, 1956.

425. Tynjanov, J. *Problema stixotvornogo jazyka.* Leningrad, 1924.

426. Valéry, P. *The art of poetry.* Bollingen series 45. New York, 1958.

427. Verwey, A. *Rhythmus und Metrum.* Halle, 1934.

428. Vildrac, C., and G. Duhamel. *Notes sur la technique poétique.* Paris, 1910. (Russian translation: *Teorija svobodnogo stixa,* V. Šeršenevič, 1920.)

429. Vinogradov, V. V. *Ocerki po istorii russkogo literaturnogo jazyka 17–19 vv.* Leiden, 1949.

430. ———. "Ponjatie sintagmy v sintaksise russkogo jazyka," in *Voprosy sintaksisa sovremennogo russkogo jazyka.* Moscow, 1950.

431. Vinokur, G. *Majakovskij novator jazyka.* Moscow, 1943.

432. Voegelin, C. F. "Meaning correlations and selections in morphology-syntax paradigms," Academia Sinica, *Bulletin of the institute of history and philology* 29.91–111 (1957).

432a. ———. "Model-directed structuralization," *Anthropological linguistics* 1:1.9–25 (1959).

433. ———. "Phonemicizing for dialect study (with reference to Hopi)," *Language* 32.116–135 (1956).

434. ———. Review in *International journal of American linguistics* 24.229–231 (1958).

435. ———. Review in *Language* 3ʳ 109–125 (1959).

436. ———, and R. C. Euler. "Introduction to Hopi chants," *Journal of American folklore* 70.115–136 (1957).

437. ———, and J. Yegerlehner. "Toward a definition of formal style, with examples from Shawnee," in W. E. Richmond, ed., *Studies in folklore,* pp. 141–150. Bloomington, 1957.

438. Wallerstein, R. C. "The development of the rhetoric and metre of the heroic couplet, especially in 1625–1645," *Publications of the Modern Language Association of America* 50.166–209 (1935).

438a. Wang Li. *Han-yü shih-lü-hsüeh* (= Versification in Chinese). Shanghai, 1958.

439. Weaver, W. "Probability, rarity, interest, and surprise," *Scientific monthly* 67.390–392 (1948).

440. Wecter, D. *The hero in America.* New York, 1941.

441. Wellek, R. "Concepts of form and structure in twentieth century criticism," *Neophilologus* 42.2–11 (1958).

442. ———, and A. Warren. *Theory of literature.* New York, 1949, 1956.

443. Wells, H. W. *New poets from old.* New York, 1940.

444. Werfel, F. *Gedichte.* Berlin, 1927.

445. Whitehall, H. "From linguistics to criticism," *Kenyon review* 18.411–421 (1956).

446. ———. "From linguistics to poetry," in N. Frye, ed., *Sound and poetry,* pp. 134–146. New York, 1957.

447. Whorf, B. L. *Language, thought, and reality,* J. B. Carroll, ed., New York, 1956.

448. Wimsatt, W. K., Jr. "The structure of the 'concrete universal' in literature," *Publications of the Modern Language Association of America* 62.262–280 (1947).

449. ———. *The verbal icon.* Lexington, 1954.

450. ———. "Verbal style: logical and counterlogical," *Publications of the Modern Language Association of America* 65.5–20 (1950).

451. ———, and M. C. Beardsley. "The concept of meter: an exercise in abstraction," *Publications of the Modern Language Association of America* 74.585–598 (1959).

452. ———, and C. Brooks. *Literary criticism, a short history.* New York, 1957.

453. Winters, Y. *The anatomy of nonsense.* Norfolk, 1943.

454. ———. "The audible reading of poetry," *The Hudson review* 4.433–447 (1951).

455. Winters, Y. *Primitivism and decadence.* New York, 1937.

456. Woodworth, R. S. *Experimental psychology.* New York, 1938.

457. Yegerlehner, J. "Structure of Arizona Tewa words, spoken and sung," *International journal of American linguistics* 24.264–267 (1958).

458. Yule, G. U. *The statistical study of literary vocabulary.* Cambridge, England, 1944.

459. Zipf, G. K. *Human behavior and the principle of least effort.* Cambridge, Mass., 1949.

460. Žirmunskij, V. *Kompozicija liričeskix stixotvorenij.* Petersburg, 1921.

461. ———. *Voprosy teorii literatury.* Leningrad, 1928.

462. ———. *Vvedenie v metriku.* Leningrad, 1925.

Index

THE M.I.T. PRESS PAPERBACK SERIES